D1407969

Classic *typefaces*

AMERICAN TYPE & TYPE DESIGNERS

DAVID CONSUEGRA

ALLWORTH PRESS
NEW YORK

To my wife Zoraida,
my sons Juan Diego and Nicolas;
and to my brother Ramón Florez

Designer and researcher: David Consuegra
Assistant designers: Juan Diego Consuegra
                     Zoraida Cadavid

Unless otherwise stated, the illustrations have been taken from the author's personal archives and research.

Allworth Press books may be purchased in bulk at special discounts for sales promotion, corporate gifts, fundraising, or educational purposes. Special editions can also be created to specifications. For details, contact the Special Sales Department, Allworth Press, 307 West 36th Street, 11th Floor, New York, NY 10018 or info@skyhorsepublishing.com.

15 14 13 12 11   5 4 3 2 1

Published by Allworth Press
An imprint of Skyhorse Publishing

307 West 36th Street, 11th Floor, New York, NY 10018.

Allworth Press® is a registered trademark of Skyhorse Publishing, Inc.®, a Delaware corporation.

www.allworth.com

ISBN: 978-1-58115-894-6

Library of Congress Cataloging-in-Publication Data is available on file.

Printed in the United States of America

ACKNOWLEDGMENTS

First and above all to Mac McGrew, whose work *American Metal Type of the Twentieth Century* (1993) has been essential to this book;

To the *Encyclopaedia of Type Faces* (1986), by Jaspert, Berry & Johnston, which was the first book to inspired me to research American type design;

To Carol Twombly, Type Design Manager of Adobe Systems, whose immediate support of the project gave me enthusiasm to make it a reality;

To all American type designers –Ronald Arnholm, Arthur Baker, Edward Benguiat, David Berlow, Charles Bigelow, Garrett Boge, Tom Carnase, Matthew Carter, Freeman Craw, Tony DiSpigna, Tobias Frere-Jones, Jonathan Hoefler, Kris Holmes, Richard Isbell, Emil J. Klumpp (through his wife), Zuzana Licko, Paul Shaw, and Carol Twombly– who generously answered questions and contributed written and graphic information, in many cases, with their original fonts;

To the staff of the Grolier Club, and to its librarian, Eric Holzenberg, who was so receptive and generous in opening their book archives to me;

To the New York Type Directors Club, and to its executive director, Carol Wahler, who were so enthusiastic and generous in allowing me to do research in their library;

To Professor Robert Sims, Professor of Modern Languages at Virginia Commonwealth University, who responded so patiently and cooperatively to my many requests for research assistance;

To the staff of Cabell Library of the Virginia Commonwealth University for their collaboration in finding so much bibliographical data;

To ITC and to Ilene Strizver, Director of Typeface Development, for providing fonts;

To Agfa/Monotype and to Allan Haley, for providing fonts;

To Colin Brignall, for his encouragement on this project;

To Sandra Kirshenbaum, editor of *Fine Print*, for sending information on various type designers;

To the Biblioteca de la Escuela de Diseño Elisava in Barcelona, and its book keepers, for their help in locating vital information;

To the Biblioteca Bergnes de las Casas in Barcelona, for its cooperation in finding information on type design;

To St. Bride Printing Library in London, and to James Mosley, its librarian, for his collaboration;

To Paul Gehl, curator of the History of Printing collection at the Newberry Library, Chicago, and to Miss Margaret Kulis, reference librarian, for their help in finding valuable biographical information;

To Rob Roy Kelly for his support and for lending his typographical research;

To Steven Heller, of the *New York Times*, for backing the project;

To Josep M. Pujol who was helpful up to the last minute in supplying additional information;

To Christopher Burke for his help in revising most of the written material;

To Nicole Potter, Senior Editor of Allworth Press, and to Monica P. Rodríguez, Editorial Assistant, for their careful editing;

To Auros Copias, Bogotá, and to its manager Hernando Ramírez, who lent their type font archive for the project, and produced the preliminary printed copies of the book;

To Reprolaser, Bogotá, and to Milton Sáenz, for lending their type font archive;

To the Biblioteca Central Universidad Nacional de Colombia, and the Biblioteca de Artes, where I have always found assistance in my search for information;

To my brother Ramón Flórez, who has always been at my side, supporting my projects;

To Luis Angel Parra, Director of Arte Dos Gráfico, Bogotá, for allowing photographs of some of his Ludlow's equipment,

To all my friends and graphic design colleagues who have been prompt in lending their books for information;

To my wife for her help in searching many volumes of biographical and graphic data and for her support on the long road completing this work; to my son Juan Diego whose help and many hours on the computer have been essential in the making of this book.

Note: The selection of the people and type foundries –both metal and digital– included in this book does not pretend to be complete. It has been based on data found to be a representative sample of what has been done in America, and which has some significance today.

Although many of the typefaces included in this book are digital versions, some of them sent by the designers exclusively for this publication, the majority of the alphabet samples presented have been carefully scanned from metal type catalogs.

The typefaces included in this book may not represent the entire œuvre of each designer. It is possible that a designer may have created other typefaces before or after the publication of this work. The aim of the author has been to present a typographical profile as significant as possible in each case.

Biographies, where possible, have been set in types created by each designer. Where there was no option, a close typeface has been selected or *News Gothic* in its default.

For the general typesetting of the book, *News Gothic* has been used, both in light, medium and bold versions.

As an homage to Morris Fuller Benton
the book has been typeset in *News Gothic*,
except for the designers' biographical data
in which each individual designer
has been represented
by their own design where possible.

Where digital versions of typefaces are available,
they have been used.
In all other cases, typefaces
have been carefully scanned
from type catalogs.

CONTENTS

PREFACE.................................... VII

INTRODUCTION..................... VIII

CHRONOLOGY OF TYPE-
RELATED EVENTS 14

COMPARATIVE AMERICAN/
EUROPEAN TYPE
CHRONOLOGY...................... 38

TYPE DESIGNS
IN ALPHABETICAL ORDER   42
Note: only those alphabets that are shown
in this book are listed

ARNHOLM, Ronald (b.1939)
VGC Aquarius 44
VGC Fovea 46
ITC Legacy 47
ITC Legacy Sans   48

BAKER, Arthur
Baker Signet 49
Visigoth 52
Amigo 52
Pelican 52
Oxford 52
Marigold 53
Kigali 53
Sassafras 53

BENGUIAT, Edward (b.1927)
ITC Souvenir 54
ITC Korinna 56
ITC Tiffany 56
ITC Bauhaus 57
ITC Bookman 57
ITC Benguiat 58
ITC Benguiat Gothic 58
ITC Barcelona 59
ITC Modern 216 59
ITC Caslon 224 60
ITC Panache 60
ITC Century Handtooled 61
ITC Cheltenham Handtooled 61
ITC Garamond Handtooled 61
ITC Edwardian Script.................. 61

BENTON, Linn Boyd (1844-1932)
Century Roman, with T.L. DeVinne. 62

BENTON, Morris Fuller (1872-1948)
Engravers Bold 64
Franklin Gothic 66
Alternate Gothic 66
Clearface 66
Commercial Script 66
News Gothic 67
Hobo 67
Cloister Oldstyle 67
Souvenir 68
Bodoni Open 68
Century Schoolbook 68
Broadway 69
Modernique 69
Parisian 69

Ultra Bodoni 70
Bank Gothic............................... 70
Stymie 70
American Text 71
Shadow 71
Tower 71
Othello 71
Empire 71

BERLOW, David (b.1954)
New Caledonia 72
FB Grotesque 73
FB Agency 74
FB Empire 75
FB Belucian 76
FB Eldorado 77

BERNHARD, Lucian (1883-1972)
Block Type................................. 78
Iniciales Bernhard 79
Bernhard Kursive 81
Lucian 81
Bernhard Fashion 81
Bernhard Gothic 82
Lilith.. 82
Bernhard Tango 82
Bernhard Tango Swash 83
Bernhard Roman Antiqua
Bold Condensed 83
Bernhard Modern Roman........... 83

BIGELOW, Charles (b.1945)
Lucida, with Kris Holmes 84
Lucida Sans, with Kris Holmes 85
Lucida Sans Typewriter,
with Kris Holmes 86
Lucida Bright, with Kris Holmes...... 87
Lucida Calligraphy, with Kris Holmes 88
Lucida Blackletter, with Kris Holmes 88
Lucida Handwriting, with Kris Holmes 88
Lucida Fax, with Kris Holmes 89
Lucida Sans Typewriter Oblique,
with Kris Holmes 89
Lucida Typewriter, with Kris Holmes 90
Lucida Casual, with Kris Holmes..... 90

BLUMENTHAL, Joseph (1897-1990)
Emerson 91

BOGE, Garrett (b.1951)
Spring 92
Florens-Flourished 93
Manito 93
Pontif, with Paul Shaw 93
Pietra, with Paul Shaw 94
Cresci, with Paul Shaw 94
Stockholm, with Paul Shaw.......... 94
Göteborg, with Paul Shaw............ 95
Uppsala, with Paul Shaw............. 95
Longhand 95

BRADLEY, William (1869-1962)
Bradley 96
Missal Initials 98
Bewick Roman 98

BULLEN, Henry Lewis (1857-1938)
Garamond 99

CARNASE, Tom (b.1939)
ITC Gorilla, with Ronne Bonder........ 100
ITC Grizzly, with Ronne Bonder 102
ITC Grouch, with Ronne Bonder 102
ITC Honda, with Ronne Bonder 102
ITC Neon, with Ronne Bonder 102
ITC Machine, with Ronne Bonder 103
ITC Pioneer, with Ronne Bonder...... 103
ITC Busorama, with Herb Lubalin ... 103
ITC Firenze 103

CARTER, Matthew (b.1937)
Auriga 104
Cascade Script 106
Snell Roundhand....................... 106
Olympian 106
Gando Ronde 107
Shelley Script Allegro 107
Shelley Script Volante 107
Bell Centennial 107
ITC Galliard 108
ITC Charter 108
Mantinia 108
Sophia 108
Big Caslon 109
Walker 109

CHAPPELL, Warren (1904-1992)
Lydian 110
Lydian Bold............................... 113
Trajanus 113
Lydian Cursive 113

CLELAND, Thomas M. (1880-1964)
Della Robbia 114

COOPER, Oswald Bruce (1879-1940)
Cooper Old Style........................ 116
Cooper Black 119
Cooper Hilite 119
Boul Mich 119
Pompeian Cursive...................... 120
Cooper Full Face 120
Bitstream Oz Handicraft 120

CRAW, Freeman (b.1917)
Craw Clarendon......................... 121
Craw Clarendon Book 124
Craw Modern 124
Craw Clarendon Condensed........ 124
Ad Lib 125
CBS Didot................................. 125
CBS Sans 125

DE VINNE, Theodore L. (1828-1914)
Century Roman 126

DiSPIGNA, Tony (b.1943)
ITC Serif Gothic, with Herb Lubalin .. 127
ITC Lubalin Graph,
with Herb Lubalin......................... 189

DWIGGINS, William A. (1880-1956)
Metrolite 129
Metroblack 132
Metromedium 132
Electra...................................... 132

Caledonia 132
Eldorado 133
Initials 133

FRERE-JONES, Tobias (b.1970)
Dolores 134
Garage Gothic 135
Interstate 135
Nobel 135
Reactor 135
Pilsner...................................... 136
HTF Gotham 136

GOODHUE, Bertram G. (1869-1924)
Merrymount 137
Cheltenham 140

GOUDY, Frederic W. (1865-1947)
Camelot 141
Village 144
Copperplate Gothic 144
Monotype 38-E 144
Kennerley Old Style.................... 144
Forum Title 145
Goudy Oldstyle 145
Cloister Initials 145
Hadriano Title 145
Garamont 180
Goudy Heavyface 146
Deepdene 146
Goudy Text 146
Lombardic Capitals 146
Goudy Sans Serif....................... 147
Trajan Title 147
Ornate Title 147
Franciscan 148
University of California Old Style 148
Goudy Thirty 148

GRIFFITH, Chauncey H. (1879-1956)
Ionic No. 5 149
Poster Bodoni 150
Excelsior 150
Janson 151
Paragon 151
Opticon 152
Bell Gothic................................ 152
Memphis Extra Bold 153
Corona 153

HAMMER, Victor (1882-1967)
Hammer Unziale 154
American Uncial......................... 155
Andromaque 155

HESS, Sol (1886-1953)
Kennerley Open Caps................. 156
Bodoni Bold Panelled................. 157
Cooper Tooled 157
Broadway Engraved 157
Hadriano Stone-Cut 158
Hess Neobold............................ 158
Stymie Extrabold 158
Spire 158
Onyx Italic 159
Post-Stout Italic 159
Postblack Italic.......................... 159
Artscript 159

HOEFLER, Jonathan (b.1970)
HTF Hoefler Text 160
HTF Champion Gothic 162
HTF Requiem............................ 162
HTF Zigurat 162
HTF Leviathan............................ 162
HTF Saracen 162
HTF Acropolis............................ 162
HTF Egiziano Filigree.................. 162
HTF Didot 163

HOLMES, Kris (b.1950)
Isadora.................................... 164
Sierra 165
Lucida, with C. Bigelow 165
Lucida Sans, with C. Bigelow 166
Lucida Bright, with C. Bigelow........ 167
Apple Chicago, with C. Bigelow 167
Apple Geneva, with C. Bigelow 167
Apple Monaco, with C. Bigelow 167
Apple New York, with C. Bigelow 168
Lucida Handwriting,
with C. Bigelow 168
Lucida Console, with C. Bigelow 168

HUXLEY, Walter (1890-1955)
Huxley Vertical 169

IRVIN, Rea (1881-1972)
Irvin 170

ISBELL, Richard (b.1924)
Americana 172
ITC Isbell 174
TF Baccarat 175

KAUFMANN, Max Richard (b.1904)
Kaufmann Script 176
Kaufmann Bold 177
Balloon.................................... 177

KLUMPP, Emil J. (1912-1997)
Murray Hill Bold 178

LANSTON, Tolbert (1844-1913)
Garamont 180

LICKO, Zuzana (b.1961)
Oakland Ten 182
Modula 184
Matrix Regular 184
Lunatix 184
Triplex 185
Totally Gothic 185

LUBALIN, Herb (1918-1981)
ITC Avant Garde, with T. Carnase 186
ITC Serif Gothic, with T. DiSpigna 189
ITC Lubalin Graph, with T.DiSpigna . 189

LUDLOW, Washington I.
Tempo Heavy Condensed 190

MERGENTHALER, Ottmar
(1854-1899)
Cheltenham 192

MIDDLETON, Robert Hunter
(1898-1985)
Cameo 194

Record Gothic 197
Delphian Open Title 197
Stellar 197
Bodoni Black 198
Tempo Heavy Condensed 198
Karnak Light 198
Lafayette Extra Condensed 199
Umbra 199
Eden 199
Mandate.................................. 200
Bodoni Campanile 200
Coronet 200
Stencil 200
Radiant 201
Samson 201
Florentine Cursive 201

MINOTT, Louis
Davida Bold 202

NADALL, Berne (1869-)
Caslon Antique 203

PAGE, William H. (1829-1906)
Antique XXX Condensed.............. 204
Gothic Tuscan Pointed 206
Ionic 206
Antique Tuscan No.8 206
Clarendon XX Condensed 206
Antique Tuscan No.11 207
Clarendon Ornamented 207
Antique Tuscan Outline 207
Skeleton Antique 208
French Antique 208
Aetna 208
Egyptian Ornamented 209
Painter's Roman 209
Celtic Ornamented.................... 209
Antique No.7 210
Teutonic 210
Gothic Tuscan Condensed No.2.. 210
French Clarendon XXX Cond. 211
Phanitalian 211
No. 129 211
No. 131 211
No. 142 212
No. 154 212
No. 500 212
No. 506 213
No. 515 213

PARKER, Wadsworth A. (1864-1938)
Goudy Handtooled...................... 214
Lexington, with C. P. Hornung 215
Gallia 215
Modernistic.............................. 215
Stymie Inline Title 215

PHINNEY, Joseph W. (1848-1934)
Jenson Oldstyle 216

PIERPONT, Frank H. (1860-1937)
Plantin 217

POWELL, Gerry (1899-)
Onyx 218
Stencil.................................... 219
Stymie Bold Condensed 219

RANSOM, Will (1878-1955)
Parsons 220

RILEY, Frank H. (1894-)
Grayda 221

ROGERS, Albert Bruce (1870-1957)
Centaur 222

RUZICKA, Rudolph (1883-1978)
Fairfield 224

SHAW, Paul (b.1954)
Old Claude............................... 226
Kolo, with Garrett Boge 229
Beata, with Garrett Boge 229
Donatello, with Garrett Boge 229
Ghiberti, with Garrett Boge 230
Bermuda Open, with Garrett Boge ... 230
Stockholm, with Garrett Boge........ 230
Göteborg, with Garrett Boge.......... 231
Uppsala , with Garrett Boge........... 231

SLIMBACH, Robert (b.1956)
ITC Slimbach 232
ITC Giovanni 233
Adobe Garamond 233
Adobe Utopia 234
Adobe Minion 234
Sanvito 235
Caflisch Script 235

SMITH, Robert (b.1910)
Park Avenue 236
Brush 237

STONE, Sumner (b.1945)
ITC Stone Sans 238
ITC Stone Serif 239
ITC Stone Informal 239

THOMPSON, Bradbury (1911-1955)
alphabet 26 240

TRAFTON, Howard A. (1897-1964)
Trafton Script 242
Cartoon 243

TWOMBLY, Carol (b.1959)
Mirarae 244
Trajan 245
Charlemagne 245
Lithos 246
Adobe Caslon 247
Myriad.................................... 248
Viva 249
Nueva 249
Chaparral 250

UPDIKE, Daniel Berkeley (1860-1941)
Merrymount 251

WARDE, Frederic (1894-1939)
Arrighi 252

WELLS, Darius (1800-1875)
Roman 254
Antique X Condensed................. 256
Gothic Extended 256
Grecian Condensed 256

Gothic Tuscan Condensed 257
Gothic Condensed Outline 257
Antique Tuscan 257
Tuscan Outline 258
Antique Light Face Extended 258
Gothic Tuscan Italian 258
Doric Ornamented 259
Painter's Roman 259

WIEBKING, Robert (1870-1927)
Artcraft................................... 260
Caslon Clearface....................... 261
Advertisers Gothic..................... 261
Munder Venezian 261

TYPE FOUNDRIES

ADOBE SYSTEMS, INC......... 262

**AMERICAN TYPE
FOUNDERS** 263

**INTERNATIONAL TYPEFACE
CORPORATION** 264

LETRASET CORPORATION .. 265

LINOTYPE COMPANY.......... 266

**LUDLOW TYPOGRAPH
COMPANY**.............................. 267

MONOTYPE COMPANY 268

PHOTO-LETTERING, INC....... 269

**GLOSSARY
OF TYPOGRAPHICAL
TERMS**................................. 270

BIBLIOGRAPHY..................... 300

INDEX................................. 302

One of my first experiences related to type dates back to my studies at Boston University, when I had to design a program cover for a Boston University Symphony Orchestra concert. I had hand lettered the text in *Caslon Oldstyle 540* capitals, taken from the book I used in my lettering class. After handing a "comprehensive" to the printer, I was surprised to be handed a printed copy in *Goudy Bold*. So, for a second design commission, this time for the presentation of Handel's *Messiah*, I decided to hand in a completely finished artwork to avoid a change in the use of the Robert Hunter Middleton's *Stellar*.

As a student of typography, I also had access to metal type and printing on a platen press. This gave me the opportunity to get acquainted with the physical aspect of type.

Later on at Yale University, I focused my interests on typography from other angles, searching for form and styles for my own work. Many of the books I consulted were prolific in examples but scarce in biographical information about type designers. At Yale, I also had the opportunity to handle metal type, and to print. My thesis *On Trademarks* was set in *Bodoni*, and printed by hand.

Later in my professional work, I developed, an approach to graphic design problem solving for the Museum of Modern Art in Bogotá, which led to mostly all-type posters. These projects and many others related to corporate image gave me the opportunity to maintain interest in typography.

As time passed, I became more and more interested in type, not only as form, but also as an essential part of history. As a professor of layout design, I started to complement graphic information with the history of typography. This gave me the opportunity to start searching for information on designers and their work.

The first book that gave me some data on this subject was the second edition of *The Encyclopaedia of Type Faces*, published by Jaspert, Berry & Johnson in 1986. Excellent as it is in displaying complete alphabets, from both Europe and America, with the type carefully grouped into three main style categories –serif, sans serif and calligraphic styles– it doesn't include any biographical data.

Sebastian Carter's book *Twentieth Century Type Designers*, published in 1987, came closer to my interests, although on account of the time boundaries Carter chose, the book only covered the life and type activities of six major American type designers. In the second edition, he covered the work of three additional designers.

Later on, through Hermann Zapf, I was referred to the second, 1993 edition of Mac McGrew's book, *American Metal Typefaces of the Twentieth Century*. This book finally gave me the opportunity to learn who the noteworthy metal type designers in America were, and which typefaces they had designed at least during the twentieth century. Unfortunately, the biographical data is very limited.

When I started to work on this project, I encountered many difficulties. Many of them related to distance, which also involves time. To develop a type project like this is a complicated enterprise, and much more so from a foreign country. Fortunately my first contacts, such as the one established with the New York Type Directors Club, gave me the opportunity to approach some type designers, and through them to start constructing a chain that slowly began to complete the picture.

The more I got into its content the more I was convinced that it was important to continue my endeavor. This book is not only on type, and technological advancements. It is essentially a book on people, an account of a great deal of work done silently by those who did research on the mechanics of type making, on the development of type as an important medium for communication, and on type as form, so important to graphic design.

As I continuously state in my lectures, history gives much credit to the invention of printing, but less to the creation of typefaces, both as means for printing and as means for designing. Without letters, graphic communication would be very difficult. Type is not only a means, it is also an end. Through history, type has played both roles. How differently a verbal statement is viewed when a letter style is improperly used, be it poetry, the cover of a book, a poster, a business card, or a street sign.

Type design is an extensive field. It is equally valuable to text or to display type. It may be based directly on calligraphy, hand drawn or designed. Its value lies more in its strength to communicate a certain spirit, an overall feeling, and a graphic character in a word, a paragraph, a page, or an entire book. To present these various instances I have tried, to the extent that it is possible, to present type as character sets, type as text and type applied to design. This will allow the reader to evaluate each designer through his or her own type designs. Unfortunately, it was not always easy to have access to a digital font, which would have permitted me to set each biography in its proper font or to present the complete works of each designer.

In scanning and carefully retouching many typographic originals, I had the opportunity to evaluate letters as if I were redrawing them. I learned more about the work of these designers than if I had just analyzed printed samples. This is what I want to share:

A good assortment of work that may enrich what we know of type and what we know of type designers.

Graphic work have been included to complement type design. I have discovered that the knowledge we may have of certain designers' work is sometimes incomplete. While a designer may be known for his graphic work, he may be ignored for his type design, or vice versa. Besides, graphic images permit a different type of visual information.

As the book contains dense information, I felt it advisable to divide the content into sections so as to permit the reader to visualize information from different points of view. Thus, the book contains an index of designers as well as an alphabetically ordered list of all the typefaces included in the book. There are two chronological descriptions of events and type designs, a comprehensive glossary of terms, sixty-two complete biographies, and data on eight firms that have been directly responsible for the development of typefaces.

The chronological development of type design was approached to both European and American events, and the appearance of other typefaces. The glossary's definitions have been extended and complemented with examples and cross-references, in order for the reader to easily access information.

Although the research has been centered on a selection of some of the most relevant contributors to type design, as well as to the work accomplished by some type foundries –metal, photo, serigraphic, and digital–, this book is above all, a recognition of their work and a way to share vital information on American type design. I hope this research may attract many other people interested in this subject, in order to complement my achievements.

From Letters to Type

Letterforms are a direct result of writing, and their evolution has been a long endeavor. At first, man drew pictures of his ideas, later he developed graphics to represent vocal sounds that expressed these ideas, and finally an arbitrary group of signs came to represent a group of definite sounds. Thanks to the Phoenicians, these groups of codes evolved into letters, which once in Greece, continued evolving formally. This group of letters, arranged in a particular order, came to be known as the *alphabet*, named after the first two Greek letters, *alpha* and *beta*.

Since alphabetical writing involved the use of letters, letters had to evolve in form and structure to be easily read. Nevertheless, while writing is done free hand, it requires a certain level of skill and a respect for the use of traditional materials and tools. Type must consider many other outside determinants which are not necessarily related to written forms and a personal approach.

Type is a regularized form which was originally cut by hand on a hard material –wood or metal– and used for printing purposes. This meant that each type containing a character of the alphabet had to maintain evenness of size and form within a running text.

Around AD 1450, to determine the formal characteristics of type, German printer and goldsmith Johannes Gutenberg, in collaboration with calligrapher Peter Schöffer, based their type design on the manuscript hand used at that time, known as *textur*. Each character was redrawn, cut, and cast maintaining its shape and legibility.

The making of metal type involved a complex process. It basically needed a punch, a matrix, and a mold, and a special alloy, that had to be soft enough to cast and hard enough to allow this piece of metal to maintain its form once cold. A punch was a vertical metal bar that had one of the characters of the alphabet –either a capital or lowercase letter, a number, or a sign– sculpted onto one of its ends.

A punch-cutter was a professional engraver, who sculpted by hand –in reverse and at actual size– each one of these characters, in this small area of the punch with the use of special tools and the help of a magnifying glass (see page 63). Once the metal bar was hardened he hit it on a softer metal with a hammer to produce a matrix, and by placing the matrix into the mold, and filling it with molten type metal, he or another person cast the metal character. It should be mentioned that a punch-cutter cut two or three punches a day, so a whole alphabet would take a long time to complete. [1]

His ability consisted of carefully maintaining a visual proportion so as to end up with a complete font, which would give the composed text a unified color and quality. Being such a costly and time-consuming procedure, printers generally used only one or two sizes and one type style.

This manual procedure did not change until the invention of the pantograph in 1834, at least concerning wood type, and it did not further change until 1885, with the invention of the automatic punch-cutter in relation to the production of metal type.

Letterforms

The present Western alphabet, which consists of twenty-six letters, was formally drawn as two different groups of signs. The first, which corresponds to a series of fairly equally high letters, has been called **capitals**; the second, made up of a group of different shaped units, has been called **lowercase letters**. While the first, basically drawn upon a two-line grid, evolved in Greece before the Christian era, the second, written upon a four-line grid, evolved after the fall of the Roman Empire around the end of fifth century AD. [2]

Capital letters, as we know them today, reached a perfect formal state during the Roman Empire around the first century, and may be seen exemplified in the inscription found at the base of the Trajan Column, a monument erected in the Roman Forum between AD 112 and 113 to honor Emperor Marcus Ulpius Trajanus's victories. As a complementary note, there were only twenty-three letters in the Roman alphabet. Letters **J**, **U**, and **W** were later added.

When Greek and early Roman letters were drawn by means of a stylus on a soft surface, such as a waxed tablet, letters were characterized by an even thickness of stroke. But once letters were transcribed into monumental inscriptions by means of a flat brush held at a 30-degree angle, their strokes acquired an uneven character. Vertical and horizontal strokes became of different width with noticeable endings or serifs, and curved strokes were characterized by an uneven stroke, which made letters more elegant and better proportioned.

Lowercase letters, as we know them today, had a different development. Approaching the fall of the Roman Empire, a conventional script, known as *Uncial*, evolved and was used for the writing of books, especially those of the Roman Church. Although written upon a two-line grid, they were executed with a different writing utensil on different material. The quill had replaced the reed pen, and papyrus had been replaced by parchment.

By the fall of the Roman Empire, writing developed into a less formal script known as *Half-uncial*, which led to the drawing of lowercase letters. Drawn upon a four-line grid, and more fluently executed, some letters started to change, slowly acquiring ascenders and descenders. Although some letters maintained a certain similarity to the capitals, others acquired a completely different shape. This script, nevertheless, was not formally kept, and by the time Charlemagne (*Carolus Magnus* or Charles I the Great) ascended to the throne in 771, letters

had lost their uniformity and clarity. With the aid of the English scholar Alcuin of York, a more uniform, calligraphic writing was developed, which came to be known as *Carolingian script*. [3]

Gothic and Roman Letters

With the development of the Gothic style in French architecture, *Carolingian script* was somewhat adapted to resemble the angularity of religious constructions. Drawn with an accented vertical stress, acute angles, and a marked absence of curves, shapes became narrow, very stiff, and characterized by an intense blackness. The distinct surface ornament, a plaited pattern, gave the script the name *textus* (plaited), or *textur*, as it was known in Germany. In France it was later referred to as *lettre de forme*, and in England as *black letter*.

So, by the middle of the fifteenth century, when Gutenberg decided to print the *Bible* using metal type, *textur* was the conventional style of letter used in manuscript books, and Latin the language. Being interested in formally competing with manuscripts, Gutenberg and Schöffer based their type on this letter style. But in Italy, as a renewed interest in classical antiquity –with its æsthetic and philosophical values– and a revived humanistic outlook, there was a change from the Gothic to the Renaissance.

This was a time when much of the work of Roman and Greek philosophers and writers became known. In Italy, handwriting had also evolved into a completely different style based on the *Carolingian script*, a style which the Renaissance men believed to be more in keeping with the classical spirit than the Gothic one. In transcribing the works of classical authors, the Renaissance humanist scribes had modified this hand, making it even more beautiful. When the first type was cut, cast, and used in 1465 the new typeface had a hint of roman.

However, these letters did not assume a fixed form until they were cut in Venice and cast as type by the French punch-cutter and printer Nicolas Jenson around 1470. By 1500, the handwriting used at the Papal Chancery had served as the basis for the appearance of the first italics in type, although Roman capitals remained as initial letters. It was not until 1537 that capitals acquired a sloped form. This means that within fifteen years of Gutenberg's initial achievement, several roman letters of lasting value and wide influence had appeared, and within eighty years, there were roman and italic versions of type.

Letters continued resembling calligraphic models, in spite of the work of masters like French engraver and founder Claude Garamond, who so successfully translated the models into metal, avoiding merely imitating the characteristics of the pen. He also brought the roman and italic forms into a working relationship.

American Type & Type Designers

The first important change came in 1693, when the French Académie des Sciences, by request of Louis XIV, appointed a special committee to study the proportions of classical Roman letters established by artists like Fra Luca de Pacioli, Albrecht Dürer, Sigismondo Fanti, and Geofroy Tory as a way to develop a "scientific" typeface that would become the property of the French nation. As copperplate engraving had superseded calligraphy, the burin replaced the pen, and pure technique became predominant. [4]

Headed by the prominent mathematician Nicolas Jaugeon, the Académie developed the master alphabet designs. These were finally engraved by Louis Simonneau [5] based on letters drawn with a ruler and a compass on a grid of close horizontal and vertical lines, which gave a precise measurement to each of their proportions. Although royal punch-cutter Philippe Grandjean, did not follow the submitted model exactly, the resulting typeface, called *Romain du Roi Louis XIV*, was a definite "transition" from the *Oldstyle*, because it had greater contrast, sharp horizontal serifs, and a vertical stress. This paved the way to the even more contrasting typefaces that followed. [6]

French punch-cutter Pierre Fournier *le jeune*, who was also influenced by copperplate engravings and followed the tastes developed in France for sharpness and contrasts, further developed the work of Grandjean. Nevertheless, his greatest contribution to type design was his proposal for a standardized type measuring system. Benjamin Franklin brought this system to America in 1786 through the acquisition of types and matrices directly from Fournier. It provided important bases for further developments in American typography. [7]

By the middle of the 1740s, the Baroque and the Rococo styles had practically disappeared in England and France. A strong reaction against both these art expressions gave way to the establishment of Neoclassicism, which would later be notable for its absence of printer's ornaments, arabesques, and borders on the printed page. The extended use of copper engraving had definitely influenced type design.

French engraver and founder Firmin Didot, and later Italian engraver and printer Giambattista Bodoni, further developed Fournier's approach to letterforms to the point of reducing their drawing to a relationship of contrasts, in which letters were constructed by opposite elements: thick and thin, line and stroke, verticals and horizontals. [8] This objective approach dehumanized the preceding letter styles and permitted them to be constructed rather than drawn and to be viewed as independent units, which could be manipulated and transformed.

Using the same approach, the nineteenth century type designers, influenced by sign painters, pushed letterforms even further, making them acquire bolder features. [9] Strokes and serifs became straight, bracketed, unbracketed, and even without serifs. *Fat face*, *Ionic*, *Egyptian*, *Clarendon* styles appeared on the market. It is important to add that all these changes were not only part of an attempt to establish clear typographical hierarchies but also a way to provide poster printers with heavy, readable-at-distance typefaces. Type was no longer in the book, but on the wall. If type sizes remained relatively small in metal type founding –that is no bigger than three inches in height– larger sizes were supplied as wood type, which was already being used in the printing of billboards and posters.

By the middle of the nineteenth century, type was approached from two different points of view: as a metal form, which had a sculpted character used for printing, and as a graphic entity. While letterforms had been entirely freed from calligraphic models, allowing the manipulation of their shapes in whatever way possible, type as a sculpted piece of metal continued being done in the same way, by hand.

It is from this perspective –taking type as a piece of metal or wood that is used for printing, and as a graphic entity– that this book has been conceived and developed.

The American Contribution

This book will investigate American contributions to technical problem solving and formal and stylistic problem solving related to type design.

While the primary function of type is to serve as a tool of visual communication, there are many contexts from which to view type and type design. The history of type can certainly be seen as part of the history of civilization. The creation of new type families can be seen as a problem solving activity, aimed at improving legibility and readability, clearer letterforms and more functional texts; it can also be viewed as a vehicle for self-expression. It can also be the result of the competition between foundries; be caused by stylistic trends; to satisfy the particular demand of a client; or as an answer to solve a particular design problem. Type design is also the vanguard of technology; technological advances require new type designs in new media.

Here, some events have been selected that appear to be significant to the development of type. They are presented in chronological order.

It is interesting to note that the first two great contributions to type production were carried out throughout the first three decades of the nineteenth century. During this time gaslight had already been installed in many places; paper was being produced mechanically; the first iron presses were being manufactured; and the electric motor had been introduced into industry. While wood engraving could be printed simultaneously with type, copperplate engraving, lithography, and mezzotint (which had also been introduced into America) needed to be printed separately.

In 1828, by taking advantage of the end grain of the wood and the wood engraving technique, Darius Wells was able to manufacture large, inexpensive and durable wood type. The earlier method, using the side grain of the wood, had limited type design to simplified shapes. He could now cut more elaborate designs, which in turn changed the development of typographical posters in America, and also influenced metal type design. Different from foundry type, letters could now be cut in sizes up to thirty inches or more.

Then, with the introduction of the combined router and pantograph, which William Leavenworth had invented in 1834, type was freed from three great limitations. First, the design could be done in a large size and simultaneously be reduced and cut to smaller sizes. This meant that only one original pattern was needed. Second, any person with some skill and concentration could do the cutting task. And third, perhaps the most important in terms of creativity, type production could now be carried out without the interpretation of an engraver. Not only Wells, but other wood type manufacturers like William Hamilton Page, who were innate designers, started to experiment with letter shapes, widths, and values, and with their chromatic aspect. They also introduced the type family concept, which was not formally developed into metal type until the first decade of the twentieth century. [10]

During the second half of the nineteenth century, when the Industrial Revolution started taking place in America, there were innumerable technical and mechanical advancements. The mechanical production of continuous paper combined with steam-driven presses stimulated mass production of newspapers and mass communication. Chromolithography was introduced as well as mechanical lithography. The three-color separation principle was already stated and applied to printing. Photography was finally being reproduced by a mechanical system, and electric light had changed human behavior in all senses. But in spite of all these advancements, the production and type handling, although aided by stereotyping, electrotyping, and mechanical casters, continued being done by hand. Armies of type compositors, type distributors, and thousands of metal characters were needed to accomplish these combined tasks.

In 1885, aiming to solve a different problem, Linn Boyd Benton was able to improve Leavenworth's combined machine, and by adapting it to the cutting of punches and matrices he brought about a complete revolution to type production. For the first time, after approximately 435 years since the invention of printing, a person other than a skilled engraver could handle the cutting of type, punches, and matrices. The minute work done by hand, by means of special tools and with the help of a magnifying glass, was now automatically done. Additionally, the original design could be drawn in a large size on paper in a frontward position, and once transferred to a backward-placed metal pattern, it would serve as a guide to produce a very reduced copy (14 pt) without any distortion. Originally, an engraver worked by looking at a frontward position original and sculpted a backwards copy of it on the end of the punch (see page 63).

The Mechanical Type Composition

The following year, with the invention of the Linotype, Ottmar Mergenthaler solved three aspects of type production. By using and arranging matrices on a line, he was able to cast a line of type, which simplified type management. Then, as a result of using matrices, he could return them to a magazine which held them in place, being able to repeat the operation as many times as needed. A printer could now simplify the setting and distribution of the type, by the use of one or two composing machines, reducing costs and time considerably. The used type could be returned to the melting pot, and converted again into useful metal. Against all predictions, handwork did not diminish. On the contrary, the reduction of time and cost lead to increased production of newspapers, magazines, and books, and more production meant more people being employed to do handwork. More printed matter also revolutionized the educational and communication world.

The mechanization of type production directly influenced foundry type. Despite the fact that metal type is a regular form in all senses, which needs to be so for both setting and printing, type sizes were not produced according to standardized measurements. Given that type foundries were private enterprises, type was produced according to measurements particular to each foundry. Type bought in one foundry could not be set with type bought from another foundry. With the establishment of the standard type measuring system of the 12-pt pica in 1886 –an important regulating system– type was finally viewed as a practical endeavor. For the sake of comparison, England adopted it eight years later.

It is interesting to note that the following year another invention took place in mechanical metal type production. In 1887, Tolbert Lanston completed the Monotype hot metal type-composing machine, with two additional characteristics. Since it was a mechanical system, which permitted the casting of individual characters, the whole process had to be planned with strictly regulated requirements. The use of a unit system in the design process permitted type to be the product of modules. Taking the em quad or em space, which is the square of any type size, as a regulating base, the surface was vertically divided into eighteen segments, each letter being assigned a particular set-width or number of horizontal segments both for capital and lowercase letters. Taking a contemporary typeface such as *Times New Roman* (1932) as a base, letter **M**, for example, would employ 18 segments, letter **A** 15, letter **B** 12, letter

C 14, etc., while lowercase letters followed a similar measurement: letter **m** would employ 18 segments, letter **a** 10, letter **b** 11, letter **c** 9, etc. This approach converted type design into a methodical undertaking, which also enabled the practical management of line breaks, justification, inter-word and inter-letter spacing.

By 1890, the ideas of the Arts and Crafts movement, which had been so influential in the appearance of the private press in America, were not as numerous. Art Nouveau had also arrived in America, but although many of its followers may have been influenced by similar principles, some people did not completely follow John Ruskin's anti-mechanical rhetoric. The advertising field was now questioning the use of an overcrowded artwork by introducing new concepts based on experiments in visual perception and market research, and trade journals protested against the overuse of decorative motifs, heavy type, crowded formats, and Art Nouveau imagery. [11] The practical side of printing also demanded a new attitude towards type production and type design. Competition between type foundries had come to a critical point. Also, Monotype being a mechanical casting system, which could cast individual types as needed, type foundries had to face type production differently in order to compete with this mass production.

When the American Type Founders was established in 1892 by the merging of twenty-four type foundries, the theories expressed in the two preceding paragraphs were put into practice. While types became standardized in size, they were also carefully selected through an in-depth analysis of all the typefaces offered by these foundries. Inconsistencies in design, outdated styles, and duplicates were dramatically reduced until only a number of useful typefaces remained. Design was formally and æsthetically channeled. This also was very significant because of the upcoming century, which was already foretelling the appearance of new art styles, and with them, new approaches to an æsthetical evaluation of form.

With the establishment of the ATF Typographic Library and Museum in 1908 under the direction of typographic historian Henry Lewis Bullen, two æsthetically related aspects were introduced to typography. Type design was not only a problem of creating new typefaces; there was a classic type legacy that should also be taken into account. The Library and Museum would introduce type designers and printers to what was done in the past. In collaboration with Morris Fuller Benton, Bullen was able to establish the basis for the future development of classical type within the type foundry. Thus, faces like *Bodoni, Cloister, Baskerville, Garamond* and *Bulmer* became available within a period of ten years. There was also an æsthetic problem within the printed page. Instead of combining styles of mixed heritage, it was better to combine variations of form genetically related. Fonts were now fully developed into type families, a concept

that had been earlier introduced by wood type manufacturers. A particular design was enhanced with a great amount of structural and formal variations, which included a treatment of width, value, and stress. Thus, a typeface was not only planned, including light, regular, bold, condensed, and expanded versions, complemented with their italics, but also a harmonic set of sizes. This provided designers and printers with the means of handling text type and typographical hierarchies with unified visual criteria, which certainly gave unity to the printed page.

The Type Design Competition

Once the problem of the standardization of type sizes was faced by all functioning foundries, including ATF, Linotype, Ludlow, Monotype, and Frederic W. Goudy (an independent type designer and type founder), competition was then channeled towards the creation of functional and æsthetically-designed typefaces. ATF had depended in the beginning on people with a keen eye for type development like Linn Boyd Benton, Morris Fuller Benton, Wadsworth Parker, Joseph W. Phinney, Henry Lewis Bullen and its manager, Robert W. Nelson. Later the company included William Bradley who developed an important advertising program for ATF through the in-house publication, *The American Chap-Book*. Mergenthaler Linotype Company appointed Chauncey H. Griffith as Director of Typographic Development in 1922, who also brought in William Addison Dwiggins and Rudolph Ruzicka. Lanston Monotype, before appointing Frederic W. Goudy as type adviser in 1920, had depended on the direct collaboration of Robert Wiebking. The Ludlow Typograph Company, which had depended on Robert Wiebking from the beginning, called type designer Ernst Frederick Detterer, who advised them to appoint Robert Hunter Middleton as its typographic adviser in 1923. Each one of them developed, with time, an important program aimed at solving specific problems stated by their consumers.

The occurrence of simultaneous events does not always permit one to see clearly from where specific changes in type design and production arise. The following events forced a new approach to type design: the development of advertising; the appearance of new mechanical composing systems such as the Ludlow (which after 1911 allowed for easier handling of headlines in newspaper layout); the structuring of the Bauhaus school in 1919, which later was very influential in a conceptual development of type and design, as in the use of sans serif typefaces; and the trend started by sans serif types imported from Europe. American type foundries, guided by their own typographic advisers, played an active role in competing with foreign foundries and with their own competitors.

In 1922, under the direction of Chauncey H. Griffith, the Linotype Company started the

American Type & Type Designers

Legibility Group, an intelligent program for creating logical, legible, and readable typefaces for newspaper text setting. As Head of Typographic Development, Griffith found that type design required more of an "engineering" than an artistic approach. Stereotyping problems for high-speed rotary letterpress printing were solved in such a way that the proposed solution became a worldwide solution for newspapers. [12] *Ionic No. 5*, introduced in 1926, became one of the most successful typefaces for more than three decades, preceding Stanley Morison's introduction of *Times New Roman* in 1932. Griffith's program, which lasted sixteen years, included the design of five typefaces for newspaper use, and of *Bell Gothic*, which was developed for the printing of telephone books nationwide. With the collaboration of William Addison Dwiggins and Rudolph Ruzicka the Legibility program was productive in developing various typefaces for newspaper and book use as well. Dwiggins also collaborated in designing various typefaces to counteract the in-coming European sans serif trend.

Lanston Monotype developed a type program with Frederic W. Goudy, which largely benefitted book production from 1920 on. Goudy was the first independent type designer in America and the first to establish a foundry –an activity no one had done since the eighteenth century. During a sixteen-year close collaboration with the firm, many of his typefaces designed and cast as foundry type were developed for the Monotype system. Many typefaces that Goudy developed for Monotype, before he entered as type advisor, were done in response to particular needs, as was the case of *Kennerley Old Style* and *Forum Title*, both used in the printing of H. G. Wells' *The Door in the Wall*, and which established Goudy's reputation as type designer worldwide. Bruce Roger's *Centaur* was later cut for Monotype, as was Frederic Warde's *Arrighi*, its complementing italic. By 1936, on Goudy's retirement, Sol Hess continued as director of the type department, developing an important program for publishing companies, printers, and department stores. For him, the practical side of typography was as important as the creative side.

In 1923, a visual and functional achievement was carried out by ATF when it published the *Type Specimen Book and Catalog 1923*. Implemented under the direction of Henry Lewis Bullen, and the collaboration of Morris Fuller Benton and Wadsworth Parker (among others), this colossal 1,148-page book, containing typefaces, color layouts, and various detailed examples, became one of the major sources for a visual and practical education for many typographers in America. It guided good sense in typographical usage for some time.

With the appointment of Robert Hunter Middleton in 1923 as typographic adviser to the Ludlow Typograph Company (he later became its director), there was a fourth effort made to develop a type design program, which this time permitted small printers to depend on an important type casting medium that was more accessible than the more expensive Linotype and Monotype machines. His typefaces, less known than those created by Goudy, Griffith, or Benton, reflected great sensitivity and diversity. He was the first one to react to the 1927 European sans serif trend started by *Futura*, *Kabel*, and *Gill Sans* by designing the first American humanist sans serif, *Stellar* in 1929, a delicate typeface which anticipated the appearance of Zapf's *Optima* (1958) by twenty-nine years. Robert Wiebking, who from the start made the new composing system a reality, complemented Middleton's collaboration with the Ludlow, both as a punch-cutter and designer.

The International Influence

The immigration of people, including illustrators, typographers, punch-cutters, engravers, photographers, inventors, and others, had taken place since the late eighteenth century. They were mainly from Germany, Scotland, England, and Czechoslovakia. This immigration continued during the nineteenth century when some of the type designers included in this book came to America. This immigration was especially important in the twentieth century between World War I and World War II. Great type designers, art directors, photographers, architects appeared, such as Lucian Bernhard, Mehemed Fehmy Agha, Alexei Brodovitch, Herbert Bayer, Leo Lionni, George Giusti, Ladislav Sutnar, and Gyorgy Kepes. Also, Gestalt psychologists, such as Max Wertheimer, Kurt Koffka, Rudolf Arnheim, and others, had a great influence on applied typography and imagery.

The Bauhaus design principles, plus the use of the grid, sans serif typefaces, asymmetric typography, and the flush-left type composition were formally imposed by art directors and designers. They also introduced an innovative use of black-and-white and color photography, full-page color reproductions, flush photographs, diagonal typography, etc. In addition to the immediate action carried out by the American type foundries and designers to counteract the sans serif trend initiated by European designs on the market, some typefaces were designed by direct request from clients, as happened with *Vogue*, designed and produced by Intertype for Condé Nast's *Vogue* magazine in 1930. [13] Throughout a whole decade, it is possible to find one or two sans serif typefaces designed for each one of the metal composition systems, including foundry type and mechanical composition. There was also the strong comeback of typefaces like *News Gothic* (1908) in the 1940s which, because of the overwhelming entrance of the European typefaces, had been put aside.

Along with other metal type production handicaps such as time consumption and the immense costs involved in production, there was the risk involved in producing a particular type design without knowing in advance if it will be a success or not. With the management of type through photography a new panorama was opened. With the support of a line film (such as the *Kodalith*, specially developed by Kodak in 1931) photocomposition to become a reality.

With the establishment of Photo-Lettering Inc. in New York, in 1936, headed by Ed Rondthaler, photographic display typesetting opened a broad field to creativity both in applied typography as in the production of new typefaces. Through the use of lenses that permitted condensing, expanding, overlapping, etc., designers like Herb Lubalin later found a way to implement his ideas. His layouts became a reality for magazines such as the *Saturday Evening Post*, which he redesigned in 1961; *Avant Garde* (1968); *Eros* (1972); *Upper & lowercase* (1973); as well as for advertising clients. Much less expensive than typecasting, photo-lettering also provided the means for experimenting with a particular design before its commercial issuing as a metal type. This was the case of Peter Dombrezian's *Dom Casual* –designed in 1950 and later cast in metal by ATF in 1952, with a bold version in 1953– and Ed Benguiat's *ITC Souvenir* –which met great success in 1970 and was commercially issued by Linotype in America and Matrotype in England, and later cast by ATF for hand composition in 1972.

From 1939 through 1962, Bradbury Thompson, one of the most influential graphic designers of postwar America, developed very innovative work in layout design, use of typography and printed color through sixty-one issues of *Westvaco Inspirations for Printers*. An experimental field for his ideas, both graphically and conceptually, it also served him as a means to present his *alphabet 26*, a logical system with a mixture of capitals and lowercase letters. With this type proposal he was in search of simplifying reading and typesetting through the use of one alphabet instead of two.

It would take too much space to enumerate all the contributions made by American designers to type development, for in some instances technical innovations were not only directed to type design but also to making typesetting accessible to other usages, such as office work, or to solve a designer's immediate needs. These innovations made people aware of type as a visual medium which could have a direct influence on their commercial relationships through a better presentation of their documents.

With the creation of the office typewriter *IBM-72 Selectric* in 1961, designed by Eliott Noyes, IBM confronted the design competition of Italian *Olivetti*. In creating its corporate identity, IBM collaborated with designers like Paul Rand, who created some of the most outstanding corporate images of the twentieth century. Different from conventional typewriters, the new machine needed less space, had a lighter touch, was æsthetically attractive, and also provided a changeable means for "printing" type. It also incorporated regulated spaces into typing, which permitted the handling of letters by units, allowing for fairly justified texts, and the making of creative typographical compositions. The ribbon was used only once, offering a perfect printing quality. And, while in other typewriters the carriage moved, in the IBM machine a mono element with the shape of a golf ball, containing a complete font, moved from one side to the other while transcribing letters onto paper. It may be said that "typography" was brought into office work, by supplying a large catalog of typefaces, which included serif and sans serif typefaces, such as *Times New Roman* and *Alternate Gothic*, from 6 to 12 pts. It offered clients, printers, and designers access to an ingenious, economic typesetting medium. In 1963, Swiss type designer, Adrian Frutiger, was appointed consultant to IBM. Thus, one of the first contemporary typefaces, *Univers*, became part of the type catalog. This new approach to type demystified typesetting, and anticipated to a certain extent the desktop publishing concept.

Although not directly related to letterforms in a typographical context, it is worth mentioning the appearance of Supergraphics introduced by architect Robert Venturi in 1962. He innovated architectural design by using giant stencil letterforms as a decoration for Grand's Restaurant in West Philadelphia, altering space and scale. Supergraphics were soon incorporated into corporate identification systems, decorating shops and boutiques, and bringing a new look to architectural environment. [14] This approach was later used by Lou Dorfsman, who conceived the idea for a horizontal 40' x 8.5' three-dimensional, typographic assemblage mural for the CBS cafeteria. Herb Lubalin collaborated by doing the overall lettering layout to scale, and Tom Carnase by doing the intricate lettering.

The Computer Age

By 1963 typography entered the computer age in America with the introduction of *Linasec* by Compugraphic Corporation. New terms like "computer-aided" and "computer-controlled" typesetting" were used for the first time. But, as it had occurred in preceding decades, other developments helped designers in a different field. *Letraset* dry transfer lettering, which made its debut in 1961, allowed for complete freedom in the making of artwork. This medium and Xerography permitted designers to work with experimental typographic layouts as presented by the group Fluxus. At the same time the personal work of French graphic designer Robert Massin combined high-contrast photography and typography in a unique way. His works *La Cantatrice Chauve* and *Delire à Deux* are still outstanding typographic accomplishments. The theory expressed by Herbert Marshall McLuhan on mass media –*The Medium is the Massage*– also had an outstanding influence on man's thinking about communication techniques.

By the end of the decade the first cathode-ray tube (CRT) was installed, and letters were visualized on the screen for the first time. *PRINT'68* exhibition in Chicago introduced participants to a series of electronic devices, which accelerated the demise of hot metal typesetting. Type generators were finally introduced in television ending previous videotaped artwork. While the International Typographic Style continued being handled and promoted by many designers in America, there also appeared a more eclectic managing of type and design as exemplified by the work of Herb Lubalin on the one hand, and Milton Glaser on the other. Both of them would be quite influential for a full decade. During this decade a completely different approach also came from a younger European generation, which was persuaded by the issues of Post-modernism. Designers like Rosemarie Tissi, and later Wolfgang Weingart, April Greiman, and Lucile Tenazas, and others, started to question the old establishment of Swiss design, influencing American graphic and typographic design. Reading habits were questioned and typographical presentations dramatically changed, transforming page layouts. Overlapped texts, and inverted paragraphs were inscribed as white texts on color shapes, and letters and ornamental elements were scattered around the page, eluding convention.

In 1969, with the setting up of the International Typeface Corporation (ITC) through a combined collaboration among Herb Lubalin, Aaron Burns and Ed Rondthaler, type development was clearly modified in America. Aimed at developing typefaces for photocomposition and digitization, ITC faced an ambitious program, which included the support of American and European type designers. Classical typefaces were redesigned to meet contemporary standards in addition to a group of original designs. The true dimension of ITC's impact on typographical development was confirmed through the publication of *U&lc* (*Upper & lowercase*), one of the most influential journals of the twentieth century. Lubalin's experiments with typography ended in the creation of special typefaces, which aided him in giving form to his typographical layouts. Thus, it may be said that type evolved from layout to serve layout. Two of these typefaces, which directly evolved from lettering and page layout, were *ITC Avant Garde Gothic*, designed in collaboration with Tom Carnase, and *ITC Machine*, designed by Carnase. The first was provided with a great number of ligatures, taken directly from the titles used on the magazine of the same name, which permitted type to maintain a lettering flavor. The second was designed to meet extreme close fit.

With the development of computer technology and the use of monitors, there appeared a need for a better readability of typography on the screen. In 1972, the Architecture Machine Group at the Massachusetts Institute of Technology (MIT) developed gray-scale fonts, which allowed for a visually sharper image on the screen.

Previous to this, type on video screen appeared chunky as a result of pixeling. In relation to this context, it is worth mentioning the work developed by Charles Bigelow and Kris Holmes who designed typefaces *Lucida* for use on low-resolution printers, and *Pellucida* for low-resolution video displays in 1984 and 1986, respectively.

In 1974, a new advancement related to type handling took place. This is the case of *Ikarus*, developed by German engineer Peter Karow in Hamburg, Germany. It permitted the conversion of scanned digital images to vectored outlines; the conversion of analogue work to digital data; and the interpolation of basic letters for yielding a family of different characteristics, among other functions. The Linotype Group of Companies and Compugraphic Corporation, among others, started to use the system for preparing digital type libraries. Also, direct communication taking place between journalists and a computerized composition system through the use of video terminals was made possible.

In 1982, type designer Charles Bigelow, Assistant Professor of digital typography at Stanford University, created a master's program in digital typography in collaboration with scientist Donald Knuth, who had created *Metafont* in 1979, a program that enabled the creation and handling of digital typefaces. Type design was eventually viewed as a science. Among his students were Carol Twombly, Dan Mills, and Cleo Huggins, who later enjoyed distinguished careers in typography and electronic design.

With the creation of *PostScript* language in 1983, developed by Engineers John Warnock and Charles Geschke at Adobe Systems Inc., contemporary designers were provided with a tool that permitted the handling of texts and images in a combined document. It also allowed for the handling of curves in type, enabling a good use of serif, sans serif, and calligraphic typefaces. Layouts could now be developed directly on the screen, permitting the designer to see the finished work before printing, something that could not be done before. One year after the creation of *PostScript*, Sumner Stone was invited to be the Director of Typography at Adobe Systems, Inc. Under his guidance, the type department developed an ambitious program for digitizing classical typefaces as well as starting to create original designs. Among the typefaces developed by the department, Robert Slimbach's *Adobe Garamond* (1987), considered one of the best contemporary revivals of Claude Garamond's classic original, must be mentioned.

By 1984, Steve Jobs and Steve Wozniak had designed Apple II, which revolutionized the computer industry with its use of windows, pull down menus, bitmapped graphics, and a mouse to handle commands. Accompanied by a number of software packages, such as *MacWrite*, *MacDraw*, and *MacPaint*, which were quickly adopted into the graphic design practice, new channels for creation were opened both in graphic and in type design. Such is the case of Zuzana Licko, who, after launching Émigré Fonts digital foundry in 1985, presented her first type designs (*Emperor*, *Oakland*, and *Émigré*), which visualized letterforms from a new perspective influenced by the computer language. Although letters were kept within a traditional structure, the simple modular elements derived from the low-resolution characteristics of screen display and dot matrix printing offered the possibility of creating fonts which were more in accordance with present times. The use of simple ratios and the minimum basic points needed to define a letter shape permitted a different access to type design, giving her the opportunity to question reading habits and to reconsider concepts on legibility and readability. Besides her own work, which continued evolving, her approach was followed by designers like P. Scott-Makela and Barry Deck who designed such typefaces like *Dead History* and *Template Gothic*. [15]

Parallel to these experiments on computer-generated fonts, Sumner Stone designed *Stone* typeface, a three-member family developed on the basis of a common letter design at Adobe in 1987. A basic structure served to define three different styles: serif, sans serif, and informal, thus showing that form and structure could be blended into one. Besides being a clarifying graphic statement, it permitted the user to employ three fonts harmonized by one basic structure, useful to set three different contents with a unified visual presentation. German designer Otl Aicher later repeated this typographical experience in 1988, and Dutch designer Lucas de Groot in 1994.

In 1991, Adobe Systems Inc. developed the multiple master technology, which enabled the management of proportion, stress, and value within a letter. A typeface could now be enlarged, condensed, expanded, or italicized without altering any of its basic attributes. Based on two or three design axes, a master design was placed in each corner. While the changes from one end to the other proved to be quite immense, the great advantages of this new technology included the possibilities of finding that intermediate point where the designer could select the shape, the value or the stress needed to adapt a particular type design to his own needs. Starting with Carol Twombly's *Viva* in 1993, there have been many designs created under the multiple master technology format. This is the case of *Nueva* (1994), and *Chaparral* (1997), both designed by Twombly, and *Adobe Minion*, designed by Robert Slimbach in 1990.

In 1995, Matthew Carter had the opportunity to develop, as part of a type design invitation extended to him by Laurie Haycock Makela, Design Director of the Walker Art Center, an alphabet for the private use of that institution. The resulting design, *Walker*, is a typeface that may be completely changed according to the designer's needs. Using a sans serif structure

as a base, the proposal includes five different serif shapes, which may be applied to the basic form in varied ways according to the needs of a specific content. This permits a contemporary typeface to acquire a particular shape related to present or past art expressions, but within the philosophy of the Center which is always committed to changing expressions in art and design.

But besides all these innovative approaches to type design, which were carried out during the last decade of the twentieth century, there also was an interest on the part of American type designers towards legacy, a legacy of both classic letterforms and those typefaces designed more recently. There have appeared, for example, two different revivals of *Caslon Old Face* (Carol Twombly and Matthew Carter), one revival of *Didot* and one of *Bodoni* (Jonathan Hoefler), various excellent digital renderings of Renaissance inscriptions (Carol Twombly, Paul Shaw, Garrett Boge, and Matthew Carter), various type designs based on lettering and calligraphy by American and European artists and designers (Paul Shaw, Garrett Boge, Tobias Frere-Jones), and various sans serif revivals (David Berlow, Tobias Frere-Jones). This shows that there is not a definite trend in American type design as a whole. While some designers have a strict attitude towards their type design work, others prefer to maintain an open approach to different styles and times.

As we may see, it is difficult to separate technology, creation, and theoretical postulates. All of them have contributed in one way or another to the development of type design.

New technologies allow for new forms of communication and new behaviors to create the appropriate environment for new technological advancements. The digital language and the computer, taken as everyday instruments, have introduced their own graphic and visual perspectives into communications.

Graphic arts, the printing industry, and the design field have all contributed to these changes. Visual communication and printed media have been substantially influenced both in their presentation and in their impact. And on the way, they have also stated new rules for type design.

Nevertheless, typographical characteristics are not necessarily oriented by technological advancements, but by reading habits which in the end have also conditioned perception.

Type as form performs four simultaneous activities. While type has a responsibility to the text, making it clear, legible, and readable, it also introduces visual characteristics on the printed page, which will or will not encourage the reader to read the printed text. The type must support the content. The proper size, color and style make content come through. Finally, type is responsible for æsthetic quality of the whole printed piece.

Each typographic style has its own particular application. It lies in the designer's sensitivity to find the proper time, the proper place, the proper style, and the proper size for using it. Type should not only be seen, but also felt.

Throughout history, typography has changed contexts, from an activity related mainly to printing, to a field characterized by the diversity of media and the overflow of information, but where typography is still essential for visual communication. It has allowed for the representation and visualization of words and content both in printing and on the screen.

The new technologies of electronic rendering, the computer, multimedia and Internet have made typography more popular than ever. They have democratized it both in form and structure to the point where typography itself must question typography's inherited structure and form.

———

[1] Warren CHAPPELL, *A Short History of the Printed Word* (New York: A New York Times Book; London: Andre Deutsch, Kingsport, TN: The Kingsport Press, Inc., 1971).

[2] Geoffrey Ashall GLAISTER, *Encyclopaedia of the Book*, 2nd ed. (New Castle, DE: The British Library & Oak Knoll Press, 1996).

[3] *Ibid.*

[4] André JAMES, *La Réforme de la Typographie Royal sous Louis XIV, le Grandjean* (Paris: Librairie Paul James, 1961).

[5] Joseph BLUMENTHAL, *Art of the Printed Book, 1455-1955* (New York: The Pierpont Morgan Library; Vermont: The Stinehour Press, 1973).

[6] *Ibid.*

[7] Hellmut LEHMANN-HAUPT, *The Book in America, a History of the Making and Selling of Books in the United States* (New York: R. R. Bowker Company, 1952).

[8] Ellen LUPTON, and Abott MILLER, *Design Writing Research, Writing on Graphic Design* (London: Phaidon Press Limited, 1996).

[9] Geoffrey DOWDING, *An Introduction to the History of Printing Types* (New Castle, DE: The British Library & Oak Knoll Press, 1998).

[10] Rob Roy KELLY, *American Wood Type, 1828-1900* (New York: Van Nostrand Reinhold Company, 1969).

[11] Ellen Mazur THOMSON, *The Origins of Graphic Design in America, 1870-1920* (New Haven: Yale University Press, 1997).

[12] Jeff LEVEL, *On Type, Face to Face with Daily News* ed. Sandra Kirshenbaum, *Fine Print, the Review for the Arts of the Book*, Vol. 15, No. 1 (1989).

[13] Mac McGREW, *American Metal Typefaces of the Twentieth Century* (New Castle, DE: Oak Knoll Press, 1996).

[14] Philip B. MEGGS, *A History of Graphic Design* (London: Allen Lane, Penguin Books Ltd., 1983).

[15] Ellen LUPTON, and Abott MILLER - *Ibid.*

1600

1605 The first part of Miguel de Cervantes' *Don Quixote de la Mancha* is printed in Madrid. The title page reflects the French influence of establishing the character of roman types being used in Europe after Geofroy Tory and Claude Garamond.

1607 The first permanent English settlement in America takes place in Jamestown, Virginia.

1609 Johan Carolus publishes the first newspaper, *Avisa Relation oder Zeitung* in Strasbourg

1610

1611 Robert Barker prints a large *folio* edition of the King James' version of *The Holy Bible*, the authorized English translation ordered by King James I in 1604. While the main text is set in *black letter*, the chapter heads, marginal notes, and the title page are set in roman type.

1618 After successful expelling the Spaniards, Holland becomes an independent state and a haven in Europe for journalists. Its maritime position transforms it into a usual place for gathering news. The Dutch press is established.

1620

1620 *The Mayflower* arrives in America to what is now Cape Cod, Massachusetts, bearing the Pilgrims who will found the Plymouth Colony.

1621 French punch-cutter and printer Jean Jannon publishes his first type specimen at the Protestant University in Sedan, showing his *Caractères de l'Université*. The Imprimerie Royal will later incorporate his types, much influenced by the work of Antoine Augereau, Claude Garamond, and Robert Granjon.

1623 In London, Isaac Jaggard and Edward Blount print the first *folio* edition of *William Shakespeare's Comedies, Histories & Tragedies* seven years after Shakespeare's death. Not being a religious text, it is set in roman letters.

1625 In America, the Dutch establish the New Amsterdam colony on Manhattan Island. When the English defeat the Dutch in 1664, it becomes New York City.

1629 In Amsterdam, the Elzevir family starts printing the vest-pocket editions of Latin classics and French literature, imitated afterwards by all printers in Europe and America. Cristoffel Van Dijck, one of the greatest Dutch type punch-cutters, has cut the typefaces employed. His types will later be bought for use by the Oxford University and the Cambridge University presses.

1630

1636 Harvard College is established by a grant from the court of the Massachusetts Bay Colony.

1637 *A Decree of Starre-Chamber Concerning Printing*, printed by Robert Barker, is issued in London limiting the activities of print shops and type foundries due to the opposition of calligraphers and illuminators.

1638 The foundation of the Harvard College in Cambridge, Massachusetts, encourages Rev. Jesse Glover to purchase a printing press while in England. Upon his death during the voyage, his widow sets up the first printing shop in America, in Cambridge, in late 1638, under the direction of Stephen Daye, who, with the help of his two sons and printer, Samuel Green, publishes *The Oath of a Free-man* and an *Almanack for the Year 1639*.

1640

1640 By suggestion of Cardinal Richelieu, the Imprimerie Royale du Louvre, known as Typographia Regia, is established for Louis XIII as a royal printing house in 1639-1640. Under the direction of Sébastien Cramoisy, the press employs Dutch printers and compositors who had come from Holland. Their first publication, in 1642, with Dutch types based on Garamond designs, will be a *folio* edition of Thomas à Kempis's *De Imitatione Christi*. The press' name will be changed, in 1871, to Imprimerie Nationale.

1640 In Cambridge, Massachusetts, Stephen Daye prints *The Whole Booke of Psalmes*, in verse, using a copy of the "Dutch press." A volume *in quarto* with 148 pages, in an edition of 1,700 copies, it is presumed to be the first book published in America.

1641 German Ludwig von Siegen invents mezzotint, an engraving technique which permits great tonal range. It will become a favored method for reproducing portraits both in Europe and in America, where it will be introduced in 1830.

1644 By this time, Paris has seventy-five printing shops.

1649 English replaces Latin in England as the official language for legal documents.

1650

1659 In Leipzig, after working for three years, Dutch type founder Anton Janson establishes the first known independent type foundry.

1660

1665 The London plague causes the court to be moved to Oxford, and there the king, lacking for news, allows Henry Muddiman to start printing the *London Gazette*. This will also become one of the printed newspapers coming to America.

1667 The Oxford University Press is established. And for it, in 1672, Bishop John Fell purchases Dutch punches and matrices cut by Dirk and Bartholomew Voskens for the fonts known as the *Fell types*. These typefaces, along with those designed by Cristoffel Van Dijck, also bought for the press, will influence much of the seventeenth century English type founding.

1670

1677 John Foster, a graduate of the College of Cambridge, prints William Hubbard's *Narrative of the Troubles with the Indians in New England*, which marks the beginning of woodcut and book illustration in America.

1680

1683 Hungarian punch-cutter and printer Miklós (Nicholas) Kis, who has worked in Amsterdam since 1680, cuts a beautiful roman typeface for the printing of his *Amsterdam Bible* (1685). Incorrectly known as *Janson Antiqua*, this typeface will serve as the basis for Linotype's revival of *Janson* (1932), designed by Chauncey H. Griffith.

1688 Miklós (Nicholas) Kis prints his *Amsterdam specimen sheet* before he returns to Transylvania in 1689-90.

1690

1690 The English James and Thomas Grover type foundry, established in 1674, issues the oldest known English decorated typeface: *Union Pearl*.

1690 In what is now known as Fairmount, William Bradford, the first printer in Philadelphia, establishes the first paper mill in America. Mennonite Bishop William Rittenhausen, a papermaker by trade, manages it.

In Boston, Richard Pierce and Benjamin Harris print *Publick Occurrences Both Forreign and Domestick*, the first American newspaper. But the governor and council suppress it immediately after being published. With a format of 6" x 9.5" folded, it has four pages. A new paper will not appear until 1704: *The Boston News-Letter*.

1692 By orders of Louis XIV, a special committee is set up by the French Académie des Sciences to study the proportions of letters established by Dürer, Fanti, Pacioli and Tory, as the basis for a "scientific" typeface property of the French nation. They will prepare drawings of Roman letters on a grid of 2,304 squares with final designs engraved on copperplates. Shifting the grid generates italic versions. This approach, which presents a complete divorce from calligraphy, will permit type founder and punch-cutter Philippe Grandjean, who is commissioned by the Académie to cut the typeface, to give shape to a new letter style.

1693 After having some differences with local authorities, William Bradford moves from Philadelphia to New York where he founds the first press in that city.

1694 Because of the successive parliamentary restriction acts, none of the cities of England, except London, York, and the two great university towns of Oxford and Cambridge, will possess permanent presses until this date.

1694 By this time, when the last inhibitory act expires in England, the printing houses of Cambridge, Boston, St. Mary's City, Philadelphia, and New York are already in operation in America.

1700

1700-1800 Many of the most impressive works of the eighteenth century, from the *Médailles* of the Imprimerie Royal of 1702 to Bodoni's *Manuale Tipografico*, represent great technical advances: better casting and fitting of types, paper with more consistent printing surfaces, and better ink and presswork. Printing will take on the look of engraving to an astonishing degree.

1700 Philippe Grandjean cuts his *Romain du Roi Louis XIV* typeface for the Imprimerie Royale. It is the first of the "transitional" typefaces, characterized by a more vertical stress, and thin unbracketed serifs, more related to engraving than punch-cutting. The first book to be printed with it is a *folio* edition of the *Médailles sur les Principaux Événements du Règne de Louis-le-Grand*, in 1702. Grandjean's work will be continued after his death in 1714 by his friend and pupil, Jean Alexandre, and finished by Louis René Luce in 1745, to include twenty-one sizes of roman with italics.

1703 Izaac Enschedé establishes what in the future will be the most famous Dutch type foundry, Enschedé en Zonen, in Haarlem. In 1815, the firm will acquire Firmin Didot's typographic material. Jan Van Krimpen (*Romulus*, 1931) will be among their future type designers.

1710

1710 English writing master George Shelley publishes *Alphabets in All Hands* (engraved by George Bickham) that will provide John Baskerville with the basis for his typeface *Baskerville*, designed in 1757.

1719 English writer Daniel Defoe produces *Robinson Crusoe*, the first story to be published serially.

1720

1720 In London, English engraver, type founder, and type designer William Caslon I sets up his own type foundry, thanks to an advancement made by William Bowyer, a city printer.

1722 William Caslon I designs, cuts and casts his 14 pts English roman and italic which will be used in William Bowyer's 1726 *folio* edition of John Selden's works. Inspired by Dutch Cristoffel Van Dijck designs, his *Caslon Old Face*, a much better and cleaner font, will dominate English printing throughout the century.

1723 Although printing ink may have been produced before, by this date Benjamin Franklin is manufacturing it for his master, Samuel Keimer of Philadelphia. Ten years later Franklin will purchase the equipment for the production of lampblack.

1730

1732 Benjamin Franklin establishes his own printing press, and starts writing, printing, and publishing, under the pseudonym of Richard Saunders, his famous *Poor Richard's Almanac*. Rich in common-sense philosophy, he will print it until 1757 (for 1758), each edition of 10,000 copies.

1733 English engraver George Bickham publishes, in parts, *The Universal Penman*, one of the finest of the eighteenth-century writing manuals.

1734 William Caslon I issues his first specimen sheet, illustrating forty-seven of his typefaces, which included Arab, Greek, Hebrew, Sanskrit, Armenian, Aramaic, Sumerian and Syrian types. By this time his work is well known abroad.

1737 French type founder, punch-cutter, and type designer Pierre-Simon Fournier *le jeune* proposes a standard type measuring system based on an ideal unit, which he calls the "typographical point" (0.0137 in.). François-Ambroise Didot will later develop it in 1783.

1740

1740 The Haas'sche Schriftgießerei AG type foundry, in Basle, comes under the direction of the Haas family from Nuremberg. In 1800, under the management of Wilhelm Haas, it will become famous for its roman, italic, Gothic, and *schwabacher* typefaces, as well as for the cutting of *Caslon* and *Bodoni*. Under Eduard and Alfred Hoffmann, Max Miedinger will become in-house designer, designing *Helvetica* in 1957. In 1972, the firm will acquire the Deberny & Peignot type foundry, the Fonderie Olive, and Berthold & Stempel.

1742 Pierre-Simon Fournier *le jeune* prints his *Modèles des Caractères de l'Imprimerie et Autres Choses Nécessaires au Dit Art*, containing typographical vignettes, music types, an elegant roman, many alphabets with decorated capitals, and a profusion of printer's *fleurons*, much in a Rococo style. The latter will become standard equipment in every office in Europe and America. He was also able to cast different ruled lines up to 14 inches, and types up to 108 pts, the largest metal type yet made.

1744 In Philadelphia, Benjamin Franklin prints, on his own press, his best-known work, Marcus Tulius Cicero's *Cato Major*, set in *Caslon Old Face* type that he had imported from England.

1745-1800 By the middle of the 1740s, the Baroque and the Rococo styles have practically disappeared in England and France. A strong reaction against both these art expressions has given way to the establishment of Neoclassicism, which will later be seen in the absence of printer's ornaments, arabesques, and borders on the printed page. There is also an extended use of copper engraving which will definitely influence type design. This is also an Age of Reason: classical learning, ancient literary rules, reason, and common sense.

1750

1750-1899 Between these two dates, noticeable changes in the world's economic structures, produced by a transition from stable agriculture and commercial society to industrialism, will take place. The use of steam power, iron, and steel, and the introduction of electricity, petroleum, and gasoline will mark further

changes. Initiated in England, the first American manifestations will take place around 1821.

1751 French philosopher Denis Diderot publishes, *in folio*, the first volume of the *Encyclopédie, ou Dictionnaire raisonée des sciences, des arts et des métiers*, which was intended to be a complete guide to useful knowledge. The entire edition of twenty-eight volumes –seventeen of text and eleven of engraved plates– will be completed by 1776. The *Encyclopédie* represents the embodiment of the spirit of the Enlightenment, which will be greatly influential in freedom of thought, both religious and philosophical.

1757 In Birmingham, English writing master and printer John Baskerville prints his first book, a *quarto* edition of Virgil's *Bucolica, Georgica, et Æneis*, in which he uses his fine typeface (*Baskerville*), and his wove calendered paper. He also issues a type specimen sheet.

1760

1763 William Caslon I and his son William Caslon II print the first English book of type specimens, which includes fifty-six alphabets by him, and twenty-seven by his son, all designed between 1738 and 1763.

1765 Joseph Jackson and Thomas Cottrell, former apprentices at William Caslon's type foundry, publish the first *Twelve-line English romans* (two inches high) in their type catalog, an idea that will be copied by other founders.

1766 After two years of work, Pierre-Simon Fournier, *le jeune* publishes, *in 16mo* (1/16), a two-volume edition of his *Manuel Typographique*. Printed by Joseph-Gérard Barbou, it includes, in addition to his own decorated letters, specimen borders by Pierre-Simon Fournier, *l'aîné*, and others. He also offers his type in six variations of the normal roman –light, bold, condensed, etc., all in the same body, introducing to printers the concept of the type family. In 1768, he will design the first hand-tooled alphabets.

1768 Italian typographer, printer, and type-cutter Giambattista Bodoni, starts working for Ferdinand, Duke of Parma at the Stamperia Reale. Three years later, in 1771, he prints his first typographical work, *Fregi e Majuscole*, a small book which closely follows Pierre-Simon Fournier *le jeune* 's *Manuel Tipographique* both in size and typographical design.

1769 Scottish inventor James Watt improves the steam engine to enable rotary motion. This invention will change transportation and industrial activities, including printing. It will also be a definite starting point of the so-called Industrial Revolution in the 1770s and 1780s.

1769 In Killingsworth, Connecticut, Abel Buell establishes what may be the first American type foundry. There, in 1781, he designs, cuts, and casts the first roman type in the United States for certain Connecticut printers, who, because of the war with England, were not able to replenish their worn-out typefaces.

Although most printing presses were imported from England, Isaac Doolittle of New Haven builds one for William Goddard of Philadelphia. From here on, other manufacturers of presses and other articles of printing-house equipment will appear in America.

1770

1770 By this date there are at least a dozen printers in Boston. One of them is Isaiah Thomas, who will later found a paper mill.

1771 Punch-cutter to the Imprimerie Royal, Louis René Luce, and printer Jean Joseph-Gérard Barbou publish Luce's *Essai d'une nouvelle typographie*, with 93 plates, showing samples of type specimens, and typographic ornaments. His types are condensed, and the large sizes present a flat serif.

1771 Christopher Sauer *the younger* starts making excellent German (*Fraktur*) type for his own use, from matrices and molds he imported from Germany. His activity in type founding will indirectly influence the development of this industry in America. He trains Justus Fox and Jacob Bay, one of whom will cast a roman letter first used commercially in 1775. Fox will continue in his trade, and after the American Revolution, type founders from England and Scotland will make their way to Philadelphia.

1772 Up to now type presses have been made entirely of wood. Wilhelm Haas of Basle builds one where most of the parts are made of iron, including a larger platen, which will enable a sheet of paper to be impressed in a single pull.

1775-1783 The thirteen colonies on the Atlantic coast start a struggle for the independence of America from England. Differences of thought and interests between the colonies and England started in the middle of the eighteenth century. The Treaty of Paris (1783) will formally recognize the United States as a nation.

1775 The Pennsylvania Assembly urges local printers to use American-made types rather than the imported ones from England. The earliest known use of American type is found in *The Pennsylvania Mercury*, published by Story & Humphreys of Philadelphia.

1776 Mary Katherine Goddard of Baltimore prints the United States' *Declaration of Independence*, set in *Caslon Old Style*, America's most popular typeface.

1780

1780 Spanish printer Joaquín Ibarra, court printer to Carlos III, prints a four-volume edition of Miguel de Cervantes's *Don Quixote de la Mancha* in Madrid, *in quarto*. He will have a great influence on raising the standard of printing both in Spain and in Europe. The type was designed by Gerónimo Gil, and produced for the Biblioteca Real.

Henry Johnson of London patents a method of casting several letters as a unit, known as a *logotype*.

1780 During the 1780s and 1790s, printing will go to Mississippi, Tennessee, Ohio, and Michigan.

1783 French printer and typographer François-Ambroise Didot establishes Didot's measuring system, based on Pierre-Simon Fournier *le jeune*'s point system proposed in 1737, and since that moment will be used in Europe. Didot divided the *pied du roi* in twelve French inches, each of which would contain 72 pts. He also introduces today's custom of identifying type sizes by their point body measure rather than by a given name.

1783 It may be assumed that by this time, each important inland town in America has its own printing press.

1784 French type founder and printer François-Ambroise Didot publishes Torcuato Tasso's *La Gerusalemme liberata*, which is the first presentation of what will later be known as *Modern* style letterforms. The preceding year, the type (*Didot*) had been cut by his second son, Firmin, just nineteen. His reduction of the alphabet to a relationship of thick and thin, vertical and horizontal elements will permit a complete departure from a classical conception of letterforms towards a new approach to typeface design.

1785 Benjamin Franklin establishes a type foundry in Philadelphia, with his grandson, which will not be too successful. Before coming to America he purchased a complete foundry from Pierre-Simon Fournier *le jeune* that would arrive in 1786, plus special tools. The pica, used since then as the standard type measure, was based upon the tools he imported. Unfortunately, French types did not receive much public acceptance in this country.

Isaiah Thomas, the eminent printer of Worcester, Massachusetts, imports "the best types obtainable" from the Caslon, Fry, and Wilson type foundries in England and Scotland. Other type sources came from Europe.

1787 With the arrival and settling of Scotsmen John Baine and his grandson in Philadelphia, who had a complete foundry and *A Specimen of Printing Types*, printed in Scotland, American type founding is established as a permanent industry.

By this time, there are ninety paper mills working in America. The Pennsylvania mills (sixty) alone produce 70,000 reams of paper annually.

1788 Giambattista Bodoni publishes, *in quarto*, his 360-page *Manuale Tipografico*, containing 100 roman, 50 italic, and 28 Greek lowercase fonts. The typeface he uses, known today as *Bodoni*, influenced by Firmin Didot's design, will spread the *Modern* style. Nevertheless, the serifs in his types are not as flat as those found in Didot's typefaces. This will be a peculiarity of modern versions of *Bodoni*.

1789-1799 The French Revolution begins with the storming of the Bastille. It will last until 1799 with Napoleon Bonaparte's *coup d'etat* and his taking control.

1789 English artist, engraver, and poet William Blake prints his book *Songs of Innocence*,

a work produced in monochrome etchings in which he combines type and image. Afterwards, it was hand colored with watercolor, or printed, thus charged with a lyrical fantasy that will innovate the art of illustrating, even though this is a unique and personal work.

1790

1790 English wood engraver Thomas Bewick publishes his *General History of Quadrupeds*, which brings renown to him and his wood engraver's technique. This will remain a major illustration method until the advent of photomechanical halftones around 1885.

The Englishman William Martin, trained as a type founder by his brother Robert Martin, who had worked at William Baskerville's printing shop, cuts his typeface *Bulmer*, based on Baskerville's design. In 1925-1926, Morris Fuller Benton will redesign this typeface, although it will not be issued until 1928.

After working for twenty-two years with Duke Ferdinand of Parma's Stamperia Reale, Giambattista Bodoni is invited by the Spanish Minister to the Papal Court to direct a series of classics. This will permit him to be recognized as printer and type designer.

The metric system is developed in France thanks to Laplace, Lagrange, and Lavoisier. It will be put into practice in 1799.

1791 Giambattista Bodoni prints a *folio* edition of Horace's works. The typography is formal, austere, and free of decoration. The text type, the equivalent of an 18-pt typeface, is widely spaced between lines. Two years later he will publish a two-volume Virgil. Beautiful as they are, the works lack scholarship.

1795 French engraver and type founder Firmin Didot develops the stereotype duplicating method that will be finished by Claude Genoux in 1829. Stereotyping will save type from wear, and make it possible to set an entire book before printing. It will also allow reprinting at will.

1796 Czech playwright and inventor, Aloysius (or Aloys) Senefelder finally succeeds in making an image on stone with ink mixture inventing the lithographic printing process. Two years later, he will design a workable press for printing. The new medium, which offers an unlimited number of impressions, will open an extraordinary field for illustration, calligraphy, and experimental display typography. It will also provide a full integration of pictures and texts.

1796 Binny & Ronaldson (perhaps the first permanent type foundry in the States) founded in Philadelphia by two Scotsmen, Archibald Binny and James Ronaldson, issues *Roman No.1*, cut by Archibald Binny, considered the first American type design. Based on the *Baskerville* cut by William Martin, who had worked with Baskerville, *Roman No.1* will be later recast in 1892 as *Oxford*, and used by Daniel Berkeley Updike in the printing of his book, *Printing Types: Their History, Forms, and Use* (1922). The press equipment employed by Binny & Ronaldson had been bought from Benjamin Franklin.

1797 Spanish painter Francisco de Goya prints the *Caprichos*, which represents one of the great graphic achievements of eighteenth-century intaglio printing (etching and aquatint).

1800

1800 French printer and type founder Pierre Didot *l'aîné*, oldest son of François-Ambroise Didot, prints the French Constitution using the typeface (*Didot*) engraved by his brother Firmin.

Charles Mahon, 3rd Earl of Stanhope, designs an all-iron press that is used at the John Boydell and George Nicol's Shakespeare Printing Office in London, where printer William Bulmer and type-cutter William Martin worked.

Gaslight is introduced thanks to English inventor, William Murdock. It will bring great advantages to working and social conditions until the advent of electric light in 1879.

1803 Aloys Senefelder succeeds in adapting his lithographic press to metal plates, by means of suitable graining. He also travels to England and prints a book with lithographs.

The first machine for the manufacturing of continuous rolls of paper, conceived by Saint-Léger Didot (son of punch-cutter and founder Pierre-François Didot) and Nicolas Louis Robert, is built by Brian Donkin in England, subsidized by Henry and Sealy Fourdrinier –hence the name of the machine. This invention will provide a true development in the printing industry as well as the use of large formats in newspapers as well as in posters. The first Fourdrinier paper machine, producing a sixty-inch paper, will arrive in New York in 1827.

English type founder Robert Thorne, apprentice to printer Thomas Cottrell, designs the first fat faces. Derived from the modern-face types of the late 18th century, they will be the first types specifically designed for the printer of posters and handbills.

1805 The first successful stereotype duplicating process is employed at Cambridge University, England, in the printing of the *New Testament*. The invention is credited to Charles Mahon, 3rd Earl of Stanhope, who, after devising a more sensitive method, using plaster, had introduced the process in this country in 1804.

1808 Printing has moved west of the Mississippi to St. Louis. Thus, as migration will continue west, printing will follow.

1809 Binny & Ronaldson type foundry issues *A Specimen of Metal Ornaments Cast at the Letter Foundry of Binny and Ronaldson*, equally considered as the first known metal type

specimen in the United States. It will also cast the first dollar sign ($), driving out the old-fashioned long *ſ* (for shillings) from American typography.

1810

1810 Steel engraving is also introduced for the making of bank notes. In 1823, it will be adopted for book illustration. But if it provided the printer with the ability to print larger editions, it did not make it possible to print larger editions cheaply. This was the age when long print runs needed to satisfy the tastes of the new middle class were of primary concern to printers.

Isaiah Thomas prints his scholarly book in two volumes, *The History of Printing in America*, which also includes European printing history.

1812 Binny & Ronaldson type foundry issues a second type catalog, *Specimen of Printing Types*, where they introduce one of the first American type designs, *Roman No.1*, recreated by Linotype as *Monticello*, and used by Theodore Low De Vinne in his book *Historic Printing Types* (1886).

Immigrant Scottish printer David Bruce, Sr., introduces stereotyping into the United States, which he brings from England, establishing the first American stereotyping firm in New York.

1813 The celebrated *Columbian Iron Press*, designed by George Clymer, of Philadelphia, appears in its final stage. The press will also be manufactured in England.

David Bruce Sr. founds the New York Type Foundry, and will be one of the first to propose the use of arithmetical progression in type sizes rather than the haphazard designations used up to that moment. His son, David Bruce, Jr., will be cutting typefaces by 1820. Throughout 1834, other type foundries will employ him. In 1902, one of his fonts will be adapted for Monotype composition by Sol Hess, as *Bruce Old Style*.

1814 The *Times* of London is the first newspaper to be printed on the Friedrich Koenig flatbed, steam-power cylinder press (1,100 c.p.h.), marking the beginning of modern printing. It will also provide ready-made circulation for commercial announcements and private advertisements.

1815 English type founder Vincent Figgins shows the first *Egyptian* (slab-serif) typefaces under the name of *antique*, as well as the earliest shaded type and the first *Tuscan* style typefaces. Though these innovations will influence the appearance of multiple variations in type design, it will not be until 1821 that William Thorowgood will first name the former typefaces as *Egyptians* in his specimen book.

1816 English type founder William Caslon IV introduces the first sans serif type in his type catalog under the name of *English Egyptian*. In 1832, Vincent Figgins will first name these designs as sans serifs typefaces.

1818 Five years after Giambattista Bodoni's death, his widow, assisted by his shop foreman, Luigi Orsi, finishes a second

two-volume edition of Bodoni's *Manuale Tipografico*, a work which had been started by Bodoni himself, with a note on the master's lifework. It contains roman and italic, Greek, gothic, Asian, and Russian fonts, lines, borders, symbols, numbers and musical notations.

In Paris manufacturer Pierre Lorilleux founds the first industrial establishment specialized in producing printing inks for fast mechanical presses. They will be used by *The Times* of London at a speed of 7,000 impressions per hour.

James Blake, John Stephenson, and William Garnett buy William Caslon IV's type foundry, establishing Stephenson, Blake & Co. in 1819. In 1905, they will also buy the typefaces of Edmund Fry and William Thorowgood foundries. Among the types they will issue are *Chisel, Playbill, Windsor, Egyptian Expanded, Fry's Baskerville*, and *Fry's Ornamented*.

In Paris, Aloys Senefelder installs a lithographic workshop. Honoré Daumier, Gustave Doré, and Jules Dupré soon take advantage of the new medium. He also publishes a *Complete Manual of Stone Printing*, which has remained a basic text on the subject.

1819 Pierre Didot *l'aîné* publishes his type *Spécimen des Nouveaux Caractères*, with Firmin Didot's *Normande* typefaces. It will influence most of the nineteenth century typographers.

Ink rollers, made of molasses, glue and tar, invented by French chemist Jean-Nicolas Gannal, begin to replace the old pelt balls that had been used for inking type from the earliest days of typography.

1820

1820 Pierre Didot *l'aîné* (François-Ambroise Didot's oldest son) cuts his *Floriated Capitals*.

English type founder William Thorowgood acquires Robert Thorne's foundry, establishing himself as an independent type founder, issuing the following year *A New Specimen of Printing Types*, in which he names for the first time the slab-serif types as *Egyptian* typefaces.

The uncontrolled putting up of posters and signs disfigure house fronts and walls more and more from this date up to the 1830s. This will eventually end with the establishment of regulated spaces in the 1840s.

1821 Around this time the first manifestations of the Industrial Revolution begin to appear in the American printing industry.

1822 French Egyptologist Jean-François Champollion finally deciphers the hieroglyphic texts of the *Rosetta Stone*, which had been erected in 195 B.C. to honor Ptolemy Epiphanes. The stone, found in 1799 in the Nile Delta, was written in Egyptian hieroglyphs, demotic script, and Greek.

The *Albion Press*, constructed in London by Richard W. Cope, as well as the American *Columbian* and *Washington* letterpresses, the latter perfected by Samuel Rust, become the basic equipment for all nineteenth-century job printing. English designer William Morris will print his works, at the Kelmscott Press on an *Albion Press*.

1823 Jonas Booth of New York prints *Abridgment of Murray's English Grammar*, by Lindley Murray, considered the first book printed on a steam-power press in America.

The *New York Advertisers* is the first American newspaper to use a steam-driven press, an improved model of the one used by the *Times* of London.

1827 Darius Wells starts manufacturing wood type on a commercial scale for use on posters. Different from other typographers using wood type, he uses end grain wood that is more resistant and permits greater detail. The following year he will issue his first wood type specimen book, marking the beginning of the American wood type industry.

1828 American scholar Noah Webster publishes *An American Dictionary of the English Language* (2 vols.), in which he proposes reforms for American spelling, such as center, color, and theater. To this day it is still the standard American dictionary.

The Andrew Jackson presidential campaign marks a turning point in the use of objects and images both as commemorative tokens, and for persuasive or propagandistic purposes.

After nineteen years of work, the Cherokee Indian Sequoyah finishes an alphabet that would transform his native culture. Edited in Georgia by Elias Boudinot, *The Cherokee Phoenix* appears as the first Indian newspaper.

Lithography is introduced into America by Barnett and Doolittle.

1829 Samuel Rust introduces the *Washington Hand Press* that uses a lever rather than a torsion screw. This improvement will make it one of the most commonly used early presses.

1830

1830 German Schelter & Giesecke type foundry issues the first sans serif font with a lowercase alphabet.

1830 From this moment and into the 1880s, wood type posters and broadsides will flourish in America and Europe.

The numerous technical and mechanical advancements, such as the use of the Fourdrinier paper making machine, the mechanical casters, and the steam-driven presses, will eventually lead to the development of web presses and the mass production of newspapers (the *New York Sun*, 1833; the *New York Herald*, 1835; the *New York Tribune*, 1841; the *New York Times*, 1851).

Isaac and Seth Adams of Boston, invent the *Adams Press*, a mechanical platen press, which will remain a favorite in America for fifty years. Almost 90 percent of the printing of good books and magazines will be done on them.

English immigrant John Sartain, portrait engraver, magazine illustrator, and publisher, introduces in Philadelphia the mezzotint engraving technique. *Graham's Magazine* will be one of the first magazines to display his work commercially in 1841.

1831 American physicist Joseph Henry develops the electric motor, thanks to the investigations of Englishman Michael Faraday. It will permit present and future inventions involved with printing to be easier to manage and more productive.

1832 English type founder Vincent Figgins issues his type catalog, *Specimens of Printing Types*, in which he introduces the term *sans serif* and the wide use of sans serif typefaces, including outline versions.

1833 On November 26, John Calhoun starts setting type for the *Chicago Democrat*, before the settlement became a city.

The first penny newspaper, the *New York Sun*, founded by Ben Day, appears in Manhattan as a competitive news medium for the "six-penny" newspapers sold by subscription. With these newspapers, there appears the concept of "news" as we know it today.

1834 William Leavenworth makes a solid contribution to the mechanical end of the wood type manufacturing trade by adapting the pantograph to the router. He is also credited with introducing the condensed concept in typeface design.

1835 Between this date and 1850, Prussian educator Friedrich Froebel works with a kindergarten teaching system he calls *Gifts and Occupations* in which he relies on the use of basic volumetric forms and colors as a way to develop sensitivity in children's perception and construction. His teaching method will later be implemented in the Bauhaus school basic courses, which with time will become one of their greatest legacies on art and design education. It is known that Frank Lloyd Wright, Wassily Kandinsky, Walter Gropius, and Le Corbusier were educated according to Froebel's method, attesting to its future impact on their work.

1836 German lithographer Gottfried Engelman perfects *chromolithographie*, the first successful method for stone printing in various colors. His son, Jean, will develop the technique in Paris. The first illustrations will appear in English books around 1839.

1836 The *New York Herald* is forced by advertisers to ban the use of display type, considering it disloyal competition for those who cannot afford to exceed the traditional one-column width ads.

1837 Alexandrina Victoria becomes Queen of England, and with her there starts a period of sixty-four years known as the *Victorian Era*. This period will be characterized by the development of photography, lithography, chromolithography, mechanical type composition systems, as well as private press movements, and Gothic and Greco-Roman style revivals in architecture and art. It will also be characterized by the Industrial Revolution.

The electrotyping method for duplicating printing forms is perfected, permitting the use of the same typesetting on various presses simultaneously.

German punch-cutter and type founder Johann Christian Bauer founds the Bauersche Giesserei, which will become the largest type foundry in Germany. In 1898, the new owner, Georg Hartmann, foresees the need for new type designs as a way to compete with mechanical composition, and requests designs from Friedrich Kleukens and Emil Rudolf Weiss. In 1916, the firm will buy the Heinrich Flinsch type foundry with fonts by F. H. Ehmcke and Lucian Bernhard. After 1927, Paul Renner, Imre Reiner, Heinrich Jost, and Max Caflisch will design for them.

1837 Samuel Morse develops the **Morse code**, a telegraph alphabet whereby letters are replaced by a system of dots and dashes, and words are represented by combinations of these symbols.

1838 Printer George F. Nesbitt publishes the second wood type specimen book in the United States, with over 225 type styles and sizes, including the first chromatic types, and various sans serif typefaces.

A Scottish printer, David Bruce, Jr., builds and patents the first commercially successful typecasting machine which produces 100 type characters per hour.

1839 French inventor Louis Jacques Daguerre discovers a method for making and fixing photographic images on silver plates, called the *daguerreotype*. This year, English Henry Fox Talbot also discovers the same principle, obtaining his first paper negative in 1841.

1839 The first self-inking treadle platen press, is designed and built by Stephen Ruggles, offering easy displacement to small printers. He will present an improved model in 1851.

1840

1840 During this decade, ornamental type becomes increasingly important in America and Europe.

Zinc is already used for simple line cuts.

1840 English painter William Sharp introduces chromolithography in America, giving birth to a popular industry of posters, book illustrations, advertisements, and calendars in Boston. It will also bring art to the middle class.

1841 The first electrotype plate is used in *Mape's Magazine* in New York. Joseph A. Adams, a wood engraver connected with *Harper's Magazine*, is responsible for its invention and early use in America.

John L. Hooper, who worked as advertising solicitor for *The New York Tribune*, establishes his own advertising office working as an intermediary between newspapers and advertisers.

1845 English engraver Benjamin Fox, of the London firm, W. Thorowgood & Besley, designs and cuts the first *Clarendon* style typeface. Although it was registered, once the ownership rights expired three years later, the design was widely copied and sold to others.

British architect and designer Owen Jones introduces Moorish ornament to Western design in his book, *Plans, Elevations, Sections, and Details of the Alhambra* (1836-1845), printed by himself in chromolithography.

1845 The first electrotype matrix is made by Thomas and Edwin Starr of Philadelphia and used in the type foundry of James Connor of New York. Starr's process largely replaces the cutting of steel punches in type foundries, especially in the case of display type.

1846 With the introduction of *papier-mâché*, stereotyping is widely used to reproduce type and images, providing the first means of retaining entire pages to reprint at will.

1846 Richard M. Hoe builds the first rotary letterpress, the *Mammoth*. Type is held on the cylinder rather than on a flat bed, and printing could reach up to 8,000 sheets per hour. He will later make these machines practical through the introduction of curved stereotype plates. With the setting of these presses in Paris and London (the *Times*), they will become the world's chief newspaper presses.

Hoe perfects the rotary lithographic press with the use of flexible metal sheets in place of stones. Although conventional stone lithographic printing continues, he will make lithography a commercially viable process. By 1860, there will be sixty firms, and by 1890, seven hundred firms. The art of lettering and the creation of the lettering profession will also result, in part, from the freedom of expression provided by this medium. Early poster images will generally be related to circuses, theater, and burlesque shows.

After designing a second model of the typecasting machine, David Bruce, Jr., establishes his own type foundry, using eight of these machines. The company will be later absorbed by ATF. His work, *History of Typefounding in the United States*, will be published posthumously.

1847 Art collector James Lenox brings to America the first *Gutenberg Bible*, reflecting a new interest in and appreciation for historical printing.

1848 John Everett Millais, William Holman, and Dante Gabriel Rossetti found the English Pre-Raphaelite Brotherhood. Being against the Industrial Revolution, they will set out in search of a medieval world that never existed. Their work will influence Edward Burne-Jones and William Morris.

1848 Platt R. Spencer develops a particular calligraphic technique for lettering known as *Spencerian script*. In 1852, he will establish the Spencerian College in Kingsville, Ohio.

1850

1850 By this date, the first mechanized lithographic press with a cylinder, flannel covered rollers for wetting, and rollers for inking is perfected.

French lithographer and photoengraver Charles Guillot makes the first etched relief plate or *"guillotage"* for letterpress of high enough quality. Nevertheless, the chief means of reproduction, wood engraving, metal engraving, and lithography will continue in use.

1850 Between this date and 1887, four monthly magazines of deservedly high reputation will begin publication: *Harper's Monthly Magazine* (1850), *Atlantic Monthly* (1857), *Century Illustrated Monthly Magazine* (1880), and *Scribner's Magazine* (1887).

1851 *The Great Exhibition of the Works of Industry of All Nations* opens at the Crystal Palace in Hyde Park, London. Designer and architect Owen Jones is appointed Superintendent of the Works as decorator and designer.

In Amsterdam, Dutch type founder Nicolaas Tetterode founds the Typefoundry Amsterdam, which, with time, will become one of the largest type manufacturers in the world. Among the typeface designers who will design for them are Sjoerd H. De Roos, Stefan Schlesinger, and Dick Dooijes.

1854 The first exhibition of Japanese art takes place at the International Exhibition in London, creating a great interest for Japanese woodcuts and their use of flat color areas. A second exhibition at the World's Fair in Paris in 1878 will spark a real cult for all Japanese things.

1854 After trying to market his product in England, Hugh Burgess immigrates to the States, where he patents and establishes the first wood pulp paper mill in Pennsylvania. Its stronger quality and easier management will make it very popular in newspaper web printing. The first newspaper to use it will be the *Boston Weekly Journal* in 1863.

1856 Owen Jones issues his work *Grammar of Ornament* (100 plates), with Day & Sons as publishers. This encyclopedic work on decoration from all periods and countries will be recognized internationally as the first comprehensive work on the subject.

German type founder Christian Emil Weber establishes the Weber type foundry in Stuttgart. The foundry program will be eventually taken over by D. Stempel AG foundry in Frankfurt. Among the type designers that will design for them are Georg Trump, Willy Schaefer, Peter A. Demeter, and F.H. Ernst Schneidler.

1857 The *Times* of London uses the first curved stereotype plates, thanks to the Italian James Dellagana who finally makes a successful plate from a papier-mâché mold. He will later patent the invention in 1861, when the *New York Times* uses it.

1858 In Berlin, German type founder Hermann Berthold founds the Institut für Galvano-Typie. In 1865 it will open as H. Berthold AG, developing as the largest type foundry in the world. In 1878, Berthold will establish a unit of measure for type that will be adopted by all German type foundries. Among the designers who will work for them are Günter Gerhard Lange, Herbert Post, Imre Reiner, and Georg Trump.

In Vienna, Alois Auer patents a press for printing newspapers from a continuous roll of paper. William Bullock will develop this idea in America by 1863.

1859 William Hamilton Page presents, in his wood type catalog of *Ornamented Clarendons*, an extensive set of type designs and a variety of ornaments, all with excellent quality in the cutting.

1860

1860 French engineer Henri Voirin is commissioned to construct a two-cylinder lithographic press for printing on metal, through the previous transporting of the image onto a rubber-covered cylinder, later known as offset lithography.

1861-1865 The American Civil War, brought about by the attempt of the Southern states (the Confederacy) to secede from the Northern states (the Union), marks a defining period in American industrial development.

1861 Although photography serves to document war for the first time, images cannot be translated into a type-compatible medium. Images not only have to be interpreted by means of wood engravings, but true war documents, in the absence of fast exposure film, are reduced to still scenes, landscapes, architecture, stiff portraits, posed groups, and corpses. *Frank Leslie's Illustrated Newspaper* (1855) and *Harper's Weekly* (1857), among others, have to depend on illustrated interpretations to present war activity.

The *New York Tribune* starts printing from curved stereotyped plates, the first used in America.

By this time there are twenty advertising agencies in New York, and ten more in other cities.

President Abraham Lincoln appoints Darius Wells postmaster of Paterson, New Jersey, a post that he will hold until 1874, one year before his death.

1865 English writer and mathematician Lewis Carroll publishes *Alice in Wonderland*, illustrated by Sir John Tenniel, innovating typographical handling through the introduction of the mouse-tail type composition.

1865 By the end of the American Civil War, there are 275 advertising agencies, which employ people to paste billboards and paint signs on buildings, barns, rocks, or whatever flat surface they may find. Web printing and lithography allows temporary fences, lampposts, and façades to be practically covered by printed matter.

William Bullock of Philadelphia invents the first rotary press that prints both sides of a continuous roll of paper at the same time, through the use of curved stereotyped plates. By 1866, the press will print 20,000 complete newspapers in one hour.

1866 French poster artist Jules Chéret returns to Paris after working as a poster and book cover designer between 1859 and 1866 in London. There he had also learned the new technique of chromolithography. Perfume manufacturer Eugène Rimmel finances the setting of a lithographic press with modern machines, and Chéret designs a new series of French colored posters, introducing the big English poster format as well. With time, he will design more than a thousand posters, which will provide him with an opportunity to experiment with different proportions.

The Holy Bible, with illustrations by Gustave Doré, French illustrator, is printed in English, in London and New York. His 229 wood engravings are reproduced in parts, using the electrotype reproduction system.

French Hyppolyte Marinoni completes his first high-speed rotary press, which prints on both sides of the paper.

1866 Thomas Mackellar, of Mackellar, Smiths, and Jordan type foundry, Philadelphia, starts editing *The American Printer*, a practical manual with valuable information on type founding in the United States.

1867 *Harper's Bazaar*, the monthly magazine for women, is founded in New York. Sold to Randolph Hearst in 1913, it will gain reputation for innovative editorial design. Fashion designer Erté was contracted, in 1924, to do covers and fashion illustration, and Alexei Brodovitch, in 1934, as art director. In 1959, under Henry Wolf, the magazine will introduce new conventions in photography, typography, and page layout.

1868 Printer Christopher Lathan Sholes perfects the typewriter that is mass-produced by E. Remington & Sons, former gun makers. Although his model has no lowercase letters, Remington will produce a typewriter with a shift key that will make it possible to move easily from upper to lowercase letters in 1878. Sholes is also credited with the "Universal" keyboard, which will be adopted by the Lanston Monotype Machine Company for their type composing machines around 1908.

1869 French physicist, chemist, and inventor Louis Ducos de Hauron discovers the principle of three-color reproduction through the use of halftone plates. The original subject is photographed three times with the use of three color filters: blue, green and red. The plates are then printed in yellow, magenta, and blue-green. He will later invent stereoscopic printing by printing an image in two complementary colors (red and green).

1869 In Philadelphia, Francis Wayland Ayer founds the first main advertising agency and names it after his father, N. W. Ayer & Son. It will also be the first agency to hire copywriters and art directors, and the first to install a public relations department.

1870

1870 The technique of making line blocks or cuts on zinc, using photography, is well advanced by this date.

1870 The Metropolitan Museum of Art in New York and the Museum of Fine Arts in Boston are both founded this year.

The printing of *ephemera* has fully evolved as a creative form with a great variety of decorative typefaces. American wood type manufacturers not only dominate both their own and the European market, but also since 1850, they have devised most of their own styles, far superior in design and execution than the Europeans.

Printer Oscar H. Harper publishes *Typography*, the first specimen book in America that shows the firm's achievement in design for ephemeral printing, with different borders and ornaments often printed in various colors.

From this year up until 1910, advertising agencies will change from space selling to full-service businesses. Art departments will begin to supply design, illustration, lettering, package design, and photography, among others, to clients. By 1875, staff artists will be supplemented with freelance workers.

1871 Around this time, thanks to the English physician Richard Leach Maddox, film exposure has been reduced to 1/100 of a second, making instant photography possible. This characteristic will change photographic documents completely.

1871 Following the establishment of the Harvard University Press, many universities in the United States will organize their own publishing departments: The University of Chicago (1891); Columbia University (1893); The University of California (1893); Princeton University (1905); and Yale University (1908).

The Chicago fire destroys, among other things, the city type foundries. Marder, Luse & Company type foundry, starting anew, decides to establish the 12-pt pica system of Mackellar, Smiths and Jordan type foundry, Philadelphia, as their standard type measurement. This initial activity will influence the American Type Founders Association to consider the use of a standard point system for the United States.

Photoengraving is commercially practical for letterpress printing. By 1880, it will be replacing wood engravings.

1874 William Hamilton Page leads the typographic field with such works as his *Chromatic Wood Types* catalog, full of original designs. Many of the alphabets are designed so that one color will overlap another, creating a third color. It is the most expensive wood type catalog and the most beautiful ever done.

1875 In London, Robert Barclay first practices offset printing, for printing on tin plate. Barclay prints from flat lithographic stones on the surface of a cylinder covered with special cardboard and from it onto sheets of metal. A few years later, he will replace the cardboard blanket with one made of rubber-coated canvas. By 1889, many metal-box decorators will be implementing this process. Nevertheless, the real significance of the offset principle will not come until 1904, when American lithographer Ira W. Rubel will apply it to printing on paper.

1875 Around this time the American Aesthetic movement, inspired by English reformer John Ruskin's ideas, takes form. Various magazines, such as *Art Amateur*, *Art Interchange*, and *Crayon* will carry his message reevaluating the value of applied arts.

1876 Belgian printer Edouard Moretus donates his type collection to the ville d'Anvers that will become the Plantin-Moretus Museum.

1876 According to the *American Printer*, there are twenty-four type foundries in the United States by this time, located in New York (7), Boston (3), Philadelphia (3), Baltimore (2), Cincinnati (2), California (2), Buffalo (1), Chicago (1), St. Louis (1), Milwaukee (1), and Richmond (1).

1878 Around this time, the Arts and Crafts movement begins in England, initiated by artist, poet, and designer William Morris, much influenced by the philosophy of Socialist reformer John Ruskin. Their books will spur the establishment of private presses in America.

Italian type founder Giovanni Nebiolo acquires G. Nazzarino's type foundry in Turin, and in 1880, the brothers Lazzaro and Giuseppe Levi join the company that will be renamed Nebiolo and Companie. Among the designers who will work with this company are Alessandro Butti and Aldo Novarese.

German inventor Karl Klietsch develops the photogravure printing process. By 1894, he will succeed in combining photogravure and doctor blade printing in the process known as intaglio printing.

1879 Thomas Alva Edison invents the incandescent light bulb, replacing gas light (1800), and initiating the era of electric illumination.

1880

1880 In Rochester, George Eastman starts industrially manufacturing the first gelatin dry photographic plates.

Stephen H. Horgan develops the first halftone printing process for reproducing a photograph. On March 4th, *A Scene in Shantytown* appears in *The New York Daily Graphic* newspaper, but he will not completely develop the process until 1897.

1881 Paris magazine *L'Illustration* prints the first photomechanical color illustrations in its Christmas issue.

German inventor Georg Meisenbach invents the line reproduction process, obtaining a patent in Germany and England in 1882.

1881 Theodore Low De Vinne starts printing *The Century Magazine* in his Theodore Low De Vinne Press. As the publishers demanded better quality in printing, De Vinne will install heavier presses, will use coated paper (not known before and specially manufactured for him), fine-line wood engravings, and halftone plates, which will make him a leading printer in the United States.

1882 Scottish architect and furniture designer Arthur Heygate Macmurdo founds the Century Guild, an Arts and Crafts movement with a less conspicuous medieval approach than that of William Morris and his future Kelmscott Press work. The cover for his book, *Wren's City Churches* (1883), and his symbol for the Guild (1884), will anticipate the Art Nouveau style.

1883 The Barnhart Brothers & Spindler type foundry, Chicago, is established under this name by the end of the year. In 1886, they will start publishing their in-house publication, *The Type-Founder*, which will continue up to 1908.

The Inland Printer starts publication in Chicago. In its first issues, it will address topics in design, layout, and illustration. It will become a leader in magazine design and the first one to change its cover design from issue to issue, at the suggestion of William Bradley, who will start doing them in 1894.

1884 The first volume of *The Oxford English Dictionary*, the most famous English dictionary, is published through a financial arrangement with Clarendon Press. Letter Z will be finished in 1928.

The *Times* of London introduces the electric printing press.

1884 Theodore L. De Vinne and Robert Hoe, among others, found the Grolier Club, a bibliophile institution. Bertram G. Goodhue will be the architect of the clubhouse, and a very active member of the Publications Committee.

1885 The Fundición Tipográfica Neufville is founded in Barcelona, after the Kramer & Fuchs Company buys the Ramírez y Rialp type foundry in the same city. Jacob de Neufville is the foundry manager. In 1971, the Neufville foundry will take over the Fundición Tipográfica Nacional founded in 1915.

1885 Linn Boyd Benton finishes his automatic punch-cutter machine through an improvement of the pantograph-router (1834). His invention will contribute to the outcome of the Linotype hot metal composing system in the production of matrices, two years later. It will also innovate in the production of foundry type.

The extensive violation of type patents, lost battles with advertising agencies, technological advancements, and the final lifting of uniform prices, will make many foundries in the United States go bankrupt.

Frederic Ives of Philadelphia invents a halftone screen for the reproduction of photographs by positioning two ruled-glass screens at right angles. The integration of text and image, in the printing process, is finally achieved.

1886 German immigrant Ottmar Mergenthaler satisfactorily demonstrates his hot metal type composing machine at the office of Whitelaw Reid, editor of the *New York Tribune*. Upon seeing it, Reid exclaimed: "*Ottmar, you've done it! A line o' type.*"

The United States Type Founders' Association adopts the American Point System (pica system), and types are identified by their point size. Not until 1898 will the English type founders adopt this point system.

Theodore Low De Vinne publishes his book *Historic Printing Types*, using James Ronaldson typeface *Roman No.1* (1812), now known as *Monticello*.

1887 Tolbert Lanston finishes the Monotype Composing Machine and the Casting Machine. Presented at the World's Columbian Exposition

in Chicago in 1893, he will start their production in Philadelphia in 1894.

The first book composed on the Linotype composing machine, *The Tribune Book of Open Air Sports*, is published and given by the *New York Tribune* to its subscribers. A note stating that the printing had been accomplished "without type" is included.

The William Hamilton Page Wood Type Company announces the production of a "New Process Wood Type" through the use of a die-cutting process.

1888 The English Arts and Crafts Exhibition Society starts activities, and English Socialist and printer Emery Walker gives an important conference on medieval manuscripts and letterpress printing, which will influence William Morris in the installment of the Kelmscott Press in 1891. Its first president, illustrator, and designer, Walter Crane, plays an active role in spreading the arts and crafts activities in Europe and in America.

1888 The Riverside Press is founded by Henry Houghton in Cambridge, Massachusetts, as a subsidiary of the publishing firm Houghton, Mifflin & Co. of Boston. The press employs Daniel Berkeley Updike for two years, and in 1896, Bruce Rogers will be appointed director of the press until it closes in 1911.

Henry Barth, president of the Cincinnati Type Foundry, invents the automatic type caster which not only cast the type, but breaks off the jets, ploughs grooves to form the feet, cuts four trimmed edges on each character at the mold/matrix interface, and delivers them in line ready for inspection. He and his son will be incorporated into ATF after its formation in 1892. His machine will later be improved by Linn Boyd Benton after Barth's death in 1905.

Brothers Max and Louis Levy of Philadelphia perfect Frederic Ives's halftone screen (1885-1886) by making finer lines with a ruling machine, etching them on glass, and filling them with black resin. The two sheets are then cemented together crosswise to make tiny clear openings. This is a direct step towards halftone reproduction and three-color separation. Copper will be preferred for halftone reproduction because of its lower price and more controllable etching qualities.

With the introduction of the *Kodak* camera and flexible film the following year, George Eastman will permit the taking of many photographs without reloading.

1889 The Linotype Company, Ltd. is founded as a manufacturing firm in Manchester, England. The first models will be installed in the offices of the *Newcastle Chronicle* (1889), the *Leeds Mercury* (1890), and in the *Globe of London* (1892). Within four years, there will be more than 250 composing machines working in this country.

1890

1890 H. J. Heinz, a nationwide manufacturing company of preserved, packed, ready-to-serve foods, is one of the first companies to build large

electric signs in New York City. These signs also mark the appearance of environmental graphics.

1891 English artist, poet, and designer William Morris founds the Kelmscott Press in Hammersmith, London, in close association with Emery Walker. By the time it will close in 1898, the press will have published fifty-three books of 200-300 copies each. Morris's typefaces *Golden Type* (1890), *Troy* (1891), and *Chaucer* (1892), all cut by Edward Prince, will also have great influence on those who follow his printing ideas.

French painter Henri de Toulouse-Lautrec designs his first of thirty-one lithographic posters that he will do during his life, in order to present Moulin Rouge's new star *La Goulone*. With its large flat color areas, he gives birth to the contemporary poster.

1892 German type founder Karl Klingspor founds the Klingspor type foundry in Offenbach, Germany. The first type issued will be a *schwabacher* type cut by Heinz Koenig. Among the type designers for this foundry will be Otto Eckmann, Peter Behrens, Walter Tiemann, Rudolf Koch, Otto Hupp, Hans Bohn, and Emil Rudolf Weiss. The firm will be bought by D. Stempel AG in 1956.

By this time Scottish architect and designer Charles Rennie Mackintosh has developed a full Art Nouveau decorative style, using elongation, abstraction, and polychromatic rhythmic forms, much influenced by the work of Aubrey Beardsley and Jan Toorop, which will become known as the *Glasgow Style*. He will also be part of the Glasgow Four that will have a great influence on Scottish and Austrian designers.

1892 To avoid being taken over by the Monotype hot metal type composing system, the union of twenty-three type foundries consolidates to form the American Type Founders Company. When starting business and discarding duplications, it had about 750 series of distinctive typefaces. Henry Lewis Bullen is appointed joint manager of the New York branch.

In New York, Ernst Vogel and W. Kurtz print the first satisfactory three-color halftones.

1893 Thomas Cobden-Sanderson, English pioneer of the Arts and Crafts movement, installs the Doves Bindery that will become the Doves Press in 1900, founded in collaboration with printer Emery Walker.

1893 Daniel Berkeley Updike founds The Merrymount Press in Cambridge, Massachusetts. For it, architect Bertram Grosvenor Goodhue will design the *Merrymount* typeface in 1895.

The Dickinson Type Foundry, Boston (now part of ATF), inspired by the Arts and Crafts movement, starts a revival of fifteenth-century types by introducing *Jenson Oldstyle*, designed by Joseph W. Phinney.

The *New York Recorder* publishes the first color page, one week before the *New York World*, directed by Joseph Pulitzer.

The World's Columbian Exposition held in Chicago, which will help change the role of the museums in American culture, presents publications in quite a different way from those of previous years. The predominance of halftone photographs over illustration announces the death of chromolithography and the birth of the photographic book.

Tolbert Lanston exhibits the first Monotype Composing Machine at the Columbian World's Fair in Chicago. Monotype machines will start production the following year.

1894 Elkin Mathews and John Lane, with Aubrey Beardsley as art director, publish the English quarterly magazine, *The Yellow Book*, which will epitomize the Art Nouveau movement. The American edition, published by Stone & Kimball, will include works by William Bradley and Frank Hazenplug, among others.

Czechoslovakian graphic artist Alfons Mucha receives the commission to design a poster for Sarah Bernhard in *Gismonda*, which marks a turning point for him as a poster designer. His decorative style, known as *le style Mucha*, will be among the best examples of Art Nouveau.

1894 In Chicago, Stone & Kimball starts publishing the *Chap-Book* magazine, which heralds with its covers the arrival of Art Nouveau in America. It will have European collaborators, such as Aubrey Beardsley, Max Beerbohm, and Lucien Pisarro, and American collaborators, such as William Bradley and Bertram G. Goodhue.

Linn Boyd Benton designs *Century Roman* for the *Century Magazine* at the request of Theodore Low De Vinne. *Century Roman* is the first text typeface to meet the requirements of legibility and readability, anticipating the work developed by Chauncey H. Griffith with his *Legibility Group* in 1922.

The Inland Type Foundry is established in St. Louis, Missouri, by three German brothers, William, Oswald, and Carl Schraubstadter.

At the suggestion of William Bradley, *The Inland Printer* commissions him to design its covers. His work, which will include twelve covers, marks the advent of Art Nouveau style in America.

1895 French brothers Louis and August Lumière revolutionize the showing of films by developing the first movie projector, which they call *cinematograph*. An audience may see the projected images on a screen. From the very start, typography will play an important role both in film titles, scene descriptions, and in actors' dialogues.

German art critic Julius Meier-Graefe and poet Otto Julius Bierbaum found the *Pan* magazine in Berlin that will promote the Jugendstil movement in this country. Among the designers who will contribute with their work are Otto Eckmann, Peter Behrens, and Emil Rudolf Weiss.

Published in London, the *Penrose Annual*, edited by William Gamble, director of the printing firm A. W. Penrose, will be one of the most important publications on all aspects of design for print and changes in printing technology from this moment on.

German art dealer Samuel Bing opens the gallery *Art Nouveau* in Paris, which in turn will give a name to the Art Nouveau style movement.

German type founder David Stempel founds a type foundry that will later become the Schriftgiesserei D. Stempel AG in Frankfurt-am-Main. In 1900, the firm will acquire the sole right in Germany to make Linotype matrices. Among the many type designers who will be commissioned by Stempel are Fritz Helmut Ehmcke, Friedrich Wilhelm Kleukens, Rudolf Koch, Paul Renner, and Hermann Zapf. It will launch the *Neue Haas-Grotesk*, designed by Max Miedinger in 1957, which will be adopted by Stempel and issued as *Helvetica* in 1960.

The St. Bride Printing Library in London is opened. Its collection, which will contain works on subjects such as paper, binding, graphic design, typography, typefaces, type specimens, calligraphy, illustration, printmaking, publishing, and bookselling, will surpass 40,000 items.

1895 In New York, the first American publication devoted entirely to the art of the poster, *The Modern Poster* by Arsene Alexandre et al., is published by Scribner's, anticipating the appearance of *The Poster* (1898) in London.

William Bradley establishes the Wayside Press in Springfield, Massachusetts, modeled after William Morris's Kelmscott Press. With Bradley, we may say that the figure of the art director in the United States appears. He also works as design consultant for the American Type Founders, producing typefaces and ornaments, writing and designing.

Architect Bertram Grosvenor Goodhue designs the *Merrymount* typeface for *The Altar Book of the American Church*, printed by Daniel B. Updike on his Merrymount Press in 1896.

The Central Type Foundry of St. Louis issues the first type catalog (727 pages), using the name of the American Type Founders Company, but by-lined it with the name of their foundry.

William Randolph Hearst purchases the *New York Journal* and determines to outsell Joseph Pulitzer's the *New York World*. The two newspapers start to compete for audience appeal through sensational headlines and exclusive "news" updates, and the introduction of color comic strips.

The *Yellow Kid*, drawn by Richard F. Outcault, today considered the first comic strip in America, appears in the *New York World*. The future use of letterers for drawing texts within the *balloons* in narrative images will lead to the creation of, over time, a trend of script typefaces such as Howard Trafton's *Cartoon* (1936). Curiously, texts will be drawn in sustained caps from here on, defying readability principles that will later be stated.

1896 The Jugendstil movement, the German equivalent of French Art Nouveau, named after the *Jugend* cultural weekly publication, appears in Munich. In addition to the curvilinear naturalistic motifs, this movement acknowledges German printmaking and medieval letterforms. It favors unique display typefaces that work

harmoniously with the image. Important type designers include Peter Behrens and Otto Eckmann, whose *Eckmann Schrift* design done in 1900 will become a typical Jugendstil typeface.

English artist Sir Edward Burne-Jones finishes illustrating the magnificent 565-page volume of the Kelmscott Press edition of *The Works of Geoffrey Chaucer*. In production for four years, it contains eighty-seven woodcut illustrations by Burne-Jones, fourteen large borders, eighteen frames and twenty-six initials. The text is set in William Morris's *Chaucer* typeface (1892).

1896 Graphic artist and art director William Bradley publishes his own short-lived literary journal, *Bradley: His Book*. During this period, he discovers, in the Boston Public Library, a collection of books printed in colonial New England, full of chapbook cuts that he will employ in his work.

Designer and typographer Bruce Rogers starts working for the Riverside Press in Cambridge, Massachusetts, a subsidiary of the publishing firm Houghton, Mifflin & Company of Boston.

1897 The Vienna Secession is formed after younger members of the Vienna Academy of Art rebel against the exclusion of foreign artists from exhibitions. Led by Gustav Klimt, the group included Koloman Moser, Alfred Roller, and Josef Hoffmann. Flat color shapes, geometric designs, distortions of letters to fit geometric figures and great symmetrical unity characterize their work.

The Lanston Monotype Corporation is founded in England through the forming of a syndicate that purchases the British rights under the direction of the Earl of Dunraven.

French symbolist poet Stéphane Mallarmé publishes *Un coup de dés jamai abolira le hasard* whose experimental typesetting anticipates the work presented by Appollinaire in his *Calligrammes* (1918).

1897 After vainly trying to persuade James Gordon Bennett to develop the halftone process in the *New York Herald*, Stephen Horgan succeeds in using it at the *New York Tribune*, in which the first halftones are printed on power presses.

Ingalls Kimball moves to New York, and establishes the Cheltenham Press. The following year he will ask Bertram G. Goodhue to design a typeface (*Cheltenham*) for him.

After working for ten years on his machine, Tolbert Lanston is finally able to introduce a perfected "monotype," thanks to John S. Bancroft's technical assistance. By this time, the Monotype composing system is widely used in book publishing and advertising.

1898 The Vienna Secession members start publishing *Ver Sacrum*, one of the most innovative and beautiful magazines at the turn of the century. From the square format to the inside layout it prefigures the functionalism of future Modernists.

The British type foundries agree to adopt the American Point System, the Caxton Type Foundry being the first to adopt it in 1899.

The publication of *The Poster* appears in London up to 1901, entirely dedicated to this medium. In it, the work of Alfons Mucha and William Bradley, among others, will appear. Sidney Ransom designs the first cover.

German type foundry H. Berthold AG issues *Akzidenz Grotesk*, reinforcing the sans serif typeface design concept. It will later serve as a model for *News Gothic* (Morris Fuller Benton, 1908), and *Neue Haas Grotesk / Helvetica* (Max Miedinger, 1957).

Gustave Peignot establishes the Peignot & Fils type foundry in Paris. His sons, Lucien and Georges, will give new impetus to French type design by commissioning *Grasset* (Eugene Grasset, 1899), and *Auriol* (George Auriol, 1902). In 1923, this type foundry will merge with Deberny type foundry, becoming Deberny & Peignot.

1898 Architect Bertram Grosvenor Goodhue starts designing, at the request of New York printer Ingalls Kimball, a typeface for his Cheltenham Press, established by him the preceding year. But while trial cuttings of *Cheltenham* will be made as early as 1899, the typeface will not be concluded until 1902. ATF will commercially issue it in 1904.

Morris Fuller Benton begins a prolific career at ATF as head of the Department of Typographic Design. He will standardize thousands of matrices that ATF had acquired when it was formed in 1892, and will draw many versions of classical types, including *Bodoni* (1910-11), the most popular in America, *Cloister Oldstyle* (1914), *Baskerville* (1915), *Garamond* (1919), and *Bulmer* (1928). He will also design original types, such as *Franklin Gothic* (1902), *News Gothic* (1908), and *Century Schoolbook* (1918).

Ottmar Mergenthaler supplements his linotype composing machine with a two-character matrix (see page 193) that enables the use of two versions of a typeface.

1899 English calligrapher and type designer Edward Johnston starts classes in calligraphy and illumination at the London Central School of Arts and Crafts. Among his students there will be Eric Gill, William Graily Hewitt, Ernst Frederick Detterer, Alfred Fairbank, and Anna Simons. Much of the interest stimulated by Johnston in letterforms will spread over type design. From 1901 to 1940, he will conduct similar classes at the Royal College of Art.

American Frank Hinman Pierpont becomes managing director of the recently established English Monotype in Salfords, England. He will stay with the firm until his retirement in 1936. Under his supervision, Monotype will adapt existing type designs to suit its machines. He will be responsible for *Plantin* (1913), considered one of the greatest Monotype's re-cuttings of the classics.

1900

1900 Englishman Thomas Cobden-Sanderson founds, in collaboration with Emery Walker, the Doves Press. Their books, unillustrated, will be in complete contrast to those of William Morris. For this reason, they will have a greater influence on fine books in Western Europe. Their finest work will be the five-volume, *Doves' Bible* (1903), set in *Doves Roman* typeface, designed by Emery Walker.

The Lanston Monotype Composing Machine is presented at the *Exposition Universelle* held in Paris.

1900 The American Type Founders Company issues their first type catalog, with the assistance of Linn Boyd Benton, Morris F. Benton, and Henry Lewis Bullen. It shows 525 series of job fonts, and thirty-seven series of body type.

Bruce Rogers starts designing The Riverside Press limited editions. During the next twelve years, he will complete sixty editions which will set a new approach to book design, and will consolidate his brilliant career as book designer and typographer.

Theodore Low De Vinne publishes *The Practice of Typography*, the first of four volumes on the subject. The other three titles will be published in 1901, 1902, and 1904.

Louis Levy of Philadelphia invents the etching machine, which works on the basis of keeping the etching fluid in continuous motion.

1901 Although only one issue of Joseph Pulitzer's *The New York World* is printed tabloid, on January 1st, it pioneers the appearance of reduced formats. In 1919, *The Illustrated News* in New York will be the first to use the new format. By 1940, there will be fifty tabloid newspapers circulating in America.

1902 Morris Fuller Benton designs *Franklin Gothic* for ATF. Considered "the patriarch of modern American gothics," it is one of the first important modernizations of traditional 19th century typefaces since he had been assigned the task of unifying all the fonts inherited by ATF in 1892.

Sol Hess is employed as the first type designer by the Lanston Monotype Machine Company.

Theories of effective advertising art based on experiments in visual perception and market research begin to be discussed in trade journals. Walter Dill Scott, a Northwestern University professor of psychology, originator of this movement, advices advertisers to follow a "scientific" program where the rules of composition, layout design, typography, and color must be treated as essential components in communicating a message.

1903 Koloman Moser and Joseph Hoffmann found the Wiener Werkstätte in order to have better control of the creation and distribution of their art and design works. Geometry becomes more important than symbolism.

1903 The American Type Founders Company adopts the standard lining system. It will enable the alignment of different sizes of type by the use of 1 pt leads or their multiples, and of all faces of a given size, whatever their characteristics.

Wadsworth Parker redesigns *Bookman* for ATF, a heavy antique typeface, much in the Mission style shared by Bertram Grosvenor Goodhue's *Cheltenham*. Elbert Hubbard's Roycroft Press, located in East Aurora, New York, will use it in the making of Arts and Crafts books.

Frederic W. Goudy establishes the Village Press in Park Ridge, outside Chicago, Illinois, in collaboration with Will Ransom. For it, Goudy will design the *Village* typeface.

1904 *Cheltenham*, designed by Bertram G. Goodhue between 1898 and 1902, becomes the first typeface to be available in both hand composition and Linotype, and the first to have a complete family. Morris Fuller Benton will design eighteen variants of *Cheltenham*, and will supervise its commercial development. Its exceeding popularity prompted many imitations, such as *Gloucester* (Monotype), *Winchester* (Stephenson Blake & Co.), and *Sorbonne* (H. Berthold AG).

Ira William Rubel, a New Jersey paper manufacturer, discovers the offset lithographic printing process when an image is accidentally transferred from the printing plate to the rubber blanket of the impression cylinder and then printed onto paper, producing a superior impression. In partnership with two other lithographers, Rubel will construct three prototypes in 1905, using metal plates, and thus challenging letterpress to print text. Offset lithography will be developed in England the following year.

William Bradley starts illustrating the first of twelve monthly issues of the *American Chap-Book*, the in-house American Type Founders' magazine.

1905 German designer Lucian Bernhard wins first prize with his poster for Priester matches and, with it, he inaugurates the *sachplakat* or object poster style, characterized by a pronounced economy of image and text.

The first group of the German Expressionist movement, Die Brücke (*The Bridge*), is formed by a group of artists who had studied at the Kunstgewerbeschule (Arts and Crafts School). Among them are Erich Heckel, Ernst Ludwig Kichner, Max Pechstein, Karl Schmidt-Rottluff, and Emil Nolde. They search for personal symbolism, and personal calligraphy. Primitive woodcut style distinguishes most of their graphic work.

1905 Initially made of three sheets, and then of eight sheets, the sixteen-sheet poster has become the standard billboard format for outside advertising.

1906 English calligrapher and typographer Edward Johnston founds the Society of Calligraphers for the advancement of lettering. Although short-lived, it has considerable influence in England and Germany. He also publishes his book *Writing & Illuminating & Lettering*. Apart from his direct pupils, Eric Gill, William Graily Hewitt, Ernst Frederick Detterer, Alfred Fairbank, and Anna Simons, his work will also influence typographers like Rudolf Koch, Hermann Zapf and Jan Tschichold.

The appearance in Edward Johnston's book, *Writing & Illuminating & Lettering,* of photo reproductions of the Trajan Column inscription –taken from a cast plaster copy of the whole column which had been in the Victoria & Albert Museum since 1864– attracts great attention to Roman classical inscriptions. The letters fine proportions are soon established as an unchangeable canon. The craft of letter-cutting is also revived in this period.

Rudolf Koch, a most influential German type designer, joins the Klingspor type foundry in Offenbach, and stays there until his death in 1934. Among his future typefaces, there will be *Koch Antiqua* (1922), *Neuland* (1923), *Kabel* (1927), *Zeppelin* (1929), and *Prisma* (1931).

Pierre Larousse, founder of the Parisian publishing house, publishes *Le Petit Larousse Illustré,* his most popular dictionary. By 1922, it will have had its 185th revised edition.

1906 Washington I. Ludlow conceives the idea of a display-typecasting machine. William A. Reade, who will also become head of the Ludlow Typograph Company, successfully develops the machine in 1911.

1907 In Paris, Spanish painter Pablo Picasso and French painter Georges Braque start painting in the Cubist manner. Subject matter is visualized from different points of view, and then composed in a series of geometric forms. Collages, letterforms, and words will later be integrated into their work.

In Munich, the Deutscher Werbund is founded by a group of artists, architects and artisans, such as Peter Behrens, Henri Van de Velde, and Hermann Muthesius, to improve the quality of German products. Peter Behrens, is called to Berlin to take charge of the AEG (*Allgemeine Elektricitäts-Gessellschaft*). Turbinen Fabrik's visual image includes architecture, design of products, and printed material, which will permit him to create the first coordinated and coherent concept of a corporate identity program.

German type foundry D. Stempel AG issues *Venus,* a sans serif typeface originally cast by Wagner & Schmidt foundry.

Punch-cutting machines, designed by American Frank Hinman Pierpont at the English Monotype Corporation, in Salsfords, displace the early Linn Boyd Benton's model (1885). Worked with less skilled labor, these devices are faster and offer a finer tolerance.

1908 The Lanston Monotype composing machine is installed in the *Times* of London, and *Modern Extended* is the typeface chosen to typeset the newspaper.

Expressionist painter Oskar Kokoschka's woodcut poster will influence Rudolf Koch in the drawing of his *Neuland* typeface, designed in 1922-23.

1908 Henry Lewis Bullen lays the foundation for ATF's famous *Typographic Library and Museum* in Jersey City, New Jersey. He will influence the revival of many classical typefaces at ATF, such as *Cloister Oldstyle, Bulmer, Baskerville, Garamond,* and *Bodoni* through the hands of Morris Fuller Benton. In 1936, the library will go to Columbia University, New York.

Morris Fuller Benton designs *News Gothic* for ATF, based on H. Berthold AG's *Akzidenz Grotesk* (1898), anticipating the appearance of *Neue Haas Grotesk/Helvetica* (Max Miedinger, 1957), also influenced by the same type design, by fifty years.

The Village Press, having been moved first to Boston (1904) and then to New York, is destroyed by fire. Frederic W. Goudy then turns to designing, cutting, and casting his own types.

The National Arts Club in New York sponsors the first annual exhibition of advertising art. Initiated by Ernest Elmo Calkins, it intends to demonstrate that advertising may have both artistic and advertising merits.

1909 Italian writer Filippo Tommaso Marinetti publishes his *Manifesto futurista* (*Manifeste du Futurism*) in *Le Figaro,* Paris, and founds the Futurist movement characterized by a great experimentation with typographic form and syntax, with Giacomo Balla, Umberto Boccioni, Gino Severini, and other painters.

1910

1910 In Berlin, Hans Sachs, in collaboration with Hans Meyer and Lucian Bernhard, founds *Das Plakat* magazine (1910-1921), later renamed *Gebrauchsgraphik* (1925), which displays posters, advertising and graphic design.

The English Lanston Monotype Corporation develops a reverse delivery mechanism for the Monotype caster that permits the type composition of languages read from right-to-left, such as Arabic and Hebrew.

1910 The National American Woman Suffrage Association, after having successful campaigns in various states, starts to employ the picture poster as a convincing tactic. The use of this type of commercial imagery reflects some of the earliest uses of the political poster, anticipating the First World War's extensive usage.

With the development of good color reproduction, photography surpasses all methods of image reproduction. Readers may, for the first time, approach reproduced art from a different perspective.

1911 A second group of the Expressionist painters, led by Wassily Kandinsky and Franz Marc, create Der Blaue Reiter (*The Blue Rider*) movement that will cultivate the abstract as a universal source of symbols. With the later presence of Paul Klee, eminent theorist and painter, color will appear as an integral component in many of his letter compositions.

1911 By this time William Bradley, as art director for various magazines, starts revising his ideas on typography and layout. In two of his articles,

written in *Printing Art,* he stresses the importance of coherence and consistency between image and type.

The Ludlow Typograph Company publicly demonstrates a machine that casts lines of type from hand-assembled matrices. Twenty of the Ludlow units will be built during the year.

Frederic W. Goudy designs *Kennerley Old Style* and *Forum Title* for Mitchell Kennerley's printing of H. G. Wells' *The Door in the Wall,* establishing his name as a type designer.

1912 English Monotype issues *Imprint,* the first Oldstyle typeface designed specifically for mechanical composition. Designed by Edward Johnston, after *Caslon Old Style,* it will be cut for the *Imprint* type journal (1913), edited by John Henry Mason, Gerard Meynell, and Johnston. Next year, Monotype will issue *Plantin,* probably developed on drawings by German Fritz Steltzer under the supervision of American Frank H. Pierpont, which will be another best-selling typeface.

Czech psychologist Max Wertheimer, in collaboration with German psychologists Kurt Koffka and Wolfgang Köhler, founds the Gestalt school of psychology, which focuses on the study of perception, memory and learning. The concept of "The whole is more important than the parts," which underlies visual theories, will have a great influence on Bauhaus art and design teachings. Kurt Koffka will introduce Gestalt theories in America in 1922. Rudolf Arnheim, a key figure in art teaching theories, will be one of Wertheimer's students.

1913 Filippo Tommaso Marinetti, one of the founders of the Futurist movement, breaks with the classical handling of typography in an article published in Giovanni Papini's *Lacerba* journal, Florence. He advocated a typographical revolution through the use of many type styles on the page and the use of three and four colors.

Franck Pick, traffic development officer of the London Underground, commissions Edward Johnston and Eric Gill to create a typeface for use on signs and advertising, as part of a global program of design. Gill does not participate but Johnston begins to work in late 1915, finishing in 1916. The *London Underground Sanserif* will become its identification typeface, influencing Eric Gill's *Gill Sans* (1928). Based on Roman classic proportions, it is still in use today.

1913 The Mergenthaler Linotype Company extends the range of its composing machine up to 60 pts, and introduces Duplex-Display, two letter faces matrices up to 24 pts. The great majority of machines continue casting up to 14 pts.

The Intertype hot metal type composing machine, a near duplicate of the Linotype, starts production. Perfected under the guidance of Hermann Ridder, it combines expired Linotype patents with some advanced details of engineering. It will be introduced in Germany in 1925.

The first commercial use of the Ludlow hot metal typecasting machine takes place in the *Chicago Evening Post*. By this time, slanted matrices (see page 191) have been developed to accommodate and to cast fluent italic type designs.

The Armory Show, which holds works of Impressionist, Post-Impressionist, Fauvist and Cubist artists, opens first in New York and then in Chicago and Boston. It introduces and determines the beginning of modern art in America.

1914-1918 The First World War takes place, causing a series of changes in world politics. Political posters will make their appearance with designers like Alfred Leete, Montgomery Flagg, and Lucian Bernhard, among others.

1914 German type foundry Wagner & Schmidt issues *Grotesk V*, a popular sans serif design widely distributed, and widely copied by Dutch, German, French, Italian, and Spanish type foundries.

1914 After being displaced in popularity by magazines as vehicles for advertising, posters re-emerge as a powerful medium of persuasion in World War I.

The American Institute of Graphic Arts (AIGA), the oldest designers' organization in America, is founded in New York by a group of members of the National Arts Club to promote greater appreciation of those arts through the exhibition of the year's best books, prints, advertisements, packaging, and other designs.

The Metropolitan Museum of Art commissions Bruce Rogers to design a private type for use by the Museum Press in its publications. The result, *Centaur*, cut by Robert Wiebking, and based on the Nicolas Jenson's 1470 model, will be considered by Daniel Berkeley Updike as one of the finest typefaces of the twentieth century. Rogers will use it the following year to print Maurice de Guerin's *The Centaur*, and hence the name. The Musée D'Orsay, Paris, will repeat this typographical experience in 1983, and the Walker Art Center, Minneapolis, in 1995.

1915 Russian painter Kasimir Malevich launches Suprematism in Petrograd. The reduction of the picture to the use of pure color geometric shapes will be a definite influence on Constructivism and the De Stijl movements.

The Fundición Tipográfica Nacional is founded in Madrid. In time, it will become one of the most important foundries in Spain. Carlos Winkow and Enric Crous-Vidal, and others, will design for it. In 1971, it will be bought by Fundición Neufville, Barcelona.

1915 After working with Doubleday, Page & Co., and with Mitchell Kennerley, Alfred A. Knopf appears in New York as an independent publisher.

1916 The Dada movement of literary and visual art content develops in Switzerland, responding to the futility of the First World War. Pioneered by Hungarian poet Tristan Tzara and German artist Jean (Hans) Arp, the movement rapidly spreads to New York, Paris, and Berlin. Besides the use of collage and photography, there will be

great experimentation with typography. It will be a forerunner of Surrealism.

1916 Although Barnhart Brothers & Spindler had sold out to ATF, they continue operating under their name. This year Richard N. McArthur joins the company as advertising manager, commissioning outside designers such as Will Ransom, Oswald B. Cooper, Carl S. Junge, George F. Trenholm, and Robert Wiebking to create new typefaces and ornaments.

1917 Russian Constructivism starts shortly before the Bolshevik Revolution. Led by Vladimir Tatlin, Alexander Rodchenko, and El Lissitsky, the movement will promote collage, photography, photomontage, the use of bold sans serif typefaces, and new printing techniques. Their ideas will have a strong influence on the educational philosophy of the Bauhaus.

De Stijl (*The Style*) magazine, founded and edited by Théo Van Doesberg, will be the basis for the De Stijl movement. In its first issue, Piet Mondrian proposes abstraction as the representation of pure spirit. It will in turn influence the Bauhaus, founded two years later. De Stijl will explore dynamic compositions, complemented by the primary colors –red, blue and yellow– in association with black, white and gray.

1918 French writer Guillaume Apollinaire presents his *Calligrammes*, or visual poems, which constitute in themselves a unique contribution to early twentieth-century typographic developments.

Ernst Keller, Swiss graphic designer and educator, and key figure in the evolution of Swiss graphic design and the International Typographic Style, starts teaching at the Kunstgewerbeschule (*School of Applied Arts*) in Zurich, and continues until 1956. Among his students, there will be Théo Ballmer (a later professor at Basle), Adrian Frutiger and Eduard Hoffmann, who will be creators of seminal type designs during the 1950s (*Helvetica* and *Univers*, 1957). The International Typographic Style will be characterized by the presence of the grid, the use of sans serif types (especially *Akzidenz Grotesk*, 1898), flush left typesetting, and photography rather than illustration.

1918 Carl Purington Rollins, who had founded the Montague Press in 1911, starts working in the Yale University Press (1916) as chief printer. For over thirty years, he will design books and supervise most of the university publications, influencing other university presses that start publishing in the United States at the same time.

Mitchell Kennerley publishes Frederic W. Goudy's book, *The Alphabet, fifteen interpretative designs drawn and arranged with explanatory texts and illustrations*. At the request of Wadsworth A. Parker, Director of ATF's Type Design Department, Goudy creates the *Cloister Initials* on the basis of the first chapter's initial **A**.

1919 German architect and educator Walter Gropius founds the Bauhaus school in Weimar. On its original staff, besides

Gropius, are Johannes Itten, Marcel Breuer, Wassily Kandinsky, Paul Klee, Lyonel Feininger, Joseph Albers, László Moholy-Nagy, and Ludwig Mies van der Rohe. There Bauhaus will exert a great influence on type design through the use of sans serif typefaces in its publications. Herbert Bayer will later design his *universal alphabet* (1925), a sans serif typeface without capital letters.

1919 Designer William A. Dwiggins publishes, under a pseudonym, for the fictitious Society of Calligraphers, *Extracts from An Investigation into the Physical Properties of Books as They Are at Present Published*, which will prove quite influential on American book design.

1920

1920 Harold M. Taylor founds the Golden Cockerel Press as part of the British private press movement. Its books are memorable for their excellent typography and illustrations by Eric Gill and David Jones, among others. The press' best publication will be *The Four Gospels* (1931) with wood engraving illustrations by Gill.

1920 By the end of the war, while European nations were exhausted, confused, and bankrupt, the United States became the richest country in the world. The following decade saw an industrial boom of enormous proportions. It was also the time of Henry Ford's *Model T* car which allowed Americans to travel all over the country. The pictorial poster immediately became one of the most effective instruments for advertising agencies, and billboards standardized their formats to a 24-sheet poster (234" x 104"). Artists such as Clarence G. Underwood, J. C. Leyendecker, and Burr Griffin were instrumental in shaping stereotyped figures both feminine and masculine which became idealized dreams for many Americans.

The Art Directors Club of New York is founded. Organized for the purpose of developing and maintaining high creative standards in visual communications, its *Advertising and Editorial Art* exhibitions will become a prestigious national event.

Frederic W. Goudy, with forty type designs to his name, is appointed as art consultant for the Lanston Monotype Machine Company, anticipating the English Monotype by assigning Stanley Morison as its consultant in 1922. Goudy will remain so until 1940, when Sol Hess will succeed him. The first results of this advisory, *Garamont* (1921) and *Italian Old Style* (1924) will be followed by many other designs.

1921 Rudolf Koch establishes his lettering workshop at the Offenbach Technical Institute where he will be very influential. Among his assistants, there will be Warren Chappell, Berthold Wolpe, Herbert Post, and Georg Salter. His work will also influence designers like Eric Gill, Alfred Fairbank, Edward Johnston, Frederic W. Goudy, Oswald Cooper, William Addison Dwiggins, Emil Rudolf Weiss, F.H. Ernst Schneidler, Walter Tiemann, and Henri Friedlaender.

George W. Jones, who ran a highly regarded printing business in London, is appointed printing adviser to Linotype & Machinery, Ltd. Under his direction, the company will develop various classic typefaces for its type composing system, such as *Granjon* (1924), *Georgian* (1925), *Estienne* (1926), and *Venezia* (1928).

Francis Thibaudeau, eminent French typographer, who will work with Deberny & Peignot type foundry until his death in 1925, publishes *La lettre d'imprimerie* (2 vols.), anticipating Maximilien Vox's work in the elaboration of a type classification (1952). He bases his grouping on the serif construction: *elzevir*, *didot*, *egyptienne*, and *antique*. The rest of the typefaces are cataloged as *écriture* and *fantasie*.

1921 Ernst Frederick Detterer starts teaching calligraphy and printing at the Art Institute of Chicago, where he will exert great influence in these fields. He had returned to this city in 1913 after studying calligraphy with Edward Johnston. One of his students will be Robert Hunter Middleton who will collaborate with him in designing *Eusebius* (1924). Alone, he will do *Eusebius Italic*. Both of these typefaces will be for the Ludlow Typograph Company.

Thomas Maitland Cleland prints his work, *The Grammar of Color*, for the Strathmore Papers Company. In this magnificent oversized book, Cleland explains the effective use of color inks on color paper through a series of foldout pages.

1922 English scholar and typographer Stanley Morison is appointed typographical advisor to the English Monotype Corporation. Morison will direct an ambitious revival of classical typefaces like *Garamond* (1922), *Baskerville* (1923), *Blado* (1923), *Poliphilus* (1923), *Fournier* (1925), *Barbou* (1926), *Bembo* (1929), *Bell* (1930), *Walbaum* (1933), *Van Dijck Roman* (1935), and *Ehrhardt* (1937). He will also introduce new typefaces like *Gill Sans* (Gill, 1929), *Perpetua* (Gill, 1929), *Centaur* (Rogers, 1929), *Arrighi* (Warde, 1929), *Emerson* (Blumenthal, 1935), *Romulus* (Van Krimpen, 1936), and *Albertus* (Wolpe, 1938).

German type designer, author, and educator Paul Renner, while working for the Deutschen Verlagsaustall, in Stuttgart, and teaching at the Frankfurter Kunstschule, publishes, in Munich, *Typographie als Kunst*, a book which will be a definite influence on Jan Tschichold's *Die neue Typographie* (1928).

German printer and typographer Hans (Giovanni) Mardersteig founds the Officina Bodoni at Montagnola di Lugano, Italy. Permission to cast type from Giambattista Bodoni's original matrices, kept in the Biblioteca Palatina, is given to him exclusively. The first book, *Orphei tragedia* by Angelo Poliziano, will appear in 1923. He will also design some typefaces, such as *Griffo* (1929), *Fontana* (1936), *Zeno* (1937), and *Dante* (1955).

German type designer Rudolf Wolf starts working as advertising manager of D. Stempel AG in Frankfurt am Main. He will work as such until 1942, and will be responsible for the foundry's type designs as well as for the revival of nineteenth-century slab-serif typefaces that he will start with *Memphis*, in 1929.

1922 German psychologist Kurt Koffka introduces American psychologists directly to Gestalt psychology in his article, *Perception: An introduction to Gestalt theory*. It is based on the study of perception, memory, and learning developed in 1912 in collaboration with Max Wertheimer and Wolfgang Köhler.

Type designer Chauncey H. Griffith becomes head of typographic development at Mergenthaler Linotype. Under his direction, the company will develop an important type design program on printing and legibility called the *Legibility Group*.

Sol Hess is appointed typographic manager of the Lanston Monotype Machine Company.

Chicago letterer Oswald Cooper designs *Cooper Black* for Barnhart Brothers & Spindler typefoundry, which becomes their best-selling typeface before their merger with ATF. Although Cooper was never interested in fashion, *Cooper Black* will establish a new trend of black faces which will be followed by designers like Robert Hunter Middleton (*Ludlow Black*, 1924, and *Bodoni Black*, 1930), Frederic W. Goudy (*Goudy Heavy Face*, 1925), Morris Fuller Benton (*Ultra Bodoni*, 1928), and Chauncey H. Griffith (*Poster Bodoni*, 1929).

Daniel Berkeley Updike prints, at his Merrymount Press, Cambridge, Massachusetts, his two-volume work *Printing Types: Their History, Forms, and Use*, which grew out of a series of lectures delivered at Harvard University between 1911 and 1926, and published by the Harvard University Press.

William Addison Dwiggins coins the term "graphic design" to describe the structural order and visual form given to his printed work.

Art Directors Annual, a New York publication specialized in advertising design, begins to appear. It will be the first publication to combine interests in advertising and other arts.

1923 In London, Oliver Simon of Curwen Press and Stanley Morison, members of The Fleuron Society, start publishing *The Fleuron: a journal of typography*, concerned with all aspects of typography, historic and modern. From 1926 to 1930 it will be edited by Morison and printed at the Cambridge University Press. Its only seven issues will be quite influential.

The first Bauhaus exhibition takes place in Weimar. With the naming of Hungarian designer, painter, writer, and photographer László Moholy-Nagy as director of basic design, graphic design acquires a definite role. That same year, his typographic manifesto expresses that typography must be communication in its purest form.

English book designer and advertising typographer Francis Meynell founds the NoneSuch Press in London. He will

innovate publishing by using machine-set production methods done by various printers. He will also publish *Typography*, a notable type-specimen book, and an essay on book production. Among the artists who will contribute to the press are Rudolf Koch, George Grosz, and Reynolds Stone.

French type foundries Deberny and Peignot & Fils establish the Fonderie Deberny & Peignot. In 1950, they will sponsor the invention of *Photon*, and in 1957, the issuing of Adrian Frutiger's *Univers*.

German type designer Rudolf Koch publishes his extraordinary work, *Das Zeichenbuch* (*The Book of Signs*, published in English in 1930), with wood engravings by Fritz Kredel.

Russian painter Wassily Kandinsky proposes a universal correspondence between the three elementary shapes and the three primary colors: the dynamic triangle is yellow, the static square is red, and the serene circle is blue. These shapes and colors will be essential visual/graphic components for structuring corporate identity imagery.

1923 Robert Hunter Middleton becomes typographic advisor for the Ludlow Typograph Company by recommendation of Ernst Frederick Detterer, who had been his teacher at the Art Institute of Chicago, and with whom he had collaborated in designing his *Eusebius*. At Ludlow he will design, among others, *Delphian Open Title* (1928), *Stellar* (1929), which anticipates Hermann Zapf's *Optima* (1958), *Tempo* (1930), *Stencil* (1937), and *Radiant* (1940).

Henry R. Luce and Briton Hadden, recent graduates from Yale University, launch *Time*, the first weekly news magazine. Luce will also create *Fortune* magazine (1930), designed by Thomas Maitland Cleland, and the large format photographic weekly publication, *Life* (1936).

The American Institute of Graphic Arts (AIGA) continues organizing *The Fifty Books of the Year* exhibition. Created in 1905, it had been sponsored by the National Arts Club.

Frederic W. Goudy opens his own type foundry, the Village Press Foundery, in Marlborough-on-Hudson, New York –something no type designer had done since the eighteenth century. Robert Wiebking had been cutting his matrices, but now is too old to do so. Thus, Goudy, already sixty-two, decides to undertake the difficult art of engraving. The first typeface entirely cut by him will be *Companion Old Style* and *Italic* (1927).

American Type Founders publishes its nationally acclaimed 1,148-page *Type Specimen Book and Catalogue 1923* under the direction of Henry Lewis Bullen in collaboration with Morris Fuller Benton and Wadsworth Parker.

1924 The Surrealist movement appears in Paris headed by French writer André Breton. Emerging as a consequence of Dada, it will challenge accepted concepts of what is normal and rational. Two of the most important exponents will be Salvador Dalí and René Magritte, whose work will certainly be influential in graphic design.

In Vienna, Viennese sociologist Otto Neurath founds the Gessellschafts-und-Wirtschaftsmuseum (Social and Economic Museum), where he will develop the *Isotype* or graphic representation of information. In less than ten years, he will be able to transform it into a universal language that will promote the use of pictographs in sign and information systems.

The 35-mm *Leica* photographic camera is put on the market. It is easy to carry, and relatively unobtrusive. Its remarkably fast shutter speeds (1/1000) will make it possible to capture faster action with less light than ever before.

1924 Charles Coiner joins the art department of N. W. Ayer & Son advertising agency. He will be quite influential as art director of Container Corporation of America's account in 1936.

1925 In Berlin, German typographer Jan Tschichold publishes his essay, *Elementare Typographie*, in a special issue of the type journal, *Typographische Mitteilungen*. In his presentation of the work of Russian painter El Lissitsky, he speaks for the first time of sans serif typefaces, the use of asymmetrical typography, and the relation between type and space.

Stanley Morison is made typographic advisor to the Cambridge University Press, which had begun a complete reform of its typographic resources under printer Walter Lewis. The press, showing that mechanical composition could be used to produce handsome and functional books, will acquire most of the types developed by Monotype under Morison's direction.

In Berlin, German publisher H. K. Frenzel starts publishing the influential design magazine, *Gebrauchsgraphik*, which will have a definite influence on American designers. Printed in German and English, it will later include texts in French and Spanish. Lucian Bernhard designs its first cover.

The *Exposition Internationale des Arts Décoratifs et Industriels Modernes*, which will lay the foundations for the *Art Deco style*, takes place in Paris. This exhibition will be a major influence on typography, especially on the use of sans serif styles with certain calligraphic characteristics. Programmed to open in 1915, it had to be postponed because of the war.

The Bauhaus school moves to Dessau and Herbert Bayer is appointed to be in charge of the typographic workshop. He will develop a fresh concept of functionalism in typography, characterized by asymmetric page layouts and by the use of sans serif letters. He will also design a *universal alphabet* (1925), with only lowercase letters, which he will present in the journal, *Bauhaus*, published in 1926.

Hungarian Constructivist László Moholy-Nagy publishes his essay, "Contemporary Typography: Aims, Practice, Criticism" in which he urges the implementation of new technologies and visual experiences of the times.

Dutch calligrapher and typographer Jan Van Krimpen becomes artistic advisor to the Dutch type foundry, Enschedé en Zonen in Haarlem. Among his future type designs will be *Lutetia* (1925), *Romulus* (1931), *Cancelaresca bastarda* (1934), *Van Dijck Roman* (1935), and *Spectrum* (1952).

1925 R. J. Smothers of Holyoke, Massachusetts, patents the earliest phototypesetting machine, employing the principles of the circulating matrix as used in the Linotype machine. Transparent alphabetical characters on glass are fastened to the edge of each matrix, and as lines are assembled, images are recorded by the use of light through a lens system on sensitized film.

Mergenthaler Linotype introduces *Ionic No. 5*, designed by Chauncey H. Griffith, as part of the *Legibility Group* that he heads. It is the first of a group of typefaces designed by Griffith (others will be *Excelsior*, 1931, *Paragon*, 1935, and *Corona*, 1941), to solve the problems of legibility, readability and printing presented by the mechanical typesetting of newspapers. In England, the *Daily Herald* will be the first newspaper to adopt *Ionic No. 5*, in 1930. Within eighteen months of release, this type design will be adopted by 3000 publications.

Caricaturist and letterer, Rea Irvin designs the cover and masthead of the *New Yorker*, which lays the foundation for the typeface *Irvin*, and which will be used by the magazine from then on as part of its typographical identity.

1926 Paul Renner invites German calligrapher and typographer Jan Tschichold to teach at the Munich School for Master Book Printers. He will be there until 1933.

The term *photocomposing*, which refers to the processes of photographic typesetting, appears in an article in the *Penrose Annual*.

1926 Joseph Blumenthal founds in New York, the Spiral Press, and designs the *Spiral* typeface (1930) for it; later recut by Monotype as *Emerson* (1935). When the press closes in 1971, he will turn his attention to the writing of the history of printing.

William Addison Dwiggins becomes head designer for publisher Alfred A. Knopf, designing more than 280 books that will stimulate American trade-book design and production. The *Borzoi Books* will become famous for Dwiggins's interest in giving each volume a distinctive appearance both inside and outside.

1927 Paul Renner, now director of the Munich School for Master Book Printers, finishes designing *Futura* for the Bauer type foundry. After three years of work, a preliminary trial made by the foundry in 1924, and subsequent commercial issue, it will be the main sans serif typeface for the next twenty-five years, sparking a sans serif phenomenon worldwide. While some of these typefaces will be close in form and structure, others will be designed as new proposals for more humanistic letterforms. In Europe, there will appear *Kabel* (Koch,

1927), *Berthold Grotesque* (H. Berthold AG, 1928), *Gill Sans* (Gill, 1929), and *Vogue* (Stephenson, Blake & Co, 1929), and in America, *Bernhard Gothic* (Bernhard, 1929), *Stellar* (R. H. Middleton, 1929); *Vogue* (Intertype, 1930); the *Metro* series (Dwiggins, 1930); *Goudy Sans Serif* series (Goudy, 1930); the *Tempo* series (R. H. Middleton, 1930); the *Sans Serif* series (Monotype); and the *Spartan* series (Linotype, 1939).

French typographer Charles Peignot starts publishing *Arts et Métieres Graphiques*, an in-house journal of the Fonderie Deberny & Peignot. Designed by Alexei Brodovitch, it will serve to launch A. M. Cassandre's typefaces *Bifur* (1929), *Acier Noir* (1936), and *Peignot* (1937).

Stanley Morison commissions Eric Gill, known as the foremost English letter-cutter, to design *Perpetua*, a serif typeface that will be issued by Monotype Corporation in 1929.

American typographic and printing historian Beatrice Warde is appointed editor of the *The Monotype Recorder*, which had been published since 1902. For this publication, Frederic Warde had produced, and will continue creating, valuable typographic ornamentation.

1927 *The Inland Printer* displays 161 typefaces brought out between 1900 and 1925 by eight of the leading foundries in the United States. Of these, it is possible to name the designers of seventy-two, almost all from the Barnhart Brothers & Spindler type foundry of Chicago. Such is the case of Oswald B. Cooper, Will Ransom, Robert Wiebking, Sidway Gaunt and George Trenholm. Unfortunately, some important type designers of this period such as Bertram G. Goodhue, Bruce Rogers, Robert Hunter Middleton and Frederic W. Goudy are left out.

Robert Hunter Middleton founds The Society of Typographic Arts in Chicago, in collaboration with Paul Ressinger, Ernst F. Detterer, Oswald B. Cooper, Edwin Gillespie, William Kittredge, among others, "to promote high standards in the typographic arts."

1928 Jan Tschichold publishes his first book, *Die neue Typographie* (The New Typography), which develops many of the ideas evolved by the Constructivists and teachers at the Bauhaus. In it, he establishes the asymmetric typographic principles, and the use of sans serif typography. He states , "sans serif is the type of the present day" and "if we aim at simplicity –we require simple and clear terms." Another three manuals will follow: *design for print* (1930), *lettering for compositors* (1931), and *typographical layout method* (1932), which will make the new style comprehensive.

1928 German poster designer, and recent immigrant Lucian Bernhard starts designing typefaces for the American Type Founders. He also designs Voltaire's book, *Candide*, the inaugural publication of Random House. Illustrated by Rockwell Kent, it was set in his typeface *Bernhard Roman*, which once redesigned, was issued as *Lucian* that same year. His first typeface for ATF, *Bernhard Gothic*, will appear the following year.

Designer William Addison Dwiggins publishes his book, *Layout in Advertising*, where he criticizes American sans serif typefaces compared to European designs. This will motivate Chauncey H. Griffith, from Mergenthaler Linotype Company, to commission him to design the *Metro* typeface series.

1929 From this year on, and up to 1960, Stanley Morison is typography consultant to London's daily newspaper, the *Times*. He also writes his famous essay, *First Principles of Typography*, for *The Encyclopaedia Britannica*, which reflects the authority he has established in this field. The Cambridge University Press will later publish it in 1936.

Eric Gill designs *Gill Sans* at the request of Stanley Morison. Different from Edward Johnston's *London Underground Sanserif* typeface (1916), Gill's design is intended for text use. Trial proofs appeared in 1928.

László Moholy-Nagy publishes his now classic book, the *New Vision* (English version, 1932).

German type designer Rudolf Wolf, advertising manager of D. Stempel AG, starts a revival of nineteenth-century typefaces designing *Memphis*, which will create a worldwide type trend. H. Berthold AG's *City* (Georg Trump, 1930), and *Beton* (Heinrich Jost, 1931) will follow it in Europe, and American Type Founders' *Stymie* (Morris Fuller Benton, 1931), Ludlow's *Karnak* (Robert Hunter Middleton, 1931-42), and Linotype's *Memphis Extra Bold* (Chauncey H. Griffith, 1938) will do it in America.

German Johannes Ostermeier improves the photoflash bulb, releasing photography from dependence on sunlight or special lighting. It also adds a useful tool to photojournalism. This year it is commercialized in Germany and brought to England and America the following year.

1929 -1940 The New York Stock Market collapses, and the Great Depression takes place. As part of a worldwide downturn in economic activity, it will bring serious consequences to American commercial projects.

1929 Russian designer Mehemed Fehmy Agha comes from France invited by Condé Nast to be art director of American *Vogue* magazine in New York. He pioneers the use of sans serif typefaces (*Vogue*, 1930), full-color reproductions, and innovative photography. He will also direct *Vanity Fair* and *House & Garden*, working for Nast until 1943.

For the Ludlow Typograph Company, Robert Hunter Middleton designs *Stellar*, the first humanist sans serif typeface, anticipating Hermann Zapf's *Optima* (1958) by twenty-nine years.

In New York, George Macy establishes The Limited Editions Club, a bibliophile publishing house organized around a yearly subscription that will commission leading illustrators, typographers, and printers. In spite of the Depression he will be able to publish on schedule, twelve books a year. Under his direction, there will also appear *The Dolphin*, which in some way will take the place of Stanley Morison's *The Fleuron* (1923). Frederic Warde will design the first issue.

1930

1930 Henry R. Luce invites Thomas Maitland Cleland, (*Della Robbia*, 1902) who had been an important book designer in the 1920s, as art director of his new monthly *Fortune* magazine. Although he only directed three issues, his layout design and covers will be maintained for ten years.

William Addison Dwiggins designs the *Metro* typeface series for the Mergenthaler Linotype Company. They will be issued as the first American sans serif typefaces to join the trend started by European type designs, *Futura* (Paul Renner, 1927), and *Kabel* (Rudolf Koch, 1927).

1931 The magazine of the British Printing Industry, *Printing Review*, is published in London from 1931 to 1959. It will include articles on design and developments in typography and layout.

Eric Gill publishes his *Essay on Typography*, set in his typeface, *Joanna* (1930), a serif companion to *Perpetua* (1929). In it, he demonstrates his belief in the merit of typographic composition with unjustified lines.

Swiss designer, teacher, and pioneer of the International Typographic Style Théo Ballmer, starts teaching at the Kunstgewerbeschule (*School of Applied Arts*), in Zurich. His rigorous use of the grid, combined with his pursuit of De Stijl principles, provides an understanding of how graphic design will be developed in Switzerland after the war.

Henry C. Beck, English draftsman for the London Underground Transport, submits a graphic interpretation of the route guide. Simplified to verticals, horizontals, and diagonals, this clear diagrammatic solution will become immensely popular after a printed trial in 1933. His work will later influence Massimo Vignelli's maps for the New York subway (1966), and the Washington Metro (1968).

1931 Philadelphia's advertising agency, N. W. Ayer & Son, establishes *The Ayer Award for Excellence in Newspaper Typography*.

An early use of the term *phototypesetting* appears in *ASME News*.

Kodak Company introduces *Kodalith*, the first high contrast lith film, so essential in the graphic arts industry, for halftone reproductions, photo-lettering, and photocomposition.

1932 London's main newspaper, the *Times*, changes its typography and masthead by introducing *Times New Roman*, produced under the direction of Stanley Morison and drawn by Victor Lardent. *Times New Roman* will become as important in the history of newspaper typefaces as was

Chauncey H. Griffith's *Ionic No. 5* in 1926. By 1933, this typeface will be available to the printing industry on Linotype and Monotype versions. Walter Tracy will redesign it in 1972, and Aurobind Patel will do it in 1990.

English calligrapher and typographer Alfred John Fairbank, student and friend of Edward Johnston, publishes his book, *A Handwriting Manual*, perhaps one of the most practical works on the drawing of the italic letter.

The London and North Eastern Railway (LNER) adopts *Gill Sans*, designed by Eric Gill in 1928, as the basis for establishing a typographic corporate identity.

1933 The Bauhaus school is finally closed under the pressure of Nazi political harassment. Jan Tschichold's ideas are considered *Kulturbolschevismus*, and he has to leave for Basle, Switzerland, where he starts to expand his typographical theories. Other professors, such as Walter Gropius, László Moholy-Nagy, and Ludwig Mies Van der Rohe will go to the United States.

1933 The Grolier Club publishes Stanley Morison's book, *Fra Luca de Pacioli of Borgo S. Sepolcro*, in a limited edition of 397 copies. Designed by Bruce Rogers, it displays Pacioli's *Classical Roman Alphabet*.

Robert Hunter Middleton is appointed director of type design for the Ludlow Typograph Company. He had been working there since 1923, when he collaborated with Ernst F. Detterer in designing *Eusebius* (1923), and its italic.

General Printing Ink Co. of New York obtains a patent for a photo-lettering machine that will be developed and manufactured by its Rutherford Machinery Division. Harold A. Horman and Ed Rondthaler were among the people who improved and persisted with this concept. In essence, the machine contained a photo-matrix slide that was moved manually to sandwich a selected character between a light source above and a projection lens below.

1934 English historian Alfred Forbes Johnson publishes his book *Type Designs: Their History and Developments*, a basic reference work on this subject.

1934 *PM* magazine (*Production Managers*), later named *AD* (*Advertising Design*), is established. It will present the work of both American and European typographers, and articles on the history of typography. Thomas Maitland Cleland will be in charge of its design, planning, and direction from 1939 to 1940.

Russian immigrant designer Alexey Brodovitch is invited by editor Carmel Snow to become art director of *Harper's Bazaar* in New York. There he will remain for twenty-five years, redefining the role of the art director and introducing new ideas in editorial graphics, typography, and photography.

The *All-Purpose Linotype* is perfected. Through manual assembling of matrices, it may cast faces up to 144 pts. This will be a direct competition with the Ludlow hot metal typecasting machine.

1935 British publisher Allen Lane founds *Penguin Books*. In collaboration with designer Edward Young (who creates its symbol), he selects *Gill Sans* (for the cover), and *Times New Roman* (for the body text), as part of the typographic approach for the pocket book editions of selected contemporary and historical literature. *Penguin Books* will do much to bring about the paperback revolution that will sweep both Europe and the United States following World War II.

At the request of Stanley Morison, German type designer Berthold Wolpe designs *Albertus* for the English Monotype. The lowercase will be added by 1938, and other weights by 1940. The City of London will use *Albertus* in its entire sign system in 1988.

Swiss designer Jan Tschichold, who has lived in Basle since 1933, publishes *Typographische Gestaltung* (English version, *Asymmetric Typography*, 1967), whose principles on asymmetrical typography and the use of sans serif typefaces will establish the foundations for modern typographic design.

1935 Works Progress Administration (WPA), instituted by President Franklin Delano Roosevelt, starts an eight-year program that brings modern typography to the American public through the commissioning of 35,000 designs (posters, informational graphics, etc.). Lester Beall's series of eight posters for the Rural Electrification Administration (1937-1941), characterized by strong colors and geometric simplicity, will be among the most significant graphic works.

From this year on, and up to 1941, Paul Rand becomes art director of *Esquire* and *Apparel Arts* magazines, enriching the conceptual role of the art director.

Russian immigrant Vladimir Zworykin invents the iconoscope, which permits an electronic analysis of images, giving birth to television in 1938.

After six years of work, Bruce Rogers finishes his typographical masterpiece, *The Oxford Lectern Bible*, published by Oxford University Press, set in his *Centaur* typeface, cut by the English Monotype.

1936 In Turin, type designer Aldo Novarese starts working for the Nebiolo type foundry. In collaboration with Alessandro Butti, he will develop *Athenaeum* (1945), *Normandía* (1949), and *Augustea* (1951). He will succeed Butti as art director in 1952.

In London, the quarterly *Typography* (up to 1939) is published by James Shand's Shenval Press, and edited by English designer Robert Harling. It will be one of the first publications to encourage display type design in England, by showing a renewed interest in nineteenth-century types.

At the Leipzig Fair, Hungarian Edmund Uher presents his *Uhertype*, the first phototypesetting machine developed in Europe.

After working thirty-nine years as Works Manager for the Lanston Monotype Corporation, American Frank Hinman Pierpont retires.

1936 New York letterer Howard Allen Trafton creates *Cartoon*. Issued by the Bauer type foundry in Germany it will give rise to a trend of alphabets evoking comic strip lettering, such as Max Kaufmann's *Balloon* (ATF, 1939), Edwin Shaar's *Flash* (Monotype, 1939), and Peter Dombrezian's *Dom Casual* (Photo-Lettering, 1952).

Linotype machines are capable of producing 4-pt size types, the smallest in mechanical typesetting.

From now and until the middle of the 1940s, many European designers and psychologists immigrate to America due to political, economic, and creative reasons. Their direct and indirect influence through their students will accelerate the spread of a new kind of typographic design –abstract, expressive, and dynamic. Among them are Herbert Bayer, Leo Lionni, Gyorgy Kepes, George Giusti, and Ladislav Sutnar. Jean Carlu and A. M. Cassandre will come from France to stay briefly. Among the psychologists are Rudolf Arnheim, Max Wertheimer, and Kurt Koffka, who will be influential in introducing Gestalt theories in America.

A commercially viable photographic display typesetting begins with the establishment of Photo-Lettering, Inc., headed by Ed Rondthaler, who had been an active participant in the improvement of the Rutherford Photo-Letter Composing Machine since 1933.

Chicago industrialist Walter P. Paepke starts a highly innovative advertising policy in collaboration with N. W. Ayer & Son advertising agency and the design direction of Egbert Jacobson. Their initiatives will place Container Corporation of America as the first company to establish a corporate identity program in the United States.

Charles Coiner, of N. W. Ayer & Son advertising agency, in Philadelphia, becomes art director of the CCA's account. He will produce a landmark series of ads that will feature the finest European /American artists and designers, and the latest techniques in printing and merchandising.

1937 French poster designer A. M. Cassandre creates sans serif *Peignot* for the Fonderie Deberny & Peignot, which brings the use of lowercase letters and small capitals onto the contemporary scene.

By this time, German typographer Jan Tschichold begins to question, and eventually reject, the principles stated in his *Die neue Typographie* (1928) as well as the use of sans serif typefaces that he now identifies with German fascist imagery.

1937 Walter Gropius, who had immigrated to the United States, and started teaching at the Harvard Graduate School of Design, invites László Moholy-Nagy, a former Bauhaus teacher, to be director of the New Bauhaus in Chicago. Moholy-Nagy introduces asymmetrical and dynamic arrangements of space, and the blending of photography and typography. In 1938, he will invite Hungarian designer Gyorgy

Kepes to teach photography and graphic design, drawing on Gestalt psychology.

For the first time, the Museum of Modern Art recognizes an American designer, Lester Beall, in a one-man exhibition. Beall was one of the first Americans to capture European experimental typography.

Chauncey H. Griffith, head of typographical development at Mergenthaler Linotype, designs *Bell Gothic*, primarily for use in the New York telephone directory. It will soon become a standard typeface for telephone books nationwide.

1938 English writer, Nicolette Gray, publishes *Nineteenth Century Ornamented Types and Title Pages*, an analysis of the English typographical trends in the Victorian Age that will influence type design and advertising.

1938 Physicist Chester Carlson formulates the basic principles of *Xerography*, a new photocopying process, which does not require special paper, works on the principle of positive and negative electromagnetic forces, and uses toner. It will be fully developed in 1947.

Austrian graphic designer and architect Herbert Bayer, who has just immigrated to the United States, organizes, in collaboration with Walter Gropius, the Museum of Modern Art exhibition, *Bauhaus 1919-1928*. It will contribute to the fame of the Bauhaus, and to the establishment of Modernism in America. Bauhaus principles will later be reflected in the Ulm Hochschule für Gestaltung founded in Ulm in 1950.

1939-1945 The Second World War occurs, causing an immense disturbance in all aspects of art, design and type production.

1939 In Berlin, German type designer Paul Renner publishes *Die Kunst der Typographie* (English and Spanish versions, 1998-2001), in which he illustrates the technical rigor he used to create *Futura*, both in form and legibility.

1939 A second fire disaster burns the Village Type Foundry to the ground, destroying much of Frederic Goudy's original type designs and thousands of matrices. Undaunted, Goudy will continue to work until his death eight years later.

Graphic designer Bradbury Thompson becomes art director of *Westvaco Inspirations for Printers*, the promotional periodical of the West Virginia Pulp and Paper Company, which he will print until 1962. He will also be one of the most influential designers in postwar America. His works will be a vehicle for experimental typography and printing.

As a consequence of war restrictions, the Pocket Book venture starts a new concept on book production and prompts technological developments in the printing industry, such as the use of offset lithography, the "perfect" binding with adhesives, and the introduction of soft covers.

The New York World's Fair opens with modernity as the overall design theme, and a decorative emphasis on streamline form. The new generation of American industrial designers

(Raymond Loewy, Norman Bel Geddes, and Henry Dreyfuss) will dominate the Fair. Immigrant Austrian designer Joseph Binder designs the World's Fair poster.

1940

1940 Type designer Sol Hess succeeds his friend and collaborator, Frederic W. Goudy, as art director of the American Lanston Monotype. He will develop an important program for many publishing companies, presses, and department stores. He will remain as such until his retirement in 1952.

1941 On January 3, Adolph Hitler, following Minister of Propaganda Joseph Goebbles' advice, orders to adopt the Roman alphabet, *Normalschrift*, as the official typeface to write the German language, instead of the *Fraktur* (*schwabacher*) type in use.

Between this time and 1975, German type designer Berthold Wolpe will create nearly 1,500 book covers for Faber & Faber, for which he makes ample use of his *Albertus* typeface (1935).

1941 Czechoslovakian immigrant designer Ladislav Sutnar starts working for Sweet's Catalog Service where he will popularize the use of the grid for organizing complex, technical information.

Paul Rand starts working as art director of William H. Weintraub advertising agency, New York. In collaboration with William Bernbach, he pioneers the integration of art and copy, a development that will change advertising during postwar years.

1942 Swiss typographer, graphic designer and educator Emil Ruder starts teaching at the Allgemeine Gewerbeschule (*School of Applied Arts*) in Basle, and will continue until 1970. His work and writings will contribute to the rational use of the International Typographic Style.

Catalan typographer Joan Trochut creates a series of modular type elements (fourteen in total), with which he is able to construct a comprehensive typography. Called *Súper Tipo Veloz*, and composed of more than fifty alphabets and a wide series of ornaments, this will present, through a series of promotional booklets, a solution to many postwar problems for small print shops.

The *European Book Production War Economy Agreement* establishes strict specifications to prevent wastage: type should not be less than 58 per cent of the page and have a maximum point size according to formats. Paper rationing will not end in England until 1949.

1942 The AIGA's *Books by Offset* exhibition, consisting of ninety outstanding works, shows the importance of this new printing technique.

1943 Bruce Rogers publishes, in a limited edition, a present classical work on this subject entitled *Paragraphs on Printing*, published by William E. Rudge's Sons in New York.

1944 In Zurich, Swiss designer Walter Herdeg edits and designs the trilingual journal *Graphis*, which will be influential in

encouraging progressive developments and fostering new talent from this moment on. It will be complemented by annual publications since 1952.

1944 Gyorgy Kepes publishes his influential text *Language of Vision*, in which perception is analyzed as the result of the immediate, biological perception rather than as a cultural conditioned intellect. The use of Gestalt psychology lends the language of vision a scientific rationale. Written at the Institute of Design in Chicago, it articulates Bauhaus principles.

Robert Hunter Middleton founds the Cherryburn Press where he will print many books, the best known of which is Thomas Bewick's three wood engraving portfolios (1945, 1970, and 1972), printed to a standard not reached by Bewick himself.

1945 In London, Stanley Morison is appointed editor of the *Times Literary Supplement*.

French Engineers René Higonnet and Louis Moyroud establish the principle of stroboscopically selecting and imaging characters from a font arrayed around and on a continuously spinning, photo-matrix disc. The flash feasibility model was also completed, though the first demonstration under the name of *Photon-Lumitype* will not take place in New York until 1950, and in Paris until 1954.

1946 Sir Allen Lane, publisher of *Penguin Books*, engages Jan Tschichold to redesign all its publications, establishing *The Penguin Composition Rules* (1947) for typographic design. During his three-year stay in London, he will design more than 500 titles in a now classical approach, with symmetrical compositions and serif typefaces.

In London, Robert Harling and James Shand's Shenval Press once again join efforts, publishing *Alphabet and Image*, a journal on typography, book design, and illustration.

1946 One year before Frederic W. Goudy dies, the Typophiles of New York, publishes, in a limited edition of 725 copies, his book *A Half-Century of Type Design and Typography 1895-1945*, a rich autobiographical type specimen book in two volumes.

Engineers John P. Eckart and John W. Maunchly invent the first electronic calculator or computer. The system, known as *ENIAC* (*Electronic Numerical Integrator and Computer*), is initially created for computing missile trajectories.

The Walker Art Center, Minneapolis, starts publishing *Design Quarterly* that will provide a useful, if variable, academic coverage of most aspects of American design.

The U.S. Government Printing Office installs the Harris-Intertype Fotosetter in Washington. *The National Gallery of Art* pamphlet will be the first publication to be filmset. Combined with offset lithography, phototypesetting fosters a decade of expressive and experimental graphic design, making printing from metal type obsolete.

Paul Rand publishes *Thoughts on Design* with over eighty examples of his work, in which he plans his conceptual approach to design.

The Type Directors Club (TDC) of New York is founded with the aim of elevating standards in typography and its related graphic arts.

1947 French graphic and type designer Roger Excoffon opens his own design studio while he continues working as art consultant to the Fonderie Olive in Marseille until 1959. For this type foundry, he will design *Banco* (1951), *Vendôme* (1952), *Mistral* (1953), *Choc* (1955), *Diane* (1956), *Calypso* (1958), and *Antique Olive* (1962).

Swiss graphic designer Armin Hoffmann starts teaching at the School of Arts and Crafts in Basle.

English type designer Walter Tracy starts working for Linotype England as head of the Department of Type Development. He will create *Jubilee* (the *Glasgow Herald*, 1953), *Linotype Modern* (the *Daily Telegraph*, 1969), and *Times Europa* (*The Times*, 1972), a redesign of *Times New Roman* (1932).

1947 The *Justowriter*, an automatic-justifying typewriter, is marketed by Commercial Controls Corporation of America. The justified copy could be typed directly with a special tape on the master plate for printing.

László Moholy-Nagy's *Vision in Motion*, a complement to *The New Vision* (1929), is published posthumously (he died in 1946). The book concentrates on the work at the Institute of Design in Chicago, and presents a broader view of the interrelatedness of art, science, and technology.

The Haloid Company, Rochester, which will later become Xerox Corporation, is interested in Chester Carlson's *Xerography*, and after buying its rights, begins its development. The following year, it will be presented in the annual meeting of the Optical Society of America in Detroit.

1948 The Alliance Graphique Internationale (AGI) is founded in Paris by A. M. Cassandre, Charles Loupot, and Maurice Moyrand, French and Swiss designers. Their first meeting will take place in Paris in 1951. The original European membership will be extended to distinguished practitioners worldwide.

1949 English typographic designer, author and educator Herbert Spencer starts publishing the journal *Typographica* (up to 1967) with illustrations of all aspects of contemporary typography. It will include thirty-two issues.

German typographer Hans Schmoller, who had worked with The Curwen Press in London, joins *Penguin Books* as the successor of Jan Tschichold, giving the publications a more stylish typographic appearance.

1949 Graphic designer Bob Cage and copywriter William Bernbach, founders of the Doyle Dane Bernbach advertising agency, New York, start changing the look of advertising through close collaboration between copywriter and art director. Their 1960s advertising campaigns for Orbach's, Levy's Bread, and especially for Volkswagen, will gain them international acclaim.

By this time, television has become the powerful visual communication language, opening new channels and establishing new patterns for advertising, publicity, and promotion. ABC, CBS, and NBC are the nationwide television networks.

1950

1950 German type foundry D. Stempel AG issues Hermann Zapf's series, *Palatino*, which he had designed two years before. This year *Michelangelo*, a display title typeface, will also appear, and the following year *Sistina*, the heaviest of the three designs.

Italian graphic designer and painter Franco Grignani, member of the second Futurist movement, starts experimenting in the field of optical dynamics, developing a personal and unique visual and typographical vocabulary. In Milan, he will do outstanding typographical work for Alfieri & Lacroix typo-lithographers.

The Ulm Hochschule für Gestaltung (*Technical College for Design*) is founded. Under the direction of Max Bill, the school, with four main divisions: product design, architecture, visual communication, and information, will reflect functionalist Bauhaus principles. When Argentinean Tomás Maldonado succeeds Bill in 1957, the school changes its curriculum, introducing sociology, psychology, and cultural history. Eventually, due to a difference in ideas, the school will close in 1968.

1950 Yale University founds the Design Department under the direction of German artist and designer Josef Albers. It is in New Haven that he will start painting his famous *Homage to the Square*.

Container Corporation of America, under the direction of Walter P. Paepcke, with the collaboration of distinguished American and international designers, starts the worldwide successful institutional campaign, *Great Ideas of Western Man*, which will continue for over three decades.

Designer Bradbury Thompson introduces his *alphabet 26*, a logical system with a mixture of capitals and lowercase letters. While vowels e and a, and consonants m and n remain in lowercase form, the rest of the letters appear as capitals.

1951 German psychologist and immigrant Rudolf Arnheim, student of Max Wertheimer, publishes his influential book, *Perception: A Psychology of the Creative Eye*. In it, he uses scientific findings to better understand the arts while preserving the role of subjectivity, intuition, and self-expression. *Visual Thinking* will follow it in 1969.

Walter P. Paepcke, president of CCA, founds the Aspen International Design Conference in collaboration with designers Herbert Bayer, Leo Lionni, Robert Hunter Middleton, and George Nelson, among others. The first round table discussion is on *"Design, a Function of Management."* Since then, many have considered it the most important annual meeting of design.

Designer William Golden, who had been art director since 1949, becomes creative director of Advertising and Sales Promotion for CBS. His pioneering corporate identity program, including CBS's eye (1951), is still considered one of the best ever done.

CBS pioneers color TV in the United States with its weekly program, *CBS Show*. Nevertheless, color television sets are not completely available.

Alvin Lustig, known for his magazine designs, covers, and striking layouts, helps establish the graphic design program at Yale University.

1952 French typographer Maximilien Vox (Samuel Théodore Monod), proposes a type classification, which continues to be the most comprehensive. An extension of Francis Thibaudeau's proposal (1921), Vox bases it more on history and style than on just serif configuration.

In Zurich, Swiss designer Walter Herdeg starts editing *Graphis Annual*, as a complement to his *Graphis* magazine published since 1944. In 1973, he will publish *Graphis Posters*, followed by further annual publications on different aspects of applied design.

Swiss typographer and type designer Adrian Frutiger starts working as a designer for the Fonderie Deberny & Peignot. Two years later, he will begin the creation and development of the sans serif *Univers* type family, which will be issued in 1957.

Hermann Zapf designs *Melior* for use in newspapers and magazines. The ellipsis used by Zapf anticipates the known super-ellipsis, conceived by Piet Hein in 1965, and described in the *Scientific American* this year. It was issued for both hand and metal type composition.

In Turin, Italian type designer Aldo Novarese becomes art director of Nebiolo type foundry. Among his typefaces, some of them designed in collaboration with Alessandro Butti, are *Microgramma* (1952), *Egizio* (1955), *Slogan* (1957), *Eurostile* (1962), *Stop* (1971), and *ITC Novarese* (1978).

1952 In New York, typographic designer Aaron Burns becomes director of The Composing Room, an important type house which sets and sells type commercially and which will be instrumental in imposing standards of advertising typography.

The Wonderful World of Insects by Albro T. Gaul is the first book to be phototypeset in America, in the Higonnet-Moyroud phototypesetting system. Set in *Scotch Roman*, and printed by letterpress from powderless-etched magnesium plates, it will be published by Reinhardt & Co. Inc, in 1953.

1953 English typographers W.P. Jaspert, W.T. Berry and A.F. Johnson publish the most comprehensive world *Encyclopaedia of Type Faces* yet published. Typefaces are grouped by styles: serif, sans serif, and calligraphic designs. In future editions (1958 and 1970), they will revise and enlarge its contents.

1953 Robert M. Jones, art director of RCA Victor Records, establishes the private press the Glad Hand Press. By often setting record album designs, using wood types, he initiates a renewed interest in nineteenth century decorative and novelty typography.

Hugh Hefner, former *Esquire* magazine staff member, starts publishing *Playboy* magazine. Marilyn Monroe appears in the first cover.

1954 German type designer Hermann Zapf publishes his *Manuale typographicum*, an extraordinary work of type, lettering, and book design that presents 100 typographical arrangements based on single-page quotations on typography.

1954 In New York, designers Milton Glaser and Seymour Chwast, and illustrators Reynolds Ruffins and Edward Sorel found the Push Pin Studio. Seymour Chwast directs the in-house publication, *Push Pin Graphic*. The studio will establish itself in the 1960s as the best-known American design group by challenging the dominant International Typographic Style. The use of bright colors, flattening outlines, and clever, sometimes bizarre image juxtapositions, exemplify their work.

1955 English typographer John Dreyfus is appointed typographical adviser for the Lanston Monotype Corporation, Ltd. with the retirement of Stanley Morison. Under his advice, Monotype will produce, in 1958, Adrian Frutiger's *Univers* (1957), which will compete with Max Miedinger's *Neue Haas Grotesk/Helvetica* (1957).

American typographer and author Beatrice Warde, defender of classical typography, publishes in London *The Crystal Goblet: Sixteen Essays on Typography*.

1955 By this time television has been described as marking "a transition from word thinking to visual thinking" (Hainline). Many leading art directors and magazine designers have been giving great attention to the interrelation of images and text to produce a faster and more dynamic delivery of information as a direct way to compete with television.

Designer Saul Bass creates the title design for Otto Preminger's film, *The Man with the Golden Arm*. By reducing the array of predictable images to a minimum of graphic elements, he establishes a new global approach to film graphic presentation and advertising. Over time, he will work with directors such as Alfred Hitchcock, Stanley Kubrick, William Wyler, and Martin Scorsese, among others, and will do extraordinary work for more than forty films.

The Type Directors Club of New York organizes the first annual typographic competition (for club members only). The following year, it will be opened to all designers.

1956 Around this time, the Pop Art movement appears in England (in America around 1961), elevating the popular advertising imagery (fast food, supermarket packaging, comic strips, journalistic photography, ordinary automobiles, etc.) to fine art. The combination of flat, coarse colors with super-enlargements of halftone screen dots and commonplace objects, and mechanical repetition of mass media, establishes a rich new vein for graphic designers. Among their most relevant American artists will be Andy Warhol, Roy Lichtenstein, Claes Oldenburg, and James Rosenquist.

Paul Klee's *Das bildnerische Denken* (*The Thinking Eye*), a collection of his classroom theories at the Bauhaus, and one of the most serious works on plastic and visual structure theories, is published posthumously in Basle (he died in 1940). The English translation will appear in England in 1961.

1956 In Cambridge, Massachusetts, while professor of Visual Design at MIT, Hungarian designer Gyorgy Kepes publishes *The New Landscape*, a new aspect of nature revealed through science and technology.

Phototypesetting developments of Higonnet and Moyroud reach the production stage with the *Photon 200* machine, in which sixteen typefaces stored in a round photo-matrix could be enlarged through a set of lenses. One of the first works to be type-composed with it will be the two-volumes (1,500 pages) of the *Funk & Wagnalls Standard International Dictionary*.

Paul Rand becomes design consultant for IBM, Cummins Engine Co., and Westinghouse Electric Corporation, creating some of his best-known corporate images.

1957 Association Typographique Internationale (ATypI) is founded in Lausanne, Switzerland by Charles Peignot (France), Hermann Zapf (Germany), Robert Hunter Middleton (USA), and John Dreyfus (England), among others, "to bring about a better understanding of typography," and to improve international copyright protection for typeface design.

Swiss type foundry Haas'sche Schriftgießerei issues *Neue Haas Grotesk*, conceived by Eduard Hoffmann and drawn by Max Miedinger, and influenced by H. Berthold AG type foundry's *Akzidenz Grotesk* (1898). In 1960, D. Stempel AG type foundry will negotiate rights and will issue it as *Helvetica*, making it one of the most popular sans serif typefaces of the twentieth century.

The Fonderie Deberny & Peignot type foundry, in collaboration with Monotype Corporation, inaugurates the *Lumitype* composing machine, commercializing Adrian Frutiger's *Univers*. Designed for both film and metal typesetting, the typeface will include twenty-one variants, all designed under Frutiger supervision.

1957 An early use of the term *photosetting* occurs in the *American Annual*.

1958 English writer Ruari McLean edits *Motif, a Journal of the Visual Arts*. Published by James Shand's Shenval Press, it will emphasize book illustration and typography.

Swiss graphic designer Josef Müller-Brockmann founds and co-edits the *Neue Graphik* (*New Graphic Design*) magazine with Richard Lohse, Hans Neuberg, and Carlo Vivarelli. A trilingual journal, it will play an important role in spreading the Swiss design principles internationally.

Swiss type designer Adrian Frutiger becomes art director for the Fonderie Deberny & Peignot type foundry.

German type foundry D. Stempel AG issues Hermann Zapf's *Optima*, a humanist sans serif typeface. Designed as *Neue Antiqua* (1952-55), it will become one of the most beautiful typefaces of the twentieth century. Quite close in design and structure, but with a larger x-height, it will overshadow *Stellar*, designed by Robert Hunter Middleton in 1929.

In their Centenary year, German type foundry H. Berthold AG enters into photo-lettering with *Dyatype*, the world's first commercial photosetting system.

1958 In Silvermine, Connecticut, Aaron Burns and Will Burtin organize the first international typography seminar, *The Art and Science of Typography*.

Print, a revised form of the earlier *Print: a Quarterly Journal of the Graphic Arts*, starts publication.

Physicist Chester F. Carlson succeeds in perfecting the xerographic printing process (1938) and makes it available for use in office work.

1959 German firm Hell Digiset GmbH, Kiel, constructs a scanner that allows for the production of halftone negatives.

In Switzerland, Swiss graphic designers Karl Gerstner and Markus Kutter publish *Die neue Graphik* (*The New Graphic Art*). An example of the Swiss Graphic Style, it is a fundamental book, outlining key developments in graphic design up to the 1950s.

1959 American *National Geographic* magazine installs the first *Linofilm* model with whole coverage. Though the phototypesetting process is more flexible, it still maintains many problems related to typeface proportions and their line justification.

Following the sudden death of William Golden, Lou Dorfsman is appointed creative director of Design for the CBS Television Network. He will continue Golden's tradition of excellence in TV graphics, promotion, and advertising.

Photo-Lettering, Inc., under the direction of Ed Rondthaler, publishes *Alphabet Thesaurus No. 1*, with 3,000 alphabets, causing a sensation in the graphic and advertising world. A second volume appeared in 1965 and a third in 1971.

1960

1960 British writer Nicolette Gray publishes her book, *Lettering on Buildings*.

English calligrapher and type designer Alfred Fairbank writes *Renaissance Handwriting: An Anthology of Italic Scripts*, in collaboration with German calligrapher and type designer Berthold Wolpe.

French engineer Pierre Bézier, former employee of Renault, who had conceived the machines for the construction of the 4CV motors in 1945, develops the bézier curves and surfaces for CAD/CAM operations, which will become the underpinning of the entire Adobe *PostScript* drawing model as well as for 3D drawing programs.

1960 Bill Garth (former president of Photon Inc.), and Ellis Hanson found Compugraphic Corporation, a digital type foundry, in Wilmington, Massachusetts.

In New York, Aaron Burns founds the International Center for the Typographic Arts (ICTA), in collaboration with German typographer Emil Ruder. He will become its president in 1961.

In Malibu, California, Theodore H. Maiman is able to generate a laser beam at the Hughes Laboratory. Nevertheless, it is not until 1972 that laser first come forward in phototypesetting as a substitute of the xenon flash tube in a *Photon 560* machine.

Educated at Pratt Institute, George Lois becomes the first director to head his own advertising agency, Papert Koenig Lois, in New York. His ninety-two irreverent, humorous, and witty covers for *Esquire* magazine will grant him the art director of the year award in 1963.

1961 *Letraset*, the first dry transfer type process, is introduced in England. Developed by John Charles Clifford 'Dai' Davies and Fred McKenzie, it will provide the graphic designer with instant headline lettering. The more than 800 future alphabets available will reflect the continuously changing typographic trends.

After working freelance for H. Berthold AG type foundry since 1950, German type designer Günter Gerhard Lange is appointed type director. He will be responsible for a dynamic design program of original typefaces as well as for licensing and adapting typefaces from other sources. Among his type designs are *Derby* (1953), *Solemnis* (1954), *Boulevard* (1955), *El Greco* (1964), and *Concorde* (1969).

Drawing upon facets of Futurism, Dadaism, the 1920s Soviet group LEF, and Russian Constructivism, a group identified as Fluxus appears in Germany. It experiments with typography, legibility, communication structure, and rules of typesetting in even the most unconventional message. Its unorthodox artistic modes of presentation will offer alternatives to Pop Art, Conceptual Art, and Performance Art. Its graphic methods will later be carried forth by "anti-art" groups such as Punk and the Situationists International. Besides its coordinator and theorist, George Maciunas, Dick Higgins, Ken Friedman, and Wolf Vostell may be mentioned.

1961 Aaron Burns publishes *typography*, a book which concentrates on the expressive potential of typography freed from the constraints of hot metal type.

IBM introduces the office typewriter, *IBM-72 Selectric*, designed by Eliot Noyes, with a mono element in the form of a golf ball that allows the user to interchange type styles within a typewritten text.

1962 Swiss designer Walter Amstutz edits and designs *Who's Who in Graphic Art*, an illustrated review of leading contemporary graphic and typographic designers, illustrators and cartoonists from all over the world. Twenty years later, he will publish a second edition with 892 pages, including *A Short History of the Graphic Arts* by Willi Rotzler, and covering a wider selection of graphic designers and countries.

English graphic designers Alan Fletcher, Colin Forbes, and Bob Gill form one of the most creative partnerships in the world of design. In 1965, Theo Crosby will enter as a partner when Gill leaves the firm, and by 1972, the group will become Pentagram.

1962 Architect Robert Venturi, one of the most controversial of the so-called Supermannerists, innovates architectural design by introducing the Supergraphics concept. Using giant stencil letterforms as a decoration of Grand's Restaurant in West Philadelphia, he alters space and scale. Supergraphics will soon be included into corporate identification systems, decorating shops and boutiques, and bringing a new look to architectural environments.

1963 The Monotype Photo-lettering Machine, a manually operated device with characters selected for exposure by dialing at the front of the unit, is inaugurated. The first application will be with display type.

In London, ICOGRADA (International Council of Graphic Design Associations), whose aims are concerned with the raising of graphic design standards, is founded. Today, it embraces more than fifty design associations worldwide and 30,000 designers.

An early use of the terms, *computer-aided* and *computer-controlled typesetting*, occurs.

In London, Letraset Limited launches its first original typeface design, *Compacta*, created by Fred Lambert.

In Amsterdam, Total Design, the first multidisciplinary design studio in Holland, is founded by: graphic designer Wim Crouwel; industrial designer Friso Kramer; and architect and graphic designer Benno Wissing, among others. It will be recognized for its commitments to the International Typographic Style. The work of Crouwel will be quite significant in type design through proposals like *New Alphabet* (1967) and *Oldenburg* (1968), among others.

1963 Compugraphic Corporation brings into the market the *Linasec*, a typesetting computer, which marks the beginning of the computer age in America. By 1970, the company will be a leader in the market.

Swiss type designer Adrian Frutiger is appointed consultant for IBM, advising on typefaces for

typewriters. Thus, *Univers* will be offered in the *IBM-72 Selectric* (1961) type catalog.

Lou Dorfsman conceives the idea for a horizontal 40' x 8.5' three-dimensional, typographic assemblage mural for the CBS cafeteria. Herb Lubalin will collaborate by doing the overall lettering layout to scale, and Tom Carnase by doing the intricate lettering.

Pantone Co., New Jersey, founded in 1953, is bought by one of its employees, Lawrence Herbert, who introduces the *Pantone Matching System* (PMS), which in a short time will become a leader among the color specification systems. One of its advantages is the possibility of checking the printed color on both glossy and matte surfaces.

Josef Albers, professor at Yale University School of Art & Architecture, publishes *Interaction of Color*, a collection of his lectures on color, and quite an influential work since then.

Designer Ben Rosen publishes *Type and Typography*, a serious reference work on the best metal type currently used in the United States. It includes many typefaces from European foundries, all in complete alphabet setting.

1964 French art director and typographer Robert Massin publishes his phototypographic version of Eugène Ionesco's *La Cantatrice Chauve* (*The Bald Soprano*), still one of the most powerful examples of typographical design. He will repeat this experience in 1966, with *Delire à Deux*.

Japanese design critic and journalist Masaru Katsumie supervises the visual design program for the 1964 Tokyo Olympics, with pictographic symbols designed by Yoshiro Yamashita. They were the first pictographs ever designed for a heterogeneous in-coming audience. Yusaku Kamekura designs all the posters, gaining international fame.

English photographer Collin Brignall joins Letraset Limited as a photographic technician in its type design studio. He will later become type designer, creating *Aachen, Lightline, Premier,* and *Revue* in 1969.

Swiss graphic designer Rosemarie Tissi, who studied at the Kunstgewerbeschule, Zurich, inspired by Post-modernism, starts breaking from the International Typographic Style by introducing a new approach to text and page layout. The following will be part of the vocabulary of the new generation of designers: the use of contrasting type weights, sometimes within the same word; the previous establishment of a grid and its subsequent violation; the use of wide letter spacing and reversed type on rectangular shapes; and the definition of the overall space as a field of tensions.

1964 *Typomundus 20*, an international exhibition of the most significant typography of the twentieth century, is organized by Aaron Burns. It is sponsored by the International Center for the Typographic Arts, founded in 1960 in New York City.

Canadian media theorist Herbert Marshall McLuhan, author of *The Gutenberg Galaxy* (1962), publishes his controversial book, *Understanding Media*, where he states, "the medium is the massage." This book, and others of his, will have a profound influence on man's thinking about his communication techniques. In 1967, he will publish *The Medium is the Massage*, a challenging graphic-visual proposal, in collaboration with designer Quentin Fiore.

The Headliners Process Lettering publishes a photo-lettering type specimen booklet with the Morgan Press Type Collection of nineteenth-century typefaces. Designed by John Alcorn, it will be one of the many phototype collections that will make the Victorian typefaces widely known.

In New York, designer Reid Miles becomes art director of *Blue Note* records. During five years, he will create a series of very innovative and imaginative typographical covers for this record firm specializing in jazz, which helped to reinforce its global identity.

Artist, illustrator, and letterer Ben Shahn publishes *Love and Joy About Letters*, a superb example of his unique brush and pen writing that reflects high understanding of letterforms.

Designer John Massey becomes director of design at CCA, introducing *Helvetica* and the International Typographic Style, and imposing a strict visual discipline upon all printed communications.

1965 In Basle, Emil Ruder becomes director of the Allgemeine Gewerbeschule and the Kunstgewerbemuseum, continuing with his teaching activities begun in 1942. Other designers, who collaborated as teachers and designers to make the school influential at an international level, are Armin Hofmann, Robert Gürtler, and Wolfgang Weingart.

Swiss graphic designer Armin Hofmann publishes *Graphic Design Manual*, a collection of his teachings, and an essential text for basic design courses.

Dr. Rudolf Hell of Kiel develops the *Hell Digiset* photosetting machine, permitting the typesetting of 6,000 characters per second in sizes from 4 to 18 points. The image is created on the line grid of a high definition cathode-ray tube (CRT), which also permits photographic copies on paper or film.

1965 At the same time as Dr. Rudolf Hell's *Digiset* phototypesetter machine is developed, Radio Corporation of America (RCA) announces *Videocomp* with similar characteristics.

Around this time, a product of the hippie movement, a particular style of poster design with an aggressive use of color known as *Psychedelia* arises in America. Although a mixture of many influences, Oriental and European, the drug-inspired palette and comic book iconography marks *Psychedelia* as a distinctively American graphic style. Victor Moscoso, Wes Wilson, and Peter Max will be among the most innovative artists.

International Business Machines (IBM) introduces a programmed composition for the paper tapes running Linotype machines. This concept forms the basis for computer typesetting, in which computers determine hyphenation, length of lines, corrections, and presentation of text.

Graphic designer Rudolph De Harak creates MacGraw Hill publisher's symbol, and starts a global visual concept for their paperback series using a basic grid system and sans serif typography. By 1967, De Harak will have designed more than 350 book jackets.

The Type Directors Club of New York organizes the first annual international typographical competition. Five years later, the TDC publishes its first yearbook.

1966 Swiss typographer Jan Tschichold finishes *Sabon* (1964-1966), a typeface based on *Garamond*. Named after French punch-cutter Jakob Sabon, who cut faces for Robert Granjon and Claude Garamond, it is the first typeface to be designed for three different type casting systems: hand composition, Monotype, and Linotype.

After his first work is completed in 1964, French graphic designer Robert Massin publishes his second extraordinary typographical experience, this time on texts from *Delire a Deux*, a theater work also by Eugène Ionesco. His unique handling of type and images remain today outstanding.

In Madrid, Spanish graphic designer Daniel Gil starts a global design program for Alianza Editorial's pocket book publications. His conceptual approach in handling content through photographed images and text will place conceptual design at its best. His more than 4,000 covers will testify plainly to this.

1966 Lou Dorfsman, director of design for the entire CBS Corporation since 1964, starts a global program of typographic information and sign systems with the construction of a new building for CBS, designed by Eero Saarinen. As part of the CBS typographical identity program, Dorfsman commissions Freeman Craw to design *CBS Didot* and *CBS Sans*.

Kodak Co. introduces a range of stabilized papers for phototypesetting. Incorporated in the photosensitive emulsion, there are developing agents that remain dormant until activated by chemical processing.

1967 Swiss typographer Emil Ruder, after twenty-one years of teaching, publishes *Typographie*, his influential design book on this subject.

French philosopher Jacques Derrida publishes *Of Grammatology*, in France (English translation, 1976), in which he introduces the concept of *deconstruction*, which will be later applied –among other theories addressed in Post-structuralism– in various U.S. art and design programs. These theories will be applied to graphic design and typography as an experimental tool to layout again many of the well-established concepts on typographical and reading hierarchies. One of the clearest intersections of Post-structuralism

and graphic design will take place in the Cranbrook Academy of Art in 1978.

1967 Pop Art painter Robert Indiana exhibits a series of paintings based on the word **LOVE**. He uses letters, numbers, and word pictures from American slang as the basis for abstract symbols in his work.

The first American cathode-ray tube (CRT) phototypesetter, the *Linotron 1010*, a third generation totally electronic machine, is installed in the U.S. Government Printing Office. Letter shapes are stored in digital form, and for the first time, typefaces may be seen on the screen.

The Cleveland Museum of Art in Ohio starts publishing *Journal of Typographic Research*.

1968 In Frankfurt am Main, Swiss type designer Adrian Frutiger is appointed typographic consultant for the D. Stempel AG type foundry. This year, he will also design *OCR-B* (*Optical Character Recognition*), a font computers can read and which, in time, will become an international standard.

In Basle, German typographer Wolfgang Weingart starts teaching at the Schule für Gestaltung (*School of Design*) as successor to Emil Ruder, with a typographical approach that defies the principles established by the Swiss School. He will propose an alternative –known as *New Wave*– that will later be followed by many American and European designers.

The student-worker uprising events in Paris of May 1968 produces a creative stimulus to a renewal of protest imagery. The use of boldly simplified forms, terse language, and deliberately crude lettering will serve as a model to others, as will be seen in the 1968 to 1970 American students' demonstrations throughout the country.

1968 In New York, Herb Lubalin creates *Avant Garde* magazine, the third of Ralph Ginsberg's publications, which continues to assure his talent as editorial designer. In 1970, its titling will give birth to *ITC Avant Garde Gothic*, a typeface designed in collaboration with Tom Carnase.

In Toronto, Canadian type designer Leslie Usherwood founds Typesettra as a trade headline and photocomposition service. Among the typefaces that he will design are *Caxton*, *Graphis Bold* (1971), and *Octavia* (1973). The firm will diversify as a type design studio in 1977.

In Chicago, the *PRINT '68* exhibition makes photoypesetting techniques popular. Initiated by Compugraphic Corporation with the presentation of a series of inexpensive machines, it will accelerate the demise of hot metal typesetting.

By this time there is a great concern for advertising directed to black audience. John H. Johnson, editor of *Ebony*, *Jet*, *Negro Digest*, and *Tan*, had encouraged national advertisers to promote their products in black markets since the appearance of these magazines.

1969 The Crosfield and Hell firms commercialize photoengraving scanners with color correction.

English typographical designer Herbert Spencer publishes *Pioneers of Modern Typography*, which displays the work of artists and designers of the inter-war period, such as El Lissitzky, Piet Zwart, Kurt Schwitters, Alexandr Rodchenko, Théo Van Doesburg, and Jan Tschichold.

1969 In New York, Herb Lubalin founds the International Typeface Corporation (ITC) in collaboration with Aaron Burns and Edward Rondthaler in order to develop typefaces for photocomposition and digitization. In this same year, they issue Lubalin's *ITC Avant Garde* and Benguiat's *ITC Souvenir*. Among the type designers that will design for the firm are Herb Lubalin, Tony DiSpigna, Tom Carnase, Edward Benguiat, Hermann Zapf, Aldo Novarese, Jovica Veljovic, Tony Stan, Matthew Carter, Ernst Friz, Leslie Usherwood, and Robert Slimbach.

CBS television introduces *Vidifont*, one of the first electronic type generators for television. Massive switcher systems are computerized; digital-effects generators create composite graphics and effects. Previous television type was videotaped artwork.

Graphic designer Rob Roy Kelly publishes his type research, *American Wood Type, 1828-1900*, the most complete work on the subject. It contains notes on the evolution of decorated typefaces and related trades of the period as well as extensive biographical data, including over 102 complete fonts.

Photo-Lettering, Inc., publishes a *Psychedelitype* catalog, which makes it possible for anyone to set type in psychedelic style.

1970

1970 Letraset, Ltd. puts into circulation its *Letragraphica typefaces* selected by leading designers from all over the world, including Herb Lubalin, Roger Excoffon, Colin Forbes, and Derek Birdsall.

The Musée des Arts Décoratifs in Paris presents the first exhibition of an American group: the Push Pin Studio. The exhibition will travel to other cities in Europe and Japan. Their work was described as intellectually diverse, articulated and above all authentic. Its impact will later be seen on the work of other illustrators.

French graphic designer Robert Massin publishes *Letter and Image*, a perceptive summary of lettering and alphabet design.

1970 Mergenthaler Linotype Co. terminates production of hot-metal line casting machines in the United States. Some 90,000 units had emerged from American factories. Manufacture of the machines continued in Germany and the United Kingdom.

Graphic designer Quentin Fiore who had designed McLuhan's *The Medium is the Massage* in 1964, produces a second typographical work, now with architect Buckminster Fuller: *I Seem to Be a Verb*, a general study of the environment, focusing (loosely) on technology rather than media.

1971 The Fundición Tipográfica Nacional, Madrid, is bought by Fundición Tipográfica Neufville, Barcelona.

1971 Compugraphic Corporation commercializes the *CompuWriter*, the earliest inexpensive direct-entry phototypesetter. It will gain immediate acceptance by the printing industry.

Allen Hurlburt, art director renowned for his publication design, especially for *Look* magazine (1953-1971), publishes his book *Publication Design*. He will later complement this work with *Layout: The Design of the Printed Page* (1977), and *The Grid* (1978).

1972 The *Times* of London changes its *Times New Roman* typeface (Stanley Morison, 1932) for *Times Europa*, redesigned by English type designer Walter Tracy, as a way to adapt it to photocomposition as well as to the new printing processes. It later reverted to the original *Times New Roman*.

In Munich, German graphic designer, typographer, and cofounder of the Ulm Hochschule, Otl Aicher, leads a visual design group in the creation of all the pictograms as well as a graphic sign system for the XX World Olympic Games, which will succeed as a worldwide visual vocabulary.

English graphic design partnership, Crosby/Fletcher/Forbes, becomes Pentagram. Relying on strong concepts, sharp wit, and an unerring graphic design style, it becomes one of the most creative and intelligent studios worldwide.

1972 The MGD Graphic Systems Division of Rockwell International introduces the *Metro-Set* cathode ray tube phototypesetter, the first to deploy successfully digital fonts with characters defined as outlines, allowing the management of all sizes up to 72 points, and eliminating the need to store a bit map for each type size.

The Architecture Machine Group at the Massachusetts Institute of Technology (MIT) develops gray-scale fonts that permit a sharper visual image on the screen. Previous to this, type on video screen appeared chunky as a result of pixeling.

Type designer Warren Chappell publishes his book, *A Short History of the Printed Word*, well illustrated with fine examples, accompanied by his own descriptive drawings.

The first use of the term *floppy disc* to describe an external magnetic computer memory formed by a flexible plastic base appears.

From this date onwards, artist and graphic designer Barbara Kruger starts designing a series of picture-text montages much influenced by Constructivism's, Bauhaus's, and Dada's visual approaches. Her use of photographs with texts set in *Futura Bold*, white on black or white on red shapes, on magazine cover designs, billboards, interior and exterior spaces, will serve to make straight forward comments on cultural, social, political, sexual, and religious concepts, while graphically integrating type, image, and content.

1973 Letraset, Ltd. opens an International Typeface Competition to enrich its original type library. It will be followed by a series of events and contests for students during the late 1970s and 1980s with the same purpose.

1973 In New York City, Joseph Blumenthal devotes himself to the mounting of the exhibition, *The Art of the Printed Book 1455-1955*, which will present 112 masterpieces of printing at the Pierpont Morgan Library.

International Typeface Corporation (ITC) starts publishing its quarterly in-house magazine, *U&lc* (*Upper and lowercase*), which will be distributed worldwide, and is issued to promote new typefaces. Under Herb Lubalin's direction, *U&lc* will become a most influential forum for typography, and a source of information for new typesetting systems.

Milton Glaser designs his **I ♥ NY** logo, which will later become part of a universal iconography.

Arthur Baker publishes *Calligraphy*, a book that explores letterforms and serves as a launch pad for his own type designs. In 1974, he will publish *Calligraphic Alphabets*, expanding on this subject.

1974 German engineer Peter Karow develops, *Ikarus*, a type-design system that permits various functions, such as the conversion of scanned digital images to vectored outlines; the conversion of analogue work to digital data; and the interpolation of basic letters to yield a family of different characteristics. The Linotype Group of Companies and Compugraphic Corporation, among others, start using the system for preparing digital type libraries.

1974 The U.S. Department of Transportation commissions an AIGA committee, led by Tom Geismar and including Ivan Chermayeff, and the staff of Cook & Shanosky Associates, to design a series of pictographic symbols for a transportation signage system to be applied across the United States.

1975 German engineer Peter Karow complements his previous investigation, *Ikarus* (1974) with a program that automatically adjusts the spaces between letters (*Kerning*), which he presents at the ATypI meeting.

Adrian Frutiger designs *Roissy*, a typeface to be used in the Charles de Gaulle Airport at Roissy. Mergenthaler Linotype will issue it as *Frutiger* the following year.

Around this time an anarchic youth movement, "punk," appears in London. Posters, record covers, pamphlets and handbills look as if they have been recycled several times, splattered with chaotic typography and collage of words and pictures. By the 1980s various record companies and fashion magazines will include their work in their publications. Through their aggressive attitude toward expression, a freedom in design is rediscovered.

1975 Two Californians, Steve Jobs and Steve Wozniak, design *Apple I*, a single-user computer, which will revolutionize the notion of storing type as mathematical formulae in digital form as introduced by German firm Hell in 1965.

The first word processors with video terminals are commercialized by the Wang, Videc, Lexitron, and Linolex companies.

1976 In Basle, German designer Wolfgang Weingart publishes a special edition of *Typographische Monatsblätter* magazine, in which he presents his work and personal typographic observations. Weingart's innovative work will energize the *New Wave* generation's interest in typography and type design.

Lanston Monotype Corporation introduces the first laser phototypesetter worldwide, called *Lasercomp*, although graphic-preparation systems had not been completely developed.

1976 Charles Bigelow and Kris Holmes establish the partnership of Bigelow & Holmes, Inc. in order to design and issue digital typefaces. Their *Lucida* series will prove quite successful.

Designers Clarence P. Hornung and Fridolf Johnson publish *200 years of American Graphic Art: A Retrospective Survey of the Printing Arts and Advertising since the Colonial Period*.

1977 Joseph Blumenthal publishes *The Printed Book in America*, an important contribution for analyzing the main publishers in the United States.

Apple Computer, Inc., is founded with the introduction of *Apple II* to the market. Incorporating all the necessary elements to function independently, it initiates the *Personal Computer* (PC) industry.

Xerox 9700 electrophotographic printer using digital fonts with a 300 dpi resolution appears.

1978 The *Nottingham Evening Post* is the first newspaper in England to allow journalists to keyboard copy directly into the computerized composition system through the use of video terminals. The *Express & Star* of Wolpverhampton will follow in 1985.

Hermann Zapf designs for ITC a set of 360 dingbats, under the name of ITC *Zapf Dingbats 100*, to be used in typography as a visual aid to information.

1978 AT&T, now owner of the Bell Telephone Company, commissions Matthew Carter to develop *Bell Centennial*, for typesetting all the U.S. telephone directories on the low resolution of the new cathode-ray tubes manufactured by Linotype, updating *Bell Gothic* typeface designed by Chauncey H. Griffith in 1937.

Designers at the Cranbrook Academy of Art, under the leadership of co-chair Katherine McCoy, are confronted by literary criticism and Post-structuralism theories, as seen in a special issue of the *Visible Language* journal on contemporary French literary aesthetics. The rejection of the well-established management of typographic and reading hierarchies will open discussions on *deconstruction*. These experiences will be repeated in 1983.

1979 American scientist Donald Knuth develops, at Stanford University, the *Metafont* computerized design system for creating fonts. He will also collaborate with Charles Bigelow in structuring a master's program in digital typography at Stanford University, California, in 1982.

1980

1980 English type designer Colin Brignall, who had been type designer for Letraset since 1974, becomes Letraset's Type Director.

In Zurich, Swiss type designer Adrian Frutiger publishes his book, *Type Sign Symbol*, followed by *The Development of the Roman Alphabet* (1981).

1981 English graphic designer and typographer Neville Brody assumes the direction of the *Face* magazine. His adoption of Post-Modernism in typography and editorial design gains him widespread acclaim.

Japanese graphic designer Takenobu Igarashi creates his *Aluminum Alphabet*, a series of three-dimensional "alphabet sculptures." Working with plied aluminum sheets of varying thicknesses joined together by screws, Igarashi liberates each letter's form of the alphabet while still maintaining its readability. With his approach, he also introduces a new reading of the form and structure of letters.

1981 Matthew Carter and Mike Parker found Bitstream, Inc. in Cambridge, Massachusetts, the first independent digital "type foundry." As director of Bitstream, Carter will recreate historical metal faces for digital composition; will introduce original faces designed on the computer; and will develop programs that will give design and production capabilities to the single user. The first typeface issued by the firm will be *Bitstream Charter* (1987).

IBM introduces the first of its personal computer (PC) models. Several system integrators and software developers will use the device as the kernel for composition systems.

1982 American engineers John Warnock and Charles Geschke found Adobe Systems, Inc., in Mountain View, California, to create pioneering software products for desktop publishing and electronic document technology.

Type designer Charles Bigelow, assistant professor of digital typography at Stanford University, California, creates a master's program in digital typography with the support of mathematician and scientist Donald Knuth, who had created the *Metafont*, a program for the creation and handling of digital typefaces in 1979. Several of his students at Rhode Island School of Design, such as Carol Twombly, Dan Mills, and Cleo Huggins will attend this program. They will later enjoy distinguished careers in typography and electronic design.

Joseph Blumenthal publishes *Typographic Years: a Printer's Journey through half a Century 1925-1975*, which, besides being autobiographical, gives an account of five decades of the development of book design in America.

1983 The Musée d'Orsay in Paris opens a competition for the design of the museum's corporate image and sign system. Swiss designers Bruno Monguzzi and Jean Widmer win the competition, and a redesigned *Didot* becomes the museum's type identity.

Letraset, Ltd. opens *Letragraphica Premier* to revitalize a program that had run successfully since 1970, when it was first created.

1983 Engineers John Warnock and Charles Geschke of Adobe Systems, Inc., develop *PostScript*, a computer page description language that enables type and images to be combined in one document. This year, also, the original development of fonts and font technology is initiated.

Philip B. Meggs, graphic designer and professor at Virginia Commonwealth University, publishes *A History of Graphic Design*, the first and most comprehensive essay on the subject.

1984 Type designer Sumner Stone becomes director of typography of Adobe Systems, Inc. until 1989. Under his guidance, the Type Department will develop an ambitious program for digitizing classical typefaces. As a consequence, Robert Slimbach will design one of the best revivals of *Garamond* (1987).

Journalist Paul Brainerd founds Aldus Corporation in Seattle. Together with a group of engineers, he develops *PageMaker*, which will allow individuals to combine text and graphics on a page using low-cost computers and laser printers, creating the basis of the desktop publishing principle.

After developing the *Lisa* software (1983), which revolutionized the computer industry with its use of windows, pull-down menus, bitmapped graphics, and a mouse, Engineers Steve Jobs and Steve Wozniak launch the *Apple Macintosh Computer*, the first computer to achieve commercial success. It is accompanied by a number of software packages, such as *MacWrite*, *MacDraw*, and *MacPaint*, which will be quickly adopted into the graphic design practice.

Designers Charles Bigelow and Kris Holmes design *Lucida*, the first typeface especially created for laser printers. In 1985, they will design *Lucida Sans*.

After founding Émigré Graphics in California, Zuzana Licko and Rudy VanderLans publish *Émigré* magazine, an experimental cultural magazine, which rebels against the coldness of the Swiss grid design and reconsiders the typographical richness of the early Modernists and Dada groups. With time, it will be one of the most influential media of new typography.

In New York, the Herb Lubalin Study Center of Design and Typography is founded to provide the means for studying innovative work and ideas of leading communicators.

1985 Aldus Corporation launches the *Desk-Top Publishing* (DTP) concept (a term coined by Paul Brainerd), with the layout program *Aldus PageMaker 1.0*, a Macintosh program that allows for a combination of graphics and text on-screen layout. Two years later, Aldus will release a version for IBM and IBM-compatible computers.

Adobe's *PostScript* is launched publicly in the *Apple LaserWriter*. Since then, it has constituted in itself the greatest revolution in the desktop publishing world, or publications assisted by computer. It is interesting to remark the eleven type designs, offered with the *LaserWriter*, each one with four series: *Courier*, *ITC Bookman*, *ITC Avant Garde Gothic*, *Helvetica*, *Helvetica Narrow*, *New Century Schoolbook*, *Palatino*, *Zapf Chancery*, *Times New Roman*, *Zapf Dingbats*, and *Symbol*.

Calligrapher-designers Jerry Kelly and George Laws mount an exhibition of Frederic Warde's typographical and calligraphic work at The Grolier Club in New York.

Zuzana Licko and Rudy VanderLans establish Émigré Fonts digital type foundry with the aim of marketing typefaces by Licko and other designers (including Jeffery Keedy, Barry Deck and J. Downer). In her first typefaces, *Emperor*, *Émigré*, and *Oakland*, which reflect the influence of computer language, Licko finds an opportunity to innovate in type design.

1986 English writer Nicolette Gray publishes her book *A History of Lettering: Creative Experiment and Letter Identity*, an important contribution on the subject.

Swiss type designer Adrian Frutiger is appointed type consultant for Mergenthaler Linotype, and Linotype-Hell AG.

Esselte Letraset acquires the International Typeface Corporation (ITC), which continues to have headquarters in New York City.

Monotype International presents *Lasercomp Express*, a machine capable of producing broadsheet newspaper pages at a rate of one per minute, with a resolution of 1,000 lines per inch. Its dual processing permits visualizing the next page while working.

1986 Mac McGrew publishes his book *American Metal Typefaces of the Twentieth Century*, the most serious account on this subject. He will complement it in a second edition (1993).

Altsys Corporation creates *Fontographer* software, the first program that allows a user to design a typeface directly on the computer.

1987 English graphic designer Sebastian Carter publishes *Twentieth Century Type Designers*, a serious work on this subject. He will complement it in a second edition published in 1995.

1987 Adobe Systems, Inc. introduces *Adobe Illustrator*, an art and design software program that exploits the graphic potential of *PostScript*. Designers may sketch ideas directly on the screen. The hard copy output is camera-ready artwork for printing.

QuarkXPress, a program for composition and page make-up and a challenger to Aldus *PageMaker*, is released by Quark, Inc., founded in Denver, Colorado in 1981.

At Adobe Systems, Inc., Sumner Stone designs the *Stone* typeface family, the first design to include a serif, a sans serif, and an informal version, all structured on one common letter design. Otl Aicher will repeat a similar typographical experience with *Rotis* in 1988, and Lucas de Groot with *FFThesis* in 1994.

1988 English graphic designer and typographer Neville Brody, one of the new generation designers to enhance the creative potential of Apple Macintosh, publishes *The Graphic Language of Neville Brody*.

It coincides with a retrospective exhibition of his work held in London at the Victoria & Albert Museum.

Albertus (1932), a typeface developed by German type designer Berthold Wolpe, is adopted by the City of London in all its sign systems, including street names.

German type designer Otl Aicher designs *Rotis* with the same structural idea of Sumner Stone (1987), a typeface with three variants: roman, sans serif and informal, using the same letter design basis.

Catalan designer Enric Satué publishes *El Diseño Gráfico: desde los orígenes hasta nuestros días*, an account of the development of Graphic Design in Europe, North America, and Latin America.

1988 Carol Twombly joins Adobe Systems, Inc., and two years later, she completes Adobe's first original display typefaces: *Trajan*, *Charlemagne*, and *Lithos*. She will continue as Adobe's Type design manager until the year 2000.

Garrett Boge founds LetterPerfect, a digital type foundry. In 1995, he invites Paul Shaw to be his design partner. Together, they will issue three important series: the Baroque Set (*Cresci*, *Pontif*, and *Pietra*) in 1996, the Florentine Set (*Beata*, *Donatello*, and *Ghiberti*) in 1997, and the Swedish Modern Set (*Stockholm*, *Göteborg*, and *Upsala*) in 1998. Their other collaborative designs include *Kolo*, *Old Claude*, *Bermuda* and *Padua*.

Agfa Gevaert buys Compugraphic Corporation and becomes Agfa Compugraphic Corporation. Their type library has over 2,500 typefaces with many original fonts, new varieties, and licensed fonts.

Steven Heller, art director of the *New York Times Book Review*, and designer Seymour Chwast publish *Graphic Style, from Victorian to Post-Modern*, an excellent graphic and historical relationship between art and graphic design.

1989 In Berlin, Erik and Joan Spiekermann found FontShop International, a mail order firm for digitized typefaces, with branches in Europe, America, and Australia. In 1990, they will open with their own fonts.

1989 *Canon Color Laser Copier* initiates the age of computer color. Printers, video screens, and other devices are transformed to full-color display and output.

Packages of typefaces (over 2,000 fonts), called *Font Libraries*, are standardized in *PostScript* for laser printers running on personal computers.

In Boston, Massachusetts, type designers Roger Black and David Berlow, cofound Font Bureau; an independent firm specialized in consulting and contracting custom typographic products and supplying fonts in *PostScript* format.

In Palo Alto, California, type designer Sumner Stone establishes Stone Type Foundry, which will specialize in the development of new *PostScript* fonts.

1990

1990 English designer Rodney Mylius collaborates in the *Letraset* exhibition in the London Design Museum. The exhibition plainly shows the company's contribution to typography during the 1960s.

1990 Adobe Systems, Inc. develops *PhotoShop*, a color image retouching and reproduction program for the Apple Macintosh computer. It will later be available for the PC and some Unix platforms.

1991 Designer Neville Brody and Editor Jon Wozencroft start publishing *Fuse*, a promotional digital publication of Font Shop International. A new issue appears every three months, including a diskette with four new typefaces and four posters designed using these typefaces. Among the contributing type designers, there will appear Phil Baines, David Berlow, Gerard Unger, Tobias Frere-Jones, Max Kisman, and David Carson.

The *Times* of London changes its typeface for the third time. *Times Millenium*, redesigned by Aurobind Patel, resolves the cultural and technological changes that have taken place since Walter Tracy designed *Times Europa* in 1972.

1991 Adobe Systems, Inc., develops the multiple master technology as a complement to *PostScript* language, which works on the basis of variable typeface attributes, such as weight, width, style, or optical size, enabling the creation of user-defined fonts in any variation without adversely affecting the letter proportions.

In Cambridge, Massachusetts, Matthew Carter and Cheri Cone found Carter & Cone Type, Inc., a digital type foundry. Their first typeface will be a new digitization of *ITC Galliard*.

1993 Carol Twombly designs *Viva*, an inline typeface, first one to be modeled with a two-axis structure.

In Minneapolis, the Walker Art Center commissions Matthew Carter to design a typeface for the Center's private use. The resulting face, *Walker* (1995-96), can be modified by the user through a series of additional and interchangeable serifs.

1994 Dutch type designer Lucas de Groot designs *FF Thesis*, repeating Sumner Stone's (1987), and Otl Aicher's (1988) experience of designing a typeface with three variants: serif, sans serif, and slab serif, all based on one common structure.

1994 Aldus Corporation joins with Adobe Systems, Inc., to strengthen research and product design. Having two competing programs on the market, the new company keeps *Adobe Illustrator* and returns *Aldus FreeHand* to its originators, Altsys Corp.

Created in early 1983, online communication has expanded into a wide network such as the Internet, which, though at one time it was restricted to universities and government employees, has now become increasingly accessible. Smaller databases and interactive publications are also available on CD-ROM's and other media. The development of the so-called "visual language" is consolidating a new approach to information that will change the world of communications into a world of hyper media visual information and interactive guidance. Type design will play an important role in the management of Web page layout. Printed and visual legibility and readability concepts will be confronted with one another.

1995 Microsoft's *True Type* challenges Adobe's *Type 1* format. Less expensive than *Type 1*, *True Type* will become widely used.

Agfa Compugraphic forms the *Creative Alliance* with more than thirty independent type designers and a type supplier to create a growing source of new and exclusive typeface designs developed for the graphic design community. Agfa also releases *Monotype CD 5.0* offering over 4,000 typefaces.

1996 H. Berthold AG declares bankruptcy and Linotype-Hell AG is purchased by Heidelberg Company, Germany.

1996 Adobe Systems Inc., develops *Adobe Type Manager Deluxe*, enabling users to handle a greater amount of typefaces without the inconveniences of the operating system font management by organizing them in groups.

In March, Agfa and Monotype announce the joint production of a *Creative Alliance CD*, including over 7,500 fonts for Mac and Windows, plus 500 new typefaces.

Microsoft Corporation releases *Word 97* with more than 150 free typefaces bundled.

1997 Microsoft and Adobe decide to merge *Type 1* and *True Type* so both font standards are supported on Windows and Macintosh platforms.

1998 English film director and writer Peter Greenaway directs his work *Pillow Book*, an extraordinary film based on the story of a Japanese writer and calligrapher that finds the human body a perfect surface for her poems. The story is developed through thirteen books of different content and meaning. Calligraphy was executed by American calligrapher Brody Neuenschwander.

1998 Adobe Systems Inc., creates *Adobe InDesign* to challenge *QuarkXpress* created by Quark, Inc., in 1987.

2000

2000 In February, Agfa/Monotype, Massachusetts, acquires ITC. Its type development department is under the direction of Ilene Strizver, and types are developed in Wilmington, Massachusetts.

2001 Adobe Systems, Inc. ceases creating multiple master typefaces.

2002 By this time Adobe and Microsoft have developed *Open Type* jointly. With a cross platform compatibility and an ability to support widely expanded characters sets and layout features, *Open Type* will provide a richer linguistic support and advance typographic control. The typical *Western PostScript font*, which was limited to 256 glyphs, may now contain more than 65,000 glyphs, allowing a single font to contain many nonstandard glyphs, such as *oldstyle* figures, true small capitals, fractions, swashes, superscript and subscript numbers, titling letters, contextual and stylistic alternate, and a full range of ligatures.

2003 By this time Adobe Systems Inc., is producing all its typefaces in *Open type* format.

Note: Only the American type designs shown in this book have been included in this type design chronology. A few additional American typefaces have been included as complementary information. The dates usually –but not always– refer to the issuing of the typeface.

1620

1621 *Caracteres de l'Université* - Jan Jannon

1680

1683 *Janson* - Miklós (Nicholas) Kis

1690

1690 *Union Pearl* - James Grover

1700

1702 *Romain du Roi Louis XIV* - Philip Grandjean

1720

1722 *Caslon Old Face* - William Caslon

1750

1757 *Baskerville* - John Baskerville

1760

1765 *Twelve-line English romans* - Thomas Cottrell

1768 *Fry's Baskerville* - Isaac Moore
Handtooled alphabets -
Pierre Simon Fournier, *l'ainé*

1780

1780 *Roman Oldstyle* - Gerónimo Gil

1784 *Didot* - Firmin Didot

1788 *Bodoni* - Giambattista Bodoni
Bell - Richard Austin
Old Face Open - Edmund Fry foundry

1790

1796 *Fry's Ornamented* - Richard Austin

1796 *Roman No. 1* - (later known as *Oxford* and *Monticello*)
Archibald Binny / Binny & Ronaldson type foundry

1800

1800 *Walbaum* - Justus Erich Walbaum

1803 *Fat faces* - Robert Thorne

1810

1810 *Thorne Shaded* - Robert Thorne

1815 *Egyptian typefaces* - Vincent Figgins
Five Lines Pica, in Shade - Vincent Figgins
English Tuscan - Vincent Figgins

1816 *Two Lines English Egyptian*, first sans serif
- William Caslon IV

1819 *Normande* - Firmin Didot

1820

1820 *Thorowgood* - Robert Thorne
Lettres Ornées - Fonds de Gillé

1828 *Roman* - Darius Wells

1830

1832 *Two-Line Great Primer Sans-serif* -
Vincent Figgins

1833 *Outline typefaces* - Vincent Figgins

1839 *Sans Serif Shaded* - William Thorowgood

1840

1840 *Antique X Condensed* - Darius Wells
Gothic Extended - Darius Wells

1845 *Clarendon* - Benjamin Fox

1846 *Grecian Condensed* - Darius Wells

1849 *Gothic Condensed Outline* - Darius Wells
Gothic Tuscan Condensed - Darius Wells
Antique Tuscan - Darius Wells
Tuscan Outline - Darius Wells

1850

1854 *Antique Light Face Extended* - Darius Wells
Gothic Tuscan Italian - Darius Wells
Doric Ornamented - Darius Wells

1859 *Antique XXX Condensed* - William Hamilton Page
Gothic Tuscan Pointed - William H. Page
Ionic - William Hamilton Page
Antique Tuscan No.8 - William Hamilton Page
Clarendon XX Condensed - William H. Page
Antique Tuscan No.11 - William Hamilton Page
Clarendon Ornamented - William Hamilton Page
Antique Tuscan Outline - William Hamilton Page

1860

1860 *Old Style Antique* (later known as
Bookman) - Alexander C. Phemister

1865 *Narrow Grotesque* - Haas Type Foundry

1865 *Skeleton Antique* - William Hamilton Page

1869 *French Antique* - William Hamilton Page
Bruce Old Style - David Bruce, Jr.

1870

1870 *Aetna* - William Hamilton Page
Egyptian Ornamented - William Hamilton Page
Painter's Roman - W. H. Page / Darius Wells
Celtic Ornamented - William Hamilton Page
Antique No.7 - William Hamilton Page

1872 *Teutonic* - William Hamilton Page

1879 *Gothic Tuscan Condensed No.2* - W. H. Page
French Clarendon XXX Condensed - W. H. Page
Phanitalian - William Hamilton Page
No. 129 - William Hamilton Page
No. 131 - William Hamilton Page

1880

1882 *No.142* - William Hamilton Page

1886 *Charlemagne* - Eleisha Pechey

1887 *No. 154* - William Hamilton Page
No. 500 - William Hamilton Page
No. 506 - William Hamilton Page
No. 515 - William Hamilton Page

1890

1890 *Golden Type* - William Morris

1891 *Troy* - William Morris

1892 *Chaucer* - William Morris

1892 *Era/Pastel* - Nicolas Werner/Gustav Schroeder

1893 *Jenson Oldstyle* - Joseph Warren Phinney
De Vinne - Gustav Schroeder

1894 *Century Roman* - Linn Boyd Benton/Theodore
Low De Vinne

1895 *Bradley* - William Bradley/Joseph W. Phinney
Merrymount - Bertram Grosvenor Goodhue

1896 *Caslon Antique* - Berne Nadall
Camelot - Frederic W. Goudy

1898 *Paris Metro Lettering* - Hector Guimard
Akzidenz Grotesk - H. Berthold AG foundry

1899 *Grasset* - Eugène Grasset

1900

1900 *Doves Roman* - Emery Walker/Thomas
James Cobden-Sanderson
Behrens Roman - Peter Behrens
Eckmann Schrift - Otto Eckmann

1901 *Auriol* - Georges Auriol
Behrens-Schrift - Peter Behrens

1902 *Della Robbia* - Thomas Maitland Cleland
Engravers Bold - Morris Fuller Benton
Franklin Gothic - Morris Fuller Benton

1903 *Brook Type* - Lucien Pisarro

1903 *Village* - Frederic W. Goudy
Copperplate Gothic - Frederic W. Goudy
Alternate Gothic - Morris Fuller Benton
Bookman - Wadsworth A. Parker / ATF

1904 *Korinna* - H. Berthold AG foundry
Arnold Böcklin - Otto Weisert foundry

1904 *Cheltenham* - Bertram Grosvenor Goodhue
Missal Initilas - Henry William Bradley
Bewick Roman - Henry William Bradley
Cloister Black - Joseph W. Phinney

1905 *Windsor* - Eleisha Pechey

1906 *Clearface* - Morris Fuller Benton

1907 *Behrens-Antiqua* - Peter Behrens
Venus - Wagner & Schmidt foundry

1908 *Ehmke* - Fritz Helmut Ehmke
Torino - Nebiolo Type Foundry
Block Type - H. Hoffmann/Lucian Bernhard

1908 *Commercial Script* - Morris Fuller Benton
News Gothic - Morris Fuller Benton
Monotype 30-E - Frederic W. Goudy

1910

1910 *Feder-Grotesk* - Jakob Erbar

1910 *Hobo* - Morris Fuller Benton
Bodoni - Morris Fuller Benton

1911 *Bernhard Antiqua* - Lucian Bernhard

1911 *Kennerley Old Style* - Frederic W. Goudy
Forum Title - Frederic W. Goudy

1912 *Imprint* - Edward Johnston
Nicolas Cochin - Georges Peignot

1912 *Artcraft* - Robert Wiebking

1913 *Plantin* - Frank Hinman Pierpoint
Caslon Clearface - Robert Wiebking

1914 *Maximilian-Gotisch* - Rudolf Koch
Maximilian-Antiqua - Rudolf Koch
Grotesk V - Wagner & Schmidt foundry

1914 *Cloister Oldstyle* - Morris Fuller Benton
Souvenir - Morris Fuller Benton
Centaur - Bruce Rogers

1915 *Ella* - Sjoerd Hendrik De Roos

1915 *Goudy Oldstyle* - Frederic W. Goudy
Baskerville - Morris Fuller Benton

1916 *London Underground Sanserif* - Ed. Johnston

1917 *Parsons* - Will Ransom
Advertisers Gothic - Robert Wiebking
Cochin - Sol Hess

1918 *Bodoni Open* - Morris Fuller Benton
Century Schoolbook - Morris Fuller Benton
Cloister Initials - Frederic W. Goudy
Hadriano Title - Frederic W. Goudy
Cooper Oldstyle - Oswald Bruce Cooper

1919 *Garamond* - Morris Fuller Benton

1920

1920 *Garamont* - Frederic W. Goudy

1921 *Deutsche Zierschrift* - Rudolf Koch

1922 *Garamond* - Lanston Monotype Corporation
Koch-Antiqua - Rudolf Koch
Erbar - Jakob Erbar
Fournier - Peter A. Demeter

1922 *Cooper Black* - Oswald Bruce Cooper
Munder Venezian - Robert Wiebking
Goudy Handtooled - W. Parker / M. F. Benton

1923 *Baskerville* - Lanston Monotype Corporation
   Blado - Lanston Monotype Corporation
   Poliphilus - Lanston Monotype Corporation
   Neuland - Rudolf Koch
   Judith Type - C. H. Kleukens
   Hammer Unziale - Victor Hammer

1924 *Italian Old Style* - Frederic W. Goudy

   1925 *Lutetia* - Jan Van Krimpen
      Phosphor - Jakob Erbar
      universal alphabet - Herbert Bayer
      Demeter - Peter A. Demeter

1925 *Bernhard Kursive* - Lucian Bernhard
   Cooper Hilite - Oswald Bruce Cooper
   Irvin - Rea Irvin
   Arrighi - Frederic Warde
   Goudy Heavyface - Frederic W. Goudy
   Kennerley Open Caps - Sol Hess

   1926 *Weiss Roman* - Emil Rudolf Weiss
      Belwe Roman - Georg Belwe
      Bauer Bodoni - Heinrich Jost
      Scriptura - Friedrich W. Kleukens
      Wilhelm-Klingspor-Schrift - Rudolf Koch

1926 *Ionic No. 5* - Chauncey H. Griffith
   Lexington - Wadsworth A. Parker
   Cameo - Robert Hunter Middleton

   1927 *Futura* - Paul Renner
      Kabel - Rudolf Koch
      Aeterna - Heinrich Jost

1927 *Pompeian Cursive* - Oswald B. Cooper
   Boul Mich - Richard McArthur / Oswald B. Cooper
   Record Gothic - Robert Hunter Middleton
   Gallia - Wadsworth A. Parker
   Deepdene - Frederic W. Goudy

   1928 *Open Roman Capitals* - Jan Van Krimpen
      Berthold Grotesque - H. Berthold AG
      Fairbank Italic - Alfred Fairbank

1928 *Lucian* - Lucian Bernhard
   Goudy Text - Frederic W. Goudy
   Modernique - Morris Fuller Benton
   Parisian - Morris Fuller Benton
   Ultra Bodoni - Morris Fuller Benton
   Broadway - Morris Fuller Benton
   Bulmer - Morris Fuller Benton
   Bodoni Bold Panelled - Sol Hess
   Cooper Tooled - Sol Hess
   Delphian Open Title - Robert Hunter Middleton
   Modernistic - Wadsworth A. Parker

   1929 *Bembo* - Lanston Monotype Corporation
      Perpetua - Eric Gill
      Gill Sans - Eric Gill
      Zeppelin - Rudolf Koch
      Kabel Swash Initials - Rudolf Koch
      Orplid - Hans Bohn
      Lux - Jakob Erbar
      Futura Black - Paul Renner
      Futura Inline - Paul Renner
      Memphis - Rudolf Wolf
      Corvinus - Imre Reiner
      Bifur - A. M. Cassandre

1929 *Lombardic Capitals* - Frederic W. Goudy
   Bernhard Fashion - Lucian Bernhard
   Bernhard Gothic - Lucian Bernhard
   Stellar - Robert Hunter Middleton
   Garamond - Robert Hunter Middleton
   Cooper Full Face - Oswald B. Cooper
   Broadway Engraved - Sol Hess
   Poster Bodoni - Chauncey H. Griffith
   Textype - Chauncey H. Griffith

1930

   1930 *Golden Cockerel Roman* - Eric Gill
      Joanna - Eric Gill

   Wallau - Rudolf Koch
   Marathon - Rudolf Koch
   Offenbach - Rudolf Koch
   City - Georg Trump
   Mona Lisa - Albert Auspurg
   Dynamo - Karl Sommer
   Motor - Karl Sommer
   Griffo - Hans (Giovanni) Mardersteig

1930 *Spiral/Emerson* - Joseph Blumenthal
   Metrolite - William Addison Dwiggins
   Metroblack - William Addison Dwiggins
   Metromedium - William Addison Dwiggins
   Initials (1930-36)- William Addison Dwiggins
   Bodoni Black - Robert Hunter Middleton
   Tempo Heavy Condensed - Robert H. Middleton
   Bank Gothic - Morris Fuller Benton
   Goudy Sans Serif Heavy - Frederic W. Goudy
   Goudy Sans Serif Light - Frederic W. Goudy
   Trajan Title - Frederic W. Goudy
   Lilith - Lucian Bernhard
   Vogue - Intertype

   1931 *Romulus* - Jan Van Krimpen
      Prisma - Rudolf Koch
      Beton - Heinrich Jost
      Futura Display - Paul Renner
      Transito - Jan Tschichold
      Weiss Initials I, II, III - Emil R. Weiss
      Capitol - K. H. Schaefer

1931 *Stymie* - Morris Fuller Benton
   Stymie Inline Title - Wadsworth A. Parker
   Excelsior - Chauncey H. Griffith
   Karnak - Robert Hunter Middleton
   Ornate Title - Frederic W. Goudy
   Goudy Sans Serif Light Italic - Frederic W. Goudy

   1932 *Times New Roman* - S. Morison/ V. Lardent
      Bell - Lanston Monotype Corporation
      Post Antiqua - Herbert Post

1932 *Franciscan* - Frederic W. Goudy
   Janson - Chauncey W. Griffith
   American Text - Morris Fuller Benton
   Lafayette Extra Condensed - Robert H. Middleton
   Umbra - Robert Hunter Middleton
   Hadriano Stone-Cut - Sol Hess
   P.T. Barnum - American Type Founders

   1933 *Walbaum* - Lanston Monotype Corporation
      Egmont - Sjoerd H. De Roos
      Egmont Inline Titling - Sjoerd H. De Roos
      Atlas - K. H. Schaefer
      Tannenberg - Erich Mayer
      Element - Max Bittrof

1933 *Park Avenue* - Robert E. Smith
   Trafton Script - Howard Allen Trafton

   1934 *Cancellaresca bastarda* - Jan Van Krimpen
      Film - Marcel Jacno
      Rockwell - Lanston Monotype Corporation

1934 *Shadow* - Morris Fuller Benton
   Tower - Morris Fuller Benton
   Othello - Morris Fuller Benton
   Bernhard Tango - Lucian Bernhard
   Bernhard Tango Swash - Lucian Bernhard
   Mandate - Robert Hunter Middleton
   Eden - Robert Hunter Middleton
   Hess Neobold - Sol Hess
   Stymie Extrabold - Sol Hess
   Pericles - Robert Foster

   1935 *Floriated Capitals* - Eric Gill
      Éclair - Fonderie Deberny & Peignot
      Bayer Type - Herbert Bayer
      Aktuell - Walter Schnippering
      Albertus - Berthold Wolpe
      Neon - G. de Milano

   Neon Ombrata - G. de Milano
   Emerson - Joseph Blumenthal/Monotype

1935 *Electra* - William Addison Dwiggins
   Opticon - Chauncey H. Griffith
   Paragon - Chauncey H. Griffith
   Huxley Vertical - Walter Huxley

   1936 *Van Dijck Roman* - Jan Van Krimpen
      Acier Noir - A. M. Cassandre
      Scribe - Marcel Jacno
      Neon - Willy Schaefer
      Allegro - Hans Bohn
      Fontana - Hans (Giovanni) Mardersteig

1936 *Bodoni Campanile* - Robert Hunter Middleton
   Kaufmann Script - Max Richard Kaufmann
   Kaufmann Bold - Max Richard Kaufmann
   Cartoon - Howard Allen Trafton
   Hauser Script - George Hauser

   1937 *Ehrhardt* - Lanston Monotype Corporation
      Flex - Georg Salter
      Peignot - A. M. Cassandre
      Claudius - Rudolf Koch/Paul Koch
      Legend - F. H. Ernst Schneidler
      Post Roman - Herbert Post
      Elizabeth Roman - Elizabeth Friedländer

1937 *Bernhard Roman Antiqua Bold Condensed* - Lucian Bernhard
   Bernhard Modern Roman - Lucian Bernhard
   Coronet - Robert Hunter Middleton
   Stencil - Robert Hunter Middleton
   Onyx - Gerry Powell
   Stencil - Gerry Powell
   Stymie Bold Condensed - Gerry Powell
   Empire - Morris Fuller Benton
   Bell Gothic - Chauncey H. Griffith
   Spire - Sol Hess

   1938 *Dorchester* - Lanston Monotype Corporartion
      Playbill - Robert Harling
      Libra - Sjoerd Hendrik De Roos
      Schadow - Georg Trump
      Weiss Rundgotisch - Emil Rudolf Weiss

1938 *Lydian* - Warren Chappell
   Caledonia - William Addison Dwiggins
   University of California Old Style - F. W. Goudy
   Memphis Extrabold - Chauncey H. Griffith
   Radiant Heavy - Robert Hunter Middleton

   1939 *Flash* - Edwin W. Shaar
      Chisel - Robert Harling.
      Tea Chest - Stephenson, Blake & Co.
      Simplex - Sjoerd Hendrik De Roos
      Stop - Walter Höhnisch

1939 *Balloon* - Max Richard Kaufmann
   Grayda - Frank H. Riley
   Onix Italic - Sol Hess
   Post-Stout Italic - Sol Hess
   Postblack Italic - Sol Hess
   Lydian Bold and *Italic* - Warren Chappell
   Trajanus - Warren Chappell

1940

   1940 *Electra* - Carlos Winkow
      Figural - Oldrich Menhart

1940 *Lydian Cursive* - Warren Chappell
   Samson - Robert Hunter Middleton
   Fairfield - Rudolph Ruzicka

   1941 *Gilgengart* - Hermann Zapf
      Nacional - Carlos Winkow

1941 *Corona* - Chauncey H. Griffith
   Artscript - Sol Hess

   1942 *Aragón* - Guillermo de Mendoza
      Ibérica - Carlos Winkow
      Súper Tipo Veloz - Joan Trochut

1942 *Brush* - Robert E. Smith
    Goudy Thirty - Frederic W. Goudy

1943 *American Uncial* - Victor Hammer

    1944 *Alcázar* - Carlos Winkow
        Post Mediaeval - Herbert Post

    1945 *Spectrum* - Jan Van Krimpen
        Stradivarius - Imre Reiner
        Hiero Rhode - Hiero Rhode
        Athenaeum - Alessandro Butti / Aldo Novarese

    1946 *Studio* - A. Overbeek
        Profil - Eugen and Max Lenz

    1948 *Rondo* - Dick Dooijes / Stefan Schlesinger
        Jacno - Marcel Jacno
        Forum I - Georg Trump
        Cezka Unciala - Oldrich Menhart
        Palatino - Hermann Zapf
        Diethelm-Antiqua - Walter Diethelm

    1949 *Monument* - Oldrich Menhart
        Normandia - Alessandro Butti / Aldo Novarese

1950

1950 *Michelangelo* - Hermann Zapf
    Parlament - Oldrich Menhart

1950 *alphabet 26* - Bradbury Thompson
Dom Casual - Peter Dombrezian / Photo-Lettering Inc.

    1951 *Festival Titling* - Phillip Boydell
        Banco - Roger Excoffon
        Vendôme - François Ganeau / Roger Excoffon
        Chaillot - Marcel Jacno
        Berling - Karl Erik Forsberg
        Sistina - Hermann Zapf
        Reiner Script - Imre Reiner
        Fluidum - Alessandro Butti
        Augustea - A. Butti / Aldo Novarese

    1952 *Raffia Initials* - Henk Krijger
        Chambord - Roger Excoffon / François Ganeau
        Melior - Hermann Zapf
        Forum II - Georg Trump
        Virtuosa - Hermann Zapf
        Saphir - Hermann Zapf
        Steile Futura - Paul Renner
        Microgramma - Al. Butti / Aldo Novarese

    1953 *Flash* - Enric Crous-Vidal
        Paris - Enric Crous-Vidal
        Mistral - Roger Excoffon
        Amati - Georg Trump
        Salto - Karlgeorg Hoefer
        Diotima - Gudrun Zapf-von Hesse
        Smaragd - Gudrun Zapf-von Hesse
        Derby - Günter Gerhard Lange
        Solemnis - Günter Gerhard Lange
        Phoebus - Adrian Frutiger

1953 *Brody* - Harold Brodersen
Eldorado - William Addison Dwiggins

    1954 *Minerva* - Reynolds Stone
        Ilerda - Enric Crous-Vidal
        Carolus - Karl Erik Forsberg
        Kompakt - Hermann Zapf
        Aldus - Hermann Zapf
        Dante - Hans (Giovanni) Mardersteig
        Trump Mediaeval - Georg Trump
        Fontanesi - Aldo Novarese
        Ondine - Adrian Frutiger

    1955 *Klang* - Will Carter
        Choc - Roger Excoffon
        Fortune - Konrad F. Bauer / Walter Baum
        Boulevard - Günter Gerhard Lange
        Columna - Max Caflisch
        Pacioli Titling - Hans (Giovanni) Mardersteig
        Codex - Georg Trump

    Signum - Georg Trump
    Egizio - Aldo Novarese
    Ritmo - Aldo Novarese
    Meridien - Adrian Frutiger

1955 *Craw Clarendon* - Freeman Craw
    Murray Hill - Emil J. Klumpp

    1956 *Diane* - Roger Excoffon

1956 *Craw Clarendon Book* - Freeman Craw
Florentine Cursive - Robert Hunter Middleton
Murray Hill Bold - Emil J. Klumpp

    1957 *Castellar* - John Peters
        Mercator - Dick Dooijes
        Cristal - Rémy Peignot
        Mercurius Bold Script - Imre Reiner
        Folio - Konrad F. Bauer / Walter Baum
        Neue Haas Grotesk / issued as *Helvetica* in 1960 - Eduard Hoffmann / Max Miedinger
        Sculptura - Walter Diethelm
        Univers - Adrian Frutiger

    1958 *Calypso* - Roger Excoffon
        Optima - Hermann Zapf
        Charme - Helmut Matheis
        Papageno - Richard Weber

1958 *Craw Modern* - Freeman Craw

1960

    1960 *Maryland* - Ricard Giralt Miracle
        Pascal - José Mendoza y Almeida
        Agitator - Wolfgang Eickhoff
        Trump Gravur - Georg Trump
        Helvetica (issued as *Neue Haas Grotesk* in 1957) - Eduard Hoffmann / Max Miedinger

1960 *Craw Clarendon Condensed* - Freeman Craw

    1961 *Eras* - Albert Boton / Albert Hollenstein

1961 *Ad lib* - Freeman Craw

    1962 *Antique Olive* - Roger Excoffon
        Eurostile - Aldo Novarese

    1963 *Compacta* - Fred Lambert / Letraset
        Gaudí - Ricard Giralt Miracle
        Hunt Roman - Hermann Zapf

    1964 *Albertina* - Chris Brand
        El Greco - Günter Gerhard Lange
        Jaguar - Georg Trump
        Apollo - Adrian Frutiger

    1965 *Friz Quadrata* - Ernst Friz

1964 *Craw Modern Italic* - Freeman Craw

1965 *Baker Signet* - Arthur Baker
Auriga - Matthew Carter
Davida Bold - Louis Minott
Rustica - Paul Hayden Duensing

    1966 *Lectura* - Dick Dooijes
        Sabon - Jan Tschichold

1966 *Cascade Script* - Matthew Carter
Snell Roundhand - Matthew Carter
CBS Didot - Freeman Craw
CBS Sans - Freeman Craw

    1967 *New Alphabet* - Wim Crouwel
        Jeanette - Hermann Zapf
        Poppl-Antiqua - Friedrich Poppl
        Serifa - Adrian Frutiger

1967 *VGC Aquarius* - Ronald Arnholm
VGC Fovea - Ronald Arnholm
Americana - Richard Isbell

    1968 *Oldenburg* - Wim Crouwel
        Firenze - Hermann Zapf
        OCR-B - Adrian Frutiger

    1969 *Countdown* - Colin Brignall / Letraset
        Aachen - Colin Brignall / Letraset
        Revue - Colin Brignall / Letraset
        Premier - Colin Brignall / Letraset

    Lightline - Colin Brignall / Letraset
    Syntax - Hans E. Meier
    Venture - Hermann Zapf
    Concorde - Günter Gerhard Lange

1970

1970 *Superstar* - Colin Brignall / Letraset
    Vellvé - Tomàs Vellvé
    Poppl-Exquisit - Friedrich Poppl
    Stop - Aldo Novarese

1970 *ITC Avant Garde Gothic* - H. Lubalin / T. Carnase
ITC Souvenir - Edward Benguiat
ITC Gorilla - Tom Carnase / Ronne Bonder
ITC Grizzli - Tom Carnase / Ronne Bonder
ITC Grouch - Tom Carnase / Ronne Bonder
ITC Honda - Tom Carnase / Ronne Bonder
ITC Neon - Tom Carnase / Ronne Bonder
ITC Machine - Tom Carnase / Ronne Bonder
ITC Pioneer - Tom Carnase / Ronne Bonder
ITC Firenze - Tom Carnase
ITC Busorama - Tom Carnase / Herb Lubalin
Gando Ronde - Matthew Carter
Olympian - Matthew Carter

    1971 *Linofilm Medici Script* - Hermann Zapf
        Antiqua Classica - S. Odermatt / R. Tissi

    1972 *Times Europa* - Walter Tracy
        Photina - José Mendoza y Almeida
        Basta - Georg Salden
        Sinaloa - S. Odermatt / Rosemarie Tissi

1972 *Shelley Script Allegro* - Matthew Carter
Shelley Script Volante - Matthew Carter

    1973 *Gaya Ciencia* - Ricard Giralt Miracle
        Chinon - Albert Boton

    1974 *Orion* - Hermann Zapf
        Present - Friedrich K. Sallwey

1974 *ITC Serif Gothic* - Herb Lubalin / Tony DiSpigna
ITC Lubalin Graph - Herb Lubalin / Tony DiSpigna
ITC Korinna - Edward Benguiat
ITC Tiffany - Edward Benguiat

    1975 *Italia* - Colin Brignall / Letraset
        Walbaum Buch - Gerard Unger

1975 *ITC Bauhaus* - Edward Benguiat
ITC Bookman - Edward Benguiat

    1976 *Victorian* - Colin Brignall (LetrasetEngland)
        Comenius Roman - Hermann Zapf
        Marconi - Hermann Zapf
        ITC Zapf Book - Hermann Zapf
        Zapf Civilité - Hermann Zapf
        Poppl-Pontifex - Friedrich Poppl
        Franklin-Antique - Günter G. Lange
        Frutiger - Adrian Frutiger

    1977 *Praxis* - Gerard Unger
        ITC Zapf International - Hermann Zapf
        Fenice - Aldo Novarese

    1978 *ITC Zapf Dingbats 100* - Hermann Zapf
        Edison - Hermann Zapf

1978 *ITC Benguiat* - Edward Benguiat
Bell Centennial - Matthew Carter
Galliard - Matthew Carter

    1979 *Romic* - Colin Brignall / Letraset
        Harlow - Colin Brignall / Letraset
        ITC Zapf Chancery - Hermann Zapf
        Tap - Georg Salden
        Imago - Günter Gerhard Lange
        Glypha - Adrian Frutiger
        Calvert - Margaret Calvert

1979 *ITC Benguiat Gothic* - Edward Benguiat
New Caledonia - David Berlow / W. A. Dwiggins

1980

1980 *Fidelio* - José Mendoza y Almeida
    Sully-Jonquières - Jose Mendoza y Almeida

Flora - Gerard Unger
Lo-Type - L. Oppenheim / E. Spiekermann
ITC Novarese - Aldo Novarese
1980 *Andromaque* - Victor Hammer / R. H. Middleton
Administer - Leslie Usherwood
1981 *Corinthian* - Colin Brignall
Swift - Gerard Unger
1981 *ITC Isbell* - Richard Isbell / Jerry Campbell
ITC Barcelona - Edward Benguiat
Caxton - Leslie Usherwood
1982 *Santa Fe* - David Quay
Poppl-Laudatio - Friedrich Poppl
Poppl-Nero - Friedrich Poppl
Vario - Hermann Zapf
Versailles - Adrian Frutiger
Icone - Adrian Frutiger
Arial - Robin Nicholas / Patricia Saunders
1982 *ITC Modern 216* - Edward Benguiat
1983 *Edwardian* - Colin Brignall / Letraset
Aurelia - Hermann Zapf
Pan Nigerian - Hermann Zapf
AMS Euler Text - Hermann Zapf
Bodoni Old Face - Günter Gerhard Lange
Expert - Aldo Novarese
1983 *ITC Caslon 224* - Edward Benguiat
Isadora - Kris Holmes
Sierra - Kris Holmes
Marbrook - Leslie Usherwood
1984 *Typeface Two* - Neville Brody
ITC Veljovic - Jovica Veljovic
ITC Symbol - Aldo Novarese
Formata - Bernd Möllenstädt
1984 *Miraræ* - Carol Twombly
Lucida - Charles Bigelow / Kris Holmes
ITC Usherwood - Leslie Usherwood
1985 *Elan* - Albert Boton
AG Buch Stencil - Günter Gerhard Lange
Swift - Gerard Unger
Zapf Renaissance Roman - Hermann Zapf
ITC Mixage - Aldo Novarese
1985 *Lucida Sans* - Charles Bigelow / Kris Holmes
Oakland Ten - Zuzana Licko
Modula - Zuzana Licko
ITC Leawood - Leslie Usherwood
1986 *Typeface Six* - Neville Brody
Boton - Albert Boton
Navy Cut - Albert Boton
Carmina - Gudrum Zapf-von Hesse
Linotype Centennial - Adrian Frutiger
1986 *Matrix* - Zuzana Licko
Citizen - Zuzana Licko
Lucida Sans Typewriter - C Bigelow / Kris Holmes
1987 *Calisto* - Ron Carpenter
Arena - Neville Brody
Zwart Vet - Max Kisman
1987 *ITC Slimbach* - Robert Slimbach
ITC Stone Sans Serif - Sumner Stone
ITC Stone Serif - Sumner Stone
ITC Stone Informal - Sumner Stone
Bitstream Charter - Matthew Carter
Lucida Bright - Charles Bigelow / Kris Holmes
1988 *Tegentonen* - Max Kisman
Rotis - Otl Aicher
Avenir - Adrian Frutiger
1988 *Visigoth* - Arthur Baker
ITC Panache - Edward Benguiat
Lunatix - Zuzana Licko
Variex - Zuzana Licko
Lucida Calligraphy - Charles Bigelow / Kris Holmes
Spring - Garrett Boge

1989 *Industria* - Neville Brody
Campanile - Neville Brody
Beowulf - E. Van Blokland / Just Van Rossum
1989 *Amigo* - Arthur Baker
Pelican - Arthur Baker
Oxford - Arthur Baker
Marigold - Arthur Baker
ITC Giovanni - Robert Slimbach
Adobe Garamond - Robert Slimbach
Adobe Utopia - Robert Slimbach
FB Grotesque - David Berlow
FB Empire - David Berlow
Triplex - Zuzana Licko
Dolores - Tobias Frere-Jones

1990

1990 *Industria Inline* - Neville Brody
Arcadia - Neville Brody
Insignia - Neville Brody
ITC Quay Sans - David Quay
Jacque Slim - Max Kisman
Scratch Regular - Max Kisman
Zwart Vet (lowercase) - Max Kisman
Agora - Albert Boton
1990 *Adobe Minion* - Robert Slimbach
Trajan - Carol Twombly
Charlemagne - Carol Twombly
Lithos - Carol Twombly
Adobe Caslon - Carol Twombly
Journal - Zuzana Licko
Totally Gothic - Zuzana Licko
Totally Glyphic - Zuzana Licko
FB Belucian - David Berlow
FB Agency - David Berlow
Florens-Flourished - Garrett Boge
Manito - Garrett Boge
Adobe Tekton - David Siegel / Francis D.K. Ching
Dead History - Peter Scott-Makela
Template Gothic - Barry Deck
1991 *Blur* - Neville Brody
Harlem - Neville Brody
New Times Millennium - Aurobind Patel
Exocet - Jonathan Barnbrook
Fudoni Bold Remix - Max Kisman
Traveller Regular - Max Kisman
Vortex - Max Kisman
Brokenscript Bold - Just Van Rossum
Mendoza - José Mendoza y Almeyda
Meta - Erik Spiekerman
Christiana - Gudrum Zapf-von Hesse
Notre Dame - Karlgeorg Hoefer
San Marco - Karlgeorg Hoefer
Omnia - Karlgeorg Hoefer
Caecilia - Peter Matthias Noordzij
1991 *TF Baccarat* - Richard Isbell
Apple Chicago - Charles Bigelow / Kris Holmes
Apple Geneva - Charles Bigelow / Kris Holmes
Apple New York - Charles Bigelow / Kris Holmes
Apple Monaco - Charles Bigelow / Kris Holmes
Stone Print - Sumner Stone
1992 *La Bamba* - David Quay / Letraset
Sho - Karlgeorg Hoefer
Oranda - Gerard Unger
ITC Syndor - Hans Edward Meier
1992 *ITC Legacy* - Ronald Arnholm
ITC Legacy Sans - Ronald Arnholm
Myriad - Carol Twombly
Poetica - Robert Slimbach
Matrix Script - Zuzana Licko
Lucida Blackletter - Charles Bigelow / Kris Holmes
Lucida Handwriting - C. Bigelow / Kris Holmes
Lucida Fax and *Italic* - C. Bigelow / Kris Holmes

Lucida Sans Typewriter Oblique - Charles Bigelow / Kris Holmes
HTF Didot - Jonathan Hoefler
Garage Gothic - Tobias Frere-Jones
1993 *Optima Cyrillic* - Hermann Zapf
1993 *Sanvito* - Robert Slimbach
Caflisch Script - Robert Slimbach
Mantinia - Matthew Carter
Sophia - Matthew Carter
Viva - Carol Twombly
ITC Century Handtooled - Edward Benguiat
ITC Cheltenham Handtooled - Edward Benguiat
ITC Garamond Handtooled - Edward Benguiat
FB Eldorado - David Berlow / William A. Dwiggins
HTF Hoefler - Jonathan Hoefler
Interstate - Tobias Frere-Jones
Reiner Script - Tobias Frere-Jones / Imre Reiner
Nitrogen - Tobias Frere-Jones
Reactor - Tobias Frere-Jones
1994 *FF Thesis* - Lucas de Groot
Palatino Cyrillic - Hermann Zapf
Greek Palatino - Hermann Zapf
1994 *Kigali* - Arthur Baker
Big Caslon - Matthew Carter
Nueva - Carol Twombly
Dogma - Zuzana Licko
Lucida Typewriter - C. Bigelow / K. Holmes
Lucida Casual - Charles Bigelow / Kris Holmes
Lucida Console - Charles Bigelow / Kris Holmes
Old Claude - Paul Shaw / Garrett Boge
1995 *ITC Mithras* - Bob Anderton
1995 *Sassafras* - Arthur Baker
Walker - Matthew Carter
ITC Edwardian Script - Edward Benguiat
Base Nine and Twelve - Zuzana Licko
Soda Script - Zuzana Licko
Pilsner - Tobias Frere-Jones
Kolo - Paul Shaw / Garrett Boge
Arepo - Sumner Stone
1996 *ITC Kallos* - Phill Grimshaw
Braganza - Phill Grimshaw
Charlotte Sans - Michael Gills
Gilgamesh - Michael Gills
Elysium - Michael Gills
ITC Lenox - Alexander Rühl
1996 *Pontif* - Paul Shaw / Garrett Boge
Pietra - Paul Shaw / Garrett Boge
Cresci - Paul Shaw / Garrett Boge
Filosofia - Zuzana Licko
Mrs Eaves - Zuzana Licko
ITC Juanita - Luis Siquot
Adobe Jenson - Robert Slimbach
Kepler - Robert Slimbach
1997 *Chaparral* - Carol Twombly
Base Monospace - Zuzana Licko
Beata - Paul Shaw / Garrett Boge
Donatello - Paul Shaw / Garrett Boge
Ghiberti - Paul Shaw / Garrett Boge
Bermuda - Paul Shaw / Garrett Boge
1998 *Zapfino* - Hermann Zapf
1998 *Tarzana* - Zuzana Licko
Göteborg - Paul Shaw / Garrett Boge
Stockholm - Paul Shaw / Garrett Boge
Uppsala - Paul Shaw / Garrett Boge
Longhand - Garrett Boge
2000 *Solex* - Zuzana Licko
HTF Gotham - Tobias Frere-Jones
2002 *Fairplex* - Zuzana Licko

Note: Only the alphabets shown in this book are listed below

A

HTF Acropolis - Jonathan Hoefler 162
Ad Lib - Freeman Craw 125
Advertisers Gothic - Robert Wiebking 261
Aetna - William Hamilton Page 208
FB Agency - David Berlow 74
alphabet 26 - Bradbury Thompson 240
Alternate Gothic - Morris Fuller Benton 66
American Text - Morris Fuller Benton 71
American Uncial - Victor Hammer 155
Americana - Richard Isbell 172
Amigo - Arthur Baker 52
Andromaque - Victor Hammer/R. H. Middleton . . 155
Antique X Condensed - Darius Wells 256
Antique XXX Condensed - William H. Page. . . . 204
Antique Light Face Extended - Darius Wells . . . 258
Antique No. 7 - William Hamilton Page. 210
Antique Tuscan - Darius Wells 257
Antique Tuscan No. 8 - William Hamilton Page. . . 206
Antique Tuscan No. 11 - William Hamilton Page . . 207
Antique Tuscan Outline - William Hamilton Page. . 207
VGC Aquarius - Ronald Arnholm 44
Arrighi - Frederic Warde 252
Artcraft - Robert Wiebking 260
Artscript - Sol Hess 159
Auriga - Matthew Carter 104
ITC Avant Garde Gothic - H. Lubalin / T. Carnase . 186

B

TF Baccarat - Richard Isbell 175
Baker Signet - Arthur Baker 49
Balloon - Max Richard Kaufmann. 177
Bank Gothic - Morris Fuller Benton 70
ITC Barcelona - Edward Benguiat 59
ITC Bauhaus - Edward Benguiat 59
Beata - Paul Shaw/Garrett Boge 229
Bell Centennial - Matthew Carter 107
Bell Gothic - Chauncey Hawley Griffith 152
FB Belucian - David Berlow/Lucian Bernhard . . . 76
ITC Benguiat - Edward Benguiat 58
ITC Benguiat Gothic - Edward Benguiat 58
Bermuda - Paul Shaw/Garrett Boge 230
Bernhard Fashion - Lucian Bernhard 81
Bernhard Gothic - Lucian Bernhard 82
Bernhard Kursive - Lucian Bernhard 81
Bernhard Modern Roman - Lucian Bernhard . . . 83
Bernhard Roman Antiqua Bold Condensed -
Lucian Bernhard 83
Bernhard Tango - Lucian Bernhard 82
Bernhard Tango Swash - Lucian Bernhard 83
Bewick Roman - William Bradley. 98
Big Caslon - Matthew Carter 109
Block Type - H. Hoffmann/after Lucian Bernhard . 78
Bodoni Black - Robert Hunter Middleton 198
Bodoni Bold Panelled - Sol Hess 157
Bodoni Campanille - Robert Hunter Middleton . . 200
Bodoni Open - Morris Fuller Benton 68
ITC Bookman - Edward Benguiat 57
Boul Mich - Richard McArthur/Oswald Cooper . . 119
Bradley - William Bradley/Joseph W. Phinney. . . 96
Broadway - Morris Fuller Benton 69
Broadway Engraved - Sol Hess. 157
Brush - Robert E. Smith 237
ITC Busorama - Tom Carnase/Herb Lubalin. . . . 103

C

Caflisch Script - Robert Slimbach 235
Caledonia - William Addison Dwiggins 132
Camelot - Frederic W. Goudy 141
Cameo - Robert Hunter Middleton 194
Cartoon - Howard Allen Trafton 243
Cascade Script - Matthew Carter 106
Adobe Caslon - Carol Twombly 247
Caslon Antique - Berne Nadall 203
Caslon Clearface - Robert Wiebking 261
ITC Caslon 224 - Edward Benguiat. 60
CBS Didot - Freeman Craw 125
CBS Sans - Freeman Craw 125
Celtic Ornamented - William Hamilton Page . . . 209
Centaur - Bruce Rogers 222
ITC Century Handtooled - Edward Benguiat . . . 61
Century Roman - L. B. Benton/T. L. De Vinne . . . 62
Century Schoolbook - Morris Fuller Benton 68
HTF Champion Gothic - Jonathan Hoefler 162
Chaparral - Carol Twombly 250
Charlemagne - Carol Twombly 245
ITC Charter - Matthew Carter. 108
Cheltenham - Bertram G. Goodhue 140
ITC Cheltenham Handtooled - Edward Benguiat . 61
Apple Chicago - Charles Bigelow/Kris Holmes . . 167
Clarendon Ornamented - William Hamilton Page . 207
Clarendon XX Condensed - William H. Page . . . 206
Clearface - Morris Fuller Benton 66
Cloister Oldstyle - Morris Fuller Benton 67
Cloister Initials - Frederic W. Goudy 145
Commercial Script - Morris Fuller Benton 66
Cooper Black - Oswald Cooper 119
Cooper Full Face - Oswald Cooper 120
Cooper Hilite - Oswald Cooper 119
Cooper Old Style - Oswald Cooper 116
Cooper Tooled - Sol Hess 157
Copperplate Gothic - Frederic W. Goudy 144
Corona - Chauncey Hawley Griffith 153
Coronet - Robert Hunter Middleton 200
Craw Clarendon - Freeman Craw 121
Craw Clarendon Book - Freeman Craw 124
Craw Clarendon Condensed - Freeman Craw. . . 124
Craw Modern - Freeman Craw 124
Craw Modern Italic - Freeman Craw 124
Cresci - Paul Shaw/Garrett Boge 94

D

Davida Bold - Louis Minott. 202
Deepdene - Frederic W. Goudy. 146
Della Robbia - Thomas Maitland Cleland 114
Delphian Open Title - Robert Hunter Middleton . . 197
HTF Didot, Jonathan Hoefler 163
Dolores - Tobias Frere-Jones 134
Donatello - Paul Shaw/Garrett Boge 229
Doric Ornamented - Darius Wells 259

E

Eden - Robert Hunter Middleton 199
ITC Edwardian Script - Edward Benguiat 61
HTF Egiziano Filigree - Freeman Craw 162
Egyptian Ornamented - William Hamilton Page. . 209
Eldorado - William Addison Dwiggins 133
FB Eldorado - David Berlow/W. A. Dwiggins . . . 77
Electra - William Addison Dwiggins 132
Emerson - Joseph Blumenthal 91
Empire - Morris Fuller Benton 71
FB Empire - David Berlow / Morris Fuller Benton . 75

Engravers Bold - Morris Fuller Benton 64
Excelsior - Chauncey Hawley Griffith 150

F

Fairfield - Rudolph Ruzicka 224
ITC Firenze - Tom Carnase. 103
Florens-Flourished - Garrett Boge 93
Florentine Cursive - Robert Hunter Middleton . . . 201
Forum Title - Frederic Goudy 145
VGC Fovea - Ronald Arnholm 46
Franciscan - Frederic W. Goudy 148
Franklin Gothic - Morris Fuller Benton 66
French Antique - William Hamilton Page 208
French Clarendon XXX Condensed - W. H. Page. 211

G

Gallia - Wadsworth A. Parker 215
ITC Galliard - Matthew Carter 108
Gando Ronde - Matthew Carter 106
Garage Gothic - Tobias Frere-Jones 135
Adobe Garamond - Robert Slimbach 233
ITC Garamond Handtooled - Edward Benguiat . . 61
Garamont - Frederic W. Goudy 180
Apple Geneva - Charles Bigelow/Kris Holmes . . . 167
Ghiberti - Paul Shaw/Garrett Boge 197
ITC Giovanni - Robert Slimbach 233
ITC Gorilla - Tom Carnase/Ronne Bonder 100
Göteborg - Paul Shaw/Garrett Boge 231
HTF Gotham - Tobias Frere-Jones 136
Gothic Condensed Outline - Darius Wells 257
Gothic Extended - Darius Wells 256
Gothic Tuscan Condensed - Darius Wells 257
Gothic Tuscan Condensed No. 2 - W. H. Page. . . 210
Gothic Tuscan Italian - Darius Wells 258
Gothic Tuscan Pointed - William Hamilton Page . 206
Goudy Handtooled - W. A. Parker/M. F. Benton . 214
Goudy Heavyface - Frederic W. Goudy 147
Goudy Old Style - Frederic W. Goudy. 145
Goudy Sans Serif Heavy - Frederic W. Goudy . . 147
Goudy Sans Serif Light - Frederic W. Goudy . . . 147
Goudy Sans Serif Light Italic - F. W. Goudy . . . 147
Goudy Text - Frederic W. Goudy 146
Goudy Thirty - Frederic W. Goudy 148
Grayda - Frank H. Riley 221
Grecian Condensed - Darius Wells 256
ITC Grizzli - Tom Carnase/Ronne Bonder 102
FB Grotesque - David Berlow 73
ITC Grouch - Tom Carnase / Ronne Bonder 102

H

Hadriano Stone-Cut - Sol Hess 158
Hadriano Title - Frederic W. Goudy. 145
Hammer Unziale - Victor Hammer 154
Hess Neobold - Sol Hess 158
Hobo - Morris Fuller Benton 67
HTF Hoefler - Jonathan Hoefler 160
ITC Honda - Tom Carnase/Ronne Bonder 102
Huxley Vertical - Walter Huxley 169

I

Iniciales Bernhard - Lucian Bernhard 79
Initials - William Addison Dwiggins 133
Interstate - Tobias Frere-Jones 135
Ionic - William Hamilton Page 206
Ionic No. 5 - Chauncey Hawley Griffith 149
Irvin - Rea Irvin 170
ITC Isadora - Kris Holmes 164
ITC Isbell - Richard Isbell 174

J

Janson - Chauncey Hawley Griffith 151
Jenson Oldstyle - Joseph Warren Phinney 216

K

Karnak - Robert Hunter Middleton 198
Kaufmann Bold - Max Richard Kaufmann 177
Kaufmann Script - Max Richard Kaufmann 176
Kennerley Old Style - Frederic W. Goudy 144
Kennerley Open Caps - Sol Hess 156
Kigali - Arthur Baker 53
Kolo - Paul Shaw/Garrett Boge 229
ITC Korinna - Edward Benguiat 56

L

Lafayette Extra Condensed - R. H. Middleton . . 199
ITC Legacy - Ronald Arnholm 47
ITC Legacy Sans - Ronald Arnholm 48
HTF Leviatan - Jonathan Hoefler 162
Lexington - W. A. Parker/C. P. Hornung 215
Lilith - Lucian Bernhard 82
Lithos - Carol Twombly 246
Lombardic Capitals - Frederic W. Goudy 146
Longhand - Garrett Boge 95
ITC Lubalin Graph - H Lubalin/T. DiSpigna 189
Lucian - Lucian Bernhard 81
Lucida - Charles Bigelow/Kris Holmes 84
Lucida Blackletter - C. Bigelow/K. Holmes 88
Lucida Bright - Charles Bigelow/Kris Holmes . . . 87
Lucida Calligraphy - C. Bigelow/K. Holmes . . . 88
Lucida Casual - Charles Bigelow/K. Holmes . . . 90
Lucida Console - Charles Bigelow/K. Holmes . . . 168
Lucida Fax - Charles Bigelow/Kris Holmes . . . 89
Lucida Handwriting - C. Bigelow/K. Holmes . . . 168
Lucida Sans - Charles Bigelow/Kris Holmes . . . 85
Lucida Sans Typewriter - C. Bigelow/K. Holmes . . 87
Lucida Sans Typewriter Oblique -
Charles Bigelow/Kris Holmes 89
Lucida Typewriter - C. Bigelow/K. Holmes . . . 90
Lunatix - Zuzana Licko 184
Lydian and Italic - Warren Chappell 110
Lydian Bold - Warren Chappell 113
Lydian Cursive - Warren Chappell 113

M

ITC Machine - Tom Carnase/Ronne Bonder 103
Mandate - Robert Hunter Middleton 200
Manito - Garrett Boge 93
Mantinia - Matthew Carter 108
Marigold - Arthur Baker 53
Matrix - Zuzana Licko 184
Memphis Extrabold - Chauncey H. Griffith 153
Merrymount - Bertram G. Goodhue 137
Metroblack - William Addison Dwiggins 132
Metrolight - William Addison Dwiggins 129
Metromedium - William Addison Dwiggins 132
Adobe Minion - Robert Slimbach 243
Mirarae - Carol Twombly 244
Missal Initials - William Bradley 98
ITC Modern 216 - Edward Benguiat 59
Modernique - Morris Fuller Benton 69
Modernistic - Wadsworth A. Parker 215
Modula - Zuzana Licko 184
Apple Monaco - Charles Bigelow/Kris Holmes . . . 167
Monotype 30-E - Frederic W. Goudy 144
Munder Venezian - Robert Wiebking 261
Murray Hill Bold - Emil J. Klump 178

Myriad - Carol Twombly 248

N

ITC Neon - Tom Carnase/Ronne Bonder 102
New Caledonia - David Berlow 72
Apple New York - Charles Bigelow/Kris Holmes 168
News Gothic - Morris Fuller Benton 67
Nobel - Tobias Frere-Jones 135
Nueva - Carol Twombly 249
No. 129 - William Hamilton Page 211
No. 131 - William Hamilton Page 211
No. 142 - William Hamilton Page 212
No. 154 - William Hamilton Page 212
No. 500 - William Hamilton Page 212
No. 506 - William Hamilton Page 213
No. 515 - William Hamilton Page 213

O

Oakland Ten - Zuzana Licko 182
Old Claude - Paul Shaw 226
Olympian - Matthew Carter 106
Onyx - Gerry Powell 218
Onyx Italic - Sol Hess 159
Opticon - Chauncey H. Griffith 152
Ornate Title - Frederic W. Goudy 147
Othello - Morris Fuller Benton 71
WTC Our Bodoni - Tom Carnase/Massimo Vignelli . 71
Oxford - Arthur Baker 52
Bitstream Oz Handicraft - Oswald Cooper 120

P

Painter's Roman - W. H. Page/D. Wells 209
ITC Panache - Edward Benguiat 60
Paragon - Chauncey Hawley Griffith 151
Parisian - Morris Fuller Benton 69
Park Avenue - Robert E. Smith 236
Parsons - Will Ransom 220
Pelican - Arthur Baker 52
Phanitalian - William H. Page 211
Pietra - Paul Shaw/Garrett Boge 94
Pilsner - Tobias Frere-Jones 136
ITC Pioneer - Tom Carnase/Ronne Bonder 103
Plantin - Frank Hinman Pierpont 217
Pompeian Cursive - Oswald Cooper 120
Pontif - Paul Shaw/Garrett Boge 93
Postblack Italic - Sol Hess 159
Poster Bodoni - Chauncey Hawley Griffith 150
Post-Stout Italic - Sol Hess 159

R

Radiant - Robert Hunter Middleton 201
Reactor - Tobias Frere-Jones 136
Record Gothic - Robert Hunter Middleton 197
HTF Requiem - Jonathan Hoefler 162
Roman - Darius Wells 254

S

Samson - Robert Hunter Middleton 201
Sanvito - Robert Slimbach 235
HTF Sarracen - Jonathan Hoefler 162
Sassafras - Arthur Baker 53
ITC Serif Gothic - Herb Lubalin/Tony DiSpigna . . 189
Shadow - Morris Fuller Benton 71
Shelley Script Allegro - Matthew Carter 107
Shelley Script Volante - Matthew Carter 107
Sierra - Kris Holmes 165
Skeleton Antique - William Hamilton Page 208
ITC Slimbach - Robert Slimbach 232

Snell Roundhand - Matthew Carter 106
Sophia - Matthew Carter 106
Souvenir - Morris Fuller Benton 68
ITC Souvenir - Edward Benguiat 54
Spire - Sol Hess 158
Spring - Garret Boge 92
Stellar - Robert Hunter Middleton 192
Stencil - Robert Hunter Middleton 200
Stencil - Gerry Powell 219
Stockholm - Paul Shaw/Garrett Boge 230
ITC Stone Informal - Sumner Stone 239
ITC Stone Sans Serif - Sumner Stone 238
ITC Stone Serif - Sumner Stone 239
Stymie - Morris Fuller Benton 70
Stymie Bold Condensed - Gerry Powell 219
Stymie Extrabold - Sol Hess 158
Stymie Inline Title - Wadsworth A. Parker . . . 215

T

Tempo Heavy Condensed - Robert H. Middleton . 198
Teutonic - William Hamilton Page 210
ITC Tiffany - Edward Benguiat 56
Totally Gothic - Zuzana Licko 185
Tower - Morris Fuller Benton 71
Trafton Script - Howard Allen Trafton 242
Trajan - Carol Twombly 245
Trajan Title - Frederic W. Goudy 147
Trajanus - Warren Chappell 113
Triplex - Zuzana Licko 185
Tuscan Outline - Darius Wells 258

U

Ultra Bodoni - Morris Fuller Benton 70
Umbra - Robert Hunter Middleton 199
University of California Old Style - F. W. Goudy . 148
Uppsala - Paul Shaw/Garrett Boge 231
Adobe Utopia - Robert Slimbach 234

V

WTC Veritas - Ronald Arnholm 45
Village - Frederic W. Goudy 144
Visigoth - Arthur Baker 52
Viva - Carol Twombly 249

W

Walker - Matthew Carter 109

Z

HTF Ziggurat - Jonathan Hoefler 162

Born in Barre, Vermont, in 1939, Ronald Arnholm's interest in lettering dates back to childhood when he watched his older brother apply pin striping and lettering on antique cars and trucks. Later on, while studying at the Rhode Island School of Design where he received his BFA in 1961, and during high school and college breaks, he was involved in sign painting in a small two-person shop. "It was during this time that I started to develop a deep interest in type. I thoroughly enjoyed analyzing the design structure of individual typefaces and incorporated them into all kinds of signage whenever I could."

In 1958, while he was in his second year at Rhode Island, he designed his first typeface for Photo-Lettering, Inc., in New York City.

Later on, during his two years of graduate study at Yale University where he received his master's degree in Fine Arts in 1963, he had the opportunity to study closely a 1470 copy of *Eusebius* by Nicolas Jenson (1420-1480), in a class on the history of typography. It was love at first sight and an inspiration for his thesis. After extensive research, and months of hard work assisted by his professors, Arnholm finished the project, which, under the name of *Jenson Roman*, became part of the Mergenthaler Linotype type library. He also received the Composing Room Award for Typographical Excellence at Yale University in 1963 for his work.

In 1965, he was awarded a prize at the National Type Face Competition, sponsored by Visual Graphics Corporation, North Miami, for his typeface *Arnholm Sans Medium*.

In 1967, he repeated the Yale University experience by designing the campus signage system for the University of Georgia, for which he received a Silver Award from the University and College Designers Association in 1975.

Between 1967 and 1974, he created a series of typefaces, *VGC Aquarius*, *VGC Arnholm Sans Bold*, and *VGC Fovea* for the Visual Graphic Corporation at North Miami, Florida, which continued to strengthen his type design creativity.

In 1980, after Sheila Levrant de Bretteville designed the new format of the *Los Angeles Times*, he was commissioned to design its four primary headline typefaces: *L.A.Times Regular, L.A.Times Regular Italic, L.A. Times Bold* and *L.A. Times Bold Italic*, which were introduced in October that year. Between 1985 and 1987, he was again commissioned by this newspaper to design a new classified typeface, which was introduced in 1989.

In 1982, he decided that his first *Jenson* type had not captured all the qualities of the original and that it needed companion italic. He went back to the original model –this time, at the Emory University Library Special Collection in Atlanta, Georgia– and after thorough research and many trial drawings, Arnholm finished *Legacy*. He feels that "the beauty and perfection of the *Jenson Roman* is due in part to its imperfection and inconsistency of details." His extensive study revealed "serif design, stroke weight and angle, and individual character curves all varied subtly from letter to letter."

He believes that "this subtle contrast between similar parts of one letter relative to another is one of the contributing factors of the mellow appearance of *Jenson*." For the italic version, since there were no models when Jenson cast his type, Arnholm chose the work of Claude Garamond (1500-1561), the French type designer. "Other forms didn't seem to work well with *Jenson*, they seemed too regular in their overall detailing."

While working on the *Jenson* type, Arnholm became intrigued with the idea of a companion series of sans serif faces having the essential structure of the old style serif types. Although he did some trial sketches, he did not begin this task until he finished satisfactorily his roman version. Both versions were finished at the end of 1992 and form part of the ITC typeface library.

Since 1963, he has taught at the Lamar Dodd School of Art, University of Georgia, Athens, where he is a professor of graphic design. He spends his time doing painting, graphic design, photography, type design, and research on visual language vocabulary and syntax. He has had one-man painting exhibitions in 1964 at the Georgia Museum of Art, Athens, in 1967 at the Carroll Reese Museum at East Tennessee State University, and in 1973 at the Visual Arts Gallery, Department of Art, at the University of Georgia.

As a type designer he has more than fifty typefaces to his credit, many of them acclaimed by world-known typographers.

Among his trademark designs, the corporate mark for American Tube and Controls was selected among the best 190 American Trademarks in the *Trademarks USA* exhibition held in Chicago in 1964.

He has received other awards, such as the Award of Distinctive Merit (1966) from the Arts Directors Club of New York; the Certificate of Merit (1970) "for an outstanding contribution to the development of the graphic art of the twentieth century" from the International Center for the Typographic Arts; and the Albert Christ-Janer Award for Creative Research (1994) from the University of Georgia Research Foundation.

VGC AQUARIUS (1967)

Created for Visual Graphic Corporation, North Miami, Florida, this fairly condensed serif typeface is certainly an experiment in the use of serifs.

The design includes a whole family of extra light, regular, medium, bold, ultra bold, black, and outline versions.

ABCDEFGHIJKLMNOPQRSTUVWXYZ
&abcdefghijklmnopqrstuvwxyz$¢£
1234567890!?

BROWN THRASHER BOOKS
(1979)

A symbol for a book series done for the University of Georgia Press. The brown thrasher happens to be Georgia's state bird.

THE MODERATOR (1962)

This trademark was designed as a graphical identification for this magazine's insight structure. The arrows were blackened down and up to signify the statement and the commentary on each one of the articles.

REFLECTION (1964)

In this acrylic painting on canvas, Arnholm expresses this visual statement through the use of typographical elements.

THE TWIST (1962)

This is a calligraphic illustration for an article written by Art Buchwald on the sixties dance craze: "It has always been my opinion that dancing should be the fast step toward seduction. If a dance discourages this, I don't see its value," wrote Buchwald.

INTEGRATION SOONER-NOT LATER (1962)

This is an illustration used in this student survey article with comments by Rev. William Sloane Coffin, Jr. for the first issue of *The Moderator*.

THE MODERATOR (1962)

This is the cover of the first issue of the Yale University students' magazine, *The Moderator*, published by the Moderator Publishing Co. Inc., in New Haven.

WTC VERITAS (1981-85)

This is a presentation of this typeface in a free composition with numbers. The design, which contains a complete family of eight variants, was designed for the World Type Center in New York. It represents "an attempt to create an original typeface."

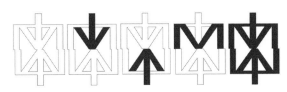

UNIVERSITY OF GEORGIA PRESS (1980)

In this symbol/trademark, Arnholm has blended typography and image since Athens, Georgia, is known as the "classic" city. While the Greek ionic column's volute gives form to the letter **G**, the vertical ornaments suggest books.

POSITIVE-NEGATIVE (1964)

In this enamel on wood painting, Arnholm has arrived at an interesting solution of this visual statement through the simple use of the two words.

CREATION (1967)

In this acrylic on canvas painting, Arnholm has once again expressed his ideas through the use of letters. The globe reinforces the visual statement.

LOS ANGELES TIMES CLASSIFIED TYPEFACE (1989)

Between 1985 and 1987, Arnholm was once again commissioned by the *Los Angeles Times* to design a new classified typeface, which was introduced in 1989.

VGC FOVEA (1967-1974)

Created for Visual Graphic Corporation at Tamarac, Florida, this roman typeface has a clear calligraphic feeling, which is accentuated by a slight slant in the construction of the letters.

THE MODERATOR (1962)

In this double spread for the first issue of *The Moderator*, Arnholm uses a classic unbalanced Swiss arrangement of the page.

AMERICAN TUBES AND CONTROLS (1962-1963)

This trademark for a manufacturer of continuous tubing was selected to be among the best 190 American Trademarks in the *Trademarks USA* exhibition organized under the auspices of the Society of Typographic Arts, Chicago, in 1964.

ITC LEGACY (1992)

A beautiful contemporary version of Nicolas Jenson's 1470 roman, it was designed in four weights for ITC, New York.

"The Jenson roman is the very first fully evolved roman typeface, which set the standard for the form of our lower case letters.

"My exposure to the Jenson roman was in history of typography class in the Yale graduate program in graphic design. We were shown a copy of a book printed by Jenson in Venice in 1470, and I was overwhelmed by its typeface.

"In the Special Collections at Emory University Library I photographed a rare illuminated copy of the 1470 Jenson *Eusebius*. The letters were photographed at a very closed range of only a few inches, using continuous tone film: letters were chosen which had the best printing impression.

"I projected the negatives in the enlarger and made pencil outlines to drawing size on tracing paper, making necessary design revisions because of the change in proportions of x-height to ascender and descender. I proceeded to create trial master drawings in ink on drafting film, working over the tracings.

"I established that *Legacy* should be a contemporary interpretation of the *Jenson* which would be suitable for wide-ranging application rather than an attempt at a precise copy, e.g., Monotype *Poliphilus*, which would result in an archaic looking type which might have rather limited potential use. My goal was to capture the spirit of the beauty, mellowness, and readability of the original. Although I could have designed the alphabets using the computer, I felt that by hand-drawing the letters I would naturally capture some of the inconsistencies that go along with punch-cutting.

"After doing hundreds of drawings I reached a point when, perhaps akin to a punch cutter, I could literally feel the design of the letters in my hands, and they began to come out like sweat.

"This work was done at a leisurely pace, with periods of months or perhaps almost a year when I might not even look at the type. This was good because I discovered that I could then clearly see what was obviously wrong with characters when I went back to work on them."

ABCDEFGHIJKLMNOPQRSTU
VWXYZ&abcdefghijklmnopqrstu
vwxyz$1234567890!?

ABCDEFGHIJKLMNOPQRSTUVW
XYZ&abcdefghijklmnopqrstuvwxyz
$1234567890!?

ABCDEFGHIJKLMNOPQRST
UVWXYZ&abcdefghijklmnopq
rstuvwxyz$1234567890!?

ABCDEFGHIJKLMNOPQRSTU
VWXYZ&abcdefghijklmnopqrstuv
wxyz$1234567890!?

ABCDEFGHIJKLMNOPQRST
UVWXYZ&abcdefghijklmno
pqrstuvwxyz$1234567890!?

ITC LEGACY SANS
(1992)

This companion to *ITC Legacy Serif*, also designed in four weights, has been praised by many typographers as one of the most legible sans-serif typefaces of this century.

"One morning in 1989, two days before Christmas, something struck me like lightning: that I should design a companion sans serif based on the skeletal structure of the *Jenson* and *Garamond*. Working in pencil on tracing paper placed over alphabet specimens of both the roman and the italic, I had both types sketched in by the end of the afternoon. I somehow realized that I had created something really good and unique.

"Next, I scanned these pencil sketches into the Macintosh, and spent several days cleaning up the bit maps of the scans, a tedious process to say the least, but one that saved me much time in the long run. This was really the only time I used the computer in the creation of *Legacy*.

"All my completed master drawings were digitized by a team of specialists at URW in Hamburg, Germany. They were not scanned; instead, points along the edges were hand-plotted. Also, the characters were unitized and side bearings determined. The medium weight of *Legacy* sans and serif roman and italic were done entirely by interpolating the book and bold weights of the serif and sans serif versions. I periodically studied many sets of proofs from URW and, surprisingly, few final revisions had to be made; the bold serif weight required not one revision.

"I am excited about the readability and legibility of the sans versions, particularly with the heaviest weights. Ultra weights have always been notoriously difficult to design, for they tend to lose the character of the typeface.

"I find it very interesting that when *Legacy* is printed out on a 300 dpi LaserWriter it looks even more like the actual *Jenson*, because the low resolution adds some of the irregularities found in the original, thickening up the slab serifs as well."

According to one type authority *Legacy* is "a magnificent sans! It has everything that a sans never had before...I'm glad I've lived long enough to see a sans serif drawn the way it should be."

ABCDEFGHIJKLMNOPQRST
UVWXYZ&abcdefghijklmnop
qrstuvwxyz$1234567890!?

ABCDEFGHIJKLMNOPQRSTUV
WXYZ&abcdefghijklmnopqrstuvwx
yz$1234567890!?

ABCDEFGHIJKLMNOPQRST
UVWXYZ&abcdefghijklmnopq
rstuvwxyz$1234567890!?

ABCDEFGHIJKLMNOPQRSTU
VWXYZ&abcdefghijklmnopqrstu
vwxyz$1234567890!?

ABCDEFGHIJKLMNOPQRST
UVWXYZ&abcdefghijklmno
pqrstuvwxyz$1234567890!?

Arthur Baker grew up in the Yosemite Valley in California and attended schools and colleges on the West Coast and in New York City, including courses at Columbia University under the famous calligrapher Oscar Ogg and private lessons with Georg Salter, Lenn Cooper, and Tommy Thompson. He has been director of calligraphic alphabet development for a number of corporations.

With his knowledge of letterforms and historical calligraphic styles, along with his own custom-designed pens and brushes, Arthur Baker has created a unique library of fonts, which include more than 300 typefaces.

Tommy Thompson says of his work, "language becomes music through the flowing pen of (his) calm and facile hand. His love of beauty is so unselfishly expressed in his work that one reads joy in each letter, each word, in the rhythm of his designs."

In 1965, Baker was prizewinner in the National Typeface Competition sponsored by Visual Graphics Corporation, North Miami, Florida, with his *Baker Signet*, a roman humanistic sans serif alphabet with a strong calligraphic feeling.

In 1973, Baker published his first book *Calligraphy*, which "was a breakthrough in the somewhat special and conservative world of calligraphy. In effect, worldwide, he has been enormously influential in the virtual explosion of interest in the art and craft of beautiful writing today. He is generous with appearances at lectures/demonstrations, gathering admirers as loyal as those who know his ideas only from books. The art of Arthur Baker is uniquely American. His adherents form a group practicing what can be truly called the New American Calligraphy, recognized as such throughout the world," writes William Hogarth in one of his introductions to Baker's books.

Many of his alphabet designs have come out of his first two books on handwriting, *Calligraphy* (1973), which includes more

than 100 original designs, and *Calligraphic Alphabets* (1974), with more than 150 complete alphabets. This is the case with *Visigoth* (1988), *Amigo* (1989), *Pelican* (1989), and *Oxford* (1989), all licensed by AGFA Monotype Corporation, Adobe Incorporated, Hewlett-Packard, IBM, Lexmark, Microsoft, and Xerox.

Many of Baker's typeface families include sx and lx styles. These distinctive variations allow greater flexibility in design, by providing different ascender and descender heights. The lx style has long, tall ascenders and regular-length descenders. The sx style has short ascenders and descenders that allow it to fit where its companion might not.

In his book, *The Roman Alphabet* (1976), Baker triumphantly demonstrates in brilliant fashion his contention that the subtlety of the work of the Roman artisans who inscribed the *capitalis monumentalis* has been unjustly ignored. Subsequent publications –such as *Calligraphic Initials* (1978), *The Script Alphabet* (1978), and *The Dance of the Pen* (1978)– give further evidence of his masterly use of the pen.

Later on, in his work, *Historic Calligraphic Alphabets* (1980), a book with eighty-eight plates, Baker challenged with great success the notion of the fixed-angle approach to the line by the tool –whether quill, reed, brush or steel nib. "Each historic hand has been reinterpreted to emphasize the ideal characteristics; each plate is the apotheosis of the work of a given period –not a mere textbook presentation of the actual surviving examples in the manner of the heavy-handed Teutonic *Schriftatlas* compilations, but a truly fresh, highly personal expression by a master of the modern form," writes Hogarth in the introduction.

"Since Edward Johnston's revival of interest in the craft of calligraphy at the beginning of the present century, there has developed a contradictory muddle of misunderstanding about historic

handwriting. Wrong assumptions have been compounded by disciples of Johnston and other enthusiasts. While craftsmanship and good intentions are laudable, such basic errors in original interpretations are unscholarly, fuzzy-minded, and even dangerous. Arthur Baker runs the risk in this book of becoming the clear-headed boy in Andersen's tale who pointed out that the Emperor's clothes didn't exist. Remember, when you return again and again to *these* interpretative pages, that the historic originals have acted on Baker's own talent and imagination to go beyond them –to add the perfect finishing touch, to summarize a style." adds Hogarth.

Besides the afore mentioned books, Arthur Baker has published *The Calligraphic Art of Arthur Baker* (1983), *Celtic Hand Stroke by Stroke* (Irish Half-uncial from the *Book of Kells*) (1983), *Calligraphic Swash Initials* (1984), *Brush Calligraphy* (1984), which show his continuous concern for handing down to others his knowledge on type and calligraphy.

In his new calligraphic work, as may be seen in *Scripsit* (2000), a triennial journal of the Washington Calligraphers Guild, Baker, working with a sponge brush and gouache, blends calligraphy with a drawing structure to obtain a sculptoric whole, where the final form, abstract in its reading, gives the feeling of being self-contained.

BAKER SIGNET (1965)

A humanistic sans serif typeface, it has a strong calligraphic feeling in its drawing. Baker won a prize with it in 1965, in the National Typeface Competition sponsored by Visual Graphics Corporation, North Miami, Florida.

A curious application may be found in the Coke logotype.

ABCDEFGHIJKLMNOPQRSTUVW XYZ&abcdefghijklmnopqrstuvwxyz $1234567890!?

CALLIGRAPHY (1973-1974)

The examples presented on this page have been selected from *Calligraphy* (1973), and *Calligraphic Alphabets* (1974), two books designed by Arthur Baker, and published by Dover Publications, Inc.

Drawn with different types of pen, they are a direct testimony of great skill and deep sensibility in shaping letters and words. They have also been a source of learning for others and a platform for his alphabets.

"In his calligraphy, rhythm, letter design, and disciplined composition are accomplished without showing human effort. Character refinement in the person of the writer will always be evident in this expression of art and joy," writes Tommy Thompson in the introduction to *Calligraphy*.

Calligraphy

Alphabet

hieroglyphica

ABCDE
FGHIK
LMNOP
QRSTU
VWXYZ

Scribebat

A abcdefghijklmnopqrstuvwxyz

A abcdefghijklmnopqrstuvwxyz

Take therefore no
thought for the
morrow: for the
morrow will take
thought for the
things of itself.

CALLIGRAPHY (1973-2000)

The examples presented on this page have been selected from *Scripsit* (2000), a triennial journal of the Washington Calligraphers Guild, plus two calligraphic examples taken from *Calligraphy* (1973), a book designed by Baker and published by Dover Publications, Inc., New York.

In his present work, executed with a sponge brush and gouache, Baker has been able to give both a new and abstract dimension to his letterforms.

A self-contained whole, each calligraphic work may be read as a sculptural piece, full of an organic quality.

ALPHABET (1987)

In this first work (24" x 18"), executed with a chisel-edged sponge brush and gouache, Baker is able to maintain the fluid calligraphic touch present in his earlier work, while he gives letters a more pictorial expression.

SCRIPTA and SCRIBE (1973)

These two earlier examples of his calligraphic work serve as a comparison to his new approach to expression.

THE ALPHABET (1987)

This horizontal calligraphic work (36" x 12"), executed with a chisel-edged sponge brush, is being cut into steel to be placed on the wall of a private library in Texas.

ABSTRACT (1987)

In these two examples (20" x 26"), all executed with a chisel-edged sponge brush, the volumetrical quality is more evident, through the handling of the gouache.

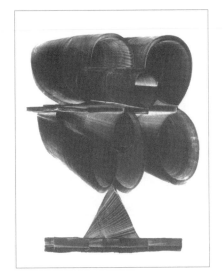

VISIGOTH (1988)

A strongly calligraphic typeface, it was designed for setting a text of Dante's *Bestiary*, published in New York by Ombondi Editions.

ABCDEFGHIJKLMNOPQRST UVWXYZ&abcdefghijklmnop qrstuvwxyz$1234567890!?

AMIGO (1989)

Structured as a roman typeface, it is characterized by a slight inclination, and a strong calligraphic drawing. This quality is more noticeable in lowercase letters.

Compugraphic Corporation licenses it.

ABCDEFGHIJKLMNOPQRST UVWXYZ&abcdefghijklmnopqr stuvwxyz$1234567890!?

PELICAN (1989)

A calligraphic roman typeface with a strong inclination in the uppercase letters, it is also characterized by an almost script lowercase alphabet.

Compugraphic Corporation licenses it.

ABCDEFGHIJKLMNOPQRSTUV WXYZ&abcdefghijklmnopqrstuvwxyz $1234567890!?

OXFORD (1989)

A calligraphic roman typeface with a slight inclination in the uppercase letters, it is characterized by the insertion, in the manner of the Uncial letters, of some majuscules (**B**, **F**, **G**, **M**, **Q**, **R**, **S**, **T** and **W**) in the lowercase alphabet.

ABCDEFGHIJKLMNOPQRSTUVWX YZ&abcdefghijklmnopqrstuvwxyz $1234567890!?

MARIGOLD (1989)

Designed exclusively for Compugraphic Corporation, this calligraphic alphabet maintains the proportions and form of the classic capital letters, with a slight inclination.

Lowercase letters are freer in their construction.

ABCDEFGHIJKLMNOPQRSTUVWXYZ&
abcdefghijklmnopqrstuvwxyz$1234567890!?

KIGALI (1994)

Designed by Baker for URW, this is a wide-bodied display type with bold, rough-edge pen strokes that taper dramatically.

Kigali also includes a *criblé* version, and a *cameo* version with letters drawn white on black squares, in the manner of the early nineteenth-century initials.

ABCDEFGHIJKLMNOPQRSTUVW
XYZ&abcdefghijklmnopqrstuvwxy
z$1234567890!?%*

ABCDEFGHIJKLMNOPQRSTUVW
XYZ&abcdefghijklmnopqrstuvwxy
z$1234567890!?

SASSAFRAS (1995)

A display type with short ascenders and descenders, it was designed for URW in 1995.

It is based on the natural inline effect created when writing with a split, metal, nibbed pen.

Baker also drew a variant with long ascenders and descenders to better retain a classical calligraphic feeling.

ABCDEFGHIJKLMNOPQRSTUV
WXYZ&abcdefghijklmnopqrstuvwxyz
$1234567890!?%*

ABCDEFGHIJKLMNOPQRSTUV
WXYZ&abcdefghijklmnopqrstuvwxyz
$1234567890!?%*

Born in New York City in 1927, Edward Benguiat got acquainted with type when he was nine or ten. His father was one of the display directors of Bloomingdale's, and as an artist he had all the drawing tools. As a boy, Benguiat used to play with them. He also knew about sign painting, showcard lettering, and speedball lettering.

At the time of World War II, he was not old enough to enter the army legally, so he lied about his age, and thus he was able to serve as a pilot in photo-reconnaissance missions over Europe. Returning to civilian life, he continued his career as an accomplished jazz drummer, playing on Manhattan's famed Swing Street with the likes of Stan Kenton and Woody Herman. He often talks about "the rhythm of type" and compares graphic design to a musical composition.

One day he stepped in for an absent lettering artist at the studio where he worked, and since then he has been doing lettering, to the point of being known as the most prolific and stylish graphic designer of the past century. His work has ranged from Spencerian scripts to casual gothics to formal romans to art nouveau and novelty display faces.

Influenced by his family –art connoisseurs and collectors–, Benguiat started to study at the Workshop School of Advertising Art in New York City, where he studied advertising, and then calligraphy with Arnold Bank and Paul Standard.

In pursuing his one main goal of becoming a significant designer of letterforms, he worked for many agencies and publishing companies in New York City, becoming associate director of *Esquire* magazine in 1953. That year he opened his own studio.

"Most people think lettering is a bore, but lettering is, in my opinion, the only true communicative art... It took every civilization, and civilizations have crumbled and all the masterful art of time that goes back before the Greeks and before the Egyptians, way back –when all this has crumbled the alphabet seems to have hung around... No one ever went crazy looking for a painting, but they went crazy over the Rosetta Stone. Communication. Now, with the advent of electronics, I don't think the alphabet's going to hold up. I really don't think it is going to hold up any more than the clock is going to hold up... Everything will go into the computer. Communication will go into the computer. A computer will give you letters looking like a computer. They may digitize them, they may do things to help them, but creativity of letterform will be based in what the computer can do. If the computer can't do it, then no matter how well you can create a letterform, it won't make any difference. The computer will take over. It's a tragedy. It's going to happen."

In 1962, Benguiat started to work with Photo-Lettering, Inc., as type design director and editor of their promotional publication *Plinc*, a position he held for some time. He was also vice president of International Typeface Corporation, where he collaborated with Herb Lubalin in giving a particular style to the *U&lc* quarterly magazine. He has also designed several fonts with Victor Caruso.

"When I design a typeface, I design it progressively. I think if Leonard Bernstein can take Beethoven's Fifth Symphony and redesign it, I think if Beethoven was alive today he would use all the stereophonic sounds, all the instrumentation, all the stereophonic equipment,

and it would possibly sound like Leonard Bernstein tries to make it. So when I design a typeface, I make believe –I don't want to tell you that I'm a warlock or a witch– but if I'm designing a face that's old and trying to revive it, I make believe, but I don't really make believe, that the person who did it is in me. Goes inside me and tells me what to do."

Benguiat is a member of the New York Arts Directors Club, the Type Directors Club, the Alliance Graphique Internationale, and the Dutch Treat Club of the Quiet Birdmen. He is often invited to lecture and to exhibit his designs in the United States and in Europe. He is at present a professor at the School of Visual Arts in New York City, where he was granted the "Professor of the Year" Award. He has received many prizes as type designer from various clubs and type associations such as the Gold Medal from the New York Type Directors Club and the recent Frederic W. Goudy Medal.

Besides his more than 300 typefaces, he has designed several logotypes for various magazines such as the *New York Times*, *Playboy*, *Reader's Digest*, *Sports Illustrated*, *Esquire*, *Photoplay*, *McCall's*, *Coronet*, *True*, *Photography*, and *Look*.

ITC SOUVENIR (1970)

Based on the font designed by Morris Fuller Benton for the American Type Founders in 1914, the new version, which has a more contemporary look, includes a complete family of four weights with their italics.

ABCDEFGHIJKLMNOPQRS
TUVWXYZ&abcdefghijklmno
pqrstuvwxyz$1234567890!?

ALPHABETS & IMAGES

Designing for Alphabets
& Images, Inc., in New York,
Benguiat used an old seal device
where he combined wood type
lettering with calligraphy.

PLINC (1962)

Benguiat describes this stylized logo
designed for *Photo-Lettering, Inc.*,
as the calligraphic equivalent of
"cutting," when jazz musicians try
to outplay each other. He refers
to this work as an egotistical
improvisation with Spencerian
flourishes.

BARCELONA '92 (1991)

Benguiat created this proposed logo
for the *1992 Barcelona Olympics*,
as an answer to what he thinks an
Olympic logo should look like. He
explored Latin influences, including
high waists for the letterforms.

PHOTO-LETTERING INC.

An example of Benguiat's
calligraphic ability is this masthead
designed for Photo-Lettering
stationery .

ESQUIRE (1953)

When Benguiat began to work
at *Esquire* magazine, one of his
"first real art jobs" was to redesign
the old logo. He managed to change
every letter substantially, yet subtly,
so as to keep the original work
recognizable.

It is interesting to compare
Benguiat's version with Tom
Carnase's, executed afterwards
(page 91).

AMPERSAND (1995)

One of Benguiat's pleasures
is to play with the ampersand (**&**)
form. This calligraphic version,
which is part of his *ITC Edwardian
Script* alphabet, shows his ability
to combine form and structure.

THE NEW YORK TIMES

After a year's work, Benguiat
handed in a new version of the old
the *New York Times* masthead.
Although he modified all the letters,
the changes were so subtle they
were unnoticeable.

INTERNATIONAL TYPEFACE
CORPORATION

Another example of Benguiat's
calligraphic ability is this masthead
designed for ITC's stationery.

ITC KORINNA (1974)

Originally cut by German type foundry H. Berthold AG in 1904, and then cut in America by Intertype in 1934, this revival typeface was done by Benguiat for ITC, in collaboration with Victor Caruso.

The font includes five weights and their corresponding oblique versions added by Benguiat to the type family in 1988.

ABCDEFGHIJKLMNOPQRS
TUVWXYZ&abcdefghijklmn
opqrstuvwxyz
$1234567890!?

ABCDEFGHIJKLMNOPQRST
UVWXYZ&abcdefghijklmno
pqrstuvwxyz
$1234567890!?

ITC TIFFANY (1974)

A roman text typeface, it has a large x-height lowercase. The italic was added by Benguiat in 1981.

It is said that the original version of *Tiffany* is to be found in earlier designs, such as *Ronaldson*, cut by MacKellar, Smiths, and Jordan type foundry in 1884, and *Caxton Old Style No. 2*, issued by the American Type Founders around 1904.

ABCDEFGHIJKLMNOPQ
RSTUVWXYZ&abcdefghi
jklmnopqrstuvwxyz
$1234567890!?

ABCDEFGHIJKLMNOP
QRSTUVWXYZ&abcdefg
hijklmnopqrstuvwxyz
$1234567890!?

ITC BAUHAUS (1975)

A roman sans serif typeface designed with four weights, it is based on the *universal alphabet*, a single alphabet proposed by German designer Herbert Bayer in 1925, while he was teaching at the Bauhaus, and which discarded capital letters.

ABCDEFGHIJKLMNOPQRSTUVW XYZ&abcdefghijklmnopqrstuvw xyz$1234567890!?

ABCDEFGHIJKLMNOPQRSTU VWXYZ&abcdefghijklmnopq rstuvwxyz$1234567890!?

ITC BOOKMAN (1975)

Named *Old Style*, this typeface was originally designed by Scottish type designer Alexander C. Phemister around 1860 for the Scottish Miller & Richard type foundry in Philadelphia.

In 1903, Wadsworth A. Parker redesigned it for American Type Founders, much in the spirit of the *mission* style later shared by Bertram Grosvenor Goodhue's *Cheltenham* (1904). Since then, it has been quite popular among printers, being issued by various American type foundries.

This is the case with the 1927 version redesigned by Sol Hess for the Lanston Monotype Machine Company, and with the 1936 version done by Chauncey H. Griffith for the Mergenthaler Linotype Company, among others.

In 1975, Benguiat drew a new version for ITC as an answer to a new *Bookman* with a truly cursive italic (not oblique).

ABCDEFGHIJKLMNOPQ RSTUVWXYZ&abcdefghi jklmnopqrstuvwxyz $1234567890!?

ABCDEFGHIJKLMNOPQR STUVWXYZ&abcdefghij klmnopqrstuvwxyz $1234567890!?

ITC BENGUIAT (1978)

A roman typeface designed with an Art Nouveau flavor, it carries all the characteristics of a Benguiat typeface: pronounced serifs, left stress in the round letters, and an accented stylized calligraphic touch. The font is also characterized by short ascenders and descenders, as well as a two-story **a** and one-story **g**.

The typeface includes two different weights with their oblique versions. The condensed styles were added in 1979.

ABCDEFGHIJKLMNOPQRST
UVWXYZ&abcdefghijklmno
pqrstuvwxyz
$1234567890!?

ABCDEFGHIJKLMNOPQRS
TUVWXYZ&abcdefghijklmn
opqrstuvwxyz
$1234567890!?

ITC BENGUIAT GOTHIC (1979)

Being a sans serif face, the overall design shows an Art Nouveau influence.

The font includes four weights, regular, medium, bold and heavy, with their oblique versions.

It is interesting to compare *ITC Benguiat Gothic* with *Kolo*, designed by Paul Shaw and Garrett Boge in 1995.

ABCDEFGHIJKLMNOPQRSTUV
WXYZ&abcdefghijklmnopqrst
uvwxyz$1234567890!?

ABCDEFGHIJKLMNOPQRSTUV
WXYZ&abcdefghijklmnopqrst
uvwxyz$1234567890!?

ITC BARCELONA
(1981)

A glyphic typeface, it is characterized by Latin serifs and a large x-height lowercase.

The bold version presents a marked difference with the regular weight, showing less contrast between the strokes, as may be seen in the serifs treatment.

ABCDEFGHIJKLMNOPQR
STUVWXYZ&abcdefghijkl
mnopqrstuvwxyz
$1234567890!?

*ABCDEFGHIJKLMNOPQRST
UVWXYZ&abcdefghijklmno
pqrstuvwxyz$1234567890!?*

ITC MODERN 216
(1982)

A stylized version of the nineteenth-century Modern typefaces, this font presents Benguiat's calligraphic touch, with a large x-height lowercase.

The font includes four weights with their corresponding italics.

ABCDEFGHIJKLMNOPQR
STUVWXYZ&abcdefghijkl
mnopqrstuvwxyz
$1234567890!?

*ABCDEFGHIJKLMNOPQRS
TUVWXYZ&abcdefghijklmno
pqrstuvwxyz$1234567890!?*

ITC CASLON 224

(1983)

A free adaptation of the classic *Caslon Oldstyle* typeface designed by English type founder William Caslon I in 1722, letterforms have a more calligraphic rendering.

The font includes four weights with their corresponding italics.

ABCDEFGHIJKLMNOPQRST
UVWXYZ&abcdefghijklmnop
qrstuvwxyz$1234567890!?

*ABCDEFGHIJKLMNOPQRST
UVWXYZ&abcdefghijklmnop
qrstuvwxyz$1234567890!?*

ITC PANACHE (1988)

This humanist sans serif typeface incorporates many of Benguiat's characteristic letterforms, such as the treatment of ovals in capital letters **O** and **Q** and the curved leg of letter **R**, much in the style of *Hobo* (Morris Fuller Benton, 1910).

The font includes four weights with their oblique versions.

ABCDEFGHIJKLMNOPQRSTUVW
XYZ&abcdefghijklmnopqrstuvwx
yz$1234567890!?

*ABCDEFGHIJKLMNOPQRSTUVWX
YZ&abcdefghijklmnopqrstuvwxyz
$1234567890!?*

**ABCDEFGHIJKLMNOPQRSTUV
WXYZ&abcdefghijklmnopqrst
uvwxyz$1234567890!?**

ITC CENTURY HANDTOOLED, ITC CHELTENHAM HANDTOOLED, ITC GARAMOND HANDTOOLED
(1993)

Even with the capabilities of current digital technology and sophisticated software design programs, Ed Benguiat prefers to continue working with his own hands.

Introduced in the nineteenth century, handtooled designs became popular additions to type families in the early twentieth century.

Being a tedious, time-consuming process, that requires a sensitive eye and careful hand, the resulting design provides a valuable range of new display typefaces, which lends a new personality to the original letterforms.

In developing the series, Benguiat was challenged with the demanding task of creating a perfectly proportioned incision on the left side of all the characters of both roman and italic versions.

The three typefaces maintain their dignity and charm.

They also include an italic version.

ABCDEFGHIJKLMNOPQR
STUVWXYZ&abcdefghijklm
nopqrstuvwxyz
$1234567890!?

ABCDEFGHIJKLMNOPQRST
UVWXYZ&abcdefghijklmnop
qrstuvwxyz$1234567890!?

ABCDEFGHIJKLMNOPQR
STUVWXYZ&abcdefghijkl
mnopqrstuvwxyz
$1234567890!?

ITC Edwardian Script
(1995)

This beautiful and sensitive calligraphic script was first used on his son's wedding invitation.

At the insistence of many people who received the printed sample, Benguiat developed a full alphabet.

ABCDEFGHIJKLMNOP
QRSTUVWXYZ&abcdefghijklmno
pqrstuvwxyz$1234567890!?

Born in Little Falls, New York in 1844, Linn Boyd Benton moved to Milwaukee in 1855 to join his father who was then editor and part owner of the *Milwaukee Daily News*. There, he learned to set type in the composing room of the paper. But, because his family moved so often, Benton's education was somewhat unusual. After attending schools in Little Falls and Milwaukee, he ended his formal education at Galesville College, at the age of sixteen.

After completing his education, Benton apparently went back to Milwaukee where he got acquainted in the office of Charles Seymour's *LaCrosse Republican* with the printing business while learning to set type and to roll the forms in the style of the day. He also had some accounting training because, in 1866, he became a bookkeeper in Northwestern Type Foundry in that city, where he worked from 1866 to 1873. In 1874, Benton and Frank M. Gove became owners of the company, and the firm became Benton, Gove, and Company. It was there that he designed a multiple mold for casting leads and slugs in 1882.

That same year, caught up in the general spirit for standardization, Benton led the way in what he called a "self-spacing type" system, later known as "point-set," that reduced the number of widths of type from 190 to 9. All widths of this new method of casting type were exact subdivisions of a 12-pt em, and although not exactly pleasing to the eye, since it was necessary to distort individual letters, it enabled a compositor to speed-up typesetting by hand as much as 30 percent.

When Gove died in 1882, and Benton sold part of his shares to Robert V. Waldo, the company changed its name to Benton, Waldo, & Co. As Benton continued to invent and perfect machines for his type foundry, he also became involved in the invention of a punch-cutting machine becauseof the lack of punch-cutters and the need for his type foundry to make over 3,000 special punches. Curiously, his aim was not for the use of this invention in a composing machine, but to improve the electrotype process in which he was working.

In 1884, his achievements in the pantographic method of cutting types in wood ended with the construction

of a machine able to cut the matrices as well as the brass punches he needed.

Benton's Automatic Punch-cutter, which he finished in 1885, was based on the pantograph principle of following the outline of an enlarged letter or other character cut in a sheet of thin brass template, while a minute router, linked to it, cuts the punch. While it was possible to cut any type size, from 6 pt to 36 pt, from a single enlarged original, certain changes of proportion had to be made if an aesthetically satisfactory reduced copy was expected from the original. This meant that it was necessary to cut several templates for intermediate sizes. But, except for this physical limitation, with Benton's machine a person needed only to make one master drawing of each character, and did not have to rely on the punch-cutter's interpretation to produce a typeface.

The matrix engraver was also capable of altering the image, compensating for the optical variations that occur when letter sizes change. For this procedure, Morris Fuller Benton used cutting slips to make certain that the operators precisely and consistently adjusted the machine for every point size. It is important to add that Linn Boyd Benton designed other machines which provided perfection to the process. Such is the case of the Wax Plate Machine, which was used to make the patterns, and the Matrix Fitting Machine, which provided final adjustments.

In one of his selling visits, Benton's partner, Robert V. Waldo, explained to the *New York Tribune*, where the first Linotype was then in use, the advantages of using punches cut by machine. Soon Philip T. Dodge, then president of Linotype and Whitelaw Reid, publisher of the *New York Tribune*, who had a large financial interest in the Mergenthaler Linotype Company, were convinced of the advantages of the invention and acquired the punch-cutter machine.

Benton's invention came at a time when Linotype was faced with an extremely delicate financial situation. If it could not provide matrices promptly enough for its new automatic typesetting machines it would go bankrupt. Some people even suggest that without Benton's invention, Linotype would not have been a

commercial success. But more than that, it was an invention which not only permitted the designer to free himself from the "interpretation" of the punch-cutter, but allowed a rapid development in type design and the growth of graphic design, in as much as it is a visual language that is strongly based on the use of typography.

While he was involved with the punch-cutter, Benton also invented a system for combining fractions (1895); a type-dressing machine (1901); another punch-cutter for his earlier "self-spacing machine" (1906); an automatic type caster (1907); and a lining device for engraving matrices of shaded letters. Once again, the Mergenthaler Linotype Company was prompt to see the advantages of many of these innovations, and established a leasing agreement with Benton.

Although his son Morris Fuller Benton surpassed his type design production, Linn Boyd Benton was also famed as a punch-cutter. Among his many achievements may be found the cutting of *Century Roman* typeface for Theodore Low De Vinne's *The Century Magazine* in 1894; and a wider version called *Century Broad-Face*, which, although designed to satisfy some printers, was only used by De Vinne.

During the first months after the merger of the twenty-three American typefoundries –including Benton, Waldo & Co.– to form ATF, the Bentons remained in Milwaukee, but as it became evident that his knowledge and experience was required in New York, he moved his foundry to this city in 1894, leaving Robert V. Waldo in Milwaukee to handle a sales office.

Robert W. Nelson, ATF's director, then asked Benton to set up a type design department, the first of its kind in a foundry. It was here that his son started to work in 1897, a few months after graduating from Cornell, and continuing until a later age with no diminution in his creativity.

Benton's mechanical genius earned him a seat on the Board of Directors and the position of Director of the General Manufacturing Department.

Linn Boyd Benton died in Plainfield, New Jersey in July 15, 1932, at the age of eighty-eight, just fifteen days after he had retired from ATF.

CENTURY ROMAN
(1894)

Designed by Benton in 1894, at the request of Theodore Low De Vinne, publisher of *The Century Magazine*, it was made only as a foundry type, handset for several years for this publication and for numerous books.

ABCDEFGHIJKLMNOPQRST UVWXYZ&abcdefghijklmnopq rstuvwxyz$1234567890!?

BENTON'S AUTOMATIC PUNCH-CUTTER (1885)

According to Maurice Annenberg's book, *Type Foundries of America* (1994), some features of Benton's pantograph may be found in a machine described in a 1631 pamphlet published by Christopher Scheimer in Rome.

Then, in Frank Denman's *The Shaping of the Alphabet* (1955), we may find a description of the process: The invention of the pantograph punch-cutting machine changed the punch-cutting process completely. The operator had only to follow the outline of a large drawing, and every movement of the lower arm was copied in reverse by the revolving cutting tool above on a much-reduced scale.

In practice, the reduction was made in two stages. From a large drawing on paper, the design was reduced to a brass pattern, and then the raised letter on the pattern served as a guide for the cutting of the punch.

The first cut was made with a coarse tool and a large, round follower in contact with the pattern. Then the operator changed to a small cutter and a proportionally smaller follower. The final cut was made with a cutter so fine that it could cut what appeared to be the inside right angle in a 6-pts letter.

Where the hand cutter checked his work through a magnifying glass, the modern punch was inspected in a projectoscope that projected its image fifty times larger on a screen where the thickness of the strokes, the length of the serifs, or any other dimension could be measured accurately. Duplicate punches will match the original exactly.

A complete series of sizes cannot be made from a set of patterns. The face of most letters gets a little wider and thicker as the size decreases. Usually no more than two or three sizes are cut from a set of patterns. The complete series will look right to the eye even though the actual proportions will change considerably between 6 pt and 36 pt.

Nevertheless, the flexibility and precision of the punch-cutting machine offers a constant urge toward over-slickness, and the interpreter must constantly fight the dexterity of the machine if he is to retain those irregularities that give the hand-cut face its character and liveliness.

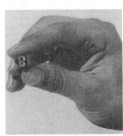

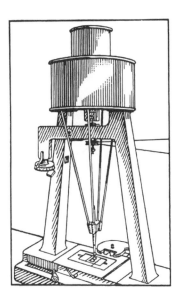

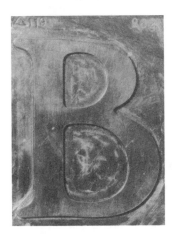

Born in Milwaukee, Wisconsin in 1872, Morris Fuller Benton entered Cornell University in 1892, when the twenty-three American type foundries –including Benton, Waldo & Co.– merged to form ATF, and graduated with a degree in mechanical engineering in 1896.

The following year, he went to work with his father, Linn Boyd Benton (1844-1932), as his assistant in the recently organized Department of Type Design at ATF, the first to exist in a foundry, having been established after a suggestion by its director, Robert W. Nelson.

Prior to coming to New Jersey, Morris Fuller Benton had helped his father to further develop the punch and matrix-engraving machines, in addition to his work on other type founding equipment.

In 1898, Benton became head of ATF's Department of Type Design, where he received the immense task of unifying and improving the varied assortment of designs inherited by ATF in 1892, when it became one large, strong company resulting from the merging of twenty-three foundries. Additional typefaces were acquired a few years later through the merging of other companies.

His first responsibilities were primarily technical, since he had to standardize the great variety of sizes and styles by applying the American Point System adopted by American type foundries in 1886, but only partially implemented by the industry. Secondly, and more importantly, he was assigned the task of conducting an in-depth study of all the typefaces offered by the type foundries, since there were duplicates, and many inconsistencies in design. As the company stabilized after the upheavals and plant closings of the merger, Morris Fuller Benton became increasingly interested in type design.

One of his first creative assignments was to redesign *Century Roman* –a design done in 1894 by his father with the assistance of Theodore Low De Vinne. He extended it slightly to meet the Typographical Union standards of the day, on which rates for typesetting were based. The resulting typeface was named *Century Expanded*, commercially issued in 1900. Showing it in his company specimen book, De Vinne commented, "The extension is upward, enabling one to get much matter in a small space."

In 1908, ATF established its Typographic Library and Museum, under the direction of typographic historian Henry Lewis Bullen, and by 1923, the library had acquired more than 12,000 volumes of type specimens, including masterpieces of early and modern printed books and works on all aspects of typography and printing. It was at Bullen's urging that Morris Fuller Benton worked on classical revivals such as *Bodoni*, *Garamond*, *Cloister Oldstyle*, and *Bulmer*.

He and his colleagues began with pencil drawings of a size preferably 96-pts or larger, which would then be inked-in for evaluation. These drawings were then enlarged to a size of ten inches, modified to meet the limits of the standard lining system and point systems, and from there back to the delineating machine. Once again the drawing was reduced to a practical size (e.g., 36-pts or less), and once again evaluated both in terms of a three-dimensional piece of metal. In short, a design had to undergo many evaluations before becoming useable type.

When the American Type Founders published the 60,000 copies of its *Specimen Book and Catalogue 1923*, all these ideas came into reality. Throughout its 1,148 pages, full of a variety of typographical compositions, this handsome 6¾" x 10" volume, many of its pages printed in two and three colors, became a major resource for compositors and layout artists. It was both a model book and a source of ideas for using sorted type, ornaments, initials, and for the disposition of paragraphs, vignettes, and other graphic materials.

Morris Fuller Benton is credited with being the most prolific type designer in American history, with more than 260 typefaces to his credit, including some original and some variants of already existing fonts, an output twice as great as that of Frederic W. Goudy, who started to design late in his thirties. Benton's designs are almost always a combined product of artistic inspiration and organized, systematic research. There is also a diversity of style found in his work that is uncommon among type designers.

Benton is also given credit for giving form to the type family concept by creating complete ranges of fonts where there only existed one weight version, although this idea seems to have come from

Robert W. Nelson, Director of ATF at that time. What is certain is that, with the growth of advertising and the appearance of the advertising designer, the production of a wider range of weights certainly made management of type hierarchies easier. This not only maintained the typographical unity on a page when employing different weights of type, but also enriched the visual and graphic alternatives of both advertising and graphic design.

Looking at the period from 1900 to 1928, we may see Benton's tremendous design achievements: eighteen variants of *Century*, including *Century Oldstyle* (1906) and the popular *Century Schoolbook* (1924); twenty-four variants of *Cheltenham*; eighteen variants of *Bodoni*; twelve variants of *Cloister*; five variants of *Garamond*; eight variants of *Stymie*; nine variants of different Goudy types, plus original designs, such as *Franklin Gothic* (1902), *Alternate Gothic* (1903), *Clearface* (1905), *Commercial Script* (1906), *News Gothic* (1908), *Hobo* (1910), *Souvenir* (1914), *Broadway* (1928), *Modernique* (1928), and *Parisian* (1928), many of which include variations of weight to complete families of their own.

From 1928 to 1934, he designed some very popular typefaces that are still in use, as is the case of *Bank Gothic* (1929), *Agency Gothic* (1932), *Shadow* (1934), *Tower* (1934), and *Empire* (1934), which were stylistic answers to the competitiveness with other foundries at their time of appearance.

Morris Fuller Benton remained at ATF for another five years after his father's death (1932), but it was a difficult period for the company. Already in the 1920s, profits had begun to decline and the 1930s brought conflict with bankruptcy. There were no younger people with younger ideas. Directors were satisfied with getting their profits.

In 1937, at the age of sixty-five, Morris Fuller Benton retired from ATF. He apparently maintained few contacts with the firm. By this time, his health was quite delicate. He and his wife moved to Millington, New Jersey.

Morris Fuller Benton died of an embolism in Morristown, New Jersey in 1948, at the age of seventy-five.

ENGRAVERS BOLD (1902)

Designed for ATF in 1902, this typeface was also cast by Barnhart Brothers & Spindler type foundry. It is characterized by triangular serifs and a high contrast between thick and thin strokes. Although it only has upper case letters, it has been quite popular in stationery.

ABCDEFGHIJKLM
NOPQRSTUVWXY
Z&$1234567890!?

AMERICAN TYPE FOUNDER'S SPECIMEN BOOK AND CATALOG 1923 (1923)

This double spread shows the layout and presentation employed in the handsome 1923 edition of the ATF catalog; many of its pages were printed in two colors.

The examples permitted the typographer to enhance his work, and to incorporate a sans serif typeface of the quality of *News Gothic* into his daily work.

CLEARFACE (1907)

A page presentation of Benton's *Clearface* (1907), as may be seen in the ATF catalog of 1912.

THE BROADWAY SERIES (1928)

In this page layout of a later ATF catalog, we may find a presentation of *Broadway* typeface. Texts illustrate some of the typeface possibilities.

It is interesting to note that Sol Hess will expand these possibilities when he designs for Monotype a lowercase and an engraved version of *Broadway* in 1928-29.

THE CENTURY FAMILY (1928)

Typographic presentation of some of the eighteen variants of *Century* developed by Morris Fuller Benton.

NEWS GOTHIC (1908)

These two double spreads from the 1923 ATF Specimen Book and catalog show in practical display the use of *News Gothic* (1908), a design that preceded the employment of the sans serif typefaces in the United States (European designs such as *Futura* and *Kabel* would not appear until 1927-28).

Benton drew *News Gothic* for ATF some time around 1908, initially in medium, condensed and extracondensed variations, as part of his work of modernizing the nineteenth-century sans serif styles inherited by ATF from its predecessors. In this process, *News Gothic* really ended up as a lighter version of *Franklin Gothic* (1902).

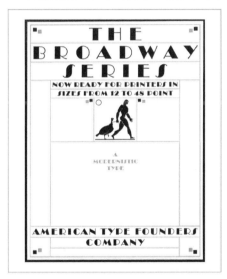

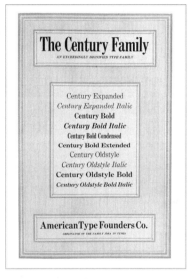

FRANKLIN GOTHIC
(1902)

Justly called "the patriarch of modern American gothics," and named after Benjamin Franklin, this typeface was one of the first important modernizations of traditional nineteenth-century designs.

It was designed after Benton was assigned the task of unifying and improving the fonts inherited by ATF after the merging of various American type foundries.

Besides its present usage, it is interesting to know that many Europeans prefer to utilize this American sans serif rather their own. It might be that they prefer the "old-fashioned" letters **a** and **g** with their two-story configuration, rather than their excessively geometric versions.

ALTERNATE GOTHIC (1903)

A condensed sans serif typeface, it was originally designed with the thought of providing four alternate widths of one design to fit various layout problems, on account of reduced space.

Sol Hess designed the italic version in 1946.

CLEARFACE (1906)

This roman typeface was designed in collaboration with his father, Linn Boyd Benton. The bold version was designed first in 1905, and cut the following year. The other weights and italics were produced in 1911.

As the name implies, the series was intended to show unusual legibility and readability, which it certainly achieved. It was very popular as a newspaper text type.

Commercial Script
(1908)

A typical Spencerian script, it was originally designed in 1895 for Barnhart Brothers & Spindler. In 1906, it was redesigned, and in 1908, it was cut and commercially issued by ATF. With heavier strokes and fewer flourishes than other scripts, it remains popular for stationery, especially for printing social invitations.

ABCDEFGHIJKLMNOPQRSTUV
WXYZ&abcdefghijklmnopqrstuv
wxyz$1234567890!?

**ABCDEFGHIJKLMNOPQRSTU
VWXYZ&abcdefghijklmnopqr
stuvwxyz$1234567890!?**

ABCDEFGHIJKLMNOPQRSTUVWXYZ&abcdefg
hijklmnopqrstuvwxyz$1234567890!?

ABCDEFGHIJKLMNOPQRSTUV
WXYZ&abcdefghijklmnopqrstu
vwxyz$1234567890!?

*ABCDEFGHIJKLMNOPQR
STUVWXYZ&abcdefghijklmn
opqrstuvwxyz$1234567890!?*

NEWS GOTHIC (1908)

Designed as part of his assignment to modernize the nineteenth-century gothics inherited by ATF from other foundries, this typeface has a much finer rendering, as part of what may be called the family of basic American gothics. It is essentially a light version of *Franklin Gothic* (1902).

Pushed aside by the popularity of the German sans serifs, such as *Futura* (Paul Renner, 1927) and *Kabel* (Rudolf Koch, 1927), it was rediscovered in the late 1940s, when it made a strong comeback.

ABCDEFGHIJKLMNOPQRSTU
VWXYZ&abcdefghijklmnopqrst
uvwxyz$1234567890!?

**ABCDEFGHIJKLMNOPQRSTU
VWXYZ&abcdefghijklmnopqrst
uvwxyz$1234567890!?**

HOBO (1910)

A very unusual typeface, for it has been drawn with virtually no straight lines. The lowercase has an extremely large x-height and practically no descenders.
Its name comes from the fact that it was continually put aside by the type foundry to the point of being called that "old hobo."

Strangely enough, regardless of its heavily mannered rendering, it has somehow become popular.

ABCDEFGHIJKLMNOPQRST
UVWXYZ&abcdefghijklmnop
qrstuvwxyz$1234567890!?

CLOISTER OLDSTYLE (1914)

A classical design, which follows Nicolas Jenson's typeface used in 1470 very closely, it was designed in 1913 and released by the Lanston Monotype Company the following year. Its heavier characteristics were introduced to compensate for the improved conditions of printing and smoother paper surfaces of that time.

Cloister Italic, released later in 1914, is based on an italic cast by Aldus Manutius in 1501, although it does not follow its source as closely as the roman does.

Numerals are drawn in *Oldstyle*.

ABCDEFGHIJKLMNOPQRRST
TUVWXYZ& abcdefghijklmnop
qrstuvwxyz$1234567890!?

SOUVENIR (1914)

An early roman typeface featuring rounded serifs and a soft, rubbery look, it has a slight contrast between thick and thin strokes, and a general lightweight.

With the advent of phototypesetting, two versions of matching heavier weights were made for this type composition medium.

One of these, drawn by Edward Benguiat in 1970, achieved such popularity, that it was later cut on matrices for use in Linotype, and by Matrotype in England, in regular and demibold weights. In 1972, American Type Founders cut it for metal type.

In 1950, we may find a similar case in *Dom Casual* (Peter Dombrezian, 1950), which was first issued by Photo-Lettering, Inc., and then by ATF in 1953.

ABCDEFGHIJKLMNOPQRS
TUVWXYZ&abcdefghijklmno
pqrstuvwxyz$1234567890!?

*ABCDEFGHIJKLMNOPQR
STUVWXYZ&abcdefghijklm
nopqrstuvwxyz
$1234567890!?*

BODONI OPEN (1918)

Drawn in 1918, this typeface was discontinued after a time and reintroduced in 1930.

It certainly is one of the most handsome versions of the classical *Bodoni*, designed by Giambattista Bodoni in 1788.

ABCDEFGHIJKLMNOPQRSTU
VWXYZ&abcdefghijklmnopqr
stuvwxyz$1234567890

CENTURY SCHOOLBOOK (1918)

This third family of *Century* was planned when Ginn & Company, publishers of schoolbooks, asked ATF to develop a typeface for maximum readability. After many studies of eyesight and reading factors dating from 1912, *Century Schoolbook* and *Italic* were designed by Benton between 1917 and 1919, and released between 1918 and 1921.

Century Schoolbook Bold was designed in 1919.

ABCDEFGHIJKLMNOPQ
RSTUVWXYZ&abcdefghijk
lmnopqrstuvwxyz
$1234567890!?

BROADWAY (1928)

Closely associated with the silent movies of the 1920s, and in particular with Charles Chaplin, this Art Deco style typeface with no lowercase alphabet, was designed by Benton in 1927 and issued commercially by ATF the following year.

In 1929, Sol Hess duplicated it for Monotype foundry, adding a lowercase alphabet with extremely short descenders. Hess had also designed *Broadway Engraved* as a complement to *Broadway* the preceding year.

It is interesting to compare *Broadway Engraved* with *Boul Mich*, a design probably sketched or suggested by Richard McArthur, BB&S's Advertising Manager. Completed by Oswald Cooper, it was brought out by this type foundry in 1927.

Cooper's version, besides being more calligraphic and elegant in feeling, has a different approach to the relationship between heavy and light strokes.

ABCDEFGHIJKLMNOP
QRSTUVWXYZ&abcdef
ghijklmnopqrstuvwxy
z$1234567890!?

ABCDEFGHIJKLMNOP
QRSTUVWXYZ&abcdef
ghijklmnopqrstuvwxyz
$1234567890!?

MODERNIQUE
(1928)

A very heavy display typeface, it is characterized by an extreme contrast between thick and thin strokes, and a strong vertical emphasis, which permits a very close fitting. Another particular feature is the use of semicircles instead of dots for letters j and i.

Unfortunately, it was gone before ATF issued its next complete specimen book in 1934.

ABCDEFGHIJKLMNOPQ
RSTUVWXYZ&abcdefg
hijklmnopqrstuvwxyz
$1234567890?!

PARISIAN (1928)

A very typical typeface of the 1920s, much related to the Art Deco style, it has some resemblance to *Broadway*, designed the preceding year. It is also lighter and more informal.

Capital letters **B** and **R** are characterized by a buckle, and lowercase letters have long ascenders and short descenders.

ABCDEFGHIJKLMNOPQRSTU
VWXYZ&abcdefghijklmnopqrstuvwxyz
$1234567890!?

ULTRA BODONI (1928)

Although completely redrawn, this typeface is certainly closer to the nineteenth-century French "fat faces," presented by Firmin Didot in 1819, than to *Bodoni*.

Also quite different from later designs like *Poster Bodoni* (Chauncey W. Griffith, 1929), and from *Bodoni Black* (Robert Hunter Middleton, 1930), Benton's *Ultra Bodoni* is characterized by shorter ascenders and by an abrupt transition between thick and thin strokes.

ABCDEFGHIJKLMNOP
QRSTUVWXYZ&abcde
fghijklmnopqrstuvwxyz
$1234567890

BANK GOTHIC (1930-1933)

A very squared typeface that anticipates Alessandro Butti's and Aldo Novarese's *Microgramma* (1952), it was designed by Benton in 1930-33, and introduced in normal weights in 1930.

Later on, Benton added *Condensed Light*, *Condensed Medium*, and *Condensed Bold* versions. These have been very popular as stationery typefaces.

ABCDEFGHIJKLMNOPQ
RSTUVWXYZ&
$ 1234567890!?()[]

STYMIE (1931)

A redesign of *Rockwell Antique* (1931), which in turn was a reissue of *Litho Antique*, introduced by Inland Type Foundry, St. Louis, in 1910, *Stymie Bold* appeared in 1931 with more refined characters and a tighter fitting.

Stymie Light and *Stymie Medium*, including their Italics, also drawn by Benton, followed the bold version in the same year.

Later on, in 1937, Gerry Powell designed *Stymie Light Title*, *Stymie Medium Title* and *Stymie Bold Condensed*.

ABCDEFGHIJKLMNOPQRSTU
VWXYZ&abcdefghijklmnopqrst
uvwxyz$1234567890!?

ABCDEFGHIJKLMNOPQRST
UVWXYZ&abcdefghijklmno
pqrstuvwxyz$1234567890!?

AMERICAN TEXT (1932)

Designed for ATF in 1932 as a modernized adaptation of the so-called *Old English*, this typeface has a strong angular appearance, as a result of holding the pen at a 45-degree angle.

ABCDEFGHIJKLMNOPQRSTUVWXY
Z&abcdefghijklmnopqrstuvwxyz
$1234567890!?

SHADOW (1934)

Designed in 1924 and issued by ATF the following year, it is a typical round, condensed gothic style popular at the time. It relies on its shadow to be read. There is no difference between capital letter **I** and number **1**, as between letter **O** and the **0** cipher.

ABCDEFGHIJKLMNOPQRSTUVWXYZ
&$1234567890!?

TOWER (1934)

Very similar to *Stymie Medium Condensed*, also designed by Benton, this typeface shows an absence of strictly round letters, emphasizing its vertical appearance. The name suggests its tallness and slimness. *Tower Bold* was undertaken by Benton but abandoned in favor of *Stymie Bold Condensed*. *Tower Italic* was designed but not cast.

ABCDEFGHIJKLMNOPQRSTUVWXYZ&abcde
fghijklmnopqrstuvwxyz $1234567890

OTHELLO (1934)

This very heavy, squared, narrow gothic letter was designed by Benton as a revision of an 1884 face of the same name issued by Central Type Foundry, St. Louis, and inherited by ATF in 1892.

It is characterized by diagonal ends on a number of strokes, and lowercase forms on capitals **M**, **N**, and **Y**.

ABCDEFGHIJKLMNOPQRSTUVWXYZ
&abcdefghijklmnopqrstuvwxyz
$1234567890!?

EMPIRE (1937)

One of the last designs created by Morris Fuller Benton, this extra-condensed sans serif face has an unusual emphasis on the vertical strokes.

It was used for a time as a headletter of *Vogue* magazine, for a smart, sophisticated look.

It is interesting to compare it with *Huxley Vertical*, designed by Walter Huxley in 1935.

ABCDEFGHIJKLMNOPQRSTUVWXYZ&$1234567890!?

Born in Boston in 1954, David Berlow lives in Westbury, Massachusetts. He obtained a Bachelor of Science degree in art at the University of Wisconsin, Madison.

His career as a type designer began in 1977 at Mergenthaler Linotype, D Stempel AG and Haas foundries, where he was involved in a number of major projects including revisions of William Addison Dwiggins's *Caledonia* and many of ITC faces released by Mergenthaler.

After leaving Linotype in 1982, he joined Bitstream, Inc., a newly formed independent type foundry, founded by Matthew Carter and Mike Parker just the year before. There he worked in the type design, technical, and marketing departments as a senior designer.

"Roger Black would come through on a strafing run, trying to get custom fonts for this or that magazine. It was too expensive and too laborious to do them, so we just told him to forget it. Then I started with the Macintosh in 1986. Designing type with it was akin to sculpting a bus through a porthole. Later we got a *Mac II*, *Fontographer*, a big monitor and a laser printer, and suddenly designing new type seemed easy. So the next time Roger came through we were ready."

"At that point, Matthew suggested we do a custom face. So we did *Belizio*, something like *Egiziano*, for Roger, who at the time was working for *California* magazine. I began to think it was time to do a business plan," comments Berlow.

Berlow went off to work on his own, and Roger Black invited him to be his partner. In 1989, he cofounded the Font Bureau with Black, an independent design firm specializing in type consulting and contracting custom typographic products and supplying fonts in *PostScript* format.

They leased Macintosh equipment and the new team went on to design the typefonts for *Smart* magazine, some for the *New York Times*, and the main fonts for the redesigned the *San Francisco Examiner*.

By 1990, Font Bureau had already designed thirteen faces that were freeof their exclusivity contracts and the firm was able to start selling them commercially.

Font Bureau has developed more than 300 new and revised designs for the *Chicago Tribune*, the *Wall Street Journal*, *Entertainment Weekly*, *Newsweek*, *Esquire*, *Rolling Stone*, Hewlett Packard and others, with OEM work for Apple Computer, Inc., and Microsoft Corporation, and has a font library consisting mostly of original designs with over 500 typefaces.

By 1992, Font Bureau, where Roger Black, David Berlow, his brother Sam, Jill Pichotta and Tobias Frere-Jones as design assistant, was employing twenty freelance type designers. "We produce about 230 faces a year, a third of which are digitized versions of typefaces found in old specimen books, a third brand-new designs for both retail and custom fonts, and a third specific client requests," says Berlow.

"There is an advantage to producing custom fonts," Black explains. "When someone designs a commercial font, he is trying to imagine what people want. In our case we know exactly what they want, and the design is clear and focused."

Font Bureau is perhaps best known for its family of *Grotesques*. A few years ago it was impossible not to find *Franklin Gothic* everywhere. Today, "People can't seem to get enough *Grots*," says Berlow. "It's the face that's eating America now." Magazines that have bought custom *Grotesques* include *Entertainment Weekly*, *PC Week*, *Esquire* and *Smart Money*, as well as newspaper *El Sol* from Madrid, and the *Chicago Tribune*.

"Reproduction is the most important thing about publication custom fonts," comments Roger Black. "It is a production problem rather than design. For instance, *Times* may be a great letterpress face but it doesn't work well offset. We just did a version of *Palatino* for *Playboy* because the text wasn't matching on their gravure and offset sections. *Newsweek* goes to ten printing plants, so we are still fine-tuning the *Scotch Roman*. We can adjust our design to whatever printing and paper a publication uses. Many newspaper people flounder around trying to make their typefaces legible by changing the printing or the plating, but with the custom faces we can tune it exactly. After all, the whole idea is to get people to read this stuff," concludes Black.

As a result of this situation, Font Bureau developed a very large group of fonts called the "readability series" leaving the choice of newspaper fonts to the production and taste they prefer.

David Berlow is currently a member of the New York Type Directors Club and the Association Typographique International (ATypI).

NEW CALEDONIA
(1979)

While he was working at Mergenthaler Linotype, Berlow was involved in a series of projects including a revision of *Caledonia*, designed by William Addison Dwiggins in 1938.

The font also includes expert small caps.

ABCDEFGHIJKLMNOPQRS
TUVWXYZ&abcdefghijklmnop
qrstuvwxyz$1234567890!?

FB GROTESQUE (1989)

Font Bureau Grotesques reintroduce the character of nineteenth-century sans serifs.

Developed in 1989 for Roger Black, Inc., The Tribune Companies and *Newsweek*, the first *Grotesques* met with immediate success.

Further weights were designed for *Entertainment Weekly* and *El Sol*, a Madrid daily, completing twelve fonts by 1993.

ABCDEFGHIJKLMNOPQRSTUVW
XYZ&abcdefghijklmnopqrstuvw
xyz$1234567890!?

ABCDEFGHIJKLMNOPQRSTU
VWXYZ&abcdefghijklmnopq
rstuvwxyz$1234567890!?

ABCDEFGHIJKLMNOPQRSTUVWXYZ&
abcdefghijklmnopqrstuvwxyz$1234567890!?

ABCDEFGHIJKLMNOPQRSTUVWXYZ&abcd
efghijklmnopqrstuvwxyz$1234567890!?

ABCDEFGHIJKLMNO
PQRSTUVWXYZ
&abcdefghijklmnopqr
stuvwxyz
$1234567890!?

FB AGENCY (1990)

ATF *Agency Gothic* was designed by Morris Fuller Benton in 1932, as a single titling face.

In 1990, David Berlow saw potential in the squared forms of the narrow monotone capitals. He designed a lowercase and added a bold version to take *Font Bureau Agency* to immediate success.

Sensing further possibilities, he worked with Tobias Frere-Jones and Jonathan Corum to expand *FB Agency* into more extensive series, offering five weights in five widths for text and display settings.

ABCDEFGHIJKLMNOPQRSTUVWXYZ&abcdef
ghijklmnopqrstuvwxyz$1234567890!?

ABCDEFGHIJKLMN
OPQRSTUVWXYZ
&abcdefghijklmnop
qrstuvwxyz
$1234567890!?

ABCDEFGHIJKLMNOPQRSTUVW
XYZ&abcdefghijklmnopqrstuvw
xyz$1234567890!?

ABCDEFGHIJKLM
NOPQRSTUVWX
YZ&abcdefghijkl
mnopqrstuvwxyz
$1234567890!?

FB EMPIRE (1989/90)

In 1937, Morris Fuller Benton designed *Empire*, a single titling of forty-seven characters that became the headletter signature of *Vogue* magazine.

In 1989, David Berlow began to draw a contemporary version of this font, adding an italic, and a lowercase font for *Publish!* magazine.

Five years later in 1994, in collaboration with Kelly Ehrgott-Milligan, Berlow completed a seven part series from the original design.

ABCDEFGHIJKLMNOPQRSTUVWXYZ&abcdefgh
ijklmnopqrstuvwxyz$1234567890!?

ABCDEFGHIJKLMNOPQRSTUVWXYZ&abcdefgh
ijklmnopqrstuvwxyz$1234567890!?

ABCDEFGHIJKLMNOPQRSTUVWXYZ&
abcdefghijklmnopqrstuvwxyz
$1234567890!?

ABCDEFGHIJKLMNOPQRSTUVWXYZ&
abcdefghijklmnopqrstuvwxyz
$1234567890!?

FB BELUCIAN

(1990)

Needing a distinctive headline style, in 1990 *Smart* magazine asked the Font Bureau to revise the work of Lucian Bernhard of 1925.

David Berlow prepared *FB Belucian Demi*, and later added *FB Belucian Book* and *Book Italic* for text, and *FB Ultra Belucian* for dynamic impact in major headlines.

It is interesting to compare *FB Belucian* with Bernhard's original *Lucian* typeface.

ABCDEFGHIJKLMNOPQ
RSTUVWXYZ&abcdefghijkl
mnopqrstuvwxyz$1234567890!?

*ABCDEFGHIJKLMNOPQR
STUVWXYZ&abcdefghijklmnop
qrstuvwxyz$1234567890!?*

ABCDEFGHIJKLMNOPQ
RSTUVWXYZ&abcdefghijkl
mnopqrstuvwxyz$1234567890!?

**ABCDEFGHIJKLMNOP
QRSTUVWXYZ&abcdefg
hijklmnopqrstuvwxyz
$1234567890!?**

FB ELDORADO
(1993)

Of William Addison Dwiggins wartime experiments, perhaps the most successful was *Eldorado*, released by Mergenthaler Linotype in 1953.

With unusual fidelity, Dwiggins followed an early roman lowercase, cut in the sixteenth century by Jacques de Sanlecque, *l'ancien*, after Robert Granjon's typeface.

Berlow, Patterson, Frere-Jones and Rickner expanded the series in 1993-94 for *Premiere* magazine, with versions not only for text and display, but a *Micro* for 6 pts and smaller, *FB 1997*.

Numerals are drawn in *Oldstyle*.

ABCDEFGHIJKLMNOPQRST
UVWXYZ&abcdefghijklmnopqrst
uvwxyz$1234567890!?

ABCDEFGHIJKLMNOPQRST
UVWXYZ&abcdefghijklmnopqrst
uvwxyz$1234567890!?

ABCDEFGHIJKLMNOPQR
STUVWXYZ&abcdefghijklm
nopqrstuvwxyz$1234567890!?

ABCDEFGHIJKLMNOPQRS
TUVWXYZ&abcdefghijklmno
pqrstuvwxyz$1234567890!?

LUCIAN BERNHARD

Born near Stuttgart, Germany, in 1883, as Emil Kahn, he adopted the pseudonym of Lucian Bernhard when he arrived as a freelance designer in Berlin in 1901.

Largely self-taught, Bernhard studied for brief periods at the Akademie der Kunst, Munich, and later in Berlin. In 1898, at the age of fifteen, he visited the Munich Flaspalast Exhibition of Interior Decoration and was so impressed by the use of color that he decided to paint everything in his house with brilliant colors. Reproached by his father, he left his home in Munich and went to Berlin.

Trying to survive economically as a poet he decided to participate in a poster contest sponsored in 1905 by the Berlin Chamber of Commerce for *Priester* matches. Winning first prize, he signed an exclusive design contract through one of the judges, Ernst Growald, advertising agent and codirector of the Berlin printing company Hollerbaum & Schmidt.

Without much awareness on his part, Bernhard had defined the contemporary poster by reducing content to a visual language. His design approach was deeply influenced by the work of the Beggarstaff Brothers, particularly in the simplified forms, use of flat colors, and in the strength and placement of illustrations. This masterpiece of economy, or *sachplakat* (object poster), became the archetype for much subsequent advertising, such as the work of Hans Rudi Erdt, Julius Gipkens, and Julius Klinger.

In 1907, the Deutscher Werkbund was founded in Munich, and Bernhard became one of its members.

Many of his best-known posters, such as those designed for *Stiller* shoes, *Adler* typewriters, and *Manoli* cigarettes, date from 1908-1910. His first logotypes, which also date from this time, exhibit the same simplicity of approach.

In 1910, Bernhard collaborated with Hans Sachs and Hans Meyer in the establishment of the magazine *Das Plakat*, which later became, in 1925, the

worldwide publication, *Gebrauchsgraphik*. Its first cover was designed by him.

During these first years of poster design, Bernhard developed a broad brushstroke sans serif lettering style, which gradually took on a unique character. To avoid being copied, as happened with *Block Type* (Hoffmann, 1908), Bernhard matured his letterforms, and created his first typeface, *Bernhard Antiqua*, for the Flinsch type foundry in Frankfurt, in 1911.

Two years later, he created a second typeface for the same type foundry named *Bernhard Fraktur*, which was well received because of the German spirit it represented.

With the outbreak of World War I, Bernhard was enlisted as a soldier designer in 1914. During this time he made considerable use of his typefaces on text posters both commercially for *Manoli* cigarettes as well as propagandistic for the German government, and the Bank of the Reich.

In 1919, Bernhard designed *Flinsch Privat*, a gothic typeface for Flinsch. As this type foundry was later absorbed by Bauer, Bernhard continued designing for the latter.

His success as a poster designer culminated in his appointment as head professor of advertising and poster design at the Akademie der Kunst, in Berlin, between 1920 and 1923, a post he did not fulfill because of his trip to America.

In 1923, Roy Lathan, owner of a lithographic firm in New York, invited him to work in the United States for a tour of six months giving lectures on design. Although this was never carried out, Bernhard stayed in America for the rest of his life.

Because Bernhard continued working for his studio in Germany, he used the trip time to create new typefaces. This was the case of *Bernhard Schönschrift*, designed for Bauer in 1924, which appeared in America as *Bernhard Cursive* in 1925; *Zarte Bernhard Antiqua*, known in America as *Bernhard Roman*, and used in Voltaire's

Candide, the inaugural publication of Random House, New York, in 1928; and *Bernhard Handschrift*, a wide brush typeface known in America as *Bernhard Brushscript*, also designed in 1928.

He also opened Contempora in 1928, the first international interior and graphic design studio in collaboration with Rockwell Kent (New York), Paul Poiret (Paris), Bruno Paul (Munich), and Erich Mendelsohn (Berlin). But as a consequence of the Depression, the project was closed one year later.

In 1929, he started a closed collaboration with American Type Founders in New Jersey, designing *Bernhard Gothic* (1929-31), his proposal to the European sans serif trend that had started with *Futura* (Paul Renner, 1927), *Bernhard Fashion* (1929), *Bernhard Tango, Bernhard Tango Swash* (1934), and *Bernhard Modern Roman* (1937), the last of his designs to be published.

Back in 1930, Bernhard had designed for Bauer his own version of *Block Type* as *Bernhard Negro* (an abbreviation of *Neue Grotesk*), also his last typeface for this type foundry.

Between 1933 and 1934, apart from the occasional design conferences, he taught at the Art Students League and New York University.

But Bernhard had become disillusioned with the increased emphasis on specialization in design and turned his attention to painting and sculpture.

He was a member of the Deutscher Werkbund; the American Institute of Graphic Arts (AIGA); and the New York Society of Illustrators. His work has been exhibited in the Deutsches Museum, the Hague (1913); the Rochester Memorial Art Gallery, New York (1950); the Walker Art Center, Minneapolis (1984); the Brooklyn Museum, New York (1986), and the Museo de Arte Universidad Nacional, Bogota (2003).

Lucian Bernhard died in New York City, in May 1972, at the age of eighty-nine.

BLOCK TYPE (1908)

This heavy sans serif typeface, drawn by H. Hoffmann, and issued by the H. Berthold AG type foundry in Berlin, is based on the lettering Bernhard used in the posters he designed at this time.

When the typeface was released, Bernhard was quite surprised to see his own lettering cast in metal.

ABCDEFGHIJKLMNOPQRSTUV WXYZ&abcdefghijklmnopqr stuvwxyz$1234567890!?

VERTEX (1912)

The *sachplakat* or object poster held such power that printers convinced advertisers to reduce their images to the size of postage stamps, which were then placed on envelopes and other items of mass distribution.

Hollerbaum & Schmidt, Berlin, printed the original poster in 1912, in orange, blue, brown and black, on a 37" x 24.4" vertical format.

MANOLI CIGARETTES (1911)

This trademark for *Manoli* cigarettes, Berlin, anticipates the simplicity of design of the postwar graphic identity.

UNIVERSAL FILM ASSOCIATION
Berlin (1919)

This emblem, still in use in newsreels, presents a structure where we may notice a disguised swastika.

AMERICAN GAS (1933)

A quite simplified image which anticipates modern trademarks.

INICIALES BERNHARD (1912)

This curious typeface was found in a Spanish typeface catalog, under his name. It was probably designed for the Flinsch Type Foundry, Frankfurt.

MANOLI CIGARETTES (1915)

This horizontal format poster for *Manoli* cigarettes (36.8" x 27.4"), was designed in Berlin and printed, as was most of his work, by the Hollerbaum & Schmidt printing press. It is also an example of the Berlin's horizontal poster.

The *Manoli* trademark was designed by Bernhard in 1911.

DAS IST DER WEG ZUM FRIEDEN (1912)

"This is the way to peace –the enemy wills it so! Therefore subscribe to the war loan!"

This red and black vertical poster (18.5" x 25.7"), designed for the Seventh War Loan, employs an illustration approach that recalls the woodcut technique.

The type design, *Bernhard Fraktur*, was produced by the Flinsch type foundry, Frankfurt, in 1913.

PRIESTER MATCHES (1905)

With this prizewinning poster in the 1905 competition, held by the Berlin Chamber of Commerce for *Priester* matches, Bernhard, without much awareness on his part, had defined the contemporary poster by reducing content to a visual language.

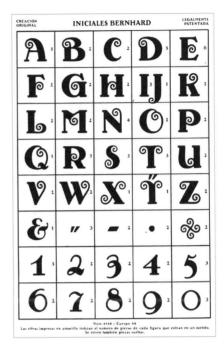

BERLINER MESSE (1926)

This trademark designed in collaboration with Fritz Rosen evokes the Berlin entrance monument.

KEUFEL + ESSEN CO. (c.1926)

This handsome trademark, still in use, was designed for a precision tools manufacturer.

CONTEMPORA INC. (1928)

This abstract symbol designed for his graphic and interior design studio, Contempora, established in New York in collaboration with Rockwell Kent (New York), Paul Poiret (Paris), Bruno Paul (Munich), and Erich Mendelsohn (Berlin), exhibit the simplicity found in contemporary design.

TOPS! PEPSI-COLA (1955)

An extraordinary horizontal poster (11" x 27,9") maintains the same simplicity of all his work.

ADLER TYPEWRITERS (1909)

This is another of his popular blue and red chromatic combination posters (18.5" x 13.5") designed for *Adler* typewriters.

Printed by Hollerbaum & Schmidt lithographers, Berlin, it uses the Berlin horizontal format.

STILLER SHOES (1907/1908)

This horizontal format poster (37.5" x 27.5"), characteristic of the Berlin format, was designed for the *Stiller* shoe factory.

Printed in red, blue, yellow, gray and black, it clearly exemplifies Bernhard's direct graphic approach.

The work was printed by Hollerbaum & Schmidt lithographers in Berlin.

BOSCH-LICHT (1911)

This lithographic vertical format poster (18.5" x 26.5"), designed for *Bosch-Licht* batteries, contains all the elements of the *sachplakat* or object poster created by Bernhard.

Hollerbaum & Schmidt lithographers printed it in Berlin.

KONKURRENZ-FLIEGEN (1909)

This quite attractive black-on-red silhouette vertical format poster (34" x 45.2"), was designed for a flight competition held by the Deutsche Flugplatz-Gesellschaft in Berlin, and printed by Hollerbaum & Schmidt lithographers in Berlin.

Bernhard Kursive
(1925)

This calligraphic typeface was designed for the Bauer type foundry in Germany, as *Bernhard Schönschrift*, one year after Bernhard left this country for the United States.

It is characterized by long ascenders and short descenders, as well as one floor **g** and **a**.

Numerals are drawn in *Oldstyle*.

ABCDEFGHIJKLMNOP QRSTUVWXYZ&abcdefghijkl mnopqrstuvwxyz$1234567890!?

LUCIAN (1928)

This roman typeface with a strong calligraphic quality and quite long ascenders and short descenders, was designed for the Bauer type foundry in Germany.

Originally issued as *Bernhard Roman*, it was used in setting the text of Voltaire's *Candide*, inaugural publication of Random House in New York, in 1928.

There are bold and open versions. The light version has some differences with the other weights, especially in the length of the lower horizontal stroke of letters **E** and **L**, and a lower case **p** with the same upper stroke found in letter **q**.

It is also interesting to compare Bernhard's original design with *FB Belucian*, developed by David Berlow in 1990.

ABCDEFGHIJKLMNOPQR STUVWXYZ&abcdefghijklmn opqrstuvwxyz$1234567890!?

ABCDEFGHIJKLMNOPQR STUVWXYZ&abcdefghijklmn opqrstuvwxyz$1234567890!?

BERNHARD FASHION (1929)

The second design done by Bernhard for ATF, this delicate Art Deco style sans serif has been, since then, very popular in fashion advertising and social printing.

It is also characterized by a quite small x-height, as well as very low cross bars in the letters **E**, **F**, and **G**, and a **B** and an **S** which seem upside down because of their reversed structure.

A bold version was tried but never completed.

Numerals have *Oldstyle* characteristics.

ABCDEFGHIJKLMNOP QRSTUVWXYZ&abcdefghi jklmnopqrstuvwxyz$1234567890!?

BERNHARD GOTHIC (1929-30)

The first design done by Bernhard for ATF, it is one of the first contemporary American sans serif typefaces. It was designed to counter the importation of such new European designs as *Futura* (Renner, 1927), *Kabel* (Koch, 1927), and *Gill Sans* (Gill, 1928).

It is characterized by long ascenders and short descenders, as well as other details such as a lower cross bar in the letters **B**, **E**, **F**, and **G**, which probably prevented it from achieving the popularity of other sans serifs of the same period.

It is interesting to compare this typeface with *Stellar* (Middleton, 1929) in letters **V**, **W**, **X**, **Y**, and **Z** in both upper and lower case letters.

Numerals have *Oldstyle* characteristics.

ABCDEFGHIJKLMNOPQRSTU
VWXYZ&abcdefghijklmnopqrstu
vwxyz $1234567890!?

ABBCDDEEEFFGHHIJKKLMNO
PPQRRSSTUVWXYZ&aabcdeefg
hijkklmnopqrrsstuuvwxyz
$ $1234567890?!

Lilith (1930)

Although Bernhard was in the United States, he kept his working relations with Germany.

This shaded fat face, with a slight inclination, was cut by the Bauer type foundry in Germany. It was later issued by ATF.

The ascending **b**, **h**, and **k** are looped; the **l** and **t** have cleft tops.

ABCDEFGHIJKLMNO
PQRSTUVWXYZabcdef
ghijklmnopqrstuvwxyz
1234567890

BERNHARD TANGO (1934)

Although it was designed in 1931, it was not cut until 1934.

It is a formalized italic with a number of unusual cursive features, such as the way up-strokes of letters **B**, **P**, and **R** start from the bottom serif separated from the main stroke.

Numerals are drawn in *Oldstyle*.

ABCDEFGHIJKLMNOPQRS
TUVWXYZ&abcdefghijklmnopqrstu
vwxyz$ 1234567890!?

BERNHARD TANGO SWASH (1934)

A companion design for *Bernhard Tango* (1934), this is a typeface with a size considerably larger than normal.

ABCDEFGHIJKLM
NOPQRSTUVWXYZ

BERNHARD ROMAN ANTIQUA BOLD CONDENSED (1937)

Although living in the United States, Bernhard designed this typeface for the Bauer Type Foundry in Germany, as a display typeface to accompany *Bernhard Roman*, designed in 1928.

ABCDEFGHIJKLMNOPQRSTUVWXYZ&
abcdefghijklmnopqrstuvwxyz
$1234567890!?*

BERNHARD MODERN ROMAN (1937)

In 1937, Bernhard redrew several characters of *Bernhard Booklet* (1935) and *Italic* (such as capitals **G**, **K**, **M**, **Q**, **V**, and **W**, and lowercase letters **g**, **s**, **v**, **w**, and **y**), at the request of American Type Founders.

One may see the original design in Mac McGrew's book *American Metal Typefaces of the Twentieth Century* (1996).

Reissued as *Bernhard Modern Roman* and *Italic*, it has a very precise drawing, large ascenders and short descenders.

In 1938, Bernhard added the bold and italic versions to the type family.

Numerals have some *Oldstyle* characteristics.

ABCDEFGHIJKLMNOPQRST
UVWXYZ&abcdefghijklmnopqrst
uvwxyz$1234567890!?

ABCDEFGHIJKLMNOPQRSTU
VWXYZ&abcdefghijklmnopqrstuvw
xyz$1234567890!?

Born in Detroit, Michigan in 1945, Charles Bigelow developed an early interest in typography, Linotype composition, and letterpress printing, as a result of his experience as a writer and editor of the Cranbrook School's literary magazine, *Opus*, in 1962-63.

In 1966-1967 Bigelow studied calligraphy with Lloyd Reynolds at Reed College in Oregon, where he graduated, and later studied typography with Jack Stauffacher at the San Francisco Art Institute, becoming his assistant the following year.

He also studied graphic arts, vision research, linguistics, and computer science at the San Francisco Art Institute, Portland State University, Rochester Institute of Technology, and Harvard University.

In 1974-75, he worked as Art Director of the *Oregon Times* magazine, and in 1972-73, as Media Specialist on the Oregon Environmental Council.

In 1976, Charles Bigelow established a partnership with Kris Holmes as Bigelow & Holmes, which has proven, thus far, to be a quite fruitful design relationship.

Between 1977 and 1978 Bigelow worked as research project director in the Oregon Arts Foundation, and between 1978 and 1980 he worked at Rhode Island School of Design, first as a "designer in residence" and later as assistant professor of graphic design. In this position, he was involved in many type design projects as well as programming and inviting several internationally known lettering designers and designers who were involved in developing new forms of creating type through digital language.

Such is the case with the Dutch type designer Gerard Unger (b.1942); Icelandic lettering artist and scholar Dr. Gunnlauger Briem; Swiss lettering artist and type designer Hans Edward Meier (b.1922), teacher at the Zurich School of Arts and Crafts; John Benson (b.1939), the famed Newport stonecutter, and Swiss lettering artist Andre Gürtler (b.1936), teacher at the Basel School of Arts & Crafts.

With his associate Kris Holmes in the design studio of Bigelow & Holmes in Menlo Park, California, specializing in letter form research and design, he has designed a number of typefaces such as *Lucida* (1984), which was the first typeface for use in low resolution printers; *Pellucida* (1986) for low resolution video displays; *Lucida Typewriter* (1986); *Lucida Bright* (1987), designed for setting the *Scientific American* magazine; and *Leviathan* (1977-78), for the Arion Press in San Francisco, and later licensed to the German type foundry, H. Berthold AG.

With Hans E. Meier and Kris Holmes, he developed *Syntax Phonetic* (around 1979), a sans serif for American Indian languages.

He was associate editor of *Fine Print*, a magazine dedicated to the arts of the book, between 1979 and 1985; and typographic adviser to Dr-Eng Rudolph Hell. He was also assistant professor of digital typography at Stanford University, Palo Alto, California, in the Department of Computer Science and Art, where, in 1992, he created a master's program in digital typography with the support of the distinguished mathematician and computer scientist, Donald Knuth (b.1938), creator of the *Metafont* digital program (1979).

Several of his students from the Rhode Island School of Design, such as Carol Twombly, Dan Mills, and Cleo Huggins (among others) were selected by Bigelow to join the program, which, though in existence for only a few years, produced a group of highly skilled, imaginative, and knowledgeable persons who have enjoyed distinguished careers in typography and electronic design.

In 1987, Charles Bigelow received the F. W. Goudy Distinguished Award in Typography from the Rochester Institute of Technology, and a MacArthur Foundation Fellowship Prize between 1982 and 1987.

He is member of the ATypI, the Society of Newspaper Designers, and the Type Directors Club of New York.

Among the many typefaces designed in collaboration with Kris Holmes, we find *Galileo* and *Italic* (1987) done for *Scientific American*; *Lucida Blackletter* (1992); *Lucida Handwriting* (1992); *Lucida Fax* and *Italic* (1992); *Lucida Sans Typewriter Oblique* and *Bold* (1992).

For Apple Computer, Inc., they have designed *Apple Chicago* (1991), *Apple Geneva* (1991), *Apple New York* (1991), *Apple Monaco* (1991), *Apple Chancery* (1994), *Textile* (1998), and *Capitals* (1998).

Charles Bigelow has written several articles on typefaces, type design, type technology, the aesthetics of type, and digital typography for publications such as *Publish!*, *Fine Print*, *Visible Language*, *Byte*, and *Scientific American* which plainly show his versatility and authority on these subjects.

He has also lectured, participated in typography symposiums, shared panels at international conferences, given several seminars on digital typographic design, and taken part in various font design workshops.

At present, he continues designing, writing, and lecturing on the subject he knows best: typography.

LUCIDA (1984)

This serif face, designed in collaboration with Kris Holmes, was the first typeface structured for the laser printer.

It was later complemented with other versions, until it completed a whole family of eighty members.

ABCDEFGHIJKLMNOPQRSTU
VWXYZ&abcdefghijlmnopqr
stuvwxyz$1234567890!?

LUCIDA SANS (1985)

Designed in collaboration with Kris Holmes, it was part of the *Lucida* family designed for low-resolution laser printers.

It is interesting to note that it is the calligraphic treatment in the drawing of the letters that permits an uneven treatment in the strokes, resulting in a more humanistic sans serif typeface.

ABCDEFGHIJKLMNOPQRSTUV
WXYZ&abcdefghijklmnopqrs
tuvwxyz$1234567890!?

ABCDEFGHIJKLMNOPQRSTU
VWXYZ&abcdefghijklmnopq
rstuvwxyz$1234567890!?

ABCDEFGHIJKLMNOPQRS
TUVWXYZ&abcdefghijkl
mnopqrstuvwxyz
$1234567890!?

ABCDEFGHIJKLMNOPQRS
TUVWXYZ&abcdefghijkl
mnopqrstuvwxyz
$1234567890!?

LUCIDA SANS
TYPEWRITER (1986)

Designed in collaboration with
Kris Holmes, this sans serif,
a somewhat condensed version
of *Lucida*, was rendered with
the spirit of typewriter designs.

It is interesting to note the serifs
placed on letters I,i,1,J, and j,
which permit a greater legibility
in words like Iliad, lilith,
or Illinois.

ABCDEFGHIJKLMNOPQRSTUV
WXYZ&abcdefghijklmnopq
rstuvwxyz
$1234567890!?

**ABCDEFGHIJKLMNOPQRSTUV
WXYZ&abcdefghijklmnopq
rstuvwxyz
$1234567890!?**

LUCIDA BRIGHT
(1897)

A roman typeface with a large
x-height, it was designed
in collaboration with Kris Holmes,
his partner, for setting the
Scientific American magazine.

It is interesting to note that the
ascenders surpass the capitals
in height.

ABCDEFGHIJKLMNOPQRST
UVWXYZ&abcdefghijklmno
pqrstuvwxyz$1234567890?

*ABCDEFGHIJKLMNOPQRST
UVWXYZ&abcdefghijklmno
pqrstuvwxyz$1234567890?*

**ABCDEFGHIJKLMNOPQR
STUVWXYZ&abcdefghijk
lmnopqrstuvwxyz
$1234567890!?**

***ABCDEFGHIJKLMNOPQ
RSTUVWXYZ&abcdefghij
klmnopqrstuvwxyz
$1234567890!?***

Lucida Calligraphy (1988)

Designed in collaboration with Kris Holmes, this interesting handwritten version of *Lucida* continues complementing the type family.

Letterforms present, in Holmes's words, "the dynamic effect that comes from twisting the pen angle during the writing of a stroke, to give an asymmetrical, flaring emphasis to the terminations."

Numerals are drawn in *Oldstyle*.

ABCDEFGHIJKLMNO
PQRSTUVWXYZ&abcd
efghijklmnopqrstuvwx
yz$1234567890!?

Lucida Blackletter (1992)

Designed in collaboration with Kris Holmes, this is another side version of *Lucida*, which not only maintains an overall flavor of the basic letter structure, but also introduces Holmes's ability in the handling of the pen.

Numerals are drawn in *Oldstyle*.

ABCDEFGHIJKLMNOPQR
STUVWXYZ&abcdefghijklm
nopqrstuvwxyz
$1234567890!?

Lucida Handwriting (1992)

Designed in collaboration with Kris Holmes, this calligraphic version of *Lucida* has a more casual feeling than *Lucida Calligraphy*.

It is interesting to note that although this is a sans serif alphabet, some letters maintain a serif.

ABCDEFGHIJKLMNOPQ
RSTUVWXYZ&abcdefg
hijklmnopqrstuvwxyz
$1234567890!?

LUCIDA FAX (1992)

Designed in collaboration with Kris Holmes, and for use with the limited tonal qualities of fax reproduction, this serif typeface maintains its clarity by means of large counter spaces.

The italic has some noticeable changes in the use of a more calligraphic approach to the letterform, as well as one one-story letters *g* and *a*.

ABCDEFGHIJKLMNOPQRST
UVWXYZ&abcdefghijklmn
opqrstuvwxyz
$1234567890!?

*ABCDEFGHIJKLMNOPQR
STUVWXYZ&abcdefghijkl
mnopqrstuvwxyz
$1234567890!?*

LUCIDA SANS TYPEWRITER OBLIQUE (1992)

Designed in collaboration with his associate Kris Holmes, the oblique version of *Lucida Sans Typewriter* appeared six years later.

It is interesting to note the serifs placed on letters *I, i, l, J*, and *j*, which permit a greater legibility in words like *illegal, lilith, illustration,* or *Illinois.*

*ABCDEFGHIJKLMNOPQRSTU
VWXYZ&abcdefghijklmno
pqrstuvwxyz
$1234567890!?*

**ABCDEFGHIJKLMNOPQRSTU
VWXYZ&abcdefghijklmno
pqrstuvwxyz
$1234567890!?**

LUCIDA TYPEWRITER
(1994)

To complement the preceding *Lucida Typewriter Sans* version designed in 1986, and *Lucida Typewriter Sans* designed in 1992, Charles Bigelow and his partner, Kris Holmes, designed this serif version with its bold and italic companions.

ABCDEFGHIJKLMNOPQR
STUVWXYZ&abcdefghi
jklmnopqrstuvwxyz
$1234567890!?

**ABCDEFGHIJKLMNOPQR
STUVWXYZ&abcdefghi
jklmnopqrstuvwxyz
$1234567890!?**

LUCIDA CASUAL
(1994)

Designed in collaboration with Kris Holmes, this casual script seems to be a roman version of *Lucida Handwriting*, but with some freedom of stroke.

It includes an Italic version.

ABCDEFGHIJKLMNOPQRS
TUVWXYZ&abcdefghijklm
nopqrstuvwxyz
$1234567890!?

Born in New York in 1897, the son of a German immigrant, Joseph Blumenthal went to Cornell University for one year before enlisting when the United States joined World War I in 1917.

At the age of twenty-six he decided that he would prefer a life "somewhat in the world of the book," and wrote a letter to every publisher in New York for a job. He was lucky: he got an answer, and a job as a traveler for Ben Huebsch, who later founded the Viking Press. At this time he first became aware of the ability of fine printing to dignify great literature. He noticed in particular the work of Francis Meynell at the NoneSuch Press, London; of Bruce Rogers at the Riverside Press, Cambridge, Massachusetts; and Daniel Berkeley Updike at the Merrymount Press, also in Cambridge.

It is noteworthy to remember that all these printers produced their fine work, not from private presses but at commercial workshops operating at the height of their powers. But of the three, it was Updike whom Blumenthal emulated, although different from him in that Updike could not set a line of text, while he himself ran his typographic press.

After working with a few well known printers, such as William E. Rudge of the Montague Press as compositor, and briefly for A. G. Hoffman at the Marchbanks Press, Blumenthal, in partnership with Hoffman, set up his own workshop, the Spiral Press, in New York, in 1926. Like any other small printing houses, it produced work for cultural institutions like museums, universities, foundations, book clubs, book shops, and art galleries. Virtually all of the editions of Robert Frost's poetry for the Random House publishers in New York were products of the Spiral Press. Frost considered himself the best-printed poet in America.

He later designed some books for George Macy's Limited Editions Club, such as Theodore Dreiser's novel, *Sister Carrie* (1900), illustrated by Reginal Marsh and set in *Janson* type, designed by Chauncey H. Griffith in 1932.

Blumenthal commented, "The Spiral Press thrived in its modest way from the beginning. It was my belief in 1926,

since strengthened by time, that the market for fine printing is not limited, except as it is limited by the capacity to produce it."

In 1930, as a result of the Great Depression, business was badly affected and Blumenthal was forced to sell his stock and machinery, keeping only the Spiral. He then went to Europe to travel, and also to design his first typeface: *Spiral*. He made his drawings, and went to the Bauer type foundry in Frankfurt, where punch-cutter Louis Hoell, who had cut types for Emil Rudolf Weiss, cut a 14-pt size from them that year.

After several sets of smoke-proofs and refinements of the punches, Blumenthal was satisfied, and trial fonts were cast by Bauer and proofed at Dr. Willi Wiegand's Bremer Presse in Munich. With Wiegand Blumenthal learned how to operate a hand press. *Spiral* typeface was initially used for a limited edition of Ralph Waldo Emerson's essay *Nature*, printed on a hand press at Croton Falls in 1932, and privately published.

It is interesting to add that around this time he briefly visited Rudolf Koch at his Offenbacher Werkgemeinschaft (famous type and calligraphy workshop) where other Americans, such as Warren Chappell, Frederic Warde and Victor Hammer had studied.

The first version of *Spiral* had no italics; but from Germany, Blumenthal went on to England, where Stanley Morison offered to cut the type for Monotype composition. In 1934, the roman version was cut, and the following year, the italic. The typeface's name was then changed to *Emerson*.

Unfortunately, *Emerson* was not a very successful typeface in its Monotype version, ranking fortieth among the company's text faces between Hans (Giovanni) Mardersteig's *Fontana* (1936), and Frederic W. Goudy's *Goudy Modern* (1918). It was best used by Blumenthal himself, both in the short period when the Spiral Press was working with a hand-press at Croton Falls up the Hudson River, and when he returned to New York City as a general printer in 1934.

Besides Robert Frost's poetry books, of which the last, *In the Clearing*, was printed at the Spiral Press in 1962,

it is worth mentioning an *Ecclesiastes* illustrated by Ben Shahn, and printed in 1965. This work, as well as others of this type, brought several of America's most prominent graphic artists to the Press. Blumenthal also designed and printed for W.H. Auden, Pablo Neruda, William Carlos Williams, Robinson Jeffers, and Franklin Delano Roosevelt.

In 1966, four years before he closed his printing endeavor, Blumenthal was able to organize an exhibition at the Pierpont Morgan Library in New York on the work done at the Spiral Press under the title of *The Spiral Press through Four Decades*. The exhibition included a catalog with a checklist of all the publications.

Blumenthal closed the Spiral Press in 1971 and devoted himself to writing on typography and mounting the highly praised exhibition of *The Art of the Printed Book 1455-1955,* which gathered "the most significant masterpieces of typography [112 books] through five centuries, from the collection of the Pierpont Morgan Library in New York," and which opened there in 1973.

In 1977, he published, through David R. Godine in Boston, *The Printed Book in America*, a very important contribution to the history of American printing in which he analyzes the performance of the main publishers in the United States.

In 1982, he published in New York another book, *Typographic Years, a Printer's Journey through Half a Century 1925-1975*, a printer's autobiography that gives an excellent account of five decades of development of book design in America and Europe. The book was printed by the members of the Grolier Club, New York.

In 1989, one year before he died, he accomplished his last work, *Bruce Rogers: A Life in Letters (1870-1957)*, which was printed by W. Thomas Taylor, Austin, Texas.

Blumenthal was awarded the American Institute of Graphic Arts' Lifetime Achievement Award in 1952.

Joseph Blumenthal died in West Cornwell, Connecticut, in 1990, at the age of ninety-three.

EMERSON (1935)

Initially cut in the Bauer type foundry by Louis Hoell in 1930, and named *Spiral* after his press, it lacked an italic version.

In 1934, Stanley Morison offered to cut the type for Monotype composition, and in 1935, after adding an italic version, the name was changed to *Emerson*, after Ralph Waldo Emerson, whose essay, *Nature*, Blumenthal printed at his Spiral Press.

Numerals are drawn in *Oldstyle*.

ABCDEFGHIJKLMNOP QRSTUVWXYZabcdefg hijklmnopqrstuvwxyz 1234567890

Garret Boge was born in Spokane, Washington in 1951, and when he was twenty-six years old, his family moved to Chicago.

In 1969, after graduating from high school, he went to the University of Chicago where he concentrated on a common-core coursework in the humanities. From 1972 to 1974, Boge returned to Evergreen College in Washington where he first encountered calligraphy through a workshop conducted by Willard McCarty, an advanced student of Lloyd Reynolds from Reed College in Portland. This gave him sufficient knowledge to freelance as a calligrapher in Seattle, Washington, and later in Portland, Oregon.

In the mid 1970s, realizing a keen affinity to calligraphy, Garret Boge moved to Portland, then as now, a vibrant center for calligraphy, and forged a joint academic degree with the Oregon School of Arts & Crafts and Marylhurst College, both centers of study for calligraphy and design. Upon graduation he was recruited to the lettering department of Hallmark Cards in Kansas City, where he spent three years honing his commercial lettering skills and learning the principles of type design in it's specialized Type Group.

In 1982, working with Hallmark's talented creative professionals, and attending master classes with Hermann Zapf at Rochester Institute of Technology, served to advance his skills and dedication to lettering and typography.

Boge left Hallmark in 1983 to open his own design and lettering studio in Kansas City, offering hand lettering and typography services to the advertising and design community. In 1986, with the advent of the Macintosh computer, he soon embraced digital technology, seeing it's potential for realizing his original type designs, thereby establishing one of the first independent foundries of the desktop era.

In 1987, Boge released his first text face, *Visage*, and a year later his first display family, **Spring**, while building a clientele for custom font services, including his former employer, Hallmark's Type Group.

In 1988, Garret Boge returned to his native northwest, relocating the studio/foundry to Gig Harbor, Washington, and specializing in type design and font production under the new name LetterPerfect. The first specimen sheet, released in 1990, showed twelve original and revived display faces of which **Spring, Spumoni, Florens Flourished** and **Manito** have since found wide acceptance. Custom font clients during this same period included Hallmark Cards, Reader's Digest, the New Yorker, Pepsi-Cola, Esteé Lauder, Cronan Design, and LA Style Magazine.

In 1991, Boge accepted a six-month contract with Monotype Corporation in Salfords, England, to assist with the font production of the Microsoft Windows system fonts (**Times New Roman, Arial, Courier,** and **Symbol**).

In addition to the technical acumen of working with leading font engineers and the rich typographic legacy at Monotype, this afforded him opportunities to acquaint himself with London's typographic resources and to instill in him a more historical appreciation of type design. One contact in particular has proven to be seminal: he joined Professor Michael Twyman's tour to Rome and Florence to study inscriptions with his Reading University typography course. (This valuable experience would resurface a few years later, prompting the launch of the **Legacy of Letters Tour** program.)

Returning to Gig Harbor in 1992, Boge resumed original design work and production commissions, which included projects for Apple Computer Inc. (the **Espy** screen font family for System 7.0), Microsoft Corporation and Aldus Corporation (both requiring customized display fonts for collateral and packaging). By this time, the LetterPerfect font range reached a total of forty-two faces comprising both original and revived designs.

In 1993, Boge put the LetterPerfect Foundry on hold for two years, accepting the position of Director of Typography for ElseWare Corporation in Seattle —a startup software company developing a font compression technology for Hewlett

Packard printers. Overseeing the aesthetic quality of type for this technology allowed him to glean insights into the engineering, multi-platform, and related industry concerns that mass-market fonts pose.

In 1995, he resumed full-time direction of LetterPerfect, now based in Seattle. This same year, he also brought on Paul Shaw, New York lettering designer and longtime collaborator, as an associate partner. This has proven fortuitous, giving LetterPerfect a bicoastal marketing reach, and initiating a brand identity with two distinctive lines of fonts reflecting their respective strengths: **Vive la Font** —lively, contemporary, display designs; and **Legacy of Letters**— carefully researched historical designs. With this latter program they have collaborated on twenty designs, which have their roots in historical type and lettering, including the **Kolo** family (Viennese Secession), the **Early Christian Set**, the **Baroque Set**, the **Florentine Set**, and the **Swedish Modern Set**.

As an adjunct to their interest in history and travel, and their research on Legacy font series, LetterPerfect launched the **Legacy of Letters Tour** program in 1997, offering small group guided tours to centers of historical lettering and printing. Michael Twyman, Boge's earlier mentor in the study of inscriptions has since signed on as a guide resource with the Legacy tour program, bringing full circle the historical inspiration he helped to spawn in Boge years earlier.

Beyond his work at LetterPerfect, Garrett Boge teaches typography and lettering at Cornish College of the Arts in Seattle, regularly speaks and participates at industry forums and writes articles for trade press. Industry accolades have included winning the Agfa Type Excellence Contest in 1987 for best digital logo design, Graphic Design USA award for the **Kolo** typeface in 1996, and winning the 1998 Serif Magazine Type Design Competition for the **Florentine Set** of typefaces (the last two in collaboration with Paul Shaw).

Spring (1988)

While Boge maintained a working contact as a calligrapher for Hallmark's Type Group, he established himself in 1986 as one of the first independent foundries. In 1988, he designed *Spring*, a fluid calligraphic alphabet, his second design and his first display family.

ABCDEFGHIJKLMNOPQR
STUVWXYZ&abcdefghijklmno
pqrstuvwxyz$1234567890!?

Florens-Flourished
(1990)

Part of his first specimen sheet issued in 1990, this is Boge's second calligraphic display alphabet.

It also includes a regular version.

ABCDEFGHIJKLMNOP
QRSTUVWXYZ&abcdefghi
jklmnopqrstuvwxyz$1234567890!?

ABCDEFGHIJKLMNOPQRSTUVW
XYZ&abcdefghijklmnopqrstuvwxyz
$1234567890!?

MANITO (1990)

A free-drawn letter created with a wide pen and angular, sturdy forms to simulate roughhewn woodcut letters, *Manito* has an additional quality of popular signs lettering.

It is named after a Native American word for "Great Spirit."

ABCDEFGHIJKLMNOPQRST
UVWXYZ&$1234567890!?

PONTIF (1996)

Baroque inscriptions still abound in Rome as testimony to the influence of the Renaissance Popes, who commissioned inscriptions throughout the Holy City.

Pontif typeface, the first of the *Baroque Set* designed in collaboration with Paul Shaw, evokes the formal qualities of refinement and authority from this period.

ABCDEFGHIJKLMNOPQR
STUVWXYZ&ABCDEFGHIJK
LMNOPQRSTUVWXYZ
$1234567890!?

PIETRA (1996)

The massive five-foot tall mosaic letters gracing the interior of cupola of San Pietro in Vatican City are the most compelling use of lettering in Baroque architecture.

Based on the inscription **TU ES PETRVS ET SVPER HANC PETRAM ÆDIFICABO ECCLESIAM MEAN ET TIBI DABO CLAVES REGNI CÆLORVM** (*Thou art Peter [petrus, rock] and upon this rock I will construct my church and I will give unto thee the keys of the kingdom of heaven*), designed by calligrapher Ventura Sarafellini in c.1605, the *Pietra* typeface, second design of the *Baroque Set*, structured in collaboration with Paul Shaw, presents a beautiful and particular form which differentiates it from the familiar Roman capital letters.

It includes small caps.

ABCDEFGHIJKLMNOPQR
STUVWXYZ&ABCDEFGHI
JKLMNOPQRSTUVWXYZ
$1234567890!?

CRESCI (1996)

Regarded as the preeminent Vatican scribe of the late fifteenth century, Milanese Giovanni Francesco Cresci, an official "writer" to the Vatican Library in Rome, was the creator, or at least the chief teacher, of a new style of calligraphy which replaced the older, more rigid chancery cursive. He was responsible for a shift toward the Baroque lettering.

Cresci's second alphabet of capitals, published in *Il perfetto scritore* (1570), is the model for the *Cresci* typeface, the third typeface of the *Baroque Set*, designed in collaboration with Paul Shaw.

ABCDEFGHIJKLMNOPQR
STUVWXYZ&ABCDEFGHIJ
KLMNOPQRSTUVWXYZ
$1234567890!?

STOCKHOLM (1998)

Designed in collaboration with Paul Shaw, *Stockholm* is the first design of the *Swedish Set*.

Inspired by post-World War II Swedish calligraphy, it is an italic face based on the work of Kerstin Anckers. It is also characterized by a 45-degree pen angle employed in the construction of the letters which gives them an elegant form.

ABCDEFGHIJKLMNOPQRST
UVWXYZ&abcdefghijklmnop
qrstuvwxyz$1234567890!?

GÖTEBORG (1998)

Designed in collaboration with Paul Shaw, *Göteborg* is the second design of the *Swedish Set*.

Inspired by post-World War II Swedish calligraphy, it is a roman face based on the work of Erik Lindgren.

It is interesting to note that the free strokes surpass the upper and lower horizontal guidelines common in typographical faces.

Numerals are drawn in *Oldstyle*.

ABCDEFGHIJKLMNO
PQRSTUVWXYZ&abcdefgh
ijklmnopqrstuvwxyz
$1234567890!?

UPPSALA (1998)

Designed in collaboration with Paul Shaw, *Uppsala* is the third design of the *Swedish Set*.

Inspired by post-World War II Swedish calligraphy, it is an uncial face based on the work of Herbert Lindgren.

The present sample presents an expert version with small caps.

ABCDEFGHIJKLMNOPQRSTU
VWXYZ&ABCDEFGHIJKLMNO
PQRSTUVWXYZ$1234567890!?

LONGHAND (1998)

This script type design was developed on the basis of a legible and flowing writing hand.

The design preserves an irregular soft edge to the character shapes, suggesting a writing tool's contact on paper. The two variations, light and bold, evoke the use of two different writing tools.

ABCDEFGHIJKLMNOP
QRSTUVWXYZ&abcdefghi
jklmnopqrstuvwxyz
$1234567890!?

ABCDEFGHIJKLMNOP
QRSTUVWXYZ&abcdefghi
jklmnopqrstuvwxyz
$1234567890!?

Born in Boston, Massachusetts, in 1869, Henry William Bradley was fascinated by type, printing and illustration as a child. Son of a newspaper artist who died during the Civil War, he found a job in Ishpeming, Michigan, as a printer's assistant, and later as a foreman of the local newspaper. In his spare time, he earned some extra money by designing posters.

In 1886, he moved to Chicago and started his career as an artist, discovering his skill as a pen-hand and ink illustrator. By 1890, his work was appearing in *Frank Leslie's Illustrated Newspaper* and in the *Inland Printer*.

Short of money to attend art classes, he relied on magazines, and local bibliophiles. He became aware of Japanese art and how Eastern concepts of design were assimilated into contemporary illustration, and he learned about the Owen Jones and Christopher Dresser theories on art and decoration.

However, it was William Morris with his Arts and Crafts movement, and the emerging English art movement influenced by Oscar Wilde's ideas that molded his vision of art and illustration.

His early work was indebted to all these artists as well as Herbert P. Horne and Walter Crane. But it was not until 1894 that his work matured into a definite Art Nouveau style, in a series of twelve covers for the *Inland Printer* and several posters for the *Chap-Book*, thanks to Aubrey Beardsley's work which served as a catalyst. These works marked the beginning of Art Nouveau in America, and along with the posters designed by Edward Penfield for *Harper's New Monthly Magazine*, started a craze for poster design in this country.

Bradley then moved to Springfield, Massachusetts, with the idea of setting up his own press, modeled after Morris' Kelmscott Press, where he could publish his own periodical.

In 1895, Bradley founded the Wayside Press, but much of his first year was spent on commissions for the *Chap-Book*, the *Chicago Sunday Tribune*, the *Echo*, and *Harpers' Bazaar*. His book design achieved such unity of type and illustration that it established him as a true American pioneer.

Shortly after, in 1896, he published the first issue of *Bradley: his book*, an art and literary magazine that became both a critical and financial success. He considered applied art, decoration, and design for the home to be part of the craft revival. Although many of all his plans were never realized, the Wayside Press produced much outstanding work from 1896 to 1898.

As early as 1891, Bradley had designed several typefaces for the *Inland Printer*, and in 1895, the American Type Founders bought the right to the lettering he had created for one of the *Inland Printer* covers. Bradley drew upon his study of Colonial American and eighteenth-century English printing, and introduced into his work *Caslon Roman* type, which he combined with woodcuts and ornaments. But as he found his health threatened by his work, he sold the Wayside Press in 1898 to the Harvard University Press at Cambridge, Massachusetts, and continued to work for them as a designer.

In 1899, he began to accept freelance commissions. He created new layouts for the *Bookman* and *Harper's Weekly* and, at the turn of the century, he arranged a new editorial prospectus for the *Ladies' Home Journal*. Although this project was never printed, it allowed him to create for the *Journal* a series of home interiors to be called the *Bradley House*.

His interest in the English Arts and Crafts movement is clearly seen in his approach to decoration, which set him apart from his contemporaries Frank Lloyd Wright and Gustav Stickley, and linked him more closely to the English craftsmen and architects M. H. Baillie Scott and C. F. A. Voysey.

He continued to do illustration, and in 1901 he completed a series of covers for *Collier's Weekly*. Though this work differs from his preceding style, he kept a decorative approach with strong contour outlines and symmetrical compositions.

Between 1904 and 1905, he designed an advertising campaign for the American Type Founders, which involved the illustrating of twelve monthly issues of *The American Chap-Book*. In these publications, he continued to express his ideas about the merger of art with business.

Bradley's dedication to type design and layout demanded more and more of his attention, and by 1907, when he became art editor of *Collier's Weekly*, his career as an artist had practically come to an end. From 1910 to 1915, he was simultaneously art director of *Century, Good Housekeeping, Metropolitan, Success, Pearson's* and *National Weekly*.

By this time, Bradley was convinced of the need to change the use of ornament. He insisted on consistency and flow in publication design, liberating the publication from ornament and changes of style from page to page. In two of his articles, written in *Printing Art*, he stressed the importance of coherence and consistency between image and type.

In 1915, he was also art supervisor for a series of motion pictures financed by William Randolph Hearst, and from 1918 to 1920 he wrote and directed his own motion picture, *Moongold*. During the 1920s, he was back working for Hearst as art supervisor of all his publications. This task limited time for his own work, and although he ran an art service in New York from 1912 to 1914, this work could not match the originality of his earlier designs.

By the time "Art Nouveau was being rediscovered by the younger generation, and the arts and crafts had become a fashion pursuit, Bradley himself was scarcely aware of his early achievements. He was somewhat surprised by the recognition he received during the 1950s until his death in 1962," writes Roberta W. Wong in her introduction to *Will Bradley: His Graphic Art* (1974).

ATF commissioned a series of type ornaments and Strathmore Papers asked him to decorate a selection of paper samples for an advertising campaign. In 1955, the Typophiles published a little book of his reminiscences.

He was a member of the Society of Arts and Crafts of Boston, the Graphic Group, and the American Institute of Graphic Arts.

Pressman, illustrator, typographer, printer, advertising and publication designer, Henry William Bradley died in Pasadena, California, in 1962, at the age of ninety-four.

BRADLEY (1895)

Credited to Joseph W. Phinney, this typeface is based on lettering by William Bradley for the Christmas cover of *Harper's Bazaar* magazine. It is a very heavy form of black letter, based on ancient manuscripts, but with novel forms for many letters.

A curious application may be found in the **Firestone** logotype.

ABCDEFGHIJKLMNOPQRSCUVWXY
Z&ÆŒææ abcdefghijklmnopqrstuvwxyz
$1234567890£ •!?

BRADLEY HIS BOOK (1896)

In this prospectus cover, Bradley shows the clear influence of William Morris.

HARPER'S BAZAAR (1896)

In this Easter *Harper's Bazaar* cover, Bradley shows a masterly dominion of composition and ornament, clearly related to the Pre-Raphaelites' work.

PEGASUS (1895)

For this handsome, highly intricate abstract poster, designed in two colors (red and black) for the *Chap-Book*, Bradley used the flying horse figure as a leitmotif.

ADVERTISEMENT (1905)

This two-color advertisement (red and black), forms part of a series of ads printed in one of the pages of the *Printer Man's Joy* magazine.

SPRINGFIELD BICYCLE CLUB TOURNAMENT (1895)

This two-color poster (red and black) was designed for this Springfield, Massachusetts, event. The repetition of the bicycle club's symbol gives a feeling of lightness to the whole.

TYPOGRAPHICAL VIGNETTES

The first, as well as the chap book cuts, are examples of the vignettes used by Bradley in his typographical compositions.

VICTOR BICYCLES (1899)

Bicycle manufacturers were the first American advertisers to use the poster to promote their products and the first to engage artists such as William Bradley and Maxfield Parrish to design them. By 1900, bicycling had become the most popular American sport.

This horizontal poster (40" x 26"), designed for the Overman Wheel Co., was originally printed in Boston. In 1899, *Le Maitres de l'Affiche* in Paris issued it in a facsimile form. This monthly publication, printed by the Imprimerie Chaix, Paris, issued thirty-eight copies of this design.

THANKSGIVING (1895)

In this three-color cover (blue, red and black) for the Thanksgiving issue of the *Chap-Book*, Bradley uses the repetition of the figure to create an emphasis of content.

MISSAL INITIALS
(1904)

Issued by American Type Founders, these initials have been ascribed to Bradley.

Derived from fifteenth century drawings, each letter was designed to fill a square area.

ABCDEFGHI
JKLMNOPQR
STUVWXYZ

BEWICK ROMAN
(1905)

Designed by Bradley in 1904, this typeface was issued by ATF the following year.

It is a singular display type with a number of unusual characteristics, such as the uneven lengths of the upper and lower horizontal strokes in capital letters, and the placement of serifs on only one side of some lowercase letters.

ABCDEFGHIJKLMNOPQRSTUV
WXYZ&abcdefghijklmnopqrstu
vwxyz §1234567890?!

Born in Ballart, Australia in 1857, Henry Lewis Bullen started an apprenticeship for training in typography, stone lithography, and bookbinding at fourteen. Once he completed his training in 1865, he left for the United States, settling in New York City.

By that time, the printing industry had a slow period and many compositors were out of work. After looking for a job without much success, Bullen left for the middle states, where he wandered for the next five years.

He returned to the East, working in New York City and Trenton, New Jersey. By 1880, he ended up in Boston, where he abandoned the duties of a type compositor to become the editor of promotional advertising material for Golding & Company, a manufacturer of printing presses and typographical material. In this new job he was a great success; he combined his duties with the selling of foundry type, and was promoted to sales manager in 1883. Although he patented the Standard composing stick and the Little Giant brass rule and lead cutter, both patents were held in the Golding name. In his own words, "he had a few dollars in the bank."

In 1888, he went back to Australia, but returned to America in 1892 to work in New York for the newly formed American Type Founders Company. Robert W. Nelson was appointed general manager of the company in 1895, and Bullen as general advertising manager and assistant sales manager under his orders.

Bullen knew that ATF's main idea was to consolidate the type manufacturing business under one roof, but as he analyzed the project, he also realized that several of the foundries had type libraries that were not considered typographical equipment or part of the sale, and that they would, in time, become scattered or disappear into

other hands. He presented a plan, which Nelson approved, that all this loose type material and catalogs be collected and stored in one place as the nucleus for a future national printing collection.

During the next few years, he was a busy person, working and assembling the *1895 Collective Specimen Book*, the *1897 Specimen Book for the New York Area*, and the 1897 *Desk Book for Boston*.

In 1899, Bullen left ATF, and signed a seven-year contract with the F. Wesel Manufacturing Company in New York. Nevertheless, in spite of the commercial success, their relations were not harmonious, and by 1905 he obtained a release from his contract to join the United Printing Machinery Company of New York. This time, financial difficulties arose, and Bullen went into seclusion for many months.

Fortunately, his old friend Henry O. Shepard, publisher of the *Inland Printer*, offered him the opportunity to publish. During the 1906-1907 period, he wrote a series of articles under the title of "Discursions of a Retired Printer." In the first of these articles, he revived the plan for establishing a national printing library and suggested that ATF be the sponsor, and that people could also donate books, thus helping the plan get started.

Bullen's idea must have been a great success, for in 1908, when he rejoined ATF, he volunteered to be librarian of the combined collections, his own and that of ATF.

ATF's Typographic Library and Museum contained more than 12,000 volumes related directly or indirectly to printing and its allied arts.

In addition to serving as a working reference collection for the company, Bullen built the library, "to serve as a model of art and craftsmanship to students of typography...to memorialize or honor predecessors in our profession or printers now living...

[and to] enhance the appreciation by the general public of printing as an art and influence." To this end, he bought examples of the great books in printing history.

Bullen worked on evenings and weekends to catalog the books, using his own standard card system. He remained in charge of the Typographic Library and Museum for over twenty-five years.

The *Type Specimen Book and Catalogue 1923*, published by ATF, included the story and illustrations of the collection; the project was nationally acclaimed. The typographical content became reality with the cooperation of Morris Fuller Benton, who as head of the type design department at ATF,had the responsibility of redesigning and unifying many of the type designs. It was through Bullen's urge that Benton worked on classical revivals, such as *Bodoni, Garamond, Cloister Oldstyle* and *Bulmer*.

But the Great Depression years came and the many visitors that once had filled the exhibition rooms were now absent.

In 1933, the library, which had remained in Jersey City while the rest of the organization moved to Elizabeth, was ordered closed and classified as an expense liability. Bullen stayed with his books, printing a fifty-nine page mimeograph sales catalog titled "Duplicates of Type Specimen Books for Sale."

In 1934, the entire collection, with the exception of duplicates, was packed and assigned to Columbia University in New York City, which purchased it in 1941.

After sixty-six years in the printing industry, working as compositor, salesman, promoter, engineer, and a librarian without remuneration, Henry Lewis Bullen died in New York City in 1938, at the age of eighty-one.

GARAMOND (1917-1931)

This typeface, as well as *Cloister Oldstyle* (1904), *Bodoni* (1909) and *Bulmer* (1926), were type revivals executed by Morris Fuller Benton while he worked as a type designer for ATF. It was at Bullen's urging that these, and other classic designs, were implemented for the ATF library.

ABCDEFGHIJKLMNOPQRS TUVWXYZ&abcdefghijklmno pqrstuvwxyz$1234567890!?

Born in New York City in 1939, Tom Carnase received an art education at the New York City Community College, and began his career in 1959 as an associate designer with the design division of Sudler & Hennessey, Inc., where he stayed for five years.

By this time he did the intricate lettering for the three-dimensional horizontal assemblage mural 40' x 8.5', which Lou Dorfsman had conceived for the CBS cafeteria, and for which Herb Lubalin had done a sketch to scale.

In 1964, Carnase worked as a freelance designer, and in collaboration with with Ronne Bonder, he established Bonder & Carnase Studio, Inc., an art studio where he worked until the end of 1968.

In 1969, he became vice president and partner of Lubalin, Smith, Carnase, Inc., an independent agency dedicated to creating and licensing design for equipment manufacturers (similar to ITC).

But it was with the publication of *U&lc* (*Upper & lowercase*), the in-house quarterly journal of ITC, and for some time one of the only places in which calligraphy regularly appeared, that Carnase found a rich field for his calligraphic work in 1973.

Being an expert in Spencerian hand lettering, a tightly drawn classicist style that became a modern idiom, he, as well as Tony DiSpigna, was responsible for executing many of Lubalin's designs. *Idea* magazine, the Japanese international advertising journal published throughout the world, called him "an original master in letterforms." He contributed much of his talent in bringing ideas to life, such as the logos for *New York Magazine* and L'eggs Products, Inc.

In 1979, he opened Carnase Computer Typography studio as an independent designer, managing the business as a design consultant.

In 1980, Carnase was cofounder and president of World Type Center, an independent type design agency. As an in-house publication they issued *Ligature*, under his direction. For WTC, he designed *Carnase Text* (1982); *WTC Goudy* (1982); *Favrile* (1985); *WTC Our Bodoni* (1989) (in which this page has been set) in collaboration with Massimo Vignelli; and *WTC 145*; as well as some revised versions of *Bodoni, Futura*, and *Goudy*, all including complete families.

Carnase's typography is another of his commercial interests as a designer. As a creator of more than fifty alphabets, he has said, "Fine typography is the result of an attitude. Its attraction comes from love and care in its planning. Designs of swirling patterns, strange marbled and curious free-form shapes, trapped in texture, are sophisticated examples of expressionism."

Among his best-known alphabets, we may find *ITC Avant Garde Gothic* and *ITC Busorama*, both designed in 1970, in collaboration with Herb Lubalin. He later designed five variations of *ITC Avant Garde Gothic* (*Extra Light, Book, Medium, Demi Bold* and *Bold*), which have enriched the type family.

He also works in packaging, exhibition design, editorial design and corporate identity, and among his many logotypes one may find the mastheads of *New York Magazine* and *Esquire*.

He has lectured widely in the USA to schools and Art Director's Clubs, and is a member of the New York City Community College Advisory Commission.

He has also held teaching positions at the University of Cincinnati, the Pratt Institute, the Herron School of Art, Parsons School of Design, the Cleveland Institute of Art, the University of Monterrey in Mexico, and the Rochester Institute of Technology.

In 1968, he had a one-man exhibition of lettering and type design in New York City. Since then, he has participated in international exhibitions organized by the U.S. Information Agency.

His works and articles on design and calligraphy have appeared in such magazines as *Graphis, Vision, Art Direction, Printers Ink, CA, Creativity, Graphics Today, Type World, Ligature, HOW, Graphics Monthly, Printing News*, and in the book *Who's Who in Graphic Arts* (1982).

He has received many awards since 1961, most of them for type design in the New York exhibits.

He is a member of the New York Art Directors Club, the New York Type Directors Club, the Society of Publication Designers, and the Frank Lloyd Wright Building Conservancy.

Among his clients are ABC, Apple Computer, CBS, the Coca-Cola Company, American Express, L'eggs Products, Condé Nast Publishing, Crown Publishing, Doubleday Publishing, The National Geographic Society, Random House, L'Oreal, and Shiseido Cosmetics.

ITC GORILLA (1970)

Designed in collaboration with Ronne Bonder for display composition, it resembles some Art Nouveau typography, such as *Adcraft Black*, cut by Barnhart Brothers & Spindler in 1900, and introduced later by the same company, as *Plymouth Bold*.

ABCDEFGHIJKLMNOPQRST
UVWXYZ@abcdefghijklmno
pqrstuvwxyz$1234567890!?

1776-1976 (1976)

This calligraphic illustration was executed for the July issue of ITC's *Upper & lower case* journal, to commemorate the bicentennial anniversary of the Independence of the United States.

THE ART DIRECTORS CLUB, INC.

Calligraphic masthead designed for the Art Directors Club, Inc.

NEW YORK

Calligraphic masthead designed for the *New York Magazine*.

DINNER (c.1980)

This masthead is another example of Carnase's sensitive handling of calligraphy.

BIG CITY

Logotype. The block letters clearly represent a group of buildings, but, they don't interfere with the reading.

1234567 (1979)

Announcement designed for the anniversary of the National Broadcasting Corporation (NBC).

ESQUIRE (1979)

Masthead designed for *Esquire* magazine. It is interesting to compare it with the one designed by Ed Benguiat (page 55).

INTER TEXT

Logotype.

NEW YORK LOTTERY

Logotype.

SCRUPLES (1979)

Calligraphic title created for Judith Krantz's book *Scruples*.

LIGATURE (1982)

Masthead designed for *Ligature*, the Typographic Communication Journal published by the World Typeface Center, Inc, under the direction of Carnase himself.

GRUMBACHER

Logotype designed for an art materials firm, where the rendering of the graphic whole, represents the ink and oil liquid quality.

GREAT TRADITIONS

Logotype. The lettering handling resembles the old fashion nineteenth-century signs.

ITC GRIZZLY (1970)

Designed in collaboration with Ronne Bonder for display composition, it is characterized by slanted oblique terminals in many of the letters.

ITC, H. Berthold AG, Bitstream Inc., Compugraphic Corporation, Linotype, and Varityper have commercialized it.

ABCDEFGHIJKLMNOPQRST
UVWXYZ&abcdefghijklmnopq
rstuvwxyz$1234567890!?

ITC GROUCH (1970)

Designed in collaboration with Ronne Bonder for display composition, it is a very heavy roman typeface with a marked calligraphic quality.

ITC, H. Berthold AG, Bitstream Inc., Compugraphic Corporation, Linotype, and Varityper have commercialized it.

ABCDEFGHIJKLMNOPQ
RSTUVWXYZ&abcdefghij
klmnopqrstuvwxyz
$1234567890!?

ITC HONDA (1970)

Designed in collaboration with Ronne Bonder for display composition, it is a condensed sans serif with a strong gothic calligraphic feeling. It has only one weight.

ITC, H. Berthold AG, Bitstream Inc., Compugraphic Corporation, Linotype, and Varityper have commercialized it.

ABCDEFGHIJKLMNOPQRSTUVWXY
Z&abcdefghijklmnopqrstuvwxy
z$1234567890!?

ITC NEON (1970)

Designed in collaboration with Ronne Bonder, this display typeface recalls neon sign lettering.

ABCDEFGHIJKLMNOP
QRSTUVWXYZ&
$1234567890!?

ITC MACHINE (1970)

Designed in collaboration with Ronne Bonder for ITC, this typeface permits a very tight kerning. The straight cutting of the curves gives the letters a particular appearance.

It was handsomely used on the cover of ITC's *U&lc* journal issue of 1978, as seen on page 187.

ABCDEFGHIJKLMNOPQRSTUVWXY
Z&$1234567890!?

ITC PIONEER (1970)

Designed in collaboration with Ronne Bonder for titling composition, it is a volumetrical sans serif with only one weight. ITC, H. Berthold AG and Bitstream Inc. have commercialized it.

ABCDEFGHIJKLMNOPQR
STUVWXYZ&
$1234567890!?

ITC BUSORAMA (1970)

Designed in collaboration with Herb Lubalin, this sans serif typeface is characterized by the use of curved strokes whenever there is an oblique.

ABCDEFGHIJKLMNOPQRSTUVW
XYZ&$1234567890!?

ABCDEFGHIJKLMNOPQRSTUV
WXYZASV&$1234567890!?

ITC FIRENZE (1970)

A contemporary version of *Century Bold*, this serif letter has all the Carnase characteristics of hand-drawn letters.

Lowercase letters and numbers have a heavy round form.

ABCDEFGHIJKLMNOP
QRSTUVWXYZ&abcdef
ghijklmnopqrstuvwxyz
$1234567890!?

Born in London in 1937, son of Harry Carter, (typographer, historian, and archivist to the Oxford University Press), Matthew Carter's career has been closely connected to the changes in typesetting technology that have taken place over the last forty years. On leaving school in 1955, he spent a year in Holland as a trainee in the type foundry of Joh. Enschedé en Zonen where he studied under P. H. Rädisch, the punch-cutter of Jan Van Krimpen's types.

In 1961, while working in London as a freelance designer, he used the skills he had acquired in Holland to cut a semi-bold typeface of Monotype *Dante* under the direction of John Dreyfus. The punches for *Dante* had been cut by the French punch-cutter Charles Malin to Giovanni Mardersteig's designs between 1946 and 1952, but Malin had died before the semi-bold was undertaken.

In 1963 Carter had his first experience of phototypesetting technology when he became typographical adviser to Crosfield Electronics, the British distributor of the *Photon/Lumitype* machine. Two years later he moved to New York to join Mergenthaler Linotype as staff designer reporting to Mike Parker, director of typographic development, with the particular responsibility of designing typefaces that exploited the advantages of photocomposition over hot metal typesetting, such as the joining script *Snell Roundhand*.

During the six years he spent in New York he also designed *Cascade Script*, *Helvetica Compressed*, *Helvetica Greek*, a *Hangul* for the Korean Language, *Olympian* for newspaper text, and the Video series of sans serifs for the first Linotype digital typesetters.

Back in London between 1971 and 1981, he continued to work in association with the Linotype companies. To this period belong *Shelley Script*, *Cadmus Greek*, *Bell Centennial* for typesetting the U.S. telephone directories, a caption face for *National Geographic*, and the *Galliard* family of classical romans. He also designed faces for Pentagram's corporate identities for *Lucas* and *Nissan*, and a titling alphabet for gallery guides at the Victoria & Albert Museum in London.

In 1981, Carter and Mike Parker were among the four cofounders of Bitstream, Inc., the first independent digital type foundry, in Cambridge, Massachusetts. Here Carter was responsible for the overall design standards of the company, and produced their first original typeface design, *Bitstream Charter*. From 1980 to 1984, he was typographical adviser to Her Majesty's Stationery Office (the British government printer), and was elected a Royal Designer for Industry in 1982. He also served as consultant to IBM's Printer Planning Division on the adaptation of type to laser printers.

At the end of 1991, Carter and another of Bitstream's cofounders, Cheri Cone, left to form their own company, Carter & Cone Type, Inc., in Cambridge, Massachusetts, to design, manufacture and sell typefaces in industry standard formats. Their first project was a new digitization of *ITC Galliard* complete with Expert Sets. They have also released for the retail market *Mantinia*, *Sophia*, *Big Caslon*, *Alisal* and *Miller*, and have produced types on commission for Apple, Microsoft, *Time*, *Wired*, *U.S. News & World Report*, *Sports Illustrated*, and the *Washington Post*.

In 1993, Laurie Haycock Makela, design director of the Walker Art Center, commissioned a typeface for the Center's exclusive use that would be "open to interpretation." The resulting face can be modified by the user by adding a range of interchangeable serifs to the basic letterforms, or by joining adjacent letters together with horizontal linking strokes.

A more recent project, completed in 1997, was the design of two typeface families, *Verdana* (sans serif) and *Georgia* (serif) for Microsoft. These families, both of which include Greek and Cyrillic versions, were designed for optimum legibility on screens. They have been widely distributed with Microsoft's Web browser and other applications.

Matthew Carter has received many distinctions for his work: the Frederic W. Goudy Award for outstanding contribution to the printing industry (1986); the honorary degree of Doctor of Fine Arts from the Art Institute of Boston (1992); a Gold Award from the Tokyo Type Directors Club for *Sophia* (1994); the Robert Hunter Middleton Award from the American Center for Design (1995); the Chrysler Award for Innovation in Design (1996); the American Institute of Graphic Arts Medal (1996), and the Type Directors Club Medal (1997). He is a member of AGI, chairman of the Type Designers' Committee and member of the Board of Directors of ATypI, and a long-standing member of Yale University's graphic design faculty.

AURIGA (1965)
Completed for, and released by Mergenthaler Linotype in 1970.

ABCDEFGHIJKLMNOPQRSTUV
WXYZ & abcdefghijklmnopqrstu
vwxyz£$1234567890!?

MANTINIA (1993)

Double spread from brochure presenting *Mantinia* typeface.

The original is printed in brick red and black.

BIG CASLON (1994)

Double spread from brochure presenting *Big Caslon* typeface.

The original is printed in brick red and black.

WALKER (1996)

Double spread from the brochure presenting *Walker* typeface.

About this typeface designer Santiago Piedrahita says, "You are not typesetting a font, the font is created in the process of designing the piece."

SOPHIA (1993)

Colophon from the brochure presenting *Sophia* typeface.

The original is printed in brick red and black.

MANTINIA (1993)

Colophon from brochure presenting *Mantinia* display typeface. The original was printed in brick red and black.

WALKER (1996)

Cover design of brochure presenting *Walker* typeface.

The original was printed in light green and black.

THE CONCERT room had both an organ and a harpsichord, refreshments on a sideboard, and excellent home-brewed ale. Guests left at twelve, to walk safely home under a full moon. This picture of Caslon's comfortable and cultured domestic life is reflected in his types, or rather in the harmonious smaller sizes it is.

SOPHIA™ WAS DESIGNED BY MATTHEW CARTER. IT WAS SUGGESTED BY HYBRID ALPHABETS OF CAPITALS, UNCIALS AND GREEK LETTER-FORMS FROM 6TH-CENTURY CONSTANTINOPLE. SOPHIA WAS FIRST SHOWN, TOGETHER WITH FACES BY ZUZANA LICKO & ED FELLA, IN 'DESIGN QUARTERLY' № 158.

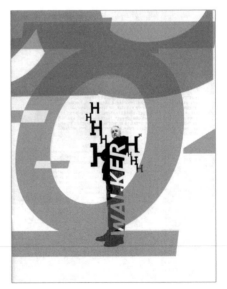

CASCADE SCRIPT
(1966)

An informal script, one of the first
scripts developed by Linotype's
Linofilm phototypesetter.

ABCDEFGHIJKLMNOPQRSTUV
WXYZ&abcdefghijklmnopqrstuv
wxyz$1234567890!?

Snell Roundhand
(1966)

Based on the hand of Charles Snell,
English writing master
of the seventeenth century.

A formal script steeply slanted
with joining letters.

ABCDEFGHIJKLMN
OPQRSTUVWXYZ&abc
defghijklmnopqrstuvwxyz
$1234567890!?

OLYMPIAN (1970)

A newspaper text face released
both for Linotype metal composition
and for the *Linofilm*.

The original series included
a TTS unit-cut version.

ABCDEFGHIJKLMNOPQR
STUVWXYZ&abcdefghijkl
mnopqrstuvwxyz
$1234567890!?

ABCDEFGHIJKLMNOPQRS
TUVWXYZ&abcdefghijklmn
opqrstuvwxyz$1234567890!?

Gando Ronde (1970)
Another script, this one French in inspiration, was designed for *Linofilm* in collaboration with Hans-Jurg Hunziker.

Numerals are drawn in *Oldstyle*.

ABCDEFGHIJKLMNOPQRST UVWXYZ&abcdefghijklmnopqrstuvwxy z$1234567890!?

Shelley Script Allegro

Shelley Script Volante (1972)

A formal script commissioned by Linotype and named for the English writing master George Shelley, whose work *Alphabets in All Hands* (1710), so influenced John Baskerville.

The face has three alternative sets of capitals, *Andante*, *Allegro*, and *Volante* that range from the plain to elaborately flourished.

ABCDEFGHIJKLMNO PQRSTUVWXYZ&abcdefghijk lmnopqrstuvwxyz$1234567890!?

ABCDEFGHIJKLMN OPQRSTUVWXYZ&abcdef ghijklmnopqrstuvwxyz$1234567890!?

BELL CENTENNIAL
(1978)

Commissioned by AT&T for setting the U.S. telephone directories by high-speed digital CRT techniques.

Its name celebrates the hundredth anniversary of the first Bell Telephone directory.

ABCDEFGHIJKLMNOPQRSTUVWXYZ&ab
cdefghijklmnopqrstuvwxyz$1234567890

**ABCDEFGHIJKLMNOPQRSTUV
WXYZ&abcdefghijklmnopqrstuv
wxyz$1234567890!?**

ITC GALLIARD
(1982)

A family of classical romans and italics in four weights based on the types of the seventeenth-century French punch-cutter Robert Granjon.

The face was taken over by ITC and released for wider distribution as *ITC Galliard* in 1982.

ABCDEFGHIJKLMNOPQRS
TUVWXYZ&abcdefghijklmno
pqrstuvwxyz$1234567890!?

ITC CHARTER (1987)

Designed at Bitstream as a contemporary seriffed face that would reproduce well over a range of output resolutions.

The face was acquired by ITC and released as *ITC Charter* in 1993.

ABCDEFGHIJKLMNOPQRSTU
VWXYZ&abcdefghijklmnopqrs
tuvwxyz$1234567890!?

MANTINIA (1993)

An elegant titling face of classical Roman capitals, inspired by lettering in the painting and engravings of Andrea Mantegna, artist of the Italian Renaissance.

The year of its appearance it received an award from the New York Type Directors Club.

ABCDEFGHIJKLMNOPQ
RSTUVWXYZ&ABCDEFGHIJ
KLMNOPQRSTUVWXYZ
$1234567890!?

SOPHIA (1993)

A titling face inspired by hybrid alphabets of capitals, uncials and Greek letter forms from sixth-century Constantinople.

It received a Gold Award from the Tokyo Type Directors Club in 1994.

The alphabet includes alternative characters, ten joining characters to form ligatures, and Greek letters.

AABCDEEFFGGHIIJKKLM
MNOPQRRSTUVWXXYZ&
ÆŒ!?$1234567890
♣£¥§+←→ºªA

CLASSIC TYPEFACES
108

BIG CASLON (1994)

Based on William Caslon's type specimen of 1734, which might be cut by Caslon himself, this contemporary version shows its grandeur.

This is the first time Caslon display typefaces are digitized.

One of the main characteristics is the lowercase large x-height.

Numerals are drawn in *Oldstyle*.

ABCDEFGHIJKLMNOP
QRSTUVWXYZABCDEFG
HIJKLMNOPQRSTUVWXYZ
&abcdefghijklmnopqrstuvw
xyz$1234567890!?

WALKER (1995-96)

Founded in 1879, the Walker Art Center, Minneapolis, has always been committed to contemporary art and design.

In 1994, its design director, Laurie Haycock Makela, found the opportunity for the Center to have its own typographical identity through the design of its own typeface. Other art institutions had typefaces for their own use: the Musée D'Orsay's *Didot*, Seattle Art Museum's *Bodoni*, and Metropolitan Museum of Art's *Centaur*.

After much research and conversations, Matthew Carter came up with a unique typeface in every sense of the word: *Walker*.

Walker, being a font that has variable serifs in its design structure, permits any designer to work with the typeface by adding or reducing the distinctive serifs at will to adjust it to a specific content. Although the basic form has a sans serif structure, the typeface may become seriffed, square serif, half serif, or whatever combination a designer may choose.

ABCDEFGHIJKLMNOPQRS
TUVWXYZ&$1234567890
!?()@%

HE MB ME NE
E⋮ EH EH EH
HHHHH

1 2 3 4 5 6 7 8 9 0

Born in Richmond, Virginia in 1904, Warren Chappell became aware of art as a discipline in 1915, when he was faced with three unrelated events, which brought into focus the creative impulses that made him a successful designer and illustrator of books: Boardman Robinson's illustrations for a series of reports on the war in Europe made for the *Metropolitan* magazine; his acquaintance with sculpture at school, which influenced his sense of volume in his drawings; and the death of his grandfather, who had become a lettering artist and designer in the late 1860s. Chappell would write later on: "Perhaps I've always wanted to do something for letterforms, to carry his efforts a step higher."

When he began his professional training, rather than an art school, he chose the liberal arts courses at the University of Richmond, Virginia, where he lived, and where he graduated in 1926. On the advice of Joseph Pennell, who taught at the Art Students' League, he took some drawing classes during the summer.

After finishing college, he attended the Arts Students' League of New York full time in 1928, where he studied with Allen Lewis, a distinguished woodcut illustrator, who laid more emphasis on the art of the book than Pennell had. Impressed by his aptitudes, Lewis introduced Warren to George Grady of the Strawberry Hill Press in New York, who offered him a part-time job. There he acquired a practical experience in typography and printing, and incidentally, a powerful urge to cut punches for typecasting.

Through Grady's advice, he went to Offenbach, Germany, where Rudolf Koch, in addition to designing types for the Klingspor type foundry, had established a flourishing workshop, the Offenbacher Werskgemeinschaft, at the Technische Lehranstalt. This workshop was already attracting talent and visitors from many parts of the world.

To finance this venture, Chappell worked three years as promotional art director for *Liberty Magazine*. In 1931, he and his wife Lydia arrived in Offenbach, and between

that year and 1932, he was part of the group integrated under the direction of Koch.

Koch exerted a powerful influence not only on him, but on many who were to become leading figures in type design in the postwar years, such as Friedrich Heinrichsen, calligrapher; Berthold Wolpe, type designer and calligrapher; Fritz Kredel, woodcutter; Frederic Warde, calligrapher; Joseph Blumenthal, typographer; Victor Hammer, calligrapher and Imre Reiner, calligrapher. Others were Richard Bender, whose job was to clean drawings for reproduction; Sir Francis Meynell, book designer; and Peter and Edna Beilenson, printers. Under the supervision of Koch, of his son Paul, and that of Gustav Eichenauer, Chappell learned all the type cutting skills he wanted to acquire, as well as all the nuances of writing with a flat pen, minutely appraising its part in the creation of design.

On returning to New York, Chappell opened a studio. Despite the Great Depression, he was kept busy on freelance work during the next three years. He also taught at the Art Students' League from 1933 to 1935, where he shared his lettering experience with his cousin, Oscar Ogg. In 1935, he published his first book, *Anatomy of Lettering*, a handsome work dedicated to Koch.

That same year, Chappell assisted Boardman Robinson in the building and opening of the Colorado Springs Fine Arts Center, where he studied illustration with him in 1936. Back to New York in 1937, he was commissioned by the American Type Founders Company to design a different sans serif typeface: *Lydian*, a calligraphic roman letter that anticipated many of the future humanist sans serif faces, and became an immediate success. The bold and italic versions were added the following year.

In 1939 Chappell designed a new typeface, *Trajanus*, for D. Stempel AG type foundry in Frankfurt, Germany, which also became available in Linotype.

In 1940, he complemented *Lydian* with a cursive version, and in 1946 with a bold condensed version. Nine years later, in 1955, Chappell executed a third design,

Eichenauer, for the Klingspor type foundry in Offenbach, Germany, which although proof-cut by Gustav Eichenauer, remained uncut when the foundry merged with D. Stempel AG in 1956.

Warren Chappell was one of the most outstanding figures in the fields of type design, graphic art, and book illustration, and also a distinguished writer and editor on the subject of the printed word. He was active in the field of lettering and type design, and, since 1940, illustrated more than ninety books, mainly for Alfred A. Knopf and Random House. He often said, "I do not consider myself a writer –I'm a draftsman."

He lectured at Columbia University, New York University, and at other colleges and professional meetings around America. Since his debut into book illustration resulting from his handsome edition of Jonathan Swift's *Tale of a Tub*, his fine eye and hand lent distinction to many books. He also contributed with various articles to *The Dolphin*, *Virginia Quarterly Review*, and *Hornbook*. In his books for children, which include *They Say Stories*, *The Nutcracker*, and *Sleeping Beauty*, he usually wrote the narrative, drew the illustrations, and designed the publication format.

In 1972, he published *A Short History of the Printed Word* for André Deutsch Limited in London, which is a clear account of the development of this art up to the time of publication, and in 1975, *The Living Alphabet*, which deals mainly with the origins of the Roman alphabet.

Some of his work may be seen in the Hamill Collection at the Newberry Library, Chicago, as well as in the book illustration and lettering collection at the Alderman Library of the University of Virginia in Charlottesville.

Warren Chappell died in Charlottesville, Virginia in 1992, at the age of eighty-eight.

LYDIAN (1938)

A sans serif with a very strong calligraphic drawing, it became one of the most popular typefaces of the period.

Named after Chappell's wife, Lydia, it was primarily used for display and for advertising. The lighter weight and italic were issued in 1938, and the bold and italic in 1939.

ABCDEFGHIJKLMNOPQRSTUVW
XYZ&abcdefghijklmnopqrstuvwxyz
$1234567890!?

HOLLIS HOLLAND

Bookplate (*ex libris*) designed for Hollis Holland's personal library.

ELSEWHERE

Two bookplates (*ex libris*) designed for Alfred E. Hamill's personal library.

LITTERA SCRIPTA MANET

Calligraphic rendering of the Latin poet Horace's maxim: *Littera scripta manet –the written word remains*.

This simple but pregnant phrase was used by Chappell many times. Ten years earlier he used it for his entry in the celebrated Peabody Institution exhibition, *Calligraphy & Handwriting in America, 1710-1962*.

CYMBELINE (1944)

Chapter ornamental vignette for the Modern Library edition of *The Tragedies of Shakespeare* printed in 1944.

MOZART (1960)

Vignette illustration of the child Mozart, for his book *They Say Stories*, published by Alfred A. Knopf in 1960.

LITTERA SCRIPTA MANET (1972)

The written word remains (Horace) - Calligraphic rendering for the frontispiece of his book *A Short History of the Printed Word*, published by André Deutsch and printed in the Klingspor Press, Inc., Tennessee, in 1972.

MITTAT IN ME LAPIDEM

Send over me a stone. Calligraphy rendering executed with a wide brush by request of Paul Standard.

The expression refers to an ancient Nordic custom of putting stones over a tomb found along the road.

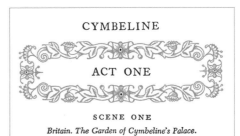

THE LIVING ALPHABET (1759)

Title page for his book *The Living Alphabet*, set in *Trajanus*, and published in Charlottesville by the University Press of Virginia.

EICHENAUER (1955)

Proof of roman type designed by Warren Chappell and cut in lead by Gustav Eichenauer in 1955. It was never casted because of the closing of the Offenbach fype foundry.

TRAJANUS (1939)

Cartouche designed for *Trajanus* typeface.

WARREN CHAPPELL PRINTER'S MARK (1972)

Printer's mark used by Warren Chappell in his book *A Short History of the Printed Word*, published by André Deutsch and printed by the Klingspor Press, Inc., Tennessee, in 1972.

INITIAL (1941)

One of the initials designed for William Saroyan's *Fables*, published by Harcourt, Brace, in 1941.

The rendering of the letter reminds us of the sixteenth-century initials based on *The Dance of Death* (1523-26) illustrations by Hans Holbein.

MOZART

Lettering from a book jacket.

ILLUSTRATIONS (1972)

Illustrations of the woodcutting process for his book *A Short History of the Printed Word*, published in London by André Deutsch in 1972.

THE TRAGEDIES OF SHAKESPEARE (1944)

Title page designed for the Illustrated Modern Library edition of *The Tragedies of Shakespeare*.

THE BORZOI BOOK OF FRENCH FOLKTALES (1958)

Front and book spine of the book jacket for *The Borzoi Book of French Folktales*, published by New York publisher Alfred A. Knopf in 1958.

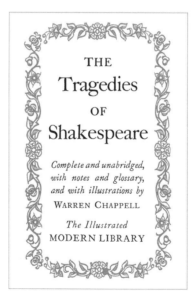

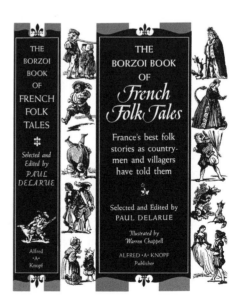

LYDIAN BOLD (1939)

The bold and italic versions were designed one year after *Lydian* (1938).

Lydian Bold Condensed and *Italic* were designed in 1946, but not marketed until 1949.

They present a more vertical emphasis than the preceding designs, where the lowercase letters give the appearance of a simplified black letter.

ABCDEFGHIJKLMNOPQRSTUV
WXYZ&abcdefghijklmnopqrstuvw
xyz$1234567890!?

TRAJANUS (1939)

Named after the Roman Emperor Marcus Ulpius Trajanus (c.53-117), it is a roman letter in the Venetian style, with a nervous pen-drawn, contemporary quality. While the ascenders are long, the descenders are short.

Designed for the D. Stempel AG type foundry, in Frankfurt, it was issued commercially in 1945.

Trajanus appeared at a time when foundry type was rapidly being supplanted by the two-dimensional technology of the photographic lens and of offset printing. Thus, the type as a solid piece of metal was almost completely replaced by its photograph, and as Chappell expressed it, "With the sculptural quality gone from the type, the lure of type design was gone for me."

In 1975, Chappell used *Trajanus* for his book *The Living Alphabet*, which deals mainly with the origins of the Roman alphabet, and which was published by the University Press of Virginia, Charlottesville, where he was artist in residence.

Numerals are drawn in *Oldstyle*.

ABCDEFGHIJKLMNOPQRSTU
VWXYZ&abcdefghijklmnopqrstu
vwxyz$1234567890!?

ABCDEFGHIJKLMNOPQRSTUVW
XYZ&abcdefghijklmnopqrstuvwxyz
$1234567890!?

LYDIAN CURSIVE (1940)

Although it gives the appearance of having been drawn with the same type of pen as the regular series, it is much more free and calligraphic, with a style unmatched by other American scripts, and reminiscent of the *Chancery script*.

The lack of flourishes was a product of the mechanical limitations of all foundry types.

ABCDEFGHIJKLMNOPQRST
UVWXYZ&abcdefghijklmnopqrstu
vwxyz$1234567890!?

Born in Brooklyn, New York in 1880, Thomas Maitland Cleland moved with his family to Manhattan a few years later. When he was fifteen, he entered the New York Artist Artisan Institute, where he took drawing and a course of applied ornamentation. But he was a poor student, and spent more time in a popular vaudeville theater across the street than he did in classes.

By watching a fellow student rendering an ornamental drawing with ink, he learned that such graphs could be reproduced by a photomechanical process and printed. Through this friend, Cleland also learned about the **American Bookmaker** magazine, where he published his first drawings. It was the beginning of his professional career.

Through Walter Crane's book **The Decorative Illustration of Books**, he learned about William Morris and his Kelmscott Press, of Aubrey Beardsley, and the wood engravings of the English illustrators. Later on, he also became acquainted with the ornamental and decorative printing of William Bradley at the Wayside Press. His interest in his work led him to designing, and with time he developed a good knowledge of the craft.

Soon after, with the help of Lewis Hatch, who worked at Charles Scribner's old shop, Cleland was able to get some small commissions for lettering and binding, and finally to be hired as designer of the Caslon Press in New York, which, under the direction of Frederic T. Singleton, did commercial printing. His work attracted the attention of some enthusiasts who induced him to bring to Boston his modest equipment, and to establish the Cornhill Press there.

Although the press only ran a year, he was able to meet Daniel Berkeley Updike, then involved in the establishment of the Merrymount Press in Cambridge. With him, Cleland developed a taste for typography and design, as well as doing some work, such as the title page of **The Humanist's Library**.

Soon after his return to New York, David Bruce's New York Type Foundry commissioned Cleland to design his first typeface: **Della Robbia**, in 1902. Bought by ATF in 1900, this type foundry continued operating until 1906.

But his liking for the theater had not died entirely, and after winning a scholarship, he entered the American Academy of Arts. Besides amateur acting, he designed and painted a number of scenarios, created costumes and stage-directed various ballets. His final failure in directing Rafael Sabatini's play **Scaramouche** in New York turned him back to design.

In 1904, he traveled to Italy, where he learned more about painting and ornamental design. One year later, he married and came back to Italy once again. By this time, regularly engaged in design and bookbinding, he was offered the art editorship of **McClure's Magazine** in 1907, but he only worked there for one year. His experiments with typography and printing led others to imitate him.

In 1914, he designed and supervised the printing of an elaborate wine list for the Hotel Claridge. The quality of the design attracted the attention of John A. Kingman, in charge of advertising for the Locomotive Company of America, who commissioned him to design a catalog for this company. It marked a new era in commercial art in America and a distinctive phase in his career.

Cleland was again a printer in the complete sense of the word, with his own equipment. He was able to turn out a large variety of commercial work with his own illustrations and decorations. With the same quality as that of Bruce Rogers and Daniel Berkeley Updike in their field of book design, Cleland's work also helped America stand out in this type of work.

After a year in the army, Cleland returned to design and to printing production. In 1921, he did **The Grammar of Color** for the Strathmore Paper Company, Westfield, Massachusetts, a work of the highest quality. Nevertheless, with its publication, he felt that there was a conflict between the printer and the artist, and after selling his workshop he turned to painting, illustration, and design.

During the 1920s, big business moved to the forefront of American life, and profits, advertising, and consumer credit lifted the nation toward unprecedented prosperity. In this environment, Cleland provided American industry with an apt graphic expression. His designs projected an atmosphere of tradition, authority, and wealth. Architects also aimed for this type of visual imagery by clothing banks, financial institutions, and corporate offices with columns and marble and granite exteriors.

In 1925, Cleland did some work for **Westvaco Inspirations for Printers**, a post later held by Bradbury Thompson in 1939.

In 1929, after five years of preparation, he printed **The Decorative Work of T. M. Cleland** at the Pinson Printers. Despite the good reception, it was also the time of the stock market crash, and the subsequent Great Depression changed everything. The following year, Henry R. Luce hired Cleland as art director of his new monthly magazine, **Fortune**. Though he directed only three issues, his format and graphic cover design approach were maintained for ten years.

Among other assignments involving periodical design, his most stimulating experience was the planning and direction in 1939-40 of the **PM** (Production Managers) journal, edited by Robert L. Leslie, and later renamed **AD** (Advertising Direction).

As the Depression deepened, and Modernist design made inroads during the 1930s, Cleland's romanticism seemed outdated. He continued to be active, but became a traditionalist in the graphic arts field rather than the innovator of the 1920s. Fortunately, Cleland continued to secure various assignments in book illustration well into his last days.

People who knew him remembered his aristocratic bearing, his cultivated tastes, and his pride at being self-educated.

Thomas Maitland Cleland died in Danbury, Connecticut, in 1964, at the age of eighty-four.

DELLA ROBBIA (1902)

Designed from the rubbings of a stonecut found in Rome, the font is named after Luca Della Robbia (1400-1482), a Florentine sculptor. Letters have an inscriptional quality, with little variation of thickness.

Morris Fuller Benton later designed a light version for ATF.

ABCDEFGHIJKLMNOPQRS
TUVWXYZ&abcdefghijklmno
pqrstuvwxyz$1234567890!?

THE GRAMMAR OF COLOR
(1921)

Title page designed for *The Grammar of Color*, published by Strathmore Papers Co. in 1921.

For this undertaking, Cleland increased his press equipment and staff in order to reach his goals.

Not only did he print the elaborate color forms, but he also wrote the text and enlivened it with decorative illustrations and diagrams. Through a series of foldout pages, Cleland explained the effective use of colored inks on colored paper.

CADILLAC (1927)

Philip Meggs says in an article on Cleland, "In his commercial work, such as railroad and automobile advertisements, Cleland was endowed with the cavalier grace of the eighteenth century, in a supreme indifference to anachronism," as may be seen in these two pages from a product brochure designed for *Cadillac* automobiles.

In these images, Cleland also "projected American industry with an ambiance of tradition and permanence, authority and wealth. Architects created a similar idiom by cladding banks, financial institutions, and corporate offices in imposing granite exteriors, with pediments and columns," adds Meggs.

INITIALS (1916-1919)

Series of ornamental initials designed to accompany different texts. The first two are based on Christophe Plantin's alphabets, the second and third evoke Geofroy Tory's initials, and the fourth and fifth evoke the *criblé* initials of the sixteenth century.

Besides these graphic influences, we may see in the first initial a curious mixture of Oriental ornaments and Renaissance images, such as Raphael's *Three Graces*.

FORTUNE MAGAZINE (1930)

In 1930, Henry R. Luce, publisher of the new monthly magazine *Fortune*, hired Cleland as art editor. Cleland not only established its format but a design style that remained for a decade, even if he only designed three issues. The illustrations show the first two covers.

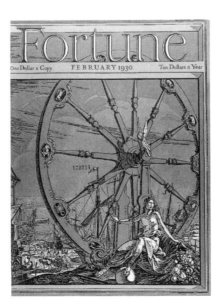

Born in Mount Gilead, Ohio in 1879, Oswald Bruce Cooper was raised in Kansas but left at the age of eighteen to study illustration at the Frank Holme School of Illustration in Chicago. There he had the opportunity to meet Frederic W. Goudy, one of the most prolific American type designers and director of Holme's Type Department.

Goudy not only became a good friend of his, but also helped him to earn his tuition fees and to discover his love for lettering by assigning jobs setting type for correspondence booklets. Through Goudy's Village Press, he was also part of the circle of typographers and illustrators who gathered together in its setting. Among these were Will Ransom, William Addison Dwiggins, and cartoonist Harry Hershfield. Soon he was appointed as lettering teacher, a position he enjoyed, regardless of the low payment he received for it.

While teaching at Holme's, he also met Fred Bertsch, who ran an art service agency next door to the school. Bertsch was so enthusiastic about Cooper's work that they became partners in 1904 as Bertsch & Cooper. They offered a full service typeshop, including typesetting, book and magazine layouts, copy writing and design. As setting up a typeshop was an expensive business even then, they established their reputation through lettering for small local businesses and later for well known established companies.

With time, they finally came to have a full service shop, giving Cooper the opportunity to express himself in other fields, such as copy writing. "...He had a gift for language, and through its discipline a power of clear and forthright expression...His text sought to persuade, not stampede," wrote Paul Standard in *The Book of Oz Cooper* (The Society of Typographic Arts, Chicago, 1949). With this mixture of well-written texts, lettering, typography, and illustration,

he eventually became one of the leading practitioners of the Chicago Style, which also permitted him to create individuality within the bounds of conventional advertising.

Cooper came to type design almost in the same accidental way as he had done with lettering. For him "types too dexterous, like tunes too luscious, are predestined to short careers. If William Caslon had improved his types as much as they have been since then improved by others, they would not have endured, for sleek perfection palls on the imperfect persons who buy and use type."

His first type was drawn and cut in 1913 by one of Morris Fuller Benton's staff artists at American Type Founders, without Cooper's knowing it, and without his permission. It happened that Benton had been impressed by one of his advertisements done for the Packard Motor Car Company, and as the art was not signed, he had ordered the face to be redrawn and founded in metal under the name of *Packard*. When he knew that Cooper had drawn it, he paid him a fee and attributed the design to him.

It was not until 1918 that Cooper had complete control over his type design. That year he designed a face initially called *Cooper* and later renamed *Cooper Old Style* for the Barnhart Brothers & Spindler type foundry. It was the first typeface with a rounded serif. An italic version was created in 1924.

Urged by Richard N. McArthur, sales manager of BB&S, to complete the type family, Cooper designed the famous *Cooper Black* in 1922, an ultra black version of *Cooper Old Style*. This not only became an immediate success but was one of the most popular faces used in advertising during that period.

Being a refined calligrapher, he was unhappy about the popularity of this design and used to refer to it as a type

"for farsighted printers and farsighted customers." It was followed by *Cooper Hilite* (1925), a variant with simulated highlights in white. The family was further extended with *Cooper Black Condensed* and *Cooper Black Italic*, both designed in 1926.

In 1927, he received a rough with some letters drawn, probably submitted by Richard McArthur. He completed the alphabet that became *Boul Mich*. That year he also designed a cursive typeface, *Pompeian Cursive*, as an American alternative to *Bernhard Kursive*, designed by Lucian Bernhard in 1925, and recently imported.

In spite of the economic success of his typefaces, and the fact that they initiated trends, as happened with *Cooper Black* which was followed by *Goudy Heavyface* (Goudy, 1925), *Ultra Bodoni* (Benton, 1928), *Poster Bodoni* (Griffith, 1928), and *Bodoni Black* (Middleton, 1930), Cooper did not really respond to trends. Yet his last face, *Cooper Fullface*, designed in 1929, before BB&S closed, was in fact consistent with dominant styles and a precursor of *Goudy Stout*.

Cooper continued to design letterforms, although he did not design more alphabets, and to exert his efforts in defending what he had created. Seeing his work pirated in Europe and at home inspired him to fight for copyrights and to try to convince Washington that patents should be awarded for typefaces. He reproached his colleagues about copying, arguing "the way to become a master is by cultivating your own talent."

In 1939, Cooper worked on the corporate identity for the *Chicago Daily News*, one of his last assignments.

Oswald Bruce Cooper died in Chicago, Illinois in 1940, at the age of sixty-one.

COOPER OLD STYLE (1918)

Produced by Barnhart Brothers & Spindler in 1918, it is an *Oldstyle* letter with innovative rounded serifs, long ascenders, and a close fit.

The italic version, designed in 1924, retains the irregularity of hand lettering.

ABCDEFGHIJKLMNOPQRSTU
VWXYZ&abcdefghijklmnopqrst
uvwxyz$1234567890!?

THE BOOK OF OZ COOPER
(1949)

Calligraphic title page done by Cooper himself for the edition of *The Book of Oz Cooper*, published by the Society of Typographic Arts of Chicago. It is interesting to note his printer's mark, much in the style of Renaissance printers.

A BOOK YOU SHOULD OWN
(1909)

This advertisement shows sans serif lettering well before the sans serif typeface style came into vogue.

GERMAN POSTERS (1913)

In this poster Cooper has used a bold sans serif typeface quite "appropriate to the poster style of Ludwig Holwein," comments Allan Hailey.

The visual division of the vertical format into two squares is also interesting.

OZ (1949)

Personal printer's mark, much in the style of Renaissance printers, used for the edition of *The Book of Oz Cooper*, published by the Society of Typographic Arts of Chicago.

ADVERTISING TYPOGRAPHERS ASSOCIATION OF AMERICA

This is an interesting use of a contrasted image of a type compositor at work.

CLOSING VIGNETTE (1949)

Raymond F. DaBoll used this calligraphic vignette as a closing ornament to the presentation article for the edition of *The Book of Oz Cooper*, published by the Society of Typographic Arts of Chicago.

TYPE ORNAMENTS (1949)

Calligraphic type ornaments employed by Cooper in his publications.

BERTSCH & COOPER (c.1904)

One of the announcements designed by Cooper to publicize his advertising firm in partnership with Fred Bertsch.

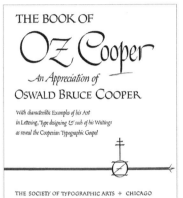

THE BOOK OF

Oz Cooper

An Appreciation of

OSWALD BRUCE COOPER

*With characteristic Examples of his Art
in Lettering, Type designing & such of his Writings
as reveal the Cooperian Typographic Gospel*

THE SOCIETY OF TYPOGRAPHIC ARTS + CHICAGO

1949

AN INTERESTING DISPLAY OF
GERMAN POSTERS
•• FROM THE COLLECTION OF ••
MISS LUCIE HARTRATH
AT THE PALETTE
& CHISEL CLUB
59 E·VAN BUREN STREET
CHICAGO·UNTIL MARCH I
YOU ARE INVITED

A BOOK YOU SHOULD OWN

THE FURNISHING of a home is a problem that confronts every man and every woman. To help solve this problem there is no book so simple, so direct, so suggestive, or so convincing as "The Furnishing of a Modest Home" by Fred H. Daniels, Director of Drawing, Newton, Mass. ❦ Every page carries conviction that the author knows what he is talking about, that his judgment is sound, and that his tastes are correct. He goes to none of the extremes of the Arts and Crafts movement. He advocates sincerity, solidity, and restfulness. He lays down principles that are sound and always have been. ❦ The book is beautifully printed, consists of 114 pages, and is profusely illustrated. ❦ The price is $1.00 per copy, postpaid.

ATKINSON, MENTZER & COMPANY

Boston, 100 Boylston St. 18 W. Washington St., Chicago
New York, 30 W. 36th St.   331 & 315 S. Preston St., Dallas

Bertsch & Cooper design advertisements, books, booklets and posters, originate type faces, and draw special ornament and decorative borders to be used along with type. Their studio is equipped to supply typography befitting their designs. 59 E·Van Buren St· Chicago

QUOUSQUE TANDEM ABUTERE, CATALINA (1924)

This is the first showing of *Cooper Oldstyle Italic* produced by the Barnhart Brothers & Spindler type foundry in Chicago, in 1924.

The text, by the way, is a classical paragraph cited by many typographers, as is the case of Giambattista Bodoni in his *Manuale Tipografico* (1788), with the error of Cooper in citing Catalina and not Catilina.

NEW QUARTERS (1927)

A 1927 advertisement for the Peoples Trust and Savings Bank of Chicago showing a free rendering of a classic letter style.

ALMANACS (1930-34)

A series of typographical designs for the almanac designed and produced by the advertising firm of Bertsch & Cooper, Chicago.

All the type was hand drawn, as was customary by Cooper.

FIFTY BOOKS OF 1923 (1923)

A two-color poster (originally red and black), designed for the American Institute of Graphic Arts annual book exhibition at the Newberry Library in Chicago.

PACKARD MOTOR CAR (c.1913)

Advertisement designed for the Packard Motor Car Company of Detroit.

The lettering was considered sufficiently original to be granted a design patent, and be eventually cut as *Packard* by the American Type Founders.

Quousque tandem abutere, Catalina, patientia nostra? quamdiu nos etiam furor iste tuus eludet? as Cicero said, and Caslon, and Bodoni, and Robert Bruce's Sons, and Hal Marchbanks.

Venerable phrases these, lending a flavor of erudition to generations of type specimens, and now finding themselves paraded in the vulgar panoply of an "advertising" type. Indignity! For this, Reader, is a kind of pre-view of a new face—Cooper Italic. The designer is conscious of its crudity, and of its irreverence for the best traditions. But he believes that there are enough good types already—that the need is for poor types that can be used! And since he admits this to be a poor one, there now remains to be found out only whether it is usable or not. Barnhart Brothers & Spindler are casting it in thirteen sizes, and the designer dares to hope they will sell enough to pay them for their trouble. He acknowledges with appreciation the services of Mr. Charles R. Murray and Mr. R. N. McArthur, of the foundry, in acting as godfathers to this and to the other members of the Cooper family, one of which—the Black— is especially in demand amongst far-sighted printers with near-sighted customers.

ANNOUNCING NEW QUARTERS

LARGER AND MORE CONVENIENT
FOR THE FRIENDS AND CUSTOMERS
OF THE

BOND AND REAL ESTATE LOAN DEPARTMENTS

OF THE

PEOPLES TRUST AND SAVINGS BANK

OF CHICAGO

EARLE H. REYNOLDS
PRESIDENT

MICHIGAN BOULEVARD AT WASHINGTON STREET

EXHIBITION
Fifty Books of 1923

Volumes selected by
the AMERICAN INSTITUTE
OF GRAPHIC ARTS
from the
publications of the year

The Newberry Library
November 21 *to* December 15, 1923
Daily, 9 A.M. *to* 10 P.M. [*except Sunday*]

All works of taste must bear a price in proportion to the skill, time, expense and risk attending their invention and manufacture. Those things called dear are, when justly estimated, the cheapest. They are attended with much less profit to the artist than those which everybody calls cheap. A disposition for cheapness and not for excellence of workmanship is the most frequent and certain cause of the decay and destruction of arts and manufactures. —RUSKIN

Packard 2-38 Coupe

Ask the man who owns one
PACKARD MOTOR CAR COMPANY DETROIT

COOPER BLACK

(1922)

An ultra black version of *Cooper Old Style*, it is a representative of Cooper's unique style. Although Cooper was never interested in trends, it started a new trend in advertising typography, as could be seen in typefaces like *Goudy Heavyface* (Goudy, 1925), *Ultra Bodoni* (Benton, 1928), *Poster Bodoni* (Griffith, 1928), and *Bodoni Black* (Middleton, 1930).

It became Barnhart Brothers & Spindler foundry's best-selling type before its merging with ATF, seven years later, and ATF's all time second-bestselling type after Goudy's *Copperplate Gothic* (1903).

Cooper Black Italic was completed in 1926, and soon joined the ranks of the bestselling types.

That same year, Cooper designed *Cooper Black Condensed*, which he described as "condensed but not squeezed."

Numerals are drawn in *Oldstyle*.

ABCDEFGHIJKLMNOPQ
RSTUVWXYZ&abcdefgh
ijklmnopqrstuvwxyz
$1234567890!?

ABCDEFGHIJKLMNOPQ
RSTUVWXYZ&abcdefghi
jklmnopqrstuvwxyz
$1234567890!?

COOPER HILITE (1925)

Part of the *Cooper Black* family, it was designed by cutting a white line which produces the effect of a highlight. It follows a practice done by Morris Fuller Benton with the *Goudy Handtooled* typeface in 1922.

It is also interesting to compare *Cooper Hilite* with *Cooper Tooled*, adapted by Sol Hess for Monotype in 1928, for the white line is placed on the opposite side. This shows how competition was practiced by type foundries who wanted to offer the same or similar designs in their catalogs.

Numerals are drawn in *Oldstyle*.

ABCDEFGHI JKLMNOPQ
RSTUVWXYZ&abcdef
hijklmnopqrstuvwxyz
$1234567890!?

BOUL MICH (1927)

Not designed by Cooper, but completed by him, it has his calligraphic touch.

The name relates to a fashion advertisement for the smart shops on Chicago's Michigan Boulevard Avenue.

It is interesting to compare it with *Broadway Engraved*, a variation of *Broadway* (Oswald Cooper), designed by Sol Hess in 1928.

ABCDEFGHIJKLMNOPQRS
TUVWXYZ&1234567890

Pompeian Cursive (1927)

This cursive typeface was drawn for Barnhart Brothers & Spindler to provide an American alternative to *Bernhard Kursive*, the popular German face designed by Lucian Bernhard in 1925, and which had been most instrumental in opening the doors to the importation of European typefaces.

Although Cooper had drawn a substantially different cursive typeface, the foundry insisted that it be more like the German face with just enough differences to make it distinctive.

Numerals are drawn in *Oldstyle*.

ABCDEFGHIJKLMN
OPQRSTUVWXYZ&
abcdefghijklmnopqrstt uvwxyz?!
$1234567890

COOPER FULL FACE (1929)

Barnhart Brothers & Spindler produced this innovative typeface shortly before the foundry was closed in 1929. Production was taken over by ATF, where it was renamed *Cooper Modern*.

According to Cooper, "it differs from *Bodoni* in that its serifs are rounded. And its main stems are drawn freely, with a suggestion of curve in almost every line. It is unusual in that it combines the sharp contrast of main and minor lines (as in *Bodoni*) with the free rendering (as in *Caslon*) of pen drawn characters."

The present digitization of the typeface was developed by David Farey in 1991 and released one year later by ITC.

**ABCDEFGHI
JKLMNOPQ
RSTUVWXY
Z&abcdefghi
jklmnopqrst
uvwxyz$123
4567890!?**

BITSTREAM OZ HANDICRAFT

Although not cast as a typeface, this Bitstream digital version is based on Cooper's lettering used on the ad found on page 117, designed for the advertising firm he established with Fred Bertsch.

Numerals are drawn in *Oldstyle*.

ABCDEFGHIJKLMNOPQRSTUVWXYZ&abcdef
ghijklmnopqrstuvwxyz$1234567890!?

Born in East Orange, New Jersey, in 1917, Freeman Craw was enthusiastic about art from an early age. Initially interested in portrait painting, he was not satisfied with the prevalent school of fashionable portraiture.

While attending Cooper Union in New York, where he studied from 1935 to 1939, he considered a shift to illustration. Again, he was not impressed with the style that was in vogue. By the end of his senior year, he felt that graphic design offered a unique medium for artistic expression. He then began to see the possibilities in letterforms, particularly the negative portion of them, as can be seen in many of his designs.

Upon graduation, he became a designer with the American Colortype Company in New York City until 1943, when he joined the Tri-Arts Press, also in New York City, as art director. In 1958, he became vice president of the company, being responsible for most of the interesting printed material in the United States. In 1968, he left the company to establish Freeman Craw Design as a specialist in design-for-printing.

He has designed several typefaces for the American Type Founders, such as **Craw Clarendon**, **Craw Clarendon Book** and **Craw Clarendon Condensed** (1955-60), **Craw Modern** (1958-64), and **Ad Lib** (1961). For Photo-Lettering, Inc., and for other film type systems he has designed **Classic**, **Chancery Cursive**, **Craw Canterbury**, as well as **CBS Didot** and **CBS Sans** for use on CBS television and in print. He has received special commissions for

architectural graphics (such as the alphabets designed for the CBS building), marks, logos, etc. for IBM and other companies.

He has designed promotional material for Mohawk Paper Mills and publications for the College Board, and is busy in diverse projects, such as designing new typefaces.

He considers himself "a hopeless Francophile," heavily influenced by the School of Paris painters like Degas, Braque, Picasso, and particularly Modigliani. He has traveled through France often, just to "soak it all in." His travel journals reflect his constant awareness of design.

While Craw was discussing the responsibilities of an art director with Eugene M. Ettenberg in an article for **American Artist**, the question arose as to how one identifies "a good idea." He immediately came to the word **appropriate**, for he thinks his continual search..." is for appropriate type, paper, design, and color."

Photography has also engaged Craw's attention. In an award-winning brochure designed to promote **Poseidon**, a line of Mohawk paper, he combined a fascinating series of his photographs of weatherworn posters and billboards that he had discovered in various cities in France. The abstract segments are not just intriguing but aesthetically good pieces of art.

German type director and designer Olaf Leu shares Freeman Craw's concerns about the future, as to what they feel are the inadequacies of

typographic design instruction in our universities and art schools.

He has had one man exhibitions of his work at Cooper Union, New York City in 1953; at the Society of Typographic Arts, Chicago, in 1956; at the BBDO advertising agency, New York City; at the American Type Founders under a traveling exhibition in 1961; in London at the Society of Typographic Designers and The Royal College of Art; and at the Rochester Institute of Technology in 1984; among others.

He is represented in the graphic art collections of the New York Museum of Modern Art and the Cooper-Hewitt Museum. He has given lectures and has served as judge in exhibitions for graphic arts groups throughout the United States. He has been an active member of the New York Type Directors Club, and has served on their board of directors.

He has received many awards, including those of the American Institute of Graphic Arts, Type Directors Club Medal, the Frederic W. Goudy Award, Honorary degree from Cooper Union, the Match Book Industry, the Direct Mail Advertising Association, Financial World Annual Reports and Fifty Books of the Year.

He is also an honorary member of the Gutenberg Museum in Mainz, Germany.

CRAW CLARENDON
(1955)

In 1955, ATF commissioned Freeman Craw to develop an American version of the *Clarendon* letter. Since then, it has been quite influential in advertising design and architectural graphics.

ABCDEFGHIJKLMNOPQRS TUVWXYZ&abcdefghijklmn opqrstuvwxyz$1234567890

"SIT DOWN AND FEED..."

Frontispiece designed for the Society of Scribes calligraphic calendar, for which the theme was food and drink.

TYPE DIRECTORS CLUB

Device taken from the announcement designed for an early Type Directors Club lecture series.

IDEAS

Lettering for *Vogue* magazine.

TRI-ARTS PRESS

Mark designed for the Tri-Arts Press, typographers and printers. This design preceded the design of the *Craw Modern* typeface.

**JOURNAL
OF COMMUNICATION ARTS**

Trademark designed for the *Journal of Communication Arts*. This mark preceded the design of the *Craw Clarendon Condensed* typeface. The inner spaces are colored for emphasis.

CHICAGO SYMPHONY

Symbol mark designed for the Chicago Symphony, Chicago Orchestral Society.

SPECIMENS

Book spine and title page lettering designed for a Stevens-Nelson's catalog of handmade papers.

NOËL (1976)

Greeting card designed for 1976. The screened letters allow the word **NOËL** to be read from front to back.

PAGE 2

Typographical illustration designed for a twenty-four page booklet.

SPECIMENS

MOHAWK SUPERFINE

Cover for the Mohawk Paper Mills specimen portfolio.

NUANCE

Product logo designed for the Mohawk Paper Company.

ROCKEFELLER UNIVERSITY REUNION 1959-1984 (1984)

Typographical logo designed for the Rockefeller University Reunion in New York.

The exchange of a letter for a number allows for a double reading.

JAP

Monogram designed for personal stationery.

MG

A monogram designed for dancer Martha Graham.

GOOO (Craw) **MODERN** (1958)

A mail piece designed for ATF to present *Craw Modern* typeface.

MPC

Monogram designed for personal stationery.

BIRTH OF A TYPEFACE (1964)

This folder cover design, used to display a Mohawk cover paper, served as a launch pad for the design of the *Craw Modern Italic* typeface.

Overprinting of large lowercase "**c**" creates other colors and shapes.

COLLEGE BOARD REVIEW (1985)

Cover design for the 137th issue of the *College Board Review* magazine.

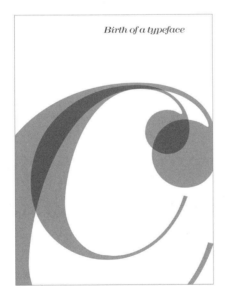

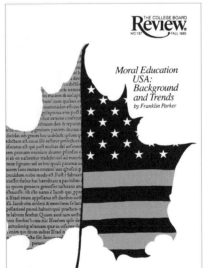

CRAW CLARENDON BOOK (1956)

Freeman Craw proposed both *Clarendon* and *Craw Clarendon Book* at the same time.

The *Book* weight was cut a year after the heavier version.

ABCDEFGHIJKLMNOPQRS
TUVWXYZ&abcdefghijklm
nopqrstuvwxyz$1234567890

CRAW MODERN (1958)

A contemporary interpretation of the modern roman style, it is a very wide typeface, with large x-height and short ascenders and descenders, otherwise somewhat the character of a nineteenth century modern roman.

Craw Modern Bold followed, and in 1964 *Craw Modern Italic* was introduced.

The similarities of form between this and the *Craw Clarendon* face do not make these type designs belong to the same family.

ABCDEFGHIJKLMNO
PQRSTUVWXYZ&abc
defghijklmnopqrstuvw
xyz$1234567890?!#%()

ABCDEFGHIJKLMNO
PQRSTUVWXYZ&abc
defghijklmnopqrstuvw
xyz$1234567890?!#%()

CRAW CLARENDON CONDENSED (1960)

Craw designed a condensed version of *Craw Clarendon* to supply the need in advertising for a heavy condensed face that could be used in narrow spaces, maintaining its visual impact and legibility.

ABCDEFGHIJKLMNOPQRSTUVWXY
Z&abcdefghijklmnopqrstuvwxyz
$1234567890

AD LIB (1961)

Freeman Craw designed this irregular, novel gothic letter, in response to the newfound freedom of photo-lettering techniques. The effect was achieved by cutting the letters out of a black sheet of material with a razor blade.

The original font presented alternate designs for a number of characters as an integral and natural part of this informal letter style.

Unlike conventional typefaces, *Ad Lib* alternate characters were included to avoid repetition of the same identical letter in a word or headline.

ABCDEFGHIJKLMNOPQ RSTUVWXYZ&abcdefghi jklmnopqrstuvwxyz $1234567890!?#%()

CBS DIDOT (1966)

When CBS constructed a new headquarters building in 1966, designed by architect Eero Saarinen, Lou Dorfsman, who was then director of design for the entire CBS Corporation since 1964 supervised all aspects of the typographic information and sign system of the buildings.

CBS Didot typeface not only became an accompanying typeface to the famous "eye," designed by William Golden in 1951, but, since then, part of the Corporate Identity Program.

The classic, early nineteenth-century letter style contrasts beautifully with the blackness of the symbol.

ABCDEFGHIJK LMNOPQRSTUV WXYZ

CBS SANS (1966)

This sans serif typeface was also designed to accompany the CBS symbol in the ad layouts, and for sign system inside the headquarters building.

The typeface, as designed by Freeman Craw, did not include a lowercase alphabet.

ABCDEFGHIJKLM NOPQRSTUVWX YZ1234567890

Born in Stamford, Connecticut in 1828, Theodore Low De Vinne was the son of a Londonderry Irish immigrant, who taught him Greek and Latin. He started at the age of fourteen as an apprentice of typography in the office of the *Gazette*, in Newburgh, New York.

In 1847, he went to New York City, and, after working in various printing offices, he began in 1849 as a type compositor for Francis Hart of Francis Hart & Co., one of the leading printers in the city.

In 1850, he was promoted to foreman of the composing room, and in 1859, Hart made him junior partner. Thus, he was aware of any advancement in printing.

Printer, researcher, and type connoisseur, De Vinne was a leader of the typographic printing movement in the United States during the second half of the nineteenth century, being recognized as the greatest scholar-printer of this country.

As well as being a practical printer, he was a distinguished writer, and by 1856, he had begun to write about printing, not only on the economic aspects of the business, but on the aspects of typographic style and the history of the craft.

Around 1860, he gathered New York printing house owners to form a union named "Typothetæ," which by 1887, merged as "United Typothetæ," naming De Vinne as their first president. In 1864, he created the first patronage syndicate of the United States. In and out of these groups, he worked for years to make printing a profitable craft, and the relations between employers and employees as harmonious as possible within the changing industrial conditions.

In 1873, contrary to Hart's timid advice, De Vinne started to print the juvenile magazine *St. Nicholas*, whose performance of literary and artistic quality was then unsurpassed. This was soon followed by *Scribner's Monthly*, which later became the *Century Magazine*. When Hart died

in 1877, De Vinne purchased the whole of the company and changed the name to Theodore Low De Vinne & Co.

In 1881, as the publishers of the *Century Magazine* demanded a degree of excellence in its printing then unknown, De Vinne was able to install, with their cooperation, heavier presses, and to start using hard packing, coated paper (invented by S. D. Warren & Company of Boston, largely at his insistence), fine-line wood engravings, and later on halftone plates. These innovations placed him as a leading printer in the United States. The magazine also allowed him to project his ideas about printing.

In 1884, he was cofounder of The Grolier Club in New York, a bibliophile association which gathered publishers, known artists and great lovers of the printed word. He was engaged, that same year, in its first publication, a reprint of the *Star Chamber Decree of 1637 Concerning Printing*.

Of the fifty-five Club publications issued before his death in 1914, forty-five were printed at the De Vinne Press. He was also the author and editor of some of them, such as *Title Pages as seen by a Printer* (1901), and *Notable Printers of Italy during the Fifteenth Century* (1910).

In 1894, because of his dissatisfaction with the types then available for magazine and bookwork, De Vinne commissioned Linn Boyd Benton to design and cut *Century Roman* typeface for use in the *Century Magazine*. As he wrote later, "Readers of failing eyesight rightfully ask for types that are plain and unequivocal, that reveal the entire character at a glance, and are not discerned with difficulty by body marks joined to hairlines and serifs that are but half seen or not seen at all." Interestingly enough, *Century* appeared much before *Cheltenham*, designed by Bertram Grosvenor Goodhue in 1904, which shared the same concern for better reading typefaces.

Benton's type design shows the influence of the modern typefaces

then popular, but without the hairlines of the true modern face. Its popularity has made *Century* an enduring typeface that has been expanded through the years, thanks to the work of people like Morris Fuller Benton, who designed eighteen variations of the face; Sol Hess; Charles E. Hughes; and finally Tony Stan, who between 1975 and 1980 brought the basic design up-to-date.

When De Vinne retired in 1908, type was mechanically set on Linotype machines, high-speed cylinder and rotary presses operated by electricity had been installed, and more than three hundred employees worked in the business. The firm was renamed as The De Vinne Press, managed by his son, Theodore B. De Vinne. It finally closed in 1923.

As a printer, De Vinne reached the highest standards of his time. Among his best-known works we may find the early books of The Grolier Club, *The Book of Common Prayer*, the "Jade" book, and *The Century Dictionary*, in ten volumes (1889-1906), considered by many critics as his finest achievement.

As a writer, he is even better remembered through such works as *The Profits of Book Composition* (1864); *The Printers' Price List* (1869); *The Invention of Printing* (1876); *Historic Printing Types* (1886); *Christopher Plantin* (1888); *The Practice of Typography*, in four volumes (1900, 1901, 1902, 1904); *Title Pages as seen by a Printer* (1901); *Plain Printing Types* (1902), an account of his long study of type founders' specimen books; *Types of the De Vinne Press* (1907); and *Notable Printers of Italy during the Fifteenth Century* (1910).

Theodore Low De Vinne died in New York City, in 1914, at the age of eighty-six.

CENTURY ROMAN
(1894)

Designed in 1894 by Linn Boyd Benton at the request of Theodore Low De Vinne, publisher of *The Century Magazine*, it was planned as a more readable typeface, and as a substitute for the design previously used. Originally made as a foundry type, it was handset for several years.

ABCDEFGHIJKLMNOPQRST UVWXYZ&abcdefghijklmnopq rstuvwxyz$1234567890!?

Born in Forio d'Ischia, Italy in 1943, Antonio DiSpigna immigrated with his family to the United States, where he studied and first graduated from New York City Community College in 1964, and then from Pratt Institute in 1967.

Soon after he finished his studies, he took a job with Bonder & Carnase, Inc., but after two years, he joined the Lubalin & Carnase, Inc. studio. His talents as a designer were mainly employed in all areas of visual communications, such as corporate identity, point-of-sale, packaging, advertising, editorial design, architectural design, sales promotion, television, films, magazine, and book publishing.

In 1973 he opened his own design office, where he worked independently until 1978, when he joined Herb Lubalin Associates Inc., as vice president and partner. In 1974, while working there, he designed with Herb Lubalin **ITC Serif Gothic**. "The letterform was originally conceived as a logo suggestion for a French shirt company, designed by Lubalin and sketched by Tom Carnase. It was turned down. So, during a slow period one time, I went back to the logo to develop other letters. We thought it was an interesting idea, to take a sans serif letterform and add minute serifs to it, but at the same time to give it an identity of its own. Designed as a display face, it is still legible and useable at small point sizes, but I would not set an encyclopedia with it."

In those days, alphabets were pumped out so fast (the **Serif Gothic** family was produced in a deadline-pressured nine months time), that there was not much opportunity to think of a good name. To DiSpigna it is a misnomer, although he thinks a name doesn't mean too much anyway.

In several of Herb Lubalin's layouts for **U&lc** (**Upper & lowercase**), the 1973 in-house publication of ITC, DiSpigna, like Tom Carnase, found a rich field for his sensitive Spencerian hand lettering. Several of Lubalin's ideas and sketches came into graphic form through DiSpigna's hands.

In 1980, he resumed independent activities as Tony DiSpigna, Inc., while also teaching. He is a full time professor at Pratt Institute and an associate professor in the New York Institute of Technology, currently teaching packaging, typography, typographics, visual communications, editorial and book design. He has also taught at the School of Visual Arts, and given seminars at several institutes, such as Syracuse University, George Washington University, the Design Centre (England), and the College of Art & Design (Ireland).

For him there is a definite relationship between human characters and the characters of an alphabet. "There is a definite connection," he says, "even in the nomenclature. Typeface. Body copy. Headline." To him, "A ligature is not just a ligature. It's like two people getting married. Sometimes it's a beautiful marriage. Sometimes it results in a poor relationship."

Logos have been the beginning point for other typefaces; including **ITC Avant Garde Gothic**, designed for the magazine of the same name by Lubalin and Carnase. A logo, by its nature, requires a unique look. That is why DiSpigna says that the evolution from logo to alphabet is not unusual, as long as the design serves as a viable display face. While Lubalin would verbalize or rough sketch the concept for a logo, it was usually up to him or Carnase to pin it down. "...One of us was the left

hand; the other was the right hand. One without the other couldn't have evolved anything... Not that Herb wasn't able to pin it down in letterform. He knew what we were capable of doing and relied on us to develop it while he would be going on to other things."

He feels strongly that a good designer will always have an eye for good typography. A poor designer can always be spotted by his misuse of type. He likes tight spacing; for him characters should be touching, especially in a logo. One of the things he reminds his students is that a person doesn't stop to read individual letters in a logo, like **Coca-Cola**. The reader sees only an image. Spacing is a matter of preference in text use, for display it definitely should be tight.

Among his typefaces we may find **ITC Serif Gothic** (designed with Lubalin in 1974); **Playgirl**, designed in the 1970s for **Playgirl** magazine; **Fattoni**, designed in 1968 but still not released; **ITC Lubalin Graph** (also with Lubalin, in 1974); some exclusive typefaces, such as **Channel WNET 13**, designed for Public Television Stations in New York; and various corporate typefaces for the Coca-Cola Company and the Louis Dreyfus Corporation.

He has also participated in exhibitions of lettering and typography in New York in 1969, and has won several awards, including a silver award at the "One Show" and three merit awards from the Type Designer's Club in 1973; creativity awards from Art Direction in 1974 and 1975; four certificates of excellence from the American Institute of Graphic Arts (AIGA) in 1974; an excellence award from New York Type Directors' Club; and "Andy" awards in 1975 and 1976.

ITC SERIF GOTHIC
(1974)

This was designed in collaboration with Herb Lubalin, after the latter felt the need for a typeface that filled the gap between Gothic and Roman.

It was first used in 1966, in a bold version, to redesign a poster for a page of *U&lc* magazine. DiSpigna later added the regular weights.

ABCDEFGHIJKLMNOPQRSTUV
WXYZ&abcdefghijklmnopqrst
uvwxyz$1234567890!?

CAVALLUCCIO MARINO (1984)

Symbol designed for the "Sea Horse" Beach Restaurant, in his hometown Forio d'Ischia, Italy.

LOVE & FRIENDSHIP (1983)

Symbol designed to express love and friendship.

PEACE DOVE (1981)

Spencerian symbol designed for a writers' organization against nuclear proliferation.

ECCO (1987)

Graphic identification designed for Ecco Computer Store.

USA (1976)

Design for a postage stamp celebrating the Bicentennial of the United States (1776-1976).

POSEIDON GARDENS (1984)

Symbol designed for Poseidon Gardens, a summer resort on the island of Ischia, Italy.

EVE (1970)

Proposed symbol designed for *Playgirl* magazine.

CHRISTMAS (1976)

Calligraphy executed for a personal Christmas card.

**SARAH VAUGHAN
SONGS OF THE BEATLES** (1970)

Spencerian script for a record album cover design for Atlantic Records.

YELLOW PAGES (1979)

Cover designed for the New York "Yellow Pages" telephone book.

**SOME THINGS YOU DECIDE
WITH YOUR HEART** (1978)

Sketch of a headline done for a proposed advertising campaign promoting Oneida products catering to newlyweds for David Deutsch Advertising Agency.

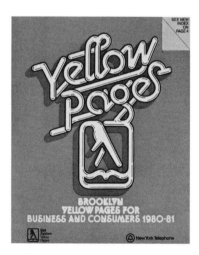

Born in Martinsville, Ohio in 1880, the son of a doctor, William Addison Dwiggins's interest in art took him at the age of nineteen to Chicago. There, at the Frank Holme School of Illustration, he studied lettering with Frederic W. Goudy and illustration with Frank and Joseph Leyendecker, illustrators of the *Saturday Evening Post.*

After a brief experience as a newspaper printer in rural Ohio, he followed Goudy to Hingham, Massachusetts, where he helped him at his Village Press. When Goudy moved to New York, Dwiggins stayed in Hingham. Although he had, for many years, a studio in Boston, he lived the rest of his life in Hingham.

In addition to his lettering and illustration, Dwiggins also brought his design sensibilities to the art of puppetry, for which he served as playwright (he wrote three marionette plays), director, stage manager, scenic designer, inventor, and creator of marionettes. On performing nights the first floor of his studio was transformed into a theater.

His early associations with Frederic W. Goudy and Daniel Berkeley Updike –as well as his fifteen-year career in advertising, which included work for Strathmore Paper Company and for *Direct Advertising* (the organ of the Paper Makers Advertising Club), plus a brief experience as acting director of Harvard University Press during World War I– provided him with a basic understanding of book design, paper, and printing.

In 1923, he met New York publisher Alfred A. Knopf, for whom he started to design books three years later. After 1928 he became Knopf's principal designer. Over the years Dwiggins completed more than 280 books, establishing a house style through a harmonious use of page design, ornamentation, illustration, binding, cover, and jacket design. He also introduced the practice of adding in the colophon a note on the type in which the book was set.

In *The Structure of a Book*, written as the introduction to the 1926 AIGA *Fifty Books of the Year* exhibition catalog, Dwiggins stated, "The text of the book is the thing for which everything else exists. In it are involved all the questions of paper, type, and page design. The design of the book begins here and works outward to the cover."

Besides Knopf, who was his main employer, Dwiggins also designed for The Limited Editions Club (two of their books were included by *AIGA Fifty Books of the Year* exhibition), and for Random House, where he designed his most celebrated book, H. G. Wells' *The Time Machine* in 1931. In it he was innovative with the introduction of the double-page title spread, and the printing of the text in two colors.

In time, Dwiggins became a successful and respected illustrator besides being a graphic designer –a term he reputedly coined in 1922– an accomplished type designer and a design critic. Through his work, especially for Knopf, and his writings, Dwiggins, more than any other designer (including Bruce Rogers) is responsible for the increased quality of American trade book design since World War I.

His *Extracts from an Investigation into the Physical Properties of Books as They Are at Present Published*, written anonymously for the fictitious Society of Calligraphers in 1919, some years before he started to work for Knopf, proved so effectively that book design, despite the Great Depression, improved notably in America.

Many of his books and jackets were decorated with his characteristic calligraphy, often drawn with a flexible nib –he was one of the pioneers of the twentieth-century revival of calligraphy– as well as with ornaments and vignettes through a unique confluence of Oriental and Mexican motifs quite harmonious with Art Deco decorative elements and Cubist sculpture compositions.

Despite his interest in lettering Dwiggins did not design a typeface until 1928, when the publication of his

Layout in Advertising, the product of twenty years in the field, prompted an invitation from Harry L. Gage of the Mergenthaler Linotype Company.

Accepting Gage's challenge to design a better sans serif than *Futura* (1927), and the other then-fashionable types, Dwiggins answered with trial drawings of *Metro*. The design was accepted, cut, and released (with *Metrolite* and *Metroblack* as additional weights) in 1929-30.

Dwiggins's association with Linotype lasted twenty-seven years until his death. He had a lasting friendship with Chauncey H. Griffith, vice president in charge of typographical development, with whom he frequently discussed problems of the legibility and readability of text types.

Dwiggins liked his work and liked to work. "I like to design type. Like to jiggle type around and see what comes out. Like to design ornaments. Like paper. Like ink on paper. Like bright colors. Handicapped by clock," he once said.

Electra, his first book type, a crisp and clear roman typeface, appeared in 1935. Four years later, Dwiggins produced *Caledonia*, his most successful typeface, a mixture of *Scotch Roman* and *Bulmer* typefaces. It has an elegant appearance with a large x-height. Although he did not cut his own types, he made careful pattern drawings, working with ten-inch tall size letters.

For Linotype, Dwiggins designed several typefaces, many of which did not go beyond an experimental stage, although they were used in limited editions books. He designed *Eldorado*, the last of his sixteen type designs to be released during his lifetime, in 1953. *Falcon* was issued by Linotype, after his death in 1961.

William Addison Dwiggins died in Hingham, Massachusetts, on Christmas Day 1956, at the age of seventy-six.

METROLITE (1930)

Designed to fill a perceived need for a good advertising sans serif, *Metrolite* follows the classical proportions employed by Eric Gill's *Gill Sans* and Edward Johnston's *London Underground Sanserif.*

Unfortunately the design was issued too late and failed to supplant *Futura* (1927) or *Gill Sans* (1929).

ABCDEFGHIJKLMNOPQRST
UVWXYZ&abcdefghijklmnop
qrstuvwxyz$1234567890!?

TRAVELS (1948)

Double-page spread from Jonathan Swift's book *Travels into Several Remote Nations of the World of Lemuel Gulliver*, printed by the Peter Pauper Press in 1948. Both the illustration and initial are by Dwiggins.

It is also worth mentioning the use of two elongated horizontal formats in contrast to a serene vertical rectangle in the middle, and the subtle ornamental borders which harmonize with the graphic quality of the illustrations.

BOOK SPINES (1931-1934)

Dwiggins always took complete care of the graphic presentation of a book, designing all its components: cover, binding, title page, illustrations, initials, and vignettes.

"Shelf backs are merely splashes of gold arranged musically. The designer's eye is on the effect they will make in the bookcase...books as house furnishings."

These book spines were designed for several books published by Alfred A. Knopf.

VIGNETTE (1937)

A particular characteristic of Dwiggins was his care in giving the necessary feeling to an illustration.

For *A Short History of Music* by Alfred Stein he designed an image in the manner of the figures on Greek vases.

INITIALS (1948)

These initials, based on *Electra*, were designed for the edition of Jonathan Swift's book *Travels into Several Remote Nations of the World of Lemuel Gulliver*, published by the Peter Pauper Press in 1948. It is interesting to note the great influence that Mexican reliefs played upon Dwiggins illustrations.

TRAVELS (1948)

Illustrations elaborated for Jonathan Swift's book *Travels into Several Remote Nations of the World of Lemuel Gulliver*, printed by the Peter Pauper Press in 1948. The care with which Dwiggins harmonized borders and illustrations is exemplified in each illustrated page of the book.

THE TIME MACHINE (1931)

Frontispiece designed for H. G. Wells's book *The Time Machine*, published by the Random House, New York, in 1931. Besides the creative use of the double page spread, where he reorders information, it is interesting to see the influence of African, Cuban, Oriental, and Egyptian art in the ornamental elements he places around the page.

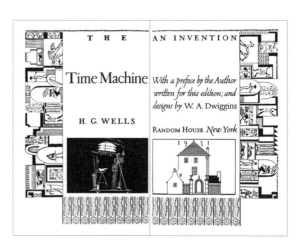

PAPER CURRENCY (1932)

Binding designed for *Towards a Reform of the Paper Currency* particularly in its point of its design. It was printed in turquoise blue and black.

THE BARLY FIELDS (1938)

This simple cover for Robert Nathan's *The Barly Fields*, exhibits Dwiggins interest for various styles: an ikebana flower arrangement with a cubist sculpture approach. It is interesting to note the inclusion of the initials R N (Robert Nathan), on the vase, a Dwiggins custom, as may be seen in other works.

ALFRED A. KNOPF'S PUBLISHER'S DEVICES (1936-1942)

In these three variations (1936-1939-1942) of the Alfred A. Knopf's publisher's devices using the Borzoi dog (originally designed by Rudolf Ruzicka in 1922), we see Dwiggins's interest in a live graphic image.

VIGNETTES

An example of the stencil vignettes with which Dwiggins continually complemented printed pages.

AN OMNIBUS (1952)

Cover illustration for the binding of Stephen Crane's *An Omnibus*.

VIGNETTE (1952)

Vignette for Stephen Crane's *An Omnibus*. Dwiggins used to incorporate the author's name within the illustration he designed for a book.

A NEW DICTIONARY OF QUOTATIONS (1942)

Title page illustration executed for H. L. Mencken's *A New Dictionary of Quotations*.

THE CHARLATANRY OF THE LEARNED (1937)

Binding illustration executed for Johann Burkhard Mencken's book *The Charlatanry of the Learned*.

THIS IS MY BELOVED (1945)

Cover illustration for Walter Benton's book *This is My Beloved*, as seen in a later edition published by Alfred A. Knopf in 1970.

Note the contrast between the pen and the brush-executed ornaments.

DEFY THE FOUL FIEND (1934)

Binding illustration for John Collier's book *Defy the Foul Fiend*, published by Alfred A. Knopf in 1934.

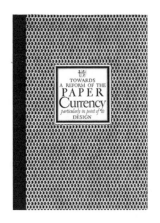

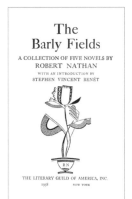

METROBLACK (1930)

Metroblack was the second face designed by Dwiggins to add to the *Metro* family. Less mechanical than the European imports, they were promoted as being less monotonous and more legible.

ABCDEFGHIJKLMNOPQRST
UVWXYZ&abcdefghijklmnop
qrstuvwxyz$1234567890!?

METROMEDIUM (1930)

Metromedium was the third typeface of the *Metro* family. It completed the set of typographical hierarchies. The *Metro* series was employed to set headlines of the *San Francisco Chronicle*.

ABCDEFGHIJKLMNOPQRST
UVWXYZ&abcdefghijklmnop
qrstuvwxyz$1234567890!?

ELECTRA (1935)

More than any other of his typefaces, *Electra* reflects the warmth and distinction of Dwiggins' personal lettering. The intent was to work into *Electra*'s letter shapes, wherever possible, some of the twentieth-century spirit: electricity, high-speed steel, streamlined curves. *Electra* innovated type design introducing an inclined roman instead of italic.

Cut by Linotype for mechanical typesetting, it was used in the text of the *San Francisco Chronicle*.

ABCDEFGHIJKLMNOPQRS
TUVWXYZ&abcdefghijklmnop
qrstuvwxyz$1234567890!?

ABCDEFGHIJKLMNOPQRST
UVWXYZ&abcdefghijklmnopqrs
tuvwxyz$1234567890!?

CALEDONIA (1938)

Caledonia was inspired by the work of Scottish type founders, and in particular by a transitional typeface known as *Bulmer*, cut by William Martin for William Bulmer around 1790.

Named for the ancient name of Scotland, it has touches of both Bulmer's *Martin* and Wilson's *Scotch*, and also "something of the simple, hardworking, feet-on-the-ground quality of *Scotch Modern*."

It was cut by Linotype for mechanical typesetting. The digital version was designed by David Berlow in 1979, and issued as *New Caledonia*.

ABCDEFGHIJKLMNOPQR
STUVWXYZ&abcdefghijklmn
opqrstuvwxyz$1234567890!?

ELDORADO (1953)

Dwiggins's last type design, *Eldorado* was developed through the war years, completed in 1951, and commercially issued by Linotype in 1953. It was suggested by an uncommonly compact and distinctive eighteenth-century face used in Madrid by the Spanish printer Antonio de Sancha.

In its anatomy, *Eldorado* retains something of the treatment of curves, arches and junctions, as well as flavor, of the Spanish typographic tradition.

David Berlow designed *FB Eldorado* digital version, in 1993.

Numerals are drawn in *Oldstyle*.

ABCDEFGHIJKLMNOPQRST
UVWXYZ&abcdefghijklmnopqr
stuvwxyz$1234567890!?

INITIÁLS (1930-1936)

These four complete alphabets were designed as initials for the use of the Plimpton Press.

In each one we can appreciate Dwiggins's masterly handling of structure and style. He moves easily from a classic letter to a calligraphic form in the German style, or to a letter composed of his own graphic elements; but in the end, all show Dwiggins's way of solving a problem: through calligraphy, and the use of a pen.

ÁBCDEFGHIJKLMN
OPQRSTUVWXYZ

ABCDEFGHIJKLMN
OPQRSTUVWXYZ

ABCDEFGHIJKLMN
OPQRSTUVWXYZ

ABCDEFGHIJKL
MNOPQRSTUV
WXYZ

Born in New York in 1970, Tobias Frere-Jones was raised in a family of writers and printers. By the end of his high school sophomore year at St. Ann's in Brooklyn, New York, he became obsessed with the concept of drawing letters. They filled hundreds of notebook pages, on which he drew during class. "Somewhere between high school and deciding where I would go to college, drawing typefaces took over all the other disciplines."

At fourteen, he was already exhibiting paintings, sculpture, and photography in New York City, and at sixteen, he designed his first alphabet, and won the best-of-age category in The Type Shop of New York's "Alphabet Design Contest" in 1986.

Clear about his goals, he enrolled in 1988 in Rhode Island School of Design's graphic design program, expecting to become, within four years, a type designer. But as it happened, he learned all about type, how to spec, and use them, but not how to draw them.

So he entered Inge Druckery's class, where he had to draw inscriptional letters, plus an independent course where he assigned himself the task of drawing a serif typeface, based on Nicolas Jenson's 1470 roman, by means of the Ikarus type design program, the first to make digitizing type possible. As his advisor, Krzysztof Lenk, could not go beyond Frere-Jones' achievements, so he arranged for Matthew Carter, then chief designer at Bitstream, Inc. in Boston, to complete the junior year evaluation.

During a travel course to Europe, he had the opportunity to meet Erik Spiekermann at FontShop International in Berlin, and to show him his second complete alphabet, Dolores, which he had drawn for his brother's rock band. He was so enthusiastic about it that there was an immediate contract and production. Since then, the typeface has done well commercially.

He also interviewed for an internship with David Berlow at the Font Bureau digital type foundry in Boston, and was offered the position. Knowing Dolores, Berlow was interested in developing new type projects.

This is how the adaptation of the letterforms used on parking garage receipts gave form to Garage Gothic.

Since he still had to finish his senior year at Rhode Island, Frere-Jones had to split his time between working in Boston at Font Bureau, and at Providence on his thesis. While he was assigned to develop full character sets from original headline designs by Neville Brody, he started working on his project, in which he focused on the developing of four typefaces. One of these, Reactor, was finally developed for FUSE #7, digital magazine in 1993, at Brody's invitation.

Upon graduation in 1992, Frere-Jones was hired as Senior Designer by the Font Bureau type foundry, and he began to work on his third typeface, Nobel, based on the work by S. H. De Roos with a cross between Kabel and Futura. This work highlights an important distinction between influence and copy, and between revival and originality.

"Starting with a historical model does not always result in a revival," points out Frere-Jones. Archipelago, for example, which bears resemblance to Hermann Zapf's Optima, began as a revival of Robert Hunter Middleton's Stellar. At the end, it includes so many different influences that it is difficult to point out the original source.

Two of the most commercially successful typefaces –created for Font Bureau– are not revivals: Garage Gothic was derived from environmental graphics –such as the parking garage receipts–, and Interstate was based on the alphabets used on Federal Highway Administration signs. Based on the manuals published by the government –the original design was developed by Travis Brooks in the 1960s– Frere-Jones created twelve versions, including Kate Moss Four and Kate Moss Ten. The final result has its own distinctive personality.

This is also the case of Pilsner, which began from a French beer label; Cafeteria, his best selling design, came from the handwriting on supermarket sale signs; Nitrogen was based on the lettering that American illustrator Ben Shahn created for the

book Once Thrice Dice; and the retail face Reiner Script, is based on a 1951 typeface by German type designer Imre Reiner.

But on the other hand, many of his faces had begun from discussions about legibility, perception, and other issues tied to type design.

He is such a hard critic of his own work that he does not release anything that has no public utility. "I try to keep myself interested and amused," he explains. "What often wins out over any concern is drawing; what I'm interested in is drawing, because I enjoy it, not because I am going to save the world of typography."

As a senior designer at the Font Bureau type foundry in Boston, he was responsible for designing (and redesigning) fonts for magazines like Rolling Stone, Business Week, and Martha Stewart's Living. He has a keen sense of what is appropriate.

In 1996, Frere-Jones joined the Yale School of Art as a Critic, where he has had the opportunity to share type concepts with Matthew Carter. Three years later, he left Font Bureau to return to New York, where he began to work with Jonathan Hoefler at The Hoefler Type Foundry, Inc. In collaboration with Hoefler he has developed several typographic projects for The Wall Street Journal, Martha Stewart's Living, Nike, Pentagram, GQ, Esquire, The New Times, Business 2.0, The New York Times Magazine, The Cooper-Hewitt Museum, The Whitney Museum, The American Institute of Graphic Arts Journal, and Neville Brody.

He has lectured at Rhode Island School of Design, Yale School of Art, Pratt Institute, Royal College of Art, and Universidad de las Americas. His work has been featured in How, ID, Page, and Print, and is included in the permanent collection of the Victoria & Albert Museum, London. His work in collaboration with Jonathan Hoefler earned the two a profile in Time Magazine.

He has designed over two hundred typefaces for retail publication, custom clients, and experimental purposes. He has expressed, "The day we stop needing new type will be the same day we stop needing new stories and new songs."

DOLORES (1989)

Frere-Jones's first commercial face, it is a freely drawn serif typeface, named after his brother's rock band.

Published by FontShop International, Berlin, in 1989, it is still commercially successful.

ABCDEFGHIJKLMNOPQR
STUVWXYZ & abcdefghijk
lmnopqrstuvwxyz?!

GARAGE GOTHIC (1992)

Based on the type employed on parking garage receipts, this typeface was developed by Frere-Jones after he obtained a position as Senior Designer at Font Bureau, Inc., under David Berlow's direction.

ABCDEFGHIJKLMNOPQRSTUVWXYZ&abcdefghijklm nopqrstuvwxyz 1234567890?!

INTERSTATE (1993)

Based on the Federal Highway Administration's "Standard Alphabets," originally designed in the 1960s by Travis Brooks, Frere-Jones developed a new type design with cleaner forms, better spacing, and punctuation.

He completed twelve versions, including a lightline set which he called *Kate Moss Four* and *Kate Moss Ten*.

Font Bureau published it in 1993.

ABCDEFGHIJKLMNOPQRST UVWXYZ&abcdefghijklmnop qrstuvwxyz$1234567890?!

ABCDEFGHIJKLMNOPQRST UVWXYZ&abcdefghijklmnop qrstuvwxyz$1234567890?!

NOBEL (1993)

Based on the designs of Dutch type designer S. H. de Roos, it is a cross between *Kabel* (Koch) and *Futura* (Renner).

On a trip to Holland, Frere-Jones discovered De Roos's obscure typeface, and through a friend, got hold of a specimen catalogue which contained every character of *Nobel* ever made. While maintaining the essential form, Frere-Jones introduced subtleties that changed the entire typeface.

ABCDEFGHIJKLMNOPQRSTU VWXYZ&abcdefghijklmnopqrstu vwxyz₤$1234567890?!

REACTOR (1993)

As part of a group of four typefaces, in which Frere-Jones was working at that time, this design was an attempt to develop a self-destroying font, one that throws off "clumps of mud two or three characters ahead and behind."

The face was introduced in Neville Brody's *FUSE #7* digital magazine in 1993.

ABCDEFGHIJKLMNOPQRSTUVW XYZ1234567890

ABCDEFGHIJKLMNOPQRSTU VWXYZ

PILSNER (1995)

Inspired by the logotype of a French beer label, this typeface is another of what Frere-Jones considers environmental graphic influences.

Some characters remind us of Berthold Wolpe's *Albertus* (1932).

ABCDEFGHIJKLMNOPQRST UVWXYZ&?!abcdefgghijklmn opqrstuvwxyz1234567890

HTF GOTHAM (2000)

Designed in collaboration with Jesse Ragan, *HTF Gotham* is an adaptation of "basic building lettering" found on a number of mundane buildings whose façades exhibit a distinctively American form of sans serif.

The shape of letterforms was often determined by the practical business of legibility, rather than by any sort of stylistic agenda –although inevitably, even the draftsman's vision of "basic building lettering" was influenced by the prevailing style of the time.

Cast iron plaques regularly feature this kind of lettering, as do countless painted signs and lithographed posters, many dating back as far as the Work Projects Administration of the 1930s.

Unlike the signage upon which it was based, *HTF Gotham* includes a lowercase, obliques, a full range of weights, and a related condensed design. Without sacrificing its appeal at display sizes, *HTF Gotham* has also been crafted as book face.

ABCDEFGHIJKLMNOPQR STUVWXYZ&abcdefghijkl mnopqrstuvwxyz $1234567890!?

ABCDEFGHIJKLMNOPQR STUVWXYZ&abcdefghijkl mnopqrstuvwxyz $1234567890!?

ABCDEFGHIJKLMNOPQR STUVWXYZ&abcdefghijkl mnopqrstuvwxyz $1234567890!?

Born in Pomfret, Connecticut in 1869, Bertram Grosvenor Goodhue derived a love and ability for drawing from his mother, who was also a painter. From her he also learned about St. Francis and St. Augustine, which probably gave the original stimulus for his love and knowledge of the Middle Ages. He had little formal schooling, but read and sketched constantly.

In 1884 he went to New York City, where he started working at Renwick, Aspinwall & Russell's architecture firm, certainly the best place in America to learn Gothic details. Goodhue soon gained a reputation as a draftsman because of his freedom of thought and great facility with pen and ink, in spite of being left-handed. At this time, Goodhue did his first book decorations, and, drawn into the companionship of a group of young men interested in good bookmaking, he produced those fine drawings that may be found in publications of Copeland & Day.

After winning several design competitions, Goodhue left Renwick's office and started to work with Cram & Wentworth in Boston, where he became head draftsman in 1899. After Wentworth died, Goodhue was taken into the partnership, and the firm became, as it remained for many years, Cram, Goodhue & Ferguson. It must have been soon after this event that he met Daniel Berkeley Updike, only a few years older and beginning to make a name for himself as a typographic designer with Houghton, Mifflin & Co., a Boston publishing house.

In 1891, and following William Morris' tradition, Goodhue designed the cover for the *Knight Errant*, a magazine that exemplified all the tendencies that were related to the Gothic revival in England and the Arts and Crafts movement. This is but one of the many examples in book design in which he was active in this period.

In 1892, Updike asked Goodhue to design borders and end-papers for an edition of *The Book of Common Prayer* that was printed by Theodore Low De

Vinne on his press in Boston. A year later, Updike started the Merrymount Press, and for *The Altar Book of the American Church*, published in 1896, and the first important work of the new press, he had Goodhue design a special typeface, which he called *Merrymount*.

For several years, Goodhue did occasional borders and cover designs for him, but his architectural work left him little time for this type of outside activity. Many of his page borders, title pages, and bookplates reveal the influence of Morris, although as time went on, Goodhue experimented with other styles.

With Cram's literary activity and fervor for a return to beauty and sacrifice in the church, and with the great craftsmanship in which Goodhue clothed his Gothic fantasy in design, their firm flourished and took the lead in ecclesiastical architecture. This is how they built All Saints' in Ashmont; St. Stephen's in Cohasset; and St. Stephen's in Fall River. Goodhue could now satisfy his urge to travel. He visited Canada, Mexico, Persia, Germany, and China, and many of his recollections are found in texts and drawings in current magazines.

In 1903 the firm won a competition to design several buildings at the U.S. Military Academy at West Point, New York, and they opened a second office in New York City with Goodhue in charge. He was primarily responsible for the Gothic design of St. Thomas' Church (1906). His architectural engagements became so pressing that the time available for book decoration was limited, yet many of his best designs were produced during these years.

Busy as he was in his architectural engagements, Goodhue found some time out for one more type venture. His good friend Ingalls Kimball, head of the Cheltenham Press in New York City, was dissatisfied with the types then in use, especially those available on the composing machines, and convinced him to collaborate on a design better suited to the needs and tastes of the time.

Goodhue's first effort in typographic design with Updike was under the inspiration of William Morris, and the *Merrymount* typeface, like Morris's *Golden Type*, was based on Nicolas Jenson's type of 1470. The same Jenson-Morris descent may be seen in *Cheltenham*, with its even color, its blunt serifs, and its dignified, well proportioned capitals. As with his architectural designs, Goodhue was not satisfied only with copying. He constantly reshaped his material to fit modern usage.

Cheltenham was commercially issued in 1904, and for a decade it was to rule the domain of ephemeral printing, as the *mission* style had dominated the domestic scene, with its austerity in furniture and architecture, product of Morris's ideas. It was also the first typeface to be available in both hand and mechanical composition (Linotype), and the first to have a complete family.

After 1913, when the architectural firm was dissolved, Goodhue became progressively independent from the past, and although some designs are within the Romanesque and the Byzantine styles, like St. Bartholomew's Church (1920) in New York City, the next buildings, like the Nebraska State Capitol (1920), and the National Academy of Sciences (1924), do not reflect a definite preceding historical style.

Goodhue was a member of The Grolier Club in New York, a bibliophile institution founded in 1884 by Theodore Low De Vinne and Robert Hoe, among others. Goodhue's unerring taste was of great value, not only in the design of the Clubhouse, of which he was the architect, but his active membership on the Publications Committee.

He delighted in black letter and in all the quirks of Latin abbreviations, as may be seen in some of the calligraphic examples, done by pen or in stone relief lettering, as in St. Bartholomew Church's façade.

Bertram Grosvenor Goodhue died in New York City in 1924, at the age of fifty-five.

MERRYMOUNT
(1895)

His first typeface, it was designed for Daniel Berkeley Updike's Merrymount Press, in Boston.

Based on the Jenson's type of 1470, it reflects the influence of William Morris's ideas. It was employed in an impressive edition of *The Altar Book of the American Church*, which established Updike's reputation as a printer.

ABCDEFGHIJKLMNOPQRST UVWXYZ&abcdefghijklmnopq rstuvwxyz$1234567890?!

INITIALS

This ornamental alphabet resembles fifteenth- and sixteenth-century French initials.

THE CHELTENHAM TYPEFACE
(1899)

This drawing, found in Frank Densman's book, *The Shaping of Our Alphabet* (1955), was taken from the files of the Mergenthaler Linotype Company. It is probably one of Goodhue's original sketches for the *Cheltenham* typeface.

Although he followed Morris's ideas, the face is more balanced and less angular than his.

INITIALS

The first two historiated initials, where Goodhue uses his *Cheltenham* type, form part of a group of initials that closely follow the ornamental letters of *The Alphabet of Death*, designed by German artist Hans Holbein, around 1530.

The other two initials, which are part of the group of initials presented in the opposite page, follows the same pattern but do not use *Cheltenham* type.

SONNETS
FROM THE PORTUGUESE

Designed for Daniel Berkeley Updike, this page layout uses his *Merrymount* typeface, with the same formal characteristics of William Morris's work.

CORNELII TACITII DE VITA

Designed for Daniel Berkeley Updike, this page layout uses his *Merrymount* typeface, created for large format pages and rough surface paper.

THE CHELTENHAM TYPE
Quaint enough will be this type lacking exactly what chiefly gives the Italic, its qualities of dash & zip; i.e. the kerns. J.
THE CHELTENHAM FONT
¶ It is in characters not differing in any material item from these (the designer trusts) that this new font will be cut.

CORNELII TACITI DE VITA ET INCIPIT FELICITER

Clarorum virorum facta tum, ne nostris quidem aetas omisit, quotiens gressa est vitium tiam recti et invidiam. pronum magisque in ad prodendam virtutis tantum conscientiae pretio ducebatur. potius morum quam adrogantiam aut obtrectationi fuit: adeo virtutes facillime gignuntur. at nunc narraturo quam non petissem incusaturus. tam cum Aruleno Rustico Paetus Thrasea, dati essent, capitale fuisse, neque in ipsos saevitum, delegato triumviris ministerio in comitio ac foro urerentur. scilicet illo senatus et conscientiam generis humani pientiae professoribus atque omni bona tum occurreret. dedimus profecto

CALLIGRAPHY (1901)

A very curious example
of Goodhue's calligraphic work,
using black letters, as curious
as is the cited text.

STEVENSON'S ATTITUDE
TO LIFE

Cover design for a hard cover edition
of John F. Genung's book,
Stevenson's Attitude to Life.

ROBERT BROWNING

Title page for a book containing
the work of English poet Robert
Browning, designed for Thomas
& Crowell publishers in New York.

As in the preceding example,
there is a marked symmetry
in the composition.

EVERY DAY'S DATE (1897)

Calligraphic title designed
for the frontispiece of a Gregorian
Calendar.

The whole text, which is drawn
using black letters, reads:
"Every Day's Date being a perpetual
Calendar according to the Gregorian
System to which is added a table
of Holy Days to the end of the
Twentieth Century compile by
Charles William Canfield Ph.D,
decorated by Bertram G. Goodhue
and printed at the press of Fleming
Schiller and Carnrick in the Steeple
Building, New York, MDCCCXCVII".

The entire text composition
is structured in the shape
of a chalice.

INITIALS

These four historiated initials
form part of another group designed
by Goodhue.

Different from the preceding page
examples, these initials resemble
sixteenth-century Renaissance style
work.

MARCUS TULLIUS CICERO

Goodhue, using his *Cheltenham*
type, designed a classic page layout
for Marcus Tulius Cicero's *Cato
Major*.

It is interesting to note the
employment of sustained capitals
on the text above.

THE LOVE-SONNETS
OF PROTEUS

Another page layout design using
his *Merrymount* typeface,
this also follows the ornamented
pages by William Morris.

MARCVS TVLLIVS CICERO DE SE-
NECTUTE *CATO MAJOR* CAP. XXII
APVD XENOPHONTEM AVTEM MO
RIENS CYRVS MAJOR HAEC DICIT:

NOLITE arbitrari, O mei carissimi
filii, me, cum a vobis discessero,
nusquam aut nullum fore. Nec
enim dum eram vobiscum animum meum videbatis, sed eum
esse in hoc corpore ex iis rebus
quas gerebam intellegebatis. Eundem igitur esse creditote, etiam si nullum videbitis. 80. Nec
vero clarorum virorum post mortem honores per-
manerent, si nihil eorum ipsorum animi efficce-
rent, quo diutius memoriam sui teneremus. Mihi
quidem persuaderi numquam potuit animos dum
in corporibus essent mortalibus vivere, cum ex-
cessissent ex eis emori; nec vero tum animum
esse insipientem cum ex insipienti corpore eva-
sisset ; sed cum omni admixtione corporis libera-
tus purus et integer esse coepisset, tum esse
sapientem. Atque etiam, cum hominis natura
morte dissolvitur, ceterarum rerum perspicuum est
quo quaeque discedat, abeunt enim illuc omnia
unde orta sunt; animus autem solus nec cum

CHELTENHAM
(1904)

The second typeface designed by Goodhue, it was done by request of Ingalls Kimball, director of the Cheltenham Press in New York City, who also supervised its production.

The original drawings were made fourteen inches high, and were subject to much experimentation and revision.

Although trial cuttings were made as early as 1899, the typeface was not completed until 1902, and commercially issued and patented in 1904 by Kimball. This, by the way, places *Cheltenham* as one of the first scientifically designed typefaces.

The thin lines were strengthened to compensate for the type of paper then in use. Ascenders were drawn unusually long, and descenders short, as the result of Goodhue's personal theories on readability.

He stated that we read lowercase characters by word shapes rather than by individual letters. He also believed that words get their characteristic shapes more from the ascending than from the descending strokes. Unfortunately, the great popularity that the face had as a display type in advertising did not include bookwork.

Cheltenham was also the first typeface to be made available both in hand type and Linotype matrices, as it was the first to be cut in all variations –regular, medium, and bold; extra condensed, regular, and wide; inline and outline.

Although the original drawings were executed by Goodhue himself, Morris Fuller Benton, as head of the type design department at ATF, collaborated in the adaptation of the original drawings to the appropriate specifications for typesetting. Many of the variations which transformed the face into the first true large type family were also done by Benton. Amounting to twenty-four different variations, they were all designed between 1904 and 1913.

Curiously enough, though many of the *Cheltenham* variations are out of use, *Cheltenham Bold* continues to be useful in printing.

For a full decade to come, *Cheltenham* was to rule the domain of ephemeral printing, as much as *mission* style dominated the domestic scene.

ABCDEFGHIJKLMNOPQR
STUVWXYZ&abcdefghijklmn
opqrstuvwxyz$1234567890!?

ABCDEFGHIJKLMNOPQRS
TUVWXYZ&abcdefghijklmnopqr
stuvwxyz$1234567890!?

ABCDEFGHIJKLMNOPQR
STUVWXYZ&abcdefghijklm
nopqrstuvwxyz
$1234567890!?

ABCDEFGHIJKLMNOPQRS
TUVWXYZ&abcdefghijklmn
opqrstuvwxyz$1234567890!?

Born in Bloomington, Illinois in 1865, son of a school inspector, Frederic William Goudy showed an early aptitude for lettering.

In 1889 he went to Chicago, where he began working as a clerk in various places, one of which was a bookshop. This job led him to the rare book department of A. C. McClurg, where he had the opportunity o study the typographical publications of English presses, such as Kelmscott, Doves, Eragny, and Vale.

In 1895, Goudy and a friend, C. Lauron Hooper, established the Booklet Press in Chicago, with equipment bought from William Bradley. Through a connection with Stone & Kimball, they came to print the the *Chap-Book*, and the press then changed its name to Camelot Press. Soon, however, Goudy sold his share, and in 1896, while waiting for a new job, he drew his first alphabet and sent it to the Dickinson Type Foundry, already a part of the American Type Founders. Besides buying it, they issued it as *Camelot*.

After working as a cashier for the *Michigan Farmer* magazine in Detroit, Goudy decided to start as a freelance lettering artist for several department stores as well as for Herbert S. Stone. By this time, Ingalls Kimball had ended his partnership with Stone, and had gone to New York to organize the Cheltenham Press. Meanwhile, Goudy had joined the teaching staff of the new Frank Holme School of Illustration as a lettering tutor.

During this time, Goudy designed several typefaces for various department stores. One of these was too expensive to be cut and cast and became the house type of his second printing venture, the Village Press, established at Park Ridge, Chicago, in 1903, in collaboration with Will Ransom.

In 1904, in spite of the clientele he had built up in Chicago, he moved to Hingham, Massachusetts, drawn by the ideals of a new craft society, which had started in this town. William Addison Dwiggins, whom he had taught at the Frank Holme School, shortly followed him.

Although Dwiggins stayed there for the rest of his life, Goudy soon found it difficult to break Bostonian social barriers and to establish himself professionally, and decided to move to New York in 1906. Unfortunately, in 1908 a fire destroyed his workshop and the Village Press' equipment. Paradoxically enough, this disaster made him turn again to type design.

In 1911, shortly after this incident, Goudy was given the opportunity to design an edition of H. G. Wells' book, *The Door in the Wall*. As he was not satisfied with the *Caslon* typeface in which proofs had been made, he suggested the design of a new typeface, which became *Kennerley Old Style*, engraved and cast by Robert Wiebking. Produced by the American Lanston Monotype and by the English Caslon, both *Forum Title* and *Kennerley Old Style* established Goudy's reputation both in America and overseas. This year he also started publishing *Typographica*.

In 1914, Goudy visited England with the idea of interesting the Caslon type foundry in a new typeface. Though they could not undertake the cutting on account of the coming war, they were interested in buying his design. Their enthusiasm so impressed Clarence Marder of ATF, who was with Goudy, that on returning to America he persuaded Robert W. Nelson, the president of ATF, to commission Goudy to produce a new typeface. *Goudy Old Style* became as successful as *Kennerley*, although one of its best variants, *Goudy Catalogue*, was actually drawn by Morris Fuller Benton.

From 1915 to 1924, Goudy taught lettering at the Art Students League in New York.

In 1918, he designed two handsome display types, *Hadriano Title* and *Goudy Open*, a decorated face based on *Goudy Modern*. That year he also started publishing the magazine *Ars Typographica*, which served him both as a teaching platform for printers and to present his new designs.

Two years later, the Lanston Monotype Company of Philadelphia, anticipating the English Monotype, asked for some advice from Goudy about their type design policies. The first results were *Garamont*, and *Italian Old Style*, one of Goudy's best text types. This association proved to be a fruitful sixteen-year relationship through which many of Goudy's typefaces were cut by and for Monotype's composing system. In 1936, Sol Hess succeeded him in his position as art director.

In 1923, Goudy moved from New York City to Marlborough-on-Hudson, where he found a larger space to make of the Village Press a foundry, both in fact and in name. He also acquired an engraving machine, and by adapting a Monotype caster, he was able to cut his own patterns and supervise every stage of the production of his types. In 1927, he cut *Deepdene*, considered a true American typeface in spite of the clear influence of the Dutch types.

In 1928, he designed *Goudy Text*, the first and perhaps the best known of a series of black letter and semi-black letter faces, on which he worked for the rest of his life. To this group also belong *Medieval* (1930) and *Franciscan* (1932), which became the Grabhorn Press private type. There were also the uncial typefaces influenced by the work of Victor Hammer, such as *Friar* (1937) and *Goudy Thirty* (1942).

Besides these special types, Goudy continued doing romans. In 1937, he cut one of the most elegant of his typefaces, *University of California Old Style*, initially designed as a private typeface. Fortunately he had sent the master patterns to Monotype, for a second fire in 1939 burned the Village Press to the ground. Once again Goudy overcame this disaster with great fortitude. The typeface was first used to print his account in *Typologia* (1940), and then in a second edition of *The Alphabet* (1942).

One year before he died, the Typophiles published, in New York, *A Half-Century of Type Design and Typography*, quite an interesting and enriching typographical autobiography.

Goudy died in Deepdene, near Marlborough-on-Hudson, New York, in 1947, at the age of eighty-two.

CAMELOT (1896)

The first of Goudy's designs, it was initially drawn without a lowercase alphabet and cast by the Dickinson Type Foundry in Boston.

In 1900, the face was produced by ATF, with a lowercase probably drawn by Joseph W. Phinney, who had worked as designer with the Dickinson Foundry.

ABCDEFGHIJKLMNOPQRS
TUVWXYZ&abcdefghijklmn
opqrstuvwxyz$1234567890!?

INITIAL (1911)

Decorated letter drawn by Goudy for the edition of H. G. Wells' book of short stories *The Door in the Wall*, published by Mitchell Kennerley in 1911.

VIGNETTE (1922)

Vignette used on the title page of *The Alphabet*, printed by Mitchell Kennerley in 1922.

THE DOOR IN THE WALL (1911)

Cover designed for H. G. Wells's book of short stories *The Door in the Wall*, printed by Mitchell Kennerley, New York, where Goudy first presented his *Kennerley Old Style* typeface.

Forum Title, also designed for this work, was used for the book's title page.

THE VILLAGE PRESS MARK (1912)

According to Goudy, this was the latest Village Press mark designed by him in 1912. It appeared on the cover of the second issue of *Typographica*, in 1912.

GOUDY'S PERSONAL SEAL (1918)

This elaborate seal first appeared in his book *The Alphabet* (1918), edited by Mitchell Kennerley.

Goudy used it again in 1946, on the cover and title page of his book *A Half-Century of Type Design and Typography, 1895-1945*, printed by Paul A. Bennett for the Typophiles, New York.

The seal was printed in red with a stem in green, simulating a flower.

HADRIANO (1910)

In 1910, while visiting the Louvre Museum in Paris, Goudy was impressed by a second century marble inscription. Based on a rubbing of four letters **R, I, A, N,** and **O**, of the name HADRIANO, he reconstructed the whole alphabet in 1918.

THE ALPHABET (1918)

Opening page from his book *The Alphabet*, printed in 1918 by Mitchell Kennerley, New York.

After seeing the decorated **A** initial designed for the first chapter, Wadsworth Parker, suggested that Goudy completed the alphabet, which appeared that same year as *Cloister Initials*.

THE INLAND PRINTER (1901)

Cover design for *The Inland Printer* magazine, July 1901, a publication of the Inland Printer Company, Chicago.

THE DOOR IN THE WALL
And Other Stories

BY
H · G · WELLS

ILLUSTRATED
WITH PHOTOGRAVURES FROM
PHOTOGRAPHS BY

ALVIN LANGDON COBURN

NEW YORK & LONDON
MITCHELL KENNERLEY
MCMXI

The Alphabet

Chapter I. *What Letters Are*

A LETTER is a symbol, with a definite shape & significance, indicating a single sound or combination of sounds, and providing a means, through grouping, for the *visible* expression of words—that is, of thoughts. Originally, letters were adaptations of natural forms employed in picture-writing, but by a process of evolution, [actually degradation,] they have become arbitrary signs with little resemblance to the symbols from which they are derived. These arbitrary shapes have passed through their periods of uncertainty and change; they have a long history and manifold associations; they are classics, and should not be tampered with, except within limits that just discretion may allow.

An ornamental form once found is repeated, the eye grows accustomed to it and expects its recurrence; it becomes established by use; it may be associated with fundamental ideas of life and nature and is handed on and on, until finally its origin and meaning are, perhaps, lost. Just so, the pictorial significance of individual letters is so deeply buried in oblivion that special study and research would be necessary to resurrect their original form or meaning—an undertaking not essential here.

Language itself, as an organized system, was of necessity slow in developing; the next steps, the approaches toward a more or less phonetic alphabet, were equally lingering; for speech existed long before it was discovered that the human voice could be represented by symbols—thus

[9]

APOLOGIA
FOR THE VILLAGE PRESS
(1933)

Initial page designed for his book *The Story of the Village Press*. Printed by the Press of the Woolly Whale, New York, it was set in *Goudy Antique*. The upper line and monogram were printed in red.

FLEURONS (1933)

According to Goudy's own words in his book, *A Half Century of Type Designs and Typography, 1895-1945*, printed by Paul A. Bennett for The Typophiles, New York, in 1946, he couldn't recall when he started to produce *fleurons* for sale. But, since "the Continental specimen is dated 1934, a number of them must have been made a year or so earlier. They are not really 'types,' but they are engraved and cast just like type."

AMPERSANDS (1936)

According to Goudy, "In 1936 I was honored by a request of the Typophiles to contribute something to its volume in preparation on *Ampersands*. I had been on making ampersands for my types for years without giving much thought to their origin, except that for the greater number of them I endeavored to convey the idea of 'et' in each." Goudy's contribution ended with the drawing and engraving of sixty-five ampersands.

ARS TYPOGRAPHICA (1934)

Cover design for Volume I, No. 4, of *Ars Typographica*, printed by the Press of the Woolly Whale, New York. Since Goudy was the editor, he used this magazine from the first issue (1918) not only as a platform for teaching typography to printers, but also as a way to present his new type designs.

DEVELOPMENT
OF THE LETTER g (1936)

In his book *The Alphabet*, published by the Grolier Club, New York, Goudy presents the development of the letter **g** from the seventh century uncials to the twentieth century (his own version). Goudy, by the way, took this graphic development from Johnston's book, *Writing and Illuminating and Lettering* (1906).

THE INLAND PRINTER (1890)

Cover design for the *Inland Printer* magazine, June edition of 1890, a publication of the Inland Printer Company, Chicago.

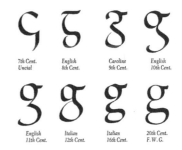

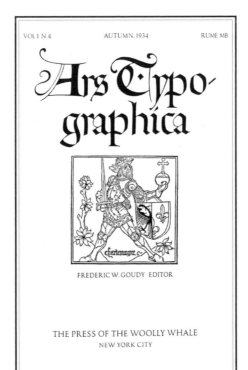

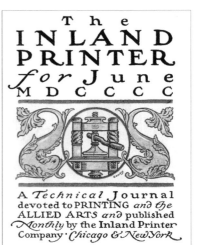

VILLAGE (1903)

Designed as a commission from Kuppenheimer & Company, a clothing store, as a private typeface for their advertising, it was never produced, due to the costs of production.

That same year, Goudy and Will Ransom established the Village Press, and after revising the drawings, it became its private typeface. Robert Wiebking cut the 16-pt size matrices.

Numerals are drawn in *Oldstyle*.

ABCDEFGHIJKLMNOPQRS
TUVWXYZ&abcdefghijklm
nopq $1234567890❦?!

COPPERPLATE GOTHIC (1903)

While Goudy was in Hingham, he designed this typeface for Marder, Luse & Company type foundry. Taken by ATF, it became an all-time best seller. It is a rather conventional gothic with minute serifs, imitative of the work of nineteenth-century engravers.

The original drawings, burned in the 1939 fire, were much treasured by Goudy. The other weights and widths were designed shortly after by Clarence C. Marder of ATF, except for the shaded version, which was designed by Morris Fuller Benton.

A curious application may be found in the **SINGER** sewing machines logotype.

ABCDEFGHIJKLMNOPQRS
TUVWXYZ&$1234567890!?

ABCDEFGHIJKLMNOPQRST
UVWXYZ&$1234567890!?

MONOTYPE No. 38E (1908)

Designed for *Life* magazine as a text type, it was set in Monotype. Goudy's lack of knowledge of the mechanical restrictions of Monotype delayed its production beyond the time needed.

Once it was released, Gimbel Brothers opened a big department store in New York and used it for their advertising.

ABCDEFGHIJKLMNOPQR
STUVWXYZ&abcdefghijklm
nopqrstuvwxyz $1234567890!?

KENNERLEY OLD STYLE (1911)

In 1911, Mitchell Kennerley, a New York publisher, asked Goudy to design H. G. Wells's book *The Door in the Wall*.

As the trial proofs were not satisfactory, Goudy undertook the task of designing a special typeface, which became a complete success.

For the title page, Goudy designed *Forum Title* as an accompanying typeface.

ABCDEFGHIJKLMNOPQRST
UVWXYZ&abcdefghijklmnopq
rstuvwxyz ctst$1234567890❀!?

FORUM TITLE
(1911)

Originally designed by Goudy as an accompanying typeface to *Kennerley Old Style*, it was used on the title page of H. G. Wells's book, *The Door in the Wall*.

The letters are based on a rubbing of the letters of an inscription on the Arch of Titus in the Roman Forum, hence the name. Their form reflects inscriptional lettering at its best. Both this face and *Kennerly Old Style* were drawn within one week's time.

GOUDY OLDSTYLE
(1915)

This typeface, drawn in 1915, was Goudy's twenty-fifth design, but his first for ATF. Letterforms were based on a few characters he had copied from a portrait, probably painted by Hans Holbein.

The design of *Goudy Oldstyle Italic*, issued in 1918, presented some problems for Goudy, who had only designed two italic alphabets. The slight inclination used became standard in most of his typefaces.

LOISTER INITIALS (1918)

In 1918, Mitchell Kennerley published Goudy's book *The Alphabet*. In the first chapter, there appeared an attractive ornamental initial **A**.

At the suggestion of Wadsworth A. Parker, head of the specimen department at ATF, who was attracted by its design, Goudy completed the whole alphabet that same year. According to Parker, they were the best initials ever made.

ATF cast them in 36- to 144-pt sizes.

HADRIANO TITLE (1918)

In 1910, while visiting the Louvre Museum in Paris, Goudy was impressed by a second century marble inscription. Based on a rubbing of four letters **R**, **I**, **A**, **N** and **O**, of the name HADRIANO, he reconstructed the whole alphabet in 1918.

The name on the inscription became the name of the font.

Robert Wiebking cut the matrices.

ABCDEFGHIJKLMN
OPQRSTUVWXYZ&
1234567890

ABCDEFGHIJKLMNOPQRST
UVWXYZ&abcdefghijklmnopqr
stuvwxyz$1234567890!?

ABCDEFGHIJKLMNOP
QRSTUVWXYZ&
$1234567890!?*

GOUDY HEAVYFACE (1925)

When Harvey Best became president of Lanston Monotype Machine Company, he was very much interested in the design of a very heavy black type, probably to compete with the commercial success of *Cooper Black* designed by Oswald Cooper in 1922.

Although Best wanted a blacker letter, Goudy felt that to produce it, letters would be left with no white at all in the "counters."

ABCDEFGHIJKLMNOPQ
RSTUVWXYZ&abcdefg
hijklmnopqrstuvwxyz
$1234567890!?%*

DEEPDENE (1927)

Named after Goudy's modest estate at Marlborough-on-Hudson, New York, it was used in 14 pt to print a Simon & Schuster's edition of *The Bible as Living Literature.*

Goudy cut the original matrices on his own matrix-engraving machine. Although based on Dutch types, this is considered by many to be a true American creation.

ABCDEFGHIJKLMNOPQRST
UVWXYZ&abcdefghijklmnopq
rstuvwxyz$1234567890?!%*

GOUDY TEXT (1928)

This typeface was designed and cut by Goudy in 1928, after some letters he had used on the No. 5 issue of *Typographica* as well as on his book, *Elements of Lettering.*

Based on Gutenberg's *42-line Bible* type, it evolved into a freely rendered Gothic letter. The original name *Goudy Black* was changed to *Goudy Text* by Harvey Best, president of Lanston Monotype, and presented in an elaborate eight-page booklet printed in three colors.

ABCDEFGHIJKLMNOP
QRSTUVWXYZ&Eabcdefg
hijklmnopqrstuvwxyz$1234567890!?

LOMBARDIC CAPITALS (1929)

Cut by Goudy in 1929, the letterforms are based on drawings he had made in 1921, and were presented as initials in his book, *Elements of Lettering.*

Derived from early Italian decorative letters, they were specially designed to serve as alternate capitals with *Goudy Text* lowercase letters or as initials.

ABCDEFGHIJKLMN
OPQRSTUVWXYZ

GOUDY SANS SERIF

(1930)

In 1929, Goudy experimented with a letter called *Goudy Gothic*. That year, the Lanston Monotype Company convinced him to complete the design, which was commercially issued the following year. In 1930, a lighter weight was introduced, and in 1931, the italic version.

Designed as an answer to the sans serif typefaces coming from Europe, it proved somewhat disappointing to Goudy as well as to Monotype.

"The most I can say for it is that it is a simple, sincere effort to provide a sans-serif letter that might hold its own in the revival of sans-serifs brought in from English and German foundries some years ago. Foundries usually listed these letters as 'lining gothics' and usually showed capital forms only; occasionally a lower-case was added, not always in complete harmony with the capitals. Without reference, however to the classic Greek models of these lining gothics, I attempted to give to my type a definite expression of freedom and a personal quality not always found in this kind of letter."

In 1930, Goudy designed a lighter version, and in 1931, an italic to accompany it, although according to him, sans serif faces did not need italics.

The digital version was issued by Compugraphic Corporation.

ABCDEFGHIJKLMNOPQRSTU VWXYZ&abcdefghijklmnopq rstuvwxyz$1234567890!?

ABCDEFGHIJKLMNOPQRSTUV WXYZ&abcdefghijklmnopqrstuv wxyz$1234567890!?

ABCDEFGHIJKLMNOPQRSTUVW XYZ&abcdefghijklmnopqrstuvwx yz$1234567890!?

TRAJAN TITLE (1930)

One of Goudy's favorite designs, based on the inscription of the Trajan Column, it was developed based on the title page lettering of The Limited Editions Club's book, *Rip Van Winkle*.

Once the book was printed, Goudy completed the alphabet, which was issued later by the Monotype Company.

ABCDEFGHIJKLMN OPQRSTUVWXYZ& 1234567890

ORNATE TITLE (1931)

According to Goudy, this decorative typeface was used very successfully by the Eucalyptus Press at Mills College, California, in several of its publications.

ABCDEFGHIJKLMN OPQRSTUVWXYZ&

FRANCISCAN
(1932)

This typeface was originally cut as *Aries*, in 1925, as a private type for the Aries Press of Spencer Kellogg, at Eden, New York.

In 1932, it was redesigned for Edwin Grabhorn, an eminent St. Francis printer of the Grabhorn Press, San Francisco. He used it for several distinctive and award-winning books, such as *The Spanish Occupation of California*, printed in 1934.

The first appearance of the face was in *Good King Wenceslas*, a carol printed by Dr. John Mason Neale in 1932.

Numerals are drawn in *Oldstyle*.

ABCDEFGHIJKLMNOO
QRSTUVWXYZ & abcdefg
hijklmnopqrstuvwxyz
1234567890

UNIVERSITY OF CALIFORNIA OLD STYLE (1938)

In 1936, Samuel T. Farquhar, manager of the University of California Press, wrote Goudy about the wish the Regents of the University had for a private font for their press.

The typeface was first used in 1940, to print Goudy's *Typologia*, as the Press contribution to the celebration of the 500th anniversary of Johannes Gutenberg's invention of movable type.

In 1958, the Lanston Monotype Company issued the typeface commercially as *California*.

Numerals are drawn in *Oldstyle*.

ABCDEFGHIJKLMNOPQR
STUVWXYZ & abcdefghijkl
mnopqrstuvwxyz$1234567890

ABCDEFGHIJKLMNOPQRSTUV
WXYZ & abcdefghijklmnopqrstuvwx
yz$!?1234567890

GOUDY THIRTY (1953)

Originally conceived for a college in the West, its production fell through due to war restrictions.

Then, when Monotype suggested that the company might bring out a type after he had passed on, to be called "Goudy Thirty," Goudy reconsidered the idea and started working on it.

Based on a Roman letter, Goudy "gothicized" it, retaining every feature of interest and legibility of its forbears.

Completed in 1942, it was not released until 1953 –long after Goudy's death in 1947.

ABCDEFGHIJKLMNOPQR
STUVWXYZ & abcdefghijklmn
opqrstuvwxyz $1234567890!?

Born in Irontown, Ohio in 1879, Chauncey Hawley Griffith started his career as a journeyman compositor and pressman.

In 1906, he joined the Mergenthaler Linotype Company as part of their sales staff. In 1915, his initiative made him sales manager and assistant to the president, before taking charge of the company's type development program.

Once he became vice president of typographic development for the Mergenthaler Linotype Company of New York in 1922, he was responsible for the appearance of new designs, especially text types for the newspaper-printing world.

The introduction of Linotype technology in 1886 had made mechanical typesetting a reality; even so, there were very few new typefaces to use with it during the 1920s. Most of the newspaper texts were set in a derivative of *Modern* style typefaces, even less suited for newspapers than for other kinds of printing.

With a clear vision of the problem, Griffith oversaw the production of what turned out to be an overwhelmingly successful technical solution to the problem.

Through "engineering" more than a design approach to letterform, he overcame the tortuous process of stereotype plate-making and high-speed rotary letterpress printing.

Theodore Low De Vinne had made a considerable contribution to legibility and readability, when he and Linn Boyd Benton designed the *Century Roman* typeface for the magazine of the same name. But in spite of the successive variations, even the wider versions of *Century* were not open enough, nor fitted to what Griffith had in mind. Moreover, the *Century* typefaces were the creation and property of American Type Founders.

Taking as a model the heavy-stroked, slab-serif typeface *Egyptian/Clarendon* genre of the Victorian era, commonly known as *"Ionic"* or *"Antique,"* which has a vertical axis and uniformly weighted strokes, Griffith and his design group established as the *Legibility Group*, came up, in 1925, with a new type design known as *Ionic No. 5*.

Although the final version did not have the sufficient contrast that Griffith and his design group thought it did, the new typeface was a commercial hit for Mergenthaler Linotype; it is said that within eighteen months from its debut in the Newark, New Jersey, *Evening News* in 1926, more than 3,000 newspapers were using it all over the world. In 1930, the *Daily Herald* adopted it in England.

Starting in 1922, under Griffith's direction, the *Legibility Group*, which later included the collaboration of William Addison Dwiggins and Rudolph Ruzicka, was a definite force into the design of readable letters.

In 1929, Griffith designed *Textype*, which was originally intended as a newspaper typeface. His smaller x-height and longer ascenders than most newspaper typefaces made it popular for magazines and other publications, as well as for a certain amount of advertising and general printing. It also included small caps.

In 1931, following the same style but with a better contrast between thick and thin, and more economy of space, the Mergenthaler Linotype introduced *Excelsior*, and soon afterwards a narrower version named *Excelsior No. 2*. With time, both typefaces came to be considered the most influential of newspaper faces of all time.

In 1935, meeting the specialized requirements of some kinds of American newspaper printing, the Mergenthaler Linotype introduced two new typefaces, *Paragon* and *Opticon*.

In 1936, Griffith became vice president of Mergenthaler Linotype, and the following year he extended his concern for legibility and readability to the printing of telephone directories. Thus, he developed *Bell Gothic* for the New York Bell Telephone Company, a typeface that would be in use for more than forty years, and would become very popular in this type of publications.

Finally, in 1941, Mergenthaler Linotype released the last member of their news-text typeface quintet, *Corona*, which Griffith called "a composite of the entire *Legibility Group*, with especial emphasis on the factor of space economy," further noting that it had "the reading visibility of any other face of at least one point larger, and the space economy of the average face one point smaller in size."

Besides this program, Griffith and Mergenthaler Linotype also worked on the revival of such classic designs as *Granjon*, *Baskerville*, and *Janson*, and an extensive number of Oriental scripts.

After fifteen years of research and concern for legibility and readability, Griffith and his *Legibility Group* offered a solution to what he called "fundamentally an engineering problem requiring the analysis of each letter and its behavior characteristics under the conditions imposed on it."

Chauncey Hawley Griffith died in Butler, New York in 1956, at the age of seventy-seven.

IONIC No. 5 (1925)

Ionic is a general name for a type style closely related to the Victorian *Egyptian/Clarendon* typefaces.

As a product of understanding letterform as a problem of "engineering" more than a design approach, *Ionic No.* revolutionized newspaper typesetting in the 1920s.

ABCDEFGHIJKLMNOPQR
STUVWXYZ&abcdefghijklm
nopqrstuvwxyz$1234567890?

POSTER BODONI (1929)

Similar to *Ultra Bodoni*, designed by Morris Fuller Benton for the American Type Founders in 1928, this display type, characterized by heavier hairlines, was designed by Griffith for Mergenthaler Linotype as a competitive answer.

ABCDEFGHIJKLMNOP
QRSTUVWXYZ&abcdef
ghijklmnopqrstuvwxy
z$1234567890!?

ABCDEFGHIJKLMNOP
QRSTUVWXYZ&abcdef
ghijklmnopqrstuvwxyz
$1234567890!?

EXCELSIOR (1931)

Following *Ionic No. 5*, Griffith corrected the letter stroke contrast and width, creating *Excelsior*.

According to John E. Allen, editor of the *Linotype News*, it "cleaves more closely to the traditional design of the roman letter."

Interestingly enough, one year later, English typographer Stanley Morison designed *Times New Roman*, a typeface that will be destined to become as important in the history of newspaper typefaces as was *Ionic No. 5*, designed five years before.

ABCDEFGHIJKLMNOPQRS
TUVWXYZ&abcdefghijklmno
pqrstuvwxyz$1234567890!?

ABCDEFGHIJKLMNOPQRS
TUVWXYZ&abcdefghijklmno
pqrstuvwxyz$1234567890!?

JANSON (1932)

At the same time that Griffith was interested in solving legibility and readability problems for newspaper text typesetting and printing, he and Mergenthaler Linotype were also focusing their aims on the revival of the classics.

Janson was based on the 1660 printing samples attributed to Anton Janson. These actually were the work of Hungarian punch-cutter Miklós (Nicholas) Kis, used by him in the printing of the *Amsterdam Bible*.

ABCDEFGHIJKLMNOPQR
STUVWXYZ&abcdefghijklm
nopqrstuvwxyz$1234567890!?

ABCDEFGHIJKLMNOPQRS
TUVWXYZ&abcdefghijklmnopq
rstuvwxyz$1234567890!?

PARAGON (1935)

In 1935, Griffith designed this typeface. It is a slightly narrower face than *Excelsior*, to meet the specialized printing requirements expressed by some American newspapers.

ABCDEFGHIJKLMNOPQRS
TUVWXYZ&abcdefghijklmn
opqrstuvwxyz$1234567890!?

ABCDEFGHIJKLMNOPQRS
TUVWXYZ&abcdefghijklmno
pqrstuvwxyz$1234567890!?

OPTICON <small>(1935)</small>

Designed for Linotype, it is essentially the same as *Excelsior*, but with stems and thick lines weighted slightly, for printing on hard-surfaced paper.

ABCDEFGHIJKLMNOPQ
RSTUVWXYZ&abcdefghij
klmnopqrstuvwxyz
$1234567890!?

BELL GOTHIC <small>(1937)</small>

Developed primarily for use in the New York City telephone directory, it soon became standard for telephone books nationwide. The two weights were used in the setting of surnames, names, and numbers, and bold listings.

Bell Gothic came to supplant holdovers from the nineteenth century, known as **numbered typefaces** used extensively for setting telephone directories.

Bell Gothic was adapted for newspaper typesetting, as *Furlong* and *Market Gothic*. The former, with special figures and other characters, was used for setting racetrack publications, and the latter, in 1941, with other special characters for stock market information.

It is interesting to note how Griffith introduced serif capital I to solve the difficulties in reading sans serif letters of identical form, such as is found in words like **Illinois** or **Iliad**.

In 1978, Matthew Carter was commissioned by AT&T to redesign this typeface to resolve problems involved in the high digital CRT techniques in the printing of telephone directories.

It was then issued as *Bell Centennial*, to honor Alexander Graham Bell's centenary.

ABCDEFGHIJKLMNOPQRST
UVWXYZ&abcdefghijklmnopqr
stuvwxyz$1234567890!?

ABCDEFGHIJKLMNOPQRST
UVWXYZ&abcdefghijklmnopq
rstuvwxyz$1234567890!?

ABCDEFGHIJKLMNOPQRST
UVWXYZ&abcdefghijklmnop
qrstuvwxyz$1234567890!?

MEMPHIS EXTRA BOLD (1938)

Memphis was the Linotype copy of the popular German square-serif *Memphis*, designed by Rudolf Wolf in 1929. Introduced by the D. Stempel AG type foundry, it did much to revive interest in nineteenth-century typefaces.

Linotype introduced *Memphis Light* and *Bold* in 1933, *Italics* in 1934, *Medium* in 1935, and other variations up to 1938. Griffith designed *Memphis Extra Bold* around 1938.

It is also interesting to note that *Stymie* was the correspondent typeface family issued by ATF, designed by Morris Fuller Benton in 1931, and later complemented by the Lanston Monotype Company, with variations designed by Sol Hess, Gerry Powell, and Wadsworth Parker.

ABCDEFGHIJKLMNOPQRS TUVWXYZ&abcdefghijklmn opqrstuvwxyz$1234567890?

ABCDEFGHIJKLMNOPQRS TUVWXYZ&abcdefghijklmn opqrstuvwxyz$1234567890!?

CORONA (1941)

Patterned after *Century Schoolbook*, and the last of the news-text quintet designed by the Legibility Group, *Corona* was also created to compensate for the shrinkage of the type image in the stereotype matrices used to do the printing plates of most American newspapers of the day.

The *San Francisco Chronicle* used it for more than fifty years.

ABCDEFGHIJKLMNOPQ RSTUVWXYZ&abcdefghij klmnopqrstuvwxyz $1234567890!?

ABCDEFGHIJKLMNOPQRS TUVWXYZ&abcdefghijklmn opqrstuvwxyz$1234567890!?

Born in Vienna in 1882, Victor Hammer was apprentice to the architect and town planner Camillo Sitte in 1897. A year later he studied at the Vienna Akademie der bildenden Künste (Vienna Academy of Fine Arts). He first did portrait painting, both in oil and tempera, and also worked in mezzotint, an engraving technique he fully mastered. Throughout his life, he continued doing portraits, biblical painting, and allegorical subjects.

Towards 1910, he began to experiment with a quill pen, and this, with an increased interest in bookbinding, introduced him into the world of the book, which led him to dedicate his entire life to type and typography. He soon modeled his own handwritten script in uncials, rather than in Roman or black letters, as a result of a personal feeling.

After the First World War, he lived in St. Martin im Innkreis, Austria, where in 1921 he met N. Schuricht, a punch-cutter who had worked for K. K. Hof-und Staatsdruckerei in Viena, and who cut the first of his types, HAMMER UNZIALE. The typeface, including a set of initials, was issued by the Klingspor type foundry in 1923. Although it was commercially successful, Hammer was not satisfied with the cutting, and decided to learn the art of punch cutting himself. It was then that he met Rudolf Koch, with whom he had a lasting friendship.

In 1922, Hammer moved to Florence, Italy, where he remained until 1933, though he returned several times to St. Martin. Four years later, Koch's son Paul, who had just finished his work on Koch's Peter Jessen Schrift capitals, came to work in Florence and cut the punches for

Hammer's next type, SAMSON. This was used to print an edition of John Milton's SAMSON AGONISTES (1931), the first work to be done by Hammer's first printing venture, the Stamperia del Santuccio. In this press, Hammer set out to produce the type of books he had always wanted to print.

After leaving Florence in 1933, Hammer began a period of wandering to various cities, such as London, Kolbsheim, Grundlsee, and Vienna.

During this period he continued to print, and for the edition of Hölderlin's FRAGMENTE DES PINDAR, finished in 1935 at Kolbsheim, he used the first type for which he cut the punches himself.

PINDAR UNCIAL was the first of his uncials to have an accompanying set of roman capitals, thus marking an important step away from the purely Carolingian minuscule, which employs one-story letters. Even so, he maintained the B, and the R, which he never changed.

In 1939, forced by the Nazis to leave his post as professor at the Vienna Academy of Fine Arts, he moved to America, abandoning most of his possessions, including all his printing equipment, and his uncial types.

In America, Hammer found a teaching post at Wells College in Aurora, New York, where he directed both the Wells College Press, used for teaching purposes, and the Hammer Press, for his own work. Not having his uncial types, Hammer used roman faces designed by others, his favorite being Joseph Blumenthal's Emerson (1935).

In the Hammer Press he was able to print seventeen titles,

such as Pedro Antonio de Alarcón's THREE-CORNERED HAT (1944), a book with color woodcuts by Fritz Kredel.

Between 1940 and 1943, Hammer cut AMERICAN UNCIAL, his best-known face, in which the letters are close to the Roman letter structure, and where the lower case b is finally decapitalized.

With the collaboration of the Society of Typographic Arts in Chicago and Robert Hunter Middleton, it was possible for him to complete the project, although the face was not produced commercially until after the war in 1952, as NEUE HAMMER UNZIALE, by the D. Stempel AG German type foundry, who finally absorbed the Klingspor type foundry.

In 1948, Hammer retired from Wells College, and went to live in Lexington, Kentucky, where he completed his handsome edition of Hölderlin's Gedichte, typeset in AMERICAN UNCIAL, as well as many other books.

In 1958 he cut his last type, Andromaque, a curious uncial with the inclusion of several Greek letters. Although the Fonderie Deberny & Peignot cast it in 1959, it was never released. The typeface was finally redrawn and completed by Robert Hunter Middleton in 1980, and cast by Paul Hayden Duensing.

Hammer's revival of uncial forms provided inspiration for many other leading figures of his generation, who went on to experiment with the uncial form, such as Goudy (FRIAR, 1937); De Roos (LIBRA, 1938); Menhart (CESKA UNCIALA, 1948); and Lange (SOLEMNIS, 1954).

Victor Hammer died in Lexington, Kentucky in 1967, at the age of eighty-five.

HAMMER
UNZIALE (1923)

Designed while Hammer was in St. Martin im Innkreis in upper Austria, this first typeface was cut by N. Schuricht, and issued in 1923. Elmer Adler used it for the Pinson Printer's 1932 edition of the English epic *Beowulf*. In 1945, Charles Nussbaumer cut a new version.

ABCDEFGHIJKLMNOPQRSTU VWXYZ&abcdefghijklmnopq rstuvwxyz$1234567890!?

american uncial (1943)

Designed and cut by Hammer in 1943, the punches were executed while he was professor of fine arts at Wells College in Aurora, New York. The type was cast by Charles Nussbaumer of the Dearborn type foundry in Chicago, and commercially issued by the D. Stempel AG German type foundry in 1952.

The first major application of this typeface was the edition of Friedrich Hölderlin's *Gedichte*, printed by Hammer on his own press, the Stamperia del Santuccio, in 1948.

abcdefghijklmnopq
rstuvwxyza
$1234567890!?

andromaque (1958/1980)

This cursive form of an uncial, which mixes the Greek letter forms of **a, e, k, l, m, n, s, t, z** with the Roman forms of the other letters, was originally cut by Hammer in 1958 in 12 pt for an edition of Jean Racine's play *Andromaque* (1667) –hence the type's name.

Years later, his widow, Carolyn Hammer, requested that Robert Hunter Middleton completed cutting the punches for the 14-pt size alphabet that Hammer had started before his death.

The font was finished in 1980, cast by Paul Hayden Duensing, a Michigan type founder who is also a type designer (*Rustica*, 1965; *Sixteen Century Roman*, 1967), and used by Middleton in his own 1980 Christmas card.

abcdefghijklmnopqrst
uvwxyz

Born in Philadelphia, Pennsylvania in 1886, Sol Hess obtained a scholarship at the age of thirteen to study for three years at the Pennsylvania Museum School of Industrial Art.

After finishing his studies, he started to work in November 1902 with the Lanston Monotype Company in Philadelphia, as a type designer redrawing and readapting all Monotype typographical material. His strong point was the development of type families, as well as the adaptation of many designs to the new mechanical and standard requirements of hot composition. This was the case with *Bruce Old Style* (1902), derived from a face produced by the Bruce's New York Type Foundry, around 1869.

In 1909, Hess redesigned this typeface to fit a new development in the machine, and *Bruce Italic* became the first kerned italic for Monotype casting. This plain and very legible design turned into a quite popular typeface for magazines and other works involving extensive reading.

In 1917, he undertook another classical adaptation with *Cochin*, originally issued by the Fonderie Deberny & Peignot in Paris around 1915, completing the family by adding an italic, and other variations, such as *Cochin Bold* and *Italic* (1921), *Cochin Open* (1927) and *Cochin Tooled* (1928), which lacks a lowercase. To compete with Monotype, ATF copied the French face in 1925. Both Monotype and ATF replaced the French *Oldstyle* figures with the more usual lining figures.

In 1922, Sol Hess was appointed typographic manager of the Lanston Monotype Machine Company, further developing the company's typographic program.

In 1940, at the age of fifty-four, he succeeded his friend and collaborator Frederic W. Goudy, already

seventy-one, as art director of the Lanston Monotype Company. During the fifty years he worked with the company, he carried out commissions for many leading American companies, including the Curtis Publishing Company, Crowell-Collier Co., Sears Roebuck, Montgomery Ward, Yale University Press, and the World Publishing Company.

In 1939, as art director of the *Saturday Evening Post*, he undertook a new typographic styling for the magazine by creating two fonts for its private use: *Post-Stout Italic* and *Postblack Italic*. *Post Stout* was a filled-in version of the earlier face, *Post Shaded Italic*, designed in 1910 and used on the magazine's headings for several years. A greater modification was achieved with *Postblack*, but after some trials in both roman and italic, the roman was abandoned. This typeface, as well as *Post-Stout Italic*, was adopted by the magazine and used extensively.

Many of Hess's typefaces were designed before the war, but not released until 1948, as was the case with *Artscript*, "an attempt to convert into rigid metal the graceful penmanship of the ancient scribe... based on the writing of Servidori of Madrid (1798)."

Among his fifty-one original type designs and more than twenty adaptations, we may find *Hess Title* (1910); *Kennerley Open Caps* (1925); *Bodoni Bold Panelled* (1928); *Broadway* (lowercase) and *Broadway Engraved* (1928); *Hadriano Stone-Cut* (1932); *Pendrawn* (1933); *Hess Neobold* (1934); *Spire* (1937); *Tourist Gothic* (1938); *Artscript* (1939); *Onyx Italic* (1939); and *Goudy Bible* (1942-43), a revision of *Goudy Newstyle* (1921) which he did in collaboration with Bruce Rogers for the printing of an American folio edition of *The Oxford Lectern Bible* (1948), designed

by Rogers for the World Publishing Company.

In 1952, after spending a lifetime as a type designer and type director for the Lanston Monotype Machine Co. in Philadelphia, the Graphic Arts Forum in its annual Christmas meeting honored Hess for his contributions to the development of Monotype typefaces. That same year he was also selected by *The Trade Compositor*, official publication of the International Typographic Composition Association, as the *Type Man of the Year*.

"Working drawings for every matrix shown in the *Monotype Specimen Book*, either personally or under his close personal supervision –650 pages of typefaces, signs, rules, and borders," said Wilfred J. Bancroft, former Monotype treasurer, "made Sol Hess one of the most important men in the development of practical typography." According to Bancroft, two of the main features of Hess's work were his enthusiasm for producing related typefaces –type families– and the simplicity and freedom from effort and strain shown in his designs, an example of which is *Hess Old Style No. 242*. He also increased the popularity of typefaces like *Broadway*, designed by Morris Fuller Benton in 1928, by creating an accompanying lowercase as well as an elegant variation, *Broadway Engraved*.

Hess was also a well-known lecturer at many schools and colleges, societies and clubs, and a writer of technical articles for various magazines. His booklet, *Origin and Development of Printing Types*, is a well-known work.

He was a member of the American Institute of Graphic Arts and the Philadelphia Graphic Arts Forum.

Sol Hess died in Philadelphia, Pennsylvania in 1953, at the house of a friend, at the age of sixty-six.

KENNERLEY OPEN CAPS (1925)

In 1920, the Lanston Monotype Company produced the *Kennerley Old Style* typeface designed by Goudy in 1911, for use in its composing machines. In 1925, Hess created an alternative design by opening a white line. Approved by Goudy, the variation gave the original design a more elegant appearance.

ABCDEFGHIJKLMNOP QRSTUVWXYZ& $1234567890

BODONI BOLD PANELLED (1928)

Designed by Hess in 1928 for the Lanston Monotype Company, as a variation of *Bodoni Bold*, it maintains a particular sense of blackness, due to the contrast produced by the inline cutting.

The font has no lowercase, points or figures.

ABCDEFGHIJKLMNOP
QRSTUVWXYZ&

COOPER TOOLED (1928)

This version of *Cooper Hilite* (Cooper, 1925) was designed by Sol Hess for the Lanston Monotype Company, as part of the competing policies of many foundries to offer similar designs to their clients.

If we compare the two typefaces, we may find a difference in the highlights placement.

Numerals are drawn in *Oldstyle*.

ABCDEFGHIJKLMNO
PQRSTUVWXYZ&ab
cdefghijklmnopqrst
uvwxyz$1234567890

BROADWAY ENGRAVED (1929)

In 1928 the American Type Founders issued *Broadway*, designed by Morris Fuller Benton the preceding year.

Hess duplicated the design for Monotype, and added a lower case with virtually no descenders.

The following year (1929), he did a variation for this company, adding a white line on the left side of the heavy strokes. Both designs are good examples of the Art Deco style's influence on typography.

It is quite interesting to compare *Broadway Engraved* with *Boul Mich* (Cooper, 1927), by observing how two similar approaches may end in two different typefaces.

ABCDEFGHIJKLMNOP
QRSTUVWXYZ&abcdef
ghijklmnopqrstuvwxy
z$1234567890!?

ABCDEFGHIJKLMNOP
QRSTUVWXYZ&abcdef
ghijklmnopqrstuvwxy
z$1234567890!?

HADRIANO STONE-CUT (1932)

In 1932, while Hess was at Lanston Monotype as art director, he experimented with *Hadriano Title* (Goudy, 1918), by removing part of the black areas on each of the caps. This also added a shading quality to the letterforms.

Goudy was so pleased with the visual effect that he immediately ordered the cutting of the matrices.

Numerals are drawn in *Oldstyle*.

ABCDEFGHIJKLMN
OPQRSTUVWXYZ
&1234567890

HESS NEOBOLD (1934)

This narrow, bold, and very squarish gothic display typeface with small serifs was designed by Hess for attention-getting, in the style of the day.

ABCDEFGHIJKLMNOPQRSTUVWXY
Z&$1234567890?!

STYMIE EXTRABOLD (1934)

Sol Hess designed this typeface for Monotype in 1934, a year before Morris Fuller Benton drew *Stymie Black*.

These heavy versions differ slightly from each other and from the lighter face.

ABCDEFGHIJKLMNOPQ
RSTUVWXYZ&abcdefg
hijklmnopqrstuvwxyz
$1234567890

SPIRE (1937)

A modernization of the old modern roman extra-condensed style, it follows the trend established by *Huxley Vertical* (Huxley, 1935), characterized by extremely elongated letters. Although it doesn't include lowercase letters, there are several alternate round characters.

A commercial use of the face may be found in the LM cigarettes package logotype.

ABCDEFGHIJKLMNOPQRSTUVWXYZ&
$1234567890

ONYX ITALIC (1939)

Onyx was an original typeface created by Gerry Powell in 1937 for American Type Founders.

Two years later, Hess designed the italic version for Lanston Monotype.

ABCDEFGHIJKLMNOPQRSTUVWXYZ&abcd efghijklmnopqrstuvwxyz$1234567890

POST-STOUT ITALIC (1939)

In 1939, a new typographic styling of the *Saturday Evening Post* was undertaken, under the direction of Sol Hess, Lanston Monotype's art director.

This new face was produced and adopted extensively by the magazine, from the masthead to the article titles.

ABCDEFGHIJKLMNOPQ RSTUVWXYZ

POSTBLACK ITALIC (1939)

A refinement of *Post Oldstyle Italic*, patented by Herman Ihlenburg in 1903, *Postblack Italic* was the result of a previous trial of roman and italic versions.

While the roman was abandoned, *Postblack Italic* and *Post-Stout Italic* were produced and adopted by the *Saturday Evening Post* in 1939 and used extensively.

ABCDEFGHIJKLMNOPQ RSTUVWXYZabcdefghijk lmnopqrstuvwxyz

Artscript (1948)

A delicate calligraphic letter, this design was issued by Monotype as "an attempt to convert into rigid metal the graceful penmanship of the ancient scribe...based on the writing of [Santiago María de] Servidori of Madrid (1798)."

Although designed in 1939, it was not released until 1948, on account of war restrictions.

Numerals are drawn in *Oldstyle*.

ABCDEFGHIJKLMNOP QRSTUVWXYZ&abcdefghijk lmnopqrstuvwxyz$1234567890?!

Born in New York in 1970, Jonathan Hoefler found himself at age of twenty-three torn between his studies of music and graphic design.

While attending Parson School of Design, he went to work in 1989 for publication designer Roger Black in New York. With him he understood the great difference between solving a client's specific need and a class project. "I found I could make up a fake annual report for some second-rate art director from the 1960s at school and get lousy advice, or make up real magazines for Roger and hear what the client had to say. It wasn't a difficult choice."

After working with Black for a year, Hoefler went freelance, founding the Hoefler Type Foundry which specialized in custom type design for such publications as *Rolling Stone*, *Harper's Bazaar*, the *New York Times Magazine*, and *Sports Illustrated*. Today most of his type designs are slowly being made available in all platforms.

In one of his vacation tours to the Caribbean he took with him Bruce Rogers's *Paragraphs on Printing*, a text that has been quite inspirational. "The fact that there are interlocking arabesques in *Hoefler Text* has very much to do with Bruce Rogers. *Hoefler Text* overall is influenced by Rogers, much as Riverside *Caslon* or the *Fell* types influenced him."

From 1991 to 1993, he undertook an ambitious project to develop a complete family typeface as part of Apple's *Quick Draw GX*. Other designers such as Matthew Carter, Charles Bigelow, Kris Holmes, and David Berlow participated on the project, designing their own typefaces.

The final result is a "synthesis of all my favorite styles," such as the types designed by Kis, Garamond, Caslon, Figgins, Thorowgood –and of course Hoefler. Besides the use of a tall x-height he has paid attention to letter fitting.

The *Hoefler Text*, which was promoted in his booklet *Every Art Director Needs His Own Typeface*, consists of various extended families –roman, italic, swash, black, black italic, small caps, engraved, ornaments, and arabesques–

which amount to 3,143 glyphs in total, with almost 10,000 kern pairs for the lot. He muses that his *Text* is "the world's largest typeface."

His way to approach type design is "read a lot, both about lettering and type design in general, and study relevant historic typefaces."

Once he has the nucleus of a design on paper he moves to the Mac and Adobe Illustrator, the software in which he draws his entire letter forms. Once he moves the characters to *Fontographer* he draws a line above and below the character at the top and bottom boundaries of the em square, copies the lines and letters to the clipboard, and pastes them into the appropriate character slot. The lines ensure that the characters retain their proportion during the cut and paste. Like Tobias Frere-Jones, Hoefler prefers to work with *Fontographer 3.5*, which enables him to see his completed letters immediately combined into words, and helps in fine-tuning the letter spacing.

Hoefler is not dogmatic about a working procedure. In *Adobe Illustrator*, he's likely to have some reference figure in the background (template) layer, possibly a scanned pencil sketch. On his typeface, *Fetish*, he worked directly in *Illustrator*, making visual references to his notebook, and on his *Saracen Italic*, he used reference characters (**n**, **k**, **n**) from other of his fonts, such as *Ziggurat Italic*, one of the *Rolling Stone* magazine set.

He usually starts the design of a new typeface with the **H**,**O**, **D**, **n**, **o**, **p** letters, a combination which have become a key for his design for they carry the general proportion (ratio of height and width), including x-height, stem weight, angle of stress and the shape of the serifs. He then works out the proportion, weight and general feel of the new type, as well as spacing.

Hoefler has just begun his career as a type designer. But if it is true that he has based his designs on specific models from the past his final product shows a masterly handling where things are in better shape than he found them. This is not only true of his classical designs but of his typefaces based on

nineteenth-century wood type. Even his experimental types –*Fetish*, *Gestalt* and *Enigma*– reveal a solid understanding of proportion and rhythms of the Latin alphabet.

All his custom-design projects begin differently. In the case of *House & Garden* magazine, Hoefler started with a sample presented on his portfolio where the letters were "sort of a mix of *Garamond* and *Janson*." And he adds, "Too often, the art director thinks that one design is all that's needed. Later, I have to force-fit italics, bolds, or condensed designs into the parameters created for the first typeface —usually not an easy proposition."

Hoefler's list of custom-design projects continues to expand. "Every project grows," he says. "Even if the art director only wants one weight to begin with, they almost always come back for more designs."

He has been named one of the forty most influential designers in America by *I.D. Magazine*, and his publishing work includes award-winning original typefaces designed for *Rolling Stone*, *Harper's Bazaar*, the *New York Times Magazine*, *Sports Illustrated*, and *Esquire*; his institutional clients range from the Salomon R. Gugenheim Museum to the rock band They Might Be Giants.

His work has been exhibited internationally and is included in the permanent collection of the Cooper-Hewitt National Design Museum (Smithsonian Institution) in New York.

In 2002, The Association Typographique Internationale (ATypI) presented Jonathan Hoefler with its most prestigious award, the Prix Charles Peignot for outstanding contributions to type design.

Hoefler sees his work as an investigation into the circumstances behind historical form. In each of his designs, he attempts to interpret the critical and aesthetic theories which gave form to a particular style of letter, and to draw out this internal logic into the foundation for a family of original designs.

HTF HOEFLER
(1993)

Perhaps his best-known work, it was originally designed for Apple Computer. It is now part of the Macintosh operating system.

It consists of various extended families –roman, italic, swash, black, black italic, small caps, engraved, ornaments, and arabesques.

ABCDEFGHIJKLMNOPQR STUVWXYZ&abcdefghijklm nopqrstuvwxyz$1234567890!?

MUSE (1997)

Cover design of *Muse No. 1*, the type specimen book of the Hoefler Type Foundry, where he presents *HTF Didot* typeface, a historical revival in the French neoclassical style.

SPECIMEN OF TYPES (1992)

Cover of his portfolio of type design much in the manner of the *Printers Ornaments* designed by Frederic Warde for the English Monotype in 1928.

BANDED ORNAMENT (1997)

One of the many ornaments released by The Hoefler Type Foundry to complement type designs.

BANDED ENDPIECES (1997)

Some of the alternative endings designed to enrich type designs.

FETISH 338, FETISH 126 (1997)

An experimental type design, the *Fetish* family is the result of "quoting freely from a large formal vocabulary drawn from styles as disparate as Gothic, Victorian, Coptic, Moorish, Celtic, and Byzantine."

"*Fetish* parodies the notions of 'fanciness' in which not only professional designers but the lay public participate," comments Hoefler.

GRAZIA BODONI (1989)

Described by Hoefler as a "humanist" *Bodoni*, this typeface is a refined, narrower version of the classical typeface. "This is the first design I think of as an original design. It's like the work I'm doing now," he says.

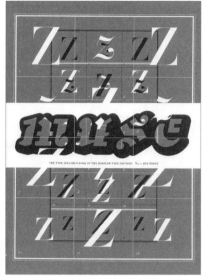

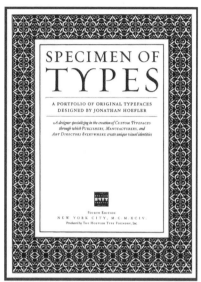

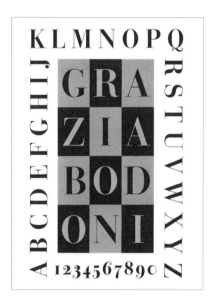

HTF CHAMPION GOTHIC (1990)

Designed for *Sports Illustrated* magazine, these six headline typefaces (*Bantamweight*, *Featherweight*, *Lightweight*, *Welterweight*, and *Middleweight*, plus a *Heavyweight* based on a related but later nineteenth century extended gothic style) are rationalized variants of the Gothic typefaces used for handbills in the nineteenth century.

This design typifies Hoefler's visual logic as well as his attention to detail.

HTF REQUIEM (work in progress)

This old style roman-titling font is inspired by the work of Italian calligrapher Ludovico Vicentino Degli Arrighi's *Il modo de temperare le penne* (1523).

TYPE WIDTH VARIATIONS (1997)

Instead of following the traditional morphology of *condensed*, *normal* and *wide*, *Champion Gothic* typefaces follow a practice first used by American wood type makers in the nineteenth century.

Because they are "cut in series," conceived from the outset as a family of variations, typefaces are without the usual hierarchy between the 'normal' font and its derivatives: each typeface is autonomous.

HTF ZIGGURAT, HTF LEVIATHAN, HTF SARACEN, HTF ACROPOLIS (1991-1994)

This group of typefaces was modeled on nineteenth-century wood types to create a set of matched display types for *Rolling Stone* magazine.

The first design *Ziggurat*, a slab serif typeface, was followed by *Leviathan*, a Gothic sans serif, *Saracen*, a Latin serif, and *Acropolis*, a type known as Grecian.

Unlike the original wood types Hoefler plans to design accompanying italics.

HTF EGIZIANO FILIGREE (1990)

"It's not really my design," says Hoefler. "It is more of an exercise in craftsmanship," a category into which he also lumps digitization of *Ehmcke*, *Schneidler Titling*, *Raleigh Gothic*, and the *Kennerley* type family.

The heavy slab-serif harmonizes with Jan Tschichold's citation set in italics.

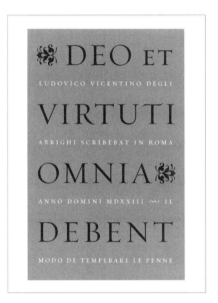

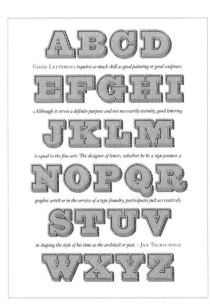

HTF DIDOT (1992)

"In researching historical material for the *HTF Didot* typefaces, I was introduced to some remarkable typographic experiments begun by Enlightenment thinkers at the turn of the seventeenth century.

There is a shocking modernity in their writings, in which aesthetic decisions are substantiated in historical, cultural and scientific terms; Louis René Luce's catalog of 1771 (*Essai d'une nouvelle typographie*), includes a thousand-word essay on the foundation of serifs in his types, discussing how and why they differ from traditional designs.

Although these writings were certainly complicit in great acts of self-promotion, they remain valuable reference works, and superb typographic specimens."

HTF Didot was presented in *Muse No.1*, a periodical type specimen that is issued by the Hoefler Type Foundry to introduce new type projects.

Considered by Hoefler himself a typeface placed between a revival and a loose interpretation of Firmin Didot's classical typeface, *HTF Didot* is certainly a very delicate typeface which preserves the beauty of the original and places itself as one of the beautiful works of American serious contributions to type design.

Originally developed for *Harper's Bazaar* magazine in 1992, and commercially available in 1997, *HTF Didot* has been designed in the classical tradition where each size was cut independently. In this way, *HTF Didot* has been drawn with individual tuned designs each for use at a specific size.

To preserve the faces' delicate features, each of the six master designs (light, medium, bold, light italic, medium italic, and bold italic) is provided in seven master versions, each for use over a specific range of sizes: below 10 pt, 11-15, 16-23, 24-41, 42-63, 64-95, 96, and above.

Numerals are drawn in *Oldstyle*.

ABCDEFGHIJKLMNOPQRST
UVWXYZabcdefghijklmnopqr
stuvwxyz$1234567890!?

ABCDEFGHIJKLMNOPQRST
UVWXYZabcdefghijklmnopqrs
tuvwxyz$1234567890!?

ABCDEFGHIJKLMNOPQRS
TUVWXYZabcdefghijklmnop
qrstuvwxyz$1234567890!?

ABCDEFGHIJKLMNOPQRS
TUVWXYZabcdefghijklmnopq
rstuvwxyz$1234567890!?

ABCDEFGHIJKLMNOPQRS
TUVWXYZabcdefghijklmnop
qrstuvwxyz$1234567890!?

Born in Reedley, California in 1950, Kris Holmes majored in art at Reed College, Portland, Oregon in 1971. There she also learned calligraphy from Lloyd Reynolds and Robert Palladino. She later studied modern dance at the Alwin Nikolai School and the Martha Graham School in New York City.

From 1976 to 1978, she taught lettering, arts courses, graphic design, and advanced lettering at Portland State University and the Museum Art School in Portland. During this time, she was also the recipient of an Oregon Arts Commission Artist in the Schools grant. Her work for this grant included traveling to various elementary schools in Oregon, and teaching the history of writing to grades one through six. In 1976-77, Kris Holmes worked as technical illustrator for the Tektronix Corporation in Portland, Oregon.

In 1977, she received a grant from the Jackson Foundation in Oregon, to prepare a multilingual calligraphic series on women storytellers. "In rewriting their words, I tried to work more as a scribe concentrating on clarity, legibility and expressiveness than as a writing master demonstrating virtuosity and inventiveness."

That year she also designed, in collaboration with Charles Bigelow, the typeface *Leviathan* for the Arion Press of San Francisco. This was a set of initial capitals to be used in Arion's edition of Herman Melville's *Moby Dick*. At this time, she also designed, in collaboration with Bigelow and Hans Edward Meier, supplemental designs for *Syntax-Antiqua*, which included special characters to accommodate Native American languages.

From 1978 to 1980, she was a type designer for Compugraphic Corporation in Wilmington, Massachusetts. "The amount of free form expression in a design often depends on its intended function. Types used for display can be wild, but types used for text must be disciplined. Digital resolution also influences a design. Types for high resolution can be complex and delicate, but types for low resolution must be simpler and sturdier."

From 1980 to 1984, she was a type designer for Hell Digiset GmbH in Kiel, Germany. For Hell Digiset, she designed two revivals, *Baskerville* and *Caslon*, with their italics. She also designed two original faces for Hell Digiset, *Sierra*, a roman type, with a calligraphic accent, and *Isadora*, a delicate script typeface, which was later issued by ITC in 1989, in the *ITC Typographica Series*.

During the summer of 1979, she took a special course in calligraphy and type design with German type designer and calligrapher Hermann Zapf at the Rochester Institute of Technology.

In 1982, Kris Holmes obtained a Bachelor of Liberal Arts degree in Extension Studies, *cum laude*, from Harvard University.

Since 1976, she has been partner with Charles Bigelow in Bigelow & Holmes, Inc. They designed the typeface family *Lucida*, the first typeface design for low-resolution laser printers. They have continued to expand this typeface family to include such variations as serif, sans serif, calligraphic, casual and blackletter. They have also designed special versions of *Lucida* to be used in mathematics, fax and monospace texts. Multi-lingual alphabets included in the *Lucida* are Greek, Hebrew, Cyrillic, Arabic, and Thai. The *Lucida* typeface family is currently used in Java, Solaris, and Lucent technologies. In 1987, the serifed version of the *Lucida* family, *Lucida Bright*, was chosen for setting the redesign of *Scientific American*.

Kris Holmes's illustrations have appeared in *Scientific American, Seybold Report, Computer Graphics*, and *Fine Print*. Her lettering and calligraphy may be seen in *Fine Print, International Calligraphy Today, Publish!*, and *Scriptura '84*.

It is worthy of mention that her calligraphic work is part of the permanent collection of the Klingspor Museum in Offenbach, Germany.

Her type design has been reviewed in books and periodical publications, such as *Scientific American, HOW* magazine, *Digital Review*, Mac World, *Typographic i, Art Direction*, and *Fine Print*, among others.

In partnership with Charles Bigelow, she has designed True Type versions of *Monaco, New York, Geneva*, and *Chicago* for Apple Computer. She also designed *Apple Chancery* for Apple Computer in 1991. These typefaces have been distributed to tens of millions of users.

In 1998, she codesigned typefaces *Textile* and *Capitals* for Apple Computer.

For Microsoft, Bigelow & Holmes have designed the series *Windings 1, 2, 3*. These were designed in 1982, and have been distributed to 100 million users.

ISADORA (1983)

Named after the American founder of modern dance, Isadora Duncan, this delicate script alphabet was released by ITC in 1989.

"While the capitals show Classical and Renaissance structure, the lowercase letters display the influence of the eighteenth-century mercantilist hands," comments Kris Holmes.

ABCDEFGHIJKLMNOPQRS TUVWXYZ&abcdefghijklmnop qrstuvwxyz$1234567890!?

SIERRA (1983)

Created for Hell Digiset GmbH, Germany, this roman typeface was designed to be used for both display and text setting on the same high-resolution equipment as *Isadora*.

"Derived from hands I developed from writing Native American texts, the designs evoke the dynamic effect that comes from twisting the pen angle during the writing of a stroke, to give an asymmetrical, flaring emphasis to the terminations," comments Kris Holmes.

ABCDEFGHIJKLMNOPQRSTUV
WXYZ&abcdefghijklmnopqr
stuvwxyz$1234567890!?

*ABCDEFGHIJKLMNOPQRSTUV
WXYZ&abcdefghijklmnopqrst
uvwxyz$1234567890!?*

LUCIDA (1984)

Designed in collaboration with Charles Bigelow, it was the first original typeface designed for use in low-resolution laser printers.

They later added *Pellucida*, which was conceived as a series of bitmap display screen fonts.

ABCDEFGHIJKLMNOPQRS
TUVWXYZ&ÆŒ§abcdefgh
ijklmnopqrstuvwxyz
$¥£1234567890!?

*ABCDEFGHIJKLMNOPQRST
UVWXYZ&abcdefghijklmn
opqrstuvwxyz
$1234567890!?*

LUCIDA SANS (1985)

A sans serif typeface designed in collaboration with Charles Bigelow, her partner, it was created for use in low-resolution laser printers.

Now available in many computer platforms, *Lucida Sans* includes several non-Latin scripts such as Greek, Hebrew, Arabic, Cyrillic, and Thai.

ABCDEFGHIJKLMNOPQRSTU
VWXYZ&abcdefghijklmnop
qrstuvwxyz
$1234567890!?

ABCDEFGHIJKLMNOPQRST
UVWXYZ&abcdefghijklmno
pqrstuvwxyz
$1234567890!?

ABCDEFGHIJKLMNOPQR
STUVWXYZ&abcdefghijk
lmnopqrstuvwxyz
$1234567890!?

ABCDEFGHIJKLMNOPQR
STUVWXYZ&abcdefghijk
lmnopqrstuvwxyz
$1234567890!?

LUCIDA BRIGHT
(1987)

A roman typeface with a large x-height, it was designed in collaboration with Charles Bigelow, for setting *Scientific American*.

It is interesting to note that ascenders surpass capitals in height.

ABCDEFGHIJKLMNOPQRST UVWXYZ&abcdefghijklmno pqrstuvwxyz$1234567890?

APPLE CHICAGO
(1991)

Designed in collaboration with Charles Bigelow for Apple Computer, Inc., this sans serif is evocative of the 1920s typography, with large x-height lowercase letters and very short ascenders.

It is also characterized by a wide **M** and a narrow **O**, as well as by an overall vertical stress.

Additionally, there is a clear difference between the letter **O** and the zero **0**.

ABCDEFGHIJKLMNOPQRST UUWXYZ&abcdefghijklm nopqrstuvwxyz $1234567890!?

APPLE GENEVA
(1991)

Designed in collaboration with Charles Bigelow for Apple Computer, Inc., this light sans serif is characterized by a large x-height lowercase.

ABCDEFGHIJKLMNOPQRSTU VWXYZ&abcdefghijklmnopqr stuvwxyz$1234567890!?

APPLE MONACO
(1991)

Designed in collaboration with Charles Bigelow for Apple Computer, Inc., it is a somewhat condensed version of *Geneva*.

It differs from it in the calligraphic lowercase that resembles *Lucida Sans Italic* lowercase, as well as in the use of serifed letters I, i, J, and j, which permit a greater legibility in words like lilith, Illinois, or Iliad.

ABCDEFGHIJKLMNOPQRSTUV WXYZ&abcdefghijklmnopq rstuvwxyz$1234567890!?

APPLE NEW YORK (1991)

Designed in collaboration with Charles Bigelow for Apple Computer, Inc., this is a crisp serif face with a calligraphic touch.

ABCDEFGHIJKLMNOPQR
STUVWXYZ&abcdefghij
klmnopqrstuvwxyz
$1234567890!?

LUCIDA HANDWRITING (1992)

Designed in collaboration with Charles Bigelow, this free-hand version of *Lucida* is a lively pen-drawn letter with connecting strokes.

ABCDEFGHIJKLMNOPQ
RSTUVWXYZ&abcdefgh
ijklmnopqrstuvwxyz
$1234567890!?

LUCIDA CONSOLE (1994)

Designed in collaboration with Charles Bigelow, this is a low, wide sans serif typeface with large x-height lowercase letters, and ascenders that surpass caps in height.

It is interesting to note the presence of horizontal strokes in upper case letters I and J, and lowercase letters i, j, and l, which permit a greater legibility in words like lilith, Iliad, or Illinois.

ABCDEFGHIJKLMNOPQRSTU
VWXYZ&abcdefghijklmno
pqrstuvwxyz
$1234567890!?

WALTER HUXLEY

Born in New York City in 1890, Walter Huxley graduated from the Art Institute of Chicago, where he taught for two years.

In 1928, he was cofounder and director of Huxley House in New York City, worked for the American Type Founders Company, and attended the Art Students League.

He was also chairman of the Advertising Typographers Association of America, Inc., a member of the New York Typographical Union No. 6, and a member of the American Institute of Graphic Arts (AIGA).

In 1934, he designed *Huxley Vertical,* a condensed Art Deco style type design sans serif, which was released by ATF the following year. It is interesting to compare it with *Empire*, designed by Morris Fuller Benton two years later, which, differently from *Huxley Vertical*, it is characterized by a modulated stroke.

Walter Huxley died in Falls Village, Connecticut in 1955, at the age of sixty-five.

HUXLEY VERTICAL (1935)

A delicate narrow sans serif face with an apparent even weight, it is characterized by low cross strokes extended to the left.

Expressive of the pre-World War II "modernism," it is a typeface still in use. It was very popular as a volumetric type in building façades.

ABCDEFGHIJKLMNOPQRSTUVWXYZ&
$1234567890!?

REA IRVIN

Caricaturist, illustrator, and letterman, Rea Irvin was born in San Francisco in 1881 and attended the Hopkins Art Institute in that city.

In 1925, Harold Ross founded the New Yorker, and invited Irvin as his first employee with the title of art director.

Ross and Irvin would select the submitted cartoons and drawings, slowly giving form to the magazine's style ~urban, urbane, and above all, witty.

This New York City magazine, which later became a major influence on the quality and level of sophisticated writing and humor in the United States, was the perfect publication for Irvin's type of work.

He did many covers, which in time became models in art courses, as a way to show students how to tell an anecdote without using words.

Among his colleagues may be listed many of the most famous cartoonists: James Thurber, Peter Arno, Saul Steinberg, Gluyas Williams, John Held, Otto Soglow, George Price, Charles Addams, Gardner Rea, Chon Day, Cobean, Whitney Darrow Jr., Alan Dunn, Robert Day, William Steig, Carl Rose, Mary Petty, and Helen E. Hopkinson.

By this time, Irvin and his wife were living in Newtown, Connecticut, and he commuted between there and New York.

In 1930, Irvin also experimented with comic strips. His short~lived Sunday color page the Smythes, done for the New York Herald Tribune, maintained the same sophisticated humor as his cartoons.

When Harold Ross died in 1951, Rea Irvin had a conflict with the magazine's editorial staff. He still submitted drawings occasionally, but they were not accepted. "He would not consider working for anyone else," commented his wife Dorothy.

Irvin and his wife moved permanently to Estate Le Grange near Fredericksted, in the American Virgin Islands, where they bought a house in 1948. He kept busy doing little drawings for his friends, and murals for the tennis club, the country club and his home.

Lee Lorenz, in his article "Cover Stories" (the New Yorker, December, 1997), would say, "More than anyone else, Rea Irvin invented the look of the New Yorker; he designed the magazine's distinctive headline typeface, and drew the trademark Regency dandy which adorned the inaugural issue's cover. An artist of rare subtlety, he could suggest a complete personality by the cock of an eyebrow or the slope of a jaw."

The first issue, published in February 1925, contained an illustration by Irvin of a Regency aristocratic gentleman observing a butterfly with his monocle. This character later became the identification image for the magazine, under the name of Eustace Tilly, while the masthead, drawn in very particular and informal lettering, gave base to a complete alphabet that was used in the publication's headlines.

The alphabet, known as Irvin, was later cut and issued by the American Lanston Monotype Company, Philadelphia, as a private typeface for the New Yorker. It has continued being used as part of the publication's typographical identification.

Rea Irvin died in 1972 in Estate Le Grange, the American Virgin Islands, at the age of ninety~one.

IRVIN (1925)

This very unusual and informal roman typeface started as the *New Yorker*'s masthead.

Harold Ross, editor of the magazine, suggested that Irvin completed the alphabet that has been used since then as part of the publication's typographical identity.

ABCDEFGHIJKLMNOPQRS
TUVWXYZ&
$1234567890?!()

CLUBS WE DO NOT CARE TO JOIN, The Darwin Club

In this drawing, Irvin caricatures the way certain people behave.

EUSTACE TILLY (1925)

A simplified black and white version of the 1925 cover illustration of the aristocratic gentleman looking at a butterfly through his monocle, this became the symbol of the *New Yorker* under the name of *Eustace Tilly*.

PREDICAMENT IN CONNECTICUT (1933)

Curious behavior of the Litchfield Hounds, following their Broadway runs in *"Uncle Tom's Cabin."*

THE NEW YORKER'S MASTHEAD (1925)

The particular shape of the letters used in the magazine's masthead gave form to a complete alphabet known as *Irvin*, after its author's name. It has continued being utilized throughout the *New Yorker*, as a display type in many of its headlines.

THE NEW YORKER (1925)

The magazine's first issue cover, which appeared in February 1925 designed by Irvin, outlines from the start the characteristic personality of the magazine.

THE NEW YORKER (1936)

Of this cover, says Lee Lorenz, "The popeyed Negro in the chicken coop is a cliché right out of blackface vaudeville, and Irvin treats the Negro figure in a correspondingly broad manner –one that makes 'Amos 'n' Andy' look like 'The Cosby Show'."

February 21, 1925 THE Price 15 cents

NEW YORKER

The third of four brothers, Richard L. Isbell was born in Kingsville, Canada, in 1924. Both parents were U.S. citizens. The family returned to the States when he was three years old and settled in Detroit, Michigan.

From an early age, he wanted to be an artist, an illustrator. Thus, from 1936 to 1943, he attended a special program of art classes for gifted students that were offered every Saturday at the Detroit Institute of Arts. He also attended Cass Tech High School (a magnet school in Detroit), known at the time as the best high school for the arts in the country. At Cass, Isbell was first introduced to the beauty of letter design, having the opportunity to take all the lettering classes offered.

In 1943, Isbell left school during his senior year and joined the U.S. Marines. After basic training, he was sent overseas and joined the First Marine Division in Australia. Later on, he was assigned to the Fifth Regiment Intelligence Section as a scout and observer. During his tour in the South Pacific, he made several drawings that toured the United States, traveling combat art.

In 1945, he was discharged from the Marines. He immediately went to work at the Fisher Body Division of General Motors, Detroit, in the graphic illustration section. After a year's work, he resigned to freelance in lettering and design.

Early in 1947, he joined New Center Studios, Detroit –owned by Art Greenwald, an ex-lettering artist and a tough taskmaster for details– where he started as a lettering and design artist, and where he worked for a period of nine years. It was there that

he created, in 1955, his first alphabets for *Mercury* and *Pontiac* automobiles. Marv Collins also worked with the New Center Studios. He was a great lettering artist and became Isbell's mentor.

In 1956, he left this post to join a group of artists from the New Center Studios, forming with them the Art Group Studios. He worked there for four years, and had the opportunity to design many special alphabets for automotive clients.

In 1960, he left the Art Group and joined, as graphic director, Headliners International of Detroit, where he worked for fifteen years, designing over fifty alphabets.

During this time, he also created various *Oldsmobile* announcement ads, and in collaboration with Jerry Campbell, Isbell designed many special alphabets for clients, banks, automotive, and related businesses.

In 1965, Isbell joined the General Motors' design staff, where he designed the new *Chevrolet* signature and an alphabet for model recognition. He also designed the new *Buick* and *Cadillac* signatures, two alphabets for model recognition; the *Saturn* signature; the *Geo* trademark; as well as the General Motors corporate signature.

In 1966, he created *Americana* for American Type Founders. Besides its accentuated calligraphic and wide letter form characteristics and an extremely large x-height lowercase, it included a new punctuation mark: the *interabang* (‽) or *interrobang* as his author calls it.

Invented by Martin K. Speckter, an advertising-agency president and a printer by hobby, this sign (‽) permits a double exclamation

and interrogation possibility in those sentences where there is a sense of ambiguity.

Delighted in its possibilities, ATF planned to include it in all new types that the firm would cut. If it had gained wide acceptance, it would have been the first punctuation mark to enter the printed language since the introduction of the quotation mark during the late seventeenth century.

In 1975, as partner with Jerry Campbell, Isbell designed *ITC Isbell*. Aaron Burns named it after its creator, and ITC did complete publicity about the new typeface.

From 1976 to 1988, he was instructor of lettering and design at the Center for Creative Studies, School of Art and Design in Detroit. He also lectured at the New York Type Directors' Club, the University of Michigan, Michigan State University, and Wayne State University.

In 1991, he designed a new typeface called *Baccarat* for Tracy Headliners, which continues showing his delicate calligraphic treatment.

Today, after forty-five years of graphic work, Richard Isbell dedicates his time to landscape painting and woodcarving.

AMERICANA (1966)

Designed as part of an assignment to "return to elegance," it features short, slightly concave serifs, and short ascenders. Letters are quite wide and capitals are lower than the ascenders.

With the alphabet signs, Richard Isbell included the *interabang*, invented by Martin K. Speckter, which permits a graphic accent for ambiguous sentences.

ABCDEFGHIJKLMNOPQR
STUVWXYZ&abcdefghijkl
mnopqrstuvwxyz
$1234567890?!‽

AIRTEMP (1962)

This logotype was designed as part of the *Chrysler Airtemp* model during the 1960s.

DECALS & OTHER THINGS (1977)

Calligraphic logotype designed for CIA, a firm that produces decals.

BODY HEAT (1979)

Using the *ITC Benguiat* alphabet as a graphic support, Isbell gives it a special treatment for letterforms, creating a visual feeling of temperature.

CHEVROLET (1988)

Being designed when Isbell joined the General Motors' design staff, this logotype has the structure of an existing, well-designed alphabet.

GENERAL MOTORS (1992)

Designed when Isbell joined the General Motors design staff, this logotype is part of the firm's corporate identity.

BUICK MOTOR DIVISION (1989)

A stylized, wide version of a *Clarendon* alphabet, this identification logo shows his ability to create new alphabets.

IMPACT

The breaking of the letters creates a visual impact.

DETROIT

Masthead designed for this Detroit's publication.

TV AND MOVIE STAR

A logotype designed for a TV and movie star product store.

SEVILLE (1989)

Logotype signature designed for this *Cadillac* model recognition.

GRAPHIC ARTISTS ASSOCIATION (1978)

This calligraphic logotype, executed with a free brush stroke, carries on the form and structure with a sense of freedom related to the institution.

ITC ISBELL (1980)
Designed for ITC while Isbell
was a partner to Jerry Campbell,
this serif typeface continues with the
calligraphic treatment he has given
to all of his typefaces as well as the
use of a large x-height lowercase.

ABCDEFGHIJKLMNOPQRST
UVWXYZ&abcdefghijklmnop
qrstuvwxyz$1234567890!?

ABCDEFGHIJKLMNOPQRST
UVWXYZ&abcdefghijklmnopq
rstuvwxyz$1234567890!?

ABCDEFGHIJKLMNOPQR
STUVWXYZ&abcdefghijkl
mnopqrstuvwxyz
$1234567890!?

ABCDEFGHIJKLMNOPQRS
TUVWXYZ&abcdefghijklm
nopqrstuvwxyz
$1234567890!?

TF BACCARAT (1991)

This handsome, condensed, humanistic sans serif, designed in 1991, and commercialized by Treacy Headlines in 1998, is characterized by short ascenders and descenders and a large x-height lowercase.

Other interesting features are found in the use of a lowercase **u** instead of a capital letter **U**, and a separated, horizontal stroke in the letters **E** and **F**.

ABCDEFGHIJKLMNOPQRSTUVWXYZ
&abcdefghijklmnopqrstuvwxyz
1234567890

RICHARD ISBELL

KAUFMANN

Born in Philadelphia in 1904 Max Richard Kaufmann became a designer, typographer, and lettering artist.

He was an art consultant for **Liberty** and an art director for **McCall's**, and later for Hill & Knowlton publishers in New York City.

In the mid-1930s, there was an interest in the lettering that accompanies comic strips —an extremely informal lettering.

This typographical trend, in which several type foundries were interested, started with **Cartoon** a design created by Howard Allen Trafton in 1936, and commercially launched by the Bauer type foundry in Frankfurt, Germany.

In the United States, the American Type Founders Company commissioned Max Kaufmann, who had designed **Kaufmann Script** in 1935 for them, to design a "cartoon" typeface. **Balloon** was launched in 1939, which like **Cartoon** didn't include a lowercase alphabet.

That same year, the English Lanston Monotype Corporation also produced its own cartoon typeface. Designed by Edwin W. Shaar, and different from the other typefaces, **Flash** included a lowercase alphabet.

Max Richard Kaufmann was also a member of the American Institute of Graphic Arts AIGA.

Kaufmann Script (1936)
Issued by ATF, this calligraphic sans serif is characteristic of the "modernistic" style of the 1930s.

The connecting strokes are well managed to provide the appearance of a smooth, flowing, hand lettering while reflecting a contemporary look and a high degree of legibility.

ABCDEFGHIJKLMNOPQRSTUVWXYZ
&abcdefghijklmnopqrstuvwxyz
$1234567890!?

Kaufmann Bold (1936)

An accompanying version to *Kaufmann Script*, this design is an interesting graphic experience for making a calligraphic stroke bolder.

ABCDEFGHIJKLMNOP2RST UVWXYZ&abcdefghijklmnopqrs tuvwxyz$1234567890!?

BALLOON (1939)

Based on the calligraphy employed in comic strips, it is a sans serif drawn with a round lettering pen. In fact, the working name in the foundry for the series was *Speedball Light*, *Bold*, and *Extra Heavy*, after these popular types of pens.

The typeface name comes from the *balloons* employed in comic strips.

It is also important to recall that these types of scripts were the result of a trend started in 1936 with *Cartoon*, a typeface designed by Howard Allen Trafton for the Bauer type foundry in Germany.

ABCDEFGHIJKLMNOPQRSTUVWXYZ &$1234567890!?

ABCDEFGHIJKLMNOPQRSTUVWXYZ &$1234567890!?

ABCDEFGHIJKLMNOPQRSTU VWXYZ&$1234567890!?

Born in 1912 in Spring Hill, a suburb of Mobile, Alabama, Emil J. Klumpp first attended local schools and then Spring Hill College, which he left in 1930 to take art training at the American Academy of Art in Chicago.

In 1933, after he had finished his art training, he began his professional career in the art department of a Chicago printing firm. Subsequently, he worked in the art department of the Washington Post as a lettering artist, heading Eastern sales operations for two of the nation's leading photo-lettering companies.

Emil Klumpp returned to Chicago where he freelanced in lettering and lettering design until 1941. Shortly before Pearl Harbor, he became a civilian instructor and manager at an Air Service Command Depot in Mobile, Alabama.

During the War, he was an instructor in industrial supervision and management training for the U.S. Government. Once the war had ended, Klumpp moved to New York, where he headed the New York studio of Lettering, Inc., a photo-lettering firm based in Chicago. There, he also helped establish Headliners, Inc., also dedicated to photo-lettering.

In 1955, Jan van der Ploeg of American Type Founders asked Klumpp to supply a contemporary face that could be used for display, job, and social printing. He felt that ATF should "come out with something new in style." This was the time when Park Avenue (Robert Smith, 1933) and other like typefaces were beginning to saturate the market.

After talking with some friends —Herb Rear, John Schaedle, Freeman Craw— Klumpp started to work on a face that he first felt should be a connected script. After drawing a complete alphabet, he had it photostatted, and from these, he worked on fitting and spacing. Curiously enough, some of the test words chosen came out with no connections between them, and Klumpp started to question if the face should have a connecting structure. After much work with the ATF production department, the typeface was finally finished.

Named after a well-known advertising area in New York, Murray Hill was produced by ATF in 1955, and first shown at a meeting of the Mobile Advertising Club in Mobile, Alabama on December 9th that year in the presence of Klumpp himself. The immediate success of the design prompted the production and issuing of Murray Hill Bold the following year (1956).

As Klumpp explained, "there are generally three primary elements in printed-page advertising: illustrative material, headline or display material, and body material. Illustration is not neglected by any means, and certainly deserves all the attention given to it. But, generally, I believe body typography is given far less attention than it should. I recommend more attention to typography, but no less to illustration. The headline and other display type, I feel, should receive not only more, but different attention than it is generally given in preparation.

"Functionally, the headline performs more like illustration than body type. Sometimes display is illustration and rarely body. My suggestion to the thoughtful is to review and consider display perhaps differently than heretofore —as a major function in itself. But be sure to co-ordinate it properly with the other two functions of illustrations and body."

In August, 1961, Klumpp joined the American Type Founders' Type Division as regional manager, becoming later that same year sales manager and director of typeface design, succeeding Jan van der Ploeg, who had been promoted to the position of manager of foreign sales.

In 1966, he worked with Bauer Alphabets and became a member of APA, while continuing to give lectures on type and type design.

Klumpp was known here and abroad as a lettering artist, a type designer, and an authority on type, having designed typefaces for both metal and photocomposition. For photo-process lettering he designed more than sixty alphabets.

In his position as director of typeface design, he directed and assisted the design of several faces for ATF. Included among these are: Americana, Catalina, Century Nova, and Caslon 641.

He was a well-known author and lecturer on lettering and type and won many awards for his graphic designs.

He also was a member of the Artists' Guild of Chicago; the Society of Typographic Arts, also in this city; the Type Directors Club of New York; the Sales Executive Club of New York; and Sales & Marketing Executive International.

Emil J. Klumpp spent his retirement years in Avenel, New Jersey, where he died in 1997 at the age of eighty-five.

Murray Hill Bold
(1956)

Klumpp designed this flowing, modern script alphabet, with non-connecting letters, for American Type Founders in 1955, with a bold version added in 1956.

Its name comes from a New York telephone exchange, serving a well-known advertising area.

ABCDEFGHIJKLMNOPQ
RSTUVWXYZ&abcdefghijklmn
opqrstuvwxyz$1234567890!?

DESIGN YOUR HEADLINES
(1955)

"I was reasonably happy with the first doodles so I quickly drew these few letters (**A**) and next day ordered enough Photostats to paste up a few words and letter combinations (**B**). The drawings were crude, but showed promise of working out. To check further, the first letters were enlarged two or three times, traced, and inked with particular emphasis on making the connections meet (**C**). Many words (**D**) were pasted up from new Photostats, trimmed to present pieces of type.

"Each stat deludes myself if I allowed any spacing or fitting adjustments. Some letters were tested up and down and twisted, however. Curiously, many words chosen at random came out with no connections in them and I began to wonder if I wanted connections at all. A few words were selected to submit to Mr. Jan van der Ploeg," says Klumpp.

THE ANNOUNCEMENT
OF THE CENTURY (1955)

These lines were the first sketches of *Murray Hill*, composed of pasted-up Photostats and submitted by Klumpp to Jan van der Ploeg of American Type Founders.

"I don't think it was what he expected but he was not displeased, rather he seemed interested. He took the sample back for consideration and to get some reactions on it. In about ten days, he called and said we ought to get together and go over this type and find a name for it.

"Then the real test came. We had the technical people go over our selections and they pointed out half dozen or more ink traps, which were marked for alteration. Happily, the matrix people were enthused with the design, which certainly helped very much."

MURRAY HILL BROCHURE
(1956)

Two pages of the brochure issued by Warwick Typographers, Inc.

MURRAY HILL BROCHURE
(1956)

A cover of the brochure designed to present *Murray Hill* to customers. It is interesting to note the positive and negative word samples.

MURRAY HILL BOLD
BROCHURE (1956)

A cover of the brochure designed to present *Murray Hill Bold* to customers.

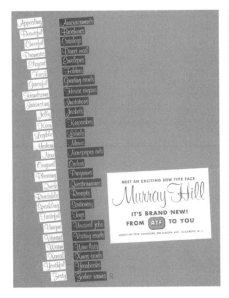

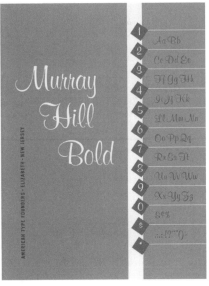

Born in Troy, Ohio in 1844, Tolbert Lanston was the son of Nicholas Randall Lanston. During his boyhood, he moved to Iowa with his parents.

While he attended the district schools and helped with the farm work, he displayed marked mechanical skill and inventive ability, until the outbreak of the American Civil War, when he enlisted and served throughout its duration.

Once the war ended, Lanston went to Washington, D.C., where he obtained a clerical position in the U. S. Pension Office. He continued there for twenty-two years while he studied law and was admitted to the bar.

He always found time to exercise his mechanical ingenuity. He was granted a patent for a sewing machine, a water faucet, and a window sash.

Around 1883, after finishing and patenting several other inventions, he became greatly interested in machines for composing type, probably as a result of the work Ottmar Mergenthaler was then doing in Washington.

Presumably Lanston devoted all of his available time between 1883 and 1887 to this matter, for he was granted in June 7, 1887, three patents: one "for producing justified lines of type," another for a "type forming and composing machine," and another "for a new form of type." William S. Bancroft aided Lanston in the technical implementation. Around the same time, Lanston obtained a British patent for the same mechanisms.

After he resigned from the U. S. Pension Office, he organized the Lanston Type Machine Company, in Washington, and he assigned all his patents to it. He then undertook the difficult task of converting all his ideas into a practical and successful machine, concerning both procedure and manufacturing. Around 1890, he finally arranged his machine to cast types from melted metal.

A few years prior to the introduction of his invention, he reorganized his company, and under the new name of Lanston Monotype Manufacturing Company, established a plant in Philadelphia.

In 1893, he exhibited his invention at the World's Columbian Exposition in Chicago. He started its production in 1894 in Philadelphia, although the first machine was not constructed until 1898.

In 1900, the Lanston Monotype Composing Machine was exhibited at the Paris Fair, and in 1908, it was installed for the *Globe* of London. This, by the way, helped to open up a European market for mechanical composition.

While the Linotype composing machine preceded the Monotype, there was room for both, and while the Linotype was more successful in the United States, the Monotype was better received in Europe. One of the reasons for this was the fact that it produced movable type, and was better suited for the good composition of books. The book faces cut by the English Monotype Company were sometimes considered superior to those produced and available in the United States.

The Monotype actually consists of two machines: one for composing type, and one for casting it. As each letter is cast, one by one, at a rate of 150 characters per minute, it is pushed into a line and each line is added to the previous one.

In 1896 Lanston was awarded the Elliott Cresson gold medal by the Franklin Institute of Philadelphia, for his invention. Over and above his basic patents of 1887, he was granted further patents in 1896, 1897 –when finally he was able to introduce his perfected "monotype" composing machine–

1899, 1900, 1902, and 1910. Shortly after securing his last patent he was stricken with paralysis, and was an invalid until his death three years later.

To seek capital for his enterprise, four Monotype machines were shipped to London in 1897. While crossing the Atlantic, the Earl of Dunraven learned of the machine and moved to form a syndicate to secure British rights for £220,000. That same year, the Lanston Monotype was founded with a capital of £550,000. In 1904, the firm was established in Paris.

In 1931, the name of the company was changed to the Lanston Monotype Corporation, and in 1975, to Monotype International which attended to worldwide operations.

Although the Monotype had been invented in 1887, the system was still limited in its production in America in 1894. Shortly after, British owners took charge of the Lanston Monotype Manufacturing Company, transferring its major production to England in 1900.

In 1905, the Monotype machine was able to cast up to 12-pt running text and up to 24-pt manually. In 1907, the keyboard was improved, permitting a faster handling of type composition.

It is interesting to note that the Monotype system was widely used for letterpress printing throughout the world up to the mid-1970s, when it was finally replaced by photocomposition and computerized composition systems.

Tolbert Lanston died in Washington DC in 1913, at the age of sixty-nine, one year after the first original *Old style* typeface, *Imprint*, was issued by the English Monotype in London.

GARAMONT (1920)

When Frederic W. Goudy joined Lanston Monotype Company as art advisor, he persuaded the company to cut its own version of *Garamond*, rather than copying the foundry face.

To preserve a difference with other versions, he suggested calling it *Garamont*. Both spellings here, by the way, were used during Garamond's lifetime.

ABCDEFGHIJKLMNOPQR
STUVWXYZ&abcdefghijklm
nopqrstuvwxyz$1234567890

THE MONOTYPE MACHINE
(1893)

The Monotype machine is composed of two individual and different machines that are managed by two different operators for the **keyboard** and the **composition caster**.

The **keyboard** has two banks of keys, representing seven complete sets of alphabet characters and figures, punctuation marks, spaces, and justification keys. Usually, the left-hand bank is used for roman and small caps, and the right-hand bank, for italic and bold faces.

Through the use of the **keyboard**, the operator prepares the perforated tape on a machine similar to a typewriter that contains all the information in an arrangement of minute holes. When the operation is near the end of the line, he decides if a word needs to be hyphenated or not. He then pulsates a key that divides the remaining space among the spaces between the words, and automatically justifies the line.

Once the operation is completed, the perforated tape is transferred by hand to the **composition caster**, which produces a separate character for each type required in a wide range of styles and sizes which go from 4¼-point to 14-point or 24-point, if a special attachment is additionally used.

Types are cast in rapid succession, and are automatically assembled into words and lines of words, evenly spaced to occupy a predetermined width. Harder metals are used for this single-type composition than are used in line composing machines.

The matrix case contains up to 272 separate matrices and space blanks, arranged in 16 rows with 17 matrices in each row.

Among the great advantages of the Lanston Monotype Composing Machine over the Linotype, we may find that the machine produces individual characters, supplying the printer with the equivalent to a metal type. Corrections are made on individual letters rather than on a complete line. Composed lines can go up to 60 picas, compared to the 42 picas of the Linotype.

On the other hand, the major disadvantage is that the composition might become disordered and the work completely lost. This made the Linotype system preferable over the Monotype for composing newspaper texts.

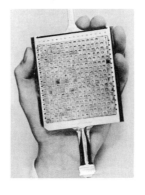

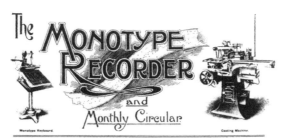

ZUZANA LICKO

Born in Bratislava, Slovakia in 1961, Zuzana Licko immigrated to the United States in 1968, where she studied graphic communications at the University of California, Berkeley.

In 1984, a year which coincides with the birth of the Macintosh computer, she met Rudy VanderLans (b. 1955), who besides having been trained at the Royal Academy of Fine Arts at the Hague in the rules of Swiss typography, had learned the limitations of its rigid system while working in the **San Francisco Chronicle**. With him, she cofounded Émigré Graphics, one of the first independent digital type foundries in the United States to be established on personal computer technology. It has been, since then, a door to a new type design approach.

With the publishing of the **Émigré** magazine in 1984, originally founded by VanderLans and others as an experimental cultural magazine for Dutch immigrants living in California, a center of debates about legibility, design philosophy, and the use of new technology was formed. By 1986, Licko and VanderLans started to apply their own ideas on design, broadening the publication's scope to focus on international artists.

In the same radical vein as other art publications done in the first decades of the twentieth-century, such as **Hard Werken**, **Émigré** was produced by small groups of fine artists and writers with no preconceptions about design, functionality, or legibility. One of the aims of VanderLans was to rebel against the coldness of the Swiss design approach, and to return to the experimental proposals of early Modernists such as Dada.

With pronounced economical limitations, VanderLans employed inexpensive, unconventional methods and materials. Before the introduction of computer language into graphics, he achieved the visual effects present in the magazine by using a typewriter and photocopies. Collage and torn images were combined with a free layout and dramatic scale contrasts.

With the introduction of Macintosh's graphic programs, Licko and VanderLans found the ideal tool to reach their design approach, and a way to reevaluate visual tradition. "It was especially exciting to sit behind this machine right at the beginning, when no one else had really exploited it yet. There were no visual standards and no existing language to copy or be spared by," says VanderLans.

By creating some of the earliest illustrations for **MacWorld** magazine and the new computer magazines in the mid-1980s, VanderLans and Licko were able to solve the economic problems of the early editions of **Émigré** as well as to get acquainted with the immense possibilities inherent in the computer as a production tool for their work.

In their book, **Émigré (The Book): Graphic Design into the Digital Realm**, published in 1993, they expressed their thoughts: "We had already printed the first issue of **Émigré** magazine, but it was the Macintosh that made it economically possible to continue publishing. It also inspired us to design and manufacture original typefaces, an area dominated by only a few large type foundries."

In 1985, Zuzana Licko and Rudy VanderLans established Émigré Fonts with the aim of marketing typefaces designed by her and other designers, including Jeffery Keedy, Barry Deck and J. Downer. Licko found, in the crudeness of this first stage (which was rejected by some designers), an extraordinary opportunity to innovate letterform designs. Her first three typefaces, **Emperor**, **Oakland**, and **Émigré 8**, reflect the simple modular elements derived from the low-resolution characteristics of screen display and dot matrix printing.

Although, with the introduction of **PostScript**, it became possible to use curves, Licko remained restrained, keeping her faces simple, such as **Modula** (1985), **Citizen** (1986), **Matrix** (1986), and **Triplex** (1989), sometimes creating new designs simply by smoothing over the stepped, bitmapped profile of earlier typefaces. She has expressed regret that the new computers' technology

has not continued to develop a unique, expressive style.

By 1987 Licko was already dedicated to typeface design and worked for Adobe Systems, Inc., while VanderLans had quit the **San Francisco Chronicle** to work entirely for Émigré Graphics. By 1989, with a new scope in mind, they started to develop a more aggressive approach to design, and to concentrate on graphic design. They are credited, along with a few other pioneers such as April Greiman, with bringing graphic design into the digital age.

The advantage of not coming from the traditional, calligraphic background of other type designers permitted Licko to approach type design from a digital point of view. She expressed that "the digital concept of combining predetermined units as distinct elements to form a coherent image" which has been common in mosaics, embroidery, and weaving throughout history, is an appropriate aesthetic for the medium. She feels that the difficulty of some people getting used to her typefaces is part of a reading tradition: "You read best what you read most."

Her work, as that of her partner VanderLans, is a continuous endeavor against the preconceived rules of symmetry, grids, and classical balance. Their personal and unreserved subjectivity is headed towards producing new aesthetics of form and composition. They, as all the new typographers, react against the neutrality and inexpressiveness of the sans serif, and base their experiments on the premise that no typeface is inherently legible; rather, as Licko expresses "it is the reader's familiarity with faces that accounts for their legibility."

Among the thirty-six typefaces Zuzana Licko has designed, we should also mention **Variex** (1988), **Journal** (1990), **Totally Glyphic** (1990), **Matrix Script** (1992), **Dogma** (1994), **Base Nine and Twelve** (1995), **Soda Script** (1995), **Filosofia** (1996), **Mrs Eaves** (1996), **Base Monospace** (1997), **Tarzana** (1998), **Solex**, and **Fairplex** (2002).

OAKLAND TEN (1985)

One of Licko's first typefaces, she found in the crudeness of computer bit-mapped images an extraordinary opportunity to innovate on letter structure.

Keeping the basic letter structure, this first approach permitted her to achieve new elements on the computer's limited vocabulary.

ABCDEFGHIJKLMNOPQRSTUVWX
YZabcdefghijklmnopqrstuv
wxyz1234567890

DO YOU READ ME? (1990)

Rudy VanderLans designed this special type issue for *Émigré* magazine No. 15.

DESIGN CIRCUS (1990)

This poster/flyer was designed for an exhibition of Rudy VanderLans's work at the Columbus Society of Communicating Arts.

OKLAND TEN (1985)

Graphic presentation of *Okland Ten*.

MODULAR REGULAR (1985)

Graphic presentation of *Modular Regular*. The type's name later changed to *Modula*.

STARTING FROM ZERO (1991)

This cover design for *Émigré* magazine No. 19 presents a more austere VanderLans design.

It was originally printed in yellow and black.

ÉMIGRÉ (1984)

A logo designed for *Émigré Graphics*.

The 1937 Morris Fuller Benton's *Empire* typeface has been enhanced by open strokes that stand for the accents present in the original spelling, ÉMIGRÉ.

TOTALLY GOTHIC (1990)

A presentation of Totally Gothic typeface, complemented with the text from an interview with Zuzana Licko.

Beginning with a gothic type, she transcribed it point by point, and then worked it on Fontographer. The new forms clearly reaffirm her statement.

ÉMIGRÉ MAGAZINE (1988)

Glenn Suokko created this cover design for a special issue on Dutch designers.

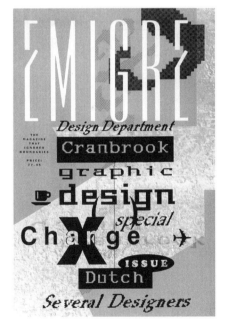

"typefaces are not intrinsically legible. rather, it is the reader's familiarity with faces that accounts for their legibility. studies have shown that readers read best what they read most. legibility is also a dynamic process, as readers' habits are everchanging. it seems curious that blackletter typestyles, which we find illegible today, were actually preferred over more humanistic designs during the eleventh and fifteenth centuries. similarly, typestyles that we perceive as illegible today may well become tomorrow's classic choices."

MODULA (1985)

In this condensed Art Deco style sans serif typeface, Zuzana Licko has introduced an angular ending in various upper and lowercase letters so as to clearly define them.

Some letterforms also change from the regular to the condensed version, such as capital letters **M**, **N**, **P**, and **R**. Lowercase letter **g** also changes from one storey to a two-storey configuration.

ABCDEFGHIJKLMNOPQRSTUVWXYZabcdefghijklmno
pqrstuvwxyz1234567890

ABCDEFGHIJKLMNOPQRSTUVWXYZ&abcdefghijklmno
pqrstuvwxyz$1234567890?!

MATRIX REGULAR (1986)

The design of *Matrix*, a latin serif typeface, is based upon the proportions of Licko's *Émigré Fourteen* bitmap design.

"*Matrix* was designed when the personal computer was very crude and memory space was very expensive. To ensure legibility for text applications, the basic elements are derived from classical forms. The characters' proportions are based on a few simple ratios and the points required to define the letterforms are limited to the essentials. The 45-degree diagonals, used in *Matrix*, are the smoothest diagonals that digital printers can generate. *Matrix* thus consumes relatively little memory space to store in the printer and facilitates fast printing."

Numerals are drawn in *Oldstyle*.

ABCDEFGHIJKLMNOPQRSTUVWXYZ
&abcdefghijklmnopqrstuvwxyz
$1234567890!?

ABCDEFGHIJKLMNOPQRSTUVWXY
Z&abcdefghijklmnopqrstuvwxyz
$1234567890!?

LUNATIX (1988)

It is interesting to note that, apart from extreme oddities in the construction of the letters, there is particular unity of form and structure that makes this typeface present a new approach to letter form and structure.

ABCDEFGHKLMNOPQRSTU
VWXYZabcdefghijklmnop
rstuvwxyz1234567890

Triplex is Licko's first sans serif text design. It evolved from her work with geometric typefaces. Traces of her earlier *Citizen* design are still visible.

Numerals are drawn in *Oldstyle*.

ABCDEFGHIJKLMNOPQRSTUVWXYZ&
abcdefghijklmnopqrstuvwxyz
$1234567890!?

ABCDEFGHIJKLMNOPQRSTUVWXYZ
&abcdefghijklmnopqrstuvwxyz
$1234567890!?

TOTALLY GOTHIC
(1990)

This typeface is Licko's twentieth-century interpretation of the blackletter style.

"Why did letterpress type start to look a certain way, and why was it eventually accepted as being legible? Not because people were reading the type off the bed of a letterpress! They were still reading it off the printed page. That did not have anything more to do with casting lead than it does with computer chips today, but that's where it came from, and that's what we've gotten used to. It's the same with blackletter, which was at one point more legible to people than today's *Helvetica*. So, two hundred years from now, who knows?" says Zuzana Licko.

While in the light version numerals are drawn in *Oldstyle*, the bold version presents substantial differences in form and structure although it preserves the same overall look and feeling.

ABCDEFGHIJKLMNOPQRSTU
VWXYZabcdefghijklmnopqr
stuvwxyz1234567890

ABCDEFGHIJKLMNO
PQRSTUVWXYZabc
defghijklmnopqrs
tuvwxyz
1234567890

Herbert Frederick Lubalin, the younger of fraternal twins, was born in New York City in 1918 to a German-Russian family. Left-handed and color-blind, as was his brother, his child drawings always presented people with purple hair. Being a good art student in high school, despite his inability to draw recognizable images, his drawing teacher encouraged his feelings for design and lettering.

In 1935, Lubalin entered Cooper Union School of Art, from which he graduated in 1939, with an award for Professional Achievement. The turning point was a class of calligraphy. His love for letters and typography grew to the point of making him a master of typographic language.

In the 1930s, layout was secondary to copy. Large agencies employed one art director to whom layout artists reported. The concept of a graphic designer had not yet evolved. However, the Second World War had begun, and many changes came into being in terms of communication. Television had already appeared and there was an audiovisual impact on the consumer. Also, with the threat of war in Europe, many great designers immigrated to the United States, such as Herbert Bayer, M. F. Agha, and Alexey Brodovitch. With them, many American designers and photographers came onto the scene: William Golden, Richard Avedon, Bradbury Thompson, and Paul Rand.

Better schools in the States adopted the Bauhaus teachings, the simplicity of the De Stijl and the discipline of the Wiener Werkstätte. Young art school graduates and rebellious layout people began to use new concepts of design, and layout men became art directors working as a team with copywriters. By the end of the war, a new generation of artists and designers appeared as well as a different attitude from the client.

In 1945 Lubalin became art director at Sudler & Hennessey, Inc., a studio specializing in pharmaceutical ads.

He worked with twenty people, including illustrators, photographers, comprehensive people, letterers and retouchers who followed through on Lubalin's tissues –a 18" x 24" tracing paper pad roughs– which reflected the whole solution.

In time, the agency became Sudler, Hennessey & Lubalin, Inc., with Lubalin as creative director, and a staff of more than forty people. He would say, "The most intriguing thing about advertising is writing a headline." His responsibility is to educate the consumer about the aesthetics of good graphics, for advertising offered the most exciting form of communication.

In 1961 he redesigned the *Saturday Evening Post* magazine and later, in 1972, he did a few other issues before it folded. In this year, Lubalin designed *Eros*, a Ralph Ginsberg publication of ninety-six pages, which was the first magazine with a mature approach to love and sex, and which secured his reputation as an editorial designer.

In 1964 he established Herb Lubalin Inc., for which the main commissions were logos and typeface design for architectural, editorial, and industrial clients. This year he also designed *Fact*, another of Ginsberg's controversial publications.

In 1968, he designed *Avant Garde*, the third of Ginsberg's publications, which continued to confirm his talent as an editorial designer and which gave birth, in 1970, to the famous *ITC Avant Garde Gothic* typeface –one of the most successful typefaces of the twentieth century– designed in collaboration with Tom Carnase.

In late 1969, in association with Aaron Burns, his partner in Lubalin, Burns & Co., Inc., and Edward Rondthaler from Photo-Lettering, Inc., he established the International Typeface Corporation, which became the world's largest supplier of typefaces. For ITC, he drew two other important typefaces: *ITC Serif Gothic* (1972), and *ITC Lubalin*

Graph (1974), in collaboration with Tony DiSpigna.

But it was in 1973, through ITC's quarterly publication, *U&lc* (*Upper & lowercase*), that Lubalin found his true place as editor and designer. Through his work, *U&lc* became a major influence on the typographic industry worldwide through the 1970s and 1980s, and a perfect place for type creation.

In 1976-1981, Lubalin was a professor of design at Cooper Union, and in 1979, he had a one-man exhibition at the George Pompidou Center for the Arts in Paris.

With new technologies, Lubalin felt freer to do what he wanted. The result excited him, not the technology. "We read words, not characters, and pushing letters closer or tightening space between lines doesn't destroy legibility; it merely changes reading habits."

All things surrounding him reflected Lubalin's personal style. He was an innovative typographer who rejected the functionalism philosophy held by his European counterparts in favor of an exuberant, eclectic approach. A gifted communicator, he combined words and images to express his ideas with great visual impact.

His work was featured in many publications, such as *Idea*, *Print*, and *Gebrauchsgraphik*, among others, and received numerous international awards, such as the Art Directors Club of New York Hall of Fame (1977), and the AIGA medal (1981).

Herbert Frederick Lubalin died of cancer in New York City in 1981, at the age of sixty-three.

ITC AVANT GARDE GOTHIC (1970)

Originally the masthead of the *Avant Garde* magazine, it evolved into a complete font. It was the first typeface released by ITC.

Tom Carnase and Ed Benguiat later developed other weights and italics.

ABCDEFGHIJKLMNOPQRSTU
VWXYZ&abcdefghijklmnop
qrstuvwxyz$1234567890!?

DIMENSION (1966)

A logo designed for the radio division of the Columbia Broadcasting System (CBS).

MORE TO COME (1971)

An animated sequence designed for the on-air television spot for the Public Broadcasting System (PBS).

Ernie Smith, who worked at Lubalin, Smith, Carnase, Inc. (1967-1975), designed the PBS logo.

AVANT GARDE (1968)

The *Avant Garde* magazine masthead which gave birth to the alphabet of the same name. The typeface was commercialized by ITC in 1970.

Tom Carnase developed the complete alphabet and ligatures.

THE BIBLE (1966)

A calligraphic logo designed for John Huston's film, *The Bible*.

THIRTEEN

A logo designed for Channel 13, New York Public Broadcasting Station (PBS). Lubalin refused to use numbers.

MOTHER & CHILD (1966)

Logo designed in collaboration with Tom Carnase for an unpublished magazine of Curtis Publications.

A winner of several prizes, it forms part of the New York Museum of Modern Art's permanent design collection.

AMERICAN BUSINESS (1976)

The masthead logo designed for a business magazine.

It is an outstanding graphic example which incorporates the two money symbols (¢ $) without interfering with the overall word reading.

THE AGONY AND THE ECSTASY (1965)

A calligraphic logo designed for Carol Reed's film, *The Agony and the Ecstasy*, based on Michelangelo's life.

Hal Fiedler did the calligraphy.

COME TO JAZZ (1978)

A cover for ITC's *U&lc* quarterly publication, dedicated to American jazz.

The alphabet used, *Machine*, was designed by Tom Carnase in 1970.

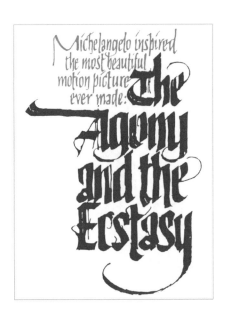

HERB LUBALIN

A typographic self-portrait created for an exhibition at the American Institute of Graphic Arts.

COOPER UNION

A logo designed for the alumni newsletter for the Cooper Union for the Advancement of Science and Art.

FAMILIES (1980)

Being an outstanding example of a typogram, it was designed as the masthead for a family magazine published by *Reader's Digest*.

The publication had only a few issues.

THE SOUND OF MUSIC (1965)

A calligraphic logo designed for Robert Wise's film, *The Sound of Music*.

NEW YORK (1966)

Lubalin's proposal designed as a graphic corporate image for the city of New York.

Although the design was accepted, it was only used once on a white sanitation truck.

MARRIAGE (1965)

A typogram for a poster presenting *Stettler* typeface, designed by Wayne J. Stettler (1934), one of the fifteen award-winning typefaces from the National Typeface Competition sponsored in 1965 by Visual Graphic Corporation, North Miami, Florida.

In this competition Ronald Arnholm, Arthur Baker, and Louis Minott also participated, among others.

THE NEXT WAR (1972)

An antiwar typographic poster designed by Lubalin for an American Institute of Graphic Arts exhibition.

It is a direct example of his concern for the copy, which he also wrote.

In the original poster, the insect's illustration was printed in color, which contrasted with the overall blackness.

UPPER & LOWER CASE (1976)

This cover, highlighting the bicentennial anniversary of the United States Independence (1776-1976), was done for a 1976 issue of *U&lc* magazine.

Tom Carnase did the calligraphy.

ITC SERIF GOTHIC
(1974)

A handsome glyphic typeface, it was based on a logo designed for a French shirt company that had been sketched by Lubalin and drawn by Tom Carnase.

Turned down by the client, Tony DiSpigna completed the alphabet, which was issued by ITC in 1974.

ABCDEFGHIJKLMNOPQRSTU
VWXYZ&abcdefghijklmnop
qrstuvwxyz$1234567890!?

**ABCDEFGHIJKLMNOPQRSTU
VWXYZ&abcdefghijklmnop
qrstuvwxyz$1234567890!?**

ITC LUBALIN GRAPH
(1974)

Essentially a slab serif version of *ITC Avant Garde Gothic*, the roman version was designed by Lubalin and drawn by Tony DiSpigna and Jose Sundwall.

Ed Benguiat drew the italic version in 1981.

It is also interesting to compare *ITC Lubalin Graph* with *Karnak Light*, designed by Robert Hunter Middleton between 1931 and 1942.

ABCDEFGHIJKLMNOPQRS
TUVWXYZ&abcdefghijklm
nopqrstuvwxyz
$1234567890!?

**ABCDEFGHIJKLMNOPQ
RSTUVWXYZ&abcdefghi
jklmnopqrstuvwxyz
$1234567890!?**

With the invention of the **Linotype** in 1885 by Ottmar Mergenthaler, and the **Monotype** in 1887 by Tolbert Lanston, the hot metal text type composition had been accomplished, including the possibility of disposing of fresh material every time there was new composing to be done. Nonetheless, the problem for casting display type continued.

Up to this time, titles and advertising ads were set by using wood type. With the full development of display type cast, the use of wood type progressively declined.

In 1906, Washington I. Ludlow had the idea for a display typesetting machine, and brought it to William A. Reade for its development. For this purpose, the Ludlow Typograph Company was established in Chicago.

The original idea included a set of matrix bars nearly two feet long, each of which carried the entire alphabet, points, and figures. These bars were wedge-shaped, and the wide letters were on the wide part, with the progressive narrower letters following in order towards the thinner end of the bar. When each bar was positioned with the desired character in place over the mold, the line was cast. This machine, which was less expensive and easier to manage than a keyboard machine, such as the Linotype or the Monotype, was intended for setting body text, 8, 10, and 12 pt.

In spite of the difficulties, especially in making the matrix bars, this model was brought to completion and five machines of this type were built during 1909. But in the way it was conceived it was not commercially attractive.

Meanwhile, during the experimental period, Reade became convinced of the need for equipment in the composing room which could produce display type and job composition in a more effective way.

Making a new start, he conceived the idea of setting lines of individual matrices by hand, directly from copy, and casting slug lines by means of a simpler and more flexible mechanism.

The new model, which did not have any resemblance to the original idea, went into production, and the first individual matrices, which were engraved, were set publicly in January 1911. This was the real start of the Ludlow Typograph Company.

The casting mechanism was redesigned and twenty machines were built during that year. Nevertheless, it soon became evident that the true task of the company was not to make machines, but to provide clients with an adequate variety of matrices. Newspapers, for which the new mechanism was initially intended, would not and could not use a system for which matrices were available in few sizes and type styles.

The manufacturing of such large point size matrices became a real problem, for while type founders only needed a matrix for one given character, the Ludlow Company had to manufacture matrices of any given character by the thousands.

A type founder could engrave a matrix directly, at a low cost, but to produce a large quantity of matrices, when there were no machines available for this purpose, was a different situation. The Ludlow Typograph Company therefore had to design and build its own presses.

The accuracy with which matrices were produced largely contributed to the success of the Ludlow type casting system. A great deal of other special machinery also had to be designed and built.

Early in 1912, fonts for 36 pt **Caslon Bold** were produced, and late in 1913, matrices for 24 pt **Caslon Light** were completed. By this time, a slanted matrix had been devised for the production of italics and script faces. Angled matrices were a unique Ludlow feature which permitted greater flexibility in design, better character fit and joins, and a stronger, more durable slug for printing.

In this year, the first machine with the new principle was successfully installed at the **Chicago Evening Post** daily newspaper, and the following year, two machines were installed in the composing room of the **Cleveland Press**. This was the first plant to carry out the entire slug make-up of the paper, a practice which soon became common in all newspapers.

In 1916, the first building —later owned by the company— was leased as a factory. While the general offices remained in Cleveland, an office was maintained in Chicago.

In 1917, an arrangement was made with the Mergenthaler Linotype Company whereby this organization would handle the sales of the Ludlow equipment. Sales were handled according to these terms until January 1, 1919, when the Ludlow Typograph Company organized its own department of sales and service field representatives.

As the Ludlow system began to catch on in the newspaper field, parallel sales efforts were concentrated on the commercial printers. In 1918, Saul Brothers Co., in Chicago, carried out the first installation of a plant devoted exclusively to producing commercial job printing.

In 1920, the Ludlow Typograph Company undertook the manufacture and sale of the Elrod strip material caster, invented by Benjamin S. Elrod in 1917, which permitted the casting of lead, rules, and borders. After extensive experimentation, an electrically heated model was placed in the market in 1929. The range in size of the Elrod product was increased, to cast strips from 1 to 36 pt in thickness.

As a complement, Philip P. Merrill, vice president and general manager of the company, conceived the idea of the Ludlow slug aligning matrix. This principle of holding slugs in an accurate vertical alignment with each other permitted the making of charts, another of the particular advantages of the Ludlow system. The first ruleform matrices were produced in 1923.

In consequence of these activities and the ability of the equipment to deliver the performance offered, the Ludlow Typograph Company entered in the 1920s in the strong position of general acceptance throughout the printing industry.

Two other persons were essential in the success of the Ludlow composing machine: Robert Wiebking, who helped the company in the making of the matrices, and Robert Hunter Middleton, who started in the company in 1923, and who largely contributed to the development of American typography with his type designs.

Middleton not only was responsible for the selection of the type designs needed and requested by printers all over the world (Ludlow did considerable export business), but also for the design, the adaptation of typefaces for the Ludlow system, and for the supervision of their production in various sizes and weights.

TEMPO HEAVY CONDENSED (1930)

Designed in 1930 by Robert H. Middleton, head of the type design department at Ludlow, it was the company's answer to the popularity of the European sans serifs in the late 1920s.

With twenty-five variations, the *Tempo* family grew to be the largest font in the Ludlow matrix library.

ABCDEFGHIJKLMNOPQRSTUVWXYZ
&abcdefghijklmnopqrstuvwxyz
$1234567890!?

THE LUDLOW HOT METAL
TYPE CASTING MACHINE (1911)

The main difference between the Linotype and the Ludlow hot metal type casting machines lies in that while the Linotype is a half-mechanical system, the Ludlow is a completely manual system.

The Linotype is divided in three main parts: the **composing machine** where the matrices are assembled in lines through the use of a keyboard; the **casting mechanism**, in which the lines are justified and cast as slugs; and the **distributing mechanism**, which returns the matrices to the matrix magazine after casting.

This whole process is done by hand in the Ludlow composing machine. The operator arranges matrices in a special composing stick, locks them in place, and puts them in the casting device to obtain one line at a time. While the freshly cast line is held in the mold, the foot of the slug is trimmed to assure great accuracy in the metal's height to paper. The machine also has a system that allows the operator to repeat a line as many times as needed. After each line is cast, matrices can be reused for the next line.

While the Linotype system matrices are flat, in the Ludlow system the matrices have a **T** shape. They have the same size (except for thickness) for all type sizes in the 4 pt through 48-pts range. Another size matrix accommodates the 60 to 72-pt sizes. Being the same size, matrices are uniformly easy to pick up, hold and transfer to the composing stick.

Matrices also differ in position for the casting of italics and cursive typefaces. In the Ludlow type composing machine, the matrices are slanted and placed at a 17-degree angle, a characteristic which permits greater flexibility of design, better character fit and joins, and a stronger, more durable slug for printing.

Ludlow type composing machines cast both 6 pt and 12 pt slugs. For the range of sizes above 12 pt, Ludlow lines are cast on a 12 pt slug with an overhang on both sides sufficient to accommodate the extra size. The overhang is 11 pt thick, giving the slug sufficient strength to print without support. The Ludlow slugs are assembled, however, with supporting slugs that fit exactly under the overhanging section of the face.

The Ludlow Typograph Company also believed that whatever was normally set by hand in a well-operated composing room could be produced more efficiently and economically with the Ludlow.

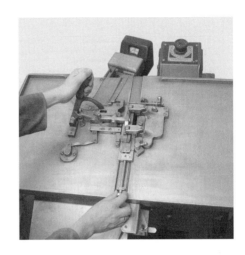

abcdefghijklm

Born in Hachtel, Germany in 1854, Ottmar Mergenthaler came from a family of teachers. Nevertheless, at the age of fourteen, showing an early disposition for mechanics, he began a four-year apprenticeship with his uncle Louis Hahl in watch and clock making in Bietigheim, Württenberg.

Once he finished, he immigrated to the United States. He went first to Baltimore and then to Washington, where he began to work in the scientific instrument shop of his cousin August Hahl in 1872.

When Hahl transferred his business to Baltimore in 1876, Mergenthaler went with him, and shortly after they were called to correct defects in the model of a newly devised typewriting machine made by Charles T. Moore for use in making lithographic transfers. After many trials, results were not completely satisfactory, particularly in obtaining clean type from the papier-mâché molds, and research was headed towards a machine that would eliminate typesetting.

By 1880, Mergenthaler had become a partner in the company. After taking up permanent residence in Baltimore, he opened his own shop. James O. Clephane, who collaborated in the preceding work, once again offered financial support to his research.

By 1883, after he had obtained perfect impressions within the matrix by the use of regular type, he came up with the idea of stamping matrices into type bars and casting type metal into them in the same machine. From this idea Linotype was developed.

By July 1884, with the collaboration of Moore, who had conceived the idea of the type slug, the first direct-casting machine was completed, except for the automatic justification of a line, which was achieved thanks to Jacob W. Shukers the following year. Meanwhile, Clephane and his associates had organized The National Typographic Company of West Virginia, for the manufacturing of this machine.

After the careful examination of the mechanism, three newspaper journalists, Whitelaw Reid from the *New York Tribune*, Melvin S. Stone from the *Chicago Daily News*, and Walter N. Haldeman from the *Courier Journal*, in Louisville, decided to be present during a private testing of the device.

On July 3, 1886, Mergenthaler himself, now thirty-two years old, satisfactorily presented the first of twelve machines –made for the *New York Tribune*– in the office of the editor, Whitelaw Reid. Seeing the machine working, he exclaimed: "Ottmar, you've done it! A line o' type." From there on, the "Blower" –as it was named after its pneumatic system–, was known as *Linotype*.

Before all the machines were delivered, Mergenthaler had carried out nine more improvements. They included the suppression of the air column, the transporting of the matrices by gravity from the magazine to the composing compartment, and the use of an arm to return the matrices back to the magazine. The use of the independent matrix became a reality, thanks to Linn Boyd Benton's invention of the automatic punch-cutter (1885). This invention also enabled the Linotype Company to develop its own matrices and type designs from there on.

By this time, the control of the National Typographic Company and its subsidiary, the Mergenthaler Printing Company, organized in 1885, passed into the hands of a group of newspaper owners. An entire change of policy was put into effect which caused Mergenthaler's resignation in 1888. But as his pride and passion was the Linotype, and not being able to withstand his break with the company, he continued improving his invention.

Mergenthaler's initial machine did not have all the advantages we now associate with it. It was his model –the *Square Base Model I*–, introduced in 1890,

which marked the advent of the modern Linotype. It was the first machine to have a 90-character keyboard that in turn managed 180 different characters, and the first to use matrices similar to the ones later implemented.

In 1897, Mergenthaler improved the measurement of the line to 42-ems, eliminating the need to set two separate slugs and bring them together for measurements wider than 30-picas.

In 1898, with the invention of the two-character matrix, it was not only possible to double the variety of typefaces, but also to easily handle roman and italic, or regular and bold, when composing a text.

By this time he had moved to Deming, New Mexico, to write his memoirs, but a fire destroyed his property, and all his possessions. Thus, he had to return to Baltimore where he died in 1899, at the age of forty-five.

Constant dedication and never-ending anxiety had undermined his health to the extent that he succumbed to tuberculosis after desperately fighting it for five years.

Mergenthaler had finally achieved his goal by developing the *Simplex Linotype*, and assembling of the machine started a regular production in the United States. The first models were installed in England at the offices of the *Newcastle Chronicle* (1889), the *Leeds Mercury*, (1890), and in London, at the *Globe* (1892). In Latin America, the first machines were installed in the first decade of the twentieth-century.

For his great invention he was awarded a medal by the Cooper Union in New York. The Franklin Institute in Philadelphia gave him the John Scott and the Elliot Cresson medals.

Thanks to the Linotype there was an increment in book, magazine, and newspaper production, definitely revolutionizing the educational and communication world.

CHELTENHAM
(1904)

Designed by Bertram Grosvenor Goodhue between 1899 and 1902 and commercialized in 1904, this was the first original type design produced by the Mergenthaler Linotype Company in association with the American Type Founders.

It also was the first type design to include a complete family.

ABCDEFGHIJKLMNOPQRS
TUVWXYZ&abcdefghijklmnopq
rstuvwxyz$1234567890!?

TYPE COMPOSING ROOM (1910)

In spite of the mechanical composing machines, such as the Linotype and the Monotype, manual composition continued to be used for several years. In the photograph we may see the Vacher & Sons printing shop in the first decade of the twentieth century.

THE LINOTYPE MACHINE (1884)

An early version of the Mergenthaler Linotype Composing Machine is now at the Smithsonian Institution in Washington.

LINOTYPE MACHINE (c.1900)

The machine, which requires only one operator, has three main parts: the **composing machine**, in which matrices are assembled in lines; the **casting mechanism**, in which typefaces are justified and cast in slugs; and the **distributing mechanism**, which returns the matrices to the matrix magazine after casting.

The composing mechanism has a keyboard, with each key being connected to its channel in the magazine. Matrices are made of brass and vary in thickness according to the type set-width. The type character is stamped into the edge of the matrix body. In two-letter (duplex) matrices, a character is usually stamped in two different variations, e.g., roman and italic or regular and bold. The matrix magazines are positioned vertically over the keyboard.

By means of a keyboard, the operator allows the matrices to descend to the founding compartment where they are arranged and justified. Each matrix has the character stamped on one of its sides, enabling the compositor to read a line before sending it to be cast. Once this operation is completed, the operator founds the line and redistributes the matrices back to the magazine. The slug takes a few seconds to come out.

The speed of composing certainly surpasses the difficulties in correcting any mistake.

LINOTYPE COMPOSING MACHINE (1930)

LINOTYPE COMPOSING ROOM (1930)

A typical linotype composing room, as could be found in any newspaper.

Born in a town near Glasgow, Scotland, in 1898, Robert Hunter Middleton immigrated with his family to North America in 1908 to join his father who worked in a coal mine in Birmingham, Alabama. Later on, the family moved to Eldorado, Illinois, and then settled in Danville.

In 1920, Middleton entered the Chicago Academy of Fine Arts with the intention of becoming an artist. However, he left there after a month to attend the School of the Art Institute of Chicago, where, thanks to German designer, letterer, and teacher Ernst Frederick Detterer (1888-1947), young Middleton was able to find his true vocation.

Detterer had been greatly influenced by the European private press movement, had studied briefly with Edward Johnston, and was now invited to create a new curriculum in the printing and typographic arts of the Art Institute of Chicago. Middleton, after taking several classes with Detterer –who became his mentor– changed his study of art to lettering and type design.

His first assignment was a project in which Detterer invited him to participate. In 1923, the Ludlow Typograph Company, commissioned Detterer to develop a typeface based on Nicolas Jenson's 1470 font. "Although I enjoyed helping Detterer it never occurred to me that there might be such a job on a permanent basis. After all, how many type designers were there in the world then –ten, maybe fifteen, at most?"

But in spite of the fact that Detterer took Eusebius's **De Praeparatione Evangelica**, printed by Nicolas Jenson in 1470 as his model –which was the same book used by Bruce Rogers for his **Centaur** (1914) typeface and the same engraver, Robert Wiebking–, Detterer's typeface called **Eusebius** (1924) was far closer to **Cloister Old Style** than to **Jenson**. Middleton collaborated on the roman, and designed the italic on his own; Detterer was so impressed with his abilities that he gave the young designer a recommendation for a steady job with the Ludlow Typograph Company. A beautiful limited edition of **The Last Will and Testament of the Late Nicolas Jenson** was printed using a 16-pt trial font in 1928.

The Ludlow Company was just starting –it had been founded in 1906. And in order to compete with more established type and matrices suppliers like Monotype, Linotype, and American Type Founders, it needed a large type library that provided new and original designs as well as types which served as formal equivalents to those produced by these companies.

Now, since the company's profits rested more on the sale of matrices than of machines, huge amounts of matrices in different styles and sizes were needed. Fortunately, Middleton was greatly helped by Robert Wiebking, Ludlow's master punch and matrix engraver, who had designed his own pantographic machine to carry out these activities.

Through him, Middleton met Frederic W. Goudy, who became a life-long friend and mentor. He helped him to further appreciate a carefully planned type library, the value of exceptional design, and how to work with independent designers.

Middleton entered the company when he finished college, at the age of twenty-five. In a short time, he became a master at both the art and craft of type design. His original creations helped establish a reputation for Ludlow over three decades. He also became a master at rendering "alternative" typefaces that blended with the already popular designs.

This is the case of **Record Gothic** (1927-60), **Tempo** (1930-42), **Karnak** (1931-42), and the highly praised versions of the classical **Garamond** (1929) and **Bodoni** (1930) typefaces. In addition to the mentioned fonts, Middleton created many original designs, such as **Cameo** (1926), **Delphian Open Title** (1928), **Stellar** (1929), **Umbra** (1932), **Eden** (1934), **Coronet** (1937), **Radiant** (1940), and **Samson** (1940).

In 1933, he was appointed Director of Type Design for the Ludlow Typograph Company, and later on, director of the whole company. During this time, Middleton published two interesting works: **Chicago Letter Founding** (1937), and **Making Printer's Typefaces** (1938).

In 1944, Middleton founded the Cherryburn Press, where he made some fine limited editions.

The best known is the printing of three portfolios of Thomas Bewick's wood engravings (1945, 1970, and 1972), which Middleton brought to a quality standard never achieved in Bewick's lifetime. Thus, he greatly contributed to the revival of interest in his work.

After devoting his entire professional life to the Ludlow Typograph Company, Middleton retired in 1971, at the age of seventy-three, with a creative portfolio of more than 100 typefaces, all with a high quality of form and structure. Unfortunately, by that time phototype was beginning to replace metal composition, and Ludlow was unable to make the transition from one technology to the other. With his departure, the company's type development program ceased to exist.

Although Middleton wanted to be an artist, his practical side made him single out a predictable career. "I have never felt that my role was to create great personal typefaces. I never intended to follow the role of my friend Fred Goudy, or Bruce Rogers. I was employed by a corporation and given a great deal of freedom, but I also felt a responsibility to their particular needs and to the needs of their customers."

While he worked at Ludlow, he was cofounder of the Chicago Society of Typographic Arts in 1927, and the first president of the group to collaborate in the organization of the International Design Conferences in Aspen in 1951. He was involved in establishing the Institute of Design (the New Bauhaus) in Chicago in 1937. He was member of the Twenty-seven Chicago Designers organized in 1934, and member of the Caxton Club since 1945. He was also one of the first American members of the Association Typographique Internationale (ATypI), founded in Lausanne, Switzerland in 1957, and an important member in building up that organization.

Robert Hunter Middleton died in Chicago, Illinois, in 1985, at the age of eighty-seven.

CAMEO (1926)

Derived from a heavy version of *Caslon*, Cameo is an elegant display incised typeface, which according to a 1926 Ludlow ad, was "designed and punches [were] produced in our own plant."

Apparently, this typeface was the first, or one of the first, so produced for the Ludlow composing system.

ABCDEFGHIJKLMNOPQR STUVWXYZ&abcdefghijkl nopqrstuvwxyz1234567890

MAKING PRINTER'S TYPEFACES (1938)

This symbol interlacing the letter **P** and a punch might have been designed by Middleton himself for the edition of his book, *Making Printer's Typefaces*, edited by the Black Cat Press in 1938.

VICTOR HAMMER
CHAPIN LIBRARY,
Williams College
THEODORE C. WETZEL
K. K. CHAPIN,
GORDON WILLIAMS (1940-1970)

Middleton followed the long tradition of engraving bookplates in boxwood. He began to engrave these pieces in 1940, continuing until the late 1970s. He printed many of them at his private workshop, the Cherryburn Press, usually constructing beautiful small boxes to contain them.

THE ART INSTITUTE OF CHICAGO (1930s)

This inscription was designed in classical roman capitals and cut into the wall of the Morton Wing of the Chicago Art Institute.

METAL PATTERN (1933)

Hand-inscribed metal pattern executed by Middleton to guide the engraver of a brass foundry type.

It was used by the Newberry Library bindery by Ernst Detterer and by Robert Hunter Middleton in 1933.

SOCIETY OF TYPOGRAPHIC ARTS

This is another clear example of Middleton's handling of calligraphy.

**TRANSYLVANIA
HANS CONRIED
JOSEPH GRAVES
THE UNIVERSITY OF CHICAGO
ROBERT PECK BATES**
(1940-1970)

These are other examples of his work on boxwood which he began in 1940, continuing until the late 1970s.

BASKERVILLE (1966-1967)

Final tracing paper drawings made prior to inscribing metal patterns for a *Baskerville* type, designed and drawn by Middleton for the Ludlow Typograph Company between 1966 and 1967, but never engraved or produced.

NATION

These letters, designed to be cut in brass, form part of a classical inscriptional alphabet.

TYPE

Middleton continued to experiment with calligraphy although he usually expressed these letters in forms that were related to the typefaces he designed. This is why there is such a strong calligraphic feeling in their shapes when his alphabets are carefully examined.

ANDROMAQUE (1980)

Originally cut by Victor Hammer in 12 pt only, his wife Carolyn Hammer asked Middleton to cut a 14-pt size. When redrawing it, Middleton returned to the second and third-century Roman cursive bookhand that had inspired the original design.

Middleton cut the steel punches and made the copper matrices; Paul Hayden Duensing cast the type.

An early use of *Andromaque* appeared on Middleton's 1980 Christmas cards.

MONOGRAMS

This is another example of his calligraphic experiments.

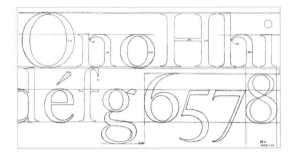

RECORD GOTHIC (1927)

Designed to compete with *News Gothic* (M. F. Benton, 1908), it was offered only in small sizes.

During the 1950s, when typographers rediscovered the traditional American gothics, it was offered in larger sizes.

In 1956, as director of Ludlow's design department, Middleton completed the type family with eighteen variants.

ABCDEFGHIJKLMNOPQRSTUVW
XYZ&abcdefghijklmnopqrstuvwx
yz$1234567890!?

DELPHIAN OPEN TITLE (1928)

A quite dignified and delicate design based on inscriptional lettering, it has been popular for titles and as initials.

Being an incised typeface, there are various inline letters which make of *Delphian* a mixture of two related styles.

It may also be considered an Art Deco style typeface. It only has caps.

ABCDEFGHIJKLMNOPQR
STUVWXYZ&
$1234567890!?

STELLAR (1929)

Designed as a less severe alternative to the monotone sans serif typefaces that were coming into great popularity both in Europe and in America, this delicate and well-shaped typeface has a moderate thick-and-thin contrast, known as humanistic sans serif.

Named *Stellar* in honor of Edwin Bryan Frost, the University of Chicago astronomer, it constituted a new type style.

Middleton's calligraphic sensitivity and keen sense of form are subtly combined.

It also preceded the appearance of *Optima* by twenty-nine years, a typeface designed by Hermann Zapf in 1958.

Lowercase letters have long ascenders and descenders and the sloping strokes are cut off at an angle, which recalls *Kabel* (Koch, 1927).

ABCDEFGHIJKLMNOPQR
STUVWXYZ&
$1234567890!?

ABCDEFGHIJKLMNOP
QRSTUVWXYZ&
$1234567890!?

BODONI BLACK (1930)

Similar to *Ultra Bodoni*, designed by Morris Fuller Benton in 1928, this typeface is characterized by curved serifs and softer treatment in their union to the thin and thick strokes.

It also presents a slight curving at the top of the lowercase stems.

ABCDEFGHIJKLMNO
PQRSTUVWXYZ&ab
cdefghijklmnopqrstuv
wxyz$1234567890?!

TEMPO HEAVY CONDENSED (1930-1942)

This typeface was designed as an answer to the sans serif trend which gained popularity in the late 1920s.

It is interesting to compare *Tempo* with *Futura* (Paul Renner, 1927) in order to analyze their subtle differences.

Middleton designed the entire series. The *Light*, *Medium*, and *Bold* weights were introduced in 1930, the *Heavy* in 1931, and other variations over the next decades.

ABCDEFGHIJKLMNOPQRSTUVWXYZ
&abcdefghijklmnopqrstuvwxyz
$1234567890!?

ABCDEFGHIJKLMNOPQRSTUVWX
YZ&abcdefghijklmnopqrstuvwxyz
$1234567890!?

KARNAK LIGHT (1931-1942)

Derived from *Memphis* (Wolf, 1929), and designed between 1931 and 1942, it is one of the extensive American slab serif families, created to compete with European foundries' typefaces produced at that time.

Although not displayed here, Ludlow's 17-degree slant matrices characterize the italic version.

It is also interesting to compare it with *ITC Lubalin Graph*, designed by Herb Lubalin and Tony DiSpigna in 1974.

ABCDEFGHIJKLMNOPQRST
UVWXYZ& abcdefghijklmn
opqrstuvwxyz1234567890

LAFAYETTE
EXTRA CONDENSED (1932)

An extra condensed typeface, it is characterized by an uneven stroke treatment and the use of Latin serifs. Although it had some use in newspaper headings, after 1940 Ludlow's catalog didn't include it for its outdated appearance.

Lafayette's formal approach may have been influenced by wood type design, if we compare it with one of the alphabets issued by James Edward Hamilton in his 1889 wood type catalog, and shown by Rob Roy Kelly in his book, *American Wood Type 1828-1900*.

ABCDEFGHIJKLMNOPQRSTUVWXYZ
abcdefghijklmnopqrstuvwxyz&
$1234567890?!

UMBRA (1932)

Very much in the Art Deco style, it is essentially a shadow version of *Tempo Light*, in which the basic letter in white is defined by a strong shadow drawn to the right of it.

It is another of the typefaces designed to compete with the European models, such as *Gill Shadow* (Eric Gill, c.1930), and *Semplicitá Ombra* (Nebiolo, 1931).

ABCDEFGHIJKLMNOPQRST
UVWXYZ&$1234567890!?

EDEN (1934)

A modern thick-and-thin display type, severely squared and compact, it causes difficulties in reading when set in a long text. It is one of those letters that may be drawn by holding a narrow pen horizontally.

It was popular in architectural typography.

ABCDEFGHIJKLMNOPQRSTUVWX
YZ&abcdefghijklmnopqrstuvwxyz
$1234567890

ABCDEFGHIJKLMNOPQRSTUV
WXYZ&abcdefghijklmnopqrstuv
$1234567890

Mandate (1934)

Middleton designed this connecting script for Ludlow in 1934.

One of its particularities is the close relationship between letters that maintains the flow of writing.

Some of the capitals extend below the base line.

ABCDEFGHIJKLMNOPQR
STUVWXYZ&abcdefghijklmn
opqrstuvwxyz$1234567890!?

BODONI CAMPANILE (1936)

A somewhat condensed *Bodoni*, it was copied one year later by Gerry Powell, who designed *Onyx* for ATF.

The italic was designed by Middleton in 1942.

ABCDEFGHIJKLMNOPQRSTUVWXYZ&abcdefg
hijklmnopqrstuvwxyz$1234567890

Coronet (1937)

This popular script was designed, taking advantage of the 17-degree matrices of the Ludlow system.

Not exactly a connecting alphabet, letters have a charming grace and swing.

It is also one of the few scripts to have two weights. The bold version was quite popular in newspapers in the setting of certain types of ads.

ABCDEFGHIJKLMNOPQR
STUVWXYZ&abcdefghijklmnopqrs
tuvwxyz$1234567890!?

STENCIL (1937)

As a heavy *Clarendon* letter with segmented strokes, it has been popular as a stencil typeface.

Although Middleton's version reached the market first (Middleton's in June and Powell's in July), Gerry Powell's version, done for ATF, and slightly more condensed, gained more popularity.

There remains the question of why the two faces were issued under the same name if they were produced by two competing type foundries.

It is interesting to compare Middleton's version with Powell's, as seen on page 219.

ABCDEFGHIJKLMNO
PQRSTUVWXYZ&
$1234567890

RADIANT (1938)

A precise, thick-and-thin sans serif letter, it expresses the modern spirit of the 1940s while breaking away from the monotone appearance of the regular sans serif typefaces of that time.

Being a designed typeface, it shows a calligraphic touch as do other Middleton fonts.

It is interesting to compare it with *Stellar* (1928), also designed by Middleton.

ABCDEFGHIJKLMNOPQRSTUVWXYZ
&abcdefghijklmnopqrstuvwxyz
$1234567890?!

ABCDEFGHIJKLMNOPQRSTUVWX
YZ&abcdefghijklmnopqrstuvwxyz
$1234567890?!

ABCDEFGHIJKLMNOPQRSTUV
WXYZ&abcdefghijklmnopqrstu
vwxyz$1234567890?!

SAMSON (1940)

Being a very bold, sturdy typeface, derived from lettering done with a broad pen, it maintains much of that feeling.

Its name expresses power and strength.

It was quite popular in newspaper advertising.

ABCDEFGHIJKLMNOPQRS
TUVWXYZ&abcdefghijklm
nopqrstuvwxyz
$1234567890?!

Florentine Cursive
(1956)

This delicate, formal cursive design, certainly more elegant than *Coronet*, has also been popular for announcements, title pages, and the like.

Numerals are drawn in *Oldstyle*.

ABCDEFGHIJKLMNOPQRS
TUVWXYZ&abcdefghijklmnopqrstuvwxyz
$1234567890!?

Born and educated in Brooklyn, New York, Louis Minott was awarded the New York City St. Gaudens Medal for art upon graduation from high school.

A graduate of Cooper Union School of Art, Minott has been a lettering artist on the staff of one of the major art studios in New York City and of a studio specializing in lettering.

In 1945, he opened his own design studio. He has serviced major advertising agencies in New York since then, collaborating with their art directors in styling lettering for headlines, logos, and related areas.

In 1965, Minott participated in the National Type Face Competition sponsored by Visual Graphics Corporation, North Miami, Florida, where he won one of the prizes with *Davida Bold*.

Among the other fifteen participants were Markus J. Low (*Basilea*), Vladimir M. Andrich (*Andrich Minerva Italic*), Richard D. Juenger (*Jana*) –who received first, second, and third prizes respectively– Ronald Arnholm (*Arnholm Sans Medium*), Arthur Baker (*Baker Signet*), and Wayne J. Stettler (*Stettler*).

Lucian Bernhard, Alvin Eisenman, Paul Rand, and Bradbury Thompson comprised the selection jury, and Arnold Bank, Lester Beall, Will Burtin, Lou Dorfsman, Robert M. Jones, Herb Lubalin, Klaus Schmidt and Carl Zahn (among others) the twelve-judge panel.

It is interesting to note that Herb Lubalin later designed a typographical poster using each one of the award-winning typefaces. In the section dedicated to his work, we may see the typogram he created to announce *Stettler* typeface.

DAVIDA BOLD (1965)

This handsome ornamental display typeface was a winner in the National Type Face Competition sponsored by Visual Graphics Corporation, North Miami, Florida, manufacturers of the Photo Typositor, the Posteriter, and film type fonts.

ABCDEFGHIJKLMNOPQRST
UVWXYZ&$1234567890!?

Born in Louisville, Kentucky in 1869, Berne Nadall manifested his talent for art at a very early age. His mother was an artist of the French school, and no doubt he received his first lessons from her.

When his mother died, he was placed under the instruction of H. Clay Woolford, a well-known artist of the South. For some reason they did not understand each other, and he made little progress. However, when he started to study with Al. Legras, a classmate of the famous Carl Brenner, his progress was almost immediate.

From these private classes, he went on to study at the Louisville School of Design for a term. In less than a year he was working for the Louisville daily papers, the *Post*, the *Daily Commercial*, and others.

It was during his connection with the *Post* that he cartooned the "Newman Ward Granite Steal," an exposé of a swindle on the city, and the result was a suit for damages in the sum of $200,000 against his newspaper.

As a consequence of this incident, he left Louisville for Chicago, where he was employed for a time as a designer and decorator, obtaining various commissions from printers and publishers.

It is probable that during this time he worked at the Camelot Press, for there is a note written by Frederic W. Goudy when he refers to his first type design *Camelot* (1896) in his book, *A Half-Century of Type Design and Typography, 1895-1945*, printed in 1946.

"While operating the Camelot Press, my associate C. Lauron Hooper and I had working for us a young man named Berne Nadall. He was employed to set type, but as a type compositor he wasn't much better than myself. He was, however, something of a decorative designer and did the odds and ends of such work we needed. When I left the Press, I remembered his work, and tried my own hand at design also."

During this period he did good work designing initials, head and tailpieces, page ornaments and titles, until he finally found a place at Barnhart Brothers & Spindler type foundry in Chicago. This proved to be an incentive for greater effort and a closer study of design in its application to the type founder's needs. He soon decided to go abroad to fulfill his typographical goals.

He first went to Birmingham, England, and afterwards to Paris, where he spent some months probably visiting type foundries and printers. From there, he returned to Birmingham and dedicated himself to working diligently.

By the end of 1896, he went back to America, and he remained continuously working with the exception of a brief visit to Chicago and his old home, Louisville, in the early part of 1899. Besides the time dedicated to his studies, he found many commissions for designing typefaces and ornaments for English type founders. In this work he founded, to his advantage, the possibilities and limitations of the type founding business. Unfortunately, there are no remaining examples of his work.

According to an article in *The Inland Printer*, his work for Barnhart Brothers & Spindler type foundry was not extensive, but showed some originality in his treatment of it and some talent in letter design. For this firm he designed a considerable number of borders and ornaments, all of which were well received by printers.

Among his type designs we may find *Mazarin* and *Mazarin Italic* (which were introduced as part of the *Jenson* trend started by William Morris, and presented by BB&S as "a revival of the *Golden Type*, redesigned by our artist" in 1895); *Tell Text* (which was also an adaptation of Morris' *Troy* and *Chaucer* types, introduced by BB&S in 1895); *Fifteen Century* and *Italic* (later known as *Caslon Antique*), and a lightface known as *Nadall*. This last font was probably cut lighter than the designer intended, and did not prove to be durable when printed.

It is interesting to note that although he was a rather obscure type designer, his typeface *Caslon Antique* not only continues to be used one hundred years after it was designed, but his treatment of drawing it has been imitated by other designers.

Very little is known of this designer after 1900, except that he was in England and that he was expected to come back to America.

CASLON ANTIQUE
(1896-1898)

Although not part of the *Caslon* family, this typeface design is a rendering of a crude face cut about 1475 in Venice.

Initially brought by BB&S, in Chicago, as *Fifteenth Century* and *Italic*, it has been very popular for simulating quaint American types of the eighteenth and nineteenth centuries.

ABCDEFGHIJKLMNOPQRST
UVWXYZ&abcdefghijklmnopqrst
uvwxyz$1234567890!?

Born in Tilton, New Hampshire in 1829, William Hamilton Page left his home at fourteen to begin a two-year apprenticeship at a printing shop in Bradford, Vermont.

In 1846, he came back to New Hampshire, then moved to Concord, and finally settled in Boston.

Beginning in 1850, he worked for two years as foreman of the *Spy* in Worcester, Massachusetts, and then moved to New York City, where, while employed at the *New York Tribune*, he worked in the Franklin Pierce presidential campaign of 1852. From this city, he went to Norwich, Connecticut, to work for Edmund Clarence Stedman of the *Norwich Tribune*, and in 1855, he met John Cooley in South Windham, Connecticut, where he became familiar with wood type manufacturing.

His first job was as a wood type finisher, since he had a better knowledge of wood type making than Cooley or his foreman. As a result of substantial experience with printing, and some knowledge of machine tools and wood engraving, he soon saw that improvements could be made.

In 1856, he purchased the equipment of the defunct H. & J. (Horatio and Jeremiah) Bill & Company, and in partnership with James Bassett founded Page & Bassett. One year later, the company moved to Greenville, a town close to Norwich.

In 1859, Basset withdrew from the firm and Page took Samuel Mowry, owner of his own company Mowry & Sons, as a new partner.

With Mowry's capital, the new William Page & Company was able to expand and relocate into a multistoried building, built on the banks of the Shetucket River, with forty employees and seventeen wood type cutting machines.

His type catalog, *Ornamented Clarendons* (1859), which illustrates

an extensive set of designs with an excellent quality in the cutting, permitted Page to arrange with the James Connor's Sons type foundry in New York for a twenty-year distribution of his type, and publication of his designs in the the *Typographic Messenger*.

During the American Civil War, Page perfected his machinery, and consolidated his markets, placing his firm as the main wood type manufacturer in the States.

In 1869, the now flourishing William Page & Company made arrangements for a better salary, and eventually directed its employees to produce in nine hours labor what was done in a ten-hour work day. It was also during this time that, due to the manpower shortage, Page & Company found women so adept to do its work that the company continued hiring them until the business was sold in 1891.

Up to 1872, Page had concentrated on wooden products –types, borders, tint blocks, and bleachers' stamps– and in 1872, he started advertising printers' goods, including country presses, card cutters, mitering machines, and inks.

In 1874, Page printed his most expensive and beautiful wood type catalog *Chromatic Wood Types*, which placed him at the head of the wood type manufacturing business, as well as a type designer, for practically all the designs are his. The catalog (13¾" x 18"), was printed in several colors in an edition of 1,000 copies.

In 1876, after Samuel Mowry retired from the firm, the company was reorganized as the William H. Page Wood Type Company, and moved its headquarters nearer to Norwich, Connecticut.

During this period, Page explored an overseas market, and the company began to exhibit wood type in international expositions.

In 1878, the Page Company was awarded medals at the Paris Exposition; in 1880, at Sidney; and in 1881, at the Melbourne Exposition.

In 1879, Page started publishing his *Page's Wood Type Album*, a triennial publication carrying news of the trade, advertisements, and examples of new designs. He followed the layout pattern of the newsletters published for many years by type founders, like the *Typographic Messenger* of James Connor, the *Typographic Advertiser* of L. Johnson, and the *Printer's Monthly Bulletin* published by the Boston Type Foundry.

In the 1880s, George Case Setchell was brought into the company. Their combined work enabled Page to produce die-cut types by 1887. However, by this time strong competition had arisen from the Hamilton Manufacturing Company of Two Rivers, Wisconsin, and the Page company was finally sold to Hamilton in 1891.

After the sale, all the equipment and the stock were moved to Two Rivers and as part of the selling agreement, Page was to become stockholder in the Hamilton Company.

Page was a self-educated man, with a broad range of interests that he enriched throughout his life. He was also a better than average "Sunday painter," and liked to do ornamental gardening. As a business man, he was quite shrewd and imaginative, backed by a great deal of physical energy. His aim for perfection is well demonstrated in his type specimen books, and his originality by a number of inventions registered under his name. His company, catalogs, designs, and business procedures are good representatives of the era.

William Hamilton Page died in his home in Mystic, Connecticut, in 1906, at the age of seventy-seven.

ANTIQUE XXX CONDENSED (1859)

First shown by William Page in his type specimen catalog of 1859, this extra condensed typeface allowed type manufacturers to create designs that permitted the setting of long texts in reduced spaces.

ABCDEFGHIJKLMNOPQRSTUVWXYZ&\$1234567890

DIE-CUT WOOD TYPE ORNAMENTS (1890)

In the 1880s, George Case Setchell was brought into the company, and, in a combined effort, the Page Company started producing die-cut types. This was one of the samples shown in his 1890 type catalog.

POINTING HANDS (1872)

William Hamilton Page was one of the first, if not the first, to incorporate pointing hands in his type catalogs, these have been very popular since then.

It is interesting to note the presence of both left and right hands, which permitted different placements within a page.

THE TYPE FAMILY VARIATIONS (1880's)

As a design became popular, the number of value and width variations increased.

By the 1840s, both primary and secondary faces were cut in "series," and by the 1880s, these series included almost all the variations shown here.

MOSAIC (1874)

This is one of the 24-line *Etruscan No.2* typefaces produced by Page, which is still very popular in circus posters.

MAY (1890)

This is an example of the 12-line *Chaldean* typeface.

CHARME EDITIONS (1872)

This is an example of the 16-line *Arabian* typeface, a variation of the so-called *Tuscan* types, patented by Page in 1872.

WOOD TYPE ALBUM (1879)

This is a page containing wood types and ornament samples from Page's *Wood Type Album*, printed in 1879.

TYPOGRAPHICAL BORDERS (1906)

These routed borders, shown by Hamilton in 1906, are believed to be designs by William Page.

We may easily notice the great amount of work and time consumed in elaborating these designs on wood. Page also had them die-cut.

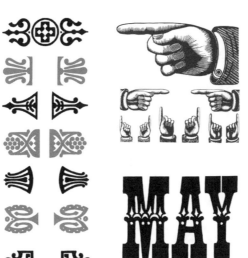

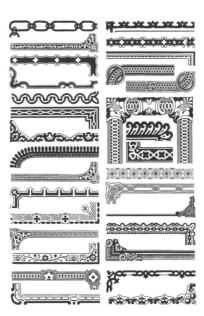

GOTHIC TUSCAN POINTED
(1859)

William Hamilton Page and John Cooley were the first to show this typeface design, in their 1859 typeface specimen.

It certainly exhibits a clear influence of wrought iron work.

Today, it may be in found as *Ironwood*, in Adobe's digital version.

ABCDEFGHIJKLMNOPQRST UVWXYZ&$1234567890?!

IONIC (1859)

Page first showed this alphabet in his type specimen of 1859. Lowercase letters and figures are missing.

According to Rob Roy Kelly, in his book, *American Wood Type: 1828-1900*, "this design is one of the most beautiful proportioned display faces from this period."

ABCDEFGHIJK LMNOPQRST UVWXYZ&

ANTIQUE TUSCAN NO. 8
(1859)

This exotic alphabet was first shown by Page in his 1859 type specimen.

Even though this design includes several characteristics of the European *Tuscans*, such as fishtail serifs and median bulges, Rob Roy Kelly considers it as one of the first American *Tuscan* typefaces.

Today, it may be in found as *Mesquite*, in Adobe's digital version.

ABCDEFGHIJKLMNOPQRSTUVW XYZ&$1234567890?!

CLARENDON XX CONDENSED (1859)

This condensed typeface design, first shown by Page in his 1859 type specimen, is believed to have originated as a wood type, produced by the Page Company.

Once again, these condensed versions were quite useful, although not so legible, in narrow spaces.

ABCDEFGHIJKLMNOPQRSTUVWXYZ&abcdefghij klmnopqrstuvwxyz$1234567890

ANTIQUE TUSCAN No.11 (1859)

Also called *Gothic Tuscan Condensed*, this typeface was first shown by William Page in his 1859 type specimen book. Lowercase letters and figures are missing.

It may still be seen in circus posters.

ABCDEFGHIJKLMNO
PQRSTUVWXYZ&

CLARENDON ORNAMENTED (1859)

Page showed this ornamented typeface in his catalog of 1859.

The font was complemented with a second block-set to be printed in two colors, and has been, since then, very popular in circus posters.

Today, it may be in found in Adobe's digital version as *Rosewood*.

ABCDEFGHIJKLM
NOPQRSTUVWXYZ
&$1234567890!?

ABCDEFGHIJKLMN
OPQRSTUVWXYZ

ANTIQUE TUSCAN OUTLINE

(1859)

An interesting variation of *Tuscan Antique* was first shown by William Hamilton Page in his 1859 type specimen.

The present sample was taken from a Vanderburgh, Wells & Company catalog.

ABCDEFGHI
JKLMNOPQR
STUVWXYZ&
1234567890!

SKELETON ANTIQUE (1865)

This typeface was first listed by Page in his type specimen catalog of 1865.

These light styles of *Antiques* were very popular with the type founders during the last quarter of the nineteenth century.

It is interesting to note the resemblance that it has with the *Typewriter* type design.

ABCDEFGHIJKLMNOPQRS
TUVWXYZ&abcdefghijklmn
opqrstuvwxyz$1234567890

FRENCH ANTIQUE (1869)

Although it is based on a European design, Rob Roy Kelly considers this interpretation peculiarly American, originating with the wood type manufacturers.

The European *French Antique* was not so condensed and had a different serif to letter-height ratio.

William Hamilton Page presented it in the *Typographic Messenger*, during 1869.

ABCDEFGHIJKLMNOPQRSTUVWXYZ&abcde
fghijklmnopqrstuvwxyz$1234567890!

AETNA (1870)

This typeface was shown by William Hamilton Page as an 1870 type specimen.

The design is typical of those that replaced the older *Fat Face Romans* during the second half of the nineteenth century.

Retaining a Roman quality, but sturdier on account of its formal treatment, the face was well received by job printers.

It is also curious to note the different serif treatment of letters E, F, L, T, and Z.

ABCDEFGHIJKL
MNOPQRSTUVW
XYZ&
$1234567890

EGYPTIAN ORNAMENTED (1870)

First listed by William Hamilton Page in his type specimens of 1870, this design was widely used in the last twenty years of the nineteenth century, and is commonly associated with Frontier events, such as the **WANTED** posters, etc.

ABCDEFGHIJKLMNOPQRSTUV
WXYZ&$1234567890

PAINTER'S ROMAN
(1870)

Cut both by William Hamilton Page and Darius Wells, this alphabet appeared during the 1870s and was always marked as a special font.

Two of its most noticeable characteristics are the curved vertical strokes and the curved serifs.

Today, it may be in found as *Juniper*, in Adobe's digital version.

ABCDEFGHIJKLMNOP
QRSTUVWXYZ&
$1234567890!?

CELTIC ORNAMENTED
(1870)

Based on a *French Clarendon* typeface, this design was patented by William Hamilton Page around 1870.

The alphabet does not include lowercase letters or figures, but it was sold with a second block-set for printing in two colors.

Today, it may be in found as *Pepperwood*, in Adobe's digital version.

ANTIQUE No.7 (1870)

With similar characteristics to the *French Antique* typeface found on page 208, this design is wider and heavier.

William Hamilton Page showed it as an 1870 type specimen.

ABCDEFGHIJKLMNOPQRSTUV
WXYZ&abcdefghijklmnopqrstu
vwxyz$1234567890

TEUTONIC (1872)

This typeface, with a curious blend of *Latin* and *Oldstyle* serif typefaces, was first shown by William Hamilton Page as an 1872 type specimen.

ABCDEFGHIJKLMN
OPQRSTUVWXYZ&
abcdefghijklmnopqrst
$1234567890

GOTHIC TUSCAN CONDENSED No.2
(1879)

This alphabet was first shown by Page in his *Page's Wood Type Album*, July 1879, and listed as *No.124*.

ABCDEFGHIJKLMNOPQRST
UVWXYZ!

FRENCH CLARENDON XXX CONDENSED
(1879)

Based on a *French Clarendon* typeface, this ultra condensed design was first shown by Page in his *Page's Wood Type Album*, July 1879. Today, it may be in found as *Ponderosa* in Adobe's digital version.

ABCDEFGHIJKLMNOPQRSTUVWXYZ&$1234567890!?

PHANITALIAN (1879)

Also known as *No. 132*, this alphabet, first shown by Page in his *Page's Wood Type Album*, October 1879, presents letters with a curious bone-like appearance.

ABCDEFGHIJKLMNOPQRSTU VWXYZ&!

No. 129 (1879)

Known also as *Latin*, *Peerless Condensed*, *Old Style Antique*, this particular Latin serif condensed design was first shown by Page in his *Page's Wood Type Album*, October 1879.

Today it may be in found as *Birch*, in Adobe's digital version.

ABCDEFGHIJKLMNOPQRSTUVW XYZ&abcdefghijklmnopqrstuvw xyz$1234567890!?

No. 131 (1879)

Also known as *Peerless*, this Latin serif type design was first shown by Page in his *Page's Wood Type Album*, October 1879.

A lowercase was not always included with this typeface.

It is interesting to note the heavy treatment of extreme horizontals, and the unevenness of design as a whole, regardless of the presence of a certain formal unity.

ABCDEFGHIJKLM NOPQRSTUVWXY Z&1234567890$!

No. 142 (1882)

Also known as *Beveled*, this sans serif typeface, with uneven strokes, was first shown by William Hamilton Page as an 1882 wood type specimen.

It is interesting to note the convex treatment of strokes and the angular cutting of their ends.

ABCDEFGHIJKLMNOPQRSTUVWXYZ
&abcdefghiiklmnopqrstuvwxyz
$1234567890

No. 154 (1887)

Patented by William Hamilton Page in 1887, this barrel-shaped sans serif is one of the seventeen styles designed for the die-cut wood types issued by Page & Setchell.

It is interesting to note the great formal experimentation carried on by Page on the letterforms, not only in this alphabet but also in other examples shown on these pages.

ABCDEFGHIJKL
MNOPQRSTUVW
XYZ&
$1234567890

No. 500 (1887)

Patented by Page in 1887, this is another one of the seventeen styles designed for the die-cut wood types issued by Page & Setchell.

Page's experimentation with serifs, angular endings, and diagonal cross bars is noticeable.

ABCDEFGHIJKLMNOPQRST
UVWXYZ&
$1234567890

No. 506 (1887)

Patented by William Page in 1887, this is another one of the seventeen styles designed for the die-cut types of Page and Setchell.

It is interesting to note the certain resemblance that *Othello*, designed by Morris Fuller Benton in 1934, has with this design.

ABCDEFGHIJKLMNOPQRS
TUVWYXZ&abcdefghijklmn
opqrstuvwxyz1234567890

No. 515 (1887)

William Page patented this typeface in 1887. No lowercase was designed for this face, and figures are missing.

This is another one of the seventeen styles designed for the die-cut types of Page and Setchell.

We may also see that an interesting variation of the same design was issued under the same name in 1887.

In 1997, Argentinean-born designer Luis Siquot, who also designed *ITC Juanita*, found inspiration in this typeface to create *ITC Florinda*. Finding it difficult to design a lowercase alphabet, Siquot added small caps.

ABCDEFGHIJKLMN
OPQRSTUVWXYZ
&1234567890$.!'·

ABCDEFGHIJKLMN
OPQRSTUVWXYZ

Born in 1864, Wadsworth A. Parker was a printer and typographer who had been in charge of the specimen design and printing department at David Bruce's New York Type Foundry. He became manager of the American Type Founders Company type specimen department in 1906, when the Bruce Company merged with it.

One of the first examples of his work at ATF was related to the production of *Bookman*. He not only chose the typeface but the name. In 1901, the New York Type Foundry had brought out *Bartlet Oldstyle*, the American version of *Old Style*, designed by Alexander C. Phemister for the Scottish foundry Miller & Richard in Philadelphia. When the company merged with ATF, Parker revised the font and designed a group of swash letters for both the roman and the italic alphabets. ATF then issued it as *Bookman* in 1903.

Bookman was the the first typeface to correspond to the spirit of the Mission style present in architectural woodwork, furniture, and interior decoration, later shared by *Cheltenham*, designed by Bertram G. Goodhue in 1904. *Bookman* was extensively used by Elbert Hubbard's Roycroft Press, in Aurora, New York, among others, in the making of arts and crafts books.

In 1918, Parker became aware of the capital letter A that Frederic W. Goudy had included in the introduction of his book, *The Alphabet*. Interested in the resemblance that this capital letter had with sixteenth-century ornamented initials, such as those engraved by Geofroy Tory and Jean Tornesius, Parker asked Goudy if he would complete for ATF the remaining letters of the alphabet in the same spirit and character.

That same year, Goudy completed the *Cloister Initials*, which Parker considered "the best Goudy initials ever made."

As ATF began to fulfill its program of improving type design as well as the specimen material, the Type Design Department came to be regarded as one of the finest letterpress printing operations in the world.

The craftsmanship involved in the production of the *ATF Specimen Book and Catalogue 1923*, with over 300 typefaces, fully confirms this statement. Each page was designed and printed with a remarkable skill that allowed a close appreciation of intricate borders and the precision of the cutting and casting of type.

The printing and design quality of the *ATF Specimen Book and Catalogue 1923* is a monument, not only to Parker and his printing staff, but also to Linn Boyd Benton, who was in charge of type production, and to his son, Morris Fuller Benton, who was hired in 1897 to set up the type design department.

Parker's contribution also extended to designing several type variations with well-established typefaces, such as *Goudy* and *Stymie*. He also produced some original designs, such as *Gallia* (1927), and *Modernistic* (1928).

He was an active member of the American Institute of Graphic Arts.

Wadsworth A. Parker died in Petersburg, Virginia, in 1938, at the age of seventy-four.

GOUDY HANDTOOLED
(1922)

Credited to Wadsworth Parker as well as to Morris Fuller Benton, this typeface is an attractive variation of *Goudy Bold*, designed by Frederic W. Goudy in 1916.

ABCDEFGHIJKLMNOPQRS
TUVWXYZ&abcdefghijklmn
opqrstuvwxyz$1234567890!?

LEXINGTON
(1926)

Parker drew this shaded and decorative font in 1926, from a design submitted by Clarence P. Hornung.

It has some characteristics present in *Tuscan* style alphabets, such as the bifurcated vertical strokes and the curled serifs.

It was recast in 1954 and copied in one size by Los Angeles Type Foundry.

ABCDEFGHIJKLMNO
PQRSTUVWXYZ&
$12345678

GALLIA (1927)

A unique roman decorative letter, it has a particular Art Deco feeling with swash endings.

It is a severe thick-and-thin style, with main strokes divided into three lines of different thickness.

ABCDEFGHIJKLMNO
PQRSTUVWXYZ&
$1234567890!?

MODERNISTIC
(1928)

A quite novel Art Deco display typeface, it is characterized by a delicate hairline and thick ornamented strokes with Modern style serifs.

ABCDEFGHIJKLMN
OPQRSTUVWXYZ
1234567890

STYMIE INLINE TITLE (1931)

A variation of *Stymie Bold* designed by Morris Fuller Benton in 1890, it is quite a handsome display typeface. It may also be considered an Art Deco style typeface.

It only has caps.

ABCDEFGHIJKLM
NOPQRSTUVWX
YZ$$1234567890

Born in Nantucket in 1848, Joseph Warren Phinney worked with the Dickinson Type Foundry in Boston, where he was responsible for the specimen-printing department, and where he entered into partnership with George J. Pierce, Alexander C. Phemister, and A. C. Converse after the great Chicago Fire, in 1872, had destroyed the entire plant.

In 1879, Michael Dalton, one of the owners of the firm, died, and by 1890 the firm came under the control of Phinney, who had been manager for many years.

When the Dickinson Company merged with the American Type Founders in 1892, Phinney became the principal advisor in developing ATF's typeface library. He also became a vice president of the new corporation and managed its Boston office.

Phinney was a man of considerable perception, and while he was at the Dickinson Foundry, had tried to issue William Morris' *Golden Type* (1890) commercially. On Morris' refusal, he went to produce his own version under the name of *Jenson Oldstyle* in 1893.

Three years later he issued *Camelot*, the first type sent to him from Chicago by a young promising designer named Frederic W. Goudy. This typeface was issued by ATF in 1900, and patented under Goudy's and Phinney's names, probably due to the fact that the lowercase was drawn by Phinney.

Being considered as America's leading authority on type design, Phinney's first task was to carefully

examine the immense number of typefaces offered by the fourteen type foundries which initially formed the new enterprise, and to narrow these down to the finest type designs, and then to adopt the point-and-pica system of measuring as the universal standard.

In 1923, ATF published its *Specimen Book and Catalogue 1923*, a 6¾" x 10" volume, with 1,148 pages and more than 300 typefaces shown in a clear and attractive typographic presentation. Each type specimen was presented with a brief showing of every available size plus a complete font in a 14- to 18-pt size range. Main families included twenty-four special inserts, printed in two or three colors on colored paper stock.

When Phinney left the Dickinson Type Foundry in Boston, he also persuaded Robert W. Nelson (1851-1926) to invest in the new company. Nelson soon became ATF's general manager, making a substantial contribution to the prosperity of the company. He became its president in 1901.

One of Nelson's policies was to bring together the most talented men who worked independently, to work under the same roof. This is how Linn Boyd Benton and his son, who were with the Benton, Waldo & Co., type foundry in Milwaukee, and Robert Wiebking, who was with the Barnhart Brothers & Spindler type foundry in Chicago, came to work with ATF.

Although Phinney's contribution as a type connoisseur was better than his contribution as a type designer, he had some typefaces to his credit.

In 1895, he completed a typeface based on William Bradley's calligraphy for the Christmas cover of the *Inland Printer*, under the name of *Bradley*. In 1901, he designed an eccentric novelty called *Abbott Oldstyle*, which resembles *De Vinne Roman*, designed by Frederic W. Goudy in 1898, and did not last long.

According to some authors, he contributed to shaping up *Cheltenham Old Style*, created by Bertram G. Goodhue in 1899, and to design its italic version, before its final version was produced in 1902.

Phinney is also credited with three black letter alphabets (also attributed to Morris Fuller Benton), which basically differ in the particular rendering of the letters: *Engravers Old English* (1901), *Flemish Black* (1902), and *Cloister Black* (1904).

In 1896, ATF issued *Satanick*, openly based on *Troy* (1891), and *Chaucer* (1892), types designed by William Morris, and *Vertical Writing*, a hand script produced by the ATF branch in Boston.

In 1897, at the suggestion of Charles H. Taylor of *The Boston Globe*, Phinney converted the *Quentell* alphabet, designed by N. J. Werner in 1895, into a more suitable face for newspaper titling.

Joseph Warren Phinney died in 1934, at the age of eighty-six.

JENSON (1893)

Though a comparatively crude typeface, it by itself did much to start the late nineteenth-century movement toward better types and typography in America.

Designed by Phinney while he was at the Dickinson Type Foundry, it is based on William Morris' *Golden Type* (1890).

ABCDEFGHIJKLMNOPQRST
UVWXYZ & abcdefghijklmnopqrs
tuvwxyz $1234567890?!

Born in New Haven, Connecticut in 1860, Frank Hinman Pierpont spent most of his professional life in England, working for the English Monotype Corporation.

During his youth, he labored in farming during his school holidays, and as a clerk in general stores, a practice that accustomed him to hard work.

In 1880, he was trained as a mechanic in Hartford, Connecticut with Pratt & Whitney Co., and in 1885, he joined the patent lawyer, Albert H. Walker. There he gained his first knowledge of composing machinery from the preparation of Patent Office drawings for the Paige Typesetter and Distributor.

At the end of 1894, a question of German patents took him to Berlin, where his keen discernment as an engineer became evident. The Ludwig Loewe Company had acquired the European rights of the American Typograph, a slug-casting machine invented by John R. Rogers (former collaborator of Ottmar Mergenthaler), which had been designed to compete with the Linotype. Pierpont, joining that company, radically redesigned the machine.

In 1896, he became director of the Typograph Setzmaschinen-Fabrik, assisting in marketing the Typograph machine, which made its debut four years later, in 1900.

The idea of mechanical composition had absorbed incredible sums in experimental work. To the average printer, it would have remained as a "mad idea" had it not been for the tremendous pressure of demand for the printed word caused by increased global literacy and the steady rise of wages. And one of the less obvious but very important problems concerned the manufacture of matrices.

With the invention of the matrix-cutting machine by Linn Boyd Benton, things became manageable, but if it was to function as an accurate machine, it required highly skilled operators, with a low rate of output.

In late 1897, the Lanston Monotype Corporation was formed in London, and not being in the position

of manufacturing the machines in England, the company procured them from the Lanston Monotype Manufacturing Company in America.

In 1899, the London office was moved to Salfords, Redhill, Surrey, and Pierpont was invited to come from Germany to take the position of works manager for the Lanston Monotype Corporation.

He brought with him a group of four of his ex-Typograph employees: Frank and William Demming, the former as tool room manager and the later as plant engineer; Fritz Max Steltzer who became head of the type drawing office, and Théodor Bisser, a punch-cutter. Seltzer remained in this position until his retirement in 1940.

Between 1900 and 1912, in collaboration with Monotype's manager Harold Duncan, Pierpont developed and improved many different Monotype machines used in type production, such as a punch-cutter which worked eight times as fast Linn Boyd Benton's pantograph, and which could be operated by semi-skilled operators.

It should also be mentioned that for Monotype as for many other type composing firms the production of new typefaces was impractical, unnecessary, and undesirable, since the demand of customers was to copy the designs originated by type founders of type for hand composition.

In 1912, Pierpont supervised the cutting of *Imprint*, a roman typeface based on *Caslon Old Face* designed by Edward Johnston for the *Imprint* typographical journal, which appeared in 1913. *Imprint* was directed by Edward Johnston, Gerard T. Meynell, and John Henry Mason, who had been called by Monotype as consultant in the cutting of the typeface. *Imprint* was also the first original *Old Style* typeface produced for mechanical composition by the foundry.

That same year, only eight months after the issuing of *Imprint*, Pierpont, in collaboration with Fritz Steltzer, and Théodor Bisser, developed *Plantin*, a new classic typeface named after the famous Antwerp printer, Christophe Plantin.

The model was a type used in an *Index characterum* printed in 1905, listing the types used by the Plantin-Moretus Press in Antwerp, and collected by Max Rooses, its director. The complete font, the work of Robert Granjon, a close contemporary of Claude Garamond, was never used by Plantin, although he used some of the letters to augment the *Garamond* font he had.

Pierpont's strong ideas about the intended purpose of a typeface always directed the adaptation process. Thus, *Plantin* pioneered typefaces designed to consume less paper and were well suited to print on art papers.

Plantin met with great success; it was the sixth bestselling typeface in Monotype's history of supplying sets of matrices for hot-metal composition. Shortly after, a lighter version was made, which was more suitable for printing on smooth and coated papers.

The appointment of Stanley Morison as adviser to Monotype was indeed a troublesome situation for Pierpont, who, being in his fifties, felt his position threatened by a young man of only twenty-four. Nevertheless, and in spite of their differences, Morison's program owed much to Pierpont, for it certainly was with his help that he was able to fulfill his program of type revivals carried on until Pierpont's retirement in 1936.

It is interesting to note one of Pierpont's comments when he received the first drawings of Eric Gill's *Gill Sans* in 1927, "I can see nothing in this design to recommend it and much that is objectionable." For a person accustomed to classical serif typefaces, a sans serif must have been beyond his comprehension. But thanks to Morison's influence, a deal was struck between Gill and the foundry; the typeface was produced with an excellent quality, and it became an immediate success.

In 1937, Frank Hinman Pierpont was appointed to the Board of the Monotype Corporation Ltd. as a consulting engineer. He died soon afterwards in London, at the age of seventy-seven, one year after his retirement.

PLANTIN (1913)

A roman typeface, it was named after the Antwerp printer, Christophe Plantin.

Cut by Théodor Bisser, probably after drawings by Max Steltzer, it was produced for the English Monotype under Pierpont's supervision. It is also characterized by a large x-height.

ABCDEFGHIJKLMNOPQR
STUVWXYZ&abcdefghijklm
nopqrstuvwxyz$1234567890!?

FRANK H. PIERPONT

BORN IN NEW YORK CITY IN 1899, GERRY POWELL MAINTAINED A STUDIO AS A TYPOGRAPHER AND INDUSTRIAL DESIGNER.

LATER ON, HE WAS DIRECTOR OF TYPOGRAPHY FOR THE AMERICAN TYPE FOUNDERS COMPANY, WHERE HE DESIGNED SUCH TYPEFACES AS ONYX (1937) AND STENCIL (1937). THIS LAST FACE WAS ISSUED WITH THE SAME NAME AS THE ONE DESIGNED BY ROBERT HUNTER MIDDLETON, ONLY ONE MONTH LATER, IN 1937.

HE ALSO COMPLETED THE FAMILY OF OTHER TYPE DESIGNS SUCH AS SPARTAN, THE AMERICAN VERSION OF FUTURA DESIGNED BY PAUL RENNER IN 1927; AND OF STYMIE DESIGNED BY MORRIS FULLER BENTON IN 1931. HE CREATED STYMIE BOLD CONDENSED AND SPARTAN BOLD CONDENSED IN 1937 AND 1940 RESPECTIVELY.

HE WAS ALSO A MEMBER OF THE AMERICAN INSTITUTE OF GRAPHIC ARTS (AIGA).

ONYX (1937)

Designed as a modernization of *Modern Roman Bold Extra Condensed*, this typeface could well be considered a condensed version of *Ultra Bodoni*.

Two years later, Sol Hess designed *Onyx Italic* for the Lanston Monotype Company.

ABCDEFGHIJKLMNOPQRSTUVWXYZ&abc
defghijklmnopqrstuvwxyz$1234567890!?

STENCIL (1937)

As a heavy *Clarendon* letter with segmented strokes, it has been popular as a stencil typeface.

Designed the same year as the version done by Robert Hunter Middleton, and commercialized in July, one month later, it is narrower and bolder in appearance.

Unlike Middleton's design, it has remained on the market.

ABCDEFGHIJKLMNOPQR
STUVWXYZ&
$1234567890!?

STYMIE BOLD CONDENSED (1937)

Between 1935 and 1936, Sol Hess designed *Stymie Light Condensed*, *Medium Condensed*, and *Medium Extrabold Condensed*.

The following year, Gerry Powell designed *Stymie Bold Condensed*, which represented the last major member of the family, although it departs a little more than the others from the type family characteristics.

ABCDEFGHIJKLMNOPQRSTUVWXY
Z&abcdefghijklmnopqrstuvwxyz
$1234567890

Born in St. Louis, Michigan, in 1878, Will Ransom was the son of teachers who moved to Washington DC on account of their work. Here he developed his interest in music, art, and printing, and even became a cellist, thanks to his mother.

He felt the impact of William Morris and the Arts and Crafts movement, of Aubrey Beardsley and *fin-de-siècle* decadence, and of Dana Gibson's illustrations. During these years, he wrote out and illuminated manuscript volumes of Alfred Tennyson's poetry and his own writings, using a quill pen for the calligraphy and Art Nouveau style decorations.

One of his first jobs was with the Snohomish (Washington) *Weekly Tribune*, where he spent several years writing, keeping books, and helping with the presses. His music was kept up and he became part of a piano trio.On free evenings, he was allowed to use a press, where he constantly tried out new techniques: wood engraving, leather binding and tooling, and writing on vellum. Thanks to his friend John Bird, all these combined talents finally resulted in the setting up of the Handcraft Shop in 1901, where he printed Alfred Tennyson's *Lady of Shalott* and Oscar Wilde's *Ave Imperatrix*.

By 1903, Ransom had saved enough money to attend an art school. Guided by Irvin Way, a bibliophile, publisher, and bookseller of Chicago, whose books he had admired and who knew Frederic W. Goudy, Ransom entered the Art Institute of Chicago.

He not only watched Goudy working at the Fine Arts Building, but went out to Park Ridge to visit him and his wife. There he met Oswald Cooper, who taught lettering at the Frank Holme School of Illustration, Frank Holme himself, and William Addison Dwiggins.

By the end of the year, Ransom had decided to quit school and start to work. When Goudy suggested that he join efforts to set up a private press, he offered to obtain the funds for the enterprise as well as for the cutting of a typeface. The Village Press was founded in 1903; Robert Wiebking did the cutting of the *Village* typeface, and the American Type Founders did the casting.

But, shortly after the first book was printed –*Printing* by William Morris and Emery Walker– Goudy bought him out of the business and Ransom was once again by himself. This also coincided with the Goudys moving to Hingham, Massachusetts, in 1904.

Ransom worked for the next nine years as a bookkeeper in Chicago. In 1911, encouraged by his wife to return to art, he set up shop as a freelance artist and letterer. Among his clients were several bookstores and publishers, especially the Morris Bookstore and the Brothers of the Book. The latter, run by Laurence Woodworth, was actually a limited edition venture, and Ransom was entrusted by Woodworth with part of the program.

In 1917, Ransom designed his most successful typeface, *Parsons*, named for the advertising manager of Carson, Pirie, Scott, & Co. department store, who used Ransom's work for most of his major ads, and who was fond of his style of lettering. Being a typical fashion typeface, *Parsons* was also a favorite for silent movie scene descriptions, as may be seen on many of Charles Chaplin's films.The typeface also included bold and italic versions.

In 1921, Will Ransom decided to try again at running his own press. Woodworth had died in 1918, and with him, Brothers of the Book. But funds were scarce, and authors subsidized many of Ransom's publications.

In 1922, "Will Ransom, Maker of Books" published the initial book in a series of seven "First Writers." He set the type and printed by hand, and drew special borders and initial letters when needed. But, once more, sales were slow and expenses high, so by 1925, he had to sell his equipment and return to commercial work. He later became director of typography for the Faithorn Company, a post in which he could design an occasional book and a great variety of commercial printing.

In 1927, he was asked to write a series of articles (fifteen in total) on private presses for *Publishers' Weekly*. He traced the history of this movement, and after two years of work, these articles became *Private Presses and Their Books*, which compiles the work of some 300 presses. R.R.Bowker Company, New York, printed it in 1929, just before the Great Depression.

In 1930, Ransom left Faithorn Company and started to struggle for freelancing once more. That same year, he became director of the book department at the Printing House of Leo Hart in Rochester, New York, where, during a five-year stay, he produced a number of limited editions, in addition to a considerable number of trade books and advertising printing. Among the former we may find William Shakespeare's *Venus and Adonis*, illustrated by Rockwell Kent; John Fenimore Cooper's *The Last of the Mohicans* for the Limited Editions Club; and William Addison Dwiggins's edition of *The Travels of Marco Polo*.

From Chicago, Ransom moved to Buffalo, where he worked with a printing house as a freelance designer. There, in 1937, he began the monthly articles for *Bookbinding and Book-Production*, continued until 1945, in which he expressed most completely his philosophy on design and bookmaking.

In 1939, preparations were made for the celebration of the 500th anniversary of the invention of printing. Being a member of the American Institute of Graphic Arts (AIGA), Ransom was invited to New York as its executive secretary. He also had the chance to work for the Limited Editions Club, for whom he designed several books through the years, as well as for J.J. Little & Ives Co. publishing company.

In 1941, Will Ransom entered the last and most fruitful period of his professional career, when he became art editor of the University of Oklahoma Press, at Norman, with the rank of associate professor. He designed several hundred books, which made the Press a leader among the university presses of the country in design and production.

He had time to keep up his correspondence and record of press books, and to publish, from 1945 to 1950, a series of *Selective Check Lists of Press Books*, which extended his earlier work up to the end of the Second World War. P. O. Duschnes in New York published it.

Ransom was a generous man, whose letters and journals reveal his knowledge and opinions of many of his contemporaries who made American printing history.

Will Ransom died in Norman, Oklahoma, in 1955, at the age of seventy-seven.

PARSONS (1917)

Based on the distinctive lettering Ransom had designed for the Carson, Pirie, Scott & Co. store in Chicago, it is characterized by long ascenders that surpass caps height, and short descenders.

Produced by Barnhart Brothers & Spindler in Chicago, it was named for I. R. Parsons, advertising manager of the store.

ABCDEFGHIJKLMNOPQRST UVWXYZ & abcdefghijklmnopq rstuvwxyz 1234567890 $

FRANK H. RILEY

Born in St. Joseph, Missouri in 1894, Frank H. Riley studied art in Highland Park, Illinois, with J. Marchand, André Lhote, L. Ritman, and L. Kroll, and worked as a freelance designer, typographer, and artist in Chicago.

He was a member of the faculty in the Art Institute of Chicago and also worked for Oswald Cooper, at Bertsch & Cooper, for several years.

While he was in New York City, he was influenced by the work of Frederic W. Goudy, and later studied with André Lhote in Paris.

In 1939, he designed *Grayda*, a quite unusual script, and in 1942, *Contact Bold Condensed*, a narrow and vigorous serif letter, both for American Type Founders. *Contact Bold Condensed* was not released until 1948 because of wartime conditions.

Frank H. Riley was a member of the American Institute of Graphic Arts (AIGA).

Grayda (1939)

This is a very unusual script, which was designed for American Type Founders.

Lowercase letters are weighted at top and bottom, giving strong horizontal emphasis; they are close fitting but not connected.

The *Narrow* version is presented here.

ABCDEFGHIJKLMNOPQRSTUV WXYZ abcdefghijklmnopqrstuvwxyz 1234567890

Born in Linwood, Indiana in 1870, Albert Bruce Rogers came from a family of English origin. With an early desire to become an artist, at the age of sixteen he went to nearby Purdue College in Lafayette (now a University) where he became aware of fine books. After graduation, he became a newspaper artist, and a landscape painter for a short time.

His early commercial work, like that of many of his generation, was influenced by the work of Morris's Kelmscott Press, which had just appeared. These books were bought directly from Morris by his friend Joseph M. Bowles, who worked in an Indianapolis art shop, and published *Modern Art*, a magazine for which Rogers did some work and lettering.

In 1895, Bowles and the magazine were taken to Boston by the Louis Prang chromolithography firm; it needed a designer, and Rogers joined them. Once in Boston, he met Daniel Berkeley Updike, founder of the Merrymount Press (1893). He introduced him to George H. Mifflin, who in turn invited him to join the Houghton, Mifflin & Co. as designer at the Riverside Press in 1896.

In 1899, Rogers persuaded Mifflin to set up a department for the production of fine books for collectors in the Riverside Press. A number of Rogers's best works, which appeared as the Riverside Press Editions, were doubtlessly influenced by the work of Updike at the Merrymount Press, which had been producing fine books since 1893.

In 1902, when Rogers was entrusted with the three-volume folio edition of *The Essays of Montaigne* (1902-1904), he suggested using a new typeface. Named *Montaigne*, after this author, it was not only his first design, but also the first one based on the type used by Nicolas Jenson in the printing of Eusebius de Cesarea's *De Præparatione Evangelica* in 1470.

Although disappointed with the punchcutter's interpretation of his drawings, it was satisfying enough for Rogers to decide to give up illustration and painting and dedicate all his time to typography. In 1912, after sixteen years of work at the Riverside Press, he left the company to become a freelance designer for the rest of his life.

That year he went to England during the summer, but he did not find a job as good as he had with Houghton, Mifflin & Co. Thus, he returned to a difficult four-year period in the United States.

In 1914, he was commissioned by Henry Watson Kent, secretary of the Metropolitan Museum of Art in New York, to design a private type for use by the Museum Press for ephemeral printing.

Once again, Rogers returned to the Jenson model, with a result much closer to his ideals. Being allowed to use his design, he decided to present it in a limited edition of Maurice de Guerin's *The Centaur* –hence the type's name– printed at the Carl Purington Rollins's Montague Press in 1915.

Between 1916 and 1919, Rogers took another trip to England, invited by Emery Walker who was interested in printing fine editions in the tradition of the Kelmscott and Dove Presses. Rogers helped Walker establish the Mall Press and, through a commission brought with him from the Grolier Club, he printed that part of Albrecht Dürer's *Geometry* which deals with the design of letters, under the title *On the Just Shaping of Letters*.

After the association with Walker, Rogers was invited by Sidney Cockerell, former secretary of Morris and now director of the Fitzwilliam Museum in Cambridge, to come to advise the Cambridge University Press on the use of typography. Thanks to Roger's report, which, by the way, was quite unflattering, the press begun a complete reform of its typographic resources, which included most of Monotype's typefaces.

In 1919, Rogers returned to the United States, where he became adviser to the Harvard University Press, spending the next ten years on book design, notably for William Edwin Rudge at Mount Vernon outside New York City. For him, Rogers designed around one hundred titles.

Approached by the American Lanston Monotype to adapt the *Centaur* typeface to their composing system, Rogers preferred to entrust the English Monotype with his work. In 1928, he traveled to England in the company of Frederic Warde to closely supervise the recutting.

Warde's *Arrighi* italic, based on Ludovico Degli Arrighi's first italic shown in Bladius Palladius's *Coryciana* (1524), and cut to accompany *Centaur*, was also redrawn under Rogers's supervision. The first edition of *Centaur*, accompanied by *Arrighi*, was John Drinkwater's *Persephone* (1926), printed and published by William Edwin Rudge at his Mount Vernon Press in New York.

Among the very many books Rogers designed, there is a consensus concerning the three outstanding works, all set in *Centaur*: the T. E. Shaw (Lawrence of Arabia) translation of Homer's *Odyssey*, which was printed at Emery Walker's works in 1932; Stanley Morison's essay *Fra Luca de Pacioli of Borgo S. Sepolcro*, the Renaissance Italian writing master piece, printed by the Grolier Club in 1933; and his masterpiece, a folio edition of the *Oxford Lectern Bible*, which after four years of work, was published in England by Oxford University Press in 1935.

In 1943, William Edwin Rudge published his *Paragraphs on Printing*, a present classic on this subject.

Rogers was acclaimed by figures such as Daniel Berkeley Updike "as the most distinguished designer of books of our time" and the author of one of the finest typefaces of this century, *Centaur*, a revival of Nicolas Jenson's type.

Albert Bruce Rogers died in 1957 in New Fairfield, Connecticut, at the age of eighty-seven.

CENTAUR (1914)

Modeled after the 1470 Nicolas Jenson typeface, it was cut by Robert Wiebking in 1914 and used in a limited edition of Maurice de Guerin's *The Centaur*, printed by Carl Purington Rollins's Montague Press. Frederic Warde designed a companion italic, known as *Arrighi*, in 1925.

ABCDEFGHIJKLMNOPQRST
UVWXYZ&abcdefghijklmnopq
rstuvwxyz$1234567890!?

BRUCE ROGERS'S PRINTER'S MARKS (1904-1920)

These are three different graphic identifications used by Rogers in his publications. While the first two are subtle formal variations of the Aldine dolphin and anchor, the third one is an allegorical image of a faun with the scythe of Chronos, with Bruce's thistle plant in the background.

This image closely follows the mark of printer Simon de Colines, who managed the Henri Estienne workshop around 1510.

THE USE OF INITIAL LETTERS

In these ten examples we may see Rogers's didactic presentation of the relationship of an initial with the running text.

While the letter **W** (perhaps by Rogers) presents an influence of William Morris's *Kelmscott Chaucer*, the **O** is a *Cloister Initial* by Frederic W. Goudy.

TYPOGRAPHIC VIGNETTES

Rogers was undoubtedly a master in creating ornaments with type. These are two of the many typographic examples created by him at the Riverside Press.

INITIALS (1917/1933)

These two initials belong to two works sponsored by the Grolier Club.

The first one appears in chapter one of Albrecht Dürer's book, *On the Just Shaping of Letters*, published in 1917, and the second, in chapter one of Stanley Morison's book, *Fra Luca de Pacioli of Borgo S. Sepolcro*, published in 1933.

This initial, by the way, is a redrawing of the wood engraving that appeared in Luca Pacioli's book, *Arithmetica Geometria Proportioni e Proportionalitá*, printed in Venice in 1494.

UTOPIA (1934)

The title page designed for the New York Limited Editions Club's English edition of Sir Thomas Moore's *Utopia*. The original printing was done in red and black.

FRA LUCA DE PACIOLI (1933)

This is the title page of the 1933 edition of Stanley Morison's essay, *Fra Luca de Pacioli of Borgo S. Sepolcro*.

Originally printed in red and black, it reflects a clear influence of Morris's work.

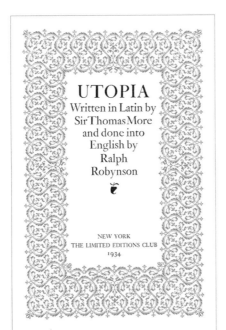

UTOPIA
Written in Latin by
Sir Thomas More
and done into
English by
Ralph
Robynson

NEW YORK
THE LIMITED EDITIONS CLUB
1934

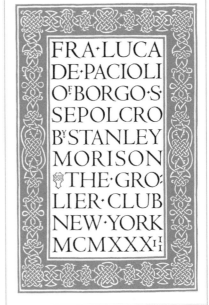

FRA·LUCA
DE·PACIOLI
OF·BORGO·S·
SEPOLCRO
BY·STANLEY
MORISON
THE·GRO-
LIER·CLUB
NEW·YORK
MCMXXXIII

Born in Czechoslovakia (then Bohemia) in 1883, Rudolph Ruzicka was brought to the United States by his parents when he was eleven. Despite his difficulty in learning English, he completed seven years of schooling in three years, and studied art at a settlement house on Saturdays.

In 1897, Ruzicka went to work for a La Salle Street wood-engraving shop as an unpaid apprentice. Meanwhile, he attended Saturday afternoon classes at Hull-House and continued his art training in evening classes at the Art Institute of Chicago.

In 1903, he went to New York City and worked for the American Banknote Company and studied at the New York School of Art. In his spare time, he experimented with wood engraving, especially with chiaroscuro prints. He worked for the Calkins & Holden advertising agency from 1906 on, but opened his own wood engraving and printing shop in 1910.

In 1907, a meeting with printer and historian, Daniel Berkeley Updike gave him a commission to engrave William Addison Dwiggins's title page as well as an invitation to visit him.

In 1910, while visiting Dwiggins, he accepted Updike's invitation. Updike not only was cordial, but appreciative and critical of his work. The following year, he began his first of twenty-nine views of Boston that the Merrymount Press sent as New Year's keepsakes, which he continued doing until Updike's death in 1941.

In 1915, at the age of thirty-two, Rudolph Ruzicka illustrated two books: *The Fountains of Papal Rome*, by Mrs. Charles MacVeagh, published by Charles Scribner's, and *New York*, a book commissioned by the Grolier Club, which asked him to do a volume on New York. After two years of preparation, Ruzicka completed the thirty colored wood engravings –in a book of large *octavo* format– that constitute this second work.

Emile Fecquet of Paris was engaged to print the ten full-scale illustrations, and Theodore Low De Vinne of New York to do the letterpress work. The book also contains a historical treatise by Ruzicka on color printing from wood engravings. The work had great significance at a time when photomechanical processing was claiming an overemphasized importance.

A new commission came from the members of the Carteret Book Club of Newark, New Jersey. The book, *Newark: A Series of Engravings on Wood*, published in 1917 in a generous *quarto*, contains five full-page illustrations with color printed by Ruzicka himself and twelve black-and-white engravings printed by Updike at the Merrymount Press.

In 1930, the Limited Editions Club published *The Fables of Jean de la Fontaine*, a book of copperplates, and the Lakeside Press in Chicago published Henry David Thoreau's *Walden* with thirty-eight black and white brush drawings reproduced in photo-engravings.

Besides the mentioned books, Ruzicka also worked in many other media: aquatints (*Washington Irving*, 1921), rubber plates, type metal, and woodcuts. He also designed many book jackets and a great deal of advertising and commercial printing.

All these works, eloquent expressions of his skill and mastery of lettering and design, attracted the attention of Chauncey W. Griffith, director of typographic development of the Mergenthaler Linotype Company. Through the suggestion of his friend, William Addison Dwiggins, Griffith commissioned Ruzicka to design a new typeface for the Linotype machine in 1935.

Ruzicka spent the first five years of what would become a forty-year relationship with the company developing the new typeface. Named after this Connecticut town, *Fairfield*

was issued in 1940. He also designed a series of *fleurons* for Linotype.

In addition, in 1935, he had the first large exhibit of his work at the American Institute of Graphic Arts in New York, where he received the Institute's Gold Medal.

Once again, Ruzicka concentrated on what might be considered his most brilliant work: *Three Monographs in Color* (1935). He designed and illustrated these *quarto* volumes for the International Printing Ink Company. The work, divided in *Color Chemistry*, *Color as Light*, and *Color in Use*, has charts, formulas, decorations, prints, and color juxtapositions, all prepared by him at I.P.I. and MIT.

In 1948, the Grolier Club held an exhibition of his work, this time with a catalog that documented his many achievements.

In 1951, he received another commission from Mergenthaler Linotype to design a newspaper typeface. *Primer*, which was intended primarily for high-speed production of books, magazines, and newspapers, is characterized by a reduced contrast between thick and thin strokes. Introduced commercially in 1953, it was used by Ruzicka when he redesigned the *Harvard Business Review* that year.

In 1968, while he was in Hanover, New Hampshire, in close relationship with Edward C. Lathem, Dartmouth College's librarian, the Friends of the Library published his portfolio, *Studies in Type Design*, containing ten alphabets "with random quotations."

Ruzicka also designed and coordinated the typographical management of the fifty-four volume *Encyclopaedia Britannica* series, *Great Books of the Western World*.

Rudolph Ruzicka died in 1978, at the age of ninety-five.

FAIRFIELD (1940)

Commissioned by C. W. Griffith for Linotype to replace Morris Fuller Benton's *Century Schoolbook*, this modernized typeface retains *Oldstyle* characteristics.

Ruzicka feels that to invite continuous reading "type must have a subtle degree of interest and variety of design."

ABCDEFGHIJKLMNOPQRST
UVWXYZ&abcdefghijklmnopqr
stuvwxyz$1234567890!?

A FONT OF TYPE (1968)

"A Font of Type" is taken from his *Studies in Type Design*, published by the Trustees of Dartmouth College, with a calligraphic text taken from Walt Whitman's *Leaves of Grass* (1855).

PRINTER'S CASE (1922)

An illustration of the old two type cases done for Daniel Berkeley Updike's book, *Printing Types: Their History, Form and Use* (1922), and included by Warren Chappell in his book, *A Short History of the Printed Word* (1972).

FORT TICONDEROGA

A bookplate (or *ex libris*) designed for the Fort Ticonderoga Library, and engraved on boxwood.

METAL TYPE (1922)

An illustration of the plan and nomenclature of a metal typeface done for Daniel Berkeley Updike's book, *Printing Types: Their History, Form and Use* (1922), and included by Warren Chappell in his book, *A Short History of the Printed Word* (1972).

THE BORZOI BOOKS (1922)

This symbol, with the borzoi-hunting dog, was designed for the Borzoi Books, a division of Alfred A. Knopf publishing company.

One should look at some of the graphic variations that William Addison Dwiggins did of this device on page 131.

ROBERT WOODS BLISS

A bookplate (or *ex libris*) designed for the library of Robert Woods Bliss, at Dumbarton Oaks, Delaware.

BOSTON ATHENÆUM

A bookplate (or *ex libris*) designed for the Howard W. Lang Fund at the Boston Athenæum Library.

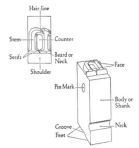

This latent mine–these unlaunch'd voices–passionate powers,
Wrath, argument, or praise, or comic leer, or prayer devout,
(Not nonpareil, brevier, bourgeois, long primer merely,)
These ocean waves arousable to fury and to death,
Or sooth'd to ease and sheeny sun and sleep,
Within the pallid slivers slumbering.

& a b c d e f g h i j k l m n o p
q r s t u v w x y z ⚏ 1967

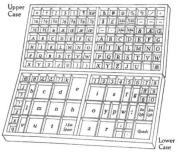

EX LIBRIS

FORT TICONDEROGA

BORZOI BOOKS

QVOD SEVERIS METES

EX LIBRIS
ROBERT WOODS BLISS
DUMBARTON OAKS

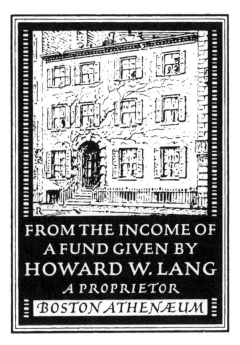

FROM THE INCOME OF
A FUND GIVEN BY
HOWARD W. LANG
A PROPRIETOR
BOSTON ATHENÆUM

Born in Ann Arbor, Michigan in 1954, Paul Shaw is a self-taught calligrapher, letterer, typographer, and graphic designer. He graduated from Reed College in 1976 with a Bachelor in Arts in American Studies, and went on to earn both an Master in Arts (1978) and a Master in Philosophy (1980) in American History from Columbia University. His unfinished dissertation is a biography of American designer William Addison Dwiggins.

Shaw had always been fascinated by letterforms from childhood, drawing them at first and later discovering the secrets of the broad pen in high school. While in graduate school he opened Paul Shaw/Letter Design in 1983, in order to help pay his tuition. The studio was such a success that within a few years he had dropped out of school to concentrate on design full time.

In the past fifteen years he has worked for a wide variety of clients creating calligraphy, hand lettering, and custom typefaces for an equally diverse set of projects. Among his clients have been Campbell Soup, Rolex, Clairol, Avon, Lord & Taylor, GRP Records, McCaffrey & Ratner, New York Methodist Hospital, Vignelli & Associates, Robilant & Associati (Milano), Bernhardt/Fudyma, *Modern Bride*, and the City of New York.

His most visible work has been the logo for Origins and its companion typeface. His work has won awards from the New York Art Directors Club, the Type Directors Club, the American Institute of Graphic Arts (AIGA), *How* magazine, *Print* magazine, and *Letter Arts Review*.

Shaw's work has been shown in group calligraphy exhibitions internationally including Paris, London, Venice, and Moscow. He has had one-man shows in St. Paul, Minnesota and in Asolo, Italy.

From 1981 to 1987, Shaw organized the *Calligraphy and Lettering in the Graphic Arts* annual competitions and exhibitions sponsored by the Society of Scribes, Ltd., in New York City.

In the 1980s he also coordinated a series of calligraphy and illustration exhibitions in New York, Washington, DC , and Cambridge, Massachusetts, by the loose-knit group known as the Circle of Friends. The Circle of Friends included type designers Michael Harvey (England), Jovica Veljovic (former Yugoslavia), Jean Evans (USA), and Julian Waters (USA), among its members.

Shaw conceived of the international calligraphy exhibition *Calligrafia nel mondo della grafica* organized by Dalilah Sottile in Asolo, Italy in 1998. That same year, he and Peter Bain cocurated *Blackletter: Type and National Identity*, the first-ever American exhibition devoted to the subject of blackletter typefaces. The exhibition, held at Cooper Union School of Design, New York, was accompanied by a monograph of the same name co-edited by Shaw and Bain.

Paul Shaw is the author of *Black Letter Primer* (1981) and *Letterforms* (1986) as well as numerous articles for *Fine Print, Design Issues, Letter Arts Review*, and *Print* magazines. Among his articles have been profiles of type designers W. A. Dwiggins and Morris Fuller Benton, calligrapher and book jacket designer Georg Salter, and reviews of type designs by Peter Matthias Noordzij, Frank Blokland, Timothy Donaldson, Jean-François Porchez, and others.

Since 1980, Paul Shaw has taught calligraphy, lettering, and typography at several New York-area design schools. He is currently at Parsons School of Design. He has also taught calligraphy workshops in Chicago, Washington, DC, New York, and Milan, Italy. Shaw has lectured in Chicago, Washington, DC, New York, London, Copenhagen and Oslo.

Since 1995, Paul Shaw has been partner with Garrett Boge in the digital type foundry LetterPerfect. Together they have designed a number of typefaces beginning with *Kolo*, a four-member family based on the lettering of the Vienna Secession. Their other designs include the Baroque Set of *Cresci, Pontif*, and *Pietra*; the Florentine Set of *Beata, Donatello*, and *Ghiberti*; *Old Claude*; and *Bermuda*. In 1998, Shaw and Boge completed a trio of typefaces inspired by modern Swedish calligraphy – *Stockholm, Göteborg*, and *Uppsala*, for Agfa. The three faces are independent and do not constitute a family. *Stockholm* is a roman, *Göteborg* is an italic, and *Uppsala* is an uncial.

Shaw is a member of numerous calligraphic organizations including the Society of Scribes, Ltd., the Society of Scribes and Illuminators, the Associazione Calligrafica Italiana and Letter Exchange. He is also a member of the Type Directors Club, AIGA, the American Center for Design, and ATypI (Association Typographique Internationale). Currently, he is serving on the board of directors of the Type Directors Club.

Shaw is the principal of Paul Shaw/ Letter Design. He lives and works in New York City.

OLD CLAUDE (1994)

Drawn to simulate an old cut of the classic Garamond type designs of the sixteenth century.

The pronounced rough edges and coarse letter shapes create the effect of letterpress printing with old foundry type onto handmade paper.

ABCDEFGHIJKLMNOPQR STUVWXYZ&abcdefghijklm nopqrstuvwxyz$1234567890!?

PAUL SHAW / LETTER DESIGN
(1995)

In this announcement card for his Letter Design studio in New York, Paul Shaw uses a calligraphic composition that is reminiscent of Islamic writing.

JEFFREY C. KEIL (1994)

Dinner program cover for the Thirty-third Annual Charter Award Dinner at St. Francis College.

PONTIF (1996)

Graphic comparison between the original inscriptional letters from the Biblioteca Ambrosiana in Milan, dedicated to Pope Sixtus V, designed by Luca Horfei of Fano (c.1590), and *Pontif* typeface, one of the three typefaces that complete the *Baroque Set* designed in collaboration with Garrett Boge in 1996.

NUMBERS (1996)

Calligraphy for the South Florida Calligraphy Guild.

THE FLORENTINE SET (1997)

Double spread from the brochure presentation of the *Florentine Set* showing a rubbing of the Berto di Lionardo tombstone (1430) in Santa Croce, Florence, graphic source for the *Ghiberti* typeface.

A NEW YEAR'S WISH FOR PEACE, HAPPINESS AND LOVE (1990)

This typographic design sent by Paul Shaw and Peter Kruty on Christmas (1990), was selected as one of the best typographic examples in *Typography Twelve*, the Annual of the Type Directors Club (1991).

KOLO (1996)

Typographic presentation of *Kolo* typeface, designed by Paul Shaw and Garrett Boge in 1996, and based on the Art Nouveau lettering used by Koloman Moser, a Vienna Secession artist in his graphic work.

PAUL SHAW / LETTER DESIGN
(1995)

This typographic announcement was sent by Paul Shaw / Letter Design, as a presentation of his calligraphic and typographic work.

The lettering is based on the work of Bernardo Rosellino, a fifteenth-century Florentine artist.

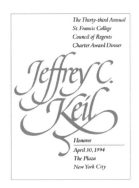

A new year's wish for peace, happiness, and love.

PAUL SHAW

227

98 (1998)

This creative and subtle use of two typographic signs exemplifies Shaw's work.

SEASON'S GREETINGS (1987)

Calligraphic Christmas card designed for R.R. Bowker Company, New York..

PRIVATE PLEASURES (c.1986)

Calligraphy for the Kordet Group.

SIMPLY THE BEST (1995)

Calligraphy done for Clairol.

HANDWRITING IS THE TONGUE OF THE HAND (c.1992)

Calligraphic announcement for Paul Shaw / Letter Design.

TRUE PAIN (1994)

Calligraphic writing done for *Weavings*, with a quotation from the *Diary of a Country Priest* (1936) by George Bernanos.

Best wishes for the New Year from Paul Shaw / Letter Design

Handwriting is the tongue of the hand.
ABU HAIYAN AL-TAWHIDI

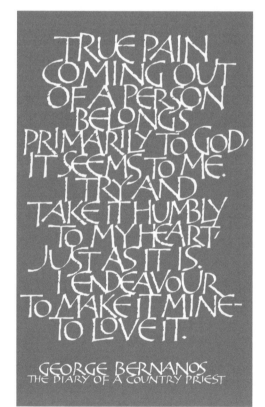

KOLO (1995)

Named after Koloman Moser (1868-1918), founding member of the Vienna Secession movement, this display typeface, designed in collaboration with Garrett Boge, is based on the sinuous nature of the Art Nouveau lettering and its myriad forms.

The typeface is presented in its normal and extended forms, which present subtle differences.

ABCDEFGHIJKLMNOPQRST
UVWXYZ&$1234567890!?

ABCDEFGHIJKLMN
OPQRSTUVWXYZ&
$1234567890!?

BEATA (1997)

A delicate design, *Beata* is modeled on the inscription by Bernardo Rossellino for the tomb of Beata Villana in Santa Maria Novella, erected in 1460.

This first of the *Florentine Set*, a collection of historically inspired titling typefaces, it was designed in collaboration with Garrett Boge.

ABCDEFGHIJKLMNOPQRSTU
VWXYZ&$1234567890!?

DONATELLO (1997)

Inspired by the lettering on the *Cantoria* by Luca Della Robbia in the Museum dell'Opera di Duomo, in Florence, *Donatello* is the second of the *Florentine Set*, a collection of historically inspired titling typefaces.

This classically proportioned design, with subtly tapered strokes, was designed in collaboration with Garrett Boge.

ABCDEFGHIJKLMNOPQRST
UVWXYZ&$1234567890!?

ABCDEFGHIJKLMNOPQR
STUVWXYZ&
$1234567890!?

GHIBERTI (1997)

Derived from inlaid marble and cast bronze Florentine inscriptions, *Ghiberti* is the third of the *Florentine Set*, a collection of historically inspired titling typefaces.

This bold design, marked by wedge-shape terminals, was designed in collaboration with Garrett Boge.

ABCDEFGHIJKLMNOPQRS
TUVWXYZ&$1234567890!?

BERMUDA OPEN (1997)

Designed by Paul Shaw and Garrett Boge, in the vein of freely drawn showcard lettering, this typeface offers a jaunty, fun, and friendly appearance.

The drawings were made with a *Speedball* B-series pen nib, the stock tool of the showcard letterer.

The variations presented here are *Bermuda Open* and *Bermuda Dots*, with their corresponding small caps.

ABCDEFGHIJKLMNOP
QRSTUVWXYZ&ABCDE
FGHIJKLMNOPQRSTU
VWXYZ$1234567890!?

ABCDEFGHIJKLMNOP
QRSTUVWXYZ&ABCDE
FGHIJKLMNOPQRSTU
VWXYZ$1234567890!?

STOCKHOLM (1998)

Designed in collaboration with Garrett Boge, and inspired by post-World War II Swedish calligraphy, *Stockholm* is an italic face based on the work of Kerstin Anckers.

It is important to note the 45-degree pen angle employed in the construction of the letters which give them an elegant form.

ABCDEFGHIJKLMNOPQRS
TUVWXYZ&abcdefghijklmn
opqrstuvwxyz$1234567890!?

GÖTEBORG (1998)

Designed in collaboration with Garrett Boge and inspired by post-World War II Swedish calligraphy, *Göteborg* is an italic face based on the work of Erik Lindgren.

It is interesting to note that the type has swash capitals.

Numerals are drawn in *Oldstyle*.

ABCDEFGHIJKLMNOP
QRSTUVWXYZ&abcdefghijk
lmnopqrstuvwxyz$1234567890!?

uppsALA (1998)

Designed in collaboration with Garrett Boge and inspired by post-World War II Swedish calligraphy, *Uppsala* is an uncial face based on the work of Herbert Lindgren.

The present sample includes an expert version with small caps.

ABCDEFGHIJKLMNOPQR
STUVWXYZ&ABCDEFGHIJ
KLMNOPQRSTUVWXYZ
$1234567890!?

ROBERT SLIMBACH

Born in Evanston, Illinois, in 1956, the son of a photoengraver and printer, and a keen gymnast, Robert Slimbach went to the University of California at Los Angeles on an athletic scholarship.

After graduating, he worked producing silk-screen posters and prints, many incorporating hand lettering. "I had no formal training in lettering and typically would refer to old *Letraset* type catalogs as a reference for hand-drawn titles in my prints."

In 1983, mainly to supplement his income, he joined Autologic, Inc., where his first job was recreating metal typefaces for digital technology. He also began to study classic typefaces, and the designs of German designers Hermann Zapf (b.1918) and Georg Trump (1896-1985). He also started to develop his own original designs encouraged by Autologic design director Sumner Stone.

In 1985, he moved to Ventura as a freelance type designer. His first typeface came about as a result of a worldwide talent search by ITC in the mid 1980s. Shortly after, International Type Corporation released *ITC Slimbach* in 1987, a squarish roman and italic typeface. By that time, Slimbach had left Autologic to work full time on his own designs.

While working on his second typeface, *ITC Giovanni*, also issued by ITC, Slimbach learned that Sumner Stone had come to work with Adobe Systems, Inc., then a small growing company. His call for advice on his new typeface ended up, one month later, with an invitation from Stone to work full-time at Adobe as an in-house type designer.

Once at Adobe, Slimbach designed *Adobe Utopia*, a transitional typeface, and the much-admired *Adobe Garamond*, both in 1989. The following year he created *Adobe Minion*, which is certainly a modern classic. This same year he designed a chancery face called *Poetica*, and collaborated with Carol Twombly on *Myriad*, a lively, sans serif face.

In 1993, he designed *Sanvito*, a freer italic typeface, which shows his interest for scripts, followed by *Caflisch Script*, based on Swiss designer Max Caflisch's handwriting.

In 1996, Slimbach designed Adobe's first multiple master historical revival, *Adobe Jenson*. For it, Slimbach used Adobe's interpolation technology to reproduce the changes in style and proportion necessary when creating various sizes from a single size of a metal typeface.

His next typeface was *Kepler*, a modern style typeface. Using the multiple master technology, Slimbach was able to modify character shapes and weights creating a design in which the character contrast is stronger and more dramatic in larger sizes. He was also able to create a friendlier modern design, which would read well at different sizes.

Although he is enthusiastic about the creative control offered by the computer, he is an accomplished calligrapher, and his preparatory work is always done on paper.

Asked about what he thinks makes a typeface timeless, Slimbach answered *U&lc* (*Upper & lower case*) journal, "Many of the qualities which make a composition typeface timeless can also be found in timeless examples from other creative fields, such as art, literature, and architecture. Timeless expressions speak to the universal humanity within all of us, without a need for interpretation. They transcend the fashion of the day, while encompassing the spirit of the day. They utilize the current technology without being limited by it. They successfully balance utility and beauty. They possess originality and vision, without abandoning the ideals of the past. They obey the universal principles of harmony, balance, and clarity; simply put, timeless expressions possess grace.

"It is difficult to predict which types will be popular in the next century; however, if a type designer has mastered the craft, understands the classic principles of letter design, and has creative insight into the modern age, this may be enough to produce a timeless typeface or two."

ITC SLIMBACH (1987)

This is Robert Slimbach's first type design, which was the result of a worldwide search done by the International Typeface Corporation in the 1980s.

ABCDEFGHIJKLMNOPQRST
UVWXYZ&abcdefghijklmnop
qrstuvwxyz$1234567890!?

ITC GIOVANNI (1989)

This is the second typeface designed by Slimbach, which was also created for ITC.

It includes three weights with their italics.

ABCDEFGHIJKLMNOPQRST
UVWXYZ&abcdefghijklmnop
qrstuvwxyz$1234567890!?

*ABCDEFGHIJKLMNOPQRST
UVWXYZ&abcdefghijklmnopqr
stuvwxyz$1234567890!?*

ADOBE GARAMOND (1989)

A highly praised roman typeface; it is modeled on Claude Garamond's original designs, researched at the Plantin-Moretus Museum in Antwerp, Belgium.

Because each size of a punch-cut face is a different design, a particular size was chosen as a model.

Being the *Vraye Parangone* model (around 18-point) selected, Robert Slimbach developed the whole alphabet.

ABCDEFGHIJKLMNOPQRS
TUVWXYZ&abcdefghijklmnop
qrstuvwxyz$1234567890!?

*ABCDEFGHIJKLMNOPQRSTU
VWXYZ&abcdefghijklmnopqrstuv
wxyz$1234567890!?*

ROBERT SLIMBACH

233

ADOBE UTOPIA
(1989)

This is a Transitional typeface, which was designed as a family.

It includes three weights with their italics.

ABCDEFGHIJKLMNOPQRST
UVWXYZ&abcdefghijklmnop
qrstuvwxyz$1234567890!?

ABCDEFGHIJKLMNOPQRST
UVWXYZ&abcdefghijklmnop
qrstuvwxyz$1234567890!?

ADOBE MINION
(1990)

Named after one of the typefaces used in the early days of type founding, this roman text typeface has a close resemblance to *Sabon* (Jan Tschichold, 1966), but with a sharper look and more condensed.

It includes a complete family of three weights with their italics.

Designed and issued before the appearance of Adobe's multiple master technology, it was reissued as a three-axis face in 1992.

ABCDEFGHIJKLMNOPQRST
UVWXYZ&abcdefghijklmnopq
rstuvwxyz$1234567890!?

ABCDEFGHIJKLMNOPQRST
UVWXYZ&abcdefghijklmnopqr
stuvwxyz$1234567890!?

SANVITO (1993)

Named after Bartolomeo Sanvito, a fifteenth-century calligrapher, this calligraphic typeface shows Slimbach's continuous interest in scripts.

ABCDEFGHIJKLMNOPQRSTU VWXYZ&abcdefghijklmnopqrs tuvwxyz$1234567890!?

ABCDEFGHIJKLMNOPQRSTU VWXYZ&abcdefghijklmnopqr stuvwxyz$1234567890!?

CAFLISCH SCRIPT (1993)

This is a script typeface based on the handwriting of the Swiss type designer Max Caflisch (b.1916).

ABCDEFGHIJKLMNOPQRSTUVW XYZ&abcdefghijklmnopqrstuvwx yz$1234567890!?

ABCDEFGHIJKLMNOPQRSTUV WXYZ&abcdefghijklmnopqrstu vwxyz$1234567890!?

ROBERT E. SMITH

Born in Chicago, Illinois in 1910, Robert E. Smith was a lettering designer associated with American Type Founders from 1933 to 1942 and created two of its most popular script typefaces, Park Avenue in 1933, and Brush in 1942. The latter was designed as an attempt to replace designs from the early part of the twentieth century.

In 1939, he was art director of the New York World's Fair, and subsequently worked in New York City as a freelance artist.

He was also a member of the American Institute of Graphic Arts, Chicago.

Park Avenue (1933)

This is a distinctive script cut by ATF around 1933, which is not quite a joining script although some letters seem to be so.

It has been one of the most successful design projects for replacing the delicate traditional scripts with more contemporary interpretations.

*ABCDEFGHIJKLMNO
PQRSTUVWXYZ&abcdefg
hijklmnopqrstuvwxyz$1234567890?*

Brush (1942)

Designed in 1942 as one of ATF's group of contemporary scripts, it was intended to replace designs from the early part of the twentieth century.

It has a hand-lettered, freely drawn appearance, with letters joined skillfully so the connections are not obvious.

The availability of the face on Monotype matrices gave it a much greater range of popularity and usefulness.

ABCDEFGHIJKLMNOP2
RSTUVWXYZ&
abcdefghijklmnopqrstuvwxyz
$1234567890!?

Born in Venice, Florida in 1945, Sumner Stone edited his high school paper and was attracted to the hot-metal Linotypes at the local printer's.

Then, when he went to Reed College in Portland, Oregon, he studied calligraphy with Lloyd Reynolds, who encouraged his interest in letterforms. From there, he went to Hallmark Cards as a lettering artist, and was also inspired by the film made by German calligrapher and typographer Hermann Zapf (b.1918), who served as a consultant. This situation led Stone to work for Hallmark in Kansas City for two years.

He moved to Sonoma, California, where he established his own design studio under the name of Alpha and Omega, which he ran for nine years. At the same time, he went back to college at Sonoma State University, where he obtained a master of arts in mathematics.

He became interested in the design of typefaces on the computer, which, in 1979, led him to start working in the field of digital type as director of typography for Autologic, Inc., in Newbury Park, California. This firm was one of the earliest manufacturers of digital typesetting equipment in the United States.

During this time, Stone tried to interest the company in establishing a more creative typeface development program. Even though he was unsuccessful in his endeavor, he was able to license some typefaces from suppliers such as ITC and Letraset.

He then became director of typography at Camex, Inc. in Boston, Massachusetts before taking the position of director of typography with Adobe Systems, Inc., in Mountain View, California in 1984.

Stone's main interest at Adobe was to digitize classic typefaces. His persistence and dedication in searching for original sources materialized in the revival of *Garamond* which was created by Claude Garamond in 1541. It was considered the first typeface to be designed as a true printing typeface. Modern versions have been based on a 1615 recutting by Jean Jannon, and on an 1897 revival of Jannon's face. Morris Fuller Benton and Thomas Maitland Cleland based their 1917 version for ATF on Jannon's typeface. From these sources, Linotype and Intertype also developed their versions.

Stone and his staff researched until they found the original punches and matrices in the Plantin-Moretus Museum at Antwerp. Because each size of a punch-cut face is a different design, a particular size must be chosen as a model. The group selected the *Vraye Parangone* model (around 18-point). The result, developed by Robert Slimbach, was a beautiful version which has repaired the damage done by several previous generations of typesetting technology.

After three years of work at Adobe, he developed the *Stone* family typefaces in 1987. According to him, after innumerable nights and weekends working on the design, his wife and children came to refer to it as "your other family." The *Stone* family, which consists of three different sub-families, *Stone Serif*, *Stone Sans Serif*, and *Stone Informal*, was also the result of his analysis of multiple letters and memos he received which had been produced on laser printers. He began to realize the need for a typeface that could offer a variety of forms appropriate for each type of personal and business communication.

With this design, Stone extended the current definition of a type family. In other type designs, such as Adrian Frutiger's sans serif *Univers* or Hermann Zapf's serif *Palatino*, all the variations are maintained within the characters of the font. However, Stone's typeface is a new proposal.

Based on a single model, the three designs share typographic characteristics such as x-heights, cap heights, and stem weights. Using the mathematical formulae inherent in *Adobe PostScript*, the *Stone* family represents two important advances in typesetting technology: using a shared model, and being the first typeface professionally designed for use by and in the desktop publishing environment.

At the end of 1989, Stone left Adobe to found Stone Type Foundry, Inc. in Palo Alto, California, which specializes in the development of new PostScript fonts. It also publishes Stone Type Foundry's own magazine, *Edge*, which functions much as ITC's *U&lc* (*Upper & lowercase*).

Their first release, *Stone Print* (1992), is a redrawn, condensed version of *Stone Serif*, which was designed for the American graphic design magazine, *Print*, and *Silica* (1993), a lively slab-serif alphabet. These two faces have been created by a combination of drawing on paper and screen using the *FontStudio* and the *Fontographer* programs.

In 1995, Stone designed *Arepo*, which was drawn as a display version of *Stone Print*, and intended for use at large size. It was also influenced by other two projects in which he had collaborated: *Trajan* (Carol Twombly, 1989), and *ITC Bodoni* (1994).

Sumner Stone has also written a book, *On Stone: The Art and Use of Typography on the Personal Computer*, published by Chronicle Books in 1991.

ITC STONE SANS
(1987)

Based on a basic model, this typeface it shares various characteristics such as x-height, cap height, and stem weights.

In 1988, ITC was given the license for the complete family, which includes *Stone Serif*, *Stone Sans*, and *Stone Informal*.

ABCDEFGHIJKLMNOPQRSTU VWXYZ&abcdefghijklmnopqr stuvwxyz$1234567890!?

ITC STONE SERIF
(1987)

A condensed version of *Stone Serif* (1987), it is a text typeface designed for American *Print* magazine, and developed with the assistance of book designer Bob Ishi, whose name in Japanese is also "stone."

"Each design is a manifestation of an underlying skeletal set of letterforms. Thus, though there are numerous differences, each typeface has many characteristics in common with the others. However, to do their job properly the typefaces needed to be distinct from one another. In the design process, several nuances in the basic form were introduced. For example, the lowercase a has similar forms in the *Serif* and *Sans* and a different form in the *Informal* [a]. The lowercase g has similar forms in the *Sans* and *Informal* and a different form in the *Serif* [g]. The variant forms are appropriate to the function of each style and help distinguish the styles when used together," explains Stone.

The International Typeface Corporation bought the license in 1988.

ABCDEFGHIJKLMNOPQRST
UVWXYZ&abcdefghijklmn
opqrstuvwxyz
$1234567890!?

*ABCDEFGHIJKLMNOPQRST
UVWXYZ&abcdefghijklmnop
qrstuvwxyz$1234567890!?*

ITC STONE INFORMAL (1987)

A condensed version of *Stone Serif* (1987), it is a text typeface designed for the *American Print* magazine.

It was developed with the assistance of book designer Bob Ishi.

The International Typeface Corporation bought the license in 1988.

ABCDEFGHIJKLMNOPQRST
UVWXYZ&abcdefghijklmno
pqrstuvwxyz$1234567890!?

*ABCDEFGHIJKLMNOPQRSTU
VWXYZ&abcdefghijklmnopqrs
tuvwxyz$1234567890!?*

Born in Topeka, Kansas in 1911, Bradbury Thompson graduated from Washburn College there in 1934, with a degree in economics. His career in graphic design began as the designer of his college yearbooks.

Following a four-year stay at Capper Publications where he designed books and magazines, Thompson came to New York City in 1938, as art director of Rogers-Kellogg-Stillson, Inc., and worked with them until 1941. It was there that he began his association with Westvaco, the house organ of the West Virginia Pulp and Paper Company, and started his noteworthy series of *Westvaco Inspirations for Printers*.

From the first issue, designed in 1939, until the last one done in 1962, the sixty-one issues became Thompson's experimental field for his ideas both graphically and conceptually. Analyzing this work we may see his interest in color and typography as a visual language for communication. His separate use of process colors and the use of typography as image, became a personal approach to graphic design that was an influence for more than a generation.

He made type dance, fly, or shout. With the use of overlapped and multiple color images, he brought motion to the static page. He made use of old engravings –many of them from Diderot's 1747-1772 *Encyclopédie* and the *Iconographic Encyclopédie* of 1851– coupled with Renaissance and Baroque typefaces. He also expressed himself in the spirit of modern painters like Pablo Picasso, Joan Miró, and Stuart Davis.

His iconoclastic side also challenged the traditional use of capital and lowercase letters. In 1944, his experiments led to replacing capital letters with large lowercase letters or with boldface.

In 1950, he introduced his *alphabet 26* –a logical system where there are no capitals and lowercase letters but a mixture of both. While vowels e and a, and consonants m and n appear in

their lowercase shape, the rest of the letters remain as capitals.

Besides doing *Westvaco Inspirations*, Thompson was associate chief of the U.S. State Department's Office of War Information between 1939 and 1962, and art director of its publications *Victory*, *USA*, and *America*, from 1942 to 1945.

He was art director of *Mademoiselle* from 1945 to 1959, and design director of *Art News* and *Art News Annual* from 1945 to 1972. He designed the formats of thirty-five other magazines, including *Harvard Business Review, Progressive Architecture*, and *Smithsonian*.

In 1956, he started teaching at the Yale University School of Art and Architecture, and since 1968, was a member of the board of trustees of Washburn University.

He also worked for the U.S. Postal Service where he designed over 120 stamps. As a design coordinator of the Citizen's Advisory Committee, he influenced countless designs. He referred to his stamps as "visual haiku, distilling a great deal of history, emotion, and information." They are exquisite combinations of beautiful images and good typography.

In book design, Bradbury Thompson turned out several outstanding works, such as *Homage to the Book* (1968), a portfolio of sixteen broad sheets designed by various international book designers such as Joseph Blumenthal, Hermann Zapf, Jan Tschichold, Norman Ives, Alvin Eisenman, Paul Rand, and George Trump, and a booklet designed by him, exalting the developments of typography and printing since the invention of typography by Johannes Gutenberg, both published by Westvaco.

Beginning in 1958, he also designed a set of twenty-four classics of American literature to be given by Westvaco, as a way to present its papers, and as a Christmas gift to its clients. Among these works, it is worthy to mention *American Cookery*, an interpretation of

eighteen-century typography enhanced with period imagery; Edgar Allan Poe's *Tales*, where he carefully integrated type, paper, color, and illustration to achieve a balance between the visual and the written elements; Stephen Crane's *Red Badge of Courage*, where he uses an unusual graphic element, a bullet hole drilled through the volume; and Benjamin Franklin's writings, set in large size type. Each volume had a concise analysis of the concept of design, which made the reader aware of his design intent.

According to Alvin Eisenman, Thompson's masterpiece and also the most important book of the century is *The Washburn College Bible* (1979), which includes sixty-six works of art as a complement to each of the biblical books. The text, set flush left, was carefully measured in lines which reflect the cadences of speech –a presentation that not only facilitates reading, but is a great typographical accomplishment that breaks away from the traditional justified columns.

An equally great achievement is *The Art of Graphic Design* (1988), in which he expresses his ideas on design and typography through the presentation of his best works.

In 1956 and 1976, he had one-man exhibitions, organized by the AIGA, and other shows in different towns of America. He received many awards including the NSAD gold T-square in 1950; the AIGA gold medal in 1975; the ADC Hall of Fame in 1977; and the Pimny Power of Printing Award in 1980. His work may be found in the collection of the New York Museum of Modern Art.

Bradbury Thompson died in New York City in 1995, at the age of eighty-four.

aLPHabeT 26 (1950)

Created in 1950, it was introduced through *Westvaco Inspirations* Nos. 180 and 213. This alphabet is a logical system where there are no capitals and lowercase letters, but a mixture of both.

While letters **a**, **e**, **m**, and **n** remain as lowercase letters with the same height as capitals, the rest of the characters are set as capitals.

aBCDeFGHIJKLmnOPQRS TUVWXYZ

ALPHABET AS EYE CHART

The two **O**s upon the human face create a clear visual pun.

DANCE (1958)

The photographs of a model and the letters **D-A-N-C-E**, literally dance around the four edges.

LEARNING NEVER ENDS (1980)

Using the work of Josef Albers as an example, we find Thompson's first haiku typographical statement.

AMERICA'S LIBRARIES (1982)

Repeating the same visual approach, we find another excellent example.

LOVE (1984)

In this stamp, Thompson creates a graphic statement also used by Robert Indiana and Milton Glaser.

WASHBURN COLLEGE BIBLE (1979)

A contemporary design based on the sign found upon a Christian mausoleum built around A.D. 350 by Constantine, the first Christian Emperor, for his daughter.

LINDENMEYER CORPORATION (1981)

Mixing Jenson's printer's mark, and Michelangelo's family mark, Thompson created a new image.

SOCIETY OF ILLUSTRATORS (1960)

In this graphic identity, he uses letter **S** to evoke a human figure, and letter **I** as a drawing surface.

ART NEWS (1970)

In this logotype, the mixture of upper and lowercase letters establishes a tension of content.

WESTVACO (1968)

In this logotype, Thompson creates a phonetic visual guide by adding a line over lowercase letter **a**.

AFRICAN MASKS (1958)

The word **WESTVACO** becomes a mask, creating a visual harmony with content.

PHOTO AND TYPE AS TEAMMATES (1958)

"Interfusing the two arts in graphic design can be a playful as well as a serious game," says Thompson.

ALPHABET 26 (1950)

Through *Westvaco Inspirations*, Thompson had the opportunity to present *alphabet 26*, a typographical proposal that combines upper and lowercase letters.

BORN IN 1897 IN NEW YORK CITY, HOWARD ALLEN TRAFTON RECEIVED HIS FIRST ART INSTRUCTION FROM HIS FATHER. HE BEGAN COMMERCIAL ART WHEN HE WAS TWELVE, RECEIVING HIS FIRST COMMISSION FROM A HABERDASHER. HE ALSO SERVED IN THE AMERICAN EXPEDITIONARY FORCE IN WORLD WAR I.

HE BECAME A WELL-KNOWN NEW YORK LETTERER AND COMMERCIAL ARTIST, AND AN INSTRUCTOR AT THE ARTS STUDENTS LEAGUE IN 1935 AS WELL AS AT THE PRATT INSTITUTE.

TRAFTON WAS AN INFLUENTIAL TEACHER AND PRACTITIONER, AND HIS CLASSES WERE POPULAR, ATTRACTING UP TO 350 STUDENTS. MANY OF HIS STUDENTS CAME FROM THE ADVERTISING WORLD. AMONG THEM, WERE SAUL BASS, ARTHUR WEITHAS, JOHN GROTH, WILLIAM RONIN, BOB PLISKIN, AND GENE FEDERICO.

ALTHOUGH MANY OF HIS STUDENTS WERE INTERESTED IN COMMERCIAL ART, HE DID NOT BELIEVE IN GIVING WHAT WAS CONSIDERED A COMMERCIAL ART COURSE. "I DON'T TRY TO TEACH MY STUDENTS TO DO FINISHED WORK. THEY CAN LEARN ALL ABOUT PRINTING, HALF-TONE REPRODUCTION, AND THE REST OF IT IN ANY AGENCY. WHY MAKE A COURSE OUT OF IT AND CALL IT PROFOUND? I TRY TO TEACH THEM THE FUNDAMENTALS OF ART -COLOR, COMPOSITION, ARRANGEMENT- AND THESE ARE THE SAME WHETHER YOU'RE GOING TO MAKE AN EASEL PAINTING OR AN ADVERTISEMENT."

BEFORE HE CONCENTRATED ON TEACHING, HOWARD TRAFTON HAD WON MEDALS FROM THE NEW YORK ART DIRECTORS' CLUB FOR THREE CONSECUTIVE YEARS.

HIS CALLIGRAPHIC WORK, AS EXEMPLIFIED BY **TRAFTON SCRIPT** (1933), CUT BY THE BAUER TYPE FOUNDRY IN GERMANY, NOT ONLY SET THE PATTERN FOR A NUMBER OF COMPETITIVE SCRIPTS THAT FOLLOWED, BUT ALSO SET AN ALTERNATIVE TYPE OPTION FOR SOCIAL ANNOUNCEMENTS, WHERE THE **WEDDING TEXT**, A BLACK LETTER FACE, WAS THE STANDARD TYPEFACE.

THAT SAME YEAR, ROBERT SMITH DESIGNED **PARK AVENUE** AND MAX RICHARD KAUFMANN, **KAUFMANN SCRIPT**, BOTH FOR ATF. IN 1934, ROBERT HUNTER MIDDLETON DESIGNED **CORONET**, AND IN 1940, SOL HESS AND FRANK H. RILEY BOTH COMPLETED THEIR OWN VERSION, **STYLESCRIPT**, AND **GRAYDA**, RESPECTIVELY.

IN THE MID-1930S THERE WAS AN INTEREST IN THE LETTERING THAT ACCOMPANIED COMIC STRIPS -AN EXTREMELY CASUAL FORM OF LETTERING.

THIS TYPOGRAPHICAL TREND, WHICH VARIOUS TYPE FOUNDRIES WERE INTERESTED IN, STARTED WITH THE DESIGN OF **CARTOON**, DONE BY TRAFTON IN 1936. THIS, BY THE WAY, WAS ONE OF THE FEW FACES BY AMERICAN DESIGNERS THAT WAS NOT CUT AND CAST IN THE UNITED STATES. IT WAS HAND CUT AND CAST BY THE BAUER TYPE FOUNDRY IN GERMANY. ITS ACCEPTANCE WAS SO IMMEDIATE THAT THE FOUNDRY PRODUCED AN ADDITIONAL BOLD VERSION.

IN THE UNITED STATES, THE AMERICAN TYPE FOUNDERS COMPANY WHICH HAD COMMISSIONED MAX KAUFMANN TO DESIGN **KAUFMANN SCRIPT** IN 1936, ASKED HIM TO DESIGN A "CARTOON" TYPEFACE. THE RESULT, **BALLOON**, WAS ISSUED IN 1939. BOTH OF THESE TYPEFACES USE ONLY CAPS.

THAT SAME YEAR, THE ENGLISH LANSTON MONOTYPE CORPORATION ALSO PRODUCED THEIR OWN CARTOON TYPEFACE, **FLASH**, DESIGNED BY EDWIN W. SHAAR, WHICH INCLUDED A LOWERCASE ALPHABET.

IN 1950, PHOTO-LETTERING, INC., ALSO ISSUED **DOM CASUAL**, DESIGNED BY PETER DOMBREZIAN, WHICH WAS LATER CAST IN METAL BY ATF IN 1952.

TRAFTON WAS ALSO A MEMBER OF THE AMERICAN INSTITUTE OF GRAPHIC ARTS (AIGA).

HOWARD ALLEN TRAFTON DIED IN NEW YORK CITY IN 1964, AT THE AGE OF SIXTY-SEVEN.

Trafton Script
(1933)

A delicate script with letters not quite connected, this typeface has large, flourished capitals and small lowercase letters with long ascenders and descenders.

The Bauer type foundry in Germany cut it.

ABCDEFGHIJKLMNOPQR
STUVWXYZ& abcdefghijklmnopqrstuvwxyz
$1234567890

CARTOON (1936)

Drawn with a wide pen, *Cartoon* is an informal letter which preserves the freedom of hand lettering.

It resembles comic strip lettering, hence its name. *Cartoon* was cut by the Bauer type foundry in Germany which also cut his other typeface, *Trafton Script*.

The bold version doesn't have the same freshness of the regular weight.

ABCDEFGHIJKLMNOPQ
RSTUVWXYZ&
$1234567890!?

ABCDEFGHIJKLMNOPQR
STUVWXYZ&
$1234567890!?

Within the world of type design few women have dedicated their time to this task. One exception is Carol Twombly, born in Bedford, Massachusetts, in 1959, and the youngest of five children.

Initially interested in sculpture, she went to Rhode Island School of Design where she found that graphic design offered her a language in which the positive and negative relationships gave her the opportunity for an immediate expression.

Encouraged by Charles Bigelow, her type design professor and Kris Holmes, his partner, Carol Twombly got involved in the design of letters. Such class assignments as those intended to solve different contents by type, started to show her the true dimension of typography.

By this time, Bigelow invited Gerard Unger (b. 1942), a Dutch type designer who had started to design digital type, to teach at the school for one semester. This experience reinforced her interest in type design. While she studied, she worked freelance with the firm Bigelow & Holmes. With Kris Holmes she began to study calligraphy and to execute the precise outline letter drawings that such software as *Ikarus* requires.

In 1982, after an additional year of freelancing in a graphic design studio in Boston, Twombly moved to Palo Alto, California. There she attended, with other students from the Rhode Island School of Design, a master's program in digital typography that Charles Bigelow had created at Stanford University with the support of the mathematician and computer scientist Donald Knuth (b. 1938), creator of the *Metafont* digital

program (1979). It was then when Carol Twombly finally considered the possibility of a career in type design. Today, she thinks of herself as a graphic designer who specializes in type, "someone who comes up with new ways of making letters for different purposes."

She submitted her first typeface, *Miraræ*, designed soon after graduating from Stanford University, in the 1984 International Typeface Competition sponsored by Morisawa & Co., Ltd., of Japan, and won first prize. Soon afterwards, and at the company's request, she included a bold version.

By this time she also began to work as a part-time designer at Adobe Systems Inc., in Silicon Valley. This eventually turned into a full-time job, and by 1988, she was one of the two in-house type designers at Adobe.

She thinks that "ultimate uses of the type –text or display– should be determined first" and that "the underlying shapes should be based in well-proportioned, legible skeletons where details play an important part." She also thinks that manipulating forms is not enough to achieve excellence in the design of a type. For her, some experiences with metal type gives the designer certain notions of form and letter relations that otherwise are difficult to acquire. Twombly's approach, rather than that of a scholar, is that of a visual artist who relies on her trained eye and skilled hand. "If a type is well-received and widely used by the public then it is a success."

In 1990, she designed *Trajan* and *Charlemagne*, the first based on the Trajan column inscriptional capitals and the second on the capital letters

of the Carolingian period; her serious analysis of the letter form and the clear dominion of type design have made them popular among designers. In terms of time, each typeface has taken her about six months to a year to develop, the classical letters being harder to design due to the research they demand.

These designs were followed by *Lithos*, a freer sans serif typeface based on Greek inscriptional lettering. It became a success within a few weeks of being commercialized. In 1990, she designed *Adobe Caslon*, and after two year's work she finished *Myriad*, a lively sans serif upon which she worked with a group of designers that included Fred Brady, Robert Slimbach, and Sumner Stone.

Myriad was followed by *Viva* (1993), an open display type, where her calligraphic ability determines the handsome resemblance of the typeface. This was later followed by *Nueva* (1994), a typeface that was originally conceived as a lowercase for *Charlemagne*, and by *Chaparral* (1997), a slab-serif type that combines nineteenth-century designs with sixteenth-century book lettering.

In 1994, she received the Charles Peignot Award from the Association Typographique Internationale for her outstanding contribution to type design.

After being type design manager of Adobe Systems, Inc., for several years, Carol Twombly left Adobe, in order to develop her own work. As she has expressed it, she finds a close relation between lettering and carving. This gives her the opportunity to approach sculpture.

MIRARÆ (1984)

A text typeface, and her first design, was the winner in the 1984 International Typeface Competition sponsored by Morisawa & Company, Ltd., of Japan.

Used for photo-typesetting, it has a large x-height, an accented calligraphic rendering, and a slight inclination.

ABCDEFGHIJKLMNOPQRST
UVWXYZ&abcdefghijklmnop
qrstuvwxyz$1234567890!?

TRAJAN (1990)

Named after the Roman Emperor, Marcus Ulpius Trajanus, *Trajan* is based on the classical letterforms of the Roman inscription on the Trajan Column (112-113 A.D.).

In the process of translating the inscriptional letters into digital type, Carol Twombly found that the forms which appeared perfect when chiseled into stone were not suited to printing on paper.

To give the characters an even color and unified appearance when printed in various sizes and resolutions, she modified serif details, hairline thicknesses, and stem and bowl weights while retaining as much of the subtlety and character of the inscriptional forms as possible.

She also completed the alphabet by adding missing letters, numerals and punctuation marks.

ABCDEFGHIJKLMNOPQ
RSTUVWXYZ&
$1234567890!?

ABCDEFGHIJKLMNOPQ
RSTUVWXYZ&
$1234567890!?

CHARLEMAGNE (1990)

Inspired by capitals such as those found in the tenth-century Carolingian manuscript *The Benedictional of St. Aethelwold* (963-984), written by the scribe Godeman, who later became Abbot of Thorney, this display typeface has an accented calligraphic rendering.

The manuscript belongs to the well-known Winchester School, a name given to the style of illumination characteristic of manuscripts originating in southern England during the period from 950 to 1100.

Carol Twombly began the design of this typeface by making a series of sketches, which captured the exuberance of the manuscript's title lettering. She then scanned the drawings and reworked the letterforms until she completed a regular design.

The bold version was a careful modification on-screen of the regular weight.

ABCDEFGHIJKLMNOPQ
RSTUVWXYZ&
$1234567890!?

ABCDEFGHIJKLMNOPQ
RSTUVWXYZ&
$1234567890!?

CAROL TWOMBLY

245

LITHOS (1990)

This sans serif display type, with only uppercase letters, is based on Greek inscriptional lettering dated from 400 B.C.

"I played with the letters on the screen for quite a while through a few intermediate stages until I began to come up with a combination of clean forms and playful, idiosyncratic shapes that had an underlying connection to the Greek models (for example the Y). Of all the three initial weights I found that the extralight weight was the most difficult to design," comments Twombly.

The typeface includes five different weights.

ABCDEFGHIJKLMNOPQRS
TUVWXYZ&$1234567890!?

ABCDEFGHIJKLMNOPQRS
TUVWXYZ&$1234567890!?

ABCDEFGHIJKLMNOPQR
STUVWXYZ&
$1234567890!?

ABCDEFGHIJKLMNOP
QRSTUVWXYZ&
$1234567890!?

ADOBE CASLON
(1990)

A revival of the classical *Caslon Old Face* designed by William Caslon I in a period of about twenty years, *Adobe Caslon* is the result of a careful study of rare specimen sheets printed for the William Caslon type foundry in 1738 and 1786.

For an analytical study, photographic samples of the same letters were made from 9-, 10-, 11-, and 14-pt samples enlarged to the same x-height.

After a careful comparison, Carol Twombly found that the proportions of x-height to capital height and the length of the ascenders and descenders varied only slightly from size to size within this text range.

Following a series of accurate sketches of every letter at each size, she made drawings for a "master" design that incorporated common elements from the four original text sizes.

The careful treatment of both light and heavy strokes permits the font to maintain a clean appearance in either high- or low-resolution printers.

The typeface includes twenty-two variations, a complete set of swash letters, alternative fonts, ligatures and typographical ornaments.

ABCDEFGHIJKLMNOPQ
RSTUVWXYZ&abcdefghijkl
mnopqrstuvwxyz
$1234567890!?

*ABCDEFGHIJKLMNOPQRS
TUVWXYZ&abcdefghijklmnop
qrstuvwxyz$1234567890!?*

**ABCDEFGHIJKLMNOPQ
RSTUVWXYZ&abcdefghijkl
mnopqrstuvwxyz
$1234567890!?**

*ABCDEFGHIJKLMNOPQRS
TUVWXYZ&abcdefghijklmnop
qrstuvwxyz$1234567890!?*

MYRIAD (1992)

Co-designed with Robert Slimbach, *Myriad* is a beautiful and delicate sans serif typeface, which includes an extensive family varying from light to black, and from condensed to semi-extended with its italics.

One of Adobe's first multiple master typefaces, *Myriad* combines the power of *PostScript* language software technology and the most sophisticated electronic design tools.

The actual drawing, digitization, and design work was split between Slimbach and Twombly and was completed in two years.

Each designer was responsible for different "master designs" in the roman and italic fonts. They then exchanged work during final design stages to give the *Myriad* family a unified appearance.

Once it met the design team's standards, they carefully selected the fifteen "instances" that would become the "primary fonts" of all the *Myriad* family.

Final testing and production was done on the master designs before release.

ABCDEFGHIJKLMNOPQRSTUV
WXYZ&abcdefghijklmnopqrst
uvwxyz$1234567890!?

*ABCDEFGHIJKLMNOPQRSTUVW
XYZ&abcdefghijklmnopqrstuvw
xyz$1234567890!?*

**ABCDEFGHIJKLMNOPQRSTUV
WXYZ&abcdefghijklmnopqrst
uvwxyz$1234567890!?**

***ABCDEFGHIJKLMNOPQRSTUV
WXYZ&abcdefghijklmnopqrstu
vwxyz$1234567890!?***

VIVA (1993)

The first multiple master typeface to be designed especially for display use, *Viva* is an inline typeface that through its two "design axis" structure, allows variations of weight and width without losing the proportions of the original letterform –but with a twist.

The design began with the idea of a light *outline* transforming into a heavy *inline* in which the change in the typefaces' weight would change its style as well. The final version permitted a typeface that, as the weight is increased, only one side of the split-outline forms change, as if each letter casts a longer "shadow."

ABCDEFGHIJKLMNOPQR
STUVWXYZ&abcdefghij
klmnopqrstuvwxyz
$1234567890!?

ABCDEFGHIJKLMNOP
QRSTUVWXYZ&abcdef
ghijklmnopqrstuvwx
yz$1234567890!?

NUEVA (1994)

This design started as sketches dating back to 1988 as a possible lowercase design to *Charlemagne* (1990).

Several years later, Twombly resumed the design with drawings and digital experiments until *Nueva* came into its own with a contemporary kinetic lowercase and a set of capital forms to match.

The face constitutes an extensive multiple master family which ranges from light condensed to bold extended.

ABCDEFGHIJKLMNOPQRSTUVW
XYZ&abcdefghijklmnopqrstuv
wxyz$1234567890!?

ABCDEFGHIJKLMNOPQRSTUV
WXYZ&abcdefghijklmnopqrs
tuvwxyz$1234567890!?

CHAPARRAL (1997)

Being a hybrid slab serif typeface, *Chaparral* combines the legibility of the heavy-serifed faces popularized in the nineteenth century, with the grace of the sixteenth-century roman book lettering.

The original inspiration for *Chaparral* was a page of "humanist" style lettering from a sixteenth-century manuscript book by Marcantonio Flaminio.

As Twombly worked to digitize her sketches, she realized that the typeface was a good candidate for adapting it to be a friendly, readable slab serif style face.

It is a multiple master typeface, which allows variations in weight from light to bold while maintaining optimum legibility at all sizes from 7 to 72 points.

ABCDEFGHIJKLMNOPQRST
UVWXYZ&abcdefghijklmnopq
rstuvwxyz$1234567890!?

*ABCDEFGHIJKLMNOPQRSTU
VWXYZ&abcdefghijklmnopqrst
uvwxyz$1234567890!?*

**ABCDEFGHIJKLMNOPQRST
UVWXYZ&abcdefghijklmnop
qrstuvwxyz$1234567890!?**

***ABCDEFGHIJKLMNOPQRST
UVWXYZ&abcdefghijklmnopq
rstuvwxyz$1234567890!?***

Born in Providence, Rhode Island in 1860, Daniel Berkeley Updike was a printer and a leader in the revival of traditional printing typefaces in the United States. Through the Merrymount Press, he exerted great influence on the improvement of the graphic arts in the United States during the first third of the twentieth century.

Upon the death of his father in 1877 and after working as an assistant in the Providence Athenæum, Updike went to Boston to the publishing firm of Houghton, Mifflin & Company in 1880. There he worked between 1880 and 1893, both in its Boston office and in the Riverside Press in Cambridge, where he spent the last two years preparing copy for advertisements. This work made him well-known for his taste in typographical arrangements.

His first publication was *On the Dedication of American Churches* (1891), a book done for the Episcopal Church in collaboration with Harold Brown. The following year, Updike collaborated with Bertram Grosvenor Goodhue in designing and decorating the end papers of an edition of *The Book of Common Prayer* printed by Theodore Low De Vinne on his press in Boston.

As Harold Brown stood ready to finance the production of *The Altar Book of the American Church* for use in the Episcopal Church, Updike left Houghton, Mifflin & Company in 1893, and went to Boston as "typographic adviser." This was the beginning of the Merrymount Press, a name adopted in 1896. His original purpose was merely to design books since he did not derive much pleasure from the actual process of printing.

For *The Altar Book*, published in 1896, and the first important undertaking of the new press, which reflected the work of William Morris' Kelmscott Press, he had Goodhue design the decorated borders and a heavy Roman typeface called *Merrymount*. By the time the volume appeared, Updike had designed nineteen other books. To reduce costs, he reluctantly invested in type and ornaments, and thus became a printer. John Bianchi, formerly of the Riverside Press, was in charge of the composing room, and later became his partner in 1915.

Unlike other English private presses such as Kelmscott, Doves, and Ashendene, which established a style based on specially cut typefaces, Updike employed a number of historic types from the seventeenth, eighteenth, and nineteenth centuries. Besides three black letter typefaces useful in ecclesiastical work, most of the printing was done in historic roman and italic typefaces. He used *Caslon Old Face, Scotch Roman, Janson Antiqua, Bell, Poliphilus, Blado Italic, Lutetia*, and *Bodoni*, finding a richer inspiration in the Renaissance and eighteenth- century printing. He also acquired *Oxford*, a typeface cut by Archibald Binny in 1796.

In 1904, Herbert P. Horne designed for him *Montallegro*, a lighter Roman typeface modeled on an early Florentine face. It was used in Horne's translation of Ascanio Condivi's book, *The Life of Michelangelo Buonarroti*, and later on, in the eight volumes of *The Humanist's Library*, edited by Lewis Einstein, and published between 1906 and 1914. These series included title pages designed by William Addison Dwiggins, and Thomas Maitland Cleland, who often worked with Updike in other projects.

The restriction in the number of typefaces, compared to those employed by an average printing office of his time, is one more proof of the importance he paid to the typographical design on a page, and this restriction gained him the reputation as one of the most careful printers in America. These were sufficient reasons to be selected to print a *folio* edition of *The Book of Common Prayer* (1930), in its revision of 1928, which is considered by many as his masterpiece. Unlike *The Altar Book* of 1896, it is without decoration; here Updike relied solely on *Janson* type, carefully printed in black and red upon handmade paper.

His statement that "the modern printer's problem is to produce books mechanically well made, tasteful without pretension, beautiful without eccentricity or sacrifice of legibility" is best seen in the many books that he privately printed for the Club of the Odd Volumes, the Grolier Club, or for the Limited Editions Club.

As a printer, Updike was also concerned with illustration. In several of his works, he employed people like designer and illustrator Rudolph Ruzicka, with whom he worked for many years. Ruzicka designed the Merrymount Press annual keepsakes as well as some illustrations for the *Printing Types: Their History, Forms, and Use*. This scholarly text is a collection of the lectures he gave during the years 1911-1916 at Harvard University Business School on the history and technique of printing. It was published by Harvard University Press and printed at the Merrymount Press in 1922. He also wrote and printed *Some Aspects of Printing Old and New* (1941), and *Notes on the Merrymount Press & Its Work* (1934).

Updike was founder of the Boston Society of Printers in 1905, and its president between 1912 and 1914. He was honorary member of the American Institute of Graphic Arts, which awarded him a gold medal for his work. He received his Master of Arts degree from Brown University in 1910, and from Harvard University in 1929.

Daniel Berkeley Updike died in 1941 at his home in Boston, Massachusetts, at the age of eighty-one.

MERRYMOUNT
(1895)

This typeface was designed by Bertram Grosvenor Goodhue upon the request of Daniel Berkeley Updike for his recently established the Merrymount Press in Boston.

Based on Nicolas Jenson's type of 1470, it reflects the influence of William Morris' ideas.

Numerals are drawn in *Oldstyle*.

ABCDEFGHIJKLMNOPQRST UVWXYZ&abcdefghijklmnopq rstuvwxyz$1234567890?!

Born as Arthur Frederick Ward in Wells, Minnesota in 1894, he changed his name to Frederic Warde in 1926. Before he finished his service in the army (1917-1919), he met Beatrice Becker whom he later married in 1921.

He obtained a position with the MacMillan Company through May Lamberton Becker, Beatrice's mother, and a children's book critic for the New York Herald Tribune. Soon after, he was employed as the supervisor of Monotype composition by the Printing House of William Edwin Rudge, first in New York in 1919, and later at the new plant in Mount Vernon, just north of the city.

In 1920, during his early period with Rudge, Warde spent some time at the Lanston Monotype Company's school in Philadelphia. There he learned the finer points of machine operation in order to better supervise the strict requirements of Bruce Rogers, who had just begun to work with Rudge.

Through Rogers, he was introduced to William A. Kittredge, formerly of the Riverside Press, and now art director of Franklin Printing Company in Philadelphia. He was to have a lasting friendship and correspondence with him.

By 1921, Warde had achieved a good reputation as a man of great technical expertise and one who could be depended upon to produce type composition of the highest quality. His knowledge of paper, ink, and presswork together with his typographical taste lent a particular distinction to his work.

Although he was very reserved, he became friends with Rogers and began to socialize with Rogers' circle of friends. Beatrice obtained, through him and after graduating from Barnard College, the position as assistant to Henry Lewis Bullen, director of the American Type Founders Company's Typographic Library and Museum.

By 1922, Warde began to accept public engagements, both in New York and Philadelphia. Through Kittredge's influence, Warde applied for the position as director of printing at Princeton University Press, where he began to work in August. His reputation as a perfectionist became well known. His essay, Book Printing

in America as One of the Fine Arts, which appeared in the New York Times Book Review, brought him greater gains in his career. In 1924, three of the books he designed were selected by the American Institute of Graphic Arts "Fifty Books of the Year" exhibition, and four others were selected the following year.

In June 1924, he had his first exhibit, Survivals in the Fine Arts of Printing, at the Princeton University Museum. It was accompanied by a catalog, which he wrote, designed, and printed. He also corresponded with Stephenson, Blake & Company, England, for the cutting of a type he had designed, but which was never executed.

Late that year, he and Beatrice decided to resign from their jobs to travel to France, where they arrived in January 1925. There, Stanley Morison who had promised to get them work while he was in America, met them. One of these jobs involved the writing of an article on Bruce Rogers to be published in the Fleuron.

Meanwhile, Warde started to work for the Monotype Recorder whose first cover design, full of type ornaments, appeared in the second issue of 1925. The inclusion of a page of Ludovico Degli Arrighi's italic in Blodius Palladius's Coryciana (1524) as well as The Writing Book of Gerardus Mercator (1540) coincides with the beginning of Warde's search for a punch-cutter for his new italic type. This type was based upon Degli Arrighi's calligraphy as shown in the publication.

During most of 1925, Warde traveled several times to Paris in search of this punch-cutter whom he finally found in George Plumet of G. H. Plumet, as we may read from a letter to Bruce Rogers telling him about his typographical adventure. The R. Ribadeau-Dumas type founders did the casting, and Bruce Rogers used it in the printing of Robert Bridge's poem, the Tapestry, printed in the Fanfare Press in 1925.

Throughout 1925, 1926, and part of 1927, Warde traveled around Europe, looking for a fine printer in France, Germany, and Holland. His principal connection was with the Officina Bodoni

in Montagnola di Lugano, established by Hans (Giovanni) Mardersteig. It was there that Warde brought his Arrighi type as well as the second version of it, which he called Brevi or Vicenza. Their first printing was a facsimile edition of the Calligraphic Models of Ludovico Degli Arrighi, in which the introduction by Stanley Morison was set in the new cut italic.

Warde returned to the United States at the end of 1927. He had already begun publishing under the Pleiad imprint, and was looking for an American copublisher / distributor. By this time, Bruce Rogers had made arrangements with the English Monotype Corporation to have his Centaur typeface cut there. As there existed the need for an italic, he relied on Warde's type to accompany his roman font.

In 1928, Warde accompanied Rogers on his trip to England, where he supervised the cutting of a third version, this time done by Charles Malin. The union of Centaur and Arrighi was a complete success, although economically speaking, it was a disaster for Warde since very few matrices were sold during his lifetime. Warde's economical situation forced him to return to the States in 1929, where he and Crosby Gaige established the Watch Hill Press in Westchester County. They had just begun to work when the stock market crash brought everything to a close.

The last years of Warde's life were spent in short and different activities. He remained with the printing house of William Edwin Rudge until Rudge's death in 1932. Then, he had other associations before joining Oxford University Press in New York as production manager.

By 1939, his separation from Beatrice brought deeper problems to his private life. Frederic Warde died that year in New York City, at the age of forty-five.

Fortunately, for Warde's work, his Arrighi type finally ended in the Cary Collection at the Rochester Institute of Technology, thanks to Joseph Blumenthal's advice and the donation by Flora Hess, the widow of Sol Hess.

ARRIGHI (1925)

Based on the calligraphy of Italian calligrapher Ludovico Degli Arrighi, this typeface was first cut in 1925 by George Plumet in Paris, and later recut in a second version known as Vicenza, the same year. A third version was cut by Monotype in 1929. Since then, it has always accompanied Bruce Rogers's Centaur, designed in 1914.

ABCDEFGHIJKLMNOPQRST
UVWXYZ&abcdefghijklmnopqrstuv
wxyz$1234567890!?

THE MONOTYPE RECORDER
(1926)

A cover designed for the publication of the English Lanston Monotype Corporation, *The Monotype Recorder*.

Warde had started this type of work in 1925, when he designed the second issue of *The Monotype Recorder*.

CALENDAR (1927)

Another one of the typographic designs Warde did for the English Lanston Monotype.

ARRIGHI TYPE (1925)

Part of a sheet of drawings in the Newberry Library, Chicago, for the *Arrighi Italic*.

The method used by Frederic Warde for the preparation of these drawings was to work over reversed photographic enlargements of the original font of *Arrighi* type, cut by hand under Warde's supervision by George Plumet in Paris.

TYPE ORNAMENT (1928)

Chapter ornament for the publication *Printers Ornaments*, designed for the English Lanston Monotype.

PRINTERS ORNAMENTS (1928)

A cover design for the publication *Printers Ornaments*, designed for the English Lanston Monotype, containing "a series of typographic ornaments applied to the composition of decorative borders, panels and patterns."

A BOOK OF "MONOTYPE" ORNAMENTS (1928)

While Frederic Warde worked for the English Monotype in London, he designed a series of publications directed to printers in which he masterfully exemplified the management of typographic ornaments.

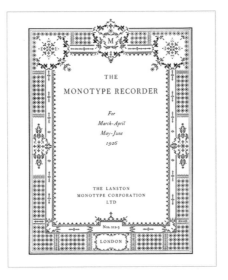

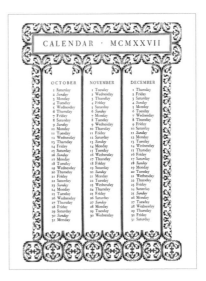

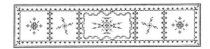

Born in Kingsborough, New York in 1800, Darius Wells was the son of a veteran of the Revolutionary War.

After his father died in 1811, Wells was an apprentice in the printing shop of William Childs in Johnstown, New York, publisher of the *Montgomery Republican*.

In 1822, he moved to Amsterdam, New York, where he founded the town's first newspaper, the *Mohawk Herald* in a partnership with Asa Childs. Four years later, Wells and Childs established a small printing shop in New York City.

It was during these years that Wells became interested in making wood type. His first experiments were done at home during a period of convalescence from a serious illness. These trials were quite important since Wells worked on the end grain of the wood like the wood engravers, rather than on the side grain as was customary for printers who carved large letters for their own use. Based on the fact that there is a font of wood type entirely carved by hand and stamped with "D. Wells, N.Y.," on the bottom, it is probable that he carved wood type by hand for the market.

His new partnership with David Bruce, Jr., whose purpose was to find a method for the mass production of large wood type, did not endure. However, it was during this time that Wells invented the lateral router, a machine that enabled him to make the mass production of letters practical.

In 1827, Wells was finally producing wood letters in quantity. In March of 1828, he issued his first catalog of wood type specimens from the back room of George Long's *Book Store*, listing himself in the New York directory as "D. Wells, letter-cutter."

The catalog contained seven different styles and twenty-one sizes. No doubt, this event marked the beginning of the American wood type industry.

By 1831, his name appeared as "type-cutter," and by 1835, there was a well-organized company under the name of D. Wells & Company in association with Thomas Vermilyea, V. Riggs, and others, as partners in the enterprise.

In 1839, Wells made Ebenezer Russell Webb, who had been his employee for several years, a full partner. The company, known as Wells & Webb, established a plant in Paterson, New Jersey. While Webb supervised the Paterson mill, Wells operated the New York City offices. The plant in Paterson produced wood type, reglets, printer's furniture, and engravers wood, while the business operations were conducted from the New York offices.

It is important to note here that before Webb began working with Wells, he had worked with William Leavenworth (1799-1860), as the supervisor of his wooden type factory. Leavenworth, besides being credited with changing letterforms from a regular face to *Condensed*, *Extra Condensed*, and *Double Extra Condensed*, had also made quite a significant contribution to the mechanical end of the trade.

In 1834, Leavenworth introduced the pantograph, which, combined with the router, formed the basic machinery for making all end-cut wood types throughout the century.

When the business was closed down in 1839 and Webb became a partner of Wells, the new Wells & Webb firm took over the inventory including the combined router-pantograph machinery. There is no doubt that before this time, Wells had manufactured wood type in a more cumbersome process only using the router.

In the preface of the 1840 catalog, he made an important remark: "Having in the year 1827, originally established the business of Wood Letter Cutting, it

is with no small satisfaction that he [Wells] views the great improvement in Job Printing that has in consequence taken place. For want of large type, no larger posting bills than of medium size were then printed, and these exhibiting but a lean variety; while the metal type cost so much as to limit their use to a few establishments. The manufacture of Wood Type formed a new era of job printing; and the use of them, although at first opposed by a strong prejudice, has now become general. In regard to their cheapness and durability, no argument is now necessary."

In 1842, Wells & Webb moved their establishment to another address, where they opened the first general printer's warehouse in America, and offered all the implements a printer could need. During these years, they commissioned David Bruce's New York Type Foundry and the Connor Type Foundry to cast metal types exclusively for their use. It is possible that these type designs were based on original wood types of their own or on styles popular at the time.

In that same year, Webb went over to the New York office, and Wells moved to Paterson. As the firm expanded its line of products, Wells & Webb moved the Paterson quarters down the river to a building they expanded several times. Although in 1854, Wells decided to sell his part to Webb, he continued managing the Paterson plant until 1854 when he finally withdrew from the wood type business.

In 1861, Abraham Lincoln appointed Darius Wells as postmaster of Paterson, a position he held until 1874.

His health suddenly declined that year, and in 1875 he died in Paterson, New Jersey, at the age of seventy-five.

ROMAN (1828)

First shown by Darius Wells in his 1828 catalog, it is one of the oldest of the large display letters used in the United States.

This design gradually fell into disuse after 1850. It is interesting to note the imbalance form of capital letters G and K, and the narrowness of the letter U.

Other curiosities include the angular serifs on capital letters L, T and Z, and the way lowercase letter g is drawn.

**ABCDEFGHIJKLMNO
PQRSTUVWXYZ&ab
cdefghijklmnopqrst
uvwxyz œæÆ!.,;:**

DARIUS WELLS'
WOOD TYPE TECHNIQUE (1828)

The use of wood for printing, and as a material for making type had been known for hundreds of years before the nineteenth century.

In America, with the expansion of commercial printing in the first decades of the nineteenth century, it was almost inevitable that someone would perfect the process for producing the large letters so in demand for broadsides.

In 1828, Wells issued his first wood type specimen, marking the beginning of the American wood type industry.

Once wood slabs are cut, they are stacked carefully so that air may circulate freely around all surfaces. In this manner, wood is cured prior to surfacing and cutting it into type.

Wood surfaces are then polished by hand with oil and pumice, and run through a gauge to ensure a perfect type-high block prior to engraving.

The operator incises the letter on the polished wood through the pantograph and routing machinery. While the needle follows the outlines of the pattern, the router is cutting the design according to a predetermined size.

Finally, skilled engravers hand-finish the wood type, correcting any type irregularities.

WOOD TYPE SPECIMEN (1840)

A later wood type specimen cover printed by Wells & Webb, New York.

ROUTING MACHINE (1857)

An illustration of the routing machine E. R. Webb & Company used around 1857.

It represents a machine better than the original router invented by Darius Wells, in that this router is no longer stationary.

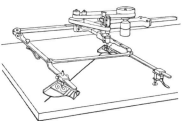

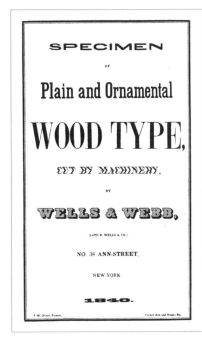

ANTIQUE X CONDENSED (1840)

Wells & Webb first showed this typeface design in their 1840 type specimen. Figures are missing.

This particular cutting is not identified by imprint, but it is believed to be more representative of the style as cut during the late nineteenth century.

ABCDEFGHIJKLMNOPQRSTUVWXYZ
&abcdefghijklmnopqrstuvwxyz

GOTHIC EXTENDED (1840)

Wells & Webb first showed this heavy extended sans serif typeface in their 1840 type specimen.

It is interesting to note that letters were always adjusted to the limits of a rectangular body as exemplified by letter **Q**. This also made typesetting easier.

ABCDEFGHI
JKLMNOPQ
RSTUVWXY
Z&1234567
890$!

GRECIAN CONDENSED (1846)

This slab serif with heavier verticals, first shown by Wells & Webb in the L. Johnson specimens for 1846, is characterized by a 45-degree cutting of curves in the intersection of vertical and horizontal strokes.

Lowercase and figures are missing.

ABCDEFGHIJKLMNOPQRS
TUVWXYZ&

GOTHIC TUSCAN CONDENSED (1849)

Wells & Webb first showed this type specimen, a mixture of serif and sans serif with curious bud terminals, in their 1849 type specimen.

First specimens included a *Modulated Outline* as well as a solid typeface.

Type founders cast this design in several sizes during the 1850s. It is believed that this type design originated as a wood type and with the Wells Company.

ABCDEFGHIJKLMN
OPQRSTUVWXYZ
&1234567890$

GOTHIC CONDENSED OUTLINE (1849)

Wells & Webb first showed this contour sans serif typeface in their 1849 catalog.

The first showing did not include a lowercase alphabet. However, later in the nineteenth century a lowercase for this design was fairly common.

Type founders issued this design under the name of *Comstock*.

ABCDEFGHIJKLMN
OPQRSTUVWXYZ
$1234567890&!

ANTIQUE TUSCAN (1849)

Wells & Webb first showed this typeface in their 1849 type specimen. This design did not include lowercase letters although they were later designed and issued in their 1854 catalog.

This design was important in American typographic styling during the nineteenth century, and especially popular with type founders from 1860 to the end of the century.

It is almost certain that this design also originated as a wood type and with the Wells Company.

ABCDEFGHIJ
KLMNOPQRS
TUVWXYZ&!

TUSCAN OUTLINE (1849)

Wells & Webb first showed this typeface in their 1849 type specimen. Figures are missing, and there was no lowercase designed for it.

This design originated in Europe and was very popular in England during the 1840s.

ABCDEFGHIJKL
MNOPQRSTUV
WXYZ&!

ANTIQUE LIGHT FACE EXTENDED (1854)

Wells & Webb first showed this extended slab serif typeface in their 1854 type specimens.

Lowercase and figures are missing.

ABCDEFG
HIJKLMN
OPQRSTU
VWXYZ&

GOTHIC TUSCAN ITALIAN (1854)

Wells & Webb first showed this type specimen in their 1854 catalog.

It was later stereotyped and mounted on wood.

Today it may be easily found in Adobe's digital version as *Cottonwood*.

ABCDEFGHIJKLM
NOPQRSTUVWXY
Z&$1234567890?

DORIC ORNAMENTED
(1854)

This ornamented wood type specimen, which combines form and character in a very particular way, has been quite popular on circus posters.

It has also been printed in two colors, enhancing its decorative characteristics.

It is interesting to mention that Mac McGrew, in his book *American Metal Typefaces of the Twentieth Century* (1996), cites this typeface as being originally a metal typeface designed at David Bruce's type foundry, under the name of *Ornamented No. 847*, around 1849.

It was also known under other names such as *Romantiques No. 2*, *Ornate No. 4*, or *Carnival*.

Today it may be in found in Adobe's digital version as *Zebrawood*.

ABCDEFGHIJKL
MNOPQRSTUVW
XYZ&
$1234567890!?

ABCDEFGHIJKL
MNOPQRSTUVW
XYZ&
$1234567890!?

PAINTER'S ROMAN
(1870)

Both William Hamilton Page and Darius Wells cut this particular display type with heavy concave main strokes, and contrasting hairlines. Although there is a relatively formal unity there are various styles mixed within the same font.

It came onto the market during the 1870s.

Today it may be in found in Adobe's digital version as *Juniper*.

ABCDEFGHIJKLM
NOPQRSTUVWXYZ
&$1234567890!?

ROBERT WIEBKING

Born in Schwelem, Germany in 1870, Robert Wiebking, a well-known matrix engraver for several American and English foundries and for the Ludlow Typograph Co., was a type designer as well. He came to America when he was just eleven years old.

He traveled with his father, Herman Wiebking, a practicing engraver of matrices who brought a matrix-engraving machine from Germany with him, and settled in Chicago. When Herman Wiebking died in his late eighties, it was Robert who developed his father's invention.

Whether by inclination or by persuasion, at fourteen, Wiebking was apprentice to the engraver C. H. Hanson, with whom he spent eight years before he considered himself qualified to start his own business. Two years later, he was ready to accept commissions for engraving punches and matrices. He also found opportunities to design type, many of them designed for the Barnhart Brothers & Spindler type foundry in Chicago.

In 1899, he did one of his first type designs for this company. Under the name of *Engravers Roman*, it was advertised as the "latest design" –"the only genuine" one. By this time, Wiebking must have been organized as a typographical firm, for in 1902, according to Robert Hunter Middleton, Wiebking cut *Tiffany Script*, the "first face engraved by Wiebking (and Hardinge) on their engraving machine brought from Germany," and which was part of a series of refined popular nineteenth-century scripts.

In 1912, he designed *Craftsman*, a roman bold typeface later known as *Artcraft*, and featured in the first ad for his short-lived Advance Type Foundry. Founded in Chicago that year, it was operated by Wiebking, Hardinge & Company.

It is interesting to note that in 1924, the second assignment of Robert Hunter Middleton (after *Eusebius*) was the adaptation of *Artcraft Italic* to the 17-degree slant of the Ludlow italic

matrices. The Ludlow Company later added a series of swash letters to the font.

While Wiebking directed the Advance Type Foundry, he also designed *Modern Text* (1913), and *Caslon Catalog* (1913), advertised as *Caslon Antique*. In 1917, he designed *Advertisers Gothic*, a sans serif typeface for the Western Type Foundry, which later absorbed the Advance Type Foundry, and was in turn, absorbed by Barnhart Brothers & Spindler in 1919.

More interesting though is his association with Frederic W. Goudy, for whom he engraved many of his first type designs. This is the case of *Pabst Oldstyle* (1902), cut for the Pabst Brewing Co., Chicago, and the first business contact with this designer; *Village* (1903) for the Village Press; *Norman* (1910), cut for private use; *Kennerley Old Style* and *Forum Title*, both cut in 1911, and used in the printing of H. G. Wells's *The Door in the Wall*. These two typefaces, by the way, established Goudy's type reputation in England. In 1918, he cut *Goudy Modern*, the last of of Goudy's typefaces for the Village Letter Foundery.

In 1914, Wiebking also engraved the matrices for Bruce Rogers's famous *Centaur*, the punches for Goudy's *Klaxon*, and in 1915, *Kennerley Oldstyle Italic*. In his own words, "no client was more exacting in his stipulations for perfection than Rogers." Later on, between 1918 and 1921, he cut other punches for Goudy: *Hadriano Title*, *Collier Old Style*, *Nabisco*, *Goudy Open* and *Italic*, and *Goudy Newstyle*. Wiebking's type production method undoubtedly greatly influenced Goudy, for he started using it himself in 1923.

Wiebking worked for a time with Barnhart Brothers & Spindler in Chicago as well as for the Laclede Type Foundry in St. Louis before he began to work with the Ludlow Typograph Company, which he did for the rest of his life. For Laclede, he designed *Laclede Oldstyle* in 1922; later recut as *Munder Venezian*, in honor

of Norman T. A. Munder, Baltimore's "dean of printers." This typeface was shown in 1925 as the highlight of the catalog printed by the BB&S foundry, which acquired the Laclede Type Foundry shortly after.

When Robert Hunter Middleton entered the Ludlow Typograph Company in 1923 as a type designer and later as director of its type design department, he found Wiebking already in his fifties. He was not only a great collaborator but also a mentor who guided him in the difficult task of creating a type library for Ludlow. Wiebking is also credited with developing a matrix-making machine for this company, which was very similar to that designed by Linn Boyd Benton in 1885.

In 1925, he did the cutting of *Marlborough*, perhaps one of his last cuttings, and his last type by Goudy. Two years before, Goudy had acquired his own engraving machine, for Wiebking was too old and sick to continue working, and he himself too old to look for another punch-cutter who could satisfy his demands for punch-cutting.

Among Wiebking type designs, we may find *Steelplate Gothic* (1907), much based on Goudy's *Copperplate Gothic*, and *Steelplate Shaded* (1918); *Artcraft* (1912), done for his own Advance Type Foundry; *Caslon Clearface* and *Italic* (1913); *Engravers Litho Bold* (1914); *Engravers Litho Bold Condensed* (1914), and *Advertisers Gothic*'s family (*Gothic Condensed* and *Outline*, 1917), all six designed for the Western Type Foundry; *Invitation Text* (1914), for BB&S; *Bodoni Light* (1923), the first Ludlow's offering of this family; and *True-Cut Bodoni*, and *Italic* (1925), designed from the original Bodoni works found in the Chicago Newberry Library. This typeface was later redesigned by Robert H. Middleton in 1936, and commercialized as *Bodoni Modern*.

Robert Wiebking died in Chicago, Illinois, in 1927, at the age of fifty-seven.

ARTCRAFT

(1912)

This roman typeface was featured under the name of *Craftsman*, in the first ad presented by Robert Wiebking's short-lived Advance Type Foundry in Chicago.

It may still be found in photo-lettering catalogs.

ABCDEFGHIJKLMNOPQRST UVWXYZ&abcdefghijklmnopq rstuvwxyz1234567890?

CASLON CLEARFACE

(1913)

Several attempts have been made to regularize *Caslon*, and to improve its so-called faults, but in the process, much of the character of the face has been lost.

In 1913, Robert Wiebking created *Clearface Caslon* with its *Italic* for the Western Type Foundry in Chicago.

The face, by the way, is lighter than the original *Caslon Old Face*, and has a larger x-height.

ABCDEFGHIJKLMNOPQR
STUVWXYZ&abcdefghijkl
mnopqrstuvwxyz
$1234567890?!

ADVERTISERS GOTHIC (1917)

This sans serif which was quite a popular novel gothic in its time, and which may still be found in photo-lettering catalogs, was designed for Western Type Foundry, Chicago in 1917, later taken over by Barnhart Brothers & Spindler in 1919.

It has practically no descenders, and caps occupy almost the entire body size. Certain distinctive characteristics are the stencil treatment of letters A, B, E, F, H, P, R, and W, and the round diagonals in letters K, M, N, V, W, X, Y, and Z.

A curious application may be found in the **MENNEN** logotype. The ampersand may have also been the basis of the (ESSO) logotype (1923).

AABCDEFGHIJKLMNOPQ
RS/TUVWXYZ&abcdef
hijklmnopqrstuvwxyz
$1234567890?!

MUNDER VENEZIAN (1922)

This sensitive Oldstyle typeface was designed for the Laclede Type Foundry in St. Louis, and first shown as *Laclede Oldstyle*. When the type foundry was acquired by Barnhart Brothers & Spindler, it was recut as *Munder Venezian* in honor of Norman T. A. Munder, Baltimore's "dean of printers."

Since Wiebking had been engraver for Frederic W. Goudy and Bruce Rogers, it is inevitable that their designs influenced him.

Nevertheless, this is his most elegant type design. In 1925-27, Wiebking added *Munder Italic*, *Munder Bold* and *Munder Bold Italic*.

ABCDEFGHIJKLMNOP
QRSTUVWXYZ&abcde
fghijklmnopqrstuvwxyz
$1234567890

ADOBE SYSTEMS INC.

Adobe Systems, Inc. was founded through the collaboration of two American engineers, John Warnock and Charles Geschke, in Mountain View, California, in 1982.

Before founding Adobe, John Warnock worked as a principal scientist at Xerox Palo Alto Research Center, and held positions at Evans & Sutherland Computer Science Corporation, the University of Utah, and IBM. He holds a bachelor's degree in mathematics and philosophy; a master's degree in mathematics; and a doctorate in electrical engineering (computer science), all from the University of Utah.

Charles Geschke was responsible for forming the Imaging Sciences Laboratory at Xerox Palo Alto Research Center (PARC) in 1980, where he directed research activities in the fields of computer science, graphics, image processing, and optics. He was also a principal scientist and researcher at Xerox PARC's Computer Science Laboratory.

In 1983, Geschke and Warnock developed *PostScript* at the Adobe Corporation. *PostScript* is a computer page description language that enables type and graphic images to be combined into one document.

In 1984, the *PostScript Language Manual* was distributed privately, and in January 1985, it was introduced publicly through the Apple LaserWriter. Since then, it has established itself as the greatest revolution in the desktop publishing world, or in publications assisted by the computer.

Based on one group of codes of the same type, *PostScript* allows not only the production of different sizes within a type design, but also to send those codes directly into the photocomposer, generate its own codes of characters, treat the images previously analyzed by a scanner, and translate the information into a binary language.

The freedom given to the creator-user is even greater since the designer may conceive and write his own description of a page layout, and obtain all the graphic and typographic effects he desires.

PostScript is the most common digital font format for electronic publishing on Macintosh, IBM, and NeXt computers. It encodes type designs as outlines made up of Bézier curves and is device-independent. It will work on any device possessing a *PostScript* interpreter,

from the 72-dpi resolution of a standard Mac screen to the 1200-lpi and more of a photographic image setter.

All the major type suppliers now produce type in this format; it no longer has to be output on their own machines, and can be combined with type from other manufacturers.

Since 1984, when Sumner Stone was director of the type design department, Adobe has had a staff of type designers and technicians who are not only considered to be among the most creative typographers of today, but have specialized skills in design and the use of tools needed to develop digital type.

Under Stone's guidance, Adobe's type designers developed an ambitious program for digitizing classical typefaces. As part of this program, Robert Slimbach designed one of the best revivals of *Garamond* in 1987.

By 1989, Adobe, Inc. was able to offer a type library of more than 200 fonts, which has grown to over 2,500 *PostScript* fonts, many of which have been created at Adobe or exclusively for Adobe. These fonts are called "Adobe Originals" and comprise both new designs and revivals of classical typefaces, setting new standards for typographical excellence.

After Stone left the company, Fred Brady became manager of new typographical development with Carol Twombly, who joined the group in 1988, and with Robert Slimbach, both Adobe's senior type designers. In time, Twombly came to manage *Adobe Originals* typeface projects assisted by a growing number of international consulting type designers.

In 1991, Adobe developed multiple master technology as a complement to *PostScript*. Two years later, Carol Twombly designed *Viva*, the first typeface to be structured using this technology.

In 1994, Aldus Corporation merged with Adobe Systems, Inc., strengthening research and product design. Having two competing programs on the market, the new company kept *Adobe Illustrator* and returned *Aldus FreeHand* to Aldus Corporation, its creators.

Besides type design, Adobe has developed a series of applications to be used by graphic designers, layout men, architects and illustrators, which help solve drafting problems and enhance creativity. Such is the case of *Adobe PageMaker* (1985), *Adobe FrameMaker* (1986), *Adobe Illustrator*

(1987), *Adobe Photoshop* (1990), *Adobe Premiere* (1991), *Adobe Acrobat/Portable Document Format* (1993), *Adobe After Effects* (1995) as well as improvements in *Adobe Acrobat* (1996), and *Adobe PostScript* (1997), which by this time was in its third generation.

Multiple master technology (1991), which works on the basis of variable typeface attributes, such as weight, width, style, and optical size, were incorporated into a growing collection of new typefaces. This technology enables the creation of user-specified fonts in any weight, width, or optical size meeting designer's needs without adversely affecting the letter proportions, unlike the results of mechanically enlarging, reducing, expanding, condensing or emboldening a typeface.

The *Adobe Type Manager Deluxe* program (1996) allows the user to organize his or her fonts into groups known as *sets*, providing the management of a large type library, as it is the case of this publication. When a user creates a set, he or she is not actually moving font files; instead, he or she is grouping representations of these files (similar to a shortcut) into a container that works best for him or her. This means, that a single font can appear in several sets without duplicating it inside the font library structure. Moreover, it improves the performance of Windows and Macintosh applications by activating or deactivating predefined sets, as opposed to standalone fonts that the user doesn't need at that moment, without removing font files from the hard drive.

In 1997, Adobe and Microsoft decided to merge *Type 1* and *True Type* fonts so both standards could be supported on both, Windows and Macintosh platforms.

In 1998, Adobe created *Adobe InDesign* to challenge *QuarkXpress*, a program for composition and page make-up, created by Quark, Inc., in 1981.

In 2001, Adobe Systems, Inc., ceased creating multiple master typefaces, and one year later, developed in collaboration with Microsoft *Open Type*, which provided a richer linguistic support and a more advanced typographic control.

Today, Adobe Systems, Inc. continues its search for new tools for the graphic design industry.

In 1892, a close study of the economic situation was held by the American type foundries. Although it was clear that the demand for type was greater than ever before, there were too many foundries –in 1885 there were thirty-four foundries in the States– leading to hard competition and profit margins practically disappearing.

By organizing a consortium, and reducing and controlling the number of establishments where type was cast, the operating costs could be reduced, and the stability of the industry restored.

Although many printers were apprehensive about this decision, and others chose to remain independent, the idea was good since more radical changes were to come with the invention of mechanical typecasting.

Ottmar Mergenthaler had created the **Linotype** in 1886, and Tolbert Lanston the **Monotype** in 1887, and newspaper production had moved towards the use of automatic typecasting. The Linotype hot metal line-casting machine was first installed in the *New York Tribune* in 1886, and by the beginning of the twentieth century, Monotype, Compositype, Universal, Thompson, and other firms were producing devices that enabled printers to produce their own display typefaces.

The new enterprise –American Type Founders– founded in 1892, and located in Elizabeth, New Jersey, absorbed other independent type foundries, such as: Boston Type Foundry; Barnhart Brothers & Spindler; Inland Type Foundry; Marder, Luse & Co.; James Connor & Sons; Cincinnati Type Foundry; AD Farmer & Son Type Foundry; Type Founders; Damon Type Foundry; Central Type Foundry; Dickinson Type Foundry; Bruce's New York Type Foundry; Keystone Type Foundry; Pacific States Type Foundry; Standard Type Foundry; Illinois Type Foundry; Damon & Peets; Great Western Type Foundry; Benton, Waldo & Co., Type Foundry; H. C. Hansen Type Foundry; and MacKellar, Smiths & Jordan, the latter being perhaps the most important type foundry in the 1860s to the 1880s. Thus, a continuous link from Binny and Ronaldson Type Foundry, down to the present organization was finally consolidated by twenty-three type foundries.

According to Henry Lewis Bullen, joint manager of the New York branch, in his *Discursions of a Retired Printer* (1906), "On starting business in 1891, it [ATF] had matrices for about two thousand series of type. Discarding duplications, it had matrices for about seven hundred and fifty series of distinctive typefaces.

"In 1900, nine years after starting, it issued a complete general specimen book, containing the salable residuum of its type faces –525 series of job and thirty-seven of body type. Not long after, it had to face the lining system proportion.

"In 1903, it issued a *quarto* (292 pages) preliminary specimen book of lining type. It now, in 1906 issues its *American Line Type Book*, and it is a safe assumption that its contents represents every series it finds salable enough to go to the expense of changing to the line system."

Thirteen of the weakest firms soon closed down, and the federation that remained lacked cohesion and a sense of direction until the appointment of Robert Wickham Nelson as general manager in 1894, and as president in 1901.

Nelson soon realized that talented men, who were underemployed on account of the group's policy of keeping the foundries separated, ran the various constituent foundries. This was the case of Joseph W. Phinney, who had been with the Dickinson Type Foundry in Boston, and who was a man of considerable perception. In 1896, he had issued the first type sent to him from Chicago by a young promising designer named Frederic W. Goudy. Two other people were Linn Boyd Benton and his son Morris Fuller Benton.

Benton Senior not only had his own type foundry –Benton, Waldo & Co.– in Milwaukee, but also had invented the automatic punch-cutting machine, so helpful to the composing machines for engraving matrices. He became ATF's chief technical advisor, responsible for setting up the first type design department to function with a type foundry. Benton Junior joined his father when his father's type foundry was absorbed by ATF in 1902, becoming one of the most prolific designers of all time, with over 260 typefaces to his credit.

Nelson was also able to foresee that if it was true that type from then on would be set by machine, display matter needed foundry type, and, with the growth of advertising and the appearance of the graphic designer, there would be an increasing need for new typefaces. He was a type man, even when ATF diversified into printing machinery. He encouraged the development of the type family, in which a design could be produced in normal, medium, bold, expanded or condensed forms without losing its character. This gave visual attractiveness and unity to a page through the use of different typographical hierarchies.

In spite of his colleagues, Nelson also backed ATF's first great success, the cutting of the *Cheltenham* family, designed by Bertram Grosvenor Goodhue in 1904, in association with the Mergenthaler Linotype Company.

In 1904 and 1905, William Bradley designed an advertising campaign for ATF that involved the illustration of twelve issues of the in-house publication, the *American Chap-Book*. In these publications, Bradley continued to express his ideas about the merger of art and business.

In 1923, ATF issued its most exotic type catalog, the *Type Specimen Book and Catalogue*, a book of 1,148 pages, many of them printed in two colors. The project, which was nationally acclaimed, was directed by Henry Lewis Bullen, who was in charge of the Typographic Library and Museum. He did this in collaboration with Morris Fuller Benton, who was in charge of the type design department, and Wadsworth A. Parker, who was in charge of the type specimen department.

With the death of Robert W. Nelson in 1926, the company's capital diminished considerably, and eventually went in bankruptcy.

In 1936, under the presidency of Thomas Roy Jones the company had a new revival, and two years later, it entered the field of offset lithography with the purchasing of the Webendorfer-Wills Company.

In 1945, the last case-bound type specimen book was issued by ATF.

During the 1960s, ATF became a subsidiary of Whitin Machine Works, but, in 1966, White Consolidated Industries, the descendant of White Machine Company, acquired both Whitin and ATF companies. It also made some successful steps toward photographic typesetting with ATF's Hadego machine.

In 1970, ATF bought the Lanston Monotype Manufacturing Company, and more recently, as a result of further negotiations, the company became known as Kingsley ATF. That same year, a large number of ATF drawings, patterns and matrices were donated to the Smithsonian Institution in Washington, DC.

In addition to type design, the firm now manufactures software packages for use within Macintosh computers including ATF's *Type Designer*. This program allows the production of *PostScript, True Type*, NeXt and IBM PC-compatible fonts, and an optical scaling program, the first of its kind, which compensates the shortcomings of departing from a single original drawing for each typeface design.

Founded in late 1969, through a joint effort between Herb Lubalin, Edward Rondthaler, and Aaron Burns, the International Typeface Corporation (ITC) soon became one of the most important type suppliers in the United States.

The prime mover in developing the ITC concept was Aaron Burns, ITC's Chairman. In 1969, he and Herb Lubalin formed the partnership Lubalin, Burns & Co., Inc. Shortly afterward, he approached Edward Rondthaler and Photo-Lettering Inc. of New York City about his idea for the creation of an international typeface design and development company. Thus, ITC was born: a jointly-owned company of Lubalin, Burns & Co., Inc. and Photo-Lettering, Inc.

The International Typeface Corporation (ITC) was established just at the time new technologies were beginning to affect the design of typefaces, typesetting methods, and what typographic designers could do and how they worked.

ITC was responsible for a far-reaching typeface development program very similar to the one carried out earlier in the century by the English Monotype Corporation. Thirty-four fully developed type families and about sixty additional display typefaces were developed and licensed during ITC's first decade.

Typefaces were developed and introduced as full families, most with four roman weights, plus matching italics. Some included condensed versions, and alternate characters. Typefaces also featured a large lowercase x-height, refined character strokes to ensure even color, controlled intercharacter spacing to reduce unnecessary and disturbing visual gaps in typesetting, and controlled counter spaces to permit the reduction and enlargements of characters while retaining design character and legibility.

In 1973, with Herb Lubalin as design director, ITC began to publish a journal, the *U&lc* (*Upper & lowercase*) periodical, which started to publicize and display his designs, many of them done in collaboration with Tom Carnase, Tony DiSpigna, and Alan Peckolick (among others).

In Lubalin's own words, and after more than three decades of designing for clients, he became his own client. The new and dynamic style he gave to this tabloid-size newsprint publication, as well as the popularity of ITC typefaces, such as *ITC Avant Garde Gothic* and *ITC Souvenir* (which, by the way, were the two first typefaces to be released) had a major impact on typographic design in the 1970s.

Through its initiative, many standard typefaces, such as *Garamond, Caslon, Baskerville, Bookman, Cheltenham,* and *Century Roman* that were originally designed for handsetting and linecasting, were reinterpreted and unitized for the newer photo-typesetting and digital systems.

In the late 1970s and early 1980s, ITC became a training ground for new typeface designers, many of whom became important designers later on.

The company continued its type program with a long list of typefaces during the 1980s. ITC designers, who were among the best of contemporary type design, included names such as Edward Benguiat, Herb Lubalin, Hermann Zapf, Aldo Novarese, Jovica Veljovic, Tony DiSpigna, Matthew Carter, Tom Carnase, Tony Stan, Leslie Usherwood, Kris Holmes, and Ernst Friz.

English type designer Colin Brignall associated with ITC as a new font scout, charged with discovering new-type design talent and new typefaces from established designers. Brignall's refined contemporary æsthetics combined with his strong historical perspective developed under his direction the Figural type family.

Successful typefaces released by ITC are both original and redrawn designs, among them we may find *Friz Quadrata* and *ITC Benguiat* in 1973; *ITC American Typewriter, ITC Korinna, ITC Tiffany,* and *ITC Serif Gothic* in 1974; *ITC Bauhaus* in 1975; *ITC Eras, ITC Kabel,* and *ITC Zapf Book* in 1976; *ITC Zapf International* and *ITC Quorum* in 1977; *ITC Clearface* and *ITC Zapf Chancery* in 1979; *ITC Fenice* and *ITC Novarese* in 1980; *ITC Galliard* and *ITC Modern 216* in 1982; *ITC Berkeley Old Style* in 1983; *ITC Caslon 224* in 1983; *ITC Usherwood, ITC Veljovic* and *ITC Symbol* in 1984; *ITC Slimbach* in 1987; *ITC Panache* in 1988; *ITC Isadora* in 1989; *ITC Oswald* in 1992; *ITC Century Handtooled, ITC Cheltenham Handtooled, ITC Garamond Handtooled,* and *ITC*

Highlander in 1993; and *ITC Edwardian Script* in 1995.

Herb Lubalin continued as editor-in-chief of the *U&lc* periodical until his death in 1981.

In 1986, Esselte Letraset acquired ITC, which continued working in New York. During this time, many of *Letraset* typefaces were commercialized by ITC.

In the late 1990s, ITC commercilized a new group of typefaces from which we can mention: *ITC Vintage* (Holly Goldsmith), *ITC Eastwood* (Martin Archer), *ITC Juanita* and *ITC Florinda* (Luis Siquot), *ITC Nora* (James Montalbano), and *ITC Jellybaby* (Timothy Donaldson).

In February 2000, Agfa / Monotype in Massachusetts, acquired ITC, including its complete library of over 1,600 typefaces. Its type development department, under the direction of Ilene Strizver, is now located in Wilmington, Massachusetts.

Two years later, Agfa / Monotype and ITC introduced the *ITC 1500* type library, the largest and most complete ITC type collection ever assembled.

Today, as part of its commitment to informing and inspiring the design community, ITC publishes the award-winning publication *U&lc Online* (*Upper & lower case: The International Journal of Graphic Design and Digital Media*), where new ITC typefaces are introduced and displayed in full use.

ITC has also released the *ITC Designer Collection*, which has provided an affordable means for graphic professionals to acquire a solid foundation of high-quality typefaces. With an assortment of 200 typefaces, the *ITC Designer Collection* includes serif and sans serif texts fonts, script designs, decorative displays, and headline fonts.

Letraset

To understand the need and advantages of such an invention as the dry-transfer lettering process known as *Letraset*, one must know that display typography and headline work was something that was done outside of a regular metal type design.

First of all, if one needed a special type of lettering, the presence of highly skilled calligraphers and designers was required. If one needed a large size type, it required a photomechanical process, since metal type was not produced in a size larger than 72 pt. Also, the use of photolettering was time-consuming, costly, and did not offer a clean presentation inside the artwork.

With the invention of *Letraset*, commercial artists, designers, and anyone interested in design suddenly found a perfect way to produce accurate, high-quality lettering incorporated in the artwork. Besides the ease inherent to the process, it permitted many advantages that no other medium allowed such as kerning, change of letter design and size within a word, non-orthogonal placement of text, etc., breaking a conventional attitude towards typography.

In 1956, Englishmen John Charles Clifford "Dai" Davies, a London-based designer and lettering artist, with Fred McKenzie, a printing consultant and part-time editor of a technical journal, developed the technique from a wet slide transfer system which had been used for some time as a children's toy, known as decalcomanias or "decals."

Bob Chudley, who had worked for Crawford's advertising agency in London and for leading department stores in the city –two areas in which the fast production of display lettering was of great importance and immediacy– foresaw the potential commercial market for developing such a medium and steered the development in its beginnings.

In 1959, Letraset Limited was formed, but its initial wet process did not make an impact on the American market. Nevertheless, two years later, in 1961, the first dry transfer type was introduced; its cleaner and easier management proved to be an immediate success. The printer's strike, which had taken place in 1959, had proved to the designer once more the need to be freed from the use of metal type in the making of an art work prior to any photomechanical process.

Alphabets were now screen-printed in reverse onto the back of a polyethylene support sheet, using a revolutionary carbon-resistant tissue film. Overprinted with a low-tack adhesive, it was possible, after shading careful pressure on the front of the sheet, and over a selected and positioned letter, to transfer it onto any surface.

The size of the *Letraset* sheets –9.8" x 14.9"– that were designed to be manageable, contained a full alphabet with a controlled frequency of characters, with sizes following the metal point system.

The type library, that included only thirty-five standard typefaces offered in a variety of point sizes, was processed from retouched enlargements of letterpress printed type.

"Dai" Davies realized that a dramatic improvement in the quality of typeface edges could only be achieved through a radical change of artwork, photographic, and screen stencil making techniques. To achieve this, Gary Gillot, a South African technician with experience in a variety of photographic and screen production methods, was employed to manage the fledgling type studio.

Gillot realized that the answer depended on the stencil. A group of young students of printing and photo techniques, after a time-consuming apprenticeship, were trained to cut perfect stencil masters of eight and then of six inches. From these originals, negatives were made.

"Dai" Davies had finally accomplished the ideals he searched for.

A network of international distributors that ensured simultaneous sales in seventy-five countries, backed the commercial success achieved in 1963.

This same year, Letraset launched its first typeface, *Compacta*, designed by Fred Lambert, followed by designs submitted by the members of the studio, thanks to their skill and typographic awareness.

In 1964, Colin Brignall, who had begun his career in press photography in London's Fleet Street and had experience in fashion and commercial photography, joined Letraset as a photographic technician in their type design studio. It was inside this working environment where he began to develop interest in letterforms, and where he began to experiment with his own ideas in type design. His first typefaces –*Aachen, Lightline, Premier*, and *Revue*– appeared in 1969.

Under Brignall's direction, Letraset not only produced a comprehensive library with classical type designs, but commissioned many type designers all over the world to create original works including more than 800 type designs, many of them, exclusive to the company, and many, designed in-house by Brignall.

The commercial success of the dry-transfer type superseded all expectations. Shares not only went up 140 times, but sales rose to £750,000 with 75 percent of the whole production going to export. This achievement granted Letraset the Queen's Award for Export in 1966.

In 1970, Letraset introduced its *Letragraphica Typefaces* collection selected by leading designers from all over the world, including Herb Lubalin, Roger Excoffon, Colin Forbes, and Derek Birdsall. By this time, Letraset products were available in over ninety countries.

In 1973, the Letraset Typeface Competition was opened to continue with the type design program. It was followed by events and contests for students during the late 1970s and early 1980s, which maintained the type library updated.

In 1980, Colin Brignall became type director of Letraset, a position he has held since then.

In 1981, the company was incorporated into the Swedish international group Esselte, and Letraset changed its name to Esselte Letraset Limited.

In 1983, Esselte Letraset issued *Letragraphica Premier* to revitalize a program that had run successfully since 1970, when it was first created.

Three years later, Esselte Letraset acquired International Typeface Corporation (ITC), which continued operating as a separate company in New York. During this time, many Letraset typefaces were commercialized by ITC.

In 1990, British designer, Rodney Mylius, organized a Letraset exhibition at the London Design Museum, which plainly displayed the company's contribution to typography during the 1960s.

As typesetting became less expensive and more flexible due to the development of digital typography, Letraset responded by diversifying into software programs for use in Macintosh computers. These included *LetraStudio* –a headline type manipulation program– and *FontStudio* –a type-designing program for creating *Adobe PostScript* format fonts.

LINOTYPE COMPANY

By the end of the nineteenth century, the development of bigger and faster printing machines had lowered the price of printed matter, encouraging the advancement of literacy on both sides of the Atlantic. This also increased the demand for newspapers, magazines, and books, and in return, created an equal demand for fast inexpensive typesetting.

But if machines were built to cast type in a faster and more reliable manner than hand setting, composition was still done by armies of hand compositors. New machines were tried to mechanize type selection through the keyboard –another important invention. But the process was slow, and type redistribution had to be done separately, and once more by hand.

In the 1880s, two Americans working independently, found an answer through a new concept: using matrices and casting type from them. Since type was always new, the time consumed in distributing type was unnecessary, and the used type always went back to the melting pot.

One of these machines was the Linotype, invented in 1886 by German immigrant, Ottmar Mergenthaler. The other one was the Monotype, invented in 1887 by Tolbert Lanston, which cast individual letters (*for additional information refer to pages 180, 192, and 268*).

In 1890, the Mergenthaler Linotype Company was founded in Brooklyn, New York; in 1895, in Manchester, England; and in 1896, in Berlin, Germany.

In the United States, the first Linotype machine was installed in the offices of the *New York Tribune* (1886), and in England, in 1899, in the *Newcastle Chronicle.* Within four years, over 800 models were at work in America, and more than 250 models were at work in the English provinces alone.

The first book to be set using the Linotype composition process was Henry Hall's the *Tribune Book of Open Air Sports*, published by this newspaper as a premium book for subscribers.

In 1904, Linotype issued its first type –which soon became its best-seller type– and first design to include a complete type family. Designed by Bertram G. Goodhue between 1897 and 1902, and initially cut by the American Type Founders for hand composition and for the Cheltenham Press, *Cheltenham* became so immensely popular that ATF and Linotype produced it in partnership.

Thanks to the Linotype composing machine there was an increase in book and magazine production of all kinds of content, which definitely revolutionized the educational and communicational world. Periodicals, such as the *Saturday Evening Post* and *Collier's*, reached audiences of millions. Many machines were also built in England and Germany having more than 6,000 machines in use, establishing basic technology for most of the printing world that would not present a substantial alteration until the 1960s.

At the beginning, both Linotype and Monotype were satisfied with the adaptations of existing typefaces. After a few decades, they both became interested in commissioning new designs.

In 1900, D. Stempel AG and Mergenthaler GmbH signed a contract whereby the former would make Linotype matrices for the English Linotype. The early years of the twentieth century saw the company issuing many new and revised typefaces under the guidance of George W. Jones, who would become their printing advisor in 1921. It was the first British company to create such a position (Monotype was to follow them with the appointment of Stanley Morison in 1922). Under Jones's direction, Linotype issued *Granjon* (1924), *Georgian* (1925), *Estienne* (1926), and *Venezia* (1928).

In 1906, the *Quick-Change Linotype* was introduced, in which the magazine could be removed from the front, allowing for "quick changes." Later in 1909, display-size matrices were developed, increasing the range of type sizes a machine could set. Two years later, Linotype introduced the use of three magazines and then four, which permitted the handling of a greater amount of type styles by just changing the position of the magazines.

In 1922, with the appointment of Chauncey H. Griffith as vice president of typographic development for the Linotype Company in New York, new designs appeared, especially those for newspaper composition. Under Griffith's guidance the *Legibility Group* was established with the main concern of improving the characteristics of type designs. In 1925, Linotype introduced *Ionic No. 5* typeface, a design that became a standard typeface in newspaper composition during the next decade. Within eighteen months nearly 3,000 newspapers had adopted it. Under his direction Linotype also issued *Excelsior* (1931), *Paragon* and *Opticon* (1935), *Bell Gothic* (1937), for the setting of telephone books texts, and *Corona* (1940).

During this period, two other great designers worked for the American Linotype. William Addison Dwiggins designed the *Metro* series in 1930, and Rudolph Ruzicka designed *Fairfield* in 1940 and *Primer* in 1953. Dwiggins later developed *Electra* (1935), *Caledonia* (1938), *Eldorado* (1953), and *Falcon*, issued after his death in 1961.

In 1932, the English Linotype issued *Times New Roman*, a typeface commissioned by the *Times* of London, cut and produced under the supervision of Stanley Morison, now type design advisor for Monotype. This typeface became as important as had been *Ionic No. 5*, nine years before.

In 1934, the *All-Purpose Linotype* was enhanced. Its manual assembly of matrices for faces up to 144 pts, permitted a certain competition with the Ludlow type-casting machine.

From 1947 on, there were several type designers who were called by the English Linotype to contribute with their designs and who also served as consultants: Walter Tracy, Hermann Zapf, Reynolds Stone, and Sem L. Hartz. Under Tracy's direction, Linotype issued *Jubilee* (1953), *Linotype Modern* (1969), and *Times Europa* (1972), a redesign of *Times New Roman* (1932).

The first *Linofilm* photocomposing machine was exhibited in London in 1955, and first installed in America in the offices of the *National Geographic Magazine* in 1959. In England, the *Linofilm* photocomposing equipment extended to book production in 1962.

During the following decades, the pace of change accelerated when Linotype and CBS, in America, collaborated for the development of cathode-ray tube (CRT) technology. The first model, the *Linotron*, was introduced in 1965, and installed in the U.S. Government Printing Office in 1967. Then, that same year, came the Computer-only *Linofilm* typesetter, an important step toward full computer compatibility, which was successfully solved by the *Linotron 505*.

In 1984, the *Linotronic 300* laser photosetter was introduced, with Linotype Laser Fonts encoded in outline form, a machine that has become pre-eminent in its field.

In 1990, Linotype AG merged with Rudolf Hell GmbH, in Kiel, to form Linotype-Hell AG. The company now manufactures a range of *Adobe PostScript* compatible image setters, and the Mergenthaler Linotype Type Library has been licensed to Adobe Systems Inc., for production in this format.

Today, Linotype has been acquired by the Heidelberg Company in Germany.

Even with the invention of the **Linotype** (Ottmar Mergenthaler, 1886), and the **Monotype** (Tolbert Lanston, 1887) machines, both for setting text-size type, there remained the need for a machine which allowed the setting of display type.

In 1906, Washington I. Ludlow projected a type composing machine for display type and took the prototype to William A. Reade, who established the Ludlow Typograph Company in Chicago, for its development.

In spite of the difficulties with Ludlow's original idea, by 1909 the project was concluded and five machines were built.

But the machine was not commercially viable as Reade visualized it, so he decided to work on a different proposal where matrices were individually set by hand on a special composer (page 191).

The new model was successfully installed at the **Chicago Evening Post**, in August 1913. Such was the satisfaction expressed by this enterprise that the following year a complete plant was installed at the **Cleveland Press** to approach an entire slug make-up of the newspaper, a practice that was soon followed by other newspapers.

In 1918, the installation of the Ludlow system made by the Saul Brothers Co., a Chicago plant devoted to commercial printing, prompted its usefulness.

This is how the Ludlow Company developed the rule form matrices which permitted the making of tables and charts, and the possibility of casting of type slugs of 30 picas long and of body size that went from 4 pt to 240 pt, as well as the repetition of a line as many times as needed.

In 1929, the Elrod strip material caster −invented by Benjamin S. Elrod in 1917− was incorporated into the Ludlow set up, allowing printing shops to produce their own typographical material, such as slugs, rulers, and borders.

As competition went on, the Ludlow Typograph Company started a design program to develop their own typefaces. Being a starting company −it had been functioning since 1911− to compete with the more established type and matrices suppliers like the Lanston Monotype, the Mergenthaler Linotype, and the American Type Founders, it needed a large type library that provided new and original designs, as well as types which served as formal equivalents or complemented type versions to these companies.

In 1923, the Ludlow Typograph Company commissioned German designer, letterer, and teacher Ernst Frederick Detterer −who had studied with Edward Johnston, and who had been invited by the Art Institute of Chicago to create a new curriculum in the printing and typographic arts−, to develop a typeface (later named **Eusebius**) based on Nicolas Jenson's 1470 font used in the edition of Eusebius de Cesarea's **De Pæparatione Evangelica**.

While studying at the Art Institute, Robert Hunter Middleton assisted Detterer in the designing of the roman version, but developed the italic on his own. Middleton's work quality so impressed Detterer that Detterer himself gave Middleton a letter of recommendation to obtain a full-time work with Ludlow.

The Ludlow Typograph Company had an additional advantage on its side −its type composing machine was less expensive, easier to operate, and widely used by small shops that could not afford either the Linotype or the Monotype, and that were usually setting short texts for all types of stationery printing. This, by the way, did not exclude the possibility of setting up a whole book using the Ludlow type composing system. We may find an example in Douglas C. McMurtrie's book **Modern Typography and Layout** −a book of 190 pages− all set by hand in Middleton's **Stellar**, and printed by the Eyncourt Press, Chicago, in 1929.

Now, since the company's profits relied more on the sale of matrices than of machines, huge amounts of matrices were needed. Fortunately, Middleton was greatly helped by German engraver and type designer Robert Wiebking, who had been with the company almost from the start, and who had designed his own pantographic machine to carry out these activities. Although he had very little faith in the Ludlow method of composition, he dedicated all of his attention to the company's engraving problems with a true and honest craftsmanship.

Wiebking's relation with the Ludlow Typograph Company grew to be friendly and profitable to both parties. As a result of this association, Wiebking and William A. Reade −the founder and president of the Ludlow Typograph Company− made an arrangement whereby the Ludlow Company purchased one of Wiebking's engraving machines.

This arrangement, together with a brief period of tutelage in engraving methods by Wiebking, launched the Ludlow Typograph Company on an independent engraving program. Wiebking lived to see the Ludlow Typograph Company succeed and to find in the "upstart" a constant and reliable client. Wiebking continued to do Ludlow matrix engraving work until his death in 1927.

The work of Robert Wiebking and Robert Hunter Middleton −who had entered the company in 1923− complemented by Douglas C. McMurtrie −who was director of typography during the 1930s− made the company a leader in the United States, for more than three decades.

The Ludlow Typograph Company's position in the field of typeface design was conscientiously kept in relation to its machine's true purpose as a composition tool. Because of this relationship between the typefaces and the machine's objective, the company developed a greater number of display or advertising typefaces than

of traditional or book faces. Among them we may find such families and individual series as **Tempo, Karnak, Eden, Stellar, Ultra Modern, Umbra, Mandate, Delphian Open Title, Mayfair, Coronet, Radiant, Samson,** and **Record Gothic.**

Of the book faces, **Caslon True-cut, Bodoni Modern** and **Italic,** and **Garamond,** all based on original sources, were also drawn and developed by Middleton. It is important to mention that Ludlow's **Garamond** was the first contemporary version of Garamond's types. Since Garamond cut no italics, the Ludlow's **Garamond Italic** was based upon the italics of Robert Granjon, whose italic types were contemporary with Garamond's roman, and are harmonious in effect.

It should also be noted that, although the Ludlow type composing system became known in the trade as a system for display typesetting, the easiness of handling the relatively large matrices for small-size typefaces, and the resulting solid, unworn type slug, were advantages often taken in consideration by printers who did short runs and imprints (small-size type and script faces were always a problem to set, print, and distribute from foundry type).

In 1933, the company designated Middleton as their director of type design. His responsibilities were heavy and numerous: to determine what typefaces were needed, and wanted, by printers all over the world (Ludlow had a considerable export business), to design or adapt these designs for the Ludlow system, and to supervise their production in various sizes and weights.

Since no unit system was involved in Ludlow, each character was individually dimensioned. Under Middleton's direction the design department at Ludlow was involved in, and actually controlled the production process at all stages, making the patterns, furnishing specifications for punch engraving, and giving final approval to the punches before matrices were made.

It should be kept in mind that the task of producing brass matrices in quantity was never easy, and even with pantographic punch-engraving machines and hydraulic punch presses, the normal production averaged about three to five new fonts a month. With the large number of sizes involved, two or three years could easily pass before a new family was complete.

Unfortunately, Middleton retired in 1971, with a creative portfolio of more than 100 designs, after devoting his entire professional life to the Ludlow Typograph Company. By this time, phototype was beginning to replace metal composition, and Ludlow was unable to make the transition from one technology to the other. With his departure, the company's type development program ceased to exist.

MONOTYPE

In the 1880s, working independently from one another, two Americans came to answer the problem of mechanical type casting, generated by the great demand of printing presses. In 1885, Ottmar Mergenthaler, a German immigrant, created the **Linotype** composing machine, and in 1886, Tolbert Lanston created the **Monotype** composing machine.

Tolbert Lanston first conceived the idea for a type-composing machine after inspecting a Hollerith Tabulator –a punch-card tabulating machine that will later revolutionize statistical computation in 1890–, and immediately formulated three principles for a successful solution: the keyboard must be separated, encoding information onto a punched tape; each piece of type must be individually produced (not as a slug, as in the Linotype machine); and each line of type must be mathematically justified.

The commercial success of the Mergenthaler Linotype urged investors to back Lanston's invention. In 1886, patents were taken out and the Lanston Monotype Machine Company was formed although the first complete machine was not finished until 1896.

Meanwhile, John Sellers Bancroft, production manager, introduced an important change to Lanston's design by replacing the original cold-stamping component with a hot metal caster, following the same principle employed by the Linotype.

In 1893, after an early model was exhibited at the World's Columbian Exposition held in Chicago, J. Maury Dove, first president of the company, commissioned William Seller's machine factory to build fifty casting machines.

Two years later, the main obstacle to the full development of the company was solved before J. Maury Dove, and Harold M. Duncan, the technical director, arrived in London. The Earl of Dunraven, a passenger on board, was clever enough to form a syndicate to purchase the British rights. As a result, the Lanston Monotype Corporation Ltd. was founded in Salfords, England in 1897, under the management of American engineer, Frank Hinman Pierpont, and production started in 1902.

Under Pierpont, who came accompanied by a group of four of his ex-Typograph employees, including Fritz Max Steltzer, who

became head of the drawing department, and Théodor Bisser, a punch-cutter, Monotype developed and improved many different machines used in type production, including the pantograph invented by Linn Boyd Benton in 1885.

The technological advances in the Monotype system during the 1910s kept the company at the forefront of mechanical type composition. By this time the machine was complemented by a new line of type designs and by 1924, the size of the typefaces went up to 24 pt through the addition of a special attachment.

From the creative point of view, the most significant contribution of the English Monotype for mechanical composition was the production, in 1912, of an original type design done for *Imprint* typographical journal founded and published by Gerard Meynell, John Henry Mason, and Edward Johnston. Known as *Imprint*, and based on *Caslon Old Face*, it proposed new parameters in type design by introducing a large x-height lowercase, and a strong italic. The following year, Pierpont supervised the production of *Plantin*, modeled after Christophe Plantin's typeface, which proved to be even more successful than *Imprint*.

In 1920, the American Lanston Monotype appointed Frederic W. Goudy as art adviser. Goudy persuaded its president, J. Maury Dove to cut its own version of the type attributed to Claude Garamond, rather than copying the foundry face. The result was named *Garamont* (1921) to preserve the distinction between the different renderings. Goudy also designed *Italian Old Style* (1924), considered one of his best text types. Stanley Morison, by the way, didn't have a very good opinion of Goudy's *Garamont*, for he developed his own version of *Garamond* for Monotype one year later. Goudy's relationship with Monotype was a fruitful, sixteen-year relationship through which many other Goudy typefaces were cut by and for the Monotype's composing system.

In 1922, Stanley Morison was appointed typographical advisor to the English Lanston Monotype, as part of an ambitious type-cutting program intended to provide a unique and important collection of book and periodical typefaces for mechanical composition.

During the 1920s and 1930s, Monotype issued, under Morison's

supervision, *Garamond* (1922), *Baskerville* (1923), *Poliphilus* (1923), *Perpetua* (1925), *Fournier* (1925), *Gill Sans* (1928), *Bembo* (1929), *Centaur* (1929), *Arrighi* (1929), *Bell* (1931), and *Times New Roman* (1932), which combined original and revival designs. The type designers –Eric Gill, Stanley Morison, Alfred Fairbank, Frederic Warde, and Bruce Rogers– were both English and American.

In 1927, the English Monotype's in-house magazine, the *Monotype Recorder*, was edited by American typographer and writer Beatrice Warde. For this publication, Frederic Warde did a series of works on typographic ornamentation.

In 1936, Sol Hess succeeded Goudy as art director for the American Lanston Monotype Company. Under his direction the company developed an important program for many publishing companies, presses, and department stores. His vision of the practical side of typography was seen during the fifty years he worked with the company.

In 1955, the English Monotype became increasingly involved with filmsetting, starting with the Monophoto filmsetter, and continuing with the Monotype filmlettering machine in 1963.

In the 1960s, the company developed increasing interest in computer-aided technology which led to setting a marketing arrangement with the Swiss GSA modular system that ended with the introduction of a computer input perforator and the development of tape conversion equipment.

The Lanston Monotype Company was finally liquidated in 1969, and the matrix-making equipment went to ATF.

In 1975, the facilities for making cellular (composition) matrices went to Hartzell Machine Works in Chester, Pennsylvania, and in 1976, Monotype introduced the world's first laser typesetting system, the *Lasercomp*, which was capable of full-page image setting. In 1983, all this equipment went to Mackenzie-Harris Corporation in San Francisco.

More recently some of these resources have gone to Giampa Textware Corp., in Vancouver, British Columbia, for conversion to electronic typesetting methods.

Today, the Monotype digital type library has over 2,500 faces, many of which are available in *Adobe PostScript* format.

The idea of entirely replacing metal for text composition was given impetus by the practical application of photography to the making of printing plates. In 1896, when E. Porzolt patented a keyboard-controlled machine that projected single characters by reflected light onto a sensitized plate, there were numerous attempts to develop a satisfactory system of setting type photographically.

Between World War I and World War II, several machines were constructed and the problem attracted considerable attention.

By 1925, the first phototypesetting machines began to be developed. R.J. Smothers adjusted the Linotype machine system to photocomposition by adapting transparent alphabetical characters on glass and fastening them to each matrix. As lines were assembled, images were recorded by a lens system on sensitized film.

This same year, Hungarian Edmund Uher also invented a photosetting machine, the *Uhertype*, which he presented at the Leipzig Fair in 1936. Controlled by a perforated tape, it produced strips of film negatives of letters which were placed on a glass cylinder.

In America, with the collaboration of Harold A. Horman, and with the establishment of Photo-Lettering Inc., in New York in 1936, there was a real opportunity to replace metal type composition. In an effort headed by Edward Rondthaler, who had been instrumental in perfecting the Rutherford Photo-Letter Composing Machine, and who held patents in mathematical devices, optics, and photocomposition, phototypography became a reality.

This technological advancement was not done overnight, for type continued to be set in metal for some time.

In 1960, Ed Rondthaler surprised the New York advertising design community when he issued his *Alphabet Thesaurus Vol.1*, displaying 3,000 alphabets, followed by a second volume in 1965, and a third in 1971.

During the five hundred years following Johannes Gutenberg's invention of typography, typefaces had been designed by printers and made by foundries. Often founders became the exclusive manufacturers of the entire output of engravers and designers. The process of casting a type took months and even years

and involved heavy financial investment. Now, with the photo-lettering process, type could be designed and redesigned in a short space of time to suit various typesetting systems.

In 1962, Edward Benguiat started to work for Photo-Lettering, Inc., using all his effort on designing, redesigning, and adjusting classical typefaces to photo-lettering new trends.

With the publishing of *Plinc*, an in-house publication under Benguiat's direction, Photo-Lettering, Inc., has continued to offer other alternatives that still find a place and demand in today's computer age.

By the end of the 1960s, metal type was virtually put aside. More than any other graphic designer, Herb Lubalin explored the creative potential of phototypography and how the fixed forms of the orthogonal blocks of metal type were being exploited by phototype dynamic and elastic qualities.

International Typeface Corporation's journal, *U&lc* (*Upper & lowercase*), founded in 1973, is proof of the wide spectrum of possibilities sought by this designer and his collaborators. By the use of special lenses, type could be enlarged, expanded, condensed, italicized, back-slanted, or outlined in large sizes without losing sharpness.

In the meantime, Photo-Lettering, Inc. had issued a *Psychedelitype* catalog in 1969, which allowed anyone to set type in a psychedelic style, so in fashion during the hippie movement.

The large costs of type design were reduced to simple film fonts, and a proliferation of type designs appeared to rival the Victorian era.

"Cutting a new typeface has always been the type founder's most hazardous gamble," explains Ed Rondthaler. "To convert a new alphabet from drawing to metal type is an expensive undertaking, and no foundry dares to embark on such a project until it is absolutely sure that the style will more than pay for itself. Photography removes the gamble. A test run of the proposed type in photo-lettering will determine its popularity and disclose any design flaws. This approach was first used in 1950, with a commercial testing of *Dom Casual* [designed by Peter Dombrezian] by Photo-Lettering for a full year before metal casting

was undertaken," adds Rondthaler. [ATF issued it in 1952, with a bold version in 1953.]

"It is often assumed that type's thirteen sizes between 6 pt and 72 pt are evenly graduated steps. Far from it. The step from 18 pt to 24 pt is 33 percent, while from 42 pt to 48 pt, it is only 14 percent. Photography carries it still further in its ability to condense, expand, oblique, compress, extend or otherwise reproportion letters to fit precisely into the allocated space. A photo-letterer with 10,000 derivatives of every character at its fingerprints has little desire to relinquish this flexibility for the typographer's thirteen-step straight jacket," comments Rondthaler.

"The challenge of Photo-Lettering's flexibility has been met by the French foundry, Deberny & Peignot, in a very interesting way. Their type designer, Adrian Frutiger, has designed a sans serif in twenty-one weights and widths, each cut in sizes up to 48 pts. This is *Univers*, the most versatile gothic to be found in metal. For metal, it is a heroic and costly achievement. But even so, it is a far match for photo-lettering's flexibility which could easily take over where metal has left off, and double, triple or quadruple the number of weights and widths.

"There is little doubt that the day of the typographic purist who sees composition only through lead-colored glasses is coming to an end," concludes Rondthaler.

In 1970, another typeface was first introduced in photo-lettering before it was cut on matrices and cast in metal. This is the case of *Souvenir*, redesigned by Edward Benguiat, whose success made it available first in Linotype in America and by Matrotype in England, and later in metal in 1972 by ATF.

In 1981, Ed Rondthaler published *Life with Letters after They Turned Photogenic*, which throws additional light on his experiences with phototypesetting.

A

Accent marks - Small graphic indications placed over, under or through a letterform (capital or lowercase), to indicate a specific pronunciation or change of stress. This occurs in languages other than English, such as Spanish, French, German, Polish, Danish, etc. Examples are á, é, ø, ô, etc.

See also Analphabetic characters; Diacritical signs

Adobe Type Manager - A technology developed by Adobe Systems, Inc. in the 1990s, which permits the user to organize fonts into groups known as sets, allowing for the management of a large type library, as is the case of this book. In creating a set, the user doesn't move font files. Instead, he groups representations of these files (similar to Windows' shortcuts) into arrangements that work best for him. Thus, a single font may appear in several sets without duplicate font files that take up disk space.

See also Multiple master typefaces; PostScript

Agate - An old name for a 5 ½-pt size typeface. It generally has been associated with the so-called "small print" in legal documents. It is used in stock exchange market reports, box scores, some classified advertising, etc. Newspaper advertising space is bought by the **agate line**. There are 14 agate lines in a column's inch. Thus, an advertising column's width occupies 28 agate lines. With the appearance of the first penny newspaper, the *Sun* (1833), founded by Ben Day in Manhattan and dependent on advertising revenues, ads were restricted to the use of the small "agate" type in a want-ad style. A larger initial or a generic illustration was used to differentiate contents.

See also Line lenght; Type sizes

Aldine Oldstyle typefaces - Also known as *Aldine Old Face*, it is a term used to refer to the typefaces created in Venice and Rome in the early 1490s, and based on the work of the Venetian printer, Aldus Manutius. These typefaces closely followed the hands of the humanists –written with broad-nib pens held at a 30-degree angle– which produced a left diagonal stress in round letters. Cut by Francesco Griffo of Bologna, the first typeface was used in 1495 in the printing of Pietro –later Cardinal– Bembo's book, *De Aetna*, and the second, in 1499 in the printing of Dominican monk, Fra Francesco Colonna's *Hypnerotomachia Poliphili*. Considered as a fine example of the old face types, it was later used as a model by Frenchmen Claude Garamond, and Robert Granjon. There is a greater contrast in stroke weight than in the preceding *Venetian Old Face* designs, capital letters are lower than lowercase ascenders, lowercase letters are narrower, and the letter e has a cross horizontal bar. In 1923 and 1926, English typographer and designer Stanley Morison directed the cutting of the two typefaces designed by Griffo for Monotype composition. The first was issued as *Poliphilus*, and the second as *Bembo*. Shortly after, Lanston Monotype in America cut it.

See also Contrast; Oldstyle typefaces; Serifs; Typeface classification; Venetian Oldstyle typefaces

Alignment - The arrangement of type upon an imaginary line so that the base of each character, excluding descenders, is on the same level. In metal type, different type point sizes cannot be set on the same line with a common base alignment because of the physical structure of the metal form and the position of the character on its body. In comparison, photocomposition as well as digital typography has a built-in alignment feature whereby the same baseline is common to all typefaces in all point sizes. Changes of size occur upwards. It is important to note that, for the sake of design, alignment may be changed to a top or center alignment.

With the great variety of proportions in various type designs, attempts at standardization were not successful until the nineteenth century, when the leading foundries instituted a system of standard alignment, and existing designs were gradually modified over several years to conform. This allowed for the mixing of two or mores styles in one line. In 1903, the American Type Founders adopted a standard lining system which permitted the alignment of different sizes by the use of 1-pt leads or their multiples.

This line of text shows a BASE line alignment.

This line of text shows a mean line alignment.

This line of text shows a CENTER line alignment.

See also Baseline; Guidelines; Leading

Alphabet - A series of letters or characters, consonants and vowels, arranged in a given order, used in a language to represent specific sounds. The letters are used "to write" sounds. The term comes from the first two letters, *alpha* and *beta*, in Greek. The number of letters in an alphabet changes from one language to another. In classic Latin there were twenty-three, in English there are twenty-six, and in Spanish, twenty-eight. It is also interesting to note that the given order of the letters in the alphabet also changes according to the application. This is the case with a type case or with the computer's keyboard, just to mention two instances.

See also Font; California type case; Keyboard; Lowercase letters; Uppercase letters

Ampersand (&) - A special character of a font, which has been the result of contracting, in one graphic whole, the Latin word *et* (and). Although its use dates back to the scribes' ligatures utilized to contract words to gain space, its origins may be traced to *graffiti* in the first century A.D. In one way or another, calligraphers and printers have used it since then. The English name refers to the words *and-per se-and*, a mixture of Latin and English. In 1936, by request of the Typophiles, New York, type designer Frederic W. Goudy, submitted a series of ampersands for a book they were doing on that subject. This series may be seen on page 143. Let us see some examples taken at random:

The ampersand is commonly used in commercial names, such as LETTERS & TYPEFACES, INC.

Anatomy of a typeface - Parts shaping a given character. They are basically main stroke or stem, hairline, arm, spine, cross bar, link, bowl, loop, shoulder, swash, apex, ear, ascender, descender, leg, tail, terminal, serifs, counters, spur, slope, and stress. It is important to note that contrast may exist between all its parts, the general weight, and the proportion between height and width.

See also each individual part; Ascender line; Baseline; Cap line; Contrast; Descender line; Guide lines; Mean line; Type nomenclature; Weight of a typeface; x-height

Analphabetic characters - Typographical characters that are used with the alphabet but lack a place in its regular arrangement. Such is the case of the diacritical signs, the reference marks, and the pi characters, among others.

See also Alphabet, Ampersand, Diacritical signs; Pi characters; Reference marks

Apex - The peak of an uppercase letter **A**. This part of the letter also changes dramatically in Art Deco style typefaces, as is the case of HUXLEY VERTICAL (Walter Huxley, 1935).

See also Anatomy of a typeface; Art Deco

Apostrophe (') - Also called **raised comma**, it is a sign of omission of a letter as well as indicative of possession. This is the case of **can't** (can not) or **John's book**. It is important not to confuse it with the **prime** which is used as a sign for feet and grades. Such as **60'**.

See also Coma; Prime and double prime; Quotation marks

Arabic numerals - A misnomer given to the ten figures from **0** to **9**, which originated in India around 264-230 BC By 200 BC the 0 had appeared, and by this time a complete inscription with all the nine numbers and the zero may be found. They are so called because Italian merchants who traded with Arab countries introduced them into Europe from Arabia around 1100. Europeans became aware of the new numbers and through Leonardo de Pisa's work they started their use of the Hindu-Arabic system for all commercial calculations. The first book to have a date in Arabic numerals was the *Calendarium* printed by German printer and type cutter, Erhard Ratdolt, in Venice in 1476. They are generally used to indicate page numbers within the body of a publication.

They are **1 2 3 4 5 6 7 8 9 10 11 12 13**, etc.

See also Cardinal numbers; Modern style figures; Oldstyle figures; Ordinal numbers; Pagination; Roman numerals; Subscript; Superscript; Title page

Arm - A horizontal or diagonal stroke that extends from a vertical stem, and is free on one end, as found in capital letters **E, F, L, K, T, Y**, and **Z**, and similar lowercase letters. Arms are also thinner than stems, although in Egyptian and sans serif typefaces they may present the same weight. In Art Deco style typefaces, middle arms and cross bars are usually placed above or below center, giving a particular design feature to the font.

See also Anatomy of a typeface; Art Deco; Contrast; Cross bar; Cross bar line; Leg; Middle arm line; Stem

Art Deco - Also known as **Style Moderne**, it emerged in France as a movement in the decorative arts and architecture during the 1920s, and developed into an international style in Western Europe and the United States during the 1930s. Its name was derived from the Exposition Internationale des Arts Décoratifs et Industriels Modernes which took place in Paris in 1925. The distinguishing features, which blend the fragmentation of Cubism and the ornamentation of Art Nouveau, and of Southeast Asian and Mayan architecture, are exemplified by simple, clean shapes, derived from natural stylized forms (human, animal, and floral), with an emphasis on the use of straight and angular shapes, and some interlaced curves. There is also an emphasis on the use of neutral colors, such as of black, white, and gray and glossy, metallic finishing. Despite Art Deco's reflecting appreciation for the machine and industrial processes –which achieved a sort of "technical appeal" for all its products– the real aim of this style was to create a sleek elegance that symbolized wealth and sophistication. Therefore, individually crafted items were highly attractive, and industrial processes were intended for limited editions. Graphic arts, advertising, and fashion design showed noticeable flourishing. In typography, Art Deco revealed a tendency to achieve a precious and sophisticated look, more decorative than strictly readable typefaces. Sans serif letters, which were more broadly used, adopted varied forms: inlined, incised, decorated, a mixture of geometry and calligraphy, or reduced to simple shapes. Cross bars and middle arms in capital letters were generally placed above or below center, and in some alphabets, angular letters had a round top. Text typefaces usually presented lowercase letters with reduced x-height, large ascenders, and short descenders. Typefaces **BROADWAY** / **Broadway** and PARISIAN / Parisian (Morris Fuller Benton, 1928), and HUXLEY VERTICAL (Walter Huxley, 1936) are typical examples. BERNHARD FASHION / Bernhard Fashion (Lucian Bernhard, 1929) also presents the reduced x-height relationship of upper- and lowercase letters of text typefaces. Art Deco became unfashionable during World War II, although there was renewed interest in design between the late 1940s and 1950s, mostly in America through the streamline style.

See also Arm; Art Nouveau; Cross bar; Cubism; Incised typefaces; Inline typefaces; Typeface classification; x-height

Art Nouveau - Also known as *Guimard* (France), *Jugendstil* (Germany), *Modernismo* (Spain), *Nieuwe Kunst* (the Netherlands), *Sezessionstil* (Austria), and *Stile Liberty* (Italy), *Art Nouveau* is the common French name for this movement, which rejected the academic revivalism that dominated nineteenth-century art and design. Deeply influenced by the aims and achievements of the Arts and Crafts movement in England, and the Vienna Secession in Austria, its main interest was also to erase the distinction between major and minor arts. This was done in order to integrate all practical-creative skills, and to recover the value of manufacturing, in view of the growing phenomenon of industrialization and mass production. Thus, a renewed interest in the study of organic forms appeared. Art Nouveau was also influenced by Japanese arts and crafts, Symbolism, the PreRaphaelites, Gothic and Greek classicism. It basically started as a movement in architecture, which was considered a total art expression. However, it later involved art and applied arts. Wrought iron, stained glass, and mosaics were the most popular media during the rise and expansion of this movement (1894-1914). Poster design and illustration were also highly developed. The flourishing of lithography and chromolithography much influenced letterforms, which acquired fluent and organic strokes. Typefaces, generally for display use, reflected a more ornamental than readable

form, and certain letters presented an asymmetrical structure. Around 1894, with the covers designed by William Bradley for the *Inland Printer*, Art Nouveau began to clearly appear as an American expression. Art Nouveau imagery was still present throughout the 1920s. During the 1960s, with the psychedelic movement in America, Art Nouveau had a late revival in the applied arts. A typical typeface design may be found in **ARNOLD BÖCKLIN** / **Arnold Böcklin** (German Otto Weisert type foundry, 1904). Influences of Art Nouveau may be found in American typefaces like ITC KORINA / ITC Korina (Ed Benguiat, 1974), and **ITC BENGUIAT** / **ITC Benguiat** also designed by Benguiat in 1978.

See also Art Deco; Jugendstil; Lithography

Ascender - A vertical stroke that rises above the body of a lowercase letter, as found in letters **b**, **d**, **f**, **h**, **k**, **l**, and **t**. In 1897, architect and type designer Bertram Grosvenor Goodhue designed the typeface CHELTENHAM / Cheltenham for Ingalls Kimball's Cheltenham Press in New York. As a result of his type research, he came to the conclusion that while we read words by blocks, ascenders are more important than descenders in determining the legibility and readability of a text. We may also find that other proposals rely on the x-height relationships between lowercase letters and capitals for greater legibility and readability.

See also Anatomy of a typeface; Descender; Legibility; Readability; Type nomenclature; x-height

Ascender line - An imaginary horizontal line that runs across the top of lowercase ascenders, and determines their relationship to uppercase letters. Ascenders are usually higher than capitals.

See also Anatomy of a typeface; Baseline; Cap line; Cross bar line; Descender line; Guidelines; Mean line; x-height

Asterisk (*) - A reference mark placed after a word or a sentence within a running text to indicate to the reader that there is further information, or a footnote. The footnote is always preceded by an identical reference mark. Its name (from the Greek *aster*, star) makes reference to its shape, although it changes depending of the typeface design (* * * * * * *). Asterisks are also preferred in mathematical texts where superscript numbers (^{123}) might present confusion. When there are other instances on the same page, other alternative marks are used, such as the dagger (†) or the double dagger (‡). Typographically, it originated in Italy as a printer's flower during the fifteenth century. The asterisk is also used to mark a person's year of birth while the dagger (†) or the cross (✝) indicate the year of death.

See also Dagger; Reference marks; Superscript

Asymmetrical typography - A modern typographic design style, it was theoretically elaborated in Germany during the 1920s. It rejects the traditional arrangement of text according to a central vertical axis (symmetry). It encourages the functional, dynamic placement of typography and visual elements as well as the use of sans serif typefaces. Asymmetric design permits the creation of visually balanced arrangements of contrasting elements. Its main theorist, German calligrapher and typographer Jan Tschichold, influenced by Paul Renner's book, *Typographie als Kunst* (1922), by the teachings of Rudolf Koch, and by Constructivists' ideas, visited the first Bauhaus exhibition in 1923. Thereafter,

he started to write a series of articles and books directed to a wide audience of printers, typesetters, and designers. Through them, he explained and demonstrated the advantages of asymmetrical typography. In 1925, Tschichold wrote an important article –a personal manifesto on modern typography– entitled *Elementare Typographie* for a special issue of the journal *Typographische Mitteilungen*, in which, referring to the work of El Lissitsky, he spoke for the first time of sans serif typefaces, asymmetrical typography, and the relation of type and space. In 1928, he laid down the theoretical principles in his book, *Die neue Typographie* (*The New Typography*), rejecting decoration in favor of rational design planned solely for communication. He advocated the use of sans serif typefaces in their full range of weights and sizes as the modern face. Furthermore, designs should be constructed on an underlying grid, and rules, bars, and boxes used for structure, balance, and emphasis, and typographical form should evolve from the text and not be put in order into a given arrangement. Moreover, the precision of photography should be preferred over illustration. In 1935, Tschichold published a major text, *Typographische Gestaltung* (English version, *Asymmetric Typography*, 1967) in Basle in which he expanded his typographical theories.

See also International Typographic Style; Sans serif typefaces; Symmetrical typography

B

Ball terminal - A circular form found at the end of upper or lower round strokes of lowercase letters such as **a**, **c**, **f**, **j**, and **r** in *Modern* and *Clarendon* style typefaces. It also appears in the ear of letter g.

acfgjr acfgjr

See also Clarendon style typefaces; Ear; Ionic typefaces; Modern style typefaces; Terminal; Tear drop terminal

Baseline - An imaginary horizontal line upon which all the letters rest, except the round letters, that usually go below this line somewhat. While in metal type its placement changes proportionally to body size, in photocomposition as well as in digital typography it is kept constant.

See also Alignment; Anatomy of a typeface; Cap line; Guidelines; Horizontal alignment; Photocomposition; Phototypography; Type nomenclature

Bauhaus - (In German this term means "building house"). This was a school of design, art, architecture, and applied arts that existed in Germany from 1919 to 1933. Initially founded in Weimar, it was closed in 1925 under political and economic pressure from the local government and reopened the same year in Dessau, where it was again closed by the Nazis in 1932. It then moved to Berlin, where it was completely shut down by the Nazis in 1933. The Bauhaus school was founded by architect and designer Walter Gropius, who was asked to merge the Weimar School of Art with the Weimar School of Arts and Crafts, to establish the Staatliches Bauhaus. The school included the teaching of basic design, painting, graphic arts, advertising, photography, typography, interior design, wall painting, textiles, etc., which Gropius envisioned as part of architecture, "the matrix of the arts." By training students equally in art and craftsmanship, the Bauhaus rejected the differences between the two, making both art and technique equally valued skills. One of the school's main aims was to improve the quality of the standards of manufacturing –which had been proposed by the Deutscher Werkbund– and the production of high quality handicrafts in combination with a design appropriate to its purpose, also proposed by William Morris and the Arts and Crafts movement. In spite of these goals, Bauhaus rejected the emphasis of the latter on individual luxury objects and focused all its efforts on the improvement and advancement of mass manufacturing and industrial production. Among the teachers were: Johannes Itten, Gerhard Marcks, Georg Muche, Lionel Feininger, Adolf Meyer, Paul Klee, Wassily Kandinsky, László Moholy-Nagy, Herbert Bayer, Josef Albers, Max Breuer, and Ludwig Mies van der Rohe. Although graphic design was not specifically included in the curriculum at Weimar, typography became a relevant part of it, making emphasis on the exclusive use of sans serif typefaces. Even though Paul Renner was not part of the staff, his **FUTURA** / Futura (1927) became associated with the school's principles. In 1937, László Moholy-Nagy founded the New Bauhaus in Chicago. In 1938, Herbert Bayer organized an exhibition at the Museum of Modern Art, which displayed the work of the Bauhaus from 1919 to 1928. Both the school and the exhibition contributed to spreading the influence of the Bauhaus's teaching principles.

See also Art Deco; Asymmetrical typography; Constructivism; International Typographic Style; Sans serif typefaces

Bicameral alphabet - That which has two alphabets joined, as is the case of the Latin alphabet, which has an upper and a lowercase alphabets. Hebrew or Arabic alphabets only contain one case.

See also Alphabet; Lowercase letters; Tricameral alphabet; Type case; Uppercase letters; Unicameral alphabet

Bitmap character - A letterform that has been described by a series of dots which simulate its form. The more the dots the more accurate will be the description of its perimeter. In the illustration below we may also appreciate that as the digital bitmap becomes less coarse the letterform not only becomes more elegant and precise, but gives the impression of changing style. As in regular halftone reproduction, dots are arranged orthogonally. In 1985, taking advantage of the bitmap aspect, American type designer Zuzana Licko created her first three typefaces *Emperor*, *Oakland Ten* (page 182), and *Émigré 8*. It is also worth citing the work of Charles Bigelow and Kris Holmes in designing fonts for low resolution printers.

ef ef ef ef

See also Digital typography; Dot-matrix printer; Fixed fonts

Black typeface - A character defined by heavier strokes than the **bold face**. Since this increment is horizontal and inwards, the letter maintains

the same height. American wood type designers made extensive use of these value variations as may be seen on page 205. Let's compare **COOPER BOLD** / Cooper Bold with **COOPER BLACK** / **Cooper Black**, both designed by Oswald Cooper in 1914 and 1921, respectively.

See also Bold typeface; Fat Face; Light typeface; Regular typeface; Typeface classification

Black letter - A name given to the group of Gothic scripts which was developed in Europe in the twelfth century. Its final form, then known as *text* or *textura*, evolved in Paris in the early thirteenth-century. It is important to know that black letter had several regional forms, such as *textura*, *rotunda*, and *bâtarde*, which were used for different purposes. The close-knit *textura* for Bibles and other liturgical books, the dagger-shaped *bâtarde* for legal documents, and the *rotunda* which had a rounded form, nearer to the Carolingian scripts on which all these letter forms were based, was used for a wide range of vernacular works. Inevitably, black letter scripts inspired the design of early printing types varying, as did the scripts, according to the place where the cutting was done. The *42-line Bible*, printed by Johannes Gutenberg between 1440 and 1456, was set in an 18-pt type based on the *textura*. The *bâtarde* evolved into different scripts, one of which developed into the modern German black letter called *Fraktur*, which due to the influence of Maximilian I, around 1517, became the national script and type, retaining a dominant position until it was abolished by Adolf Hitler in 1941 for being considered Jewish. According to Sigfrid Henry Steinberg the prevalence of black letter in Germany and other northern countries may be found in the predominance of theological over humanist writings. In England, black letter was used from the 1560s until it was abandoned on general publishing in the seventeenth century. It was again used for ecclesiastical and legal publications during the Gothic revival of art and architecture during the nineteenth century. Black letter is also known as *Gothic*, *Fraktur*, *Textura*, and *Old English*. We find a contemporary example in Frederic W. Goudy's GOUDY TEXT / Goudy Text, designed in 1928, and influenced by Johannes Gutenberg's *42-line Bible* (1456) gothic type.

See also Carolingian script; Fraktur; Gothic letter; Typeface classification

Body - In type composition, it is the metal or wooden block that carries the raised printing surface. It is the depth of the body that gives the typeface its point size. In photocomposition or in digital type composition this rectangular space is maintained for sizing and spacing the type.

In setting types with the same body size but from different styles, but also on behalf of their x-height, letters may appear to have different heights, as may be seen in comparing the following four different typefaces all set in 10 pt:

Bodoni, **Futura**, Helvetica, Americana.

The term body also denotes a block of text copy as well as the main part of a book or other publication, excluding preliminary and end material.

See also Anatomy of a typeface; End material; Face; Preliminary material; Typeface nomenclature; Type size; x-height

Body size - The apparent height of a typeface due to the fact that measurements refer to the body in which the typeface stands and not to the character shape.

Body size

When relating type designs in a composition, one must compensate for apparent heights by giving each style a different body size. This, unfortunately, will change line spacing. While in the example bellow, *Bodoni* and *Americana* typefaces are set in 11 pt, *Futura* is set in 10.5, and *Helvetica* in 10 pt. A visual unevenness remains due to the fact that while caps have been equaled in height, the different x-heights remain.

Bodoni, **Futura**, Helvetica, Americana

See also Anatomy of a typeface; Type size; Unit

Bold typeface - A character defined with heavier strokes than the regular font. This broadening of the strokes is done in a horizontal sense, both inwards and outwards. For this reason, a bold face may seem to be smaller than a regular face. Let us compare NEWS GOTHIC REGULAR / News Gothic Regular and **NEWS GOTHIC BOLD** / **News Gothic Bold**, both designed by Morris Fuller Benton in 1908. Bold faces are generally used for headings to distinguish them from related text.

See also Black typeface; Light typeface; Regular typeface; Typeface classification

Book face - Also referred to as **text type**, it is a term applied to the typographical characters employed in running texts, which usually go from 6 to 12 pt. Smaller sizes are usually employed for notes. It is useful to take into consideration that this size range may change in relation to the size of a publication, in which case it is determined by a reading relationship, as is the case of children's books in which the text type may be larger than fourteen points without losing this denomination. Gutenberg's *42-line Bible* was set in 18-pt type.

See also Display type; Typesetting specification

Bookplates - Printed labels of ownership pasted on the inside front cover of a book. Also known as *ex libris* (Latin for "from the books of"), the first examples appeared at the end of the fifteenth century. Thanks to German artist, Albrecht Dürer, who designed some around 1503, they became known in Europe. The word *ex libris* may form a part of the design. Some examples may be seen on pages 111 (Warren Chappell), and 225 (Rudolph Ruzicka).

See also Woodcut; Wood engraving

Book cover - *See* Cover

Book spine - Also called **bookbone**, it is the side portion of a book normally seen when it is placed upright on a shelf or on a table. The direction in which the information is placed (upwards or downwards) differs for a justified reason. Some designers affirm it should go downwards so that

it may be read when placed on a table, and some affirm that it should go upwards for it reads easier when placed on a shelf. A third option is horizontal, if space so permits. The author's name, the title and the printer's emblem and/or its name, and the volume number, when relevant, must go on the spine. The tooling of gold letters on the spine is found on Italian bindings around 1535 on, the wording running up the spine. Around 1708, titles were set typographically in Germany, and around 1780 in England. William Addison Dwiggins was a designer who always thought of a book as a whole entity; he would design all its parts from cover to spine. We may find four of his designs on page 130.
See also Cover

Borders - A continuous, decorative design arranged around printed matter on a page. Borders can be continuous cast strips of rulers, plain or patterned, or they can be made up of repeated border units. The individual repetitive devices (rules, dots, flowers, etc.) were normally available in metal or wood type in a range of sizes to match the point size of each typeface. This treatment of a page was a feature of the illuminator's art, and in imitation of this, it first appeared in printed books around 1472. We find some examples on pages 205, 223 and 253.

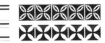

See also Rules; Printer's flowers; Typographic devices; Typographical ornaments

Bowl - In a letter, it is a curved stroke which makes an enclosed space within a character, as in capital letters B, D, P, R, and in lowercase letters a, b, g, p, and q. In the letter g, the upper part is a bowl, while the lower part is a loop.
See also Anatomy of a typeface; Link; Loop

Brackets [ ] - Also called **square parentheses**, they are punctuation marks used in pairs, generally employed to enclose quotations within quotations, such as interpolations written by the editor or the translator.
See also Parentheses; Punctuation marks

Bracketed serifs - Also called **adnate serifs**, they are letter stroke terminals that having a curved shape in the union with any stroke flow smoothly into it. We may find them in *Oldstyle*, and in *Clarendon* typefaces. An example is ITC LEGACY / ITC Legacy, designed by Ronald Arnholm in 1992.
See also Clarendon serif; Latin serif typefaces; Serifs; Square Serifs; Typeface classification; Type nomenclature

Brush script typefaces - A term used to refer to those characters that have been drawn with a brush rather than with a pen. They appeared as a product of advertising design during the twentieth century. Such is the case of *Brush Script*, designed by Robert E. Smith in 1942.
See also Calligraphic typefaces; Calligraphy; Script typefaces; Typeface classification

Bullets - Geometric graphic elements used to preface any given information, such as a list of items. They usually come in three sizes –small, medium, and large– and are generally placed at the

beginning of a line of text, centered with either the lowercase letters or with the capitals.
This is the case of ■ ○ ▲ ● □ ▣ ⊙ ▣
See also Dingbats; Pi characters

C

c - An abbreviation for caps, as in **c & lc** (caps and lowercase), or **c & sc** (caps and small caps). This abbreviation is generally used when specifying type.
See also Copyright symbol; Typesetting specifications

Cabinet - An enclosed rack to hold type cases. Formerly of wood, they are now constructed of pressed sheet steel, as seen on page 191.
See also Type case

Calendered finish - A degree of smoothness imparted to paper as a result of running it through the calenders, or hot cylinders, of a papermaking machine. Smoothness varies with the number of times the paper is calendered. In 1757, English printer and type designer John Baskerville printed his first book, an edition of Virgil's *Bucolica, Georgica et Æneis*, in which he also used his fine type (*Baskerville*), and his woven calendered paper.
See also Coated paper

California job case - A name given to a specific distribution in a type case, which puts the two old cases (the upper and the lower cases) together into one container, and which is probably the most commonly used. Being divided vertically into three major sections, the left two-thirds are filled with lowercase letters and the right third with the uppercase letters. Numbers are located in the upper part of the middle section. There are two versions of where the name came from. Some say it was developed in California, and others say that the original two old cases were transformed into one to simplify the printer's equipment during the mid-nineteenth-century Gold Rush. We may compare the California job case with the two old cases configuration as seen on page 225.

See also Foundry type; Letterpress; Type case

Calligrammes - A name given by French poet Guillaume Apollinaire to his visual poems. Published in 1918, his texts are arranged to structure a whole blend of form and content. Lines of text are ordered to give visual readings. Closely associated with Cubism, Apollinaire explored the potential fusion of poetry and painting, introducing simultaneous readings of text and image. His experiments with onomatopoeic sounds, and repeated letters to create visual statements are worthy of mention.
See also Cubism; Typogram

Calligraphic typefaces - A term used to refer to the script typefaces that present a closer

resemblance to handwriting. They came into vogue with the introduction of lithography in the eighteenth-century, and have maintained their popularity for stationery. Their appearance in hot metal types became a reality through the use of Linn Boyd Benton's automatic punch-cutter. Today, through digital type design programs, many of these designs have become a reality. We find two examples in *Shelley Allegro Script*, designed by Matthew Carter in 1965 and in *ITC Edwardian Script*, designed by Edward Benguiat in 1995. A different approach is found in *Pelican* and in *Marigold*, typefaces designed by Arthur Baker in 1989.
See also Chancery Italic; Script typefaces; Thibaudeau typeface classification; Typeface classification; Vox type classification

Calligraphy - A term derived from Greek, which refers to "beautiful writing" (*kalos*, beautiful; *graphein*, writing). The art of calligraphy requires an understanding of formal penmanship and a respect for traditional materials and tools. It is done freehand, with a certain style and with the components in proportion to each other and to the whole. From Roman times to the sixteenth century, such scripts as Half-uncial, Carolingian, humanistic, and their derivatives attained their finest forms in the service of religion, law and commerce. Both a formal and a freer cursive letters were used alternatively according to content. Printing did not eclipse interest in calligraphy, especially in sixteenth-century Italy where such writing masters as Ludovico Degli Arrighi, Giovanantonio Tagliente, Giovanni Francesco Cresci and Giovanbattista Palatino became famous, as did their English contemporaries, John Baildon and Roger Ascham, and later, George Shelley, Martin Billingsley, and George Bickham. Four classic texts on Western calligraphy are George Shelley's *Alphabets in All Hands* (1710?); George Bickham's *The Universal Penman* (1733); Ramón Stirling's *Bellezas de la Caligrafía* (1843), and Edward Johnston's *Writing & Illuminating & Lettering* (1906). On pages 50, 51, 101, 122, 123, 128, 130, 131, 139, 142, 143, 179, 195, 196, 227, and 228, we may find excellent examples of this art.
See also Brush; Calligrammes; Calligraphic typefaces; Hand lettering; Lettering; Script typefaces; Uncials

Cameo - A term applied for a typeface in which individual characters are reversed white on a solid or shaded background. These typefaces appeared in the early nineteenth century. The first examples were *Egyptians*, *Fat Faces*, and *Tuscans* reversed white on black background. Different from contemporary versions, in which letters are separated by a white line, original designs appeared on continuous black grounds with no separation between characters. The name refers to those jewels, which contain a figure or portrait carved in relief on precious stones, such as onyx, agate, etc., which having two layers of different colors –one lighter than the other– permit the differentiation between the figure and the background. English type founder William Thorowgood showed such typefaces in the specimen book of 1828. We find a contemporary example in ▦▦▦▦▦ ▦▦▦▦▦ designed by Arthur Baker in 1994.
See also Ornamented typefaces

Capital letters - Characters of larger size and different structure than lowercase letters, which are normally used in starting sentences or proper names. When a text is set in only "caps," it is said that it has been set in **sustained caps**. The name derives from the inscriptional letters at the head, or capital, of Roman columns. They are

ABCDEFGHIJKLMNOPQRSTUVWXYZ

It is interesting to note that in order to avoid the use of two different alphabets, American graphic designer Bradbury Thompson proposed an alphabet, which mixed both letters within the same font in 1944. Issued commercially in 1950, as *alphabet 26* (see page 240), he used *Baskerville* as the basis for his typeface design.

See also Carolingian script; Lowercase letters; Majuscules; Minuscules; Small caps; Trajan Column

Cap line - An imaginary line that runs across the top of uppercase letters. It is important to observe that curve letters, such as **C, G, J, O, Q, S**, and **U** go above this line and below the baseline somewhat to compensate for an optical size. Letter **A** also goes above the cap line for the same reason. The cap line is usually placed below the ascender line, although in some alphabets may be on the same level or slightly above.

See also Apex; Ascender line; Baseline; Guidelines; Proportional size

Cardinal numbers - It is the name given to a normal sequence of numbers, such as **one, two, three, four**, etc. They may be expressed graphically as 1234567890 or as 1234567890

See also Modern style numbers; Old style numbers; Ordinal numbers

Carolingian script - A name given to the round handwriting style with clubbed ascenders and a minimum of ligatures and cursive features, which was developed during the Emperor Charlemagne's reign (771-814) at the Abbey of St Martin at Tours, France, with the aid of Alcuin of York, who became Abbot of Tours after 786. At St. Martin, Alcuin had over 200 monks, many of them working at the *scriptorium*. Alcuin also introduced punctuation marks and the grouping of words into sentences, which, for the first time, began with a capital letter. Carolingian script was the standard letterform well into the eleventh century. At the end of the twelfth-century, Carolingian script had a typically Gothic character.

See also Calligraphy; Capital letters; Initials; Black letter; Gothic letter; Paragraph; Punctuation marks

Casting - *See* Typecasting

Centered type composition - *See* Symmetrical typography

Chancery italic/Script - A cursive handwriting used in administrative offices for official documents and letters. It was developed in the Papal Chancery in Rome during the fifteenth and sixteenth centuries. This design provided the model for the subsequent development of the italic typeface. The earliest

known humanist cursive dates from 1446. Although *cancelleresca corsiva* had been developed and perfected in the Papal Chancery since the pontificate of Pope Pius II, it was not until 1522 that one of its finest exponents, Ludovico Degli Arrighi, published *La Operina*, a book containing engraved specimens of the script. With this book this handwriting became familiar and named as such. Degli Arrighi's work will serve as a model for the first true italic, designed by Robert Granjon in 1566, and then for *Arrighi*, designed by Frederic Warde in 1925 as an accompanying face to Bruce Rogers's Centaur designed in 1914.

See also Calligraphy; Italics

Chapbook cuts - Crude and lively wood cuts which were very popular during the eighteenth century. They were used to illustrate paper-covered booklets known as *chapbooks*, which contained poems or ballads, sometimes of religious nature. The name refers to the chapmen who sold them on the street. In America, the chapbook era was from about 1725 to 1825. Supplies were imported from England until the 1750s, when printers in Philadelphia and Boston began making them in America. One of the best-known examples is the *American Chap-Book* magazine designed by William Bradley between 1904 and 1905, an in-house advertising publication of the American Type Founders Company. On page 97, we may see several examples of these cuts, all designed by Bradley.

See also Vignette

Character - Any individual letter, symbol, sign, or punctuation mark in the written system of a language that has been cast as a type for printing.

See also Analphabetic characters; Complete font; Foundry type; Letterpress; Type; Typeface

Chase - A steel rectangular metal frame into which metal type and blocks are locked by means of wooden wedges or small metal expanding boxes, called **quoins**, for proofing or printing. It is used in letterpress printing. The subdivided frame, invented around 1470-1480, was quite an important advancement in the art of letterpress printing for it permitted the printing of several pages at the same time. A proof of this advancement is the 1501 *octavo* edition of Virgil's *Opera* printed by Aldus Manutius in Venice and the 1629 vest-pocket editions of Latin classics and French literature by the Dutch Elzevir family.

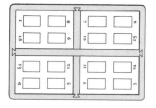

See also Format; Letterpress; Octavo; Quarto; Sextodecimo

Cicero - A European typographic unit of measure, derived from the Didot System established by François-Ambrose Didot in 1783, which measures twelve Didot points, and is slightly larger than

the American pica. Its name derives from the fact that Peter Schöfer's edition of Cicero's *De Oratore*, published in 1458, was set in 12-pt type, known since then as *cicero*. The *cicero* is also used all over Europe except in England and Ireland.

See also Didot measuring system; Pica; Point system; Type sizes

Clarendon serifs - Very heavy bracketed and squared-cut letter vertical and horizontal strokes terminals.

See also Bracketed serif; Clarendon style typefaces; Legibility Group; Serifs; Typeface classification

Clarendon style typefaces - A term used to describe the typefaces that became popular in the 1850s, and which were modified Egyptian style letters. Serifs are normally heavy, bracketed, and usually square-cut. Benjamin Fox of the London foundry W. Thorowgood & Besley originally designed and registered this style of typeface in 1845. But, no sooner had the copyright ended three years later than the market was inundated with copies and imitations. It probably owes its name to Clarendon Press in Oxford or to Britain's Earl of Clarendon for his interest in that country's Egyptian policies. A contemporary example may be found in CRAW CLARENDON/Craw Clarendon, designed by Freeman Craw in 1958.

See also Bracketed serifs; Legibility Group; Serifs; Typeface classification

Close spacing - A type set with very little area between letters and words. Some display types have been designed to allow this type of spacing. Such is the case of **MACHINE**, designed by Tom Carnase in 1970. It is also interesting to note that much of Herb Lubalin's typographical work was characterized by close spacing as may be seen on pages 187 and 188.

See also Kerning; Letter spacing

Coated paper (smooth finish) - Paper which has received sizing, a technique which decreases porosity and absorbency during its manufacturing. After the paper is calendered, a coating containing finely divided pigments and a water-based bind is deposited on the paper. These papers are specially manufactured for publications needing high-quality printing. In 1881, as the publishers of the *Century Magazine* demanded a degree of excellence in its printing which was then unknown, Theodore Low De Vinne requested the manufacturing of coated paper (developed by S. D. Warren & Company of Boston, largely at his insistence). This type of paper permitted him to print fine-line wood engravings and later on, halftone plates, which made him into a leading printer in the United States.

See also Calendered paper

Cold type - A term used generally to refer to a type that is set by means other than casting molten metal. Apparently it was coined as an opposite term to "hot composition." It refers more specifically, to describing typewritten or strike-on composition rather than photocomposition. Movable type set by hand, as well as dry transfer type, is also referred to as cold type.

See also Digital typesetting; Hot type; Movable type; Photocomposition; Transfer type

Colon (:) - A punctuation mark consisting of two points, one above the other, which is used after a word or a phrase to open a new content, as in the salutation of a letter; to start a list; to begin a direct quote, a definition, etc. Such as *Colon: a punctuation mark*. It is also used in mathematics as a sign to express division, such as 4:2=2

See also Comma; Punctuation marks; Semicolon

Colophon - A brief technical inscription placed at the end of a book, generally on the left page, which contains facts about the printer, date of production, typographical characteristics, number of issues, and type of paper. The first printed colophon appeared in the *Psalterium Romanum* or *Mainz Psalter*, printed by Johann Fust and Peter Schöffer in 1457.

See also Printer's mark

Column - A name given to the vertical arrangement of lines of a text. A page may contain as many columns as needed depending on the content. Columns may be type composed justified, flush left, flush right, or centered, according to a specific layout. The width of a column is measured in picas, and its depth or height, in points.

The term column also refers to a vertical section of a chart.

See also Agate; Centered type composition; Flush left type composition; Flush right type composition; Layout; Line length; Pica; Point

Comma (,) - A punctuation mark used to indicate a pause while reading. It separates independent clauses, words in a series, items in a list, figures, etc. Its shape changes, as in the case of a period, according to the type design. In American English, the comma, like the period, is always placed inside quotation marks. Historically, the comma was already in use in ninth-century Greek manuscripts.

See also Apostrophe; Period; Punctuation marks; Quotation marks; Semicolon

Commercial typefaces - Type designs that are issued for general use as retail typefaces. Today, they may be bought directly from a digital type foundry or as part of a design program offered for desktop publishing.

See also Custom typefaces

Complete font - A total set of characters, including capital letters, lowercase letters, special characters, numbers, signs, and punctuation marks within one size and one style. Most text typefaces include small caps. For the sake of space and standardization, the fonts displayed in this book only contain upper case, lowercase, numbers, and two punctuation marks.

See also Alphabet; Expert fonts; Font; Type nomenclature

Composing room - *See* Type composing room

Composing stick - *See* Type composing stick

Compositor - *See* Type compositor

Computerized type composition - *See* Digital type composition

Condensed typefaces - Those characters with a narrower width than a regular version, as is the case of News Gothic Condensed. A condensed version of a typeface is usually designed for saving space as well as to hold the same information in minimum-sized areas. It is important to note that certain type designs are structurally condensed and have no other widths. Such is the case of HUXLEY VERTICAL, designed by Walter Huxley in 1935.

We may assume that both condensed and extended variations in a typeface design may have appeared during the nineteenth century, and with wood types, as may be seen on pages 205 and 206.

See also Close spacing; Extended typeface; Regular typeface; Typeface classification

Constructivism - Initially influenced by Cubism, Futurism, and Suprematism, this Russian art and architectural movement started in 1913 with the counter-reliefs done by Vladimir Tatlin. This movement was further developed in 1917, shortly after the Bolshevik Revolution. In an attempt to redefine the role of the artist and contribute to the "construction" of a new Communist state, the members of the movement became divided into two main groups (often known as the *utopian* and the *utilitarian* or productivist) and directed their energies towards two different goals. While the first group was interested in personal expression, the second group was interested in making utilitarian designs for the masses. Thus, while the work of the utopians, Antoine Pevsner and Naum Gabo, remained on spatial-sculptural terms, the work of the utilitarian Vladimir Tatlin, El Lissitzky, Aleksandr Rodchenko, Varvara Stepanovna, and the Stenberg brothers, among others, covered industrial design, graphic design, theater design, photography, and film. After the group was dissolved as a consequence of their opposing ideals and the political climate of the early 1920s in Russia, Gabo, Pevsner, and others moved to the West, while El Lissitzky went to the German Bauhaus school, ensuring the spread of the Constructivism principles throughout Europe and later in America. Constructivists' graphic work embraced collage, photography, photomontage, and new printing technologies, and was typified by the use of bold lettering design and sans serif typefaces (such as *Akzidenz Grotesk* and *Venus* in all their weights), typographical rules, and a reduced and symbolic palette which stressed the use of red and black. Although Constructivists did not directly design type, their attitude towards their use of sans serif typefaces fructified through the influence of El Lissitzky in the Bauhaus, through Jan Tschichold (*Elementare Typographie* 1925), and Herbert Bayer.

See also Asymmetrical typography; Bauhaus; Futurism; Sans serif typefaces

Contour typefaces - Letterforms that, being described by outline, maintain the rest of the stroke inside. Although wrongly named, we find an early example of a contour typeface in *Gothic Condensed Outline*, a wood type issued by American Darius Wells in 1849 (see page 257). A contemporary example is **ERAS CONTOUR / Eras Contour**, designed by Albert Boton and Albert Hollenstein for Studio Hollenstein of Paris in 1961.

See also Outline typefaces; Stroke; Typeface classification

Contrast - It is the degree of difference between the thick and the thin strokes in letterforms. While *Transitional* typefaces present a greater general contrast than *Oldstyle*, *Modern* typefaces present a greater contrast than *Transitional*. Sans serif typefaces, on the other hand, present very little or no contrast at all in their strokes.

See also Modern typefaces; Modulation; Sans serif typefaces; Serifs; Transitional typefaces

Copyright symbol (©) - A pi character used at the end of a name or title to testify and ensure ownership. To meet requirements of the Universal Copyright Convention, publishers in subscribing countries must ensure that the first and all subsequent editions of a work bear the symbol ©, the name of the copyright owner, and the year of publication. Apart from this symbol, there are other equally used symbols: ® (Registered), and ™ (Trade Mark).

See also Analphabetic characters; Pi characters

Counter space - Also called counter form, it is the inside opening or white area within a letter. Counter spaces may be closed as in letters **b**, **d**, **e**, **g**, **o**, **p**, and **q**, or partially open as in letters **c**, **h**, **k**, **m**, **n**, **s**, **t**, **u**, **v**, **x**, **y**, and **z**. Letters like **e** and **a**, present both open and closed spaces. Typefaces such as Bembo and Centaur present reduced counter spaces, while sans serif typefaces such as News Gothic and Helvetica present large counter spaces.

See also Anatomy of a typeface; Type nomenclature; x-height

Cover - The harder material to which the body of a publication (book or magazine) is secured. A design is usually printed on it as a graphic presentation and identification. The cover of a machine-bound book is called a **case**. In hard-cover editions, books usually have a jacket which includes inner flaps containing a brief note about the author and the publication. On pages 45, 105, 112, 115, 122, 123, 128, 131, 142, 143, 161, 171, 179, 183, 187, 188, we may find some examples.

See also Book spine; Title page

Criblé initials - A French name applied to those decorated initials containing small white dots on their corresponding black areas. This practice was introduced by engravers to compensate for the impossibility of obtaining a solid black background due to the imperfections of early presswork during the sixteenth century. Principally, French printer, Geofroy Tory, used *criblé* initials at the beginning of chapters in his work. This practice, besides adding a texture to a given surface, permitted a more even visual reading. We find an example in **KIGALI / Kigali**, a type designed by Arthur Baker in 1994.

See also Handtooled typefaces; Incised typefaces

Croquill pen - A fine metal pen used for calligraphy and hand lettering. Originally called **crow quill pen**, for being manufactured from the quill of the crow's wing, it was cut to a fine point and used for writing with ink. Quills were also obtained from geese and swans. The steel nib was invented in the sixteenth century and has survived to the present day in a variety of forms. In 1808, the nib and the penholder became two separate elements, making nibs interchangeable and replaceable. Today, well-known letterers like Tom Carnase, Tony DiSpigna, and Edward Benguiat, among others, use this type of pen.

See also Calligraphy; Hand lettering; Reed pen; Spencerian script

Cross bar - A horizontal stroke in a letter, which joints two vertical strokes as in letters **A** and **H**. In Art Deco style typefaces, cross bars, and medium arms were placed below or above center, introducing a particular feature to the font.

See also Art Deco; Anatomy of a typeface; Type nomenclature

Cross bar line - An imaginary horizontal line placed between the cap line and the baseline (it's different from the **mean line**) that helps to determine the position of cross bars in capital letters **A** and **H**. The difference in position of this letter component makes these letters acquire a particular form which directly affects the general style of the whole font. A clear example may be found in typefaces designed in Art Deco style, such as BERNHARD FASHION / Bernhard Fashion (Lucian Bernhard, 1929).

See also Analphabetic of a typeface; Arm; Art Deco; Ascender line; Baseline; Cap line; Descender line; Guidelines; Mean line; Middle arm line; Trajan Column

Cubism - A name given to an artistic movement that emerged in France between 1907 and 1909 with the work of George Braque and Pablo Picasso. Based on the premise stated by Paul Cézanne that the painter should "treat nature in terms of the cylinder and the sphere and the cone," and the rejection of the use of the system and laws of perspective inherited since the Renaissance, these painters started to visualize subject matter from different angles by fragmenting it, and then simultaneously recomposing it in a series of rhythmic, geometric planes. Abstract forms of primitive sculpture from Africa, Oceania, and Iberia were also a definite influence on their synthetic and expressive perception of human forms. In its first stage, known as *Analytic Cubism* (1909-1912), paintings were often complex and difficult to discern. In a second stage, known as *Synthetic Cubism* (1912-1914), the group developed less complex compositions, introducing collage, and assemblage. By this time, other artists had shared the Cubist principles through their paintings (Juan Gris, Lionel Feininger, Jean Metzinger), and sculptures (Jacques Lipchitz, Aleksandr Archipenko, Raymond Duchamp-Villon). The influence of Cubism can also be seen in Futurism, Suprematism, and Constructivism. Cubist painting also incorporated letterforms and words both as visual elements and for associated meanings. Its effects on graphic design may be more easily seen in applied typography through the presence of isolated type block compositions on the printed page.

See also Constructivism; Dada; Futurism

Currency symbols - Monetary signs which form part of a complete character set, and usually include one or two crossing lines. They also are initials of the current money. The **$** is a descendant of the old symbol for the *shilling* (*ſ*).

The most frequent signs are: **$ ¢ ƒ £ ¥ €**.
See also Analphabetic characters; Punctuation marks

Cursive typefaces - A type style similar to hand-writing, but which has non-connecting letters. We find an example in ***Cascade Script***, designed by Matthew Carter in 1966.

See also Italics; Calligraphic typefaces; Script typefaces

Custom typefaces - Type designs that, created for a particular client or firm, are not commercially produced. Generally speaking, these types are commonly designed for newspapers, magazines, etc. After a time of exclusive use, custom typefaces are generally issued as retail designs or commercial typefaces. We may find two early American examples in CENTURY ROMAN / Century Roman, and in CHELTENHAM / Cheltenham typefaces. The first one was designed by Linn Boyd Benton for the

Century Magazine, by request of Theodore Low De Vinne in 1864, and the second, by Bertram Grosvenor Goodhue by request of Ingalls Kimball for the Cheltenham Press in New York in 1904.
See also Commercial typefaces; Private press

D

Dada - A name given to an artistic and literary movement reflecting a widespread protest against all aspects of western culture, especially towards the exercise of military means, which appeared during and after World War I (1914-1918). The term was coined at random by Rumanian-born poet, essay-writer, and editor Tristan Tzara, who started the movement in 1916, with German writer Hugo Ball, Alsatian-born artist, Jean Arp, and other intellectuals living in Zurich. A similar movement occurred simultaneously in New York City led by Man Ray, Marcel Duchamp, and Francis Picabia, and in Paris, where it became the inspiration for the Surrealist movement. Dadaists used novel materials, including discarded objects found on the streets, and new methods, such as allowing chance to determine their works. Worthy of mention are the collages carried out by Kurt Schwitters, and the *ready-made objects* by Marcel Duchamp. Dadaist's experiments with typography were a blend of the random Cubist *papier collés* and the Futurist *parole a libertá* with the efficiency of mechanical reproduction techniques. Widely scattered and mixed typography, with different sizes and weights, exemplified this approach to layout. On many occasions the use of red and black permitted the use of transparencies and the printing of simultaneous messages. Dadaists also innovated in photographic terms by creating *photomontage*, which in the hands of John Heartfield became a medium for political criticism. After 1922 many members of this movement moved on to either Surrealism or to Constructivism.

See also Calligrammes; Constructivism; Cubism; Futurism; Post-modernism; Surrealism

Dagger (†) - Footnote reference mark that is used as a complementary sign to the asterisk (*), or other reference mark. The footnote is always preceded by an identical reference mark. An accompanying design is the double dagger (‡). The dagger is also a sign of mortality, used to mark the year of death or the names of deceased persons.
See also Asterisk; Paragraph; Reference marks

Dash (— – -) - A horizontal stroke which varies in length depending of its use in hyphening, to join two complementary words or to separate sentences with marked difference in content in a sentence.

Its length determines the name of a dash, as is the case of **em dash** (—), **en dash** (–) and **hyphen** (-).
See also Hyphening

De Stijl (The Style) - A Dutch art movement and magazine created by painter and designer Théo Van Doesburg, in Amsterdam in 1917. It included painters, such as Piet Mondrian, Vilmos Huszár, architect Jacobus Oud, and poet A. Kok. Other associates of De Stijl were Bart Van der Leck, George Vantongerloo, Jan Wills, Robert Van t'Hoff, and Gerrit Rietveld. While working in an abstract style, they searched for equilibrium and harmony in both art and life. The most representative

painter, Mondrian, sought for clarity and order in his work that would also express his religious and philosophical beliefs. By eliminating all representational components, he reduced painting to its basic elements: straight lines and flat color surfaces, limiting his chromatic scheme to the use of primary colors –yellow, red, blue– and the neutrals –black, gray and white– which had a deep influence both on design and on architecture. The graphic and typographical design was very disciplined, and the employment of sans serif typefaces and asymmetrical designs provided a foretaste of the International Typographic Style. Van Doesberg introduced De Stijl's ideas to the Bauhaus while he lived in Weimar.
See also Bauhaus; International Typographic Style; Sans serif typefaces

Decals, Decalcomania - Transferable printed works, made possible through the use of a special printing process which permits the separation of the printed area from the supporting material by moistening the whole piece, and then sticking it to any surface, usually more rigid, such as paper, glass, plastic, etc. *Letraset* originally used this process before it became a **dry-transfer type** (see page 265).
See also Transfer type

Decorated typefaces - Those large display letterforms whose wide strokes permit heavy ornamentation. They were very popular during the first half of the nineteenth century, thanks to wood type engraving. We find an example in DORIC ORNAMENTED, a wood type issued by Darius Wells in 1854.
See also Floriated initials; Historiated letters; Initials

Descender - A vertical stem that extends below the baseline of a lowercase letter, as in the case of **g**, **j**, **p**, **q**, and **y**. In italic and calligraphic typefaces, we may find the letter *f* having a descender as well.
See also Anatomy of a typeface; Ascender; Baseline; Body size; Type nomenclature

Descender line - An imaginary horizontal line that runs across the limit of lowercase descenders, and determines how much they extend downwards from the baseline.
See also Anatomy of a typeface; Ascender line; Baseline; Body; Cap line; Guidelines

Design axis - In multiple master typefaces, it is a variable which permits innumerable formal changes between one extreme variant and another. Based on the five basic variants of a typeface: weight, width, style, stress, and size, the design axis allows for minute changes between one variant and another. In crossing variants of a different nature, the multiple master permits the possibility of simultaneously passing from a light to a bold typeface, and from a condensed to an extended variant. Some fonts are based on three design axes, allowing for changes of weight, width and size without altering the original letterform. Adobe Systems, Inc., is developing design axes that incorporate style design axes, which permits a typeface to pass from a sans serif to a serif.
See also Master design; Multiple Master typefaces; Design matrix; Type form variants

Design matrix - In multiple master typefaces, it is a design based on one of the four basic type form variants: proportion, dimension, value, and structure. Thus, every type design has four basic variants, which contemplate weight, width, size, and style. Once the two ends of the axis are determined, a design matrix permits making minute changes of shape in a typeface, supplying the user with the exact weight and width he needs for a specific design. More complex design matrices are also possible using additional design axes, for example, ranging from a small text type master to a large display master design or from a sans serif to a serif style.

See also Design axis; Master design; Multiple master typefaces

Desktop publishing - A computer set-up with which a person may control all the components of an entire document –images, texts, and output– through the use of a package of computer software, such as word processors, font libraries, drawing units, scanners, laser printers, etc., freeing the person from outside resources. With the use of a monitor he may visualize the finished layout with no need for pasting up type and illustrations.

See also Digital typography; PostScript; Printer fonts; Screen fonts

Diacritical signs - Distinguishing marks used to indicate different sounds of a letter, accents, diæresis, cedilla, etc.

See also Accent; Analphabetic characters

Didot measurement system - A type measuring system established by French printer and typographer, François-Ambroise Didot in 1783, and used extensively throughout Europe, except in England and Ireland. Based on the work of French type founder and punch-cutter Pierre-Simon Fournier, *le jeune* (1737), it has the point as unit. Twelve points make a *cicero*. Didot divided the *pied du roi* (royal foot) in twelve French inches, each of which contained 72 pts. He also introduced today's custom of identifying type by their point body measure rather than by a given name.

See also Cicero; Point; Type sizes

Die cutting - A method by which stamping cuts a shape. The die is made by fitting a steel cutting rule into the slots cut on a piece of wood, very much like heavy-duty cookie cutters. As early as 1852, this new procedure to manufacture type appeared in the wood type market. In 1879, William Hamilton Page introduced wood type ornaments die cut, and between 1887 and 1890, wood type letters. We may see an example of die cutting ornaments on page 205.

Digital type composition - Typesetting done through a computer. One of the main advantages of computer typesetting is that it can take all the variables and refinements of typography and store them in a memory bank. The working tools offer extensive possibilities including such modification formats as indenting, undercutting letters, negative leading, kerning, modification in letter proportions, etc. Variations in typefaces and point sizes are automatically base-aligned.

See also Baseline; Digital typography; Indented paragraph; Kerning; Negative leading; Phototypography

Digital typography - Characters that are drawn through a series of fine dots or lines that create the shape of each of the individual signs. The resolution of dots or lines for text size is 900 dots per linear inch; the resolution for display type is nearly 2,000.

Point sizes normally range from 4½ pt to 96 pt, with a maximum width of 80 picas. The result of this composition is a master film, in positive or negative form according to the printing needs.

See also Baseline; Bitmap character; Desktop publishing; Digital composition; Photocomposition; Phototypography

Digitization - The process of converting a drawing or a typeface contour into a set of short lines, which a computer can process to reproduce the original image. This process differs from a scanned image, which is comprised of a color or monochrome specification of each element of a grid placed over the original image. In 1960, French engineer Pierre Bézier, a former employee of Renault, developed the Bézier curves and surfaces for CAD/CAM operations, which became the underpinning of the entire Adobe *PostScript* drawing model as well as for 3D drawing programs. The Illustrating sample is by Charles Bigelow.

See also Digital typography; PostScript; Resolution

Dingbats - Representational decorations generally extracted from daily imagery. Many of them are pictograms –small pictures of objects, such as telephones, scissors, planes, envelopes, etc.– and some are abstract symbols –crowns, crosses, hearts, stars, pointing hands, etc. They both permit adding a visual interpretation to a text. In 1978, German type designer Hermann Zapf designed a series of 360 dingbats under the name *Zapf Dingbats 100*, of which the following are some samples.

See also Bullets; Fleurons; Pi characters; Typographical ornaments

Direct printing - That which is obtained from straight contact between the inked raised form and the paper or other type of material like parchment. Such is the case in letterpress. As additional information, Johannes Gutenberg printed the *42-line Bible*, in 1456, on both paper and parchment.

See also Foundry type; Indirect printing; Letterpress

Display type - Typesetting which uses the full range of type sizes and weights to ensure that the information conveyed stands apart from continuous text settings and is readable from a certain distance. It usually covers type sizes 14 pt and above, and is exemplified primarily by headlines and titles. It is important to note that from the time of the invention of printing up to the eighteenth century there was no call for display type. To be a printer meant to be a printer of books and even in books, title pages did not appeared until 1500. The casting of display types designed for jobbing or ephemeral printing that is for advertising purposes, did not take place until the second half of the eighteenth century. England took the lead in this field. The first large display metal typeface (two inches high) was cast in 1765 by English type-cutter and founder Thomas Cottrell, a former apprentice at William Caslon's type foundry.

The manufacturing of large size display typefaces, such as the wood types introduced by Darius Wells after 1828, made possible the development of poster design in America.

See also Book face; Text type; Typeface classification

Dot leader - A row of evenly spaced periods often used to link a flush-left text with flush-right numerals, as found in a **table of contents**.

See also Ellipses; Period

Dot-matrix printer - A computer-linked printing device that uses a pattern of dots to create a printed character. In 1984, Charles Bigelow and Kris Holmes designed LUCIDA/Lucida, which was the first typeface developed to cope with the low resolution of dot-matrix printers.

See also Bitmap character; Digital typography; Resolution

Double spread - A term generally used to refer to two facing pages on which matter is managed directly across as if there were only one graphic entity. William Morris regarded two facing pages as the unit. On page 130, we may see how William Addison Dwiggins made use of a double spread to unify information and graphics on the book layout for H. G. Wells' *The Time Machine*, published by Random House, New York, in 1931.

See also Layout; Page

E

Ear - Small stroke that projects from the upper right side of the bowl of a serif type lowercase letter g. Although this feature is characteristic of serifed letters, some sans serif types may also include it as is the case Lydian (g) (Warren Chappell, 1938).

See also Anatomy of a typeface; Ball terminal; Bowl; Loop; Tear drop terminal

Egyptian typefaces - Letterforms characterized by slab-like serifs similar in weight to the main strokes. They are also characterized by a fairly monotone color, short descenders, and a number of features common to *Modern* typefaces. Although the term was first used for a typeface designed in 1816 by William Caslon IV when he applied it to the first English sans serif typeface, the name *Egyptian* really described a group of display types shown in the 1815 specimen book of Vincent Figgins. Even so, it was William Thorowgood who first used the name when he printed *A New Specimen of Printing Types* in 1821. This style seems to be a product of the heightened interest in the early nineteenth century for all things that were Egyptian, encouraged after Napoleon Bonaparte's expedition to that country. Egyptian typefaces were also referred to as "antiques." According to Daniel Berkeley Updike in his book *Printing Types, Their History, Forms and Use*, they were probably called so due to the "darkness" of the typefaces. He also cites an 1806 London jest-book's text that refers to "Fashionable Egyptian Sign-Boards," in which there is a mention of the even weight of all the strokes. It is also interesting to note that around 1821 there appeared in England a reversed Egyptian type design where serifs were thicker than the main stroke, as may be seen in PLAYBILL / Playbill, a contemporary typeface designed by Robert Harling in 1938. Another example of an Egyptian style design is found in ITC LUBALIN GRAPH / ITC Lubalin Graph, a typeface designed by Herb Lubalin and Tony DiSpigna for ITC in 1974.

See also Ionic typefaces; Modern type faces; Slab serif; Serifs; Typeface classification

Electrostatic printing - That which is based on photoconductivity, as is the case of Electrofax and Xerography.

See also Xerography

Electrotyping - A duplicating system of relief printing plates achieved by depositing a shell of copper on a mold of an original form. The shell was backed with type metal and blocked to be made to type-high. It was improved by 1837. The first American to experiment in electrotypes for printing cuts was Joseph A. Adams of New York who succeeded in supplying *Mape's Magazine* with an electrotype of one of his engravings, which was successfully printed in 1841. Most probably, the simultaneous printing of *The Holy Bible, with illustrations by Gustave Doré*, done in New York and London in 1866 was possible through the use of the electrotyping process.

See also Letterpress; Stereotyping

Elementare Typographie - See Asymmetrical typography

Ellipses (...) - An omission of one or several words which is shown typographically by three dots set in a row (...). Often used when a text has not been completely quoted.

See also Dot leader; Punctuation marks

Em space (■) - A unit of space equivalent to a square of the type body and represented by an **em-quad**. Its name derives from the fact that in early fonts the capital letter **M** was usually cast on a square body. This unit is used for computing the area of a printed page no matter what size of type is used for setting the text, and for determining the width of a letter through the use of a **unit system** based on the vertical division of its surface. It is also used for determining the initial space in an indented paragraph.

See also En space; Indented paragraph; Line Lenght; Outdented paragrpah; Quads; Unit system

En space (▌) - A unit of space equivalent to half the width of an **em-space**, and represented by an en-quad. Thus, the en-space of a 10-pt typeface is 5 pts wide.

See also Em space; Quads

End matter - Those sections of a book that normally follow the **main content**, such as appendices, the glossary, the bibliography, the index, etc. These sections are usually paged in sequence after the main content, also in Arabic numerals.

See also Arabic numerals; Body; Main content; Preliminary matter

Ex libris - See Bookplates

Exclamation points (¡ !) - Punctuation marks that are used to express surprise, strong feelings, or irony. The exclamation points became part of the generally accepted punctuation marks during the seventeenth century. Just as with question marks, English has only the closing form (!), while Spanish, since the eighteenth century, has both the opening and the closing forms (¡ !), which, by the way, permit the reader to know the type of content of a given sentence in advance. Its form

seems to have evolved from the Latin word io, "joy", expressed graphically with a capital I set over a lowercase o. In 1966, Martin K. Specker created the *interabang* or *interrobang*, which was an interlacing of a question mark and an exclamation point, and which was proposed as a graphic sign to express ambiguous sentences, such as You did what‽. That same year Richard Isbell designed Americana, and included the sign in the font (see page 172).

See also Punctuation marks; Question mark

Expert font - That which includes a series of typographical characters for specialized used, such as bilingual dictionaries, science, mathematics, classical texts, etc. Expert fonts are also very useful when setting texts in a foreign language.

See also Analphabetic characters; Complete font; Font; Pi characters; Small caps

Extended typefaces - They are wider versions of regular typefaces. However, we may remember that, as in the case of condensed typefaces, there are type designs that are originally extended, such as the case of **LATIN WIDE / Latin Wide** (Stephenson Blake & Co.).

Let's compare Helvetica Light Regular

with Helvetica Light Extended

We may assumed that both condensed and extended variations in a typeface design may have appeared during the nineteenth century, and with wood types, as may be seen on page 205.

See also Condensed typeface; Regular typeface

F

Face - That flat raised part of a metal or wood type that contains the design of a character, letter or sign that receives the ink. In direct contact with a surface, generally paper, it forms the image. On page 225, there is an illustration of a metal type, drawn by Rudolph Ruzicka.

The term is also used as an equivalent to **typeface**.

See also Letterpress; Type nomenclature; Typeface

***Facsimile* typefaces** - The re-cutting of existing typefaces (usually historical), taking into account all the imperfections and idiosyncrasies of the original; rather than modeling them to a more contemporary taste. The term *facsimile* comes from the Latin words, *facere*, to make; and *similis*, similar or like. It was coined around 1655-56. Two of the best examples that may be compared are English Monotype's *Poliphilus* (1923), cut under the direction of Stanley Morison and considered a *facsimile*, and *Bembo* (1929), also cut under his direction and considered a *revival*.

See also Reissue typeface; Revival typeface

Fat faces - A name that identifies those typefaces that exhibit an extreme contrast between their thick and thin strokes. The first fat faces appeared in England in 1803, designed by English printer, Robert Thorne, as a variation on **BODONI / Bodoni**. They probably evolved in an attempt to define visual hierarchies within the printed matter. As such, they were initially seen on lottery handbills, and later in pamphlets, newspapers, etc. They were also the first typefaces directly designed for advertising purposes. Thorne's approach was soon copied by other type foundries. Although

fat faces were very popular during part of the nineteenth century, they somehow waned as the century advanced, only regaining popularity in the twentieth century when ATF commercially issued *Ultra Bodoni*, designed by Morris Fuller Benton in 1928. As a competitive design, Mergenthaler Linotype issued **POSTER BODONI / Poster Bodoni**, designed by Chauncey H. Griffith the same year.

See also Contrast; Modern style typefaces; Serifs; Shadowed typefaces; Typeface classification

Feet - In metal type, it is the base on which a type stands, being formed by a separating groove cut across the body by the dresser. On page 225, there is an illustration of a metal type, drawn by Rudolph Ruzicka, which clarifies the definition.

See also Type nomenclature

Figures - *See* Modern figures; Oldstyle figures; Subscript; Superscript

Fixed fonts - Bitmapped master fonts capable of setting a substantial range of type sizes.

See also Bitmap character; Digital typography

Floriated initials - Ornamental large letters cut in boxwood and set against a pattern of leaves, flowers, and sometimes birds, which were very popular during the twelfth century. Those initials with acanthus leaves evolved in the thirteenth-century into historiated letters. We find a contemporary example in *Cloister Initials* (page 145) designed by Frederic W. Goudy in 1918.

See also Historiated letters; Initials; Ornamented typefaces

Fleurons (❦) - A French name given to printer's flowers, and used by American designers like Frederic W. Goudy, as seen on page 143. *Fleurons* are often used as *vignettes* at the end of a text.

See also Dingbats; Printer's flowers

Flush type paragraph - A text setting where the starting line of a paragraph is not indented –as is the case of this book–, but set even with the rest of the text. Flush type paragraphs require a physical vertical separation, which, by the way, give a better readability to the page as compared to indented paragraphs, which are set without this additional space between them.

See also Indented paragraph; Justified type composition; Leading; Typesetting specifications

Flush left type composition - The arrangement of a text, lining it up vertically on the left. This is the case of all the texts of this book. Also known as **unjustified type composition**, the text column has a ragged edge on the right side. In 1931, English designer and printer Eric Gill, published his *Essay on Typography* where he plainly demonstrated his belief in the merit of typographical compositions with unjustified lines.

See also Asymmetric typography; Flush right type composition; Typesetting

Flush right type composition - The arrangement of a text, lining it up vertically on the right. Also known as **unjustified type composition**, the text column has a ragged edge on the left side. This type of composition is generally used on left marginal notes to create a better visual relation with the adjacent column.

See also Flush left type composition; Typesetting

Folio - A page number. It is important to keep in mind that preliminary pages in a book are commonly numbered using **Roman numerals**, while the main content is numbered with **Arabic numbers**. Also, even folios are always on the left-hand pages (2, 4, 6, etc.), and odd folios on the right-hand pages (1, 3, 5, etc.). The first book to have page folios (numbers) was St. Augustine's *De civitate Dei*, printed by German Johannes von Speier (da Spira) in Venice in 1470.

The term *folio* also refers to a book format resulting from folding a sheet of handmade paper or other material one time, thus reducing it to half of its original size. To fully define the proportions of a given publication, it is important to know the paper's original format, for it is difficult to clearly define its proportions by just referring to it as a *folio* or a *crown folio* edition. The Gutenberg *42-line Bible* (1456); the first edition of *Shakespeare's Comedies, Histories & Tragedies* (1623); and the first publication of the Imprimerie Royale du Louvre, Kempis' *De Imitatione Christi*, for example, were all printed *in folio*. While the *Bible* measures 11 3/4" x 16"; *De Imitatione Christi* measures 9 3/4" x 14 5/8".

See also Arabic numerals; Chase; Format; Pagination; Roman numerals

Font - The complete assembly of all the characters (upper and lowercase letters, small caps, punctuation marks, numerals and fractions, special characters, ligatures, and reference marks) in a given size, and within a particular type design. The number of characters also differs from one font to another, depending on the language, and the function for which it has been designed. A text typeface usually has more characters than a display typeface, more so if it is used to set specialized material. A font usually contains from 96 to 225 characters. In photocomposition, the definition of font is less orthodox since the potential for reductions, enlargements, and distortions enables the range of alphabet sizes to be extended endlessly.

See also Anatomy of a typeface; Complete font; Expert font; Pi characters

Foreword - A text that precedes the introduction, which is generally written by a person other than the author, in which the reasons for the book, its scope and content are explained. Different from the **Preface**, it doesn't change for a new edition.

See also Introduction; Preface; Preliminary matter

Form - A term used in letterpress to refer to type or other matter set for printing, locked up in a chase, from which either a printed impression is pulled or a plate is made. Once the form is set on the platen, which is an even metal surface, it is inked. Paper is then placed upon the form, and pressure is evenly applied to pull out copies.

See also Chase; Foundry type; Wood cut; Wood engraving; Galley proof; Letterpress

Format - Proportions of a given publication, which include position (vertical or horizontal). The word format comes from the **form** in which handmade paper was manufactured. It is useful to differentiate it from the term **size**, which refers to the dimensions of a publication, as is the case of pocketbook size. As the original paper format was folded with one, two, three, or four folds it permitted to obtain smaller

formats, such as *folio* (1/2), *quarto* (1/4), *octavo* (1/8), and *sextodecimo* (1/16).

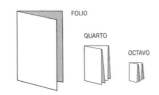

See also Chase; Folio; Proportion; Quarto; Octavo; Sextodecimo; Size

Foundry - *See* Type foundry

Foundry type - Metal type characters used in hand composition, cast individually by type founders, with the aid of a matrix, and a special alloy. From the invention of the manual caster for movable types done by Johannes Gutenberg around 1450, up until the invention of the automatic punch-cutter by Linn Boyd Benton in 1885, and the invention of the Monotype casting machine by Tolbert Lanston in 1887, the cutting and casting of individual metal typefaces was entirely done by hand. As a side note, it took six type compositors two years to produce the type needed for the printing of the 1,282 folio pages of the *Bible* done by Johannes Gutenberg in 1456.

See also Type foundry; Hand composition; Matrix; Metal type; Monotype; Type; Typecasting; Type compositor; Type metal

Fractions (1/4) - Compound characters used to express graphically a quantity that is not integral. Formed by a numerator and a denominator separated by a slash, they are cast as a unit. A standard character set only includes three of them: 1/4 1/2 3/4. **Piece fractions**, such as (1/16) or (1/32), must be built from separate component characters.

See also Expert font; Oldstyle figures; Modern style figures; Slash; Subscript; Superscript

Fraktur - A German form of **black letter** typeface believed to have been originated in Augsburg, around 1510, from designs done by Leonhard Wagner based on the fifteenth-century *lettre bâtarde*. Its name comes from the Latin, *fractus*, broken. It is characterized by a narrow and pointed letter, with uppercase letters essentially calligraphic. The first book to be printed in this type was the *Prayer Book of Maximilian I*, dated 1513. Nevertheless, it was writing master Johann Neudörfer's design of 1522 that became the commonly used one. This Fraktur type was also used by Albrecht Dürer in his book, *Triumphwagen* (1522). Fraktur types remained the German traditional letter until 1941, when Adolf Hitler ordered the use of the Roman typefaces as the *Nomalschrift* for writing the German language.

See also Black letter; Roman style typefaces

Freehand lettering - An irregular letterform structured to be more quickly written than the formal style of handwriting, such as *Chancery*. Today, it refers to a writing style frequently associated with advertising, in which letters and words are usually drawn with a brush or a similar drawing device. A good example may be found in *Murray Hill Bold* designed by Emil J. Klumpp in 1956.

See also Calligraphic typefaces; Calligraphy; Chancery; Hand lettering; Lettering; Script typefaces; Spencerian Script

Front matter - *See* Preliminary matter

Furniture - In letterpress, they are those rectangular pieces of wood, metal, or plastic, which are lower than type, and are used to fill in areas of blank spaces around the type and engravings when locking up the form for printing.

See also Chase; Letterpress; Quads

Futurism - A term coined by Italian poet Filippo Tommaso Marinetti in 1909, in his *Manifesto futurista* (*Manifeste du Futurism*) published in the French newspaper *Le Figaro*. It refers to a revolutionary artistic movement, which reflected an aggressive and controversial position against the static and irrelevant art of the past by celebrating change, originality, and innovation in culture and society. In his writing, Marinetti glorified the new technology of the automobile and the beauty of its speed, power, and movement. He also exalted violence and conflict and called for the eradication of traditional cultural, social, and political values and the destruction of cultural institutions such as museums and libraries. Among the most relevant artists of the movement were Umberto Boccioni, Giacomo Balla, and Gino Severini. Their futurist ideas extended to literature, music, dance, performance, painting, and architecture, as well as to everyday activities. Futurism was the first attempt in the twentieth-century to propose a new concept of life transfixed by new technologies. The impact on typography is most evident by the emergence of the typographer/poet, who challenged the tradition of the printed page and the predictable sequence of typographical information. Type elements and collage were used in a dynamic manner to create picture-poems, forerunners of concrete poetry. The direct influence of Futurism on typography is better seen in practice rather than particular type designs. The random placing of texts, the use of different typographic styles and sizes, and the inclusion of rules will later influence Dada and Constructivism.

See also Calligrammes; Constructivism; Dada; Rules

G

Galley - In letterpress, it is a long, shallow, three-sided metal tray that held type forms prior to printing. Type on the galley could be corrected more conveniently and economically than elsewhere. From the galley, type was transferred to the imposing stone where it was ordered. Galleys were usually stored in special compartments prior to being arranged into pages. The galley's length also helped to measure Linotype composition, and thus to know how much work was done by the compositor.

See also Foundry type; Galley proof; Hand composition; Linotype; Ludlow; Metal type; Monotype; Type composition

Galley proof - Also called a **rough proof**, it was the impression of type, usually metal type, as it had been composed, to allow for proofreading. The galley proof presented a column of as many lines as could fit in the metal tray or galley, which was around twenty-four inches long.

See also Galley; Linotype; Ludlow; Monotype; Type composition

Glossary - A set of defined terms which are used throughout a publication, usually limited to its content, as complementary information for the reader. It may or may not have cross-references or complementary images.

See also End matter

Glyphic Style typefaces - A term used to refer to those typefaces that tend to reflect lapidary inscriptions in their design rather than pen-drawn letterforms. There is a minimum of contrast in the stroke weight, and the axis of curved strokes tends to be vertical. A contemporary example may be found in **ITC SERIF GOTHIC / ITC Serif Gothic**, designed by Herb Lubalin and Tony DiSpigna in 1974.

See also Contrast; Inscriptional letters; Latin serif typefaces; Rubbing; Serifs; Typeface classification

Gothic letter - An alternative name for **black letter** –the printing typeface style used in fifteenth-century Europe. This name, by the way, was an ironic nickname given by the Renaissance humanists to the compressed, angular, and heavy style of writing. Developed as formal book lettering, the early Gothic style of tall, narrow, black letter made with great precision and even spaces resembled a woven fabric, and was appropriately named *textura* (from the Latin, *textus*, plaited). Written with an upright holding of the pen, the first simple broken letters became even more broken, and with few exceptions, they were all upright.

In America, probably because of the rigidity of letterforms, this term is also used as an alternative name for *Grotesque* types, such as **ALTERNATE GOTHIC / Alternate Gothic**, designed by Morris Fuller Benton in 1903, or **ITC AVANT GARDE GOTHIC / ITC Avant Garde Gothic**, designed by Herb Lubalin and Tom Carnase in 1970.

See also Black letter; Book face; Carolingian script; Fraktur; Typeface classification

Graphic Design - A term that refers to a communication language that combines typography, illustration, photography, and printing for the purpose of transmitting a given message, which may be of a varied nature, such as institutional, commercial, political, instructional, informational, persuasive, etc. American designer William Addison Dwiggins is given credit for the first use of the term "graphic designer" which he used in 1922 to define his work. Today, graphic design covers a wider scope including visual communication languages, as well as graphic and typographic research.

See also Type Design; Typogram; Typography

Grid - A layout device consisting of a group of crossed lines generally vertical and horizontal, and some times diagonal. They are used as guides to divide a given space to resolve rationally problems of proportion and placement of images and text. Although grids were used by calligraphers to give proportions to a text on a page, as may be seen in examples cited by Philip Meggs in his book, *History of Graphic Design* (1983), most certainly the first contemporary designer to make use of the grid was German typographer Jan Tschichold, who in his book *Die neue Tipographie* (1928), laid down the principles employed by the Swiss designers almost twenty years later when they created the International Typographic Style.

See also International Typographic Style; Layout; Proportion

Grotesque typefaces - A term used to refer to the first sans serif typefaces that appeared in Germany and England during the nineteenth century. A common characteristic is found in the use of two-storey **g** and **a** lowercase letters, and the use of a spur in capital **G**. An example may be found in **News** Gothic (1908, Morris Fuller Benton). They differ from the later sans serif typefaces, such as **Futura** (**g a**) (Paul Renner, 1927), for being less geometric in their structure. Since 1942, revivals of hand-cut nineteenth-century grotesques have come into use. They are also known as *grots*. American type designers, David Berlow has developed a series of grotesque typeface designs as custom typefaces for several American publications.

See also Custom typefaces; Humanist sans serif; Sans serif typefaces; Spur; Typeface classification

Guidelines - Horizontal lines, commonly used by type designers, which provide vertical limits for particular aspects in a letter and define its relationship to other characters. They may also be used define certain type style characteristics. Usually only four of them are mentioned, but there are seven guidelines to be considered: ascender line, cap line, mean line, medium arm line, cross bar line, baseline, and descender line. In medieval times, horizontal guidelines were drawn to contain and align each line of lettering. While the *Uncial* was written on a two-line grid, the *Half-uncial* was drawn on a four-line writing system.

See also Alignment; Anatomy of a typeface; Art Deco; Ascender line; Baseline; Cap line; Cross bar line and middle arm line; Descender line; Half-uncial; Mean line; Uncial; x-height

H

Hairline - Thin strokes present in the configuration of a typeface. They may be vertical, horizontal, or diagonal according to the letter design. Also, due to the style, they have a corresponding heavy or main stroke. We find an example in DIDOT / Didot, designed by Firmin Didot in 1784.

See also Anatomy of a typeface; Cross bar line; Contrast; Fat Faces; Hairline serifs; Modern style typefaces; Serifs; Stroke; Type nomenclature

Hairline serifs - Unbracketed type stroke terminals present in *Modern* typefaces, such as DIDOT / Didot (Firmin Didot, 1784) or BODONI / Bodoni (Giambattista Bodoni, 1788). They are usually placed at straight angles with the main stem.

See also Modern typefaces; Serifs; Thibaudeau typeface classification

Half title - A name given to the title of a book appearing on the upper right portion of the first page following the front flyleaf and preceding the full title page. The *verso* sometimes contains an illustration, called **frontispiece**, which contains images related to content or a portrait of the author.

See also Preliminary matter; Title page

Half-uncial - By the fall of the Roman Empire, a more extreme form of *Uncial* had developed, which

consisted mostly of lowercase letters. This script was based on a four-line writing system. From the sixth- to the twelfth century, the use of the *Uncial script* spread throughout Europe receiving certain national modifications in each country, such as *Insular* hand (Ireland and England), *Merovingian* (France), Lombardic (Italy), and *Visigothic* (Spain). The Irish *Half-uncial*, which developed around AD 600, was introduced later in Europe, influencing *Carolingian minuscule* letters which in turn became the basis of our lowercase roman letters. One of the finest manuscripts written in *Half-uncial* script is the *Book of Kells*, written in the Abbey of Kells in Ireland, probably in the late eighth or early ninth-century. The name comes from the Latin word *uncia*, inch, or the equivalent of $^1/_{12}$ part of the foot (11.6"). Initially, Romans used the word *uncia* to refer to the height of the letter, 0.98", but it is more likely that, in coining the term, St. Jerome had referred to "large letters," rather than to a specific size. A *Half-uncial* is then half that measure.

See also Carolingian script; Guidelines; Uncial

Hand composition - A general term used to refer to setting type by hand, by means of a **composing stick**. Once the measure is set, the line of type is justified by inserting the needed spaces. From there, lines of type are placed on a galley, and samples are pulled for proofreading, preceding type imposition for printing.

See also Composing stick; Foundry type; Galley; Galley Proof; Leading; Machine composition; Space; Type case

Hand lettering - A hand-drawn type. There is a great difference between hand lettering and calligraphy. Although one is an extension of the other, hand lettering is geared towards replacing type by hand-drawn letters with the purpose of achieving a more organic form. On pages 117, 118, 130, and 131, we may see the work of two great American letterers and calligraphers, Oswald Cooper and William Addison Dwiggins.

See also Calligraphy; Freehand lettering; Lettering; Spencerian script

Handtooled typefaces - A term used to describe a letterform that has been altered by an off-centered engraved line, with the aim of highlighting the black area. Very popular during the nineteenth century, they have maintained their attractiveness. A contemporary example is found in GOUDY HANDTOOLED / Goudy Handtooled, designed in 1922, and attributed to both Wadsworth Parker and Morris Fuller Benton.

See also Incised typefaces; Inline typefaces; Open face typefaces; Shaded typefaces; Typeface classification

Headline - The most important line of text in a piece of printing, which forces the reader to read further on or summarizes at a glance the content of the copy which follows. Newspapers usually depend on headlines to sell content. Headlines are commonly set in bold display typefaces. On page 65, we may see a newspaper front page with various headlines set in *News Gothic* (Morris Fuller Benton, 1908).

See also Bold typefaces; Display type

Historiated initials - Large capital letters embellished with detailed drawings surrounding the character and illustrating an incident in the text they introduce. These letters were usually Roman

or gothic and appeared during the thirteenth-century. There are some contemporary examples on pages 138 and 139 designed by Bertram Grossvenor Goodhue, which resemble those designed by Hans Holbein in 1530. Victorian historiated initials differ from these earlier ones in that the embellishment was inside the letterforms, generally demanding heavy *Clarendon* typefaces.
See also Floriated initials; Ornamented initials

Horizontal alignment - A typographical arrangement of characters so as to perceive an even sequence that will permit a legible and readable line. This alignment is a direct product of the strict use of a baseline when casting type. Nevertheless, if we set metal types of different size or style they will not align physically. Today, thanks to computers, this alignment is perfectly managed by software, even regardless of type size or style.
See also Alignment; Baseline; Body

Hot metal type composition - A mechanical or semi-mechanical character composition involving the use of a Monotype caster, a Linotype, a Ludlow slug-caster or comparable systems that casts fresh type for each job, after which the type is re-melted.
See also Linotype; Ludlow; Monotype; Type metal

Hot Type - That which involves a mechanical or semi-mechanical casting of types through the injection of hot molten type metal.

It has also been used as a colloquial term to define type produced by hot metal casting systems, such as the Linotype, the Monotype, or the Ludlow. Largely replaced by "cold" typesetting systems based on film and computers, many of today's typographic terms still relate to the conventions of foundry type and hot metal type setting.
See also Cold type; Foundry type; Hot metal type composition; Linotype; Ludlow; Monotype; Type metal

Humanist script - Derived from the *Carolingian minuscule*, it is the name given to the letterform, also known as *lettera antiqua*, used to copy classical texts during the late fourteenth-century in Italy. Humanism had taken place in this country as a revival of the literary heritage of ancient Rome, and Florentine scholars such as Petrarca, Niccoli, and Bracciolini had pioneer it. Humanist script presented two modalities. A more discipline humanistic form, known as *lettera antiqua formata*, was used for the writing of sumptuous manuscripts, and a small, quickly written, and often ligatured, known as *lettera antiqua corsiva*, was used for plain scholastic texts. As copyists wrote the Roman inscriptional texts, letterforms introduced forms alien to the strictly Latin tradition developing ligatures and the use of classical Roman capitals. The conventions of these capitals led, from about 1465, to the use in calligraphy of clear serifs and rounded, more carefully formed letters.
See also Carolingian script; Italics; Ligature

Humanist sans serif typefaces - A term used to refer to the typefaces that in spite of being sans serif, their proportions are based on those of the Roman inscriptional letters. There is also a contrast in weight, and strokes vary in width towards their end. An excellent example is found in LEGACY SANS / Legacy Sans, designed by Ronald Arnholm in 1992.
See also Sans serif typefaces; Serifs; Typeface classification

Hyphenation - A term that refers to the division of words at the end of a line, or indicates compound words. It becomes necessary when a text is set justified to avoid an uneven tone in the text texture due to extreme kerning. Hyphenation differs considerably from one language to another.
In word processing programs, hyphening may also be controlled to avoid too many hyphens in a paragraph or the presence of continuous hyphening from line to line.
See also Dash; Justified type composition; Texture

I

Imposition - A particular arrangement of the pages that are to be printed on one side of a sheet so that, when cut, folded and trimmed, they can be read up right, and fall in numerical sequence. This operation is repeated for the other side of the sheet. Common imposition schemes encompass two, four, eight, and sixteen pages.

This term also refers to the plan of such an arrangement.
See also Chase; Format; Letterpress

Impression - A degree of pressure required between the printing form or plate and the printing surface. The term comes from the Latin *imprimo*, to press down. An impression may be done with ink or without ink (*intaglio*).

The term **impression** also refers to each individual piece of printed matter obtained during a press run as well as to an image of any kind imposed on a surface.
See also Chase; Imposition; Letterpress

Imprint - A legal obligation, which requires that the name of the publisher, printer, date, and place of printing appear in any published work. The publisher's name and symbol normally appear on the title page; the bibliographical data are shown on the reverse of the title page, and the rest of the information appears at the end of the book, in the colophon. The first book to have the imprint and title together on the title page was the *Calendarium* of German scientist Johannes Regiomontanus, printed in Venice in 1476, by Erhard Ratdolt.
See also Colophon; Printer's mark; Title page

Incised typefaces - Also referred as **engraved**, it is a term applied to those typefaces that have been altered by engraving one or various lines along or across the main stem. They differ from the **handtooled** or the **inline typefaces** in their visual effect as may be seen in **BROADWAY ENGRAVED / Broadway Engraved**, a variation of **Broadway** (Morris Fuller Benton, 1928), drawn by Sol Hess in 1929.
See also Handtooled type; Inline typefaces; Open Face typefaces; Ornamental typefaces

Incunabula - A name given to the early period of the art of printing. The name is taken from the Latin *incunabula*, in the cradle. Thus, it refers to the books printed from 1430 to 1500. The limit for this date may derive from the earliest catalog of these books: an appendix to Johann Saubert's *Historia bibliothecae Noribergensis...catalogus librorum proximis ad inventione annis usque ad a. Chr.1500 editorum*, printed in 1643. It would be interesting to note that this term should equally apply to the

early printing in the Americas, and not only to Europe, for in these countries a similar development took place (the first typographic workshop in the Americas was established in Mexico, in 1538).

Indented paragraph - A holding of one or more lines of printed matter in from the margin, generally the left margin. Thus, the first or more lines of a paragraph are shorter than the rest. This type of setting avoids physical separations between paragraphs, counting always on an equal number of lines per page. It is also a type of setting commonly used in pocket book editions. The initial space is usually equal to one **em space** (■). Some designers make use of this indentation to create a particular visual configuration on the page by increasing it progressively. It is also used to set an initial, as we may see on page 223. Opposite to it we find a **hanging indentation** or **outdented paragraph**, in which the first line is flush left and the subsequent lines are indented one em from the left. The indented paragraph was the standard paragraph break in western prose by the seventeenth century. Outdented paragraphs are quite usual in dictionaries.
See also Em space; Flushed paragraph; Initials; Type specifications

Index - An essential part of any publication, it is an alphabetical listing of all the terms and names found in a book with page reference. As its content makes easy finding information, the more complete it is the better service it will offer.
See also General Index; End matter

Index (☛) - Special character showing a pointing hand (with an extended index), used to direct attention. A Baroque invention there may be found good examples in the wood type catalogs of William Hamilton Page (see page 205).
See also Dingbats; Pi characters

Indirect printing - That which is obtained through the transferring of the inked image onto another surface and from this onto paper or another type of material, as is the case of offset lithography. It is interesting to note that indirect printing was known in England as early as 1875, when Robert Barclay used this procedure to print lithographic-stone images onto tin plates to make metal containers, such as those used for candies, tobacco, and the like. All the advantages of this printing method did not fully developed until American lithographer, Ira W. Rubel, did offset printing of type in 1906.
See also Direct printing; Offset lithography

Initial letter - The first letter of a chapter, section, or article that is set in a type size larger than the body text. When the base of the initial is aligned with the base of the first line of the text, the initial is referred as a **raised initial**. When the top of the initial is aligned with the top of the first line of text and carry-over lines run around the lower part of the initial, this initial is said to be a **cut in initial**. When the initial is set into the text, requiring that a number of lines be indented, the initial is referred as a **drop initial**. When the initial is placed outside the measure, and aligns on top with the cap height of the first line it is referred as a **hung initial**.
The initial relationship to the running text may differ according to the book designer. There are various examples designed by Bruce Rogers on page 223.

It is interesting to note that during the reign of Emperor Charlemagne, in the ninth century, Alcuin of York introduced punctuation marks and the grouping of words into sentences, which, for the first time, began with a larger size initial letter.

This is a text with a *Doric Ornamented* raised initial.

See also Decorated typefaces; Typeface classification

Inline typefaces - A term used to refer to the letterforms in which the vertical, diagonal, and curved strokes are engraved with a thin white line, which may be either in the center or off center of the black area in the stroke. Inline types lighten the color while preserving the shape and proportion of the original design. We find an example in **NEULAND INLINE**, designed by Rudolf Koch in 1923. Different from the **incised typeface**, the white line is maintained within the stroke.

See also Handtooled typefaces; Incised typefaces; Open Face typefaces; Outline typefaces; Typeface classification

Inner space - The white area between letters. The management of these spaces is as important as the space between words or the space between lines. While newspapers work with wide parameters, advertisers work with narrower parameters, usually ending with better typographic work. Legibility and readability rely mostly on a good balance of both spaces.

See also Counter space; Justified type composition; Leading; Legibility; Readability; Side bearings

Inscriptional letters - Carved lettering usually done on marble by means of a chisel. The most famous historical carvings are found in inscriptional monuments in Rome –as is the case of the Trajan Column– and in ancient Roman foundations. English type designer and sculptor Eric Gill was one of the most notable letter carvers in England in his time. Some type designs maintain this quality in their structure, and are cataloged as **glyphic style typefaces**. Such is the case of **ALBERTUS / Albertus**, designed by German type designer Berthold Wolpe in 1932.

See also Glyphic style typefaces; Rubbing; Trajan column

Interline spacing - *See* Leading

International Typographic Style - A name given to the rational use of typography, known also as **Swiss Style**, which developed in Switzerland in the 1950s. Based on ideas expressed by Constructivism, and by the De Stijl, Bauhaus and the New Typography of the 1930s, the International Typographic Style sought to present complex information in a structured and unified manner. Ernst Keller, Théo Ballmer, Max Bill, and Max Huber had major influences on the early evolution of this style. It is characterized by the use of a grid as a formal structure of information, a preference for sans serif typefaces (especially **Akzidenz Grotesk**, later changed by **Helvetica** after its introduction in 1957). It also uses flush left typesetting, narrow text columns, photographs rather than illustrations, and simply written prose, which permits the delivering of an articulated visual and verbal message. Personal expression is also rejected in favor of the presentation of a more objective whole. The international popularity of the style extended throughout the 1950s and 1970s with major figures like Joseph Müller-Brockmann, Armin Hoffman, Karl Gerstner, and Emil Ruder, and publications such as *Neue Graphik* (1958), *Die neue Graphic* (1959), *Graphic Design Manual* (1965), and *Typographie* (1967). Swiss typographer, graphic designer and educator Emil Ruder later contributed to the logical use of the International Typographic Style through his typography class (1942-1970) at the Allgemeine Gewerbschule (*School of Applied Arts*) in Basle. During the 1970s the International Typographic Style as well as the use of *Helvetica* became strongly identified with a corporate style of design, especially in the United States. The objective approach has kept the International Typographic Style a major force in graphic design. During the 1960s and 1970s in Switzerland, Germany, and the United States, a group of designers appeared (Rosmarie Tissi in Zurich, Wolfgang Weingart in Basle, and April Greiman in California) who, being very much identified with Post-modernism, strongly challenged the International Typographic Style's postulates. Their vital and fresh innovations suggest new approaches which will certainly continue being influential in graphic design.

See also Asymmetric typography; Bauhaus; Constructivism; De Stijl; Grid; Post-modernism; Sans serif typefaces

Introduction - An opening chapter or section of a book in which the author introduces the reader to the subject matter.

See also Preliminary matter; Foreword

Ionic typefaces - A popular letter range designed for newspapers, originating in the 1830s and 40s. Similar in style to the *Egyptian* family of typefaces –but with the characteristics of a bracketed serif, a large x-height, short ascenders, and descenders the *Clarendon*'s faces– it is a letter that permits great legibility in the smaller sizes. They are also characterized by a greater differentiation between the thick and thin strokes, and quite open counters. The name *Ionic* seems to have been used by early Victorian founders as an additional name for *Egyptian* types. We may find an example in **IONIC No. 5/Ionic No. 5**, designed by Chauncey H. Griffith in 1926, the first of the *Legibility Group* typefaces. He will later develop *Excelsior*, *Paragon*, *Opticon*, and *Corona*, continuing with the same design principles.

See also Ball terminal, Clarendon typefaces; Custom typeface; Egyptian typefaces; Legibility Group; Typeface classification

ISBN - A publishing classification system used to identify all books published. The "International Standard Book Number" uses ten digits to identify the country of origin, publisher, and title. This unique code number for identifying a book eliminates the need to quote author, title, edition, and publisher in all translations. It usually appears on the *verso* of the title page, on the back book cover or on the jacket, if there is one.

See also Imprint

Italics - Letterforms that have a slant to the right. It is a cursive letter which was originally called by its designers, "*corsiva*" or "*cancellaresca*," for it was based on a fluid writing style known as *chancery script* which originated in Italy in the fourteenth and fifteenth-centuries. It is still called *kursiv* by the Germans. Italics may be divided into four main groups: the *Aldine*; the *Vicentino*; the group that is the contemporary of the *Oldstyle* typefaces; and the modernized italics. The *Aldine* italic was based on the Papal Chancery of the time, whose prototype was cut by Francesco Griffo of Bologna in 1501 for Venetian printer Aldus Manutius, and used in his edition of Virgil. Manutius only commissioned a lowercase alphabet, using small roman capitals with the italics. Vicentino Degli Arrighi's italic first appeared as metal type in *Il modo di temperare le penne* in 1525. Although capitals remained upright, there is an introduction of swash letters. Johann Singrenius of Vienna first used italic capitals around 1524. The *Oldstyle* italic originated c.1530 with French punch-cutter Claude Garamond, who was the first to consider roman and italic as part of one family, is characterized by a marked inclination in both upper and lowercase letters. It was usual in European typography until William Caslon. The modernized italics begin with the work Philip Granjean, who attempted to make the secondary type conform to the roman. Pierre-Simon Fournier, le jeune, and Firmin Didot followed his work by further introducing other changes. Italics are commonly used for book titles, quotations, or foreign words within a running text. The author has also used italics in this book to set the name of type designs (such as *News Gothic*), providing an easy recognition of their names within the running text. The term **italic** is always associated with a letter which presents a different design, especially in the lowercase alphabet (roman a, cursive *a*), while the term **oblique** refers to a simply inclined letterform (roman a, sloped *a*).

This is an example of a text set in italics

This is an example of a text set in obliques

See also Chancery italic; Humanist script; Oblique letters; Roman style typefaces; Swash letters; Typeface classification

J

Job press - A small printing press into which stock is fed by hand. The platen and bed open and close to receive the stock, which is pressed against the type form on the bed. In 1839, Stephen Ruggles designed and built the first self-inking treadle platen press, which offered easy displacement to small printers. He presented an improved model in 1851. **CHELTENHAM / Cheltenham**, designed by Bertram G. Goodhue in 1897, is a good example of a job press typeface.

See also Letterpress

Jugendstil - The German equivalent of the French **Art Nouveau** movement, emerging in 1896, and taking its name from the cultural weekly magazine, *Jugend* (1896-1914), published in Munich by Georg Hirth. That same year, Albert Langen began publishing his satirical weekly, *Simplissimus*, whose Jugendstil-inspired artists so influenced cartoons and caricatures elsewhere in Europe. In addition to the curvilinear naturalistic motifs of Art Nouveau, Jugendstil acknowledged the German printmaking tradition and medieval letterforms, producing a style more precise and austere. Its members also rejected traditional typography in favor of unique display types which worked harmoniously with images. Among the Jugendstil artists may be found Otto Eckmann, Peter Behrens, Josef Sattler, Bruno Paul, Hans Christiansen, and Henry Van de Velde. An example of their style is found in **ECKMANN /**

Eckmann, the first Art Nouveau typeface, designed by German type designer Otto Eckmann, in 1896.

See also Art Nouveau style; Plakatstil; Typeface classification; Victorian style

Justification - The action of aligning a text to a given axis, usually vertical. If the text is justified to the right, it is referred to as **flush right**, and to the left, **flush left**. If each line follows a visual vertical axis, it is referred to as a **justified centered text**. If the text is aligned to both ends, it is referred to as a **justified text**.

See also Alignment; Symmetrical typography; Flush left type composition; Flush right type composition; Inner space; Typesetting

Justified type composition - A typesetting format in which the letters and words of each line of a text are spaced to ensure that the line fully occupies the column width. The result is a column of text with even vertical edges on both sides. This type of composition demands the presence of **hyphenation** to avoid undesirable white spaces between words, product of unnecessary **kerning**. It is commonly used on newspaper type setting. The perfectly justified line became the standard typesetting after the invention of printing between 1450 and 1456, when Johannes Gutenberg finished the printing of the *42-line Bible*.

See also Flush left type composition; Flush right type composition; Flush paragraph; Hyphenation; Justification; Kerning; Linotype; Mono element; Monotype; Ludlow; Symmetric typography; Typesetting

K

Kerned letters - Type characters where a part of the letter extends, or projects, beyond the body, thus overlapping onto the adjacent character. Kerned letters are common in italic, script, and swash letters. These types of problems were avoided by the Ludlow Typograph Company in making slanted matrices at 17-degree angles for the italic versions of a typeface, as we may see on page 191.

See also Matrix; Swash; Swash letters

Kerning - A term used to refer to the physical adjustment of inter-letter spacing to produce an optical spacing or to produce a better fit. Besides the running text in which it is usually applied to single lines or to whole paragraphs, kerning is particularly useful in titling where an adjustment is necessary due to uneven formal relationships of certain letters, such as **LA, VA, TT**. Letter spacing programs, including a kerning facility, are available in most filmsetting and computerized typesetting systems.

Digital fonts are generally kerned through the use of **kerning tables**, which can specify a reduction or an increment in spacing for every possible pair of letters, numbers, or symbols.

See also Computerized type composition; Inner space; Justified type composition; Ligatures; Typesetting

Keyboard - A device consisting of buttons or keys managed by the touch of fingers used to enter data into typesetting and computer systems. Keyboards manage typewriters as well as hot metal type composing machines like Linotype and Monotype. The so-called universal keyboard, which was adopted by the Lanston Monotype Company, is credited to Lathan Sholes, inventor of the typewriter machine (1868). In 1907, Monotype (see page 181) improved the keyboard permitting a faster handling of type composition.

See also Alphabet; Linotype; Monotype

L

Latin serif typefaces - A term used to refer to the typefaces that have wedge-shaped serifs, which appeared during the nineteenth-century. Latin serifs slope towards but do not curve into the main stroke. We find an example in **LATIN WIDE** / **Latin Wide**, issued by the English type foundry Stephenson, Blake, & Company.

See also Chisel; Glyphic style typefaces; Serifs; Thibaudeau typeface classification; Typeface classification

Layout - A visual-graphic organization of a given information generally expressed by a preliminary plan on a given format, on which the basic elements (type and/or illustrations) are shown in their proper proportion and placement prior to making a finished art. It also includes outside and inside margins and leading. Evidence of the early practice of marking up a manuscript to show the printer the desired position of illustration blocks may be seen on the "copy" for the German version of Hartman Schedel's *Liber chronicarum* (*Nuremberg Chronicle*), printed by Anton Koberger in 1493, and kept in the Nuremberg City Library. During the 1950s, Swiss designers developed a rational system through the use of a grid that permitted the presentation of complex information.

See also Composition; Double page; Format; Grid; International Typographic Style; Page

Leading - An interline spacing, so called because in hand composition, it is obtained by the insertion of thin strips of metal called leads. Leads are usually 1-, 2-, and 3-pt thick; for a 6- or 12-pt thick piece of metal, is also called a **slug**. Leading is also referred to as **vertical spacing**.

Longer measures need more leading than short ones; dark faces and large sizes need more than light and small sizes. Serif types also need less vertical spacing than sans-serif typefaces. It is important to know that leading must be incremental in a progressive ratio to type size. This means that while an 8-pt text may need 2-pt leading, a 12-pt text may need 2.5 or 3-pt leading.

See also Letter spacing; Line spacing; Negative leading; Slug

Leaf - A sheet of paper in a book or a magazine. Each of its two sides is a page (*recto* and *verso*). It is important to remember that a leaf is part of a larger sheet of paper that has been folded in two or more, and, therefore, there are two or more pages which all together form a signature.

See also Folio; Octavo; Page; Quarto; Recto; Sextodecimo; Verso

Leg - The lower diagonal stroke, usually straight, in a letter, such as in **K, k**, and **R**.

See also each instance of a letter; Anatomy of a typeface; Tail

Legibility - A quality inherent in type design that permits an observer's fast perception and easiness in identifying a given character. It is important to differentiate **legibility** and **readability**, for the first deals with the structure and form of a character, and the second with the relationship that exists between characters and between lowercase and upper case letters. These two characteristics are inseparable when dealing with reading. Other factors, such as type size, type style; weight of typefaces, letter spacing, word spacing, leading, and characters per line, also have a definite influence on perception, and therefore on the legibility and readability of a given typeset text. Outside aspects, such as surface texture and color of the paper, margins, and printing quality are also strong determining factors. It is also interesting to mention that while serif letters have been proven more readable for texts; sans serif letters are more legible for signs.

See also Inner space; Leading; Legibility Group; Letter spacing; Readability; Space; Texture; Type style; Weight of a typeface; Word spacing

Legibility Group - A name given to a typographic program sponsored by the Mergenthaler Linotype Company, New York, under the direction of Chauncey H. Griffith. This group started to work towards the design of more legible and readable typefaces in 1922. Among the five typefaces that were developed we may find **Ionic No. 5** (1925), **Excelsior** (1931), and **Corona** (1941) designed by Griffith, and based on **Clarendon**. Later on, designers William Addison Dwiggins and Rudolph Ruzicka joined efforts creating **Electra** (1935), and **Fairfield** (1940), respectively.

See also Clarendon Style; Legibility; Readability

Letraset - *See* Transfer types

Letter spacing - Additional space placed between letters. Letter spacing is variable and may be adjusted to suit the designer's needs or taste. It may be used to expand the length of a line or to improve and balance typography. Although it is measured in units, letter spacing is referred to as **normal, loose, tight**, and **very tight** spacing. In order to better understand what a unit is, we may simply recall that standard typewriters are based on unit characters. This means that all characters measure the same width, be they letters, numbers, or punctuations marks. It is also important to have in mind that in loose letter spacing, it is necessary to adjust the word spacing to maintain the same spacing ratio. We may see an example:

This is a very tight line of text (- 6)

This is a very loose line of text (+9)

See also Inner space; Inter space; Kerning; Line spacing; Optical letter spacing; Word spacing

Lettering - The process of making letters with the additional aid of mechanical instruments, such as a ruler, a compass, and a triangle. During the Renaissance, nearly all artists and writing masters used compasses and rulers to help them draw letters and alphabets. Proof of this is found on the specimen sheets intended for teaching pupils. Leonardo da Vinci used compasses and rulers as an aid for the construction of his roman capital letters. A similar case is found in Fra Luca de Pacioli's book, *De Divina Proportione* (1509). Albrecht Dürer also worked with these tools in his book, *Unterweysung der Messung mit dem Zirckel und Richtscheydt* (1525), to draw the roman capitals. Other artists like Felice Feliciano (1460), Damiano da Moille (1480), Sigismondo Fanti (1514), Francesco Torniello (1517), Giovam Battista Verini (1526), and Geofroy Tory (1529), also used mechanical means for showing the construction of the roman letters. But it was not until the twentieth-century that compasses and rulers were considered writing tools. Dadaism (Kurt Schwitters), Constructivism (El Lissitzky), De Stijl (Piet Zwart, Théo Van Doesburg, Bart Van der Leck), and above all the Bauhaus was formed by artists interested in new forms of type. Bauhaus lettering teachers, Joseph Albers, Herbert Bayer, Max Bill, and Joos Schmidt developed "pure" type forms, as may be seen through the alphabets they created.

See also Bauhaus; Dada; Constructivism; De Stijl; Freehand lettering; Hand lettering; Calligraphy; Spencerian script

Letterpress - A traditional relief printing process in which type and images are raised above non-printing areas. Impression is obtained through direct contact between the inked raised surface and paper. Although supplanted by lithography, letterpress is still used in the production of high-quality limited editions. Letterpress came into being when German printer Johannes Gutenberg, after he invented the movable type around 1448-1450, started printing the *42-line Bible*, which he finished in 1456. The establishment of the press is one of the historic facts that brought the Middle Ages to an end.

See also Chase; Foundry type; Job press; Lithography; Movable type; Offset lithography; Typography

Ligatures - A typographic term that refers to the connecting link that joins two or three characters together. Cast as a unit, joint characters save space and kerning is simplified. Johannes Gutenberg introduced typographic ligatures when he found that double and triple letters looked better linked together, avoiding inner spaces when they were cast separately. Most of the early ligatures were used for Latin texts. As typography spread through Europe, new regional ligatures were added, as may be seen in the German *eszett* (ß), or double ss. Some of the most common ligatures are:

ff fi fl ffi ffl æ Æ œ Œ ſt ſh fi (*Adobe Caslon*, Carol Twombly, 1990).

See also Anatomy of a typeface; Inner space; Kerning

Light typeface - A character defined with thinner or ultra thin strokes compared to the regular face. It is interesting to note that type variations are not always created in the same order. Sometimes a light variation may come after a regular weight, as was the case of LITHOS / LITHOS, designed by Carol Twombly in 1990. It is also interesting to note that NEWS GOTHIC / News Gothic, designed by Morris Fuller Benton in 1908, is essentially a lighter version of **FRANKLIN GOTHIC / Franklin Gothic** (1902), designed by the same person.

See also Bold typeface; Regular typeface

Line length - The horizontal measurement of a typographical line of text, usually expressed in picas. It has been found that for easier reading, there must not be more than eight or nine words per line. A 66-character line (counting both letters and spaces)

is regarded as an ideal length for a single-column page. For multiple-column work, a better average is 40 to 50 characters. This, of course, must be reinforced by good leading and a good choice of a typeface, according to the content.

See also Agate; Leading; Pica; Typesetting; Weight of a typeface

Line spacing - Also called **leading**, it refers to the vertical spacing set between lines of a text. Originally, to space lines of metal type composition, it was necessary to insert thin strips of lead (of 1- to 2-pt of thickness) between them. But, besides leading, metal typefaces are also cut with a space above the ascender line, and below the descender line, which provides each character with a space of its own avoiding them to touch if the line of text is set solid. Casting machines, such as the Linotype, the Intertype, or the Monotype, could be adjusted to cast type with additional space to avoid leading. The strips of lead also act as a way to hold type together. The rectangular shape of the metal block, where the face rests, has been maintained in photo and in digital typesetting for use in sizing and spacing the type (see **body size** illustration). Line spacing is expressed graphically by a fraction; this means that an 8-pt text set solid is expressed thus: 8/8; a text set with 2-pt lead spacing: 8/10; with 4-pt lead spacing: 8/12, etc. To obtain a true solid setting, which is possible in desktop publishing, it is necessary to give a text a negative leading.

These four lines of text have been set in 10-pt with -2-pt lead, $^{10}/_8$	These four lines of text have been set in 10-pt with 2-pt lead, $^{10}/_{12}$

Longer measures need more leading than short ones, as well as dark faces and large sizes need more than light faces and small sizes. Serif types also need less spacing than sans-serif typefaces. It is important as well to have in mind that leading increments change proportionally to type size. This means that while an 8-pt text may need 2-pt leading, a 10-pt text may need 2.5 or 3-pt leading.

See also Body size; Leading; Legibility; Letter spacing; Negative leading; Readability; Shoulder; Solid composition

Link - In a two-storey letter **g**, it is that small stroke that connects the upper bowl and the lower loop.

See also Bowl; Loop; Type nomenclature

Linotype - A hot metal composition casting machine which allowed for the setting of type in slugs, by the use of matrices which were assembled through the use of a keyboard. After matrices were adjusted to a line length, they were placed in a caster and a line-of-type was thus produced. Linotype was used extensively in the letterpress printing of books and magazines for more than sixty years. Invented by Ottmar Mergenthaler in 1885, it was first tested in the office of the *New York Tribune* on July 3, 1886. One of the advantages of the Linotype over Monotype was the easiness in handling typeset material. The first book published using linotype setting was Henry Hall's *The Tribune Book of Open Air*, given by the newspaper as a premium to its subscribers.

See also Hot metal type composition; Ludlow; Matrix; Monotype; Slug

Lithography / Stone lithography - A planographic printing process in which the image and non-image areas appear together on a completely flat plate or stone. Based on the principle that oil and water do not mix, the image attracts ink while non-printing areas are covered with water. While the lithographic stone prints through direct contact with paper, offset lithography prints through a transferred image onto a cylinder covered by a rubber blanket and then onto paper. Invented by Czech playwright Alloys Senefelder in 1796, it gave birth to the modern poster as well as to lettering as a professional activity. Writing was usually done on stone with special lithographic pencils or by means of a quill pen or a fine brush. Type foundries continually tried to imitate these unusual alphabets, resulting in a great collection of typefaces available for printing. Lithography was introduced in France around 1800 and in America in 1828. Among the artists who took advantage of lithography for creating the first posters are Jules Chéret, Henri de Toulouse-Lautrec, Théophile Steinlein, Lucien Lefévre, and Alfons Mucha, among others. Designers such as Lucian Bernhard (as seen on pages 79 and 80), Ludwig Hohlwein, and William Bradley (as seen on page 97), also developed important works through this medium.

See also Calligraphy; Crowquill pen; Offset lithography

Logotype - Originally referring to a word cast as a unit, it refers today to a word that has been drawn in a distinctive and unified form to act as a device that serves as graphic and visual identification. This is the case of *Coca-Cola*. The first metal logotypes using words such as *sales*, *free*, appeared in London, cast by type founder Henry Johnson in 1780.

See also Ligature; Masthead; Typogram

Lombardic capitals - In the context of fifteenth century printing, it is a *majuscule* type in the style of the *Lombardic* Uncial manuscript hand, current in Italy about the thirteenth century, and widely used in Europe as a design for decorative capitals in rubricating. Many fifteenth-century printers used red inked Lombardic type in liturgical works. In 1928, Frederic W. Goudy designed a somewhat stylized font, called LOMBARDIC CAPITALS, later commercially issued by the American Lanston Monotype in 1933.

See also Half-uncial; Majuscules; Typeface classification

Loop - In a two-story letter **g**, it is the lower part of the letter, which is connected by a short line or link with the upper bowl.

See also Anatomy of a typeface; Bowl; Link

Lowercase letters - A typographical name derived from the fact that metal type letters were placed in two cases, the upper case being for capitals. On page 225, we may see an illustration done by Rudolph Ruzicka of the old, two-case furniture, which clarifies this fact. Lowercase letters are a b c d e f g h i j k l m n o p q r s t u v w x y z. They match well with *Oldstyle* figures.

In 1925, Herbert Bayer designed his *universal alphabet*, a sans serif typeface, which only included lowercase letters. Redrawn by Edward Benguiat –this time including both alphabets–, it was issued by ITC in 1975.

See also Bicameral alphabet; Half-uncials; Oldstyle figures; Tricameral alphabet; Upper case letters

Ludlow - A hot metal composition casting machine which allows the setting of large-size fonts or display type, by the use of matrices which, different from the Linotype, are assembled by hand in a special composing stick (see page 191). The matrices are then inserted in the casting machine, and a line of type is produced in slug-line form. The original machine designed by Washington I. Ludlow in 1906, was developed by William A. Reade through an entirely new concept in 1911. The new machine was first used commercially in the composing room of the *Chicago Evening Post* in 1913.

See also Hot metal type composition; Linotype; Matrix; Monotype; Slug

M

Machine composition - A general term given to the mechanical hot metal type composition, such as the Linotype, Monotype, or Ludlow, as opposed to hand composition. The first mechanical type composition was successfully carried out in New York, with the invention of the Linotype composing machine by Ottmar Mergenthaler in 1886.

See also Foundry type; Hand composition; Hot metal type composition; Linotype; Ludlow; Monotype

Magazine - A slotted metal container used to store brass matrices in line-casting machines, such as the Linotype. A magazine held one complete font, which was later enhanced when the two-character matrices, called **duplex** (page 193), were designed in 1898. By 1911, the Linotype Company had produced a model with four magazines, which allowed for an even greater versatility in type composing.

See also Linotype; Matrix

Main stroke - *See* Stem

Main content - The principal part of a publication, generally a book, which is preceded by the **preliminary matter** and followed by the **end matter**. It is paged in sequence after the preliminary matter but in Arabic numerals.

See also Arabi numerals; End matter; Preliminary matter

Majuscules - A French name for the upper case letters, also referred to as **major** or **capital letters**. A derivative term is used in Spanish (*mayúsculas*).

See also Capital letters; Minuscules; Uppercase letters

Master design - In the context of digital typography, it is a typeface that has the essential characteristics of a determining state: weight, width, style, and size. Thus it serves as a point of departure to vary a letterform from one state to another. Now, within the context of multiple master typefaces, a master design is placed at each end of a design axis, allowing the user to choose any intermediate state, according to his design needs.

See also Design axis; Digital typography; Multiple Master typefaces; Scalable Fonts

Masthead - The upper graphic-visual identification of a magazine or a newspaper. It usually consists of a name set in a regular typeface, drawn in a unique way or drawn with special characters. This is the case of THE NEW YORKER, designed by Rea Irvin in 1925 (pages 170 and 171), which in turn laid the foundations for the type design IRVIN. We find another case in ITC AVANT GARDE

GOTHIC, which was developed by Herb Lubalin in collaboration with Tom Carnase, from the magazine's masthead in 1970 (see page 187).

See also Logotype

Matrix - A mold employed in foundry-cast type. In line casting (Linotype or Ludlow), it is a special brass mold which, assembled in a row, serves to cast a slug. While in the Monotype casting machine, matrices are used individually; in the Linotype and Ludlow casting machines matrices are assembled for casting a slug. On pages 181, 191, and 193, we may see the three types of matrices. The Linotype two-character matrices (page 193) were introduced in 1898. It is important to add that while in the Linotype two-character matrices romans and italics were cut within the same mold –one below the other– causing that both letters would have the same width, in the Monotype and Ludlow systems each version had a separate mold, thus permitting those subtleties characteristic of italics.

The illustration below shows how the width of a two-character Linotype matrix conditions letterforms.

The term **matrix** also refers to the font negative used in phototypesetting, as well as to the impression in *papier maché* taken from a form of type for stereotyping.

See also Foundry type; Slug

Mechanical letter spacing - That in which the same space is used between all characters, as in typewriting machines. In this case, all the characters also have the same body width.

See also Inner space; Kerning; Mono element; Optical letter spacing; Unit

Mean line - An imaginary line that marks the top of lowercase letters, such as **a, c, e, g, i, j, m, n, o, r, s, x, y,** and **z**, and the top of the torso of letters like **b, d, p, h,** and **q**. Also called **x-line**, it lays the foundations for the term **x-height**, which determines the relation between lowercase and uppercase letters.

See also Anatomy of a typeface; Ascender line; Baseline; Body; Cap line; Cross bar line; Guidelines; Middle arm line; x-height

Metal type - See Foundry type

Metal type sizes - There are definite sizes in metal type which are conditioned by the material, its weight and handling, but above all, by the cost that is implied in cutting a set of matrices for each size. Although we may find intermediate sizes, the basic ones are: 4 6 8 10 12 14 16 20 24 36 48 60 72

See also Type sizes

Middle arm line - An imaginary horizontal line placed between the cap line and the baseline, different from the **mean line**, to help determine the position of middle arms in capital letters **E** and **F**. The difference in position of this letter component

makes these letters acquire a particular form which directly affects the general style of the whole font. A clear example may be found in typefaces designed in Art Deco style, such as BERNHARD FASHION (Lucian Bernhard, 1929).

See also Anatomy of a typeface; Arm; Art Deco; Ascender line; Baseline; Cap line; Cross bar line; Descender line; Guidelines; Mean line; Trajan Column

Minuscules - A French term for the lowercase letters also referred to as **minor** letters. A derived term is used in Spanish (*minúsculas*).

See also Lowercase letters; Majuscules

Modern style figures - A set of numerals that align with the top and bottom of the matching capitals in a typeface, and are best used with them. They are also called **lining figures** or **titling figures**. This is the case of *News Gothic* (Morris F. Benton, 1908) TITLING FIGURES 1234567890. Some typefaces include lining figures lower and lighter than the uppercase letters. In 1788, English punch-cutter Richard Austin cut a font of three-quarter-height lining figures for founder John Bell. Later on, during the nineteenth century, founders made these figures cap height, and titling figures became customary in commercial typography.

See also Capital letters; Cap line; Oldstyle figures

Modern style typefaces - A term used to describe the typefaces designed at the end of the eighteenth-century. Generally characterized by vertical stress and horizontal hairline serifs, they have pronounced contrasts between thick and thin strokes. As a product of Baroque and Rococo etching techniques, mechanical improvements in the printing press, better ink, and paper with more consistent printing surfaces, the punch-cutter was able to cut typefaces with a greater contrast in their strokes, and finer and more clearly defined hairlines. Letters were no longer drawn freehand, but constructed with rulers, compasses and grids. Although more difficult to read than other roman styles, their elegance, precision, and great naturalness are still impressive today. As a result, ornamental initials were replaced by large capitals from the same alphabet. The first type to present these characteristics was DIDOT / Didot, designed in 1784 by French designer Firmin Didot. In 1788, Italian Giambattista Bodoni designed BODONI/ Bodoni, much based on Didot's early types, later followed by German founder Justus Erich Walbaum and other European founders. Modern typefaces were introduced in England by type founder Robert Thorne in 1800.

See also Hairline serifs; Serifs; Transitional Style

Modernism - Although Modernism cannot be clearly defined because of the numerous movements, theories, and attitudes which have been part of it, there is general agreement that it arose as a result of the advent of the machine, of industry, and of the development of the urban world during the late nineteenth century. Modernism brought to art, applied arts, architecture, literature, and music a succession of varied movements and styles which not only represented the core of Western art (from the late nineteenth century and far into the second half of the twentieth century), but the triumph and domain of avant garde movements in Western cultures. Modernism is a complex process in art, architecture and the applied arts. This process manifests: the loss of ornament as a result of a new rationalism and functionalism; the influence of the mass media; and the use of technological processes of communication (cinema, Web printing, mechanical type composition, photography, photomechanical processes, etc.). As a consequence, there is a dynamic and controversial art, and an interest for synthesis and a non-objective approach to imagery not only as the continuation of the theories introduced by Cézanne and Cubism, but as a reawakening of the abstract (Worringer). Modernism equally presents abstraction in graphic design with the use of sans serif typefaces, a rational structure of information and the preference for photographs rather than illustrations.

See also Asymmetric typography; Cubism; Constructivism; Dada; De Stijl; Futurism; Post-Modernism

Modulation - A variation in width of the stroke produced by the use of a wide brush or a broad-nib pen as it changes of position in the drawing of a letter. This feature is a characteristic of serif typefaces. In unmodulated letterforms, such as sans serif typefaces, the stroke is always fundamentally the same width. Modulation appeared in Roman lapidary inscriptions through the use of the flat brush to draw letterforms previous to carving them with a chisel.

The example shows *Garamond* and *News Gothic*.
See also Sans serif typefaces; Serif typefaces; Serifs; Stress

Mono element - A golf-ball size sphere that held printing characters all over its surface and permitted a quick change of typefaces within the typewriter. Introduced in 1961 with the *IBM-72 Selectric* typewriter, designed by Elliot Noyes, it slowly brought typewriter fonts more into line with printing type. The machine worked with a new concept: the mono element moved instead of the carriage when a key was struck. The typewriter could perform typing intervals of nine different breadths and could write text in block format. A computer automatically calculated the spaces between the words. In 1963, Swiss designer Adrian Frutiger became consultant to IBM, introducing *Univers* (1957) in their typeface catalog.

See also Inner space; Justified type composition; Typewriter; Typewriter typefaces; Unit; Unit system

Monotype - A hot metal composition casting system which utilizes a composition keyboard and a metal caster to cast, from special matrices, individual, movable, type characters in metal, employing a softer metal alloy than the one used for casting movable type. Types were cast in rapid succession and were automatically assembled into words, and lines of words, evenly aligned to occupy a predetermined width. Invented by Tolbert Lanston in 1887, and perfected by 1891, it could set type from 4- to 18-pt or 24-pt if a special attachment was fitted. Although it was developed in America, Monotype was a more successful metal composing system in England than in the United States, where it was widely used for book text composition.

See also Foundry type; Hot type; Linotype; Ludlow; Matrix; Movable type; Unit system

Movable type - A type cast as a single-character unit. Although the term is usually limited to foundry type, set by hand in a composing stick, the Monotype casting machine also casts individual characters. German printer Johannes Gutenberg is credited with the invention of movable type between 1448 and 1450, which he used in his *42-line Bible*, finished in 1456.

See also Foundry type; Letterpress; Monotype; Relief printing; Punch; Punch-cutter

Multiple master typefaces - Fonts that have been created on the bases of a design axis which permits varying their form characteristics from one master design to another without altering the original type design. Considering that a typeface has variations of weight, width, size, style, and stress, there are master designs on each extreme side of this design axis: light to bold; condensed to extended; regular to display; vertical to oblique. This allows for infinite variations from one extreme side to the other, supplying the user with the exact typeface characteristics according to the graphic/visual design specific needs. Among the various examples we may cite VIVA/**VIVA** (Carol Twombly, 1993), which was the first multiple master typeface.

See also Design axis; Master design

N

Negative leading - Also known as **reverse leading**, it is a reduction in both the amount of interline space as in the body size. This reduction of space is possible in photocomposition and in desktop publishing where one may set a 10-pt typeface on an 8-pt body size, or $^{10}/_8$.

An advertising sentence or a title might be set with negative leading, so long as ascenders and descenders do not interfere with each other.

This is an example
of negative leading

The example has been set in *Times New Roman* $^{11}/_{9.5}$
See also Line spacing; Solid composition

New Wave - *See Post-modernism*

Nick - In foundry type, it is a concave horizontal depression on the down narrow side of the body that identifies a character as belonging to a specific typeface style, and serves to place it right way up in the composing stick. On page 215, there is an illustration of a metal type done by Rudolph Ruzicka, which clearly shows this section of a metal typeface.

See also Composing stick; Foundry type; Type nomenclature

Numerals - *See Arabic numerals; Roman numerals*

Non-lining figures - *See Oldstyle figures*

O

Oblique letters - Also referred to as **sloped romans**, they are letterforms that slant to the right, as opposed to Roman letterforms. The term **oblique** is usually applied to serif or sans serif letters which do not present a modified form in their italic version. Such is the case of **Futura**, **Univers**, or **Romic**.
See also Italic

Octavo ($^1/_8$) - The resulting format that arises from folding a sheet of handmade paper three times, thus

reducing it to $^1/_8$ of its original size. To fully define the proportions of a given publication, it is important to know a piece of paper's original format, for it is difficult to clearly define its proportions by just referring to it as a book printed *in octavo*. The first printer to use the *octavo* format was Venetian typographer and printer Aldus Manutius, who in 1501 printed Virgil's Opera (3¾" x 6"), which was considered a prototype of the modern **pocket book** editions. The entire book was set in italics, but with the capital letters in roman. This typeface, the first italic, was designed and cut by Francesco Griffo.

See also Folio; Format; Octavo; Proportion; Sextodecimo; Size

Offset lithography - A planographic printing process in which the form and the paper do not have direct contact. It uses flat photomechanical plates where ink is transferred from the printing plate onto a rubber blanket, and from it onto the paper. Although Robert Barclay had used this process in London for printing lithographic stones onto sheets of metal for metal packaging since 1875, it was American Ira W. Rubel who advanced the printing process when he applied it to printing type onto paper in 1904.

See also Direct printing; Indirect printing; Lithography

Oldstyle figures - Numerals that exhibit a variation of size, and are aligned with the lowercase letters and some of them project their forms below the baseline. Some have ascenders and some descenders. Also called **text figures**, they were the common form in European typography between 1540 and 1800. They match well with running text and small caps in size and weight. We find an example in *New Caledonia* (David Berlow, 1979):

TEXT FIGURES 1234567890.

See also Lowercase letters; Modern style figures; Small caps

Oldstyle typefaces - A term used to describe the first roman types, which originated in France, and were designed between the late fifteenth and mid-eighteenth centuries. Based on the types cut by Francesco Griffo of Bologna for Venetian printer Aldus Manutius, in 1495, they were originally designed by Claude Garamond in 1540, and later developed by Jean Jannon and Robert Granjon. Caslon Old Face, designed by English type designer William Caslon I in 1722, is considered the last of the *Oldstyle* typefaces. A moderately thick-and-thin contrast, bracketed serifs, and a handwriting style characterize them. The axis of curved strokes is generally inclined to the left, and the lowercase upper serifs are oblique. Capitals are often lower than the lowercase ascenders, and both upper and lowercase letters are narrower than *Venetians*. The lowercase **e** has a horizontal bar placed slightly above center. Examples are found in JANSON / Janson, designed by Nicolas Kis in 1690, and CASLON / Caslon, designed by William Caslon I in 1722.

See also Bracketed serifs; Venetian Oldstyle typefaces; Aldine Oldstyle typefaces; Dutch Oldstyle typefaces; Oldstyle typeface revivals

Open face typefaces - A term used to describe those typefaces that are defined by an uneven outline, which permits letterforms to maintain their shape. Their presence in typography not only permits the use of a lighter form, but also give a different visual feeling to words set with them.

Such is the case of CLOISTER OPEN FACE. Nevertheless, we may find a variation in DELPHIAN OPEN TITLE, designed by Robert Hunter Middleton in 1928, in which there is a mixture of both the open and the incised concepts within one type design.

See also Handtooled typefaces; Incised typefaces; Outline typefaces

Optical letter spacing - A term used to describe the management of inner spaces so as to obtain an even, consistent visual distance between letters. Although a time-consuming task, it is in many cases needed, especially with large display type and uppercase letters. It is important to remember that this optical spacing must be compensated by proportional word spacing.

See also Inner space; Kerning; Letter spacing; Mechanical letter spacing; Spacing

Ordinal numbers - A sequence of numbers according to their position, as is the case of **first, second, third, fourth**, etc. Ordinal numbers may be expressed in two ways: by using Roman numerals, such as I, II, III, IV, etc., or by combining Arabic numbers with the abbreviation of the corresponding placement, which may be expressed as **1st, 2nd, 3rd, 4th**, etc, or as 1st, 2nd, 3rd, 4th, etc.

See also Cardinal numbers; Roman numerals; Superscript

Ornamental typefaces - Letterforms in which strokes have been embellished for a decorative purpose. These kinds of typefaces are frequently used as initials or in short words. Such is the case of **ÐAVIÐA BOLÐ**, designed by Louis Minott in 1965. It is interesting to compare ornamental typefaces with **decorated typefaces** and **historiated initials**.

See also Decorative typefaces; Historiated initials; Initials; Thibaudeau typeface classification

Outline typefaces - Letterforms described by an outer, even contour line, with the inner part of the strokes remaining unfilled. As this line is drawn around the outsides of the letters, they are fatter than the originals, and, in consequence, have less contour definition. The earliest designs of this kind appeared as jobbing typefaces. English type founder William Thorowgood showed three examples in his specimen book of 1833. This is the case of COOPER BLACK OUTLINE / Cooper Black Outline, a variation of **Cooper Black**, designed by Oswald Cooper in 1922. It is useful to compare **outline typefaces** with **open face typefaces** and **contour typefaces**.

See also Contour typefaces; Job press; Open face typefaces

P

Page - One side of a leaf of paper (or other material) in a publication (book or magazine) once it is printed or is identified in some manner to show its sequential arrangement. The physical designation of a page comes from folding a sheet of handmade paper (originally called *format*) into two (thus, the designation of *folio*). In this way we have two pages on the front (left and right), and two pages on the back (left and right). While the front side is called *recto*, the back side is called *verso*. Two facing pages, when layout as a whole, are referred as a **double spread**. It is useful to remember that right side pages have odd numbers, and left side pages, even numbers.

See also Double spread; Folio; Format; Leaf; Pagination

Pagination - A numbering of pages, of any publication, in consecutive order. Pagination is usually done in Arabic numbers although preliminary matter pagination in a book is commonly set in Roman numerals. Although referred to as **foliation**, numbers were initially placed only on the *recto*, one number serving for both the right and the left pages. Early manuscripts were numbered in Roman numerals. The first typographic book with foliation was Johannes von Speier (da Spira)'s 1470 edition of St. Augustine's *De Civitate Dei*. The use of pagination (numbers on all pages) seems to have started with the work *Cornucopiae* by Nicolo Perotti, printed by Aldus Manutius in 1499. Pagination did not become customary until the second half of the sixteenth century.

See also Arabic numerals; End matter; Folio; Page; Preliminary matter; Roman numerals

Pantograph - A tool used by craftsmen and artists to make equal, enlarged, or reduced copies of a given design. It consists of a fixed pivot, a tracing point, and a copying (pencil) point, the three held in mathematical relationship to each other by a parallelogram of four bars. The device can be adjusted to enlarge or reduce in any desired proportion. In 1834, William Leavenworth adapted a router to the pantograph, permitting a mechanical manufacturing of wood type. When Darius Wells bought Leavenworth equipment he improved the machine, which enabled him to make the mass production of type practical (see page 255). In 1885, Linn Boyd Benton improved the pantograph by inventing the matrix-boring machine, which permitted the mechanical cutting of a matrix, and enabled the commercial success of the Linotype machine. We may see how it works on page 63.

See also Wood type

Paragraph (¶) - A number of lines of a text containing the development of a complete thought. When setting type, it is customary to break a running text into blocks of text for easy reading. Alcuin of York, head of the Carolingian Court School, in the seventh century, is attributed with the introduction of paragraphs. When there is no physical breaking within a continuous composition, the old graphic device ¶, called *parágraphos*, derived from the Greek letter *pi* (Π), and introduced in early manuscripts, is still used as a reference mark. It functioned variously as a pointer or separator. It usually occurred inside a running block of text which did not break onto a new line. This technique saved space, and preserved the visual tone and density of the page. There are three basic ways for visually determining a paragraph: by indenting or by outdenting the starting line, in which case there is no physical separation between blocks or by physically separating them, as is the case of this publication. There is also the use of display type initials at the beginning of chapters.

See also Indented paragraph; Initials; Leading; Ornamental typefaces; Readability; Reference marks; Running text

Parchment - Name given to the processed skin of animals, such as sheep, goats, and calves, used as a writing support. It was during the second century B.C. that methods were found for preparing smoother close-textured skins. Being more durable and readily available than papyrus, parchment

slowly supplanted it. Ink was a solution of soot in olive oil or Arabic gum. When made from calf or kid skin, parchment is usually called **vellum**.

Today the words parchment and vellum refer to high-quality paper made from wood pulp and rags.

See also Croquill pen; Reed pen; Uncials

Parentheses ( ) - Punctuation marks used in pairs to set off extra or incidental contents from the rest of the text. While Renaissance parentheses are drawn as lines of equal weight ( ), neoclassical parentheses ( ) are thick in the center and thin at the ends. An early use of parentheses is found in Barzizius' *Epistolæ*, printed in Paris in 1470, which is also the first book printed in France.

See also Brackets; Punctuation marks

Period (.) - A punctuation mark that is used to indicate the end of a sentence. Although its shape changes according to the type design, it is generally round.

See also Comma; Dot leader; Ellipsis; Paragraph; Punctuation marks

Photo-lettering - See Phototypography

Photocomposition - A generic term for typesetting systems that use photographic media to reproduce type on film or paper. Phototypesetting machines may produce negative or positive images of type according to the printing process requirements. One of the major differences between metal and photographic composition is in the letter's proportions from one size to another. In photocomposition, a single master drawing is used for all sizes, rather than a drawing particular to each size. This usually causes thin strokes to disappear in small sizes.

See also Baseline; Digital type composition; Foundry type; Phototypography

Phototypography - A photographic reproduction of letterforms. Taking a line negative, a high intensity light is flashed through the non-blocked areas, projecting the character forms –through a series of lenses and prisms– onto film or photosensitive paper. The exposed film or paper is then developed and becomes the master setting. Phototypography has permitted replacing the rigid quality of metal type for a dynamic new flexibility according the versatility offered by the lenses. A commercially viable photographic display typesetting began in 1936 with the establishment of Photo-Lettering, Inc. headed by Ed Rondthaler. One of the first designers to take advantage of this typesetting system was Herb Lubalin, as seen in many of his typographic layouts (pages 187 and 188). Phototypography also permitted the introduction of new type designs as it was the case of **DOM CASUAL** / **Dom Casual** (Peter Dombrezian, 1950), prior to being cut in metal by AFF in 1952.

See also Baseline; Digital typography; Digitization

Pica - A typographic unit of measurement equal to 12 pt. One pica is also closed to, but not exactly, one sixth of an inch, and six picas are equal to an inch. Picas are used to measure the length of type lines, while points are used to measure the depth of a column. The term may derive from the old name for a 12-pt letter, used on the Roman Church *Pye-books*, which contained the appropriate liturgy on a given day. From it, probably came *pye-character*, or *pi-ca*. The United States Type

Founder's Association adopted the American Point System or **pica system** in 1886. Not until 1898, the English type founders adopted this point system. In computer languages, such as *PostScript* or *TrueType* a pica is exactly one sixth of an inch.

See also Cicero; Didot point system; Em space; Point; Type measuring units; Type size; Type sizes

Pi characters - Special designs, not included on the standard font, which are used to clarify, define, or emphasize certain contents. Such is the case of mathematical signs, zodiac signs, astronomical signs, monetary signs, pointing hands, telephone symbols, etc. These are some examples:

= + ÷ ± % # © ® @ § $ £ ¥ ♂ ♀ ♀ ♄ ♀

Foreign characters, such as ñ ð ø ý á è ç õ are also included.

See also Unalphabetic characters; Bullets; Dingbats

Plakatstil - A German word for **poster style** also referred to as *sachplakat* or object poster, in which there is a marked economy of image and text. By 1896, Munich had seen the birth of the Jugendstil poster, a product of the first years of contact between design and industry. After the turn of the century, Berlin, the center of commerce, became the home of the Berliner Plakat or *Plakatstil*. Through the keen eye of Ernst Growald of the Hollerbaum & Schmidt lithographic printing company who was one of the jurors in a poster design contest for Priester matches, sponsored by the Berlin Chamber of Commerce, German designer Lucian Bernhard won first prize in 1905. With a striking, simplified image-text whole (page 79), Bernhard inaugurated a new form of poster design. His approach was followed by designers Hans Rudi Erdt, Julius Gipkens, and Julius Klinger, among others.

See also Jugendstil

Point - The smallest typographical unit of measurement. It is equivalent to $^1/_{72}$ of an inch. Twelve points equal a pica. Type body size and interline spacing is measured in points. Points are also used for vertical measurements while picas are used for horizontal measurements. In the Didot system a point is $^1/_{12}$ of a *cicero*. In computer languages, such as *PostScript* and *TrueType*, a point is precisely $^1/_{72}$ of an inch, and a pica $^1/_6$ of an inch.

See also Cicero; Interline spacing; Pica; Unit; Unit system

Point system - A typographical measuring magnitude that permits the handling of type composition. There are two major type measuring systems in use today: the English/American System, used primarily by the English speaking world, and the Didot System, used by the rest of Europe. Until the eighteenth century, there was no standardized measuring method, only vague categories of type sizes. Then in 1737, French designer and printer Pierre Fournier *le jeune* proposed a mathematical system for denoting type sizes. Later on, in 1783, François-Ambroise Didot established the Didot point system, based on Fournier's work. During the late nineteenth century, the United States and England developed their own system, which was based upon Didot's work. It was adopted in America in 1886, and in England in 1898. In the English/American System, twelve points make a **pica**, and in the Didot System, twelve points make a **cicero**.

See also Body size; Cicero; Didot measuring system; Pica

Postage stamp - Perhaps the smallest printing area for a graphic design creation, it is employed on envelopes in payment for mailing correspondence. On page 241, we may find three excellent examples designed by Bradbury Thompson for the U.S. Postal Service in 1980-1984.

See also Cover; Poster

Post-modernism - Covering architecture, art, applied arts, literature, critical theory, philosophy, etc., it can be approached as a critical response to the project, myths, progress, mastery, and originality of Modernism. It evolved in America and Europe around the mid 1960s through the theories of post-structuralism and deconstruction (Barthes, Foucault, Derrida, among others). In graphic design, post-modernism thus evolved during the mid 1960s as a rather anarchic and critical attitude towards the orthodox issues of rationalism, functionalism (e.g., the order and discipline dictated by the Bauhaus and its followers as well as the rational conception of the International Typographic Style), and the logical evolution of styles. The possibilities of internalizing dissimilar graphic and artistic sources (eclecticism), the interest in historical data (in many ways rejected by the purity and autonomy of the modern project), and its relationship with new technology and mass media may be regarded as some of the main issues of post-modern design. Also, the evaluation, revision and breaking away from the patterns inherited from structuralism (the grid, the system of oppositions, and the hierarchical relationships of image and text), are clearly seen in the management of type and layout. Reversed lines of texts, words over-spaced, mixtures of type styles, floating forms, and randomly placed blips and lines; and multiple layered and fragmented images are used interchangeably. Leading the movement were Sigfried Odermatt and Rosmarie Tissi in Zurich, and Wolfgang Weingart in Basle. Weingart's influence as a teacher at the Schule für Gestaltung in Basle spread to the United States. Although orthodox typographers like Jan Tschichold, Emil Ruder, and Karl Gerstner rejected his proposal many other designers backed it. His eclectic, anarchic approach –also known as *New Wave*– often sacrificed legibility for expression. Post-modernism has been a definite and liberating influence on type design providing a new approach to letterform. With the development of the digital age and its applicability in type design, post-modern typography has produced a skeptical and comprehensive view of technology. The use of parody, irony, quotation, and pastiche has given type a way to deconstruct formal canons, which challenge well-established concepts of legibility and readability. The work of Rudy VanderLans and Zuzana Licko (as presented on *Émigré* magazine), and that of Tobias Frere-Jones are good examples of this approach.

See also Dada; Modernism

PostScript - A page description language, and also a font format, developed by John Warnock and Charles Geschke in 1983 (also cofounders of Adobe Systems Inc.), which enables type and images to be combined in one document. In 1984, the *PostScript Manual* was distributed privately, and in January 1985, it was introduced publicly in the *Apple Laser Writer*. Since then, it has constituted the greatest revolution in desktop publishing, or publication assisted by the computer.

See also Adobe Type Manager; Desktop publishing

Preface - The author's personal remarks which sometimes conclude with a paragraph of acknowledgments. It is customary to write a new preface for each new edition, outlining the changes and additions. If previous prefaces are included, they should follow the latest.

See also Foreword; Introduction; Preliminary matter

Preliminary matter - Also called **front matter**, it refers to those book sections preceding the main content. It normally includes the false cover, the frontispiece, the title page, the publication data, ISBN, acknowledgements, dedication, the content, the foreword, the preface, and the introduction. Pagination in preliminary matter is usually set in Roman numerals; a custom derived from early printing days when preliminary matter was usually composed after the body of the book had been finished. It is worth noting that many contemporary designers/authors do not follow this rule, and use Arabic numerals all throughout the book. Others, on the contrary, start a new pagination after preliminary matter.

See also Body; End matter; ISBN; Roman numerals

Prime and **double prime** (' ") - Abbreviation signs for measurements. **Single primes** are use for feet and minutes, and **double primes** for inches and seconds. Not to be confused with the **apostrophe** (') nor with the **quotation marks** (").

See also Apostrophe; Punctuation marks; Quotation marks

Printer's flowers - Decorative (traditionally in metal) type ornaments composed of motifs based on floral or organic shapes. They are used in repeated patterns to form typographic borders to embellish chapter headings, tail-pieces, title pages, and generally to enliven printed matter. Probably the earliest use of these kind of ornaments is found in Dominico Capranica's *Arte de ben morire*, printed in Verona in 1478. Among the many American typographers who took advantage of these floral designs to enrich their typographical pages, it is worthwhile mentioning Bruce Rogers and Frederic Warde. In 1946, Frederic W. Goudy, in his book, *A Half Century of Type Designs and Typography, 1895-1945*, presented a whole page of printer's flowers that he called *fleurons* (see page 143).

See also Dingbats; Fleurons; Typographic borders

Printer font - In desktop publishing, it is a typeface that can be used on any printing device. It is important to differentiate a **printer font** from a **screen font**, in which samples only allow for a visualization of type characteristics, and cannot be printed out. In 1984, Charles Bigelow and Kris Holmes developed LUCIDA / Lucida, which was the first typeface designed for low-resolution printers.

See also Desktop publishing; Screen font

Printer's mark - Also called a **printer's device**, it may contain the printer's initials, a symbolic image or an abstract element. Today, it usually appears on the title page, accompanied by the printer's name, and appears in every book the publisher issues. The first book to contain a printer's device was the *Latin Bible* or *48-line Bible* printed by Johann Fust and

Peter Schöffer in 1462. On page 225 we may see the *Borzoi Books* device designed by Rudolph Ruzicka in 1922 for New York publisher Alfred A. Knopf, and on page 131, some graphic variations done by William Addison Dwiggins.

See also Colophon; Title page

Printer's ornaments - Letterpress blocks, bearing designs cut in relief by an engraver for printing together with the text of a book. Such ornaments were particularly popular as decorative head and tailpieces in the eighteenth century. They have remained popular since then. Some of them may be seen in the section on William Bradley (page 97).

See also Chapbook cut

Printing - *See* Letterpress; Relief printing

Private press - A small printing house which issues, for public sale, limited editions of books that have been carefully made in their own establishment. According to Eric Gill, a "private" press prints solely what it chooses to print whereas a "public" press prints what its customers demand of it. According to Joseph Blumenthal, a private press is a "sustained enterprise of a person of means, and of taste and ability, who produces books for his own aesthetic pleasure, frequently with a newly commissioned proprietary typeface and, usually, with one or more employed journeymen. Books were set by hand and printed on dampened handmade papers and customarily bound in vellum." After William Morris with his Kelmscott Press initiated the private press movement in England, many Americans decided to imitate him, establishing their own presses. This is the case of the Merrymount Press founded by Daniel Berkeley Updike in 1893, for which Bertram G. Goodhue designed *Merrymount* in 1895, and the Village Press founded by Frederic W. Goudy in 1903, in collaboration with Will Ransom. For it, Goudy also designed his own private typeface, *Village*. It is also worthwhile mentioning Joseph Blumenthal's Spiral Press (1926), Victor Hammer's Stamperia del Santuccio (1931), Robert Hunter Middleton's Cherryburn Press (1944), and Robert M. Jones's The Glad Hand Press (1953), among others.

See also Custom typefaces; Foundry type; Letterpress

Proportion - A relationship of measurements (height and width or width and height), which determines the final appearance of a given surface, as well as its direction (horizontal or vertical), according to the order of measurements. Such is the case of 8" x 11" (vertical) or 11" x 8" (horizontal). In printing, it is referred to as **format**.

See also Dimension; Format

Proportional size - The physical adjustment of certain letters of the alphabet, especially capitals, so that they may appear visually even. Curves and angles must surpass the **cap line** and **baseline** a little. Otherwise these characters will look smaller. This is the case of letters **A**, **C**, **G**, **J**, **O**, **Q**, **S**, and **U**.

See also Baseline; Cap line; Visual size

Punch - A short vertical metal bar in which each one of the characters of an alphabet –capitals, lowercase letters, numbers and signs– is sculpted actual size and in reverse in one of its ends. Once engraved, the metal bar is hardened and stamped into a bar of brass or copper, known as the **matrix**. It is important to remember that each character of

a given size requires a different punch, that is, one for 4 pt, one for 6 pt, one for 8 pt, etc.

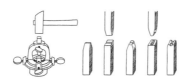

See also Matrix; Phototypography; Punch-cutter

Punch-cutter - A professional engraver who specializes in cutting punches. In precise terms there is a difference between the original punch-cutter who also designed his own typefaces, such as Francesco Griffo, Nicolas Kis, Claude Garamond, Philippe Grandjean, Pierre Fournier, Firmin Didot, and Giambattista Bodoni, and the interpreter, who cuts someone else's design. Among the contemporary punch-cutters, we may mention French Charles Malin, who cut Eric Gill's *Perpetua* (1926), Frederic Warde's *Arrighi* (1928), and Giovanni (Hans) Mardersteig's *Dante* (1954), and American Robert Wiebking, who, apart from his own designs, cut a large number of Frederic W. Goudy's types. On page 63, we may see the utensils of a punch-cutter as well as a punch-cutter working on a typeface. In 1885, Linn Boyd Benton invented the automatic punch-cutter, which enabled any person, without being a specialized punch-cutter, to cut a typeface. It not only permitted Linotype to overcome the bottleneck in production and to allow it to prosper definitely, but also to allow designers like Goudy to cut their own typefaces.

See also Matrix; Punch

Punctuation marks - A term used to refer to those small typographic marks that are employed to give a clear meaning to sentences. The term comes from the Latin *punctum*, "point." The first person to have an interest in these graphic signs was Aristophanes of Byzantium, director of the Library of Alexandria, who, around 260 B.C., revising many of Homer's works, established a punctuation system. He marked the shortest segments of discourse with a center dot called *comma*; the longer sections with a low dot called *colon*; and the longest unit with a high-placed dot he called *periodos*. He developed them from rhetoric, as a reference to rhythmical units of speech. As such, they served to regulate pace and give emphasis to particular phrases, rather than to mark the logical structure of sentences. During the reign of Emperor Charlemagne, Alcuin of York introduced punctuation marks and the grouping of words into sentences, which, for the first time, began with an enlarged letter. The approach to modern punctuation, including the comma, began with Venetian printer Aldus Manutius. Nevertheless, the contemporary use of most punctuation marks in typography only dates from the seventeenth century; some of them, like the quotation and exclamation marks, to the eighteenth century. The main punctuation marks are:

. , ; : " " ' ' ¿ ? ¡ ! - \ / ... * ( ) [ ] ~

See also Brackets; Carolingian script; Colon; Comma, Dot leader; Ellipses; Exclamation point; Hyphen; Initial letter;

Question marks; Quotation marks; Parentheses; Period; Semicolon; Slash; Virgule

Q

Quads (| **|** ■) - Blank typographical elements cast less than type height, in standard point sizes, and used as inter-letter and inter-word spacing material in hand-set type. The most usual sizes are **5-to-the-em** ($1/5$ size of em), **4-to-the-em** ($1/4$ size of em), **3-to-the-em** ($1/3$ size of em), **en**, **em**, **2-em**, **3-em**, and **4-em** quads. The word quad is an abbreviation from *quadrate*, which is never used in full. These spaces have been maintained in desktop publishing.

See also Em space; En space; Inner space; Kerning; Space

Quarto ($1/4$) - The resulting format from folding a sheet of handmade paper twice, thus reducing it to $1/4$ of its original size. To fully define the proportions of a given publication, it is important to know the paper's original format, for it is difficult to clearly define its proportions by just referring to it as a book printed *in quarto*. Between 1495 and 1496, Venetian printer and scholar Aldus Manutius issued a small *quarto* ($53/4$" x 8") of sixty pages edition of Pietro, later Cardinal, Bembo's *De Aetna*. The type was designed and cut by Francesco Griffo. In 1499, Manutius printed a *quarto* (8" x 12$1/4$") edition of Dominican monk Francesco Colonna's book, *Hypnerotomachia Poliphili*, considered one of the world's most beautifully illustrated books. The type was also cut by Griffo, and the 168 woodcut illustrations were executed by an unknown artist.

See also Chase; Folio; Format; Octavo; Sextodecimo

Question marks (¿ ?) - Punctuation marks that are used to express doubt. Some typographic historians think that the question mark derived from an abbreviation of the Latin word *quid* or *quidnam*, "what," which was represented by a *Q* over a lowercase o. This compound figure gave way to the present form, which developed in England around the seventeenth century. While in English only the closing question mark is used (**?**), in Spanish, since the eighteenth century, both question marks (¿ ?) are employed, which, by the way, permit the reader to know in advance the characteristics of the sentence. It is interesting to note that in 1966, Martin K. Specker created the **interrobang**, which was a mixture of a question mark and an exclamation point, and which was proposed as a graphic sign to express ambiguous sentences, such as You did what‽. Richard Isbell designed and included it in his alphabet AMERICANA / Americana (1966), as we may see on page 172.

See also Exclamation point; Punctuation marks

Quill pen - *See* Crowquill pen

Quotations - Written or spoken words taken from elsewhere, and included by an author in his text. Such passages are usually enclosed between quotation marks and set in italics. They may also be set in a smaller body size or as footnotes at the bottom of a page. It is most probable that German printer Johann Froben (1460-1527), who used roman and italics types, was the one who originated the use of italics for quotations.

See also Italics; Prime and double prime; Quotation marks

Quotation marks (' ') (" ") - Also called **quotes**, they are inverted commas used singly or in pairs to enclose cited texts. When there is a quoted text within another quoted text, single quotes are used. Also known as *guillemets*, they were first introduced, in 1546, by French typecutter Guillaume Le Bé although different in form « ». According to Mac McGrew in his book, *American Metal Typefaces of the Twentieth Century*, the typeface *John Alden*, cut by Keystone type foundry in 1901, is the first American font to include **reverse apostrophes** (" ") as modern quotation marks. As a side note, in the German language, open quotes are placed on the baseline („) and are drawn as common closing quotes. McGrew also notes that, according to the uniform width of all characters, typewriters have "uniquotes," a characteristic maintained today in word processors.

See also Apostrophe; Punctuation marks; Quotations

R

Readability - The quality inherent in type design that permits an observer to perceive a text as a fluid continuity of characters, and allows him or her to read words and sentences rather than isolated elements. It is important to differentiate **readability** and **legibility**. The first term deals with the relationship that exists between characters, and between lowercase and uppercase letters; the second term, refers to the structure and form of a given character. They are inseparable from each other when dealing with reading. Other factors, such as type size, letter spacing, word spacing, leading, and characters per line, also have a definite influence on perception, and therefore on the legibility and readability of a given typeset text. Other aspects, such as surface texture, color of the paper, color of the ink, margins, printing systems, and printing quality, are also strong determining characteristics.

See also Leading; Legibility Group; Letter spacing; Readability; Space; Texture

Recto - A term taken from Latin, it applies to the front side of a sheet of paper as opposed to *verso*, or back side of the same sheet. It also applies to the right side page of a book. We must also note that there are papers that have a *recto* and a *verso*, especially handmade papers, on account of their texture or their watermarks.

The term *recto* also refers to the face of a blank sheet of paper, which is first printed.
See also Page; Verso

Reed pen - A writing utensil cut from the reed, a tall straight firm-stemmed water or marsh plant. One of the ends of a dry reed was cut at an angle to manufacture writing pens, to write upon papyrus, a paper-like writing material initially used by the Egyptians. Around the second century, the croquill pen supplanted the reed, when parchment also supplanted papyrus. Both of them were essential in the development of letterforms.
See also Brush; Chisel; Croquill pen; Parchment; Uncials

Reference marks - Graphic symbols used within a running text as a way to indicate to the reader that there is further information, or a footnote. This additional information is always preceded by an identical reference mark. The most usual reference marks are asterisk (*), dagger (†), double dagger (‡), paragraph (¶), section (§), and virgule (~).
See also Asterisk; Dagger; Paragraph; Section; Virgule

Reflexive serif - That which simultaneously stops a main stroke and implies its continuation. It always involves a reversal of the pen's stroke direction. Being usually bilateral, it extends to both sides of the stem. Reflexive serifs are typical of roman typefaces.

See also Italic; Modulation; Serif; Stem; Transitive serif

Regular typefaces - Characters defined with heavier strokes than light versions. It is interesting to note that type variations are not always created in the same order. Sometimes a light variation may come after a regular weight. Let us compare News Gothic Light with News Gothic Regular, two typefaces designed by Morris Fuller Benton in 1908. Although they are more condensed, they were essentially lighter variations of **Franklin Gothic** (1902), also his.
See also Bold typeface; Light typeface; Weight of a typeface

Reissue typeface design - A type that is generally cast in its original form and often cast from the same matrix. Many decorated faces from the nineteenth-century returned to favor in the 1950s and were re-issued. We may also cite the work done by Giovanni (Hans) Mardersteig at the Officina Bodoni, at Montagnola di Lugano, who reissued Giambattista Bodoni's types by casting them from the original matrices. The first book, *Orphei tragedia* by Angelo Poliziano, appeared in 1923.
See also Facsimile typeface; Revival typeface design

Relief printing - A traditional method of obtaining a duplicate of an image by using carved surfaces where ink is applied to the raised surface. Impression is obtained through direct contact between the inked raised surface and paper or other similar material placed on top. The first printed impressions were little more than the equivalent of the modern rubber stamping. They were made from wooden charms seals, originally used for stamping on clay. These were dipped in red ink and impressed on paper. The resulting image was red with white characters. Around AD 500, artisans cut away the negative area surrounding the characters, so that the characters could be printed red surrounded by the white of the paper. This was one precedent for printing; the other was ink-rubbing. Chinese also used to take impressions from carved stones inscriptions by laying damp paper over the surface of the stone, brushing it well into the letters and then wiping ink over the back of the paper so that the text stood out white against the inked paper. The invention of block printing is attributed to Fêng Tao in the fifth-century, and the printing with movable characters (baked clay) to Pi Sheng around 1041-1048. The ink they used was comparable to the known *encre de Chine*, and was made of lampblack mixed with gum. It was quite unlike European printing ink, which depends on an oily base.
See also Foundry type; Impression; Letterpress; Movable types; Typography; Woodcut; Wood engraving; Wood type

Resolution - It is the quality of reproduction of a given original based on the number of pixels or dots per inch available on an output device. Thus, it may be **low-resolution** or **high-resolution**, and it is valued in the fineness of the grain of the typeset image. Laser printers, for example, generally have a resolution which goes from 150 d.p.i. up to 600 d.p.i. or more, and typesetting machines a resolution which is substantially greater than 1000 d.p.i. Scanners and monitors also present similar low and high resolutions. In terms of photomechanical reproductions it is valued in terms of lines per inch, depending of the type of screen, and it may go from 64 to 200 l.p.i.
See also Bitmap character; Digital typography; Digitization; Xerography

Revival typeface design - An adjustment of an existing design to more contemporary technology or to manufacturing methods. The design usually goes under a series of regulated characteristics to adapt it to newer style demands. One example may be found in SOUVENIR / Souvenir, designed by Morris Fuller Benton in 1914, and redrawn by Edward Benguiat in 1970, making it a best seller. The term also refers to those typefaces that have been designed following classical models. Generally, these typefaces are based on *Oldstyle* designs. When the revival maintains all the idiosyncrasies of the original, it is referred to as a *facsimile*, as might be the case of Monotype's *Polyphilus* (1923), cut under Stanley Morison's supervision. From 1960 to 1980, most new types and revivals were usually planned for photocomposition, and since 1980, most of them were planned for digital type composition.
See also Digital type composition; Facsimile typeface; Photocomposition; Reissue typeface design

Rhythm - In a printed page, it is a visual unevenness in pattern created by the sequence of different shapes, ascenders, and descenders in lowercase letterforms, which enhances reading. This is one of the reasons why a text set in sustained capital letters is less readable than one set in lowercase letters.
See also Capital letters; Legibility; Lowercase letters; Readability; Uppercase letters

Roman numerals - A numerical notation system developed by the Romans. Based on a combination of symbols and capital letters, the system was replaced by Arabic numerals. Roman numerals are generally used in a book's preliminary pages and to number chapters. They are: **I, II, III, IV, V, VI, VII, VIII, IX, X, XI**, etc. **L**: 50; **C**: 100; **D**: 500; **DC**: 600; **CM**: 900; **M**: 1000, etc. Some early printed books as well as some contemporary printers, such as Bruce Rogers, used to date books using Roman numerals, as may be seen on the title page of the Grolier Club edition of *Fra Luca de Pacioli of Borgo S. Sepolcro* by Stanley Morison (page 223), which is written thus: **MCMXXXIII** (1933).
See also Arabic numerals; Ordinal numbers; Preliminary matter

Roman style typefaces - Upright letterforms, as differentiated from *italics*. They are based on the book hand of the Renaissance humanists, which was developed principally in Florence, in the first half of the fifteenth century. While capital letters were based on Roman *Capitalis Quadrata*, lower-case letters were descendant of the *Carolingian script*. The name comes from the French, and it is probably based on the fact that the first roman typeface used in France, that of the Sorbonne press of 1470, was copied from the font cut and used by German printers Konrad Schweynheim and Arnold Pannartz in Rome in 1467. An earlier form, and the first roman type to be considered as such, was the typeface cut and used by these German printers at Subiaco, Italy, around 1464. Less calligraphic in style were the Venetian types of German printers, Johannes and Wendelin von Speier (da Spira), 1469, and Frenchman Nicolas Jenson, 1470. Jenson's type is still the most highly praised of all romans. They led to the Aldus Manutius typeface of 1495, which in Francesco Griffo's refined version of 1499 represented the perfect *Oldstyle* typeface. Later, between 1530 and 1550, Claude Garamond in Paris produced typefaces, which were also based on the Venetian roman. The Renaissance roman fonts were thus divided into two groups, the Venetian and the French. Roman typefaces have evolved from four distinct stages of development: **Venetian**, **Oldstyle**, **Transitional** and **Modern**.

This is an example Roman and *italic*, as seen in ITC LEGACY / ITC Legacy designed by Ronald Arnholm in 1992.

See also Aldine Old Face types; Black letter; Carolingian script; Humanist script; Italics; Oldstyle typefaces; Trajan Column; Transitional typefaces; Venetian Old Face types

Rubbing - An impression taken from a stone inscription by means of *frottage*. This is a practice used by many type designers as a way to access Roman inscriptional letters and from them, develop a complete font. Such is the case of HADRIANO TITLE developed by Frederic W. Goudy in 1918, after a rubbing (page 142) taken from a second century Roman inscription found in the Louvre Museum in Paris. We may find another example in GHIBERTI, a typeface designed by Paul Shaw and Garrett Boge in 1997, after a rubbing (page 227) of the Berto di Leonardo tombstone (1430) in Santa Croce, Florence.

See also Glyphic style typefaces; Inscriptional letters; Trajan Column

Rules - In handset metal type, strips of brass or type metal, type high, cast in point sizes and to various lengths. They are generally used to print lines and simple borders, as may be seen on page 65. They are also used to separate columns of texts in Bibles, dictionaries, newspapers, etc.

See also Borders; Typographic devices

Running text - Also referred to as **body text**, it is normal typesetting as opposed to **display type**. This term usually covers type up to 14 pt.

See also Book face; Display type

S

Sans serif typefaces - A term used to refer to those typefaces that don't have finishing terminals in their strokes and generally have strokes of even thickness. Stone cut versions of this style pre-date printing with movable type, as may be found in Greek and Roman lapidary inscriptions.

They reappeared in Rome in the third and second centuries B.C., and in Florence in the early Renaissance. Nevertheless, sans serif letterforms designed and used by Florentine architects and sculptors were not translated into metal type in the 1470s. James Mosley shows in his article, *The Nymph and the Groot: The Revival of the Sanserif Letter*, several examples which precede the first sans serif type specimen. Among these examples we may find the architectural drawings done by Sir John Soane in 1791, an engraved titling designed by John Flaxman in 1805-1806, and an engraved title page for Thomas Hope's *Household Furniture* from 1807. At different times in their history, these typefaces have been known as condensed, doric, grotesque, sans-surryphs, gothics, and monoline. Although the first type to be designed with these characteristics was made by the English printer and founder William Caslon IV in 1816, it was not until 1832 that type founder Vincent Figgins in his *Specimen of Printing Types* applied this name. By 1830, we may find many examples of sans serif types in American wood type catalogs, such as those edited by George F. Nesbitt. In 1898, the German type foundry, H. Berthold AG popularized the style with its **Akzidenz Grotesk**. We find an American example in **Franklin Gothic**, designed by Morris Fuller Benton in 1903. According to A. F. Johnson, the term sans serif "comes from the fact of being an Egyptian typeface with the serifs knocked off."

We may finally add that sans serif typefaces may be grouped in three different categories according to their features: **Grotesque** (AKZIDENZ GROTESK, H. Berthold AG, 1898), **Geometric** (**FUTURA**, Paul Renner, 1927), and **Humanist** (STELLAR, Robert Hunter Middleton, 1929).

See also Bauhaus; Humanist Sans serif; International Typographic Style; Serif typefaces; Thibaudeau typeface classification; Vox type classification

Scalable fonts - In digital typography, it is a font designed so that weight and proportions of letter-forms alter simultaneously with their size. In foundry type these were altered size to size. Small sizes were cut darker and wider than larger sizes so as to avoid visible changes in color, and to avoid closed counters from clogging with ink when printing. It is worth mentioning the interest placed by Morris Fuller Benton when cutting a typeface. For it, he used cutting slips to make certain that ATF's engraving machine operators precisely and consistently adjusted the machine for every point size. Linotype and Monotype fonts were scaled in a similar way. This is one of the problems present in photocomposition where types are reproduced from a single matrix. Thus, thin strokes tend to disappear in small sizes. Genuine scaling fonts are a recent development in digital typography. An example may be found in Jonathan Hoefler's HTF DIDOT / HTF Didot, a typeface designed in 1992, with seven master versions for use in a specific range of sizes: below 10 pt; 11-15; 16-23; 24-41; 42-63; 64-95; 96 and above.

See also Digital typography; Master design; Matrix

Screen fonts - Typefaces designed to be displayed on a monitor's screen. In 1972, the Architecture Machine Group at MIT developed the first gray-scale

fonts that permitted type contours to appear smooth and legible on the screen.

See also Bitmap character; Digital typography; Printer fonts

Script typefaces - A term used to refer to the printing characters that being based on handwriting, usually display flowing curves, flourishes and connecting strokes between letters. An early example is found in French *Civilité* designed by Robert Granjon in 1556, and based on the current handwriting used in the royal chancery since he considered *italic* to be essentially Italian. A contemporary example is found in *Gando Ronde*, designed by Matthew Carter in 1970.

See also Calligraphic typefaces

Section (§) - A reference mark used by twelfth-century scribes, to indicate, within a running text, that there started a new **paragraph**. This also saved space. It is an alternate sign for ¶.

See also Paragraph; Reference marks

Semicolon (;) - A punctuation mark, which is a combination of a **comma** and a **period**, that is used to determine a pause greater than a comma, but less than a period. It is generally used to separate complete and closely related sentences. Such as: A typeface may be identified by the name of the designer, *Goudy*; by a country, *Helvetica*; by a related name, *Charlemagne*; or by simply a name, *Myriad*. The semicolon may be found in European manuscripts of the seventh- and eighth centuries.

See also Colon; Comma; Punctuation marks

Series of typefaces - A term that generally refers to all the sizes of one particular typeface. These variations of size are designed according to use. Body text type has variations of one point, thus, 3, 4, 4½, 5, 6, 7, 8, 9, 10, 11, 12, and 14; and display type are designed with certain intervals, as follows: 18, 24, 30, 36, 42, 48, 54, 60, and 72. From this size on, display types are usually measured in lines; such as **one-line**, **two-line**, **three-line**, **four-line** type denominations. These large typefaces appeared for the first time in 1765 when English type founder, Thomas Cottrell presented a sample of his Two-line English Romans typefaces (two inches high), based on Caslon Oldstyle.

See also Book face; Display type; Initials; Type sizes

Serifs - A term given to those characteristic stroke terminals normally found in Roman typefaces. Serifs may be **unilateral** (at only one side of the main stroke) or **bilateral** (at both sides). Although we may find serifs in Greek monumental inscriptions, they were properly developed in the Roman Empire stone-carving practice through the use of the chisel after a calligrapher had drawn letterforms with a flat brush on the stone before carving. Serifs help knit letters into word shapes, in extended copy, and considerably aid legibility and readability, especially with letters that have similar structure, such as capital I and lowercase l. Let's compare a word like Illinois or Illinois, set in sans serif and serif types.

With the development of type styles, serifs have acquired five distinctive forms: **bracketed serif**, **hairline serif**, **Egyptian serif**, **slab serif**, and **wedge serif**, as may be seen in the preceding illustration.

See also Bracketed serifs; Brush; Chisel; Clarendon serifs; Egyptian serifs; Hairline serifs; Legibility; Modern serif; Readability; Reflexive serif; Sans serif typefaces; Slab serifs; Transitive serif; Tuscan typefaces; Wedge-shaped serif

Serif typefaces - A generic term used in typography to refer to those characters based on the Roman letters, characterized by modulated strokes, and the presence of stroke terminals. Such as is the case of ELDORADO / Eldorado, designed by William Addison Dwiggins for Mergenthaler Linotype in 1953.

See also Brush; Chisel; Modulation; Oldstyle typefaces; Roman style typefaces; Sans serif typefaces; Serifs

Set-width - In metal type, it refers to the width of the body upon which the type character is cast. This amount of space added on either side of a character permits a physical separation from the characters placed on either side of it. It is important to remember that this space has been maintained in digital typefaces reflecting the incidence of metal type structure. It may be modified through **kerning**.

See also Body; Body size; Kerning; Shoulder; Type nomenclature; Unit system

Sextodecimo / Sixteenth ($1/16$) - The resulting format from folding a sheet of handmade paper with four folds, thus reducing it to $1/16$ the original size or 16mo (from the Latin, *sextodecimo*). To fully define the proportions of a given publication, it is important to know a piece of paper's original format, for it is difficult to clearly define its proportions by just referring to it as a book printed *in 16mo*. Besides the Dutch Elzevir family, who first printed vest-pocket editions in 1629, French engraver and punch-cutter Pierre Simon Fournier *le jeune* used this format (4 $1/4$" x 6 $3/4$") when he published his handsome, *Manuel Typographique*, between 1764 and 1766.

See also Chase; Folio; Format; Octavo; Quarto; Size

Shaded typefaces - A term applied to those characters which usually have a white line incised on the main stem, giving the appearance of a shaded stroke. **Shaded** as well as **decorated** typefaces were designed as display fonts. Thus, they were used both on books as well as on ephemeral printing. The first shaded typefaces were designed by Pierre Fournier and presented in his *Manuel Typographique* of 1764-66. He cut nine decorated and shaded letters, the largest of the latter being approximately 84 pt and 108 pt. According to him, these were cut "expressly for posters and bills." These typefaces are also known as **inline** or **handtooled**, although there are noticeable differences among them.

See also Handtooled typefaces; Inline typefaces; Shadowed typefaces

Shadowed typefaces - A term applied to outline alphabets that have been given a strong three-dimensional quality by the use of a heavy shadow on one side of the letter following a given light source. The first shadowed letters appeared in 1815, introduced by Vincent Figgins. Its immediate popularity made every founder come out with a wide range of sizes, many with italic. Although

the original designs were **fat faces**, there also appeared sans serif characters with the same features. We find an example in GRAPHIQUE, designed by Hermann Eidenbenz in 1946, and in ITC PIONEER, designed by Tom Carnase and Ronne Bonder in 1970. We find an example of a shadowed typeface without an outline in UMBRA, designed by Robert Hunter Middleton in 1932.

See also Fat faces; Shaded typefaces; Three-dimensional typefaces

Shoulder - In metal type, it refers to the flattop or platform from which the **face** raises. Since it extends above and below the face, it also provides a physical space which separates a line of text from the immediate one below, when a text is set solid. This space has been maintained in digital typesetting. On page 225, there is an illustration of a metal type, executed by Rudolph Ruzicka, which clearly shows this part.

The term **shoulder** also refers to the stroke emerging from a stem, usually round, as in letters **h**, **m**, and **n**.

See also Anatomy of a letter; Face; Matrix; Set-width; Stem; Type nomenclature

Side bearings - *See* Set-width

Sixteenth - *See* Sextodecimo

Size - The dimension of a given surface. It may be big or small. Not to be mistaken for **proportion**. Thus, when we say **pocket size books** we are only referring to their portable characteristic, but not to their format, nor if they are vertical or horizontal, wide or narrow.

See also Format; Proportion

Slab serif - The square or rectangular stroke terminals that align horizontally and vertically to the baseline, and usually have the same or a heavier weight than the main strokes of a letterform. We may find an example in letters **H** and **T**, of typeface ITC **LUBALIN GOTHIC** / ITC Lubalin Gothic, designed by Herb Lubalin and Tony DiSpigna in 1974.

See also Anatomy of a letter; Egyptian typefaces; Serif; Thibaudeau typeface classification; Typeface classification

Slab Serif typefaces - *See* Egyptian typefaces

Slash (/) - A diagonal line that is placed between words to indicate that there is an alternative way of reading a concept, such as light and/or bold. It is also used to express fractions graphically, such as ½, and percentages, such as **%**. It may be to the right (/), or to the left (\ ) (**back slash**), as may be found in computer commands. A shorter slash known as *virgule* (⁄), was used as a **comma** in medieval manuscripts and early printed books. We may find an example in **HAMMER UNZIALE** / Hammer Unziale, a typeface designed by Victor Hammer in 1923 (page 154).

See also Fractions; Punctuation marks; Reference marks; Virgule

Slope - The angle of inclination of the stems and ascenders. Generally, *italics* slope to the right at an angle that goes from 2 to 20 degrees.

See also Ascender; Italics; Stem

Slug - A bar of **type metal** containing a line of type that has been cast as a unit in a typecasting machine, such as the Linotype or the Ludlow.

The length of these bars was between 30 and 42 picas. If a narrower type width was required, the excess metal was trimmed off. Type metal employed was softer than the used in foundry type. We may see Linotype and Ludlow slugs on pages 191 and 193.

The term **slug** is also applied to a 6-pt metal lead spacing.

See also Foundry type; Leading; Linotype; Ludlow; Type metal

Small Caps - An alternative set of capital letters available on most type designs used for text setting, but especially on **expert type fonts**. They have the same height as the lowercase x-height, and are commonly used within the body text to indicate a cross-reference. They are also used when there is a title set in sustained capitals to avoid a mayor visual emphasis within the running text or to enhance a name visually. Small caps also go well with *Oldstyle* numerals as in FIGURES 1234567890 WITH SMALL CAPS. A common example is found in stationery in the setting of a name, such as WILLIAM A. DWIGGINS. Small caps appeared in medieval manuscripts marking an opening phrase after an accompanying initial. We may find a sample of complete fonts on pages 93, 94, 95, 230 and 231.

See also Book face; Capitals; Expert type fonts; Initial; Oldstyle numerals; Tricameral alphabet

Solid composition - A term that refers to type setting with no additional spacing between the lines. It is expressed $8/8$, $10/10$, etc. Nevertheless, it is important to remember that since a character is placed upon a piece of metal or body, there is a free space above and below it, which avoids touching between lines of a text. On page 225, we may see an illustration of a metal type, executed by Rudolph Ruzicka, in which we may see these spaces more clearly.

See also Body size; Line spacing; Negative leading; Shoulder; Type setting; Typesetting specifications

Space - The horizontal distance existing between letters and words that allows for readability. In handset type, they are pieces of metal, lower than type-high, inserted between words, and sometimes between letters for proper spacing in a line of text. It is also useful to remember that since there is a set-width for each character, there is a space on each side, which avoids letters touching physically. While some letterforms have been designed with very close fitting, as is the case of ITC MACHINE (Tom Carnase, 1970) (see an example on page 187), some type styles need an optical spacing, specially with display type when set in sustained caps.

See also Display type; Em space; En space; Inner space; Letter spacing; Leading; Optical spacing; Paragraph; Set-width

Space bands - Movable wedges used in typecasting machines, such as the Linotype, for word spacing and justifying lines of type. After a row of matrices was set, space bands were forced by the operator into them to tighten the line, justifying it prior to casting. We may see them on page 193.

See also Linotype

Spacing - *See* Letter spacing; Line spacing

Speedball pen - A special lettering pen used for show-card writing and lettering. On page 230, we may see an example in BERMUDA OPEN, a typeface designed by Garrett Boge and Paul Shaw

using a *Speedball* pen. The first dip pens were manufactured by C. Howard Hunt's company, Camden, New Jersey in 1899. In 1915, Ross F. George pattented the *Speedball* pen to the Howard Hunt Pen Co., which commercialized it that year.
See also Calligraphy; Lettering

Spencerian script - A term applied to lettering that is developed in sketch form, and is very tightly drawn with a **croquill pen**. Although similar to calligraphy in its final form, it differs from it in that calligraphy is executed with a free single-stroke movement of a brush or a pen. Developed by Platt R. Spencer in Kingsville, Ohio, the first series of manuals appeared in 1848. They contained materials for writing, as well as a systematic development of skills in forming and spacing letters. In 1852, he established the Spencerian Commercial College, where he implemented his pedagogic program. Three great contemporary representatives of Spencerian script are Edward Benguiat, Tom Carnase, and Tony DiSpigna, whose skill and sensitivity helped Herb Lubalin to bring many of his ideas and sketches to reality. We may see some fine examples on pages 128, 187, and 188.
See also Calligraphy; Croquill pen; Hand lettering; Lettering

Spine - In both upper and lowercase letters **S s**, this term refers to the curve of the main stroke.
See also Anatomy of a letter; Stem; Stroke

Spur - A term generally applied to a small projection found at the lower end of a vertical stroke as a result of a calligraphic gesture. In **grotesque typefaces**, such as **Akzidenz Grotesque** (1898) or News Gothic (1908), the uppercase letter **G** is characterized by a projection or spur on the lower curve, which gives visual stability to the letterform. A spur was also employed by Philippe Grandjean in the middle left of the vertical strokes of lowercase letters **l** and old *f* to create a distinctive feature on the *Roman du Roi Louis XIV* typeface, cut for the Imprimerie Royale in 1700. This feature was later copied by other European typographers.
See also Anatomy of a letter; Grotesque typefaces; Stem; Stroke

Square sans serif typefaces - A term used to refer to those typefaces that present block-like shapes instead of round letters. They are also characterized by an even stroke. This is the case of BANK GOTHIC, designed by Morris Fuller Benton in 1930, and MICROGRAMMA, designed by Alessandro Butti and Aldo Novarese in 1952.
See also Sans serif typefaces

Stem - The main support of a letter is usually vertical or slightly inclined in italics. Curved letters do not have a stem. Besides those letters with even strokes (slab-serif typefaces), the stem is usually thicker. This gives a visual hierarchy within letterforms.
See also Arm; Anatomy of a typeface; Cross bar; Italics; Slope; Spine

Stencil printing - One of the basic printing systems, it is based on a **hollowed matrix** principle practiced on a surface and where ink passes through the openings. Examples of this principle are found in mimeograph and silkscreen printings. It is interesting to note that phototypography uses a similar principle since light, instead of ink, passes through a line negative which comes up to being a hollowed matrix.

See also Matrix; Phototypography; Stencil typefaces

Stencil typefaces - Based on cut-out plates used in hand illustration, these typefaces are segmented to allow their printing through a stencil printing procedure. They are generally related to the marking of large containers and cardboard packages. Although there was much formal experimentation on type design during the Victorian era, there is no printed example of stencil type characters during the nineteenth century. It seems that this formal variation is a product of the twentieth century, most probably as a result of the war shipping of packages. An example is found in **STENCIL**, created by Gerry Powell in 1937, which appeared one month after Robert H. Middleton's type design of the same name.
See also Stencil printing; Typeface classification

Stereotyping - The process of making a solid metal duplicate of a relief printing plate by pressing a malleable material (*papier mâché*, clay, or plaster) against the original, then using the resulting mold to cast a duplicate from molten metal. The term, coined by Firmin Didot, comes from the Greek *stereo*, solid and *týpos*, mold. The first successful stereotyping was used in 1805, at Cambridge University Press to print *The New Testament*, thanks to Charles Earl Stanhope, who had perfected the method between 1800 and 1802. In 1857, Italian James Dellagana successfully developed curved stereotyping plates, which were used in the *Times* of London.
See also Electrotyping; Letterpress

Stress - The distinctive axis orientation with which letterforms, especially round letters, are drawn. It is a direct product of the pen's nib orientation. Not to be confused with **slope**.

This angle, which is clearly seen on counter space of capital letters **C**, **G**, **O**, and **Q**, and their corresponding lowercase letters and numbers, varies from the oblique left, to the vertical and to the oblique right, as a result of the inclination of the strokes. We find three types in **Goudy Oldstyle** (O) (Frederic W. Goudy, 1915), **Bodoni** (O) (Giambattista Bodoni, 1788), and LITHOS (O) (Carol Twombly, 1990).

See also Anatomy of a typeface; Counter space; Modulation; Slope; Typeface classification

Stroke - An ink pen or pencil mark which is made in one movement and direction. Letters are generally drawn in several strokes, which may be continuous or interrupted.

Through the reduction in the number of strokes needed to draw a certain letter, medieval calligraphers came to structure lowercase letterforms as we know them today. The illustration shows the development of various lowercase letters according to calligrapher Fr. Edward M. Catich, in his book *The Origin of the Serif* (1991).

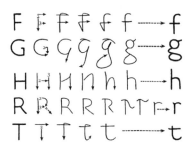

See also Anatomy of a typeface; Stress

Subscript - A name given to a small character (number or letter) which is placed after and slightly below the baseline of another character. This is the case of 2_3, generally found in chemical formulæ. Subscript characters are also useful to create additional fractions, such as $1/_{32}$.
See also Baseline; Fractions; Superscript

Superscript - A name given to a small character (number or letter) which is placed after and slightly above the center horizontal line of a character. This is the case of 2^3. This type of character is also used within a running text as an indication of a marginal note or a bibliographical reference, as well as to create additional fractions, such as $1/_{32}$.
See also Fractions; Ordinal numbers; Reference mark; Subscript

Swash - In a letter, it is a fancy flourish replacing a terminal or a serif, as we may see in *Adobe Caslon Swash* (Carol Twombly, 1990).

See also Anatomy of a letter, Calligraphic typefaces; Serif; Swash letters; Terminal

Swash letters - A term which is used to described those italic characters with pronounced calligraphic flourishes or flowing tails. We may find examples on pages 83 and 231.
See also Calligraphic typefaces; Kerned letters; Typeface classification

Symbol characters - A name given to those typographic devices which serve to add visual reading to a text and help the reader to find given information easier. Such is the case of **bullets**; **dingbats**; **pi characters**; and **reference marks**.
See also Bullets; Dingbats; Pi characters; Reference marks

Symmetrical typography - A traditional typographic style characterized by the arrangement of each line of text according to a central vertical axis. The relative importance of each line is emphasized by its placement on the page combined with the weight and size of the type selected. In 1946, *Penguin Books*, London, commissioned German type designer Jan Tschichold to redesign all their publications. By this time, he had changed his 1920s avant-garde typographical approach characterized by asymmetrical type arrangements and had returned to a classical, symmetrical typography, with the use of Roman, Egyptian, and script styles in his designs.

See also Asymmetrical typography; Serif typefaces

T

Tail - That part of the letter **Q** that extends beyond the baseline and differentiates it from the letter **O**. Some authors also apply the term tail to the leg a letter that is curved. Not to be confused with **swash**. Examples are taken from *Baskerville* and *Bodoni*.

See also each instance of a letter; Anatomy of a typeface; Baseline; Trajan Column

Teardrop terminal - A swelling found at the end of upper or lower round strokes of lowercase letters such as a, c, f, j, and r in *Oldstyle* typefaces. It also appears in the ear of letter g. Not to be confused with **serif**. Examples are taken from Adobe Caslon.

See also Oldstyle typefaces; Ball terminal; Ear; Serifs; Terminal

Terminal - In a letter shape, it is the end of a stroke not terminated with a **serif**, as is the case of the lower ending in a lowercase **t**. Terminals vary with typographical styles, and may be applied to all letters, to only some letters or to some of their parts. They may be cut at a straight angle (*News Gothic, Futura*), be rounded (*Helvetica Rounded, Benguiat Gothic, Modula*), half rounded (*Shimano*), cut at an angle (*Kabel, Samson, Grizzly, Lithos*), teardrop (*Baskerville, Times*), ball rounded (*Bodoni*), pointed (*Draylon*), wider at the end (*Stellar, Optima*), etc.

See also Anatomy of a letter; Serif; Spur; Swash; Teardrop and Ball terminals

Text - The main body of a written or printed material, as opposed to headings, footnotes, marginal notes, appendices, index, etc.

See also Book face; Display type; Text type

Textura - See Gothic letter

Texture - A term applied to the interwoven patterns of light and dark tones created within a text by the interrelation between letter shapes and the space around them. These visual patterns change dramatically when setting the same text in different styles, sizes, weight, etc., as much as they change by incrementing leading, margins, kerning, etc.

See also Inner space; Kerning; Leading; Size; Type composition; Type size; Type style; Weight of a typeface

Thibaudeau typeface classification - In 1921, French typographer Francis Thibaudeau, who had designed various type catalogs for type foundries Renault et Marcou, and Debergny et Peignot, developed a type classification based on serif construction: *elzévirs* (triangular serif); *didots* (hairline serif); *égyptiennes* (slab serif), and *antiques* (sans serif). The rest of the characters were classified under *écritures* (calligraphic), and *fantasies* (not conventional). His theories are well explained in his two-volume work, *La lettre d'imprimerie* (1921), and in his *Manuel français de typographie moderne*, published after his death in 1924. His approach has continued in use regardless of Maximilien Vox's concepts proposed in 1952, and adopted by the ATypI in 1962.

See also Typeface classification; Vox typeface classification

Three-dimensional typefaces - Those fonts that have been designed with a volumetric form. There are some shaded typefaces that may be considered three-dimensional fonts due to their visual appearance, as is the case of ▓▓▓▓▓, designed by Tony Wenman in 1972, and issued by Letraset. Nevertheless, in **▓▓▓▓**, also issued by this firm, we may find a true three-dimensional typeface.

See also Shaded typeface

Title page - A term applied to that page printed at the beginning of a book, which contains its full name or title, the author's name, the printer's name and emblem, and the place and date of printing. The title page is always found on the *recto* preceded by a blank sheet which also contains on its *recto* the book's title printed in small letters in the upper right corner, and known as **half title**. It may also be preceded by an illustration containing images related to the content or a portrait of the author. On the *verso* of the title page we may find the book's technical data, copyright, ISBN, and acknowledgments. It may or may not contain a brief biography of the author. In 1463, Peter Schöffer and Johann Fust printed, in Mainz, the first book to have a title page. The first ornamented title page appeared in 1476, designed by German printer, Erhard Ratdolt of Venice, who used it for his *Calendarium*. We may find various examples on pages 112, 117, 130, 131, 139, 142, 143, 161, 223, 253, and 255.

See also Cover; Display type; Half title; Preliminary matter

Titling typefaces - Those large size characters which don't include a matching lowercase alphabet. They are generally used as display type for headings. In foundry type, they usually fill the full face of the type, allowing the setting of capitals with little line spacing. We find a good example in CHARLEMAGNE, designed by Carol Twombly in 1990.

See also Book face; Cover; Display type; Small caps; Uppercase letters; Title page

Tone - It is the darkness of type composition taken as a mass. Apart from the type style, the weight of letterforms, the spacing of words and letters, the line spacing, the type of printing, the blackness of the ink, and the type of paper, among others, all have an incidence in the general tonality of the printed page.

See also Gothic letter; Inner space; Line spacing; Texture; Type style; Weight of a typeface

Trajan column - The name of a stone monument erected in the Roman Forum in AD 112-113 by order of the Roman Senate to honor Emperor Marcus Ulpius Trajanus's victories. It contains an inscription carved in sustained capital letters, whose letterforms have been considered a perfect canon of the Roman classical letter style. In this inscription we also find the use of a **middle point** to separate words, and quite a number of **abbreviations**. An outstanding contemporary version of these letters is found in Carol Twombly's *Trajan* typeface, designed in 1990. The inscription contains the following text:

SENATVS·POPVLVSQVE·ROMANVS·
IMP·CAESARI·DIVI·NERVAE·F·NERVAE·
TRAIANO·AVG·GERM·DACICO·PONTIF·
MAXIMO·TRIB·POT·XVII·IMP·VI·COS·VI·
P·P·ADDECLARANDVM·QVANTAE·
ALTITVDINIS·MONS·ET·LOCVS·TANTIS·
OPERIBVS·SIT·EGESTVS

A translation of the first four lines reads: "The Senate and the People of Rome to Emperor Cesar Divine Nerva, son of Nerva, Trajanus Augustus Germanicus Dacico, Maximum Pontif..."

In 1906, the appearance in Edward Johnston's book, *Writing & Illuminating & Lettering*, of photo reproductions of the Trajan Column inscription –taken from a cast plaster copy of the whole column which had been in the Victoria & Albert Museum in London, since 1864– attracted great attention to Roman classical inscriptions. The letters' fine proportions were soon established as unchangeable canon, and the craft of letter cutting was revived.

See also Capital letters; Roman style typefaces; Serifs; Type style; Typeface classification

Transfer types - A term applied to those characters carried on a supporting sheet that may be transferred to the working surface by cutting out self-adhesive letterforms (cut-out lettering) or by burnishing (pressure-sensitive lettering). Examples are found in *Letraset, Artype, Formatt, Mecanorma, Prestype*. *Letraset* dry-transferred types appeared in 1961 (see page 265). Its immediate success was backed by worldwide distribution as well as by a printer's strike two years before, which had made the elaboration of artwork difficult.

See also Decals; Phototypography; Type catalog

Transitional typefaces - A term used to refer to the letters designed during the mid-eighteenth century, which are considered a transition between the *Oldstyle* and the *Modern* style typefaces, although this classification usually refers to the work of the English printer and typographer, John Baskerville after 1757. The first true departure from the *Oldstyle* letter took place in 1692, when, by order of King

Louis XIV, a typeface was drawn and later cut by Philippe Grandjean for private use of the Imprimerie Royal in 1702. Letters were no longer regulated by the strokes of the broad-nibbed quill, but were derived from the precise forms used in copper plate engravings, and there was greater differentiation between hairlines and stems. French punch-cutter Pierre Simon Fournier further developed the work of Grandjean, as may be seen in his *Modèles de Caracteres*, printed in 1742. The typeface used in this book is considered to be the first true transitional design. Baskerville's work with wove calendered paper permitted him to reproduce characters with finer strokes, maintaining their subtle features. In transitional typefaces, the axis of curved strokes may be inclined but generally maintain a vertical stress, and lowercase letter **e** has a horizontal bar. Serifs are bracketed and lowercase head serifs are oblique. His typeface BASKERVILLE / Baskerville, exemplifies the term.

The illustration below shows the primary distinctions between oldstyle, transitional, and modern, as described by Jan Tschichold in his book *Treasury of Alphabets and Lettering* (1966).

See also Modern Style typefaces; Oldstyle typefaces

Transitive serif - That which flows directly into or out of the main stroke. Being unilateral, they only extend to one side of the stem. They are typical of lowercase italics as seen in *Times New Roman* (1932)

See also Italic; Reflexive serif; Serifs; Stem

Tricameral alphabet - That which has three different alphabets or characters –as happens with a normal font of roman type where one may distinguish **uppercase letters**, **lowercase letters**, and **small caps**.

See also Alphabet; Bicameral alphabet; California job case; Foundry type; Lowercase letters; Small caps; Type case; Unicameral alphabet; Uppercase letters

Tuscan typefaces - A name given to those letterforms in which the main stem bifurcates with serifs that curl. According to Stanley Morison, Pope Damasus invented them in the fourth century. According to Nicolette Gray in her book, *Nineteenth-Century Ornamented Types and Title Pages* (1938), these typefaces tended to acquire a bulge in the middle of the bifurcated stem during the nineteenth century. Vincent Figgins issued the first example in 1815. Between 1815 and 1817, these letterforms were subject to various changes in their shape to vary their color, shape and shadow. We find an example in ANTIQUE TUSCAN NO. 8, shown by William Hamilton Page in his 1859 type specimen book.

See also Ornamented typefaces; Serifs; Stem; Wood type

Type - A polyhedral bar of metal casting, taken from a matrix, which has the reversed image in relief, of any one of the characters of a font, and which is used in letterpress printing. The word derives from the Greek (*týpos*, mold), which is used both individually and collectively to refer to the letters of the alphabet usually within the context of printing. Types may be used singly or collectively to create words, sentences, blocks of type, etc. On page 225, we may find an illustration of a metal type, drawn by Rudolph Ruzicka.

See also Characters; Font; Foundry type; Hand composition; Letterpress; Matrix; Monotype; Typeface; Type case; Type nomenclature

Type cabinet - A wood or metal piece of furniture built to contain type cases, galley units, drawers, etc., which has a place on a slightly tilted top for the type compositor to work. There is an example on page 191.

See also Foundry type; Hand composition; Type case

Type case - A wooden tray divided into compartments for holding individual pieces of type, and from which the characters are hand-selected and placed on a composing stick to form a line of type. The individual cubicles differ in size and placement according to the number of characters needed in relation to their frequency of use. Those employed most are placed nearest to the compositor's right hand and close to the body; the left hand holds the composing stick. As this usage varies from language to language, each language favors its own particular arrangement of characters in the type case.

Type cases may also vary in number (one, two, three or four), and in arrangement (vertical or horizontal) depending of the language (Hebrew, Arab, Chinese, etc.). On page 225, we may see an illustration done by Rudolph Ruzicka of the old two type cases.

See also California type case; Composing stick; Foundry type; Letterpress; Type cabinet; Upper and lowercase letters

Typecasting - A type founding process in which molten type metal is poured into an adjustable mold to the upper orifice of which is brought a **matrix** of a letter or character. This may be considered the essential contribution of Johannes Gutenberg to printing. During the fiftteenth-century printers cast their own type and handwriting was the model they sought to imitate in print. During the eighteenth-century it became more and more usual for printers to buy their type from special type foundries. In 1838 Scottish immigrant printer David Bruce Jr. built and patented in New York the first commercially successful typecasting machine in America, which produced 100 type characters per hour. With the invention of mechanical and semi-mechanical typecasting systems such as the Linotype (1886), the Monotype (1887), and the Ludlow (1909), among others, it became possible to set body text and display type either as individual characters, words or complete lines of type with a speed and efficiency that surpassed what could be accomplished by handcasting tools.

See also Book face; Display type; Foundry type; Linotype; Logotype; Ludlow; Matrix; Type; Type metal

Type catalog - A printed sample of typefaces published by a type founder for the use of printers and designers in general. It has always served as a direct source for selection. It differs from the **type specimen book** in that it only shows a sample of the typeface, usually in complete font. With the creation of transfer types and digital typefaces, the type catalog is a direct way for commercializing a particular type design. We may find a contemporary example on page 161, issued by the Jonathan Hoefler digital type foundry.

See also Digital typography; Type specimen book; Transfer types; Type specimen sheet

Type composing room - That section of a typesetting shop or a printing plant in which type is set or composed. On page 193, we may see a photograph of a typical 1910 composing room, at Vacher & Sons' printing firm.

See also Type compositor; Typesetting

Type composing stick - In foundry type composition, it is an adjustable hand-held metal frame used to hold handset metal type as it is being composed. Since letters are in reverse, right-to-left, they are assembled upside down to allow a right-left progression by the compositor. When setting small size type, the composing stick permits the assembling of several lines, which are separated by pieces of metal or leading cut to the line length. After several lines have been composed in the stick they are transferred to a **galley**. While Henry Lewis Bullen worked in 1880 as editor of promotional material for Golding & Company, Boston, manufacturers of printing presses and typographical material, he designed the Standard composing stick, although the patent, as others of his inventions, was held by Golding. The illustration was done by Warren Chappell for his book *A Short History of the Printed Word* (1972).

See also Foundry type; Galley; Galley proof; Hand composition; Leading; Letterpress; Line spacing; Type compositor; Word spacing

Type composition - Within letterpress context, it refers to the placing together of typographic and engraving material into a form for letterpress printing on a printing press.

Otherwise, it refers to the organization of all the elements, body text, display type, illustrations, captions, etc., into a harmonic whole. The overall appearance of a printed page will then be a result of an adequate relationship between type hierarchies, type styles, type sizes, interline spacing, and margins and between these and the page.

See also Chase; Format; Foundry type; Layout; Typesetting; Wood engraving

Type composition - *See* Typesetting

Type compositor - A name given to a craftsman whose work consists of setting up type by hand or by machine, correcting machine-set composition, making up pages, imposing them, and performing all the necessary assembling of the type form for letterpress printing. On page 117, we may see a symbol designed by Oswald Cooper, which illustrates a type compositor at work. In the early days, type compositors were also in charge of casting type.

See also Composition; Foundry type; Hand composition; Letterpress; Typecasting

Type design - A creative activity originally associated with the work of punch-cutting, in which a character –letter, number, or sign– was engraved for printing. Among these punch-cutters, there were masters of design who made a beautiful piece of sculpture out of letters as well as excellent letterforms to be imitated by future designers. Such is the case of Nicholas Kis, Francesco Griffo, Claude Garamond, William Caslon I, John Baskerville, Firmin Didot, and Giambattista Bodoni, among others. Others were letter-cutters, such as Eric Gill. Among the contemporary European type designers, we must mention Edward Johnston, Rudolf Koch, Hermann Zapf, Paul Renner, Roger Excoffon, Berthold Wolpe, A.M. Cassandre, Jan Tschichold, Jan Van Krimpen, Georg Trump, Hans (Giovanni) Mardersteig, Aldo Novarese, Adrian Frutiger, Matthew Carter, and Zuzana Licko. Many contemporary American calligraphers have used their knowledge for type design, as is the case of Frederic W. Goudy, Oswald B. Cooper, William Addison Dwiggins, Robert Hunter Middleton, Warren Chappell, Freeman Craw, Arthur Baker, Ed Benguiat, Tom Carnase, Tony DiSpigna, Kris Holmes, Paul Shaw, among others. Today, a type designer is a draftsman, a combination of calligrapher and designer, who, with great letter knowledge of letterforms, is capable of creating a particular font for printing.
See also Calligraphy; Digital typography; Foundry type; Phototypography; Punch-cutter

Typeface - An alphabet created for the purpose of printing. All its components, letters, numbers, and punctuation marks are formally unified by a consistent graphic treatment or **type style**. A typeface, whatever its shape, weight or stress will have a definite influence on the visual appearance of the printed page. It is also interesting to note that a typeface, being based on the same original design, in this case *Caslon*, may have noticeable differences from one designer to another as well as from a type foundry to another. This is the case of *Caslon 540* (c. 1901), issued by American Type Founders; *ITC Caslon 224* (1983), designed by Edward Benguiat; *Adobe Caslon* (1990), designed by Carol Twombly; and *Big Caslon* (1994), designed by Matthew Carter.
See also Anatomy of a typeface; Type nomenclature; Type style

Typeface classification - An ordering system established to define typeface categories, according to periods of creation and particular designs. In 1921, French typographer Francis Thibaudeau first proposed a typeface classification on the basis of **serif characteristics**. Thirty years later, in 1952, another French typographer, Maximilien Vox (Samuel Théodore William Monod), presented a new typeface classification, this time based on **historical and stylistic characteristics**. Although not universally adopted, the British Standard Institute and the Association Typographique Internationale have recognized it. Thibaudeau's typeface classification is also considered as an alternative. However, the common problem of classifying type is that many typefaces fall into more than one category.
See also Thibaudeau typeface classification; Type nomenclature; Type style; Vox typeface classification

Type family - A generic term that refers to the complete range of variations of form and proportion of a given typeface design, which includes light, medium, bold, black, regular, condensed, extended as well as the complementary italics. The basic components of a type family are roman, italic, bold, and bold italic. One of the first American type design to have a complete family was CHELTENHAM / Cheltenham, designed by Bertram G. Goodhue between 1897 and 1902, and commercially issued by ATF in 1904. Morris Fuller Benton, besides collaborating in the adaptation of the original drawings to the appropriate specifications for typecasting, he designed twenty-four variants.
See also Type nomenclature

Type form variants - A term that refers to the changes in proportion, dimension, value, stress, and structure of a given letterform. Thus, every type design has five basic variants which include weight, width, size, stress, and style. Letterforms may then be light or bold, condensed or extended, serif or sans serif, roman or italic, plain or ornamental, full, outline, or contour, handtooled, or incise, etc. They may also be designed as book or as titling typefaces, for running text or for titles.
See also Book face; Titling typefaces; Typeface classification

Type foundry - A place where types are cut and founded for **hand composition**. Undoubtedly the first foundry in Europe was that of Johannes Gutenberg, organized around 1449, for the future printing of the *42-line Bible* (1450-1456). Originally, the earliest printers were out of necessity their own type founders, and cast types for their own use. This was the case of Nicolas Jenson, Erhard Ratdolt, or Aldus Manutius. It was not until about 1530 that these two arts were separated. Later type founders, like Claude Garamond, William Caslon, John Baskerville, Pierre François Didot, Giambattista Bodoni, Pierre Simon Fournier, Frederic W. Goudy, among others, produced types for other printers. The first American type foundry was that of Abel Buell, established in New Haven, Connecticut, in 1769.
See also Foundry type; Movable type; Type metal

Type gauge - Being commonly called **line gauge**, it is a metal ruler with a hook at one end, calibrated in points and picas on one edge, or picas on one edge and inches on the other, used to measure metal type. While Henry Lewis Bullen worked in 1880 as editor of promotional material for Golding & Company, Boston, manufacturers of printing presses and typographical material, he designed the Little Giant brass ruler and lead cutter although Golding held the patents.

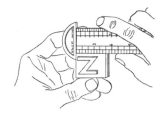

See also Metal type, Pica, Point

Type-height measurement - A name that refers to the standard foot-to-face distance of metal typefaces, measured in fractions of an inch –0.9186– in English-speaking countries. In other words, it is the distance from the printing bed or platen to the printing surface. When a wood engraving or a zinc plate is said to be "type high," it means that it has been conditioned to the proper height to be used on a letterpress-printing machine. Spaces, for example, are cast lower than type-height so they won't print, and rulers, on the other hand, are cast type-height, so they will print.

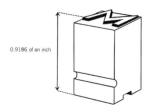

0.9186 of an inch

See also Em space; En space; Quads; Rulers; Space; Type nomenclature

Type measuring units - Basic type dimensional measurements. They are **points**, **picas**, and **units**. Points are used to measure the size of a typeface; picas, to measure the length of a line or the width of a column, and units, to measure the width of individual characters.
See also Em space; Pica; Point; Type gauge; Type size; Type sizes; Unit

Type metal - An alloy of lead (65 percent), antimony (28 percent), tin (5 percent), a small amount of bismuth, and sometimes a trace of copper, used for typographical material. The bismuth and tin keep the alloy malleable for casting purposes and the antimony ensures its hardness to withstand the printing process. Metal alloys were already in use for this purpose in the fifteenth century. No doubt the first to experiment with them was German goldsmith and typographer Johannes Gutenberg, who invented movable types between 1448 and 1450. His metal alloy was 80 percent lead, 5 percent tin, and 15 percent antimony. It is important to note that type metal used in hot metal mechanical type composition such as the Linotype, the Monotype, or the Ludlow is softer than that used for casting foundry type. The proportions of the alloy also changes according to the size and style of the type and the purposes for which it will be used.
See also Casting; Foundry type; Linotype; Ludlow; Matrix; Metal type; Monotype; Movable type

Type nomenclature - A term used to describe, as a whole, all the parts of an individual unit of type (metal or wood) used in letterpress printing. The anatomy of a letter should also be taken into account, which refers to its component parts.
See also Anatomy of a typeface; Typeface classification

Typesetter - Also known as **type compositor**, it is the person who handles hand metal type composition.

The term **typesetter** also refers to any device that sets type, be it hot metal typesetters such as

BOWL ARMS SERIFS
CROSS BAR
A B E G I
SPUR
STROKE STRESS
STEM LEG
K N O Q
TAIL
SWASH ARMS
SPINE STEM
R S T U
HAIRLINE
KERN SERIFS
ARMS ASCENDER CROSS BAR BOWL
COUNTER
Y d e f g
TERMINAL LOOP
TEAR DROP SHOULDER CROSS
TERMINAL SHOULDER WITH DROP BAR
TERMINAL
LINK g n p r t
TERMINAL
DESCENDER

Linotype, Monotype, and Ludlow, photo-lettering machines, or digital word processors which are connected to laser or ink-jet printers.
See also Desktop publishing; Hand composition; Linotype; Ludlow; Monotype; Photo-lettering; Phototypography

Typesetting - The putting of a given manuscript into type by any method or process.

The term **typesetting** also refers to typographic material suitable for printing or being incorporated into a printing plate, that may be typeset by hand, by machine (cast), by typewriter (strike-on), phototypesetting (light), or by digital typography (laser).
See also Digital composition; Handset type; Linotype; Ludlow; Monotype; Photocomposition; Xerography

Typesetting specifications - A series of typographical specifications placed on the copy or manuscript prepared by the designer/typographer, and supplied to the type compositor so its written content may be put correctly into type. These specifications deal with type style, size, weight, line measurements, spacing, hierarchies, etc. Manuscripts must be typewritten one column, double spaced, so as to allow for typographical specifications within the text, and narrow enough to permit writing notes on both margins. Today, with the computer, most of the manuscripts are handed directly to the designer in electronic files, on a disk or CD-ROM.
See also Layout

Type size - The distance, measured in points, from the highest to the lowest character, that is, from the cap line to the end of a letter descender. This is why an 8-pt typeface with short descenders may look as big as a 10-pt typeface with long descenders. It is interesting to see that a 36-pt letter is smaller than the sum of three 12-pt lines set solid, as may be seen in this example:

B This is a 36-pt initial letter as compared to three lines of 12-pt type, set solid.

See also Body; Body size; Cap line; Descender line

Type sizes - The vertical dimension of letterforms, expressed in numeric terms. From the early years of printing until the late eighteeth century, type sizes were recognized by names, but measured in points. In 1783, French type designer François-Ambroise Didot was instrumental in establishing the Didot's measuring system, a way of identifying type sizes in numeric terms rather than by name. Many of these old names were associated with the work in which they were used, such is the case with the *Cicero* (12 pt), used to set Cicero's work printed by Peter Schöffer in 1458.

Let us recall some of them: *Minikin* (3), *Brilliant* (3½), *Gem* (4), *Diamond* (4½), *Pearl* (5), *Agate* (5½), *Nonpareil* (6), *Emerald* (6½), *Minion* (7), *Brevier* (8), *Bourgeois* (9), *Long Primer* (10), *Small Pica* (11), *Pica* (12), *English* (14), *Columbian* (16), *Great Primer* (18), *Paragon* (20), *Double Pica* (24), and *Canon* (48).
See also Agate; Cicero; Point; Pica

Type specimen books - A compendium of the typefaces offered by a foundry. Different from a **type specimen sheet**, books usually present types set in different sizes so as to show printers some suggested applications. The first specimen book known to have been issued was that of Christophe Plantin in 1567. Another famous specimen book was that issued by Jean Jannon of Sedan in 1621. Perhaps the first American wood type specimen book may be that of Darius Wells, issued in 1828, which contained an assortment of wood types. It marked both the beginning of the American wood type industry as well as the time when the first typographical posters started to appear in the States. There are two other examples which are worth mentioning both for their beauty and for their importance in typographical innovations: *Ornamented Wood Types*, printed by William Hamilton Page in 1874, and the *American Type Founders Specimen Book and catalog 1923*, published by ATF.
See also Font; Layout; Letterpress; Type specimen sheet

Type specimen sheet - A typeset sample produced and supplied by the printer to show the visual properties of the typefaces with which a customer/designer may work. Johann Fust and Peter Schöffer are acknowledged for having issued the first type specimen sheet in 1459, in which they present a specimen of the *Psalter* type. In 1486, Erhard Ratdolt issued a type specimen sheet showing ten sizes of *rotunda*, three of roman and one Greek. The first well-printed display of English types is the type specimen sheet of William Caslon I issued in 1734. As for America, it is quite certain that the Binny & Ronaldson type foundry in Philadelphia issued the first known American type specimen sheet in 1809, under the name *A Specimen of Metal Ornament Cast at the Letter Foundry of Binny and Ronaldson*. On page 227, we may find a contemporary sample issued by LetterPerfect presenting *Kolo* typeface (Paul Shaw/Garrett Boge, 1996).
See also Type specimen book

Type specification - *See* Typesetting specifications

Type style - The formal and structural characteristics of a given type design. There are two main basic type styles: **serif** and **sans serif**. In addition to them, there are other variations which have to do with the **serif structure** (bracketed, hairline, slab or latin), as well as with the **letter stress** (roman and italic). **Formal** and **structural** changes in weight (light, medium, bold, extra bold, and black) as in width (condensed, regular, and extended) will affect appearance, permitting many other graphic applications than simply defining hierarchies. In creating a typeface, a type designer must consider many determining factors so as to obtain an overall unity.
See also Thibaudeau typeface classification; Type classification; Vox typeface classification

Typewriter typefaces - Those fonts based on the standard typewriters' alphabets. These styles started to appear after 1878 when the first shift-key typewriter appeared. They are usually characterized by even weight strokes although following a *Clarendon* letter style. One of the most popular designs is ITC American Typewriter, designed by Joel Kadan in 1974, which reminds us of the old *Remington* typewriter model typefaces. With the introduction of the *IBM-72 Selectric* typewriter supplied with different **mono elements**, each carrying a whole font, new type styles were incorporated into everyday typewritten texts. This was the case of *Univers* (1952), which was incorporated into the *IBM-72 Selectric*, as a result of Adrian Frutiger being appointed consultant to IBM. We may also find another example in Lucida Typewriter, designed by Charles Bigelow and Kris Holmes in 1994.
See also Mono element

Typogram - A typographic unit in which the message and the graphic configuration are joined into an expressive visual entity. Different from the **logotype**, the typogram depends exclusively on type to visually transmit a message. One of the first exponents of the typogram was Herb Lubalin, whose work on this matter gained him worldwide recognition. Various examples of his work may be seen on pages 187 and 188.
See also Logotype; Masthead

Typographer - A term that should be applied to a person qualified for his knowledge of letter designing, punch-cutting, type founding, and printing process as well as all the operations concerning the art of typography, and not only applied to a craftsman.
See also Typography

Typographic devices - Small abstract or semi-abstract graphic elements generally used in groups either to compose bigger typographical motifs or in linear arrangements to form borders. Sometimes they are presented in isolated fashion as a closing graphic accent at the end of a set text. Examples of these three variations may be seen on pages 117, 223, and 253. One of the greatest exponents of a creative use of these typographic devices was American type designer and printer Bruce Rogers.
See also Borders; Fleurons; Printer's flowers; Printer's ornaments; Vignettes

Typography - A name originally given to the art and process of working with and printing from type, which includes composition, imposition and presswork. Traditionally associated with printing from metal type (letterpress), this term is now equally applied to typesetting produced by any type composition system. With today's technology, typography has abandoned its connotation as a craft, and has become a powerful design language. In 1919, in the Bauhaus's first publication, *Staatliches Bauhaus*, Weimar, László Moholy-Nagy stated, "Typography is a tool of communication. It must be communication in its most intense form. The emphasis must be on absolute clarity."

See also Foundry type; Letterpress; Typographer

U

U & lc - An abbreviation for the words "upper and lowercase," used when specifying type in a typewritten manuscript.

U&lc is also the name of the International Typeface Corporation's journal published in New York from 1973 on, under the direction of graphic designer, Herb Lubalin.

See also Typesetting specifications; Upper & lowercase letters

Uncial - A conventional script developed around the fourth century for writing books, especially those of the Christian Church. Although the alphabet is formed of only *majuscules*, letters D, E, H, M and N (ꚰ e ҍ m n) are drawn with *minuscule* forms. Some of the factors that contributed to the great evenness and calligraphic quality of writing were the introduction of **parchment** and the substitution of the **crowquill pen** for the reed. Uncials were influenced in their shape by Byzantine art. Their name comes from the Latin word *uncia*, inch, or the equivalent of $1/12$ part of the foot (11.6"). Initially, Romans used the word *uncia* to refer to the height of the letter (0.98"), but it is more likely that, in coining the term, St. Jerome probably referred to "large letters," rather than to a specific size. A **Half-uncial** is then half that measure. We find a contemporary example in ꚰmerican uncial (Victor Hammer, 1943).

See also Croquill pen; Half-uncial; Majuscules; Reed pen

Unicameral alphabet - That which has only one case or set of characters –such as the Hebrew, the Arab and the Devanagari alphabets–, and many titling typefaces.

See also Alphabet; Bicameral alphabet; Lowercase letters; Small caps; Titling typefaces; Tricameral alphabet; Uppercase letters

Unit - The basic measuring element used to determine the width of individual characters as well as the space between characters and words. Taking the em quad or **em space** (■), which is the square of any type size, it is usually divided into equal vertical segments, normally eighteen-units-to-the-em, although it may also be divided into thirty-six or fifty-four units. In newer devices it may be divided into a thousand units.

Taking the **Times New Roman** (1932) alphabet as a base, each letter will then occupy a number of units. While the capital **M** may be eighteen units wide, and lowercase **m** will also measure eighteen units, letter **a** may measure ten units, letter **t** may measure six units, etc. It is useful to remember that depending on the type design, each character may measure different units as well as occupy a different area of the body. When typefaces are designed, each character is assigned a fixed amount of space, measurable in units. This dimension is called **set-width** and includes a small amount of space on either side to prevent the characters from touching one another. In designing a typeface, it is advisable to take into consideration the unit system, for the greater the number of units, the greater the possibilities of typographic refinement. The first firm to introduce the typographical unit system was the Lanston Monotype Company.

See also Em space; Set-width; Unit system

Unit system - A counting system first developed for the Monotype Composing machine, and used by most typesetting machines, which still permits a control of line breaks, justification, and inter-word and inter-letter spacing.

See also Em space; Letter spacing; Set-width; Unit; Unit system; Word spacing

Unjustified type composition - A name given to any type composition with irregular line lengths, product of a non-breaking word setting. This is also known as **flush left** and **flush right type composition**. This type of composition presents a ragged margin on either side of a column of text. This book has been type set with a flush left type composition.

See also Hyphening; Flush left type composition; Flush right type composition; Justified type composition

Upper & lowercase letters - A name given to the specified use of capitals and lowercase letters within any given typesetting. The name comes from the fact that type characters were placed in two different type cases (the upper and the lower cases), as may be seen on page 225.

See also Bicameral alphabet; Type case

Uppercase letters - A typographical name derived from the fact that metal type letters were deposited in two cases, being the upper case for capital letters. They are: ABCDEFGHIJKLMNOPQRSTUVWXYZ

On page 225, we may see an illustration of the old two-case piece of furniture done by Rudolph Ruzicka that clarifies this fact.

See also California job case; Capitals; Initials; Letterpress; Lowercase letters; Majuscules

V

Venetian Old Face types - A term used to refer to the first *Oldstyle* letters, originating in Venice between 1470 and 1495. Generally, they take their style and proportions from handwritten letters drawn with a pen held obliquely. Besides a gradual modeling between thick and thin strokes, a left diagonal stress on round letters, and the heavy bracketed serifs, they are characterized by the use of a sloping cross bar in the lowercase e, and the inclined top serifs on the main stem of lowercase letters (b d l). Letters are also wide and strong in color, especially for capitals. Following the

ransacking of the city of Mainz in 1462, many of the German printers went to Italy. Konrad Sweynheym and Arnold Pannartz set up a printing press at Subiaco, and later in Rome. Johannes and Wendelin von Speier (da Spira), and Erhard Ratdolt set up printing presses in Venice. By this time, the Renaissance humanists, in transcribing the works of classical authors, had rejected the gothic letter and returned to the *Carolingian script*. The scribes modified letterforms and made them even more beautiful. So, when these German printers cut their typefaces, there had already appeared a different style which definitely influenced their printing types. With French printer and punch-cutter Nicolas (Nicolaus) Jenson, who also established a printing press in Venice, the *Venetian Old Face* types reached their most exquisite form. He used them to print Eusebius de Cesarea's book, *De Præparatione Evangelica*, in 1470. Jenson's typeface later influenced Bruce Rogers' CENTAUR/Centaur, cut by Robert Wiebking in 1914, considered one of the finest typefaces of the twentieth century.

See also Aldine Old Face typefaces; Carolingian script; Transitional typeface

Verso - A term taken from Latin, it applies to the back side of a sheet of paper, as opposed to *recto*. It also refers to the face of a sheet of paper which receives a back printing. It is important to note that there are papers that have *recto* and *verso*, especially handmade papers, on account of their texture or their watermarks.

The term *verso* also applies to the left side page.

See also Page; Recto

Vertical spacing - See Line Spacing; Leading

Vignettes - Small typographic ornaments used to decorate the head or foot of a page and elsewhere. Although Gabriel Giolito in Venice initiated their use around 1540, it was Pierre-Simon Fournier who gave them an elegant application. He showed these typographical ornaments in 1742 in his *Modèles des caractères de l'imprimerie*. American type designer Bruce Rogers is considered a master in creating typographical vignettes, as may be seen on page 223. Larger size vignettes were also used by William Bradley and Frederic W. Goudy, as may be seen on pages 97, 142, and 143, respectively.

See also Printer's flowers; Type ornaments

Virgule (~) - A term derived from the French, used to refer to a graphic sign found in all dictionaries to represent either the complete word at the beginning of a text or the uninflected part of that word, such as in the case of **eager; ~ly**; or **eagle; double ~**. In Spanish, this same sign is placed over the letter **n** to transform into an **ñ**, whose sound is equivalent to the Italian **gn**.

See also Slash; Punctuation marks

Visual scaling - Variations of form needed from one type size to another to accommodate human perception. In the early days of type founding, type was hand-sculpted in metal, resulting in optimized or visually scaled letters for each point size. Visual scaling accommodates human perception by providing letters that in small sizes are generally wider and have larger x-heights than in larger sizes; they also tend to have heavier serifs, more open counter forms, looser letter fit, and less contrast between thick and thin strokes. In large sizes, where aesthetics become more important, visually scaled letters have narrower widths, thinner serifs, shorter x-heights, and more delicate and refined shapes. One example may be found in CBS DIDOT designed by Freeman Craw in 1966 as part of the CBS's Corporate Identity Program developed by Lou Dorfsman for use in CBS headquarters in New York. These letters, used on advertising and sign systems, present a higher contrast between thin and thick strokes, as may be seen on page 125. To preserve the typeface's delicate features, Jonathan Hoefler provided HTF DIDOT / HTF Didot, a typeface designed in 1992, with seven master versions, for use over a specific range of sizes: below 10 pt; 11-15; 16-23; 24-41; 42-63; 64-95; 96 and above.

See also Book face; Display type; Legibility; Letter spacing; Line spacing; Readability; Scalable fonts; Serif; x-height

Vox typeface classification - A scheme proposed by French typographer Maximilien Vox (Samuel Théodore William Monod) in 1954 for classifying type designs according to history and style. The initial typeface classification in ten groups was reworked into nine groups in the *Caractères Noël* yearbook in 1955. In 1962, the Atypl (Association Typographique Internationale) adopted his cataloguing system. According to Vox, typefaces are divided into nine groups: *humane* (Venetians); *garalde* (Garamond-Aldus); *réale* (Transitional); *didone* (Modern); *mécane* (Antique, Clarendon, Egyptians); *linéale* (sans serif); *incise* (glyphic); *scripte* (script, calligraphic); *manuaire* (manuscript); *fracture* (black letter). When a letter does not fit exactly into a category, a double name should be used.

See also Thibaudeau typeface classification; Typeface classification

W

Wedge-shaped serifs - Pronounced triangular letterform terminals present in certain lapidary inscriptions, usually a product of the use of a chisel or an incising tool. Such is the case of MATRIX REGULAR / Matrix Regular (Zuzana Licko, 1986).

See also Latin serif typefaces; Serifs

Weight of a typeface - The visual lightness or darkness of form in a typeface, resulting from the proportional relationship between the stroke's thickness and the character's size. This is the case of light, medium, **bold**, **heavy**, and **black** as seen in Helvetica (Max Miedinger, 1957)

See also Anatomy of a typeface; Black typeface; Light typeface; Regular typeface

Width of a typeface - The horizontal structural variations in a letterform, such as normal, condensed, extracondensed, and extended. It is useful to remember that a certain width may be an inherent characteristic of a typeface and not a formal variation, such as the case of the condensed HUXLEY VERTICAL (Walter Huxley, 1935), or the extended and square BANK GOTHIC (Morris Fuller Benton, 1930-1933).

See also Condensed typefaces; Extended typefaces; Square typefaces

Woodcut - A traditional engraving technique, also called **block printing**, in which illustrations or designs are cut into a block of wood, usually pear wood. The surface is cut with a knife along the **side grain** of the wood. The non-printing areas are cut away, and the remaining raised lines or solid areas become the printing surfaces. Initiated in China around 764 to 770, it became known in Europe by the fourteenth century. The first book (roll) printed by this system is the Chinese *Diamond Sutra*, printed by Wang Chieh in 868. Artistic woodcutting is known to have started in Europe with artists such as German artist Albrecht Dürer. Early printers who cut ornamental initials and title pages display type also used woodcuts, but due to the fragility of wood, they were only used for short printings. Even before Darius Wells produced wood engraved letters in 1828, many local printers used the woodcut technique for large size letters.

See also Wood engraving; Wood type

Wood engraving - An engraving technique that uses the **end grain** of a block of wood, usually boxwood, which has a more durable surface, and permits a better image rendering. Using special tools, the engraver can create very fine lines, and achieve a remarkable subtlety in the tonal range. The development and subsequent popularity for book illustration was due to English engraver Thomas Bewick, who, in 1790, published *A general history of quadrupeds*. Darius Wells employed this same technique in the manufacturing of wood letters in 1828, as we may see on page 255. For pictures with a larger dimension than 20 cm, blocks were assembled in such a way that they could be engraved separately by various engravers and bolted together again for printing. After 1860, photographs of works were printed directly onto sensitized block surfaces for engraving. Probably the first commercialized images appeared in Winkworth's *Lyra Germanica*, printed by John Leighton in 1861. Worth mentioning are the bookplates engraved on boxwood by Robert Hunter Middleton (pages 195 and 186), and Rudolph Ruzicka (page 225).

See also Bookplates; Woodcut; Wood type

Wood type - Characters that have been cut from wood by means of a mechanical router. Since they are usually larger than one inch, they are measured in lines. Thus, a 10-line face is equal to a 120-pt type. When wood type was first done, wood was used on its **side grain** (woodcut). In 1828, Darius Wells discovered that the **end grain** woodcarving was best suited for detail and resistance (wood engraving). He also innovated in the wood type cutting technique by perfecting the pantograph invented by William Leavenworth in 1834, by adding a router. A later example of this type of characters is GOTHIC TUSCAN ITALIAN, first presented by Darius Wells in his 1854 type catalog. This same year, he presented two-color printed characters as may be seen on DORIC ORNAMENTED. Later on William Hamilton Page innovated in designs and two-color printed characters.

See also Initials; Woodcut; Wood engraving

Word processor - It is a sophisticated electronic typewriter with great memory capacity. It also has a monitor where the typesetter may confront typesetting visually. It is ideal for desktop publishing.

See also Casting-off; Desktop publishing; Screen fonts

Word spacing - A term used in typesetting to refer to the adding of space between words to extend each line in order to achieve a justified setting. Computer software applies this spacing automatically (kerning) when working in desktop publishing. A regular spacing between words is a **3-to-the-em space**, although it may vary according to the type style, the type size, and to the amount of words in a line, especially in a justified type composition.

See also En space; Kerning; Justified type composition; Letter spacing; Quads

X

Xerography - An electrostatic printing system, which is based on photoconductivity and uses toner instead of ink. The term is taken from the Greek *xeros*, dry, and *graphein*, writing. Invented by American physicist Chester Carlson in 1947, it was developed by the Haloid Company, Rochester, which became Xerox Corporation. The image is scanned and transferred from a selenium-coated drum to paper. The image may be printed in black or in color depending on the printer's model. Basic resolution is 600 dpi, although it may go up to 1,200. Xerography will also set the basis for future laser printers, as will be the case of *Xerox 9700* electrophotographic printer using digital fonts with a 300 dpi resolution, which appeared in 1977.

See also Digital typography; Resolution

x-height - Also known as **mean line**, it is the basic vertical measurement of the body of a lowercase letter, without counting ascenders and descenders, and taking the letter **x** as a parameter. The reason for its use is due to the fact that all four corners of the letter touch a point of measurement (**baseline** and **mean line**). It is important to have in mind that the x-height establishes both a proportional relationship between caps and lowercase letters, as well as between lowercase letters and both ascenders and descenders.

In the illustration we may see through three different typefaces, all set in the same body size, how x-height affects type size, and the relations between its parts: Garamond (Claude Garamond, 1750); Helvetica (Max Miedinger, 1957), and Americana (Richard Isbell, 1976).

Hhpx **Hhpx** Hhpx

See also Anatomy of a typeface; Ascenders; Baseline; Descenders; Guidelines; Mean line; Type nomenclature

Z

Zapf Dingbats - *See* Dingbats

BIBLIOGRAPHY

ADOBE SYSTEMS. *Adobe Systems Incorporated Type Promotional Booklets*. Mountain View, California: 1989-1993.

AGNER, Dwight. *The Books of WAD: A Bibliography of the Books designed by W.A. Dwiggins*. San Francisco: Alan Wofsy Fine Arts, 1977.

—— *The Complete Typographer, No. 24*. Athens, Georgia: Graphic Composition, Inc., 1995.

AMERICAN INSTITUTE OF GRAPHIC ARTS. *American Type Designers and their Typefaces on Exhibit*. Chicago: 1948.

AMSTUTZ, Walter. *Who's Who in Graphic Art. Vol. 1*. Dübendorf, Switzerland. De Clivo Press, 1962.

—— *Who's Who in Graphic Art. Vol. 2*. Dübendorf, Switzerland: De Clivo Press, 1982.

ANNENBERG, Maurice. *Type Foundries of America and Their Catalogs*. New Castle, Delaware: Oak Knoll Press, 1994.

ASIMOV, Isaac. *Cronología de los Descubrimientos*. Barcelona: Editorial Ariel, S. A., 1991.

ASSOCIATION TYPOGRAPHIQUE INTERNATIONALE. *Type: A Journal of the Association Typographique Internationale*. Vol.1, No. 1. New York: 1997.

ATKINS, Robert. *Art Speak*. New York: Abbeville Press, 1990.

—— *Art Spoke*. New York: Abbeville Press, 1993.

AULT & WIBORG CO. *The Inland Printer*. Chicago: The Ault & Wiborg Co., 1900.

BAIN, Peter y Paul Shaw. *La Letra Gótica, tipo e identidad nacional*. València: Campgràfic Editors, 2001.

BAKER, Arthur. *Calligraphy*. New York: Dover Publications, Inc., 1973.

—— *Calligraphic Alphabets*. New York: Dover Publications, Inc., 1974.

—— *Historic Calligraphic Alphabets*. New York: Dover Publications, Inc., 1980.

BELANGER GRAFTON, Carol. *Historic Alphabets & Initials: Woodcut and Ornamental*. New York: Dover Publications, Inc., 1977.

BENNETT, Paul A. *Books and Printing: A Treasury for Typophiles*. Cleveland: The World Publishing Company, 1963.

—— *BR Marks & Remarks*. New York: The Typophiles, 1946.

—— *Goudy's Type Designs , His History and His Specimens*. New Rochelle, New York: The Myriade Press, 1978.

BIEGELEISEN, J. I. *Art Directors's Workbook of Type Faces*. New York: Arco Publishing Company, Inc., 1976.

BLACKBEARD, Bill, and Martin Williams. *The Smithsonian Collection of Newspaper Comics*. New York: The Smithsonian Intitution Press, and H. N. Abrams, Inc., 1977.

BLACKWELL, Lewis. *La Tipografía del siglo XX*. Barcelona: Editorial Gustavo Gili, S.A., 1993.

BLUMENTHAL, Joseph. *The Printed Book in America*. Boston: David R. Godine, in association with The Scholar Press Ltd., London, 1977.

—— *Bruce Rogers: A Life in Letters, 1870-1957*. New York: Austin W. Thomas Taylor, 1989.

BOAG, Andrew & Lawrence W. Wallis. *One Hundred Years of Type Making, 1897-1997*. Salsfords, England: The Monotype Recorder, Centenary Issue, No. 10, 1997.

BOOTH-CLIBBORN, Edward, and Daniele Baroni. *The Language of Graphics*. New York: Harry N. Abrams, Inc., 1980.

BRINGHURST, Robert. *Elements of Typographic Style*. Vancouver: Hartley & Marks Publishers, 1992.

BRUCKNER, D. J. R. *Frederic Goudy: Masters of American Design*. New York: Harry N. Abrams, Inc., 1990.

BRUNO, Michael H. *Pocket Pal: A Graphic Arts Production Handbook*. Everett, Massachusetts: Daniels Printing, 1992.

BURKE, Christopher. *Back to Basics, Stanley Morison and old face*. Berkshire, England: Monotype Typography Ltd., Quadgraphic Partnership, 1993.

CARTER, David E. *Trademarks / 5: The Annual of Trademark Design*. New York: Century Communications, Inc., 1977.

CARTER, Rob. *American Typography Today*. New York: Van Nostrand Reinhold, 1989.

CARTER, Sebastian. *Twentieth Century Type Designers*. New York: W. W. Norton & Company, 1995.

—— *Victor Hammer. Matrix 7*, Review for Printers & Bibliophiles. Manor Farm, Andoversford, Gloucestershire: The Wittington Press, 1987.

CAXTON CLUB. *RHM, Robert Hunter Middleton, the Man and His Letters*. Chicago: The Caxton Club, 1985.

CEREZO, José María. *Diseñadores en la Nebulosa*. Madrid: Editorial Biblioteca Nueva, 1999.

CHAPPELL, Warren. *A Short History of the Printed Word*. London: Andre Deutsch, 1972.

CHOUTEAU BROWN, Frank. *Letters & Lettering*. Boston: Bates & Guild Company, 1921.

CIRKER, Hayward, and Blanche. *The Golden Age of the Poster*. New York: Dover Publications, Inc., 1971.

THE COLUMBIA VIKING DESK ENCYCLOPEDIA. New York: The Viking Press, 1953.

COST, Patricia A. *Linn Boyd Benton, Morris Fuller Benton, and Typemaking at ATF - Printing History* Ns. 31/32. American Printing History Association, 1994.

CRAIG, James, and Bruce Barton. *Thirty Centuries of Graphic Design*. New York: Watson-Guptill Publications, 1987.

—— *Basic Typography: A Design Manual*. New York: Watson-Guptill Publications, 1990.

DAHL, Svend. *Historia del Libro*. Madrid: Alianza Editorial, S. A., 1972.

DARRACOTT, Joseph. *The First World War in Posters*. New York: Dover Publications, Inc., 1974.

DAY, Kenneth. *Book Typography, 1815-1965, in Europe and the United States*. Chicago: University of Chicago Press, 1965.

—— *Book Typography, in Europe and the United States* - London: Ernest Benn Limited, 1966.

DELONEY HITCHCOCK, Maureen. *Benton Types: Typefaces Designed or Adapted by Morris Fuller Benton* (260 fonts). The Press of the Good Mountain.

DENMAN, Frank. *The Shaping of Our Alphabet*. New York: Alfred A. Knopf, 1955.

DESIGN QUARTERLY. *The Evolution of American Typography. Design Quarterly*. No. 148. Minneapolis, Minnesota: Walker Art Center, 1990.

DOWDING, Geoffrey. *An Introduction to the History of Printing Types*. New Castle, Delaware: The British Library & Oak Knoll Press, 1998.

DRUCKER, Johanna. *The Alphabetical Labyrinth, the Letters in History and Imagination*. London: Thames and Hudson, Ltd., 1999.

EASON, Ron, and Sarah Rookledge. *The Rookledge International Directory of Type Designers*. New York: The Sarabande Press, 1994.

THE NEW ENCYCLOPAEDIA BRITTANICA. Auckland: Encyclopaedia Brittanica, Inc., 1991.

E. P. S. *Tecnología Tipográfica, Segundo Tomo*. Barcelona: Librería Salesiana, 1950.

EYE MAGAZINE. No. 11, Vol. 3. London, 1993.

FALK, Peter Hastings. *Who was Who in American Art*. Ed. Peter H. Falk. California: Sound View Press, 1985.

FAREY, Dave, Colin Brignall, Mike Daines, Alan Meeks, Freda Sack, and Peter O'Donnell. *Letraset & Stencil Cutting*. New York: International Typeface Corporation, and St. Bride Printing Library, London, 1996.

FAUDOUAS, Jean Claude. *Dictionnaire des Grands Noms de la Chose Imprimée*. Paris: Editions Retz, 1991.

FINE PRINT: the Review for the Arts of the Book. San Francisco: Kirchenbaum, Sandra Ed.

FOREST, Dominique. *Dibujando para las Artes Gráficas*. Barcelona: Ediciones Ceac, S. A., 1971.

FRIEDL, Friedrich, Nicolaus Ott, and Bernard Stein. *Typography, When, Who, How*. Köln: Könemann Verlagsgesellschaft mbH., 1998.

FRIEDMAN, Mildred. *Graphic Design in America*. New York: Harry H. Abrams Inc., in association with The Walker Art Center, Mineapolis, 1989.

GERSTNER, Karl, und Markus Kutter. *Die Neue Graphik*. Teufen: Verlag Arthur Niggli, 1959.

GLAISTER, Geoffrey Ashall. *Encyclopedia of the Book*. New Castle, Delaware: Oak Knoll Press, 1996.

GOTTSCHALL, Edward. *Typographical Communications Today*. New York: International Typeface Corporation, 1989.

GOUDY, Frederic W. *The Alphabet and Elements of Lettering*. New York: Dover Publications Inc., 1967.

—— *The Story of the Village Press, by its designer Frederic W. Goudy*. New York: The Press of the Wooly Whale, 1933.

THE GROLIER CLUB - *Book Decorations by Bertram Grosvenor Goodhue*. New York: The Grolier Club, 1931.

HAAB, Armin, and Walter Haettenschweiler. *Lettera 3*. Barcelona: Editorial Blume, 1968.

HALEY, Allan. *ABC'S of Type, a Guide to Contemporary Typefaces*. New York: Watson-Guptill Publications, 1990.

—— *Typographic Milestones. Upper & lowercase journal*. New York: International Typeface Corporation.

—— *Oswald Cooper. Upper & lowercase journal*. Vol. 8. No. 2. New York: International Typeface Corporation, 1991.

—— *Hot Designers Make Cool Type*. Gloucester, Massachusetts: Rockport Publishers, Inc., 1998.

HARRISON, Charles, and Paul Wood. *Art in Theory, 1900-1990, An Anthology of Changing Ideas*. Oxford, England: Edited by Blackwell Publishers, Inc., 1999.

HELLER, Steven, and Seymour Chwast. *Graphic Style, from Victorian to Post-Modern*. New York: Harry N. Abrams, Inc., 1988.

—— *Telling and Selling*. Eye magazine. No. 7. London, 1972.

—— *Pushing boundaries, with an eye on tradition*. Rockville, Maryland: Print Magazine. (March-April 1996)

HILLEBRAND, Henri, publisher. *Graphic Designers in the USA, No.1*. Tokyo: Bijutsu Shuppan-sha, and Fribourg: Office du Livre, 1971.

HOFER, Phillip. *Rudolph Ruzicka, Artist and Craftman*. Chicago: The Newberry Library Bulletin, 1978.

HORNUNG, Clarence P. *Will Bradley: His Graphic Art*. New York: Dover Publications, Inc., 1974.

——, and Fridolf Johnson. *200 Years of American Graphic Art*. New York: George Brazilier, 1976.

HOW MAGAZINE. Cincinatti: FW Books.

HUCK, Andreas M., and Erhardt D. Stiebner. *Gebrauchsgraphik, International Advertising Art*. München: Verlag F. Bruckmann KG, 1970.

HURLBURT, Allen. *Publication Design*. New York: Van Nostrand Reinhold Company, 1976.

—— *The Grid*. New York: Van Nostrand Reinhold Company, 1978.

JAMMES, André. *La Réforme de la Typographie Royal sous Louis XIV, Le Grandjean*. Paris: Librairie Paul Jammes, 1961.

JASPERT, Berry, and Johnson. *Encyclopædia of Type Faces*. England: Blandford Press, 1986.

JERVIS, Simon. *The Penguin Dictionary of Design and Designers*. London: Penguin Books, 1984.

JOHNSON, Fridolf. *Type Designs*. London: Andre Deutsch. 1966.

——— *A Treasury of Bookplates, from the Renaissance to the Present*. New York: Dover Publications, Inc., 1977.

JULIER, Guy. *The Thames and Hudson Encyclopædia of 20th Century Design & Designers*. London: Thames and Hudson, Ltd., 1993.

KELLY, Rob Roy. *American Wood Type, 1828-1900*. New York: Van Nostrand Reinhold Company, 1969.

KENNEDY, Paul E. *Modern Display Alphabets, 100 Complete Fonts*. New York: Dover Publications, Inc., 1974.

KLEIN, Manfred, and others. *Type & Typographers*. London: Architecture Design and Technology Press, 1991.

LABUZ, Ronald. *Contemporary Graphic Design*. New York: Van Nostrand Reinhold, 1991.

LAMBERT, Frederick. *Letterforms, 100 Complete Alphabets*. New York: Dover Publications, Inc., 1972.

LANSTON MONOTYPE CORPORATION. *Printers Ornaments, applied to the composition of decorative borders, panels and patterns*. London: Lanston Monotype Corp., 1928.

LANSTON MONOTYPE RECORDER. *The Monotype Recorder*. London: The Lanston Monotype Corp., 1937.

——— *The Monotype Recorder, the Centenary Issue*. London: The Lanston Monotype Corp., 1997.

LAWSON, A., and A. Provan. *100 Type Histories*. Vol. 1. Arlington: National Composition Association, 1983.

——— *100 Type Histories*. Vol. 2. Arlington: National Composition Association, 1983.

LEHMANN-HAUPT, Hellmut. *The Book in America: A History of the Making and Selling of Books in the United States*. New York: R.R. Bowker Company, 1952.

LETTER ARTS REVIEW, Magazine. Norman, Oklahoma: Karyn L. Gilman, Ed.

LEWIS, John. *Anatomy of Printing*. New York: Watson-Guptill Publications, 1970.

LIEBERMAN, J. Ben. *Type and Typefaces*. Second Ed. New Rochelle, New York: The Myriade Press, 1978.

LIVINGSTON, Alan, and Isabella. *The Thames and Hudson Encyclopædia of Graphic Design and Designers*. London: Thames and Hudson, Ltd., 1992.

LUDLOW TYPOGRAPH COMPANY. *Digitised and Hot Metal Typeface Alphabets*. Ludlow Typograph Company.

LUPTON, Ellen, and others. *The abc's of ▲ ■ ●: The Bauhaus and Design Theory*. New York: Abott Miller, editors - The Cooper Union for the Advancement of Science and Art - Princeton Architectural Press, Inc., 1993.

———, and J. Abott Miller. *Design Writing Research, Writing on Graphic Design*. London: Phaidon Press Limited, 1999.

MALONE, Dumas. *Dictionary of American Biography*. New York: Charles Scribner's Sons, 1946.

MARTÍN, E. y L. Tapiz. *Diccionario Enciclopédico de las Artes e Industrias Gráficas*. Barcelona: Ediciones Don Bosco, 1981.

MAZUR THOMSON, Ellen. *The Origins of Graphic Design in America, 1870-1920*. New Haven: Yale University Press, 1997.

McLEAN, Ruari. *Manual de Tipografía*. Madrid: Hermann Blume, 1987.

——— *Typographers on Type*. London: Lund Humphries, 1995.

McGREW, Mac. *American Metal Typefaces of the Twentieth Century*. New Castle, Delaware: Oak Knoll Books, 1996.

McMURTRIE, Douglas C. *American Type Design in the Twentieth Century*. Chicago: Robert O. Ballou, 1924.

——— *Modern Typography and Layout*. Chicago: Eyncourt Press, 1929.

——— *Notes on the History of the Ludlow*. Chicago: Ludlow Typograph Company, 1936.

——— *Type Design: An Essay on American Type Design, 1888-1944*. Pelham, New York: Bridgman Publishers, 1947.

MEGGS, Phillip B. *An Eminent Pre-Modernist: The Curious Case of T. M. Cleland*. Rockville, Maryland: Print Magazine. (March-April 1995)

——— *A History of Graphic Design*. Allen Lane. London: Penguin Books Ltd., 1983.

MEIER, Hans Eduard. *The Development of Script and Type*. Cham, Switzerland: Sintax Press, 1994.

MELCHER, Daniel, and Nancy Larrick. *Printing and Promotion Handbook*. New York: McGraw-Hill Book Company, 1966.

MERGENTHALER LINOTYPE COMPANY. *Supremacía Linotype, catalog*. Brooklyn, New York: Mergenthaler Linotype Company, 1930.

MIDDLETON, Robert Hunter. *Chicago Letter Founding*. Chicago: The Black Cat Press, 1937.

MODERATOR PUBLISHING CO. *The Moderator: An International Magazine of Student Conviction*. New Haven, Connecticut, 1962.

MONOTYPE RECORDER, The. *Frank Hinman Pierpont - 1860-1937, A Memoir and a Tribute*. London: The Monotype Corp., 1937.

MORISON, Stanley. *Pacioli's Classic Roman Alphabet*. New York: Dover Publications, Inc., 1994.

MÜLLER-BROCKMANN, Josef, and Shizuko. *History of the Poster*. Zürich: ABC Verlag, 1971.

NEUENSCHWANDER, Brody. *Letterwork, Creative Letterforms in Graphic Design*. London: Phaidon Press Ltd., 1993.

NEWBERRY LIBRARY BULLETIN. *Vol. IV. No.1*. (November 1955)

THE NEW YORK TIMES. (September 1964)

——— (May 1972)

THE NEW YORKER. *Cartoon Issue*. (December 1997)

NORTON, Robert. *Types Best Remembered, Types Best Forgotten*. Somerset, England: Parsimony Press, 1994.

OLMERT, Michael. *The Smithsonian Book of Books*. New York: Wings Books, 1995.

OSBORNE, Harold. *The Oxford Companion to the Decorative Arts*. England: Oxford University Press, 1988.

PATTERSON, Rhodes. *The Ludlow Story*. Chicago: Newberry Library, 1940.

PENDERGAST, Sara. *Contemporary Designers*. Detroit: Saint James Press, 1997.

PEDERSEN, B. Martin. *Graphis Design 92: The International Annual on Design and illustration*. Zurich Graphis Press Corp., 1992.

PERFECT, Christopher. *The Complete Typographer: A Manual for Designing with Type*. London: Little, Brown and Company, Quarto Publishing, 1992.

PHIL'S PHOTO, INC. *Homage to the Alphabet: A Typeface Sourcebook*. Washington: Phil's Photo, Inc., and Rockport Publishers, Inc., 1994.

POLK, Ralph W. *The Practice of Printing, Letterpress and Offset*. Peoria, Illinois: Chas. A. Bennett Co, Inc., 1971.

POYNOR, Rick, Edward Booth-Clibborn, and Why Not Associates. *Typography Now: The Next Wave*. London: Internos Books, 1993.

PRINT MAGAZINE. *Print, American's Graphic Design Magazine*. Rockville, Maryland: RC Publications, Inc.

RANDOM HOUSE, INC. *The Random House Encyclopedia*. New York: Random House, Inc., 1983.

RIEDEL, Hubert. *Bernhard: Werkbung und Design im Aufbruch des 20. Jahrhunderts*. Stuttgart: Institut für Auslands-beziehungen e.V., 1999.

RHODES, Patterson. *The Ludlow Story*. Chicago: Newberry Library, 1940.

ROGERS, Bruce. *Paragraphs on Printing*. New York: Dover Publications, Inc., 1979.

ROSEN, Ben. *Type and Typography: The Designer's Type Book*. New York: Van Nostrand Reinhold Co., 1963.

——— *The Corporate Search for Visual Identity*. New York: Van Nostrand Reinhold Company, 1970.

ROTHE, Anna. *Current Biography*. New York: The H. W. Wilson Co., 1947.

SATUÉ, Enric. *El Diseño Gráfico: Desde sus Orígenes hasta Nuestros Días*. Madrid: Alianza Editorial., 1989.

——— *El Diseño Gráfico en España: Historia de una Forma Comunicativa Nueva*. Madrid: Alianza Editorial, 1997.

SCRIPSIT: *Triannual Journal of the Washington Calligraphers Guild*. Vol. 23. No. 2. Washington, 2000

SERIF: *The Magazine of Type & Typography*. Chicago: Quixote Digital Typography. Don Hosek, Ed.

SNYDER, Gertrude, and Alan Peckolick. *Herb Lubalin, Art Director, Graphic Designer and Typographer*. New York: American Showcase, Inc., 1985.

SOLOMON, Martin. *The Art of Typography: An Introduction to Typo.icon.ography*. New York: Watson-Guptill Publications, 1986.

THE SOCIETY OF TYPOGRAPHIC ARTS. *The Book of Oswald Cooper: An Appreciation of Oswald Bruce Cooper*. Chicago, 1949.

SOLO, Dan X. *Decorative Display Alphabets: 100 complete fonts*. New York: Dover Publications, Inc., 1990.

SOUTHWARD, John. *Modern Printing: the Practice and Principles of Typography and the Auxiliary Arts*. Leicester, England: De Montford Press, Leicester, 1950.

SPARKE, Penny, Felice Hodges, Anne Stone, and Emma Dent Coad. *Design Source Book*. London: QED Publishing Ltd., 1986.

STEP-BY-STEP-GRAPHICS. Magazine. Peoria, Illinois: A Division of Dynamic Graphics, Inc.

THOMPSON, Bradbury. *Bradbury Thompson: The Art of Graphic Design*. New Haven, Connecticut: Yale University Press, 1988.

TINKEL, Kathleen. *Typographic Harmonies*. Peoria, Illinois: Step-by-Step Graphics, Vol. 10. No. 5. 1994.

TSCHICHOLD, Jan. *A Treasury of Alphabets and Lettering*. London: Lund Humphries, 1992.

TYPE DIRECTORS CLUB. *Typography Twelve*. New York: Watson-Guptill Publications, 1991.

TWYMAN, Michael. *Printing 1770-1970*. London: Eyre & Spottiswoode, 1970.

UPDIKE, Daniel Berkeley. *Printing Types: Their History, Forms and Use*. Cambridge, Massachusetts: Harvard University Press, 1957.

VISUAL GRAPHICS CORPORATION. *Fifteen Award Winning Type Face Designs*. Miami: Visual Graphics Corporation, 1965.

V & M TYPOGRAPHICAL, INC. *The Type Specimen Book of V & M Typographical, Inc.* New York: Van Nostrand Reinhold, 1974.

WALLIS, Lawrence W. *A Concise Chronology of Typesetting Developments, 1886-1986*. London: The Wynkyn de Worde Society and Lund Humphries, 1988.

——— *Modern Encyclopedia of Typefaces 1960-1990*. New York: Van Nostrand Reinhold, 1990.

WEMBER, Paul. *Die Jugend der Plakate, 1887-1917*. Scherpe Verlag Krefeld, 1961.

Note: Bold numbers refer to primary key references.

A

Aachen, 33, 40, 265,
ABC (American Broadcasting Co.), New York, 31, 100,
Harry N. Abrams, publishers, New York, 142,
Abridgment of Murray's English Grammar, 18,
Academie des Sciences, Paris, 9, 14,
Acier Noir, 27, 39,
HTF Acropolis, 6, 42, **162**,
AD (Advertising Design), magazine, 28, 114,
Adams, Isaac and Seth, 18,
Adams, Joseph A., 18,
Adams Press, letterpress, 18,
Addams, Charles, 170,
AD Farmer & Son Type Foundry, 263,
ADC Hall of Fame, 240,
Adcraft Black, 100,
Adler, typewriters, Germany, 78, **80**,
Adler, Elmer, 154,
Ad Lib, 40, 42, **125**,
Administer, 41,
Adobe Acrobat / Portable Document Format, software, 262,
Adobe After Effects, software, 262,
Adobe FrameMaker, software, 262,
Adobe Illustrator, software, 36, 160, 262,
Adobe InDesign, 37, 262,
Adobe Multiple Master Technology, 234, 249, 262,
Adobe multiple master typefaces, 234, 248, 249, 250,
"Adobe Originals", 262,
Adobe PageMaker, software, 262,
Adobe PhotoShop, software, 37, 262,
Adobe PostScript, computer language, 32, 36, 37, 238, 262, 265, 268,
Adobe PostScript Language Manual, 262,
Adobe Premier, software, 262,
Adobe Systems, Inc., Silicon Valley, 6, 12, 13, 36, 37, 182, 232, 238, 244, **262**,
Adobe Type Design Department, 36, 37, 262,
Adobe Type Manager Deluxe, software, 37, 262,
Advance Type Foundry, Chicago, 260,
Advertisements, **117, 118**,
Advertisers, 23,
Advertisers Gothic, 6, 38, 42, 260, **261**,
Advertising, 10, 18, 26, 30,
Advertising agencies, 18, 19, 20, 21, 29, 30, 32,
Advertising design, 26,
Advertising and Editorial Art, exhibitions (Art Directors Club), 25,
Advertising art, exhibitions, 24, 25,
Advertising Art theories, 23,
Advertising imagery, 32,
Advertising Typographers Association of America (ATA), New York, **117** (symbol), 169,
Advertising typography, 31,
AEG (Allgemeine Elektricitæts Gessellschaft), Turbinen Fabrik, Berlin, 24,
Aeterna, 39,
Aetna, 6, 38, 42, **208**,
FB Agency, 5, 41, 42, **74**,
Agency Gothic, 64, 74,
Age of Reason, 15,

Agfa Compugraphic Corp., Wilmington, 37, 226,
Agfa Gevaert, 37,
Agfa /Monotype, type founders, Mass., 264,
Agfa Type Excellence Contest, 92,
Agha, Mehemed Fehmy, 11, 28, 186,
AGI (Alliance Graphique Internationale), Paris, 30, 54, 104,
Agitator, 40,
The Agony and the Ecstasy (film, Reed), **187**,
Agora, 41,
Aicher, Otl, 13, 35, 36, 37, 41,
AIGA (American Institute of Graphic Arts), New York, 25, 26, 30, 35, 78, 91, 96, 104, 121, 127, 156, 169, 176, 186, 188, 214, 218, 220, 221, 224, 226, 236, 240, 242, 251, 252,
Air Service Command Depot, Mobile, Alabama, 178,
Akademie der Kunst, Berlin, 78,
Akademie der Kunst, Munich, 78,
Aktuell, 39,
Akzidenz Grotesk, 23, 24, 25, 32, 38,
Alarcón, Pedro Antonio de, 154,
Albers, Josef, 25, 31, 33,
Albertina, 40, 42,
Albertus, 26, 29, 30, 37, 39, 136,
Albion Press, letterpress, 18,
Alcázar, 40,
Alcorn, John, 33,
Alcuin of York, 8,
Alderman Library, University of Virginia, Charlottesville, 110,
Aldine dolphin and anchor (printer's mark), 223,
Aldus, 40,
Aldus Corporation, Seattle, 36, 37, 92, 262,
Aldus FreeHand, software, 37, 262,
Aldus PageMaker, software, 37,
Aldus PageMaker 1.0, software, 36,
Alexandre, Jean, 15,
Alphabet scultures (Igarashi), 36,
Alfieri & Lacroix, typo-lithographers, Milan, 31,
Alianza Editorial, pocket-book publications, Madrid, 34,
Alice in Wonderland (Carroll), 19,
Alisal, 104,
Allegro, 39,
Allen, John E., 150,
Alexandre, Aresene, 22,
Allgemeine Gewerbeschule (School of Applied Arts), Basle, 30, 33,
"All-purpose linotype" machine, 28,
All Saints, church, Ashmont, 137,
Almanacs, **118**,
Almanack for the Year 1639 (Peirce), 14,
Alpha and Omega, Sonoma, 238,
Alphabet, 8,
The Alphabet, fifteen interpretative designs drawn and arranged with explanatory texts and illustrations (Goudy), 25, 141, **142**, 143, 145, 214,
Alphabet and Image, magazine, London, 30,
Alphabet & Images, Inc., New York, **55**,
Alphabet Design Contest, Type Shop, New York, 134,
Alphabet of Death (Holbein), 138,
"Alphabet sculptures" (Igarashi), 36,
Alphabets in All Hands (Shelley), 15, 107,
Alphabet Thesaurus No.1 (Photo-Lettering), 32, 269,
Alphabet 26, 6, 11, 31, 40, **240, 241**,

The Altar Book of the American Church (Updike, printer), 22, 137, 251,
Alternate Gothic, 5, 12, 38, 42, 64, **66**,
Altsys Corporation, 36,
Aluminum Alphabet (Igarashi), 36,
Alwin Nikolai School, of modern dance, New York, 164,
Amati, 40,
America, magazine, 240,
American Academy of Art, Chicago, 178,
American Academy of Arts, New York, 114,
American advertising agencies, 19, 20,
American Annual, magazine, 32,
American Aesthetic movement, 20,
American Artist, magazine, 121,
American Banknote Company, New York, 224,
American book design, 25,
American Bookmaker, magazine, 114,
American Center for Design, 104, 226,
The American Chap-Book (ATF), 10, 23, 96, 263,
American Civil War, 19, 96, 180, 204,
American Colortype Co., New York, 121,
American Cookery, 240,
American design, 30,
An American Dictionary of the English Language (Webster), 18,
American Express, magazine, 100,
American Gas, **79**,
American Independence, 16,
American industrial designers, 29,
American Metal Typefaces of The Twentieth Century (McGrew), 7, 36, 83, 259,
American metal types, 16,
American newspapers, 14, 18, 19,
American paper mills, 14, 16,
American Point System, 10, 21, 22, 64,
American press, 14, 15,
The American Printer (MacKellar), magazine, Philadelphia, 20,
American printing ink, 15,
American printing presses, 15, 16, 17, 18, 19,
American publishers, 35,
American Revolution, 16,
American sans serif typefaces, 28,
American Telephone and Telegraph (AT&T), 35, 107, 152,
American Text, 5, 39, 42, **71**,
American Tube and Controls, 44, **46**,
American Type Founders' Association, 20,
American Type Founders Company, Jersey City, 6, 10, 11, 19, 20, 21, 22, 23, 24, 25, 26, 27, 38, 41, 54, 56, 57, 62, 64, 68, 71, 78, 81, 82, 96, 98, 99, 110, 116, 121, 140, 141, 145, 149, 150, 153, 156, 157, 169, 172, 176, 178, 192, 194, 201, 214, 218, 220, 221, 236, 242, 252, **263**, 266, 268,
ATF Department of Type Design, 23, 25, 62, 64,
1906 ATF American Line Type Book, 263,
ATF Collective Specimen Book of 1895, 99,
ATF Desk Book for Boston, of 1897, 99,
ATF Hadego machine, 263,
ATF Specimen Book, of 1895, 22,
ATF Specimen Book and Catalogue, 1923, 11, 26, 64, **65**, 99, 214, 263,
ATF Specimen Book for the New Yor area, of 1897, 99,
ATF Type Design Department, 64, 178, 214, 263,
ATF Type Designer, software, 263,

ATF Typographic Library and Museum, Jersey City, New Jersey, 10, 24, 64, 99, 252,
American type founding, 20,
American type foundries, 8, 15, 20, 21, 263,
ITC American Typewriter, 264,
American Uncial, 5, 40, 154, **155**,
American Wood Type: 1828-1900 (Kelly), 34, 199, 206,
American wood type industry, 18, 254,
Americana (Isbell), 6, 40, 42, **172**,
Americana (Klumpp), 178,
Amigo, 5, 41,42, 49, **52**,
Ampersands, **143**,
Amsterdam Type Foundry, 19,
Amsterdam Bible, 14, 151,
Amsterdam specimen sheet (Kis), 14,
Amstutz, Walter, 33,
Anatomy of Lettering (Chappell), 110,
Anckers, Kerstin, 94, 230,
Anderton, Bob, 41,
Andrich, Vladimir M., 202,
Andrich Minerva Italic, 202,
Andromaque (Racine), 155,
Andromaque, 5, 41, 42, 154, **155**, **196**,
Annenberg, Maurice, 63,
"Anti-art" groups, 32,
Antiqua Classica, 40,
Antique X Condensed, 6, 38, 42, **256**,
Antique XXX Condensed, 6, 38, 42, **204**,
Antique Light Face Extended, 6, 38, 42, **258**,
Antique No.7, 6, 38, 42, **210**,
Antique Olive, 30, 40,
Antique Tuscan, 6, 38, 42, **257**,
Antique Tuscan No.8, 6, 38, 42, **206**,
Antique Tuscan No.11, 6, 38, 42, **207**,
Antique Tuscan Outline, 6, 38, 42, **207**,
First Annual typographic competition (TDC), 32,
Apollinaire, Guillaume, 22, 25,
Apollo, 40,
Apparel Arts, magazine, New York, 29,
Apple I, personal computer, 35,
Apple II, personal computer, 35,
Apple Capitals, 84, 164,
Apple Computer Inc., 35, 36, 92, 100, 104, 164, 167, 168,
Apple computers, 72,
Apple LaserWriter, laser printer, 36, 262,
Apple Macintosh Computer, 36, 37,
Apple Microsoft, 104,
Apple's Quick Draw GX, 160,
Applied arts, 20,
VGC Aquarius, 5, 40, 42, **44**,
Aquatint, etching technique, 17,
Arabian, **205**,
Aragón, 39,
Arcadia, 41,
Archer, Martin, 264,
Archipelago, 134,
Architecture Machine Group (MIT), 12, 35,
Arch of Titus, Rome, 145,
Arena, 41,
Arepo, 41, 238,
Arial, 41, 92,
Aries, 148,
Aries Press, Eden, 148,
Arion Press, San Francisco, 84, 164,
Arithmetica Geometria Proportionie Proportionalitá (de Pacioli), 223,
Armory Show, art exhibition, New York, Chicago, and Boston, 25,

Arnheim, Rudolf, 11, 24, 29,
Arnholm, Ronald, 5, 31, 40, 41, 42, 43, **44**, 188, 202,
VGC Arnhold Sans Medium, 44, 202,
VGC Arnholm Sans Bold, 44,
Arno, Peter, 170,
Arnold Böcklin, 38,
Arp, Jean (Hans), 25,
Arrighi, 6, 11, 26, 39, 42, 222, **252**, **253**268,
Ars Typographica (Goudy), 141, **143**,
The Art and Science of Typography, seminar, Silvermine, Connecticut, 32,
Art Amateur, magazine, 20,
Art collector, 19,
Artcraft, 6, 38, 42, **260**,
Artcraft Italic, 260,
Art Deco, movement, 27,
Art Deco, style, 27, 69, 81, 169, 197, 199, 215,
Art Deco style typefaces, **69**, **71**, **75**, **76**, **81**, **119**, **157**, **169**, **197**, **199**, **215**,
Art departments, 20,
Art Direction, magazine, 100, 127, 164,
Art directors, 20, 22, 28, 29, 30, 31, 32,
Art Directors Annual, 26,
The Art Directors Club Inc., New York, 25, 44, 54, 100, **101**, 186, 226, 242,
Art Directors Club's Hall of Fame, New York, 186,
Art Group Studios, Detroit, 172,
Art Institute of Boston, 104,
The Art Institute of Chicago, 26, 169, 194, 195, 220, 221, 224,
Art Interchange, magazine, 20,
Artist Guild of Chicago, 178,
Art News magazine, 240,
Art News Annual, 240,
Art Nouveau, gallery, Paris, 22,
Art Nouveau, movement, 22,
Art Nouveau, style, 20, 21, 22, 58, 96, 100, 220, 226,
Art Nouveau style typefaces, **58**, **141**, **220**,
The Art of Graphic Design (Thompson), 240,
The Art of the Printed Book, 1455-1955, exhibition, New York, 35, 91,
The Art of Typography (*Die Kunst der Typographie*)(Renner), 29,
Art reproductions, 18, 19, 20, 22, 24,
Arts and Crafts Exhibition Society, London, 21,
Arts and Crafts movement, 20, 21, 96, 137, 214, 220,
Arts et Métieres Graphiques, journal, (Peignot), 27,
Artscript, 5, 39, 42, 156, **159**,
Arts Students' League, New York, 78, 110, 141, 242,
Artwork, 265,
Ashendene Press, Chelsea, 251,
ASME News, magazine, 28,
Aspen International Design Conference, 31, 194,
Association Typographique Internationale (ATypl), Lausanne, Switzerland, 32, 72, 84, 104, 194, 226, 244,
Associazione Calligrafica Italiana, Milan, 226,
Assymetric typography, 11, 27, 29,
Assymetric Typography (*Typographische Gestaltung*) (Tschichold), 29,
Atlantic Monthly, magazine, 19,
Atlas, 39,
Athenæum, 29, 40,

AT&T (American Telephone and Telegraph), 36, 107, 152,
ATypl (Association Typographique Internationale), Lausanne, Switzerland, 32, 72, 84, 104, 194, 226, 244,
Auden, W(ystan) H(ugh), 91,
Auer, Alois, 19,
Augereau, Antoine, 14,
Augustea, 29, 40,
Aurelia, 41,
Auriga, 5, 40, 42, **104**,
Auriol, George, 38,
Auriol, 23, 38,
Auspurg, Albert, 39,
Austin, Richard, 38,
Autologic Inc., Newbury Park, 232, 238,
Automatic punch-cutter, 8, 21, **63**,
Automatic type caster, 21,
Avant Garde, magazine, New York, 11, 34, 186, **187**,
ITC Avant Garde Gothic, 6, 12, 34, 36, 40, 42, 100, 127, **186**, 189, 264,
Ave Imperatrix (Wilde), 220,
Avedon, Richard, 186,
Avenir, 41,
Avisa Relation oder Zeitung, newspaper, Strasburg, 14,
Ayer, Francis Wayland, 20,
N. W. Ayer & Son, advertising agency, Philadelphia, 20, 27, 28, 29,
N. W. Ayer Award for Excellence in Newspaper Typography, 28,

B

TF Baccarat, 6, 41, 42, 172, **175**,
Bain, Peter, 226,
Baine, John, type founder, Philadelphia, 16,
Baines, Phil, 37,
Baker, Arthur, 5, 35, 40, 41, 42, 43, **49**, 188, 202,
Baker Signet, 5, 40, 42, **49**, 202,
The Bald Soprano (*La Cantatrice Chauve*)(Ionesco / Massin), 12, 33,
Balla, Giacomo, 24,
Ballmer, Théo, 25, 28,
Balloon, 6, 39, 42, 176, **177**, 242,
Ballons, 22,
La Bamba, 41,
Banco, 30, 40,
Bancroft, John Sellers, 22, 180, 268,
Bancroft, Wilfred J., 156,
Bank, Arnold, 54, 202,
Bank Gothic, 5, 39, 42, 64, **70**,
Barbou, 26,
Barbou, Jean Joseph-Gerard, 15, 16,
ITC Barcelona, 5, 41, 42, **59**,
1992 Barcelona Olympics, **55**,
Barclay, Robert, 20,
Barker, Robert, 14,
The Barly Fields (Nathan), **131**,
Barnard College, 252,
Barnbrook, Jonathan, 41,
Barnhart Brothers & Spindler, type foundry, Chicago, 21, 25, 26, 27, 69, 100, 116, 118, 120, 203, 220, 260, 261, 263,
Barnett and Doolittle, lithographers, 18,
P.T. Barnum, 41,
Baroque style, 9,
The Baroque Set, typefaces, 37, 92,**93**, **94**, 226, 227,
Baroque style, 15,

Baroque typefaces, 240,
Barth, Henry, 21,
Bartlet Old Style, 214,
Base Monospace, 41, 182,
Base Nine and Twelve, 41, 182,
Basilea, 202,
Baskerville, John, 15, 16, 38, 107,
Baskerville, 10, 15, 16, 23, 24, 26, 38, 39, 149, 164, 196, 264, 268,
Basle School of Arts and Crafts, 84,
Bass, Saul, 31, 242,
Bassett, James, 204,
Basta, 40,
Bauer, Johann Christian, 18,
Bauer / Bauersche Giesserei, type foundry, Frankfurt, 18, 27, 29, 78, 81, 83, 91, 176, 177, 242, 243,
Bauer, Konrad F., 40,
Bauer Alphabets, 178,
Bauer Bodoni, 39,
Bauhaus, school, Weimar, 18, 24, 25, 32,
Bauhaus, school, Dessau, 27, 28, 29, 57,
Bauhaus, journal, Dessau, 27,
ITC Bauhaus, 5, 40, 42, **57**, 264,
ITC Bauhaus Bold, 5, **57**,
Bauhaus 1919-1928, exhibition, New York Museum of Modern Art, 29,
Bauhaus exhibition, Weimar, 26,
Bauhaus principles, 11, 24, 25, 30, 31, 35, 186,
Baum, Walter, 40,
Bay, Jacob, 16,
Bayer, Herbert, 11, 25, 27, 29, 31, 39, 57, 186,
Bayer Type, 39,
BBDO, advertising agency, New York, 121,
Beall, Lester, 29, 202,
Beardsley, Aubrey, 21, 22, 96, 114, 220,
Beata, 6, 37, 41, 42, 226, **229**,
Beata Villana, 229,
Beck, Henry C., 28,
Becker, Beatrice (Beatrice Warde), 252,
Beerbohm, Max, 22,
Beethoven, Ludwig van, 54,
Beggarstaff Brothers, 78,
Behrens, Peter, 21, 22, 24, 38,
Behrens-Antiqua, 38,
Behrens Roman, 38,
Behrens Schrift, 38,
Beilenson, Peter and Edna, 110,
Bel Geddes, Norman, 30,
Belizio, 72,
Bell, Alexander Graham, 152,
Bell, 26, 38, 39, 251, 268,
Bell Centennial, 5, 36, 40, 42, 104, **107**, 152,
Bell Gothic, 5, 11, 29, 36, 39, 42, 149, **152**, 266,
Bell Telephone Company, New York, 36, 149, 152,
FB Belucian, 5, 41, 42, **76**, 81,
FB Belucian Demi, 76,
FB Belucian Book, 76,
Belwe, Georg, 39,
Belwe Roman, 39,
Bembo, 39, 268,
Bender, Richard, 110,
The Benedictional of St. Aethelwold (Godeman, scribe), 245,
Benguiat, Edward, 5, 11, 34, 40, 41, 42, 43, **54**, 68, 101, 186, 189, 269,
ITC Benguiat, 5, 40, 42, **58**, 264,
ITC Benguiat Gothic, 5, 40, 42, **58**,

Bennett, James Gordon, 22,
Bennett, Paul A., 142,
Benson, John, 84,
Benton, Linn Boyd, 5, 9, 10, 21, 22, 23, 38, 42, **62**, 64, 66, 126, 149, 217, 260, 263, 268,
Benton, Morris Fuller, 5, 10, 11, 16, 23, 24, 26, 28, 38, 39, 42, 43, 54, 60, **64**, 99, 114, 116, 119, 140, 141, 150, 153, 156, 157, 158, 183, 192, 197, 198, 213, 214, 215, 218, 224, 226, 238, 263, 269,
Benton, Walter, 131,
Benton's Automatic Punchcutter, 62, **63**, 192,
Benton, Waldo & Co., type foundry, Milwaukee, 62, 263,
Beowulf, epic work, 154,
Beowulf, 41,
ITC Berkeley Oldstyle, 264,
Berlin Chamber of Commerce, 78, 79,
Berliner Messe, **80**,
Berling, 40,
Berlow, David, 5, 13, 37, 41, 42, **72**, 81, 133, 134, 135, 160,
Berlow, Sam, 72,
Bermuda, 37, 41, 42, 226, 230,
Bermuda Dots, **230**,
Bermuda Open, 6, **230**,
Bernanos, George, 228,
Bernbach, William, 30,
Bernhard, Lucian (pseud. of Emil Kahn) , 5, 11, 18, 23, 24, 25, 27, 38, 39, 42, 76, **78**, 116, 120, 202,
Bernhard, Sarah, 22,
Bernhard Antiqua, 38, 78,
Bernhard Booklet, 83,
Bernhard Brush Script / Bernhard Handschrift, 78,
Bernhard Buchschrift, 78,
Bernhard Fashion, 5, 39, 42, 78, **81**,
Bernhard Fraktur, 78, 79,
Bernhard Gothic, 5, 28, 39, 42, 78, **82**,
Bernhard Handschrift / Bernhard Brushscript, 78,
Bernhard Kursive, 5, 39, 42, 78, **81**, 116, 120,
Bernhard Modern Roman, 5, 39, 42, **83**,
Bernhard Negro, 78,
Bernhard Roman / Zarte Bernhard, 28, 78, 81,
Bernhard Roman Antiqua Bold Condensed, 5, 39, 42, **83**,
Bernhard-Schönscrift, 78, 81,
Bernhard Tango, 5, 39, 42, 78, **82**, 83,
Bernhard Tango Swash, 5, 39, 42, 78, **83**,
Bernstein, Leonard, 54,
Berry, W. T., 31,
Berthold, Hermann, 19,
H. Berthold AG, type foundry, Berlin, 19, 23, 24, 27, 28, 32, 37, 38, 39, 56, 78, 84, 102, 103,
Berthold Grotesque, 27, 39,
Berthold & Stempel, type foundry, 15,
Bertsch, Fred, 116,
Bertsch & Cooper, art service agency, Chicago, 116, **117**, 118, 221,
Best, Harvey, 146,
Bestiary (Dante), 52,
Beton, 28, 39,
Beveled, **212**,
Bewick, Thomas, 16, 30, 194,
Bewick Roman, 5, 38, 42, **98**,
Bézier, Pierre, 32,
Bézier curves, 32, 262,
Bianchi, John, 251,

The 42-line Bible (Gutenberg, printer), 19, 146,
The Bible (film, Huston), **187**,
The Bible as Living Literature (Simon & Shuster, publishers), 146,
Biblioteca Ambrosiana, Milan, 227,
Biblioteca Palatina, Roma, 26,
Biblioteca Real, Madrid, 16,
Bickham, George, 15,
Bierbaum, Otto Julius, 22,
Bifur, 27, 39,
Big Caslon, 5, 41, 42, 104, 105, **109**,
Bigelow, Charles,5, 12, 35, 36, 41, 43, **84**, 160, 164, 165, 166, 167, 168, 244,
Bigelow & Holmes, Inc., digital type foundry, Menlo Park, 35, 87, 164, 244,
Das bildnerische Denken (*The Thinking Eye*) (Klee), 32,
Bill, Max, 31,
H. & J. Bill & Company [Horatio and Jeremiah], Lebannon, 204,
Billboards, 19, 23, 25, 35,
Binder, Joseph, 30,
Bing, Samuel, 22,
Binny, Archibald, 16, 17, 38, 251,
Binny & Ronaldson, type foundry, Philadelphia, 16, 17, 38, 263,
Birch, **211**,
Bird, John, 220,
Birdsall, Derek,34, 265,
Bisser, Théodor, 217, 268,
Bitmapped characters, 35,
Bitmapped graphics, 12, 36,
Bitstream Inc., digital type foundry, Cambridge, 36, 72, 102, 103, 104, 120, 134,
Bittrof, Max, 39,
Black, Roger,37, 72, 160,
Black Cat Press, 194,
Black letter, 8, 14, **71**, **88**, 146, 154, **185**, 242, 251,
Blackletter: Type and National Identity, exhibition, New York, 226,
Black Letter Primer (Shaw), 226,
Black and white photography, 11,
Black audience, 34,
Black typefaces, 9, 17, 26, 38, 70,
Blado, 26, 39,
Blado Italic, 251,
Blake, James, 17,
Blake, William, 16,
Der Blaue Reiter (*The Blue Rider*), movement, 24,
Robert Wood Bliss Library, Dumbarton Oaks (bookplate), **225**,
Block Type, 5, 38, 42, **78**,
Blokland, Frank, 226,
Blount, Edward, 14,
Blue Note, records, New York, 33,
The Blue Rider (*Der Blaue Reiter*), 24,
Blumenthal, Joseph, 5, 26, 27, 35, 36, 39, 42, **91**, 110, 154, 240, 252,
Blur, 41,
Boccioni, Umberto, 24,
Bodoni, Giambattista, 9, 15, 16, 17, 26, 38, 68, 118,
Bodoni, 10, 13, 15, 16, 23, 24, 38, 64, 68, 70, 99, 109. 120, 160, 194, 251,
ITC Bodoni, 238,
Bodoni Black, 6, 39, 42, 70, 116, 119, **198**,
Bodoni Bold, 157,
Bodoni Bold Panelled, 5, 39, 42, 156, **157**,
Bodoni Campanile, 6, 39, 42, **200**,
Bodoni Light, 260,

Bodoni Modern, 260, 267,
Bodoni Oldface, 41,
Bodoni Open, 5, 38, 42, **68**,
Boge, Garrett, 5, 13, 37, 41, 42, 43, 58, **92**, 226, 227, 229, 230, 231,
Bohn, Hans, 21, 39,
Bolshevik Revolution, Russia, 25,
Bonaparte, Napoleon, 16,
Bonder, Ronne, 40, 100, 101, 103,
Bonder & Carnase Studio, Inc., New York, 100, 127,
Book Binding and Book-Production (Ransom), 220,
Book design, 23, 27, 28, 36, 116, 129, 141, 154, 240, 251, 252,
Book designers, **91**, **96**, 110, 114, 126, 129, 141, 154, 224, 251, 252,
Book faces, 47, 48, 49, 54, 56, 57, 60, 62, **66**, **67**, **68**, 72, 77, 83, 84, 85, 87, 91, 99, 104, 106, 108, 110, 113, 114, 116, 124, 126, 132, 133, 135, 136, 140, 144, 145, 146, 148, 149, 150, 151, 152, 153, 165, 166, 167, 168, 174, 180, 184, 185, 192, 197, 217, 222, 224, 226, 230, 232, 233, 234, 238, 239, 244, 247, 248, 250, 252, 261,
Book illustration, 14, 18, 32, **130**, 224,
Book illustrators, **96**, 110, 129, **224**,
The Book of Signs (*Das Zeichenbuch*)(Koch), 26,
Booklet Press, Chicago, 141,
Bookman, 23, 38, 57, 214,
ITC Bookman, 5, 36, 40, 42, **57**,
The Bookman, magazine, 96,
The Book of Common Prayer (Updike, printer), 126, 137, 251,
Book of Kells, 49,
The Book of "Monotype" Ornaments (Warde), **253**,
The Book of OZ Cooper, 106, 116, **117**,
The Book of Signs (*Das Zeichenbuch*) (Koch), 26,
Bookplates / Exlibris, **111**, **195**, **196**, **225**,
Book Printing in America as One of the Fine Arts (Warde), 252,
Book spines, **112**, **130**,
Books by Offset, 1942 AIGA annual exhibition, 30,
Booth, Jonas, 18,
Borzoi dog, **131**, **225**,
Borzoi Books, 27, **225**,
The Borzoi Book of French Folktales, 112,
Boston Athenæum Library (bookplate), **225**,
Boston News-Letter, newspaper, 14,
Boston Public Library, 22,
Boston Society of Printers, 251,
Boston Type Foundry, 204, 263,
Boston University Symphony Orchestra, 7,
The Boston Weekly Journal, newspaper, 19,
Boton, Albert, 40, 41,
Boton, 41,
Boudinot, Elias, editor, Georgia, 18,
Boulevard, 32, 40,
Boul Mich, 5, 39, 42, 69, 116, **119**, 157,
Bowker, R. R., printers, New York, 220, 228,
Bowles, Joseph M., 222,
Bowyer, William, 15,
Boydell, John, printer, London, 17,
Boydel, Phillip, 40,
Bradford, William, printer, Philadelphia, 14,
Bradley, William, 5, 10, 21, 22, 23, 24, 42, 43, 94, 114, 141, 263,
Bradley, 5, 38, 42, **96**, 97,
Bradley: His Book (Bradley), 22, 96, **97**,
The Bradley House, 96,

Brady, Fred, 244, 262,
Braganza, 41,
Brainerd, Paul, 36,
Brambrook, Jonathan, 41,
Brand, Chris, 40,
Braque, Georges, 24, 121,
Bremer Presse, Munich, 91,
Brenner, Carl, 203,
Breton, André, 26,
Breuer, Marcel, 25,
The Bridge (*Die Brücke*), 23,
Bridge, Robert, 252,
Briem, Gunnlauger, 84,
Brignall, Colin, 33, 36, 40, 41, 264,
British Printing Industry, 28,
British type foundries, 22,
Broadway, 5, 39, 42, 64, 65, **69**, 156, **157**,
Broadway Engraved, 5, 39, 42, **69**, 156, **157**,
Brodersen, Harold, 40,
Brodovitch, Alexey, 11, 20, 28, 186,
Brody, 40,
Brody, Neville, 36, 37, 41, 134, 136,
Brokenscript Bold, 41,
Brooklyn Museum, New York, 78,
Brooks, Travis, 134, 135,
Brook type, , 38,
Brothers of the Book, limited editions, Chicago, 220,
Brown, Harold, 251,
Browning, Robert, 139,
Brown University, Providence, 251,
Bruce Sr., David, 17, 114, 156, 214, 259,
Bruce Jr., David, 17, 18, 19, 38, 254,
Bruce Italic, 156,
Bruce Old Style, 17, 38, 156,
Bruce Rogers: A Life in Letters (Blumenthal), 91,
Die Brücke (*The Bridge*), movement, 23,
Brush, 6, 40, 236, **237**,
Brush Calligraphy (Baker), 49,
Brush script typefaces, 33, **237**,
AG Buch Stencil, 41,
Buchwald, Art, 45,
Bucolica, Georgica et Æneis (Virgil), 15,
Buell, Abel, 15,
Bullen, Henry Lewis, 5, 10, 11, 21, 23, 24, 25, 26, 64, **99**, 252, 263,
Bulmer, William, 129, 132,
Bulmer, 10, 16, 23, 24, 39, 64, 99, 132,
Bullock, William, 17, 19,
Buonarroti, Michelangelo, 241,
FB Bureau Grotesque, ,
Burges, Hugh, 19,
Burne-Jones, Edward, 19, 22,
Burns, Aaron, 12, 31, 32, 33, 34, 172, 186, 264,
Burtin, Will, 32, 202,
Business Week, magazine, 134,
ITC Busorama, 5, 40, 42, 100, **103**,
Butti, Alessandro, 20, 29, 31, 40, 70,
Byte, magazine, 84,

C

CA, magazine, 100,
CAD/CAM, computer programs, 32,
Cadmus Greek, 104,
Caecilia, 41,
Cafeteria, 134,
Caflisch, Max, 18, 40, 232, 235,
Caflisch Script, 6, 41, 42, 232, **235**,
Cage, Bob, 30,

Caledonia, 5, 39, 42, 72, 129, **132**, 266,
Calhoun, John, 18,
Calenders, 18,
California / University of California Old Style, 148,
California, magazine, 72,
Calisto, 41,
Calkins, Ernest Elmo, 24,
Calkins and Holden, advertising agency, New York, 224,
Calligrafia nel mondo della grafica, exhibition, Assolo, Italy, 226,
Calligrammes (Apollinaire), 25,
Calligraphers, 14, 37,
Calligraphic Alphabets (Baker), 35, 49, 50,
The Calligraphic Art of Arthur Baker (Baker), 49,
Calligraphic Initials (Baker), 49,
Calligraphic Models of Ludovico Degli Arrighi (Degli Arrighi), 252,
Calligraphic Swash Initials (Baker), 49,
Calligraphic typefaces, 12, 16, **52**, **53**, **61**, **66**, 81, **82**, 83, 92, 93, 95, **106**, **107**, 113, **120**, 133, 146, 148, 154, 155, 159, 164, 168, 178, 201, 215, 221, 230, 231, 235, 236, 242,
Calligraphy, 19, 23, 37, **50**, **51**, 55, **101**, 111, 112, 122, 123, 139, 187, 188, 195, 196, 227, 228,
Calligraphy (Baker), 35, 49, 50, **51**,
Calligraphy and Lettering in the Graphic Arts (Shaw), exhibition, 226,
Calvert, 40,
Calvert, Margaret, 40,
Calypso, 30, 40,
Cambridge College, 14,
Cambridge University, England, 14, 17,
Cambridge University Press, England, 14, 26, 27, 28, 222,
Camelot, 5, 38, 42, **141**, 203,
Camelot Press, Chicago, 141, 203,
Cameo, 6, 39, 42, **194**,
Camera-ready artwork, 36,
Camex, Inc., Boston, 238,
Campanile, 41,
Campbell, Jerry, 41, 172,
Cancelaresca bastarda, 27, 39,
Candide (Voltaire), 27, 78, 81,
Canfield Ph.B., Charles William, 139,
Canned food, ready-to-serve, 21,
Canon Color Laser Copier, 37,
La Cantatrice Chauve (*The Bald Soprano*) (Ionesco / Massin), 12, 33,
Capital letters, 8,
Capitol, 39,
Capper Publications, Topeka, 240,
Caprichos (Goya), 17,
Carlson, Chester, 29, 30, 32,
Carlu, Jean, 29,
Carmel Snow, publisher, New York, 28,
Carmina, 41,
Carnase, Tom, 5, 12, 33, 34, 40, 42, 43, 55, **100**, 127, 186, 187, 188, 189, 264,
Carnase Computer Typography, New York, 100,
Carnase Text, 100,
Carnival, 259,
Carolingian manuscripts, 245,
Carolingian script / miniscule, 8, 154,
Caroll Reese Museum, East Tennessee University, 44,

Carolus, Johan, 14,
Carolus, 40,
Carpenter, Ron, 41,
Carroll, Lewis (pseud. of Charles Lutwidge Dodgson), 19,
Carson, David, 37,
Carson, Pirie, Scott & Co., department store, Chicago, 220,
Carter, Harry, 104,
Carter, Matthew, 5, 13, 34, 36, 37, 40, 41, 42, 43, 72, **104**, 134, 152, 160, 264,
Carter, Sebastian, 36,
Carter, Will, 40,
Carter & Cone Type Inc., digital type foundry, Cambridge, 37, 104,
The Carteret Book Club of Newark, 224,
Cartoon, 6, 22, 29, 39, 42, 176, 177, 242, **243**,
Cartoon Bold, 6, **243**,
Cartoonists, 33, **170**,
Cartoons, **171**,
Caruso, Victor, 54, 56,
Cary Collection, Rochester Institute of Technology, 252,
Cascade Script, 5, 40, 42, 104, **106**,
Caslon I, William, 15, 38, 60, 109, 116, 160, 247,
William Caslon I, type foundry, London, 16, 141, 247,
Caslon II, William, 15,
Caslon IV, William, 17, 38,
Adobe Caslon, 6, 41, 42, 244, **247**,
Caslon Antique, 6, 38, 42, **203**,
Caslon Bold, 190, 194,
Caslon Catalogue / Caslon Antique, 260,
Caslon Clearface, 6, 38, 42, 260, **261**,
Caslon Clearface Italic, 260,
Caslon Light, 190,
Caslon Old Face / Caslon Old style, 13, 15, 16, 24, 38, 60, 96, 120, 141, 160, 164, 217, 251, 261, 264, 268,
Caslon Oldstyle 540, 7,
Caslon 641, 178,
Caslon Press, New York, 114,
ITC Caslon 224, 5, 41, 42, **60**, 264,
Caslon True-cut, 267,
Cass Tech High School, Detroit, 172,
Cassandre, A. M., (pseud. of Jean-Marie Mouron), 27, 29, 30, 39,
Castellar, 40,
Catalina, 178,
Cathode ray tube (CRT), 12, 33, 34, 35, 266,
Cato Major (Cicero), 15, 139,
Caxton, 34, 41,
Caxton Oldstyle No. 2, 56,
Caxton Club, a bibliophile organization, Chicago, 194,
The Caxton Type Foundry, England, 22,
CBS (Columbia Broadcasting System), New York, 31, 34, 100, 187, 266,
CBS' Cafeteria three-dimensional typographic assemblage mural, 12, 33, 100,
CBS Corporate Identity Program, 31, 34, 125,
CBS Didot, 5, 34, 40, 42, 121, **125**,
CBS' eye (symbol) (Golden), 31,
CBS Sans, 5, 34, 40, 42, 121, **125**,
CBS Show, first color TV program, 31,
CBS television, 31, 34, 121,
CBS Television Network, 32,
CD-ROM, 37,
Celtic Hand Stroke by Stroke (Baker), 49,
Celtic Ornamented, 6, 38, 42, **209**,

Centaur, 6, 11, 25, 29, 38, 42, 109, 194, **222**, 252, 260, 268,
The Centaur (de Guerin), 25, 222,
Center for Creative Studies, School of Arts and Design, Detroit, 172,
Central School of Arts and Crafts, London, 23,
Central Type Foundry, St. Louis, 22, 71, 263,
Century Bold, 103,
Century Broad-Face, 62,
The Century Dictionary (De Vinne, designer/printer), 126,
Century Expanded, 64,
The Century Family, **65**
Century Guild, London, 20,
ITC Century Handtooled, 5, 41, 42, **61**, 264,
Century Illustrated Monthly Magazine, 19,
The Century Magazine, 20, 22, 62, 96, 126,
Century Nova, 178,
Century Roman, 5, 22, 38, 42, **62**, 64, **126**, 149, 264,
Century Schoolbook, 5, 23, 38, 42, 64, **68**, 153, 224,
Century Schoolbook Bold, 68,
Cervantes, Miguel de, , 14, 16,
Cezca Unciala 40, 154,
Chaillot, 40,
Chaldean, **205**,
Chambord, 40,
HTF Champion Gothic, 6, 42, **162**,
HTF Champion Gothic Bantamweight, 6, **162**,
HTF Champion Gothic Featherweight, 6, **162**,
HTF Champion Gothic Heavyweight, 6, **162**,
HTF Champion Gothic Lightweight, 6, **162**,
HTF Champion Gothic Middleweight, 6, **162**,
HTF Champion Gothic Welterweight, 6, **162**,
Champollion, Jean-François, 17,
Apple Chancery, 164,
Chancery Cursive, 121,
Chancery Italic Classic, 121,
Chancery Script, 113,
Channel 13, Public Broadcasting Station, New York, 187,
Channel WNET 13, New York, 127,
Chaparral, 6, 13, 41, 42, 244, **250**,
The Chap-Book, magazine, Chicago, 22, 96, **97**, 141,
Chap-book cuts, 22, **97**,
Chapin Library (bookplate), **194**,
K. K. Chapin Library (bookplate), **194**,
Chaplin, Charles, 69, 220,
Chappell, Lydia, 110,
Chappell, Warren, 5, 25, 35, 39, 43, 91, **110**, 225,
The Charlatanry of the Learned (Mencken), **130**, **131**,
Charlemagne (Charles I the Great, *Carolus Magnus*), 8,
Charlemagne (Pechey), 38,
Charlemagne (Twombly), 6, 37, 41, 42, 244, **245**, 249,
Charles De Gaulle Airport, Roissy, 35,
Charlotte Sans, 41,
Charme, 40,
Bitstream Charter, 36,
ITC Charter, 5, 41, 42, 104, **108**,
Chaucer, 21, 22, 38, 203, 216,
Cheltenham, 5, 6, 22, 23, 38, 42, 57, 64, 126, 137, **138**, **140**, **192**, 214, 264, 266,
ITC Cheltenham Handtooled, 5, 41, 42, **61**, 264,

Cheltenham Press, New York, 22, 23, 137, 140, 141, 266,
Chéret, Jules, 19, 20,
Chermayeff, Ivan, 35,
Cherokee language alphabet, 18,
The Cherokee Phoenix, newspaper, New Echota, Georgia, 18,
Cherryburn Press, Chicago, 30, 194, 195, 196,
Apple Chicago, 6, 41, 42, 84, 164, **167**,
The Chicago Daily News, 116, 192,
The Chicago Democrat, newspaper, 18,
The Chicago Evening Post, 25, 190, 267,
Chicago fire, 20,
Chicago letter founding (Middleton), 194,
Chicago Society of Typographic Arts, 194,
Chicago style, 116,
The Chicago Sunday Tribune, 96,
The Chicago Symphony (symbol), Chicago Orchestral Society, 122,
The Chicago Tribune, 72,
Childs, Asa, 254,
Childs, William, 254,
Ching, Francis D., 41,
Chinon, 40,
Chisel, 17, 39,
Choc, 30, 40,
Christiana, 41,
Christian era, 6,
Christopher Plantin (De Vinne), 126,
Chromatic wood types, 18, 20,
Chromatic Wood Types (Page), 20, 204,
Chromolitographie, 18,
Chromolithography, 9, 18, 19, 22,
Chronos, Greek god, 223,
Chrysler Award for Innovation in Design, 104,
Chudley, Bob, 265,
Chwast, Seymour, 31, 37,
Cicero, Marcus Tulius, 15, 139,
Cincinnati Type Foundry, 21, 263,
Cinematograph, 22,
Circle of Friends, calligraphers, New York, 226,
Citizen, 41, 182, 185,
City, 28, 39,
Clairol, beauty products, 226, 228,
Clarendon, 18, 38,
Clarendon Ornamented, 6, 38, 42, **207**,
Clarendon XX Condensed, 6, 38, 42, **206**,
Clarendon Press, Oxford, 21,
Clarendon style typefaces, 9, 18, 121, **123**, **124**, **149**, **150**, **151**, **152**, **153**,
Classic, 121,
Classical Roman Alphabet (de Pacioli), 28,
Claudius, 39,
Clearface, 5, 38, 42, 64, 65, **66**,
ITC Clearface, 264,
In the Clearing (Frost), 91,
Cleland, Thomas Maitland, 5, 26, 28, 38, 42, **104**, 238, 251,
Clephane, James O., 192,
Cleveland Institute of Art, Ohio, 100,
Cleveland Museum of Art, Ohio, 34,
The Cleveland Press, Cleveland, 190, 267,
Cloister Black, 38, 216,
Cloister Oldstyle, 5, 23, 24, 38, 42, 64, **67**, 99, 194,
Cloister Oldstyle Italic, 67,
Cloisters Initials, 5, 25, 38, 42, 142, **145**, 214,
Club of the Odd Volumes, 251,

Clymer, George, 17,
Coated paper, 126,
Cobean, 170,
Cobden-Sanderson, Thomas J., 21, 23, 38,
Coca-Cola, logotype, 127,
Coca-Cola Company, 100, 127,
Cochin, 38, 156,
Cochin Bold and *Italic*, 156,
Cochin Open, 156,
Cochin Tooled, 156,
Cockerell, Sidney, 222,
Codex, 40,
Coiner, Charles, 27, 29,
Coffin, William S., 45,
Colines, Simon de, 223,
Collages, 24, 25, 35,
College Board, 121,
College Board Review, magazine, 123,
College of Art and Design, Ireland, 127,
Collier, John, 131,
Collier Oldstyle, 260,
Collier's Weekly Magazine, 96, 266,
Collins, Marv, 172,
Colophon, **105**, 129,
Color comic strips, 22,
Color photography, 11, 24,
Color reproduction, 21, 24, 28,
Color television (CBS, New York), 31,
Color television sets, 31,
Colorado Springs Fine Arts Center, 110,
Colored posters, 20,
Colortype Company, New York, 121,
Columbia University, New York, 24, 99, 110, 226,
Columbia University Press, New York, 20,
Columbian Iron Press, letterpress, 18,
Columbus Society of Communication Arts, 183,
Columna, 40,
Comenius Roman, 40,
Comic book iconography, 31, 33,
Comic strips, 22, 31,
Comic strips lettering, 22, 29,
Commedies, Histories & Tragedies (Shakespeare), 14,
Commercial Controls Corporation of America, 30,
Commercial Script, 5, 38, 42, 64, **66**,
Compacta, 33, 40, 265,
Companion Old Style and *Italic*, 26,
Complete Manual of Stone Printing (Senefelder), 17,
The Composing Room, New York, 31,
Compositype, composing machine, 263,
Compugraphic Corporation, Wilmington, Massachusetts, 12, 32, 33, 35, 37, 52, 102, 147, 164,
Computer / electronic calculator, 30,
Computer age, 33,
Computer-aided typesetting, term, 12, 33,
Computer color, 37,
Computer-controlled typesetting, term, 12, 33,
Computer Graphics, magazine, 164,
Computer language, 12, 13,
Computer-only Linofilm, typesetter, 266,
CompuWriter, Compugraphic, 35,
Comstock, **257**,
Conceptual Art, movement, 32,
Conceptual design, 34,

Concorde, 32, 40,
Condé Nast, publications, 11, 28, 100,
Condensed typefaces, 15, 18, **66**, **75**, **120**, **169**, **184**, 199, **200**, **204**, 206, **208**, 211, 218, **256**,
Condivi, Ascanio, 251,
Cone, Cheri, 37, 104,
The Confederacy, Southern states, 19,
Conmemorative tokens, 18,
James Connor Type Foundry, New York, 19, 204, 254, 263,
Conried, Hans, 196,
Emperor Constantine, 241,
Constructivism, movement, 25, 27, 32, 35,
Contact Bold Condensed, 221,
Container Corporation of America, Chicago, 27, 29, 31, 33,
Contempora Inc., design office, New York, 78, **80**,
Contemporary Typography: Aims, Practice, Criticism (Moholy-Nagy), 27,
Contour typefaces, **207**, **257**, **258**,
Converse, A. C., 216,
Cook & Shanosky Ass., advertising agency, New York, 35,
Cooley, John, 204, 206,
Cooper, John Fenimore, 220,
Cooper, Lenn, 49,
Cooper, Oswald Bruce, 5, 25, 26, 27, 38, 39, 42, 43, 69, **116**, 146, 157, 220, 221,
Cooper Black, 5, 38, 42, 116, **119**, 146,
Cooper Black Condensed, 116, 119,
Cooper Black Italic, 116,
Cooper Full Face, 5, 39, 42, 116, **120**,
Cooper-Hewitt Museum, New York, 121,
Cooper Hilite, 5, 39, 42, 116, **119**, 157,
Cooper Old Style, 5, 38, 42, **116**, 119,
Cooper Old Style Italic, 118,
Cooper Tooled, 5, 39, 42, 119, **157**,
Cooper Union, New York, 121, 192,
Cooper Union School of Art, New York, 121, 186, 202,
Cooper Union for the Advancements of Science and Art, New York, **188**,
Cooper Union School of Design, New York, 226,
Cope, Richard W., 18,
Copeland & Day, publishers, London, 137,
Copper, metal, 21,
Copperplate engraving, 9,
Copperplate Gothic, 5, 38, 42, 119, **144**, 260,
Copywriters, 20, 31,
Corinthian, 41,
Cornell University, Ithaca, 64, 91,
Cornhill Press, Boston, 114,
Cornish College of Arts, Seattle, 92,
Corona, 5, 27, 39, 42, 149, **153**, 266,
Coronet, 6, 39, 42, 144, **200**, 242, 267,
Corporate identity imagery, 26, 32,
Corporate identity program, 24, 29, 31, 32, 36,
Corporate identity systems, 12, 33, 36,
Corum, Jonathan, 74,
Corvinus, 39,
Coryciana (Palladius), 222, 252,
Cottonwood, **258**,
Cottrell, Thomas, 15, 17, 38,
Countdown, 40,
Un Coup de dés jamais n'abolira le hasard (Mallarmé), 22,
Courier, 36, 92,
The Courier Journal, Louisville, 192,

Cover design, 21, **45**, **97**, **105**, **112**, **115**, **123**, **128**, **131**, **142**, **143**, **161**, **171**, **179**, **183**, **187**, **188**, **253**,
Cover Stories (Lorenz), 170,
Craftsman / Artscraft, 260,
Cram, Goodhue & Ferguson, architects, Boston, 137,
Cram & Wentworth, architects, Boston, 137,
Cramoisy, Sébastien, 14,
Crane, Stephen, 131, 240,
Crane, Walter, 21, 96, 114,
Cranbrook Academy of Art, Michigan, 35,
Cranbrook School, Michigan, 84,
Craw, Freeman, 5, 34, 40, 42, **121**, 178,
Freeman Craw Design, New York, 40, 121,
Craw Canterbury, 121,
Craw Clarendon, 5, 40, 42, **121**, 124,
Craw Clarendon Book, 5, 40, 42, 121, **124**,
Craw Clarendon Condensed, 5, 40, 42, 121, 122, **124**,
Craw Modern, 5, 40, 42, 121, 122, 123, **124**,
Craw Modern Bold, 124,
Craw Modern Italic, 5, 40, 42, **124**,
Crawford's Advertising Agency, London, 265,
Crayon, magazine, 20,
Creative Alliance (Agfa), 37,
Creative Alliance CD (Agfa / Monotype), 37,
Creativity, magazine, 100,
Cresci, Giovanni Francesco, 94,
Cresci, 5, 37, 41, 42, **94**, 226,
Elliot Cresson Medal, 180, 192,
Cristal, 40,
Cronan Design, 92,
Crosby, Theo, 33, 35,
Crosfield Electronics, phototypesetting machines, 34, 104,
Crous-Vidal, Enric, 25, 40,
Crouwell, Wim, 33, 40,
Crowell-Collier Co., Philadelphia, 156,
Crown Publishing, 100,
The Crystal Goblet: Sixteen Essays on Typography (Beatrice Warde), 31,
Crystal Palace, Hyde Park, London, 19,
Cubism, movement, 24,
Cubist paintings, 25,
Cummins Engine Co., 32,
Curtis Publications, 187,
Curtis Publishing Company, Philadelphia, 156,
Custon typefaces, 72,
Curved stereotype plates, 19,
The Curwen Press, London, 26, 31,

D

DaBoll, Raymond F., 117,
Dada, movement, 25, 27, 32, 35, 36, 182,
Daguerre, Louis Jacques, 18,
Daguerreotype, 18,
The Daily Commercial, Louisville, 203,
The Daily Herald, England, 27, 149,
The Daily Telegraph, England, 30,
Dalí, Salvador, 26,
Dalton, Michael, 216,
Damon & Peets, type foundry, 263,
Damon Type Foundry, New York, 263,
The Dance of Death (Holbein), 112,
The Dance of the Pen (Baker), 49,
Dante, Allighieri, 52,
Dante, 26, 40, 104,
Darrow Jr., Whitney, 170,

Dartmouth College, Hanover, 224, 225,
Databases, 37,
Daumier, Honoré, 17,
Davida Bold, 6, 40, 42, **202**,
Davis, John Charles Clifford 'Dai', 32, 265,
Davis, Stuart, 240,
Day, Ben, 18,
Day, Chon, 170,
Day, Robert, 170,
Day & Sons, publishers, London, 19,
Daye, Stephen, 14,
Dead History, 13, 41,
Dearborn Type Foundry, Chicago, 155,
Deberny, type foundry, Paris, 23, 26,
Fonderie Deberny & Peignot, type foundry, Paris, 15, 23, 26, 27, 29, 31, 32, 39, 154, 269,
Decals / Decalcomanias, 265,
Deck, Barry, 13, 182,
Declaration of Independence of the United States of America, 16,
Deconstruction, concept, 34, 35,
The Decorative Illustration of Books (Crane), 114,
Decorative typefaces, 20, 34, **205**, **207**, **209**, **258**, **259**,
Deck, Barry, 13, 36, 41, 182,
The Decorative Work of T. M. Cleland (Cleland), 114,
A Decree of Starre-Chamber Concerning Printing (Barker, printer), 14,
Deepdene, 5, 39, 42, 141, **146**,
Defoe, Daniel, 15,
Defy the Foul Fiend (Collier), **130**,
Degas, Edgar, 121,
Degli Arrighi, Ludovico Vicentino, 162, 222, 252,
De Groot, Lucas, 13, 36, 37, 41,
De Harak, Rudolph, 34,
Délire à Deux (Ionesco / Massin), 12, 33, 34,
Dellagana, James, 19,
Della Robbia, Luca, 114,
Della Robbia, 5, 28, 38, 42, **114**, 229,
Delphian Open Title, 6, 26, 39, 42, 194, **197**, 267,
Demeter, Peter A., 19, 38, 39,
Demeter, 39,
De Milano, G., 39,
Demming, Frank and William, 217,
Demotic script, 17,
Denman, Frank, 63, 138,
Derby, 32, 40,
De Roos, Sjoerd Hendrik, 19, 38, 39, 134, 135, 154,
Derrida, Jaques, 34,
Design, a Function of Management, conference, Aspen, 31,
Design Centre, England, 127,
Design for print (Tschichold), 27,
Design Issues, magazine, 226,
Design Quarterly, magazine, Minneapolis, 30,
Desk Top Publishing (DTP), 12, 36,
De Stijl (The Style), magazine, 25,
De Stijl, movement, 25,
De Stijl principles, 25, 28, 186,
Detroit Institute of Arts, 172,
Detterer, Ernst Frederick, 10, 23, 26, 27, 28, 194, 195, 267,
André Deutsch Limited, publisher, London, 110, 111,
David Deutsch Advertising Agency, 128,
Deutsche Zierschrift, 38,

Deutsche Flugplatz-Gesellschaft, Berlin, 80,
Deutsches Museum, The Hague, 78,
Deutschen Verlagsaustall, Stuttgart, 26,
Deutscher Werkbund, Munich, 24, 78,
The Development of the Roman Alphabet (Frutiger), 36,
De Vinne, Theodore Low, 5, 17, 20, 21, 22, 23, 38, 42, 62, 64, **126**, 137, 149, 224, 251,
De Vinne, 40,
De Vinne, Theodore B., 126,
Theodore Low De Vinne & Company, printing press, New York, 20, 126,
The De Vinne Press, New York, 126,
Diane, 30, 40,
Diary of a Country Priest (Bernanos), 228,
Dickinson Type Foundry, Boston, 21, 141, 216, 263,
Diderot, Denis, 15,
Didot, Firmin, 9, 15, 16, 17, 38, 70,
Didot, François-Ambroise, 15, 16, 17,
Didot, Pierre François, 17,
Didot, Saint-Léger, 17,
Didot, Pierre, l'ainé, 17,
Didot, 13, 16, 17, 36, 38, 109,
HTF Didot, 6, 41, 42, 160, **163**,
Didot's type measuring system, 16,
Die-cut wood type, 204, 205,
Die-cutting process, 21,
Diethelm, Walter, 40,
Diethelm-Antiqua, 40,
Digital publication, 37,
Digital Review, magazine, 164,
Digital typefaces, 34, 35, 36, 37,
Digital type foundries, 36, 37,
Digital type libraries, 12, 35,
Digital Typography, master's program, Stanford University, California, 35, 84, 244,
Diotima, 40,
Direct Advertising, magazine, Boston, 129,
Direct Mail Advertising Association, 121,
Discursions of a Retired Printer (Bullen), 99, 263,
El Diseño Gráfico: desde los orígenes hasta nuestros días (Satué), 37,
DiSpigna, Tony, 5, 34, 40, 43, 100, **127**, 186, 189, 264,
Tony DiSpigna, Inc., studio, New York, 127,
Display type, 18, 19, 24, 29, 33, **61**, **69**, **70**, **71**, **73**, **74**, **75**, **78**, **82**, **83**, **93**, **96**, **98**, **100**, **102**, **103**, **109**, **119**, **120**, **121**, **125**, **136**, **156**, **157**, **158**, **159**, **169**, **170**, **177**, **178**, **185**, **194**, **197**, **199**, **201**, **202**, **204**, **206**, **207**, **208**, **209**, **210**, **211**, **212**, **213**, **214**, **215**, **218**, **219**, **230**, **237**, **243**, **246**, **254**, **256**, **257**, **258**, **259**, **261**,
Display typecasting machine, 24,
Diskette, 37,
Dodge, Philip T., 62,
Dogma, 41, 182,
Dollar sign ($), 17,
Dolores, 5, 41, 42, **134**,
The Dolphin, magazine, New York, 28, 110,
Dombrezian, Peter, 11, 29, 40, 68, 242, 269,
Dom Casual, 11, 29, 40, 68, 242, 269,
Dom Casual, 11, 29, 40, 68, 242, 269,
Donaldson, Timothy, 226, 264,
Donatello, 6, 37, 41, 42, 226, **229**,
Donkin, Brian, 17,
Don Quixote de la Mancha (Cervantes), 14, 16,
Dooijes, Dick, 19, 40,
Doolitle, Isaac, 16,
The Door in the Wall (Wells), 11, 24, 141, **142**, 144, 145, 260,
Dorchester, 39,

Doré, Gustave, 17, 20,
Dorfsman, Lou, 12, 32, 33, 34, 100, 125, 202,
Doric Ornamented, 6, 38, 42, **259**,
Doubleday, Page & Co., 25,
Double spread, **46**, **65**, **105**, **130**, **227**, **241**,
Doubleday Publishing, Co., 100,
Dove, J. Maury, 268,
Doves' Bible (Cobden-Sanderson / Walker), 23,
Doves Bindery, Hammersmith, 21,
Doves Press, Hammersmith, 21, 23, 141, 222, 251,
Doves Roman, 23, 38,
Downer, J., 36, 182,
Doyle Dane Bernbach, advertising agency, New York, 30,
Dreiser, Theodore, 91,
Dresser, Christopher, 96,
Dreyfus, John, 31, 32, 104,
Dreyfuss, Henry, 30,
Drinkwater, John, 222,
Druckery, Inge, 134,
Dry transfer type, 32, 265,
Ducos de Hauron, Louis, 20,
Duensing, Paul Hayden, 40, 154, 155, 196,
Duke of Parma, Ferdinand, 15, 16,
Duncan, Isadora, dancer, 164,
Duncan, Harold M., 217, 268,
Dunn, Alan, 170,
Duplex-Display, two-letter Monotype matrices, 24,
Duplicate of Type Specimen Books for Sale (Bullen), catalog, 99,
Dupré, Jules, 17,
Dürer, Albrecht, 9, 14, 222, 223,
P.O. Duschnes, publishers, New York, 220,
Dutch press, 14,
Dutch printers and compositors, 14,
Dutch punches, 14,
Dutch Treat Club of the Quiet Birdman, 54,
Dwiggins, William Addison, 5, 10, 11, 25, 26, 27, 28, 39, 40, 41, 42, 43, 72, 77, 116, **129**, 141, 144, 149, 220, 224, 225, 226, 251, 266,
Dyatype, photo-lettering machine, 32,
Dynamo, 39,

E

Earl of Dunraven, 22, 268,
3rd Earl of Stanhope, Charles Mahon, 17,
The Early Christian Set, typefaces, 92,
Eastman, George, 20, 21,
ITC Eastwood, 264,
Ebony, magazine, 34,
Ecclesiastes (Bible / Shahn), 91,
Ecco, computer store, **128**,
The Echo, magazine, 96,
Eckart, John P., 30,
Eckmann, Otto, 21, 22, 38,
Eckmann Schrift, 22,
Éclair, 39,
Eden, 6, 39, 42, 194, **199**, 267,
Edge, magazine, 238,
Edison, Thomas Alva, 20,
Edison, 40,
Editorial designer, 28, 31, 34,
Edwardian, 41,
ITC Edwardian Script, 5, 41, 42, 55, **61**, 264,
L'eggs Products, Inc., 100,
Egiziano, 72,
HTF Egiziano Filigree, 6, 42, **162**,
Egizio, 31, 40,

Egmont, 39,
Egmont Inline Titling, 39,
Egyptian Expanded, 17,
Egyptian Hieroglyphs, 17,
Egyptian Ornamented, 6, 38, 42, **209**,
Egyptian style typefaces, 9, 17, 38, **70**, **71**, **258**,
Ehmcke, Fritz Helmut, 18, 22, 38,
Ehmcke, 38, 162,
Ehrgott-Milligan, Kelly, 75,
Ehrhardt, 26, 39,
Eichenauer, Gustav, 110,
Eichenauer, 110, **112**,
Eickhoff, Wolfgang, 40,
Eisenman, Alvin, 202, 240,
Einstein, Lewis, editor, 251,
Elan, 41,
Eldorado, 5, 40, 41, 77, 129, **133**, 266,
FB Eldorado, 5, 40, 42, **77**, 133,
Electra (Dwiggins), 5, 39, 42, 129, 130, **132**, 266,
Electra (Winkow), 39,
Electric light, 9, 17, 20,
Electric motor, 9, 18,
Electric signs, 21,
Electronic document technology, 36,
Electronic type generators , 34,
Electrophotographic printer, 35,
Electrotype matrix, 19,
Electrotype plate, 18,
Electrotyping duplicating process, 9, 18, 20,
Element, 39,
Elementare Typographie (Tschichold), 27,
Elements of Lettering (Goudy), 146,
El Greco, 32, 40,
Elizabeth Roman, 39,
Ella, 38,
Elrod, Benjamin S., 190, 267,
Elrod strip material caster, 190, 267,
ElseWare Corporation, Seattle, 92,
El Sol, newspaper, Madrid, 72, 73,
Elysium, 41,
Elzevir family, printers, Amsterdam, 14,
Emerson, Ralph Waldo, 91,
Emerson, 5, 27, 39, 42, **91**, 154,
Émigré, 13, 36, 182,
Émigré, magazine, 36, 182, **183**,
Émigré (The Book): Graphic Design into the Digital Realm (VanderLans / Licko), 182,
Émigré Fonts, digital type foundry, California, 13, 36, 182,
Émigré Fourteen, 184,
Émigré Graphics, 36, 182, 183,
Emory University Library, Atlanta, 44, 47,
Emperor, 13, 36, 182,
Empire, 5, 39, 42, 64, **71**, 75, 183,
FB Empire, 5, 41,42, **75**,
The Encyclopaedia Britannica, 28, 224,
Encyclopaedia of Type Faces (Jaspert, Berry, Johnson), 7, 31,
Encyclopédie, ou Dictionnaire raisonée des sciences (Diderot), 15, 240,
End grain wood, 7, 18, **255**,
Engelmann, Gottfried, 18,
Engelmann, Jean, 18,
English settlement, 14,
English Egyptian, 17,
English Monotype, 23, 24, 25, 26, 27, 29, 37,
English poster format, 20,
English Tuscan, 38,
Engravers Bold, 5, 38, 42, **64**,
Engravers Litho Bold, 260,

Engravers Litho Bold Condensed, 260,
Engravers Old English, 216,
Engravers Roman, 260,
ENIAC (Electronic Numerical Integrator and Calculator), 30,
HTF Enigma, 160,
The Enlightenment, France, 15,
Enschedé, Izaac, 15,
Enschedé en Zonen, type foundry, Haarlem, 15, 104,
Entertainment Weekly, magazine, 72, 73,
Environmental graphics, 21,
Ephemera printing, 20,
Era / Pastel, 38,
Eragny Press, Hammersmith, 141,
Eras, 40,
ITC Eras, 264,
Erbar, Jakob, 38, 39,
Erbar, 38,
Erdt, Hans Rudi, 78,
Eros, magazine, 11, 186,
Erté (pseud. of Romain de Tirtoff), 20,
Esquire, magazine, New York, 29, 31, 54, **55**, 72, 100, **101**,
Essai d'une nouvelle typographie (*Essay on a new typography*) (Luce / Barbou), 16, 163,
Essay on Typography (Gill), 28,
Essays of Montaigne (Montaigne), 222,
Esselte Letraset, London, 36, 264, 265,
Estée Lauder, 92,
Estienne, 26, 266,
Estienne, Henri, 223,
Etchings, 16, 17,
Etching machine, 23,
Ettenberg, Eugene M., 121,
Etruscan No. 2, **202**,
Eucalyptus Press, Mills College, 147,
AMS Euler Text, 41,
European Book Production War Economy Agreement, 30,
European French Antique, 208,
European sans serif trend, 11,
Eurostile, 31, 40,
Eusebius (Jenson), 44,
Eusebius, and *Italic*, 26, 28, 194, 260, 267,
Eusebius de Caesarea, 194, 222, 267,
Eustace Tilly, caricature character, 170, **171**,
Evans, Jean, 226,
Evans & Sutherland Computer Science Corporation, 262,
Eve, *Playgirl* (magazine symbol), **128**,
Evening News, Newark, 149,
Evergreen College, Washington, 92,
Every Art Director Needs His Own Typeface (Hoefler), 160,
Excelsior, 5, 27, 39, 42, 149, **150**, 151, 266,
Excelsior No. 2, 149,
Excoffon, Roger, 30, 34, 40, 265,
Exlibris / Bookplates, **111**, **225**,
Exocet, 41,
Experimental display typography, 16, 29,
Expert, 41,
Exposition Internationale des Arts Décoratifs, Paris, 27,
1900 Exposition Universelle, Paris, 23,
The Express & Star, newspaper, England, 35,
External magnetic computer memory, 35,
Extracts from An Investigation into the Physical Properties of Books as They Are at Present Published (Dwiggins), 25, 129,
Eyncourt Press, Chicago, 295,

F

Faber & Faber, publishers, 30,
Fables (Saroyan), 112,
The Fables of Jean de La Fontaine (La Fontaine), 224,
The Face, magazine, 36,
Fact, magazine, 186,
Fairbank, John Alfred, 23, 25, 28, 32, 39, 268,
Fairbank Italic, 41,
Fairfield, 6, 39, 42, **224**, 266,
Fairplex, 41, 182,
Faithorn Company, printers, Chicago, 220,
Falcon, 129, 266,
Families, magazine, **188**,
Fanfare Press, 252,
Fanti, Sigismondo, 14,
Faraday, Michael, 18,
Farey, David, 120,
Farquhar, Samuel T., 148,
Fat Face Romans, 208,
Fat Faces, 9, 17, 38, 70,
Fattoni, 127,
Fauvist paintings, 25,
Favrile, 100,
Fecquet, Emil, printer, Paris, 224,
Feder-Grotesk, 38,
Federico, Gene, 242,
Feininger, Lyonel, 25,
Bishop Fell, John, 14,
Fella, Ed, 105,
Fell types, 14, 160,
Fenice, 40,
ITC Fenice, 264,
Festival Titling, 40,
HTF Fetish, 160, **161**,
Fidelio, 40,
Fiedler, Hal, 187,
Fifteen Century / Caslon Antique, 203,
Le Figaro, newspaper, Paris, 24,
The Fifty Books of the Year, AIGA exhibition, 26, 121, 129, 252,
Figgins, Vincent, 17, 18, 38, 160,
Figural, 39,
Film exposure, 19, 20,
Film graphics, 31,
Filosofia, 41, 182,
Financial World Annual Reports, 121,
Fine Print, magazine, 84, 164, 226,
Figural type family, 264,
Film, 39,
Film titles, 22,
Fiore, Quentin, 33, 34,
Firenze (Zapf), 40,
ITC Firenze (Carnase), 5, 40, 42, **103**,
Firestone (logotype), 96,
First Principles of Typography (Morison), 28,
First Writers, book collection, (Ransom) 220,
Fisher Body Division, General Motors, 172,
Fitzwilliam Museum, Cambridge, Mass., 222,
Five Lines Pica, in Shade, 38,
Flagg, Montgomery, 25,
Flaminio, Marcantonio, 250,
Flash (Crous-Vidal), 40,
Flash (Shaar), 29, 39, 176, 242,
Flat brush, 8,
Flemish Black, 216,
Fletcher, Allan, 33, 35,

The Fleuron, a journal of typography (Morison), 26, 28, 252,
The Fleuron Society, London, 26,
Fleurons / Printer's Flowers, 15, **143**, 224,
Flex, 39,
Flexible film, 21,
Flexible lithographic metal sheets, 19,
Heinrich Flinsch, type foundry, Frankfurt, Germany, 18, 78, 79,
Flinsch-Privat, 78,
Floppy disc, 35,
Flora, 41,
Florens-Flourished, 5, 41, 42, 92, **93**,
Florentine Cursive, 6, 40, 42, **201**,
The Florentine Set, typefaces 37, 92, 226, 227, **229**, **230**,
Floriated Capitals (Didot *l'aîné*), 17,
Floriated Capitals (Gill), 39,
ITC Florinda, 213,
Fluidum, 40,
Flush left type composition, 11, 25, 28,
Fluxus, movement, 12, 32,
Folio, 40,
Fonds de Gillé, type foundry, 38,
Fontana, 26, 39, 91,
Fontanesi, 40,
Font Bureau, digital type foundry, Boston, 37, 72, 134, 135,
Font libraries, digital typefaces, 37,
Fontographer, software (Altsys), 36, 72, 160, 238,
FontShop International, Berlin, 37, 134,
FontStudio, software, (Letraset), 238, 265,
Forbes, Colin, 33, 34, 35, 265,
Ford, Henry, 25,
Formata, 41,
Forsberg, Karl Erik, 40,
Fort Ticonderosa Library (bookplate), **225**,
Fortune, 40,
Fortune, magazine, 26, 28, 114, **115**,
Forum I, 40,
Forum II, 40,
Forum Title, 5, 11, 24, 38, 42, 141, 142, 144, **145**, 260,
Foster, John, printer, 14,
Foster, Robert, sculptor, 39,
Foudrinier, Henry and Sealy, 17,
Foudrinier paper machine, 17, 18,
Foundry type, 9, 21, 34,
The Fountains of Papal Rome (MacVeagh / Ruzicka), 224,
The Four Gospels (Bible / Gill), 25,
Fournier, Pierre-Simon *l'aîné*, 15, 38,
Fournier, Pierre-Simon *le jeune*, 9, 15, 16,
Fournier, 26, 38, 268,
VGC Fovea, 5, 40, 42, **46**,
Fox, Benjamin, 18, 38,
Fox, Justus, 16,
Fragmente des Pindar (Hölderlin), 154,
Fraktur, typefaces, 16, 30,
Fra Luca Pacioli of Borgo S. Sepolcro (Morison), 28, 222, **223**,
Franciscan, 5, 39, 42, 141, **148**,
Frankfurter Kunstschule, Frankfurt, 26,
Franklin, Benjamin, 15, 16, 17, 66, 240,
Franklin Antique, 40,
Franklin Gothic, 5, 23, 38, 42, 64, 65, **66**, 67, 72,
Franklin Institute, Philadelphia, 180, 192,
Franklin Printing Company, Philadelphia, 252,
Freelance design, 20,

Fregi e Majuscole (Bodoni), 15,
French Antique, 6, 38, 42, **208**, 210,
French Clarendon, 209, 211,
French Clarendon XXX Condensed, 6, 38, 42, **211**,
French Constitution, 17,
French Revolution, 16,
Frenzel, H. K., 27,
Frere-Jones, Tobias, 5, 13, 37, 41, 42, 43, 72, 74, 77, **134**, 160,
Friar, 141, 154,
Friedman, Ken, 32,
Friedlænder, Elizabeth, 39,
Friedlænder, Henri, 25,
Friz, Ernst, 34, 40, 264,
Friz Quadrata, 40, 264,
Froebel, Friedrich, 18,
Frost, Edwin Bryan, astronomer, 197,
Frost, Robert, 91,
Frutiger, Adrian, 12, 25, 26, 31, 33, 34, 35, 36, 40, 41, 238, 269,
Frutiger, 35, 40,
Fry, Edmund, 17,
Edmund Fry, type foundry, London, 16, 38,
Joseph Fry, type foundry, London, 16,
Fry's Baskerville, 17, 38,
Fry's Ornamented, 17, 38,
Fudoni Bold Remix, 41,
Full-color display and output, 37,
Fuller, Richard Buckminster, 34,
Fundición Tipográfica Nacional, Madrid, 21, 25, 34,
Fundición Tipográfica Neufville, Barcelona, 21, 25, 34,
Funk & Wagnalls Standard International Dictionary (Funk & Wagnalls, publishers), 32,
Furlong / Bell Gothic, 152,
FUSE, digital publication, 37, 134, 136,
Futura, 11, 28, 29, 39, 65, 67, 82, 117, 129, 134, 135, 198, 218,
Futura Black, 39,
Futura Bold, 35,
Futura Display, 39,
Futura Inline, 39,
Futurism, movement, 24, 32,

G

Gage, Harry L. 129,
Gaige, Crosby, 252,
Galesville College, Milwaukee, 62,
Galileo and Italic, 84,
Gallia, 6, 39, 42, 214, **215**,
Galliard, 40, 104,
ITC Galliard, 5, 37, 42, 104, **108**, 264,
Gamble, William, 22,
Gando Ronde, 5, 40, 42, **107**,
Ganeau, François, 40,
Gannal, Jean-Nicolas, chemist, 17,
Garage Gothic, 5, 41, 42, 134, **135**,
Garamond, Claude, 8, 12, 14, 34, 62, 160, 180, 217, 233, 238, 268,
Garamond, 5, 23, 24, 26, 34, 38, 39, 48, 64, **99**, 160, 194, 217, 238, 264, 267, 268,
Adobe Garamond, 6, 12, 41,42, 36, 232, **233**, 262,
ITC Garamond Handtooled, 5, 41, 42, **61**, 264,
Garamont, 5, 25, 38, 42, 141, **180**, 268,
Garnett, William, 17,
Garth, Bill, 32,
Gaslight, 9, 17, 20,

Gaudí, 40,
Gaul, Albro T., 31,
Gaunt, Sidway, 27,
Gaya Ciencia, 40,
The Gazette, Newburg, 126,
Gebrauchsgraphik, magazine, Munich, 24, 27, 78, 186,
Geismar, Tom, 35,
Gelatin dry photographic plates (Eastman), 20,
General History of Quadrupeds (Bewick), 16,
General Motors Design Staff, 172,
General Printing Ink Co., New York, 28,
Apple Geneva, 6, 41, 42, 84, 164, **167**,
Genoux, Claude, 16,
Genung, John F., 139,
Georgia, 104,
Georgia Museum of Art, Athens, 44,
Georgian, 26, 266,
German, language, 30,
German Expressionism, movement, 23, 24,
Gerstner, Karl, 32,
La Gerusalemme liberata (Tasso), 16,
Geschke, Charles, 12, 36, 262,
Gesselschafts-und-Wirtschaftsmuseum (Social and Economic Museum), Vienna, 27,
Gestalt School of Psychology, Germany, 24,
Gestalt theory, 24, 26, 29, 30,
HTF Gestalt, 160,
Ghiberti, 6, 37, 41, 42, 226, 227, **230**,
Giampa Textware Corp., Vancouver, British Columbia, 268,
Gibson, Dana, 220,
Gifts and Occupations (Froebel), teaching system, 18,
Gil, Daniel, 34,
Gil, Gerónimo, 16, 38,
Gilgamesh, 41,
Gilgengart, 39,
Gill, Bob, 33,
Gill, Eric, 23, 24, 25, 26, 27, 28, 39, 82, 129, 199, 217, 268,
Gill Sans, 11, 24, 26, 27, 28, 29, 39, 82, 129, 217, 268,
Gill Shadow, 199,
Gills, Michael, 41,
Gillespie, Edwin, 27,
Gillot, Charles, 19,
Gillot, Gary, 265,
Gillotage, 19,
Gimbel Brothers, department store, New York, 144,
Ginn & Company, publishers, 68,
Ginsberg, Ralph, 34, 186,
ITC Giovanni, 6, 41,42, 232, **233**,
Gipkens, Julius, 78,
Gismonda (play), 22,
Giusti, George, 11, 29,
The Glad Hand Press, New York, 31,
Glaser, Milton, 12, 31, 35, 241,
Glasgow Four, 21,
The Glasgow Herald, Scotland, 30,
The Glasgow Style, 21,
The Globe, London, 21, 180, 192,
Rev. Glober, Jesse, 14,
Gloucester, 23,
Glypha, 40,
Glyphic typefaces, **59**, **114**, **136**, **189**, **246**,
Goddard, William, 16,

Goddard, Mary Katherine, printer, Baltimore, 16,
Godeman, later Abbot of Thorney, 245,
Godine, David R., publisher, Boston, 91,
Goebbles, Joseph, 30,
Golden, William, 31, 32, 186,
Golden Cockerel Press, Berkshire, 25,
Golden Cockerel Roman, 39,
Golden Type, 21, 38, 137, 216,
Golding & Company, printing presses, Boston, 99,
Goldsmith, Holly, 264,
Good Housekeeping, magazine, 96,
Goodhue, Bertram Grosvenor, 5, 21, 22, 23, 27, 38, 42, 43, 57, 126, **137**, 192, 214, 251, 263, 266,
Good King Wenceslas (Neale), 148,
ITC Gorilla, 5, 40, 42, **100**,
Göteborg, 5, 6, 37, 41, 42, **95**, 226, **231**,
HTF Gotham, 5, 41, 42, **136**,
Gothic Condensed Outline, 6, 38, 42, **257**,
Gothic Extended, 6, 38, 42, **256**,
Gothic letter / Textur, 6, 146,
Gothic style, 6,
Gothic style revival, 18,
Gothic Tuscan Condensed (Page), **207**,
Gothic Tuscan Condensed (Wells), 6, 38, 42, **257**,
Gothic Tuscan Condensed No.2, 6, 38, 42, **210**,
Gothic Tuscan Italian, 6, 38, 42, **258**,
Gothic Tuscan Pointed, 6, 38, 42, **206**,
Goudy, Frederic William, 5, 10, 11, 23, 24, 25, 26, 27, 29, 30, 38, 39, 40, 42, 43, 64, 91, 116, 119, 129, **141**, 154, 156, 158, 180, 194, 203, 214, 220, 221, 223, 260, 261, 263, 268,
WTC Goudy, 100,
Goudy Antique, 143,
F. W. Goudy Award, 54, 84, 104, 121,
Goudy Bible, 156,
Goudy Black, 146,
Goudy Bold, 214,
Goudy Catalogue, 141,
Goudy Handtooled, 6, 38, 42, 119, **146**,
Goudy Heavy Face, 5, 26, 39, 42, 116, 119, **146**,
Goudy Modern, 91, 141, 260,
Goudy Newstyle, 156, 260,
Goudy Old Style, 5, 38, 42, 141, **145**,
Goudy Oldstyle Italic, 145,
Goudy Open, 141, 260,
Goudy Open Italic, 260,
Goudy Sans Serif Heavy, 5, 27, 39, 42, **147**,
Goudy Sans Serif Light, 5, 27, 39, 42, **147**,
Goudy Sans Serif Light Italic, 5, 27, 39, 42, **147**,
Goudy Stout, 116,
Goudy Text, 5, 39, 42, 141, **146**,
Goudy Thirty, 5, 40, 42, 141, **148**,
La Goul07ue, Moulin Rouge dancer, 21,
Goya, Francisco de, 17,
Grabhorn, Edwin, 148,
Grabhorn Press, San Francisco, 141, 148,
Grady, George, 110,
Martha Graham School, modern dance, New York, 164,
Graham's Magazine, 18,
The Grammar of Color (Cleland), 26, 114, **115**,
Grammar of Ornament (Jones), 19, 114,
Grand's Restaurant, West Philadelphia, 12, 33,
Grandjean, Philippe, 9, 14, 15, 38,

Granjon, Robert, 14, 34, 77, 108, 217, 267,
Granjon, 26, 149, 266,
Graphic Arts Forum, Philadelphia, 156,
Graphic arts industry, 28, 30,
"Graphic Design", term, 129,
Graphic design, 26, 30, 32, 34, 37,
Graphic Design Manual (Hofmann), 33,
Graphic Design USA Award, 92,
Graphic designers, 33, 44, 78, 96, 100, 116,
121, 127, 129, 186, 202, 226, 240,
The Graphic Group, 96,
The Graphic Language of Neville Brody
(Brody), 36,
Graphic Style, from Victorian to
Post-Modern (Heller / Chwast), 37,
Graphics Monthly, magazine, 100,
Graphics Today, magazine, 100,
Graphik, 39,
Graphis, design magazine, Zurich, 30, 31,
100,
Graphis Annuals (Herdeg), 31,
Graphis Bold, 34,
Graphis Posters, annual, (Herdeg), 31,
Grasset, Eugène, 23, 38,
Grasset, 23, 38,
Gray, Nicolette, 29, 32, 36,
Grayda, 6, 39, 42, **221**, 242,
Gray-scale screen fonts, 12, 35,
HTF Grazia Bodoni, , **161**,
Great Books of the Western World (The
Encyclopaedia Britannica), 224,
Great Depression, 28, 78, 91, 110, 114, 129,
220,
The Great Exhibition of the Works of
Industry of All Nations, London, 19,
Great Ideas of Western Man, institutional
campaign (CCA), 31,
Great Western Type Foundry, 263,
Grecian Condensed, 6, 38, 42, **256**,
Greco-Roman style revival, 18,
Greek, language, 17,
Greek inscriptional letters, 246,
Greek Palatino, 41,
Green, Samuel, 14,
Greenaway, Peter, 37,
Greenwald, Art, 172,
Greiman, April, 12, 182,
Grid, 11, 25, 30, 33,
The Grid (Hurlburt), 35,
Griffith, Chauncey H., 5, 10, 11, 14, 22, 26,
27, 28, 29, 36, 39, 42, 43, 57, 70, 91, 116, 119,
129, **149**, 224, 266,
Griffin, Burr, 25,
Griffo, 39,
Grignani, Franco, 31,
Grimshaw, Phill, 41,
ITC Grizzli, 5, 40, 42, **102**,
The Grolier Club, New York, 21, 28, 36, 91,
126, 137, 143, 222, 223, 224, 251,
Gropius, Walter, 18, 25, 28, 29,
Grosz, George, 26,
FB Grotesque, 5, 41, 42, **73**,
Grotesques, typefaces, 72, 73,
Grotesk V, 25, 38,
Groth, John, 242,
ITC Grouch, 5, 40, 42, **102**,
Grover, James, 38,
James and Thomas Grover, type foundry,
London, 14, 38,
Growald, Ernst, 78,
Grunbacher, artist products (logotype), **101**,

De Guerin, Maurice, 25, 222,
Guimard, Hector, 38,
Gürtler, André, 84,
Gürtler, Robert, 33,
Gutenberg, Johannes, 8, 9, 148, 240, 269,
Gutenberg 42-line Bible, 6, 19, 146,
The Gutenberg Galaxy (McLuhan), 33,
Gutenberg Museum, Mainz, 121,

H

Haas, Wilhelm, 15, 16,
Haas'sche Schriftgießerei AG, type
foundry, Basle, 15, 32, 72,
Hadden, Briton, 26,
Hadriano Stone-Cut, 5, 39, 42, 156, **158**,
Hadriano Title, 5, 38, 42, 141, **145**, 158, 260,
Hahl, August, 192,
Hahl, Louis, 192,
Hainline, Wallace F., 31,
Haldeman, Walter N., 192,
Haley, Allan, 117,
A Half-Century of Type Design and
Typography 1895-1945 (Goudy), 30, 141,
142, 143, 203,
Halftone negatives, 21, 32,
Halftone photographs, 22,
Halftone plates, 20,
Halftone printing process, 20,
Halftone reproductions, 21, 22, 28, 32,
Halftone screen, 21,
Half Uncials, 8,
Hall, Henry, 266,
Hallmark Cards, Kansas City, 92, 238,
Hallmark Type Group, Kansas City, 92,
Haloid Company, Rochester, 30,
Hamill, Alfred E., 111,
Hamilton, James Edward, 199,
Hamilton Manufacturing Company, Two
Rivers, Wisconsin, 204,
Hammer, Carolyn, 155, 196,
Hammer, Victor, 5, 39, 40, 41, 42, 91, 110,
141, **154**, 194, 196,
Hammer Press, Aurora, 154,
Hammer Unziale, 5, 39, 42, **154**,
Handbills, 17,
Handcraft Shop, printing shop, Snohomish,
Washington, 220,
Hand composition, 34,
Handtooled alphabets, 15, 61, 119, 214,
A Handwriting Manual (Fairbank), 28,
Hangul, 104,
H. C. Hansen Type Foundry, 263,
Hanson, C. H., 260,
Hanson, Ellis, 32,
Hard Werken, magazine, 182,
Harlem, 41,
Harling, Robert, 29, 30, 39,
Harlow, 40,
Harpel, Oscar H., 20,
Harper's Bazaar, magazine, New York, 20,
28, 96, **97**, 160, 163,
Harper's Magazine, 18,
Harper's Monthly Magazine, 19,
Harper's New Monthly Magazine, 96,
Harper's Weekly, magazine, 19, 96,
Harris, Benjamin, 14,
Harris-Intertype Fotosetter, 30,
Francis Hart & Co., printers, New York, 126,
Hart, Francis, 126,
Leo Hart, publisher, 220,

Hartmann, Georg, 18,
Hartz Sem, L., 266,
Hartzell Machine Works, Chester,
Pennsylvania, 268,
Harvard Business Review, magazine, 224,
240,
Harvard College, Cambridge, Mass., 14,
Harvard University, Cambridge, Mass.,
Mass.,84, 164, 251,
Harvard University Business School,
Cambridge, Mass, 251,
Harvard University Graduate School of
Design, Cambridge, Mass., 29,
Harvard University Press, Cambridge,
Mass. 20, 96, 129, 222,
Harvey, Michael, 226,
Hatch, Lewis, 114,
Hauser, George, 39,
Hauser Script, 39,
Hazenplug, Frank, 22,
Headliners, Inc., Chicago, 178,
Headliners International, Detroit, 172,
Headliners Process Lettering, New York, 33,
Hearst, William Randolph, 20, 96,
Heckel, Erich, 23,
Hefner, Hugh, 31,
Heidelberg Company, Germany, 37, 266,
Hein, Piet, 31,
Heinz, Henry J., 21,
Heinrichsen, Friedrich, 110,
Held, John, 170,
Hell, Dr. Ing. Rudolf, 33,
Hell Digiset, photosetting machine, 33, 35,
Hell Digiset GmbH, Kiel, 33, 84, 164, 165,
266,
Heller, Steven, 37,
Helvetica / Neue Haas Grotesk, 15, 22, 23,
24, 25, 31, 32, 33, 36, 40,
Helvetica Compresed, 104,
Helvetica Greek, 104,
Helvetica Narrow, 36,
Henry, Joseph, 18,
Herbert, Lawrence, 33,
Herdeg, Walter, editor, Zurich, 30, 31,
Herron School of Art, Indiana, 100,
Hershfield, Harry, 116,
Hess, Flora, 252,
Hess, Sol, 5, 11, 17, 23, 25, 26, 30, 38, 39,
42, 43, 65, 66, 69, 126, 141, 153, **156**,218,
219, 242, 252, 268,
Hess Neobold, 5, 39, 42, 156, **158**,
Hess Oldstyle No. 242, 156,
Hess Title, 156,
Hewit, William Graily, 23,
Hewlett Packard, 49, 72, 92,
Hieroglyphs, 17,
Hiero Rhode, 40,
Higgins, Dick, 32,
ITC Highlander, 264,
Higonnet, René, 30, 32,
Higonnet-Moyroud, phototypesetting
system, 31, 32,
Hill & Knowlton, publishers, New York, 176,
Hippie movement, 34,
Historic Calligraphic Alphabets (Baker), 49,
Historic Printing Types (De Vinne), 17, 21, 126,
A History of Graphic Design (Meggs), 36,
A History of Lettering: Creative Experiment
and Letter Identity (Gray), 36,
The History of Printing in America (Thomas),
17,

History of Typefounding in the United States
(Bruce, Jr.), 19,
Hitchcock, Alfred, 31,
Hitler, Adolph, 30,
Hobo, 5, 38, 42, 60, 64, **67**,
Hoe, Richard M., 19,
Hoe, Robert, 21, 137,
Hof, K. K., und Staatsdruckerei, Viena, 154,
Hoefer, Karlgeorg, 40, 41,
Hoefler, Jonathan, 6, 13, 41, 42, 43, **160**,
HTF Hoefler Text, 6, 41, 42, 160,
Hoefler Type Foundry, digital type, New
York, 160, 161, 163,
Hoell, Louis, 91,
Hoffman, George, 91,
Hoffmann, Alfred, 15,
Hoffmann, Eduard, 15, 25, 32,
Hoffmann, Eduard and Alfred, 15,
Hoffmann, Josef, 22, 23,
Hoffmann, H., 78,
Hofmann, Armin, 30, 33,
Höhnisch, Walter, 39,
Holbein, Hans, 112, 138, 145,
Hölderlin, Friedrich, 154, 155,
Holland, Holis, 111,
Hollerbaum & Schmidt, printing company,
Berlin, 78, 79, 80,
Holleridge Tabulator, 268,
Hollestein, Albert, 40,
Holman, William, 19,
Holme, Frank, 220,
Frank Holme School of Illustration,
Chicago, 116, 129, 220,
Holmes, Kris, 6, 12, 35, 36, 41, 42, 43, 85,
86, 87, 88, 89, 90, **164**, 244, 262,
Holwein, Ludwig, 117,
The Holy Bible (King James version), 14,
The Holy Bible, with illustrations by Gustave
Doré, 20,
Homage to the Book (Thompson), 240,
Homage to the Square (Albers), 31,
Homer, 222,
Hommel micrometers (symbol), **80**,
ITC Honda, 5, 40, 42, **102**,
Hooper, John. L., 18,
Hooper, C. Lauron, 141, 203,
Hopkins Art Institute, San Francisco, 170,
Hopkinson, Helen E., 170,
Horace, 16,
Horfei of Fano, Luca, 227,
Horgan, Stephen H., 20, 22,
Horman, Harold A., 28, 269,
Hornbook, magazine, 110,
Horne, Herbert P., 96, 251,
Hornung, Clarence P., 35, 215,
Hotel Claridge, New York, 114,
Hot-metal type composition, 21, 24, 32, 34,
Hot-metal line casting machines, 21, 28, 34,
Houghton, Henry, 21,
Houghton, Mifflin & Co., Boston, 21, 22,
137, 222, 251,
House & Garden, magazine, New York, 28,
160,
HOW, magazine, 100, 164, 226,
Howard Lang Fund (bookplate) (Boston
Athenaeum Library), **225**,
Hubbard, Elbert, printer, East Aurora, 23,
214,
Hubbard, William, 14,
Huebsch, Ben, 91,
Huges Laboratory, Malibu, California, 32,

Hughes, Charles E., 126,
Huggins, Cleo, 12, 36, 84,
The Humanist Library (Einstein / Updike), 114, 251,
Humanist sans serif typefaces, **48**, **60**, **197**, **229**,
Hunt Roman, 40,
Hunziker, Hans-Jung, 107,
Hupp, Otto, 21,
Hurlburt, Allen, 35,
Huston, John, 187,
Huxley, Walter, 6, 39, 42, 158, **169**,
Huxley House, New York, 169,
Huxley Vertical, 6, 39, 42, 158, **169**,
Hyperion, 39,
Hyper media visual information, 37,

I

Ibarra, Joaquín, court printer, Madrid, 16,
Ibérica, 39,
IBM (International Business Machinery), 11, 12, 32, 33, 36, 49,
IBM computers, 262, 263,
IBM Personal computer (PC), 36,
IBM Printer Planing Division, 104,
IBM-72 *Selectric*, typewriter, 11, 12, 33,
ICOGRADA (International Council of Graphic Design Associations), 33,
Icone, 41,
Iconoscope, 29,
Iconographic Encyclopédie, 240,
Idea, magazine, Japan, 100, 186,
Igarashi, Takenobu, 36,
Ihlenburg, Herman, 159,
Ikarus, digital type-design program, 12, 35, 134,
Ilerda, 40,
Illinois Type Foundry, 263,
Illumination, 23,
Illuminators, 14, 33,
Illustration, 20, 22, 25, 28,
L'Illustration, Paris, 20,
The Illustrated News, newspaper, New York, 23,
I ♥ NY (Glaser), logo, 35,
Imaging Sciences Laboratory, Palo Alto, 262,
Imago, 40,
De Imitatione Christi (Kempis), 14,
Immigration of people, 11, 29,
Impressionist paintings, 25,
Imprimerie Chaix, lithographers, Paris, 97,
Imprimerie Nationale, Paris, 14,
Imprimerie Royal du Louvre, 14, 15, 16,
Imprint, 24, 38, 180, 217, 268,
The Imprint, type journal, 24, 217, 268,
Incandescent light bulb, 20,
Index characterum (Rooses), 217,
Indiana, Robert, 34, 241,
Industria, 41,
Industria Inline, 41,
Industrial Revolution, 9, 15, 17, 18, 19,
Information graphics, 29,
Iniciales Bernhard, 5, 42, **79**,
Initials, **130**, **133**, **138**, **139**, **142**, **145**, **146**, **223**,
Initials (Dwiggins), 5, 39, 42, **133**,
Ink rollers, 17,
The Inland Printer, magazine, 22, 27, 96, 99, **142**, **143**, 203,

Inland Printer Company, Chicago / New York, 142, 143,
Inland Type Foundry, St. Louis, 22, 70, 263,
Insignia, 41,
Instant photography, 20,
Institute für Galvano-Typie, Berlin, 19,
Institute of Design (the New Bauhaus), Chicago, 30, 194,
Intaglio printing / etching, 17,
Intaglio printing / photogravure, 20,
Interabang, **172**,
Interaction of Color (Albers), 33,
Interactive publications, 37,
International Calligraphy Today, magazine, 164,
International Center for the Typographic Arts (ICTA), New York, 32, 33,
1854 International Exhibition, London, 19,
International Printing Ink Company, 224,
International Typeface Competition (Letraset), 35,
ITC (International Typeface Corporation), New York, 6, 12, 34, 35, 36, 37, 54, **55**, 100, 164, 186, 232, 238, 239, **264**, 265, 269,
ITC 1500, type library, 262,
ITC Typographica Series, 164,
International Typographic Composition Association, 156,
International Typographic Style, 12, 25, 28, 30, 31, 33,
Internet, 37,
Interstate, 5, 41, 42, **135**,
Intertype, hot metal type composing machine, 24, 39, 56, 81, 238,
The Invention of Printing (De Vinne), 126,
Invitation Text, 260,
Ionesco, Eugene, 33, 34,
Ionic (Page), 6, 38, 42, **206**,
Ionic No. 5 (Griffith), 5, 11, 27, 28, 39, 42, **149**, 150, 266,
Ionic style, typefaces, 9, 149,
Iron presses, 9,
Irvin, Dorothy, 170,
Irvin, Rea, 6, 27, 39, 42, **170**,
Irvin, 6, 27, 39, 42, **170**,
Isadora, 6, 41, 42, **164**, 165, 262,
Isbell, Richard, 6, 40, 41, 42, **172**,
ITC Isbell, 6, 41, 42, 172, **174**,
I Seem to Be a Verb (McLuhan / Fiore), 34,
Ishi, Bob, 239,
Isotype (*International System of Typographic Picture Education*), 27,
Italia, 40, **265**,
Italian Old Style, 25, 39, 141, 268,
Itten, Johannes, 25,
Ives, Frederic, 21,
Ives, Norman, 240,

J

President Jackson, Andrew, 18,
Jackson, Joseph, 15,
Jackson Foundation, Oregon, 164,
Jacno, Marcel, 39, 40,
Jacno, 40,
Jacobson, Egbert, 29,
Jaggard, Isaac, 14,
Jaguar, 40,
King James I, 14,
The King James Bible, 14,
Jana, 202,
Jannon, Jean, 14, 38,

Janson, Anton, 14, 151,
Janson, 38, 160,
Janson (Griffith), 5, 14, 39, 43, 91, 149, **151**,
Janson Antiqua, 14, 251,
Japanese Art, 19,
Japanese woodcuts, 19,
Jaque Slim, 41,
Jaspert, W. Pincus, 31,
Jaugeon, Nicolas, mathematician, 9,
The Jealous Ghost (Strong), **130**,
Jeanette, 40,
Jeffers, Robinson, 91,
ITC Jellybaby, 264,
Jenson, Nicolas, 25, 44, 47, 62, 67, 134, 137, 194, 222, 251, 267,
Adobe Jenson, 41, 232,
Jenson Oldstyle (Phinney), 6, 21, 38, 43, **216**,
Jenson Roman, 44, 48, 203,
Jet, magazine, 34,
Joanna, 28, 39,
Job printing, 254,
Job printing typefaces, 263,
Jobs, Steve, 12, 35, 36,
Johnson, Alfred Forbes, 28,
Johnson, Fridolf, 31, 35,
Johnson, Henry, 16,
Johnson, John H., editor, 34,
Johnson, L., type foundry, Philadelphia, 204, 256,
Johnston, Edward, 23, 24, 25, 28, 38, 129, 143, 194, 217, 268,
Jones, David, 25,
Jones, George W., printer, 26, 266,
Jones, Owen, 19, 96,
Jones Robert M., 31, 202,
Jones, Thomas Roy, 263,
Jost, Heinrich, 18, 28, 39,
Journal, 41, 182,
Journal of Communication Arts, 122,
Journal of Typographic Research (Cleveland Museum of Art), Ohio, 34,
Journalistic photography, 31,
ITC Juanita, 41, 213, 264,
Jubilee, 30,
Judith Type, 39,
Juenger, Richard D., 202,
Junge, Carl S., 25,
Juniper, **209**, **259**,
Jugend, magazine, Munich, 22,
Jugenstil, movement, 22,
Justowriter, type composer, 30,

K

Kabel, 11, 24, 27, 28, 39, 65, 67, 82, 117, 134, 135, 197,
Kabel Swash Initials, 39,
ITC Kabel, 264,
Kahn, Emil (pseud. of Lucian Bernhard), 78,
ITC Kallos, 41,
Kamekura, Yusaku, 33,
Kandinsky, Wassily, 18, 24, 25, 26,
Karmitri Cigaretten (trademark), **80**,
Karnak, 6, 28, 39, 43, 194, **198**, 267,
Karnak Light, **198**,
Karow, Peter, 12, 35,
Kate Moss Four, 134, 135,
Kate Moss Ten, 134, 135,
Katsumie, Masaru, 33,
Kaufmann, Max Richard, 6, 39, 42, 43, **176**, 242,

Kaufmann Bold, 6, 39, 43, **177**,
Kaufmann Script, 6, 39, 43, **176**177, 242,
Keedy, Jeffery, 36, 182,
Keimer, Samuel, 15,
Keller, Ernst, 25,
Kellog, Spencer, publisher, 148,
Kelly, Jerry, 36,
Kelly, Rob Roy, 34, 199, 206, 208,
Kelmscott Press, Hammersmith, 18, 20, 21, 22, 114, 141, 222, 251,
Kempis, Thomas à, 14,
Kennerley, Mitchell, 24, 25, 142, 144, 145,
Kennerley Old Style, 5, 11, 24, 25, 38, 43, 141, 142, **144**, 145, 156, 162, 260,
Kennerley Oldstyle Italic, 260,
Kennerley Open Caps, 5, 39, 43, **156**,
Kent, Henry Watson, 222,
Kent, Rockwell, 27, 78, 80, 220,
Kepes, Gyorgy, 11, 29, 32,
Kepler, 41, 232,
Kerning, letter spacing software, 35,
Keufel & Essen, precision tools (logotype), **80**,
Keyboard, 20,
Keystone Type Foundry, Philadelphia, 263,
Kigali, 5, 41, 43, **53**,
Kimball, Ingalls, 22, 23, 137, 140,
King Black Associates, 268,
Kingman, John A., 114,
Kingsley ATF, 263,
Kirchner, Ernst Ludwig, 23,
Kis, Miklós (Nicholas), 14, 38, 151, 160,
Kisman, Max, 37, 41,
Kittredge, William A., 27, 252,
Klang, 40,
Klaxon, 260,
Klee, Paul, 24, 25, 32,
Kleukens, Friedrich Wilhelm, 18, 22, 39,
Klietsch, Karl, 20,
Klimt, Gustave, 22,
Klinger, Julius, 78,
Klingspor, Karl, 21,
Klingspor, type foundry, Offenbach, 21, 24, 110, 154,
Klingspor Museum, Offenbach, 164,
Klingspor Press, Inc., Tennessee, 112,
Klumpp, Emil J., 6, 40, 43, **178**,
Knight Errand, magazine, 137,
Alfred A. Knopf, publisher, New York, 25, 27, 110, 111, 112, 129, 130, 131, 225,
Knuth, Donald, 12, 35, 84, 244,
Koch, Paul, 39, 110, 154,
Koch, Rudolf, 21, 22, 23, 26, 27, 28, 38, 39, 82, 91, 110, 117, 135, 154, 197,
Koch Antiqua, 24, 38,
Kodak camera, 21,
Kodak Company, Rochester, New York, 28, 11, 34,
Kodalith, 11, 28,
Koenig, Friedrich, 17,
Koenig, Heinz, 21,
Koffka, Kurt, 11, 24, 26, 29,
Köhler, Wolfgang, 24, 26,
Kokoschka, Oscar, 24,
Kolo, 6, 37, 41, 43, 58, 92, 226, **227**, **229**,
Kompakt, 40,
Kordet Group, 228,
Korina (H. Berthold AG), 38,
ITC Korinna (Benguiat), 5, 40, 43, **56**, 264,
Kramer, Friso, 33,
Kramer & Fuchs, type foundry, Barcelona, 21,

Krantz, Judith, 101,
Kredel, Fritz, 26, 110, 154,
Krijger, Henk, 40,
Kroll, J., 221,
Kruger, Barbara, 35,
Kruty, Peter, 227,
Kubrick, Stanley, 31,
Die Kunst der Typographie (*The Art of Typography*) (Renner), 29,
Kunstgewerbeschule (School of Applied Arts), Zurich, 23, 25, 28, 33,
Kunstgewerbemuseum, Basle, 33,
Kuppenheimer & Co., clothing store, 144,
Kurtz, W., printer, New York, 21,
Kutter, Markus, 32,

L

Lacerba, journal, Florence, 24,
Laclede Oldstyle / Munder Venezian, 42, 260, **261**,
Laclede Type Foundry, St. Louis, 260, 261,
Ladies' Home Journal, magazine, 96,
Lady of Shalott (Tennyson), 220,
Lafayette Extra Condensed, 6, 39, 43, **199**,
Lagrange, Joseph Louis, Comte, 16,
Lakeside Press, Chicago, 224,
Lamar Dodd School of Art, Athens, 44,
Lambert, Fred, 33, 40, 265,
Lamberton Becker, May, 252,
Lamp-black, 15,
Lane, Allen, publisher, London, 29, 30,
Lane, John, 22,
The Last Will and Testament of Late Nicolas Jenson (Jenson), 194,
Howard W. Lang Fund (bookplate), Athenaeum Library, Boston, **225**,
Lange, Günter Gerhard, 19, 32, 40, 41, 154,
Language of Vision (Kepes), 30,
Lanston, Nicholas Randall, 180,
Lanston, Tolbert, 6, 10, 21, 22, **180**, 190, 263, 266, 267, 268,
Lanston Monotype Composing Machine, 10, 23, 24, 27, 28, 34, 65, 91, **181**, 190, 194, 237, 263,
Lanston Monotype Corporation Ltd., London, 6, 22, 23, 24, 25, 26, 27, 29, 31, 32, 35, 37, 38, 39, 92, 141, 144, 160, 176, 180, 217, 222, 242, 253, 264, 266, **268**,
Lanston Monotype Machine Company, Philadelphia, 6, 10, 11, 20, 23, 25, 26, 27, 30, 57, 67, 141, 146, 147, 148, 153, 156, 157, 158, 159, 170, 180, 194, 217, 222, 252, **268**,
Laplace, Pierre Simon, marquis de, 16,
Lardent, Victor, 28, 39,
Larousse, Pierre, 24,
Laser beam, 32,
Lasercomp, Monotype phototypesetter, 35, 268,
Lasercomp Express, phototypesetter, 36,
Laser phototypesetter, 35,
LaserWriter, printer (Apple), 36, 48,
The Last of the Mohicans (Cooper), 220,
Lathan, Roy, lithographer, New York, 78,
Lathem, Edward C., 224,
Latin, language, 14,
Latin, **211**,
Latin serif typefaces, **162**, **184**, **211**, **212**,
Lavoisier, Antoine Laurent, 16,
Laws, George, 36,
Layout, 12,

Layout: The Design of the Printed Page (Hurlburt), 35,
Layout in Advertising (Dwiggins), 28, 129,
Leavenworth, William, 9, 18, 254,
Leaves of Grass (Whitman), 225,
ITC Leawood, 41,
Le Corbusier, 18,
Lectura, 40,
The Leeds Mercury, England, 21, 192,
Leete, Alfred, 25,
LEF, Soviet art group, 32,
ITC Legacy, 5, 41, 43, 44, **47**, 48,
Legacy of Letters, 92,
Legacy of Letters Tour, 92,
ITC Legacy Sans, 5, 41, 43, **48**,
Legend, 39,
Legibility, 22, 27, 32, 37,
Legibility Group, 11, 22, 26, 27, 149, 153, 266,
Legras, Al., 203,
Leica, photographic camera, 27,
Lenk, Krzysztof, 134,
Lenox, James, 19,
ITC Lenox, 41,
Lenz, Eugene and Max, 40,
Leonardo, Berto di, 227,
Frank Leslie's Illustrated Newspaper, 19, 96,
Leslie, Robert L., 114,
1983 Letragraphica Premier (Letraset), England, 265,
Letragraphica, type design program (Letraset), 34, 36, 265,
Letraset, dry transfer type, 12, 32, 40, 41, 238, 265,
Letraset exhibition, London Design Museum, 37,
1973 Letraset's International Typeface Competition, London, 265,
Letraset Limited, London, 6, 33, 34, 35, 36, 37, 40, 41, **265**,
LetraStudio, software, 265,
Letter and Image (Massin), 34,
Letter Arts Review, magazine, 226,
Letter cutting, 24, 27,
Letter Exchange, London, 226,
Letterforms (Shaw), 226,
Lettering, 19, 20, 22, 79, **80**, **97**, **115**, **117**, **118**, **130**, **131**, **142**, **143**, **171**, **173**, **179**, **223**, **225**, **227**,
Lettering, Inc., New York, 178,
Lettering for compositors (Tschichold), 27,
Lettering on Buildings (Gray), 32,
LetterPerfect, digital type foundry, Seattle, 37, 92, 226,
Letterpress printing, 21, 23,
Leter spacing, 33, 35, 103,
Lettre de forme, 8,
La lettre d'imprimerie (Thibaudeau), 26,
Lettres Ornées, 38,
Leu, Olaf, 121,
Levi, Lazzaro and Giuseppe, 20,
Leviathan, 84, 164,
HTF Leviathan, 6, 43, **162**,
Levrant de Breteville, Sheila, 44,
Levy, Max and Louis, 21,
Levy, Louis, 23,
Levy's Bread, 31,
Lewis, Allen, 110,
Lewis, Walter, 27,
Lexington, 6, 39, 43, **215**,
Lexitron, electronic products, 35,

Lexmark, electronic solutions, 49,
Leyendecker, Frank and Joseph, 129,
Lhote, André, 221,
Liberty, magazine, 110,
Libra, 39, 154,
Lichtenstein, Roy, 32,
Licko, Zuzana, 6, 13, 36, 41, 43, 105, **182**,
Life, magazine, 26, 144,
The Life of Michelangelo Buonarroti (Condivi), 251,
Life with letters after they turned photogenic (Rondthaler), 269,
Lifetime Achievement Award (AIGA), 91,
Ligature, magazine, New York, 100, **101**,
Lightline, 33, 40, 265,
Lilith, 5, 39, 43, 78, **82**,
The Limited Editions Club, New York, 28, 91, 129, 147, 220, 223, 224, 251,
Linasec (Compugraphic Corp.), 12, 33,
Lincoln, Abraham, 19, 254,
Lindgren, Erik, 95, 231,
Lindgren, Herbert, 95, 231,
Line reproduction process, 20,
Linofilm, Linotype's phototypesetting machine, 32, 106, 266,
Linolex, electronic products, 35,
Linotron, Linotype's photocomposing machine, 266,
Linotron 505, Linotype's photocomposing machine, 266,
Linotron 1010, Linotype's photocomposing machine, 34,
Linotronic 300, Linotype's laser photosetter machine, 266,
Linotype, hot metal type composing machine, 10, 21, 27, 28, 29, 34, 110, 129, 137, 140, 190, 191, 192, **193**, 194, 217, 263, 266, 267, 268, 269,
Linotype Centennial, 41,
Linotype Company Ltd., Manchester, England, 21,
Linotype Duplex-Display matrices, 24, **193**,
Linotype England, 30,
Linotype Group of Companies, 12, 35,
Linotype-Hell AG, 36, 37, 266,
Linotype Laser Fonts, 266,
Linotype matrices, 22,
Linotype Modern, 30,
Linotype News, Brooklyn, 150,
Linotype's *Square Base Model I*, composing machine, 192,
Linotype & Machinery Co., London, 26,
Lionni, Leo, 11, 29, 31,
Lisa, software (Apple), 36,
Lissitzky, El (Eleazar), 25, 27, 34,
Litho Antique, 70,
Lithographic illustrations, 16, 17, 18,
Lithographic metal plates, 17, 23,
Lithographic flexible metal sheets, 19,
Lithographic posters, 19, 20, 21,
Lithographic press, 16, 17, 19,
Lithographic stones, 16, 19,
Lithography, printing process, 9, 16, 17, 18, 19,
Lithos, 6, 37, 41, 43, 244, **246**,
J. J. Little & Ives Co, publishers, New York, 220,
Little Giant brass rule and lead cutter, 99,
The Living Alphabet (Chappell), 110, **112**, 113,
Locomotive Company of America, New York, 114,
Ludwig Loewe Company, Berlin, 217,

Loewy, Raymond, 30,
Logotype, metal character, 16,
Logotypes, 45, **55**, 78, **101**, **128**, **171**, **183**, **187**, **188**, **241**,
Lohse, Richard, 32,
Lois, George, 32,
Lombardic Capitals, 5, 39, 43, **146**,
London and North Eastern Railway (LNER), 28,
London Design Museum, 37, 265,
The London Gazette, 14,
London plague, 14,
London sign system, 29,
London Underground Transport, 24, 28,
London Underground Transport, map (Beck), 28,
London Underground Sanserif, 24, 28, 38, 129,
Long, George, 254,
George Long "Book Store", 254,
Longhand, 5, 41, 43, **95**,
Look, magazine, 35,
L'Oreal, cosmetics, 100,
Lorenz, Lee, 170, 171,
Lorilleux, Pierre, 17,
L. A. Style Magazine, 92,
Los Angeles Times, 44, 46,
L.A. Times Regular and *Italic*, 44,
L.A. Times Bold and *Italic*, 44,
Lo-Type, 41,
Louis Dreyfus Corporation, 127,
King Louis XIII, 14,
King Louis XIV, 9, 14,
Louisville School of Design, 203,
Loupot, Charles, 30,
Louvre Museum, Paris, 145,
Love and Joy About Letters (Shahn), 33,
Low, Markus J., 202,
Lowercase letters, 8, 20,
Low resolution video displays, 12, 13,
Lubalin, Herb, 6, 11, 12, 33, 34, 40, 42, 43, 54, 100, 103, 127, **186**, 202, 264, 265, 269,
Herb Lubalin, Inc., New York, 186,
Herb Lubalin Associates, Inc., New York, 127,
Lubalin, Burns, & Co., Inc., 186, 264,
ITC Lubalin Graph, 5, 6, 40, 43, 127, 186, **189**,
Lubalin, Smith, Carnase, Inc., New York, 100, 127, 187,
Herb Lubalin Study Center of Design, New York, 36,
Luce, Henry R., 26, 28, 114, 115,
Luce, Louis René, 15, 16,
Luce Bosch, batteries, **80**,
Lucian, 5, 28, 39, 43, 76, **81**,
Lucida, 5, 6, 12, 35, 36, 41, 43, **84**, 86, 88, 164, **165**, 168,
Lucida, series, 35,
Lucida Blackletter, 5, 41, 43, 84, **88**,
Lucida Bright, 5, 6, 41, 43, 84, **87**, 164, **167**,
Lucida Calligraphy, 5, 41, 43, **88**,
Lucida Casual, 5, 41, 43, **90**,
Lucida Console, 6, 41, 43, **168**,
Lucida Fax, 5, 41, 43, 84, **89**,
Lucida Handwriting, 5, 6, 41, 43, 84, **88**, 90, **168**,
Lucida Sans, 5, 6, 36, 41, 43, **85**, **166**,
Lucida Sans Italic, **166**, 167,
Lucida Sans Typewriter, 5, 41, 43, 84, 86, 89, 90,
Lucida Sans Typewriter Oblique, 5, 41, 43, 84, **89**, 90,

Lucida Typewriter, 5, 41, 43, **90**,
Ludlow, Washington I., 6, 24, **190**, 267,
Ludlow, hot metal typecasting machine, 24, 28, **191**, 266,
Ludlow Black, 26,
Ludlow composing sticks, **191**,
Ludlow matrices, **191**,
Ludlow ruleform matrices, 190,
Ludlow sloping matrices, 25, **191**,
Ludlow slog-aligning matrices, 190,
Ludlow Typograph Company, Chicago, 6, 10, 11, 24, 25, 26, 28, 190, 191, 194, 196, 197, 199, 260, **267**,
Lumière Louis and Auguste, 22,
Lumitype, photocomposing machine, 32,
Lunatix, 6, 41, 43, **184**,
Lustig, Alvin, 31,
Lutetia, 27, 39, 251,
Lux, 39,
Lydian, 5, 39, 43, **110**, 113,
Lydian Bold , 5, 39, 43, **113**,
Lydian Bold Condensed and italic, 113,
Lydian Cursive, 5, 39, 43, **113**,
Lyendecker, J. C., 25,

M

MacArthur Foundation Fellowships, 84,
MacDraw, software (Macintosh), 12, 38,
MacGraw-Hill, publishers, New York, 34,
MacKellar, Thomas, 20,
MacKellar, Smiths & Jordan, type foundry, Philadelphia, 20, 56, 263,
Mackenzie-Harris Corporation, type founders, San Francisco, 268,
Mackintosh, Charles Rennie, 21,
MacMillan Company, publishers, 252,
MacMurdo, Arthur Heygate, 20,
MacPaint, software (Macintosh) 12, 36,
MacVeagh, Mrs. Charles, 224,
Mac World, magazine, 164,
MacWrite, software (Macintosh) 12, 36,
ITC Machine, 5, 12, 40, 43, **103**, 186,
Macintosh, computers, 72, 92, 182, 262, 263,
Maciunas, George, 32,
Macy, George, 28, 91,
Maddox, Richard Leach, 20,
Mademoiselle, magazine, 240,
Magazine, Linotype matrices, 10,
Magazine covers, 32, 35, **45**, **123**, **142**, **143**, **183**, **187**, **188**,
Magazine designers, 31,
Magritte, René, 26,
Mahon, Charles, third Earl of Stanhope, 17,
Maiman, Theodore H., 32,
Les Maîtres de L'Affiche, lithographic editions, Paris, 97,
Her Majesty's Stationery Office, London, 104,
Makela, Laurie Haycock, 13, 104, 109,
Making Printer's Typefaces (Middleton), 194, 195,
Maldonado, Tomás, 31,
Malevich, Kasimir, 25,
Malin, Charles, 104, 252,
Mallarmé, Stéphane, 22,
Mall Press, London, 222,
Mammoth rotary letterpress, 19,
The Man with the Golden Arm (film, Preminger), 31,
Mandate, 6, 39, 43, **200**, 267,

Manifesto futurista (Manifeste du Futurism) (Marinetti), 24,
Manito, 5, 41, 43, 92, **93**,
Manoli, cigarettes, Berlin, **79**, 80,
Mantegna, Andrea, 108,
Mantinia, 5, 41, 43, 104, 105, **108**,
Manuale Tipografico (Bodoni), 14, 16, 17, 118,
Manuale tipographicum (Zapf), 31,
Manuel Typographique (Fournier), 15,
Manutius, Aldus, printer, Venice, 67,
Mape's Magazine, 18,
Marathon, 39,
Marbrook, 41,
Marc, Franz, 24,
Marchand, J, 221,
Marchbanks Press, 91,
Marconi, 40,
Marder, Clarence, 141, 144,
Marden, Luse & Company, type foundry, Chicago, 20, 144, 263,
Mardersteig, Hans (Giovanni), 26, 39, 40, 91, 104, 252,
Marigold, 5, 41,43, **53**,
Marinetti, Filippo Tommaso, 24,
Marinoni, Hyppolyte, 20,
Market Gothic / Bell Gothic, 152,
Marlborough, 260,
Marsh, Reginald, 91,
Martin, Robert, 16,
Martin, William, 16, 132,
Maryland, 40,
Marylhurst College, Portland, 92,
Mason, John Henry, 24, 217, 268,
Massachusetts Bay Colony, 14,
Massachusetts Institute of Technology (MIT), 12, 32, 35, 224,
Massey, John, 33,
Massin, Robert, 12, 33, 34,
Match Book Industry, 121,
Matheis, Helmut, 40,
Mathews, Elkin, 22,
Matrix, type mold, 9, 10, 21, 29, 191, 193,
Matrix, 6, 41, 43, 182, **184**,
Matrix Script, 41, 182,
Matrotype, company, England, 11, 68, 269,
Maunchly, John W., 30,
Max, Peter, 33,
Maximilian-Antiqua, 38,
Maximilian-Gotisch, 38,
May 1968, student-workers uprising events, Paris, 34,
Mayer, Erich, 39,
Mayfair, 267,
The Mayflower, English ship, 14,
Mazarine, 203,
Mazarine Italic, 203,
McCall's, magazine, 176,
McArthur, Richard N., 25, 69, 116,
McCarthy, Willard, 92,
McClure's Magazine, 114,
McClurg, A.C., book department, Chicago, 141,
McCoy, Katherine, 36,
McGrew, Mac, 5, 36, 83, 259,
McKenzie, Fred, 32, 265,
McLean, Ruari, 32, 34,
McLuhan, Herbert Marshall, 12, 33, 34,
McMurthrie, Douglas, 267,
Mechanical casters, 9, 18,
Mechanical lithography, 9, 19,

Mechanical presses, 17,
Mechanical type composition, 18, 24, 27,
Medailles sur le principaux Evénéments du Règne de Louis-le-Grand (Imprimerie Royale), 14, 15,
Linofilm Medici Script, 40,
Medieval, 141,
Medieval manuscripts, 8, 21,
The Medium is the Massage (McLuhan / Fiore), 12, 33, 34,
Meggs, Philip B., 36, 115,
Meier, Hans Edward, 40, 41, 84, 164,
Meier-Graefe, Julius, 22,
Meisenbach, Georg, 20,
1881 Melbourne Exposition, 204,
Melior, 31, 40,
Melville, Herman, 164,
Memphis, 26, 28, 39, 153, 198,
Memphis Bold, 153,
Memphis Extrabold, 5, 28, 39, 43, **153**,
Memphis Light, 153,
Memphis Medium, 153,
Mendelsohn, Erich, 78, 80,
Mendoza, 40,
Mendoza, Guillermo de, 39,
Mendoza y Almeyda, José, 40, 41,
Menhart, Oldřich, 39, 40, 154,
Menken, H. L., 131,
Menken, Johann Burkhard, 131,
Mennen, children products, 261,
Mercator, Gerardus, 252,
Mercator, 40,
Mercurius Bold Script, 40,
Mergenthaler, Ottmar, 6, 10, 21, 23, 180, 190, **192**, 263, 266, 267, 268,
Mergenthaler Linotype Company, Brooklyn, 6, 10, 24, 26, 27, 28, 29, 34, 36, 57, 62, 68, 72, 77, 104, 129, 138, 150, 151, 190, 192, 217, 224, 238, 263, **266**,
Mergenthaler Linotype Type Library, 44,
Mergenthaler Linotype Typographic Development, 29, 224,
The Mergenthaler Printing Company, 192,
Meridien, 40,
Merrill, Philip P., 190,
Merrymount, 5, 6, 21, 22, 38, 43, **137**, 138, 139, **251**,
The Merrymount Press, Cambridge, 21, 22, 91, 114, 137, 222, 224, 251,
Mesquite, **206**,
Messiah (Handel), 7,
Meta, 41,
Metafont, computerized design system, 12, 35, 84, 244,
Metal box decoration, 20,
Metal engraving, 15, 19,
Metal type, 6, 30,
Metric system, 16,
Metro, series, 27, 28,
Metroblack, 5, 39, 43, 129, **132**, 266,
Metrolight, 5, 39, 41, 43, **129**, 266,
Metromedium, 5, 39, 129, 43, **132**, 266,
Metropolitan, magazine, 96, 110,
Metropolitan Museum of Art, New York, 20, 25, 109, 222,
Metropolitan Museum of Art Press, New York, 25, 222,
Metroset, cathode ray tube phototypesetter, 35,
Meyer, Hans, 24, 78,
Meynell, Francis, 24, 26, 91, 110, 217,
Meynell, Gerard, 268,

Mezzotint, 14, 18,
MGD Graphic Systems Division (Rockwell International), 35,
Michelangelo, 31, 40,
The Michigan Farmer, magazine, Detroit, 141,
Michigan State University, Ann Arbor, 172,
Microgramma, 31, 40, 70,
Microsoft Corporation, Seattle, 37, 49, 72, 92, 104, 164, 262,
Microsoft Windows System, 92,
Middleton, Robert Hunter, 6, 10, 11, 26, 27, 28, 30, 31, 32, 39, 40, 41, 42, 43, 70, 82, 116, 119, 134, 154, 155, 190, **194**, 218, 219, 242, 260, 267,
Robert Hunter Middleton Award, 104,
Miedinger, Max, 15, 22, 23, 24, 31, 32, 40,
Mies Van der Rohe, Ludwig, 25, 28,
Mifflin, George H., 222,
Miles, Reid, 33,
Millais, John Everett, 19,
Miller & Richard, type foundry, Philadelphia, 57, 214,
Mills, Dan, 36, 84,
Mills College, California, 147,
Milton, John, 154,
Minerva, 40,
Adobe Minion, 6, 13, 41, 43, 232, **234**,
Minott, Louis, 6, 40, 42, 188, **202**,
Miracle, Ricard Giralt, 40,
Miraræ, 6, 41, 43, **244**,
Miró, Joan, 240,
Missal Initials, 5, 38, 43, **98**,
Mission Style, 23, 57, 140, 214,
Missouri, 40,
Mistral, 30, 40,
MIT Visual Design Department, 32,
ITC Mithras, 41,
ITC Mixage, 41,
Mobile Advertising Club, Mobile, Alabama, 178,
Moby Dick (Melville), 164,
Model T, car (Ford), 25,
Modèles de Characteres de l'Imprimerie et Autres Choses Necessaires au Dit Art (Fournier), 15,
The Moderator, magazine, New Haven, **45**, **46**,
Modern Art, magazine, 222,
Modern Bold Extra Condensed, 218,
Modern Extended, 24,
The Modern Poster (Alexandre et al.), 22,
Modern style typefaces, 16, 17, **68**, **70**, **103**, **120**, **125**, 149, **150**, **158**, **163**, **200**, **218**, **254**,
Modern Text, 260,
ITC Modern 216, 5, 41, 43, **59**, 254,
Modern Typography and Layout (McMurtrie), 265,
Modernique, 5, 39, 43, 64, **69**,
Modernism, movement, 22, 29, 36,
Modernistic, 6, 39, 43, 214, **215**,
Modigliani, Amadeo, 121,
Il modo di temperare le penne (Degli Arrighi), 162,
Modula, 6, 41, 43, 182, **183**, **184**,
The Mohawk Herald, Amsterdam, New York, 254,
Mohawk Paper Mills, 121, 123,
Moholy-Nagy, László, 25, 26, 27, 28, 29, 30,
Möllenstädt, Bernd, 41,
Mona Lisa, 39,
Apple Monaco, 6, 41, 43, 84, 164, **167**,

Mondrian, Piet, 25,
Monguzzi, Bruno, 36,
Monitors, 12,
Mono element (*IBM-72 Selectric* typewriter), 12, 33,
Monograms, **123**, **196**,
Monophoto, filmsetter, 268,
Monotype cast type, **181**,
Monotype caster, **181**,
Monotype caster reverse delivery mechanism, 24,
Monotype CD 5.0 (Agfa), 37,
Monotype hot metal casting machine, 21, 24,
Monotype hot metal composing machine, 10, 11, 17, 21, 22, 23, 24, 65, 91, 181, 190, 194, 237, 263, 266, 267, 268,
Monotype filmlettering machine, 268,
Monotype International, London, 36, 180,
Monotype matrix case, **181**,
Monotype Photo-lettering Machine, 33,
The Monotype Recorder, journal, London, 27, **181**, 252, **253**, 268,
Monotype Specimen Book, 156,
Monotype 30-E , 5, 38, 43, **144**,
Monroe, Marilyn, 31,
Montaigne, Michel, 222,
Montaigne, 222,
Montague Press, Montague, Mass. 25, 91, 222,
Montalbano, James, 264,
Montallegro, 251,
The Montgomery Republican, Johnstown, 254,
Montgomery Ward Department Store, Philadelphia, 156,
Monthly magazines, 19,
Monticello / Roman No.1, 17, 21, 38,
Monument, 40,
Moongold (movie) (Bradley), 96,
Moore, Charles T., 192,
Moore, Isaac, 38,
Moorish ornament, 19,
More, Sir Thomas, 223,
Moretus, Edouard, printer, 20,
Morgan Press Type Collection, New York, 33,
Morisawa & Co., Ltd., type foundry, Japan, 244,
1984 Morisawa's International Typeface Competition, Japan, 244,
Morison, Stanley, 11, 25, 26, 27, 28, 29, 30, 31, 35, 39, 91, 150, 217, 222, 223, 252, 266, 268,
Morris, William, 18, 19, 20, 21, 22, 23, 38, 96, 114, 137, 138, 203, 216, 220, 222, 251,
Morris Bookstore, Chicago, 220,
Morse, Samuel, 18,
Morse's code, 18,
Moscoso, Victor, 33,
Moser, Koloman, 22, 23, 227, 229,
Mother & Child, magazine, **187**
Motif: a Journal of the Visual Arts, magazine, London, 32,
Motor, 39,
Moulin Rouge, Paris, 21,
Mount Vernon Press, New York, 222,
Mouse (computer), 12, 36,
Mouse tail type composition, 19,
Mowry, Samuel, 204,
Mowry & Sons, wood type company, 204,
Moyrand, Maurice, 30,
Moyroud, Louis, 30, 32, 134,

Mrs Eaves, 41, 182,
Mucha, Alfons, 22, 23,
Muddiman, Henry, 14,
Müller-Brockmann, Josef, 32,
Multimedia, 13,
Multiple master technology, 13, 37,
Munder, Norman T. A., printer, Baltimore, 260, 261,
Munder Venezian, 6, 38, 43, 260, **261**,
Munder Venezian Bold, 261,
Munder Venezian Bold Italic, 261,
Munder Venezian Italic, 261,
Munich Flaspalast Exhibition of Interior Decoration, 78,
Munich School for Master Book Printers, 27,
Murdock, William, 17,
Murray Hill, 6, 40, 178, 179,
Murray Hill Bold, 6, 40, 43, **178**, 179,
MUSE, type catalog, **161**,
Musée des Arts Décoratifs, Paris, 34,
Musée D'Orsay, Paris, 25, 36, 109,
Museo de Arte, Universidad Nacional, Bogota, 78,
Museum dell'Opera di Duomo, Florence, 229,
Museum of Art School, Portland, 164,
Museum of Fine Arts, Boston, 20,
Museum of Modern Art, New York, 29, 121, 187, 222, 240,
Museum of Modern Art of Bogotá (Museo de Arte Moderno de Bogotá), Colombia, 7,
Museum School of Industrial Art, Pennsylvania, 156,
Music types, 15,
Muthesius, Hermann, 24,
Mylius, Rodney, 37, 265,
Myriad, 6, 41, 43, 232, 244, **248**,

N

Nabisco, 260,
Nacional, 39,
Nadall, 203,
Nadall, Berne, 6, 38, 42, **203**,
Narrative of the Troubles with the Indians in New England (Hubbard), 14,
Narrow Grotesque, 38,
Nathan, Robert, 131,
National Academy of Sciences, 137,
National American Woman Suffrage, 24,
National Arts Club, New York, 24, 25, 26,
The National Gallery of Art, journal, Washington, 30,
National Geographic, magazine, 32, 100, 104, 266,
National Typeface Competition, Visual Graphics Corp., North Miami, Florida, 44, 49, 188, 202,
National Typographic Company, West Virginia, 192,
The National Weekly, magazine, 96,
Nature (Emerson), 91,
Navy Cut, 41,
Nazzarino, type foundry, 20,
NBC (National Broadcasting Company), New York, 31, 100,
Neale, Dr. John Mason, 148,
Nebiolo, Giovanni, 20,
Nebiolo & Companie, type foundry, Turin, 20, 29, 31, 38, 199,
Nebraska State Capitol, 137,
Negro, 78,

Negro Digest, magazine, 34,
Nelson, George, 31,
Nelson, Robert Wickham, 10, 62, 64, 99, 141, 263,
Neoclassicism, 9, 15,
Neoclassical style, 7, 161,
Neon (De Milano), 39,
Neon (Schaefer), 39,
ITC Neon (Carnase), 5, 40, 43, **102**,
Neon Ombrata (De Milano), 39,
Neruda, Pablo, 91,
Nesbit, George F., 18,
Neuberg, Hans, 32,
Neue Antiqua / Optima, 32,
Die neue Graphik (The New Graphic Art) (Gerstner), 32,
Neue Graphik (New Graphic Design) (Müller-Brockmann), 32,
Neue Haas-Grotesk / Helvetica, 22, 23, 24, 31, 32, 40,
Neue Hammer Unziale, 154,
Neuenschwander, Brody, 37,
Die neue Typographie (The New Typography) (Tschichold), 26, 27, 29,
Neufville, Jacob de, 21,
Neuland, 24, 39,
Neurath, Otto, 27,
New Alphabet, 33, 40,
New Amsterdam, colony, Manhattan, 14,
Newark: a series of engravings on wood (Ruzicka), 224,
New Bauhaus School (Institute of Design), Chicago, 29, 194,
Newberry Library, Chicago, 110, 118, 195, 260,
New Caledonia, 5, 40, 43, **72**,
The Newcastle Chronicle, England, 21, 192, 266,
New Center Studios, Detroit, 172,
*New Century Schoolbook*36,
A New Dictionary of Quotations (Mencken), **131**,
The New Graphic Art (Die Neue Graphik) (Gerstner), 32,
New Graphic Design (Neue Graphik) (Müller-Brockmann), 32,
The New Landscape (Kepes), 32,
New Process Wood Type (Page), die-cutting, 21,
New School for Social Research, New York, 91,
A New Specimen of Printing Types (Thorowgood), 17,
The New Testament, 17,
The New Typography (Die neue Typographie) (Tschichold), 17,
New Times Millennium, 41,
The New Vision (Moholy-Nagy), 28, 30,
New Wave, typographical management, 34, 35,
New York (Ruzicka, engraver), , 224,
New York, magazine, 100, **101**,
Apple New York, 6, 41, 43, 164, **168**,
The New York Advertisers, 18,
New York Artist Artisan Institute, 114,
New York City, 14,
New York City Community College, 127,
New York City Community College Advisory Commission, 100,
New York City Saint Gaudens Medal, 202,
The New York Daily Graphic, newspaper, 20,
The New Yorker, magazine, 27, 92, 170, **171**,
The New York Herald, newspaper, 18,

The New York Herald Tribune, newspaper, 170, 252,
New York Institute of Technology, 127,
The New York Journal, newspaper, 24,
New York Public Library, 81,
The New York Recorder, newspaper, 21,
New York School of Art, 224,
The New York Society of Illustrators, 78,
New York Stock Market crash, 28,
New York Subway, map (Vignelli), 28,
The New York Sun, newspaper, 18,
The New York Telephone Directory, 29,
The New York Times, newspaper, 18, 19, **55**, 72,
The New York Times Book Review, magazine, 37, 252,
The New York Times Magazine, 160,
The New York Tribune, newspaper, 18, 19, 21, 22, 62, 192, 204, 266,
New York Type Foundry, 17, 114, 156, 214, 254, 263,
New York Typographical Union No. 6, 169,
New York University, 78, 110,
The New York World, newspaper, 21, 22, 23,
1939 New York World's Fair, 29, 236,
The New York Yellow Pages, **128**,
News, concept, 18,
News Gothic, 5, 11, 23, 24, 38, 43, 64, 65, **67**, 197,
Newsweek, magazine, 72, 73,
New Wave, design movement, 34, 35,
NeXt computers, 262, 263,
Nicholas, Robin, 41,
Nicholson, William, 78,
Nicol, George, printer, London, 17,
Nicolas Cochin, 38,
Nineteenth Century Ornamented Types and title pages (Gray), 29,
Nineteenth-century typefaces, 28, 29, 31, 33,
Nitrogen, 41,
Nobel, 5, 43, 134, **135**,
Nolde, Emile, 23,
Nonesuch Press, London, 26, 91,
Noordzij, Peter Matthias, 41, 226,
ITC Nora, 264,
Normalschrift, Roman alphabet, 30,
Norman, 260,
Normande, typefaces, 17, 38,
Normandia, 29, 40,
Northwestern Type Foundry, Milwaukee, 62,
Northwestern University, Chicago, 23,
The Norwich Tribune, 204,
Notable Printers of Italy During the Fifteenth Century (De Vinne), 126,
Notes on the Merrymount Press & Its Work (Updike), 251,
Notre Dame, 41,
The Nottingham Evening Post, newspaper, England, 35,
Novarese, Aldo, 20, 29, 31, 34, 40, 41, 70, 264,
ITC Novarese, 31, 41, 264,
Noyes, Eliot, 11, 33, 35,
NSAD Gold T-square Award, 240,
Nueva, 6, 13, 41, 43, 244, **249**,
No.124, 43, **210**,
No.129, 6, 38, 43, **211**,
No.131, 6, 38, 43, **211**,
No.142, 6, 38, 43, **212**,
No.154, 6, 38, 43, **212**,
No.500, 6, 38, 43, **212**,

No.506, 6, 38, 43, **213**,
No.515, 6, 38, 43, **213**,
Numbered typefaces, 152,
Nussbaumer, Charles, 154, 155,
The Nutcracker, 110,

O

Oakland, 13, 36, 182,
Oakland Ten, 6, 41, 43, **182**, **183**
The Oath of a Free-man (Daye, printer), 14,
OCR-B (Optical Character Recognition), 34, 40,
Octavia, 34,
Odermatt, Siegfried, 40,
Odyssey (Homer), 222,
Of Grammatology (Derrida), 34,
Offenbach, 39,
Offenbach Technical Institute, 25,
Offenbacher Werkgemeinschaft (Offenbach Workshop), 91, 110,
Officina Bodoni, Montagnola di Lugano, Italy, 26, 252,
Offset lithographic printing process, 19, 20, 23, 29,
Ogg, Oscar, 49, 110,
Old Claude, 6, 37, 41, 43, **226**,
Oldenburg, Claes, 32,
Oldenburg, 33, 40,
Old English, 71,
Old Face Open, 38,
Old Style / Bookman, 57, 214,
Old Style Antique, 38, **211**,
Old Style Antique / Bookman, 57,
Old style typefaces, 24,
Old style / Venetian typefaces, **47**, **56**, **58**, **66**, **67**, 113, **137**, **144**, **146**, 148, **203**, **222**, **233**, **251**, **252**, **261**,
Fonderie Olive, type foundry, Marseille, 30,
Olivetti, typewriters, 11,
Olympian, 5, 40, 43, 104, **106**,
Ombondi Editions, New York, 52,
Omnia, 41,
An Omnibus (Crane), **131**,
WTC 145, 100,
On Stone: The Art and Use of Typography on the Personal Computer (Stone), 238,
On the Dedication of American Churches (Updike, printer), 251,
On the Just Shape of Letters (Dürer), 222, 223,
On Trademarks (Consuegra), 7,
Once Thrice Dice (Shahn), 134,
Ondine, 40,
Onyx, 6, 39, 43, **218**,
Onyx Italic, 6, 39, 43, 156, **159**, 218,
Open Roman Capitals, 39,
Open Type, 37, 262,
Oppenheim, Louis, 41,
Optical Society of America, Detroit, 30,
Opticon, 5, 39, 43, 149, **152**, 266,
Optima / Neue Antiqua, 11, 26, 28, 32, 40, 134, 197,
Optima Cyrillic, 41,
Opus, magazine, Michigan, 84,
Oranda, 41,
Orbach's, 31,
Oregon Arts Commission, 164,
Oregon Arts Foundation, 84,
Oregon Environmental Council, 84,
Oregon School of Arts and Crafts, Portland, 92,
The Oregon Times, magazine, 84,

Origins and Development of Printing Types (Hess), 156,
Orion, 40,
Ornamental typefaces, 18, **133**, **145**, **202**, **207**, **209**, **215**, **259**,
Ornamented Clarendons (Page), wood type catalog, 19, 204,
Ornamented No.847, 259,
Ornate No.4, 259,
Ornate Title, 5, 39, 43, **147**,
Orphei tragedia (Poliziano), 26,
Orplid, 39,
Orsi, Luigi, 17,
Ostermeier, Johannes, 28,
ITC Oswald, 264,
Othello, 5, 39, 43, **71**, 213,
WTC Our Bodoni, 5, 43, **100**,
Outcault, Richard F., 22,
Outline typefaces, 18, 38,
Outside advertising, 23,
Overbeek, A., 40,
Overman Wheel, Co., Boston, 97,
Oxford (Baker), 41, 43, 49, **52**,
Oxford/Roman No. 1 (Ronaldson), 16, 38, 251,
The Oxford English Dictionary, 21,
The Oxford Lectern Bible (Rogers), 29, 156, 222,
The Oxford University Press, England, 14, 29, 222, 252,
Bitstream Oz Handicraft, 5, 43, **120**,

P

Pabst Brewing Company, Chicago, 260,
Pabst Oldstyle, 260,
Pacific States Type Foundry, 263,
Pacioli, Fra Luca de, 9, 14, 28, 223,
Pacioli Titling, 40,
Package design, 20,
Packaging exhibitions, 25,
Packard, 116,
Packard Condensed, 116,
Packard Motor Car Company, Detroit, 116, 118,
Padua, 37,
Paepcke, Walter P., 29,
Page, William Hamilton, 6, 19, 20, 38, 42, 43, **204**, 259,
Page & Bassett, wood type company, 204,
The Page & Company, Greeneville, 204,
Page & Setchel, 212, 213,
PageMaker, software (Aldus), 36,
PageMaker 1.0, software, 36,
The William Hamilton Page Wood Type Company, Norwich, 21, 204,
Page's Wood Type Album (Page), 204, 205, **205**, 210, 211,
Paige Typesetter and Distributor, 217,
Painter's Roman, 6, 38, 43, **209**, **259**,
Palatino, 31, 40, 36, 72, 238,
Palatino Cyrillic, 41,
Palladino, Robert, 164,
Palladius, Blodius, 222, 252,
Pan, magazine, Berlin, 22,
ITC Panache, 5, 41, 43, **60**, 264,
Pan Nigerian, 41,
Pantograph, 8, 9, 18, 254, **255**,
Pantograph-router, 9, 18, 21, 254, **255**,
Pantone Co., New Jersey, 33,
Pantone Matching System (PMS), color specification system, 33,
Papageno, 40,
Papal Chancery, 8,
Paper, mechanical production of, 9,

Paperback books, 29, 34,
Paper Makers Advertising Club, Boston, 129,
Paper mill, 14,
Paper negative, 18,
Papert Koenig Lois, advertising agency, New York, 32,
Papier-mâché, 19,
Papini, Giovanni, 24,
Papyrus, 8,
Paragon, 5, 27, 39, 43, 149, **151**, 266,
Paragraphs on Printing (Rogers), 30, 160, 222,
Parchment, 8,
Paris, 40,
1878 Paris Exposition, 204,
Parisian, 5, 39, 43, 64, **69**,
Paris Metro Lettering, , 38,
Park Avenue, 6, 39, 43, 178, **236**, 242,
Parker, Mike, 36, 72, 104,
Parker, Wadsworth A., 6, 10, 11, 23, 25, 26, 38, 39, 42, 43, 57, 142, 145, 153, **214**, 263,
Parlament, 40,
Parrish, Maxfield, 97,
Parsons, I. R., 220,
Parsons, 6, 38, 43, **220**,
Parson's School of Design, New York, 100, 160,
Pascal, 40,
Patel, Aurobind, 28, 37, 41,
Patterson, 76,
Paul, Bruno, 78, 80,
PBS (Public Broadcasting System) (CBS), New York, 187, **187** (symbol),
PC Week, magazine, 72,
Pearson's, magazine, 96,
Pechey, Eleisha, 38,
Pechstein, Max, 23,
Peckolick, Alan, 264,
Peerless, **211**,
Peerless Condensed, **211**,
Peignot, Charles, 27, 32,
Peignot & Fils, type foundry, Paris, 23, 26,
Charles Peignot Award, 244,
Peignot, George, 38,
Peignot, Gustave, 23,
Peignot, Lucien and George, 23,
Peignot, Rémi, 40,
Peignot, 27, 29, 39,
Pelican, 5, 41, 43, 49, **52**,
Pellucida, 12, 84, 165,
Pendrawn, 156,
Penfield, Edward, 96,
Penguin Books, London, 29, 30, 31,
Penguin Books Composition Rules, 30,
Pennel, Joseph, 110,
Pennsylvania Assembly, Philadelphia 16,
The Pennsylvania Mercury, Philadelphia, 16,
Pennsylvania Museum School of Industrial Art, 156,
Penny newspapers, 18,
A. W. Penrose, publishers, London, 22,
Penrose Annual, magazine, London, 22, 27,
Pentagram, Design Studio, 33, 35,
Peoples Trust and Savings Bank, Chicago, 118,
Pepperwood, **209**,
Pepsi-Cola Company, **80**, 92,
Perception: An Introduction to Gestalt theory (Koffka), 26,
Perception: A Psychology of the Creative Eye (Arnheim), 31,

"Perfect" binding, with adhesives and soft covers, 29,
Il perfetto scrittore (Cresci), 92,
Performance Art, movement, 32,
Pericles, 39,
Perpetua, 26, 27, 28, 39, 268,
Persephone (Drinkwater), 222,
Personal computer (PC), 35, 36, 37,
Peter Jessen Schrift, 154,
Peter Pauper Press, 130,
Peters, John, 40,
Le Petite Larousse Illustré (Larousse), 24,
Petty, Mary, 170,
Phanitalian, 6, 38, 43, **211**,
Phemister, Alexander C., 38, 57, 214,
Philadelphia Graphic Arts Forum, 156,
Phinney, Joseph Warren, 6, 10, 21, 38, 43, 96, 97, 141, **216**, 263,
Phoebus, 40,
Phosphor, 39,
Photina, 40,
Photocomposing, term, 27,
Photocomposition, 28, 30, 32, 34, 35, 178, 180, 269,
Photocopying process, 29,
Photoengraving, process, 20,
Photoengraving scanners, 34,
Photo flash bulb, 28,
Photographic Arts, magazine, **101** (symbol),
Photographic book, 22,
Photographic documents, 19, 20,
Photography, 18, 19, 20, 21, 25, 28, 269,
Photogravure, printing process, 20,
Photojournalism, 28,
Photo-Lettering, Inc., New York, 6, 11, 29, 32, 34, 40, 44, 54, 55, 68, 121, 186, 242, 264, **269**,
Photo-lettering process, 28, 29, 32, 269,
Photo-lettering type specimen book, 33,
Photomechanical color illustrations, 20,
Photomechanical halftones, 16, 21,
Photomechanical reproduction, 21,
Photo-matrix, 28, 30, 32,
Photomontage, 25,
Photon Inc., 32,
Photon 200, 32,
Photon 560, 32,
Photon-Lumitype, photocomposing machine, 26, 30, 32,
Photosetting, term, 32,
Phototypesetting, term, 28,
Phototypesetting, 31, 32, 34, 35,
Phototypesetting machine, 27, 29,
Phototypography, 29, 269,
Photo Typositor, 202,
Pica, typographical measuring system, 16, 20,
Picasso, Pablo, 24, 121,
Pichotta, Jill, 72,
Pick, Frank, 24,
Pictograms, 27, 33, 35,
Picture poster, 24,
Pied du roi, measuring system, 16,
Pierce, George J., 216,
President Pierce, Franklin, 203,
Pierce, Richard, 14,
Pierpont, Frank Hinman, 6, 23, 24, 29, 38, 43, **217**, 268,
Pierpont Morgan Library, New York, 35, 91,
Pietra, 5, 37, 41, 43, **94**, 226,

Pilgrims, 14,
Pillow Book (film) (Greenaway), 37,
Pilsner, 5, 41, 43, 134, **136**,
Pimny Power of Printing Award, 240,
Pindar Uncial, 154,
Pinson Printers, New York, 114, 154,
ITC Pioneer, 5, 40, 43, **103**,
Pioneers of Modern Typography (Spencer), 34,
Pisarro, Lucien, 22, 38,
Das Plakat, magazine, 24, 78,
Plakatstil (poster style), 78,
Plain Printing Types (De Vinne), 126,
Plans, Elevations, Sections, and Details of the Alhambra (Jones), 19,
Plantin, Christophe, 115, 217, 268,
Plantin, 6, 23, 24, 38, 43, **217**, 268,
Plantin-Moretus Museum, Antwerp, Belgium, 20, 233, 238,
Plantin-Moretus Press, 217,
Platen, 16,
Playbill, 17, 39, 72,
Playboy, magazine, 31,
Playgirl, 127, 128,
The Pleiad Press, 252,
Plinc, magazine, 54, **55**, 269,
Plimpton Press, 133,
Pliskin, Bob, 242,
Plumet, George, Norwood, 252,
G. H. Plumet, type foundry, Paris, 252,
Plymouth, colony, Cape Cod, Mass., 14,
Plymouth Bold, 100,
PM (*Production Managers*), magazine, 28, 114,
Pocket book editions, 29, 30, 34,
Pocket Book venture, 29,
Poe, Edgard Allan, 240,
Poetica, 41, 232,
Pointing hands, **205**,
Poiret, Paul, 78,
Poliphilus, 26, 39, 47, 251, 268,
Political poster, 24, 25,
Poliziano, Angelo, 26,
Pompeian Cursive, 5, 39, 43, 116, **120**,
George Pompidou Center for the Arts,, Paris, 186,
Ponderosa, **211**,
Pontif, 5, 37, 41, 43, **93**, 226, 227,
Poor Richard's Almanac (Franklin), 15,
Pop Art, movement, 31, 32, 34,
Poppl, Friedrich, 40, 41,
Poppl-Antiqua, 40,
Poppl-Exquisit, 40,
Poppl-Laudatio, 41,
Poppl-Nero, 41,
Poppl-Pontif, 40,
Popular advertising imagery, 31,
Porchez, Jean François, 226,
Portland State University, Portland, 84, 164,
Porzolt, E., 269,
Poseidon Gardens, 127,
Post, Herbert, 19, 25, 39, 40,
Post Antiqua, 39,
Postblack Italic, 5, 39, 43, 156, **159**,
The Poster, magazine, London, 22, 23,
Poster Bodoni, 5, 26, 39, 70, 43, 116, 119, **150**,
Posteriter, 202,
Posters, 7, 17, 18, 20, 21, 22, 23, 25, 29, 33, 35, 37, **69**, **70**, **97**, **117**, **118**, **177**, **178**,
Post-Impressionist paintings, 25,
Post Mediaeval, 40,
Post-Modernism, 33, 36,
Post Oldstyle Italic, 159,

Post Roman, 39,
PostScript, computer language (Adobe)12, 36, 37, 248, 262,
PostScript Language Manual (Adobe), 262,
Post Shaded Italic, 156,
Post-Stout Italic, 5, 39, 43, 156, **159**,
Post-structuralism, 34, 36,
Powell, Gerry, 6, 39, 43, 70, 153, 201, **218**,
The Practice of Typography (De Vinne), 23, 126,
Louis Prang, chromolitography press, Boston, 222,
Pratt Institute, New York, 100, 127, 242,
Pratt & Whitney Co., Hartford, 217,
Praxis, 40,
Pre-Raphaelite Brotherhood, 19, 97,
Premier, 33, 40, 265,
Premier, magazine, 77,
Preminger, Otto, 31,
De Pæparatione Evangelica (Eusebius), 194, 222, 267,
Present, 40,
Press of the Wooly Whale, New York, 143,
Price, George, 170,
Priester, matches, Berlin, 23, 78, **79**,
Primer, 224, 266,
Prince, Edward, 21,
Princeton University Museum, 252,
Princeton University Press, 20, 252,
Print, magazine, 32, 84, 186, 226, 238, 239,
PRINT '68 exhibition, Chicago, 12, 34,
The Printed Book in America (Blumenthal), 35, 91,
Printer Man's Joy, 97,
Printer's case, **225**,
Printers Ink, magazine, 100,
Printer's marks, **111**, **112**, **117**, **223**,
The Printer's Monthly Bulletin, Boston, 204,
Printers ornaments, **223**, **261**, **253**,
Printing (Morris / Walker), 220,
Printing Art magazine, 96,
Printing ink, 15, 17,
Printing News, magazine, 100,
Printing processes, 35,
Printing Review, magazine, London, 28,
Printing technology, 22, 29,
Printing Types: Their History, Forms, and Use (Updike), 17, 225, 251,
Prisma, 24, 39,
Private press movement, 10, 18, 20, 25,
Private Presses and their Books (Ransom), 220,
Profil, 40,
Process colors, 20, 21, 240,
The Profits of Book Composition (De Vinne), 126,
Programmed type composition, 34,
Progressive Architecture, magazine, 240,
Protest imagery, 34,
Protestant University, Sedan, France, 14,
Providence Athanæum, 251,
Pryde, James, 78,
Psychedelia, movement, 33,
Psychedelic style, 33, 269,
Psychedelitype (Photo-Lettering Inc.), catalog, 34, 269,
Ptolemy Epiphanes, 17,
Public Television Stations, New York, 127,
Publication Design (Hurlburt), 35,
Publick Occurrences Both Foreign and Domestick, newspaper, Boston, 14,

Publish!, magazine, 75, 84, 164,
Pulitzer, Joseph, 21, 23,
Pull down menus, 12, 36,
Punch, metal typography, 8, 10, **195**,
Punch-cutter, 8, 14, 16, **63**,
Punch-cutting machine, 24, 62,
Punk, movement, 32, 35,
Purdue College, Lafayette, 222,
Push Pin Graphic, magazine, 31,
Push Pin Studio, New York, 31, 34,

Q

Quark, Inc., Denver, Colorado, 36, 37, 262
QuarkXpress, page layout program, 36, 37, 262,
Quay, David, 41,
ITC Quay Sans, 41,
Quick-Change Linotype machine, 266,
Quill pen, 6,
ITC Quorum, 264,

R

Racine, Jean, 155,
Radiant, 6, 26, 39, 43, 194, **201**, 267,
Rädisch, P. H., 104,
Raffia Initials, 40,
Ragan, Jesse, 136,
Raleigh Gothic, 162,
Ramírez & Rialp, type foundry, Barcelona, 21,
Rand, Paul, 11, 29, 30, 32,
Random House, publishers, New York, 27, 78, 81, 91, 100, 110, 129, 130,
Ransom, Sidney, 23,
Ransom, Will, 6, 23, 25, 27, 38, 43, 116, 141, 144, **220**,
Will Ransom Maker of Books, Chicago, 220,
RCA (Radio Corporation of America), 33,
RCA Victor Records, 31,
Rea, Gardner, 170,
Reactor, 5, 41, 43, 134, **136**,
Readability, 22, 27, 37,
Reading hierarchies, 34,
Reade, William A., 24, 190, 267,
Readers Digest, magazine, 92,
Reading hierarchies, 34,
Rear, Herb, 178,
Record covers, 31, 33, 35,
Record Gothic, 6, 39, 43, 194, **197**, 267,
Red Badge of Courage (Crane), 240,
Reed, Carol, 187,
Reed College, Portland, 84, 92, 164, 226, 238,
Reed pen, 6,
Reid, Whitelaw, 21, 62, 192,
Reiner, Imre, 18, 19, 39, 40, 41, 110, 134, 135,
Reiner Script (Reiner), 40,
Reinhardt & Co. Inc., publishers, 31,
E. Remington & Sons, gun makers, 20,
Renaissance handwriting: an anthology of italic scripts (Fairbank / Wolpe), 32,
Renaissance, 8,
Renaissance humanist scribes, 8,
Renaissance typefaces, 240,
Renault, cars, France, 32,
Renner, Paul, 18, 22, 26, 27, 28, 29, 39, 40, 117, 135, 198, 218,
Renwick, Aspin & Russell, architects, New York, 137,

HTF Requiem, 6, 43, **162**,
Ressinger, Paul, 27,
Revue, 33, 40, 265,
Reynolds, Lloyd, 84, 92, 164, 238,
Rhode, Hiero, 40,
Rhode Island School of Design, Providence, 36, 84, 134, 244,
R. Ribadeau-Dumas, type founders, Paris, 252,
Cardinal Richelieu (Armand Jean du Plessis, duc de Richelieu), 14,
Ridder, Hermann, 24,
Riggs, V., 254,
Riley, Frank H., 6, 39, 42, **221**, 242,
Rimmel, Eugène, perfume manufacturer, Paris, 19,
Rip Van Winkle, 147,
Ritmo, 40,
Bishop Rittenhausen, William, paper maker, 14,
Riverside Press, Cambridge, 21, 22, 23, 91, 222, 223, 251,
Riverside Press Editions, 222,
Robert, Nicolas Louis, 17,
Robinson, Boardman, 110,
Robinson Crusoe (Defoe), 15,
Rochester Institute of Technology, 84, 92, 100, 121, 164, 252,
Rochester Memorial Art Gallery, New York, 78,
Rockefeller University Reunion, New York, 123,
Rockwell, 39,
Rockwell Antique, 70,
Rockwell International, 35,
Rococo style, 15,
Rodchenko, Alexander, 25, 34,
Roger Black, Inc., 73,
Rogers, Bruce, 6, 11, 21, 22, 23, 25, 26, 27, 28, 29, 30, 38, 42, 91, 114, 129, 156, 160, 194, **222**, 252, 260, 261, 268,
Rogers, John R., 217,
Rogers-Kellog-Stillson, Inc., New York, 240,
Roissy, 40,
Roller, Alfred, 22,
Rolling Stone, magazine, 72, 134, 160, 162,
Rollins, Carl Purington, 222,
Romain du Roi Louis XIV, 9, 15, 38,
Roman, 6, 38, **254**,
Roman alphabet, 8, 30,
The Roman Alphabet (Baker), 49,
Roman classical inscriptions, 8, 24,
Roman Church, 8,
Roman Empire, 8,
Roman Forum, 8,
Roman No.1, 16, 17, 21, 38,
Roman Oldstyle, 38,
Romantiques No.2, 259,
Romic, 40,
Romulus, 15, 26, 27, 39,
Ronaldson, 56,
Ronaldson, James, 16,
Ronin, William, 242,
Rondo, 40,
Rondthaler, Edward, 11, 12, 28, 29, 32, 34, 186, 264, 269,
Rose, Carl, 170,
Rosellino, Bernardo, 227, 229,
Rosen, Ben, 33,
Rosen, Fritz, 80,

Rosenquist, James, 32,
Rosetta Stone, 17, 54,
Rosetti, Dante Gabriel, 19,
President Roosevelt, Franklin Delano, 29, 91,
Rosewood, **207**,
Ross, Harold, 170,
Router, machine, 18, 254, **255**,
Rotary letterpress, 19, 20,
Rotary lithographic press, 19,
Rotis, 36, 37, 41,
Rotzler, Willi, 33,
Royal Academy of Fine Arts, The Hague, 182,
The Royal College of Art, London, 23, 121,
Roycroft Press, East Aurora, New York, 23, 214,
Rubbings, **142**, **227**,
Rubel, Ira William, paper manufacturer, New Jersey, 20, 23,
Ruder, Emil, 30, 32, 33, 34,
Rudge, William Edwin, printer, New York, 30, 91, 222, 252,
Ruffins, Reynold, 31,
Ruggles, Stephen, 18,
Rühl, Alexander, 41,
The Rural Electrification Administration, 29,
Ruskin, John, 10, 20,
Russian Constructivism, 25, 27, 32, 35,
Rust, Samuel, 17,
Rustica, 40, 155,
Rutherford Machinery Division, 28,
Rutherford Photo-Letter Composing Machine, 29, 269,
Ruzicka, Rudolph, 6, 11, 39, 42, 131, 149, **224**, 251,

S

Saarinen, Eero, 34, 125,
Sabatini, Rafael, 114,
Sabon, Jakob, 34,
Sabon, 34, 40, 234,
Sachplakat (object poster), 23, 78, **79**, **80**,
Sachs, Hans, 24, 78,
Saint Agustine, 137,
St. Bartholomew, Church, New York, 137,
St. Bride Printing Library, London, 22,
Saint Francis, 137,
Saint Francis College, New York, 227,
St. Stephen, Church, Cohasset, 137,
St. Stephen, Church, Fall River, 137,
St. Thomas, Church, New York, 137,
St. Nicholas, magazine, 126,
Salden, Georg, 40,
Sales Executive Club, New York, 178,
Sales and Marketing Executive International, 178,
La Salle Street, advertising agency, Chicago, 224,
Sallwey, Friedrich K., 40,
Salter, Georg, 25, 39, 49, 226,
Salto, 40,
Samson (Middleton), 6, 39, 43, 194, **201**, 267,
Samson (Hammer), 154,
Samson Agonistes (Milton), 154,
San Francisco Art Institute, 84,
The San Francisco Chronicle, 132, 153, 182,
The San Francisco Examiner, 72,
Sancha, Antonio de, printer, Madrid, 133,
Sanlecque l'ancien, Jacques de, 77,
San Marco, 41,

Sans Serif, 27,
Sans serif, term, 18,
Sans Serif Shaded, 38,
Sans serif trend, 27, 28,
Sans serif typefaces, 9, 10, 11, 12, 17, 18, 23, 25, 28, 29, 34, **48**, **57**, **58**, **60**, **66**, **67**, **69**, **70**, **71**, **73**, **74**, **75**, **78**, **81**, **82**, **85**, **86**, **89**, **93**, **102**, **103**, **107**, **109**, **110**, **113**, **119**, **120**, **125**, **129**, **132**, **135**, **136**, **147**, **152**, **157**, **162**, **166**, **167**, **168**, **169**, **182**, **184**, **185**, **186**, **190**, **197**, **198**, **199**, **201**, **229**, **238**, **246**, **248**, **256**,
Santa Fe, 41,
Sanvito, Bartolomeo, 235,
Adobe Sanvito, 6, 41, 43, 232, **235**,
Saphir, 40,
HTF Saracen, 6, 43, **162**,
HTF Saracen Italic, 160,
Sarafellini, Ventura, 94,
Saroyan, William, 112,
Sartain, John, 18,
Sassafras, 5, 41, 43, **53**,
Satanick, 216,
Satué, Enric, 37,
The Saturday Evening Post, magazine, 11, 129, 156, 159, 186, 266,
Sauer, Christopher, *the younger*, 16,
Saul Brothers Co., printing firm, Chicago, 190, 267,
Saunders, Patricia, 41,
Saunders, Richard (pseud. of Benjamin Franklin), 15,
Scalable fonts, 163,
Scaramouche (play) (Sabatini), 114,
A Scene in Shantytown, photograph, 20,
Schadow, 39,
Schaedle, John, 178,
Schaefer, K. H., 39,
Schaefer, Willy, 19, 39,
Scheimer, Christopher, 63,
Schelter & Giesecke, type foundry, Germany, 18,
Fleming Schiller and Carnrick, printers, New York, 139,
Schlesinger, Stefan, 19, 40,
Schmidt, Klaus, 202,
Schmidt-Rotluff, Karl, 23,
Schmoller, Hans, 30,
Schneidler, F. H. Ernst, 19, 25, 39,
Schneidler Titling, 162,
Schnippering, Walter, 39,
School of Arts and Crafts, Basle, 30,
School of Arts and Design, Detroit, 172,
School of Visual Arts, New York, 54, 127,
Schöffer, Peter, 8,
Schraubstadtler, William, Oswald, and Carl, 22,
Schroeder, Gustav, 38,
Schule für Gestaltung (School of Design), Basle, 34,
Schuricht, N. 154,
Schwabacher typefaces, 21, 30,
Schwitters, Kurt, 34,
The Scientific American, magazine, 31, 84, 87, 164, 167,
Scorsese, Martin, 31,
Scotch Roman, 31, 72, 129,
Scott, Walter Dill, professor of psychology, 23,
John Scott Medal, 192,
Scott, M. H. Baily, 96,
Scott-Makela, P., 13, 41,
Scratch Regular, 41,

Screen fonts, 12, 34,
Scribe, 39,
Scribner, Charles, publisher, New York, 22, 114, 224,
Scribner's , book store, 114,
Scribner's Magazine, 19,
Scribner's Monthly, magazine, 126,
The Script Alphabet (Baker), 49,
Scripsit, journal, 49, 51,
Scriptura, 39,
Scriptura '84, exhibition, 164,
Script typefaces, 22, **88**, **90**, **95**, **176**, **177**, **178**, **200**, **221**, **230**, **235**, **237**, **243**,
Scruples (Krantz), **101**,
Sculptura, 40,
"Sea Horse" Beach Restaurant, Ischia, Italy, 127,
Sears Roebuck, department stores, 156,
Seattle Art Museum, 109,
Selden, John, 15,
Selective Check Lists of Press Books (Ransom), 220,
"Self-spacing" measuring system (Benton), 62,
Seller, William, 268,
Seltzer, Fritz Max, 217,
Semplicità Ombra, 199,
Seven War Loan, 79,
Senefelder, Aloysius (or Aloys), 16, 17,
Sequoyah, Cherokee Indian, 18,
Serial publications, 15,
ITC Serif Gothic, 5, 6, 40, 43, **127**, 186, **189**, 264,
Serif Magazine Type Design Competion, 92,
Serif typefaces, 11, 12, 30,
Serifa, 40,
Serifs, 8, 9,
Servidori of Madrid, Domingo María de, 156, 159,
Setchell, George Case, 204, 205,
Severini, Gino, 24,
Seybold Report, magazine, 164,
Shaar, Edwin W., 29, 39, 176, 242,
Shadow (M.F. Benton), 5, 39, 43, 64, **71**,
Shadowed typefaces, **71**, **103**,
Shahn, Ben, 33, 91, 134, 136,
Shakespeare, William, 220,
William Shakespeare's Comedies, Histories & Tragedies (Shakespeare), 14,
Shakspeare Printing Office, London, 17,
Shand, James, 29, 30, 32,
The Shaping of the Alphabet (Denman), 63, 138,
Sharp, William, lithographer, Boston, 18,
Shaw, Paul, 6, 13, 37, 41, 42, 43, 58, 92, 93, 94, 95, **226**,
Paul Shaw / Letter Design, New York, 226, 227,
Shaw, Thomas Edward (pseud. Lawrence of Arabia), 222,
Shelley, George, 107,
Shelley Script Allegro, 5, 40, 43, 104, **107**,
Shelley Script Andante, 107,
Shelley Script Volante, 5, 40, 43, 104, **107**,
Shenval Press, London, 29, 30, 32, 104,
Shepard, Henry O., publisher, 99,
Shiseido, cosmetics, 100,
Sho, 40,
Sholes, Christopher Lathan, 20,
A Short History of the Graphic Arts (Rotzler), 33,

A Short History of Music (Stein), **130**,
A Short History of the Printed Word (Chappell), 35, 110, 111, 112, 225,
Shuckers, Jacob W., 192,
Siegel, David, 41,
Siegen, Ludwig von, 14,
Sierra, 6, 41, 43, 164, **165**,
Silica, 238,
Simon, Oliver, 26,
Simon & Shuster, publishers, New York, 146,
Simonneau, Louis, French engraver, 9,
Simons, Anna, 23,
Simplex, 39,
Simplex Linotype, composing machine, 192,
Sinaloa, 40,
Singleton, Frederic T., 114,
Sign and information systems, 27, 35, 37,
Sign painters, 9,
Signs, 17,
Signum, 40,
Sixtax-Antiqua, 40, 164,
Sintax Phonetic, 84,
Siquot, Luis, 41, 213, 264,
Sister Carrie (Dreiser), 91,
Sistina, 31, 40,
Sitte, Camilo, architect, 154,
Sixteen Century Roman, 155,
Pope Sixtus V, 227,
Skeleton Antique, 6, 38, 43, **208**,
Slab serif typefaces, 17, 26, 70, 71, 153, **162**, **189**, **198**, **215**, **219**, **256**, **258**,
Slanted matrices, 25, 190, 191, 267,
The Sleeping Beauty (Perrault), 110,
Slimbach, Robert, 6, 12, 13, 34, 36, 41, 42, 43, **232**, 238, 244, 248, 262,
ITC Slimbach, 6, 41, 43, **232**, 264,
Slogan, 31,
Smaragd, 40,
Smart, magazine, 72, 76,
Smart Money, magazine, 72,
Schmidt, Klaus, 202,
Small caps, 29, **93**, **94**, **95**, **109**, **231**,
Smith, Ernie, 187,
Smith, Robert E., 6, 39, 40, 42, 43, 178, **236**, 242,
Smithsonian, magazine, 240,
Smithsonian Institution, Washington, 192, 263,
Smothers, R. J., 27, 269,
The Smythes (comic strip) (Rea Irvin), 170,
Snell, Charles, 106,
Snell Roundhand, 5, 40, 43, 104, **106**,
Snow, Carmel, publisher, New York, 29,
Society of Arts and Crafts, Boston, 96,
Society of Calligraphers (Dwiggins), 25, 129,
Society of Calligraphers (Johnston), 23,
Society of Newspaper Designers, 84,
Society of Publication Designers, New York, 100,
Society of Scribes, Ltd., New York, 122, 226,
Society of Scribes and Illuminators, London, 226,
Society of Typographic Arts, Chicago, 27, 116, 117, 121, 154, 178,
Society of Typographic Designers, London, 121,
Soda Script, 41, 182,
Soft covers binding, 29,
Soglow, Otto, 170,

Solemnis, 32, 40, 154,
Solex, 41, 182,
Some Aspects of Printing Old and New (Updike), 251,
Sommer, Karl, 39,
Songs of Innocence (Blake), 16,
Sonoma State University, California, 238,
Sophia, 5, 41, 43, 104, 105, **108**,
Sorbonne, 23,
Sorel, Edward, 31,
Sottile, Dalilah, 226,
The Sound of Music (film, Wise), **188**,
Souvenir (M.F. Benton), 5, 38, 43, 64, **68**, 269,
ITC Souvenir (Benguiat), 5, 11, 34, 40, 43, **54**, 264,
The Spanish Occupation of California, 148,
Spartan, 27, 218,
Spartan series, 27,
Spartan Bold Condensed, 27, 218,
Spécimen des Nouveaux Caractéres (Didot l'aîné), 17,
A Specimen of Metal Ornaments Cast at the Letter Foundry of Binny and Ronaldson (Binny & Ronaldson), 17,
Specimen of Printing Types (Binny & Ronaldson), 17,
A Specimen of Printing Types (Baine), 16,
Specimens of Printing Types (Figgins), 18,
Speckter, Martin K., 172,
Spectrum, 27, 40,
Speedball pen, 177, 230,
Spencer, Herbert, 30, 34,
Spencer, Platt R., 19,
Spencerian College, Kinsgsville, Ohio, 19,
Spencerian script, 19, **55**, **61**, 100, **101**, 127, **128**,
Spiekermann, Erik, 37, 41, 134,
Spiekermann, Erik and Joan, 37,
Spiral, 27, 39, **91**,
Spiral Press, Croton Falls, New York, 27, 91,
The Spiral Press through Four Decades (Blumenthal), exhibition, New York, 91,
Spire, 5, 39, 43, 156, **158**,
Sports Illustrated, magazine, 104, 160, 162,
Spring, 5, 41, 43, **92**,
Spring Hill College, Alabama, 178,
Springfield Bicycle Club Tournament, Massachusetts, **97**,
Spumoni, 92,
Spy, screen font, 92,
The Spy, Worcester, 204,
Stamperia del Santuccio, Florence, 154, 155,
Stamperia Reale, Parma, 15, 16,
Stamps, **128**, 240, **241**,
Stan, Tony, 34, 126, 264,
Standard, Paul, 54, 111, 116,
Standard composing stick, 99,
Standard lining system, 23,
Standard type measuring system, 9, 10, 20, 21, 23,
Standard Type Foundry, 263,
Stanford University Department of Computer Science and Art, 84, 244,
Star Chamber Decree of 1637 Concerning Printing, 126,
Starr, Thomas and Edwin, Philadelphia, 19,
Stauffacher, Jack, 84,
Steam engine, 15,
Steam-power cylinder press, 17, 18,
Stedman, Edmund Clarence, 204,
Steel engraving, 17,
Steelplate Gothic, 260,

Steelplate Shaded, 260,
Steel punches, 19,
Steig, William, 170,
Steile Futura, 40,
Stein, Alfred, 130,
Steinberg, Saul, 170,
Stellar, 6, 11, 28, 32, 39, 43, 82, 134, 194, **197**, 267,
Steltzer, Fritz Max, 24, 217, 268,
Stempel, David, 22,
D. Stempel AG, type foundry, Frankfurt-am-Main, 19, 21, 22, 24, 26, 28, 31, 32, 32, 34, 72, 110, 113, 153, 154, 155, 266,
Stencil (Middleton), 6, 26, 39, **201**, 219,
Stencil (Powell), 6, 39, 43, 201, 218, **219**,
Stephenson, John, 17,
Stephenson, Blake & Co., type foundry, Sheffield, 17, 23, 27, 39, 252,
Stereoscopic printing, 20,
Stereotype duplicating process, 9, 16, 17, 19, 149,
Stettler, **188**, 202,
Stettler, Wayne J., 188, 202,
Stevens-Nelson, handmade papers, 122,
Stevenson's Attitude to Life (Genung), 139,
Martha Stewart's Living, magazine, 134,
Stickley, Gustav, 96,
Stiller, shoes, Germany, 78, **80**,
Stockholm, 5, 6, 37, 41, 43, **94**, 226, **230**,
Stone, Herbert S., 141,
Stone, Melvine S., 192,
Stone, Reynolds, 26, 266,
Stone, Sumner, 6, 12, 13, 36, 41, 43, 232, **238**, 244,
ITC Stone Informal, 6, 36, 41, 43, 238, **239**,
Stone lithography, 16, 19, 20,
Stone Print, 41, 238,
ITC Stone Sans Serif, 6, 36, 41, 43, **238**,
ITC Stone Serif, 6, 36, 41, 43, 238, **239**,
Stone Type Foundry, digital type foundry, Palo Alto, 37, 238,
Stone & Kimball, publishers, Chicago, 22, 141,
Stop (Novarese), 31, 40,
Stop (Höhnisch), 39,
Story & Humpries, publishers, Philadelphia, 16,
The Story of the Village Press (Goudy), **143**,
Stradivarius, 40,
Strathmore Paper Company, Westfield, 26, 114, 115, 129,
Strawberry Hill Press, New York, 110,
Stream line, 29,
Strizver, Ilene, 37, 264,
The Structure of a Book (Dwiggins), 129,
Studies in Type Design (Ruzicka), 224, **225**,
Studio, 40,
Style Mucha, 22,
Stylescript, 242,
Stylus, writing tool, 8,
Stymie, 5, 28, 39, 43, 64, **70**, 153, 214, 218,
Stymie Black, 158,
Stymie Bold, 70,
Stymie Bold Condensed, 6, 39, 43, 70, 71, 218, **219**,
Stymie Extrabold, 5, 39, 43, **158**,
Stymie Inline Title, 6, 39, 43, **215**,
Stymie Light Condensed, 219,
Stymie Light Title, 70,
Stymie Medium Condensed, 71,
Stymie Medium Extrabold Condensed, 219,
Stymie Medium Title, 70,

Success, magazine, 96,
Sudler & Hennessey, Inc., New York, 100, 186,
Suddler, Hennessey & Lubalin, Inc., New York, 186,
Sully-Jonquières, 40,
Sundwall, Jose, 189,
Suokko, Glenn, 183,
Super-ellipsis, 31,
Supergraphics, 12, 33,
Supermannerists, 33,
Supermarket packaging, 31,
Superstar, 40,
Súper Tipo Veloz, 30, 39,
Suprematism, movement, 25,
Surrealism, movement, 25, 27,
Survivals of the Fine Arts of Printing, exhibition, Princeton, 252,
Sustained caps, 22,
Sutnar, Ladislav, 11, 30,
The Swedish Modern Set, typefaces, 37, 92, **94**, **95**, **230**, **231**,
Sweet's Catalog Service, 30,
Swift, Jonathan, 110, 130,
Swift, 41,
Swiss graphic design, 12, 25, 32,
Swiss Graphic Style, 32, 34, 36,
Symbol, 36, 92,
ITC Symbol, 41, 254,
Symbols, **45**, **46**, **79**, **80**, **112**, **117**, **122**, **128**, **131**, **142**, 171, **223**, **225**, **241**,
Symmetrical typography, 30,
ITC Syndor, 41,
Syntax, 40,
Syracuse University, 127.

T

Tabloid newspapers, 23,
Talbot, Fox, 18,
Tale of a Tub (Swift), 110,
Tales (Poe), 240,
Tan, magazine, 34,
Tannenberg, 39,
Tap, 40,
The Tapestry (Bridge), 252,
Tarzana, 41, 182,
Tasso, Torcuato, 16,
Tatlin, Vladimir, 25,
Taylor, Harold M., 25,
W. Thomas Taylor, printer, Austin, 91,
Tea Chest, 39,
Tegentonen, 41,
Adobe Tekton, 41,
Tektronix Corporation, Portland, 164,
Telephone books, 29, 35,
Television, 29, 31,
Tell Text, 203,
Template Gothic, 13, 41,
Tempo, 26, 27, 194, 198, 267,
Tempo Bold, 27, 198,
Tempo Heavy Condensed, 6, 27, 39, 43, **198**, **199**,
Tempo Light, 27, 198, 199,
Tempo Medium, 27, 198,
Tenazas, 41,
Tenniel, Sir John, 19,
Tennyson, Alfred, 222,
Tetterode, Nicolaas, 19,
Apple Textile, 84,
Text Type, 39,

Textur, 8,
Teutonic, 6, 38, 43, **210**,
Theater Guild (symbol), **80**,
FF Thesis, 36, 37, 41,
They Say Stories, 110, 111,
Thibaudeau, Francis, typographer, 26, 31,
The Thinking Eye (*Das bildnerische Denken*) (Klee), 32,
This is My Beloved (Benton), **131**,
Thomas, Isaiah, printer, Worcester, 16, 17,
Thomas & Crowell, publishers, New York, 139,
Thompson, Bradbury, 6, 11, 29, 31, 40, 42, 114, 186, 202, **240**,
Thompson, Tommy, 49, 50,
Thompson, composing machine, 263,
Thoreau, Henry David, 224,
Thorne, Robert, 17, 38,
Robert Thorne, type foundry, 17, 38,
Thorne Shaded, 38,
Thorowgood, William, 17, 38, 160,
Thorowgood, 38,
William Thorowgood & Besley, type foundry, London, 18,
Thoughts on Design (Rand), 30,
Three-color halftones, 21,
Three-color reproduction principle, 20,
The Three Cornered Hat (Alarcón), 154,
Three-dimensional drawing programs, 32,
Three-dimensional typefaces, **103**,
Three Monographs in Color (Ruzicka), 224,
Thurber, James, 170,
Tiemann, Walter, 21, 25,
ITC Tiffany, 5, 40, 43, **56**, 264,
Tiffany Script, 260,
The Time Machine (Wells), 129, **130**,
Time, magazine, New York, 26, 104,
The Times, newspaper, London, 17, 18, 19, 24, 28, 30, 35, 37,
Times Europa, 30, 35, 37, 40,
The Times Literary Suplement, London, 30,
Times Millennium, 37,
Times New Roman, 11, 12, 28, 29, 30, 35, 36, 39, 72, 92, 150, 266, 268,
Tissi, Rosmarie, 12, 33, 40,
Title pages, **46**, **65**, **112**, **117**, **130**, **131**, **142**, **223**, **253**, **255**,
Title Pages as Seen by a Printer (De Vinne), 126,
1964 Tokyo Olympics, 33,
Tokyo Type Directors Club, 104, 108,
Toner, 29,
Toorop, Jan, 21,
Torino, 38,
Tornesius, Jean, 214,
Tory, Geofroy, 9, 14, 115, 214,
Total Design, design studio, Amsterdam, 33,
Totally Glyphic, 41, 182,
Totally Gothic, 6, 41, 43, 182, **183**, **185**,
Toulouse-Lautrec, Henri de, 21,
Tourist Gothic, 156,
Towards a Reform of the Paper Currency particularly in point of its design (Dwiggins), **131**,
Tower, 5, 39, 43, 64, **71**,
Tower Italic, 71,
Tracy, Walter, 28, 30, 37, 40, 266,
The Trade Compositor, 156,
Trademarks and symbols, **45**, **46**, **55**, **79**, **80**, **112**, **117**, **122**, **128**, **131**, **142**, 171, **195**, **223**, **225**, **241**,
Trademarks USA, exhibition, Chicago, 44, 46,

Trafton, Howard Allen, 6, 22, 29, 39, 42, 43, **242**, 243,
Trafton Script, 6, 39, 43, **242**, 243,
Trajan Column inscription, 8, 24, 245,
Trajan, 6, 37, 41, 43, 238, 244, **245**,
Trajan Title, 5, 39, 43, **147**,
Trajanus, 5, 39, 43, 110, 112, **113**,
Emperor Trajanus, Marcus Ulpius, 8, 113, 245,
Transitional typefaces, 15,
Transito, 39,
Transportation signage system, 35,
Traveller Regular, 41,
Travels into Several Remote Nations of the World of Lemuel Gulliver (Swift), 130,
The Travels of Marco Polo (Marco Polo / Dwiggins), 220,
Treacy Headliners, 175,
Treadle platen press, 18,
The Treaty of Paris, 16,
Trenholm, George F., 25, 27,
Tri-Arts Press, New York, 121, 122,
The Tribune Book of Open Air Sports (Hall), 21, 266,
The Tribune Companies, 73,
Triplex, 6, 41,43, **185**,
Trochut, Joan, 30, 39,
Troy, 21, 38, 203, 216,
True-Cut Bodoni / Bodoni Modern and Italic, 260,
TrueType, Microsoft, 37, 262, 263,
Trump, Georg, 19, 24, 39, 40, 232, 240,
Trump Gravur, 40,
Trump Mediaeval, 40,
Tschichold, Jan, 23, 26, 27, 28, 29, 30, 34, 39, 40, 162, 234, 240,
Tuscan Antique, 207,
Tuscan Outline, 6, 38, 43, **258**,
Tuscan style typefaces, 17, **206**, **207**, **257**, **258**,
TV graphics, 32,
Twelve-line English romans, 15,
Twentieth Century Type Designers (Carter), 7, 36,
Twenty-seven Chicago Designers, Chicago, 194,
Two-character matrix, 23, 24,
Two-line English Egyptian, first sans serif, 38,
Two-line Great Primer Sans-serif, 38,
Two-line pica letters, 38,
200 Years of American Graphic Art: a Retrospective Survey of the Printed Arts and Advertising since the Colonial Period (Hornung / Johnson), 35,
Twombly, Carol, 6, 12, 13, 36, 37, 41, 42, 43, 84, **244**, 262,
Twyman, Michael, 92,
Type and Typography (Rosen), 33,
Type case, **193**, **225**,
Typecasting machine, 18, 19, 24, 25,
Type catalog, 15, 23,
Type classification, 26, 31,
Type composing machine, 21, 22, 23, 24,
Type design, 32,
Type design systems, 35, 36,
Type Designer's Club, 127,
Type Designs: Their History and Developments (Johnson), 28,
The Type Directors Club, New York, 7, 30, 31, 34, 54, 72, 84, 100, 108, 121, 122, 127, 172, 178, 226, 227,

TDC International Typographical Competition, 34,
Typeface Six, 41,
Typeface Two, 41,
Type family concept, 10, 64,
Type family variations, **205**,
The Type-Founder, magazine (Barnhardt Brothers & Spindler), Chicago, 21,
Type Founders, 163,
Type foundries in the United States, 263,
Type Foundries of America (Annenberg), 63,
Type nomenclature, **225**,
Type 1 (Adobe), 37,
Type patents, 21, 116,
Typesetting systems, 21, 24, 29, 35,
Typesettra, Toronto, 34,
Types of the De Vinne Press (De Vinne), 126,
Type Shop, New York, 134,
Type Sign Symbol (Frutiger), 36,
Type sizes, 16, 17,
Type slug, 190, **191**, 192, **193**, 266,
Type specimen book, 15, 30,
Type World, magazine, 100,
Typewriter machine, 11, 20,
Typewriter types, 208,
Typograms, **187**, **188**,
Typograph, composing machine, 217,
Typograph Setzmaschinen-Fabrik, Berlin, 217,
Typographia Regia, Paris, 14,
Typographica (Goudy), 141, 142, 146,
Typographica (Spencer), 30,
The Typographic Advertiser (Johnson), 204,
Typographic i, magazine, 164,
Typographic identity, 25, 27, 28, 29, 34, 36, 125, 170,
The Typographic Messenger (Connor), New York, 204, 208,
Typographic Years: a Printer's Journey through a half century 1925-1975 (Blumenthal), 36, 91,
Typographical borders, 20, 27, **161**, **205**, **213**, **253**,
Typographical design, 33, 34,
Typographical hierarchies, 10, 35,
Typographical layout methods (Tschichold), 27,
Typographical point (Fournier le jeune), 10, 15,
Typographical ornaments, **97**, **223**, **253**,
Typographical posters, 9,
Typographical vignettes, 15,
Typographie (Ruder), 34,
Typographie als Kunst (Renner), 26,
Typographische Gestaltung (Assymetric Typography) (Tschichold), 29,
Typographische Mitteilungen, journal, Berlin, 27,
Typographische Monatsblätter, magazine, Basle, 35,
Typography (Harling), 29,
Typography (Harper), 20,
Typography (Meynell), 26,
typography (Burns), 32,
Typography Twelve, annual (TDC), 227,
Typologia (Goudy), 141, 148,
Typomundus 20, exhibition, New York, 33,
The Typophiles, New York, 30, 96, 141, 142, 143,
Typothetae, New York, 126,
Tzara, Tristan, 25,

U

UFA (Universal Film Association) (emblem), Berlin, **79**,
Uher, Edmund, 29, 269,
Uhertype, phototypesetting machine, 29,
Ulm Hochschule für Gestaltung (Ulm Technical College for Design), 29, 31, 35,
FB Ultra Belucian, 76,
Ultra Bodoni, 5, 39, 43, **70**, 116, 119, 150, 198, 218,
Ultra Modern, 267,
Umbra, 6, 39, 43, 194, **199**, 267,
Uncial letters, 8, **154**, **155**,
Understanding Media (McLuhan), 33,
Underwood, Clarence G., 25,
Unger, Gerard, 37, 40, 41, 84, 244,
The Union, Northern states, 19,
Union Pearl, 14,
Unit system, 10,
United Kingdom, 34,
United Printing Machinery Company, New York, 99,
U.S. Department of Transportation, Washington, 35,
U.S. Department Office of War Information, Washington, 240,
U.S. Federal Highway Administration, 134, 135,
U.S. Government Printing Office, Washington, 34, 266,
U.S. Information Agency, Washington, 100,
U.S. Military Academy of West Point, New York, 137,
U.S. News & World Report, magazine, 104,
U.S. Pension Office, Washington, 180,
U.S. Postal Service, 240,
U.S. telephone directories, 29, 35,
United States Type Founders' Association, 21,
United Typothetæ, New York, 126,
Univers, 12, 25, 26, 31, 32, 33, 40, 238, 269,
universal alphabet, 25, 27, 39,
Universal composing machine, 263,
Universal Film Association (UFA) (emblem), Berlin, **79**,
"Universal" keyboard, 20, **181**,
The Universal Penman (Bickham), 15,
University of California, Berkeley, 182,
University of California Old Style, 5, 39, 43, 141, **148**,
University of California Press, 20, 148, 182,
University of Chicago, 92, 197,
University of Chicago Library (bookplate), **196**,
University of Chicago Press, 20,
University of Cincinnati, Ohio, 100,
University of Georgia, Athens, 44,
University of Georgia Press, Athens, 45, 46,
University of Georgia Research Foundation, Athens, 44,
University of Michigan, Ann Arbor, 172,
University of Monterrey, Mexico, 100,
University of Oklahoma Press, Norman, 220,
University of Richmond, Virginia, 110,
University of Utah, Salt Lake City, 262,
University of Virginia, Charlottesville, 110,
University of Wisconsin, Madison, 72,
University Press of Virginia, Charlottesville, 113,
University presses, 25,

Unix, computer program plataform, 37,
Updike, Daniel Berkeley, 6, 17, 21, 22, 25, 91, 114, 129, 137, 138, 222, 224, 225, **251**,
U&lc (*Upper and lower case*) (ITC), magazine, 11, 12, 35, 54, 100, 101, 103, 127, 186, **187**, **188**, 232, 238, 264, 269,
U&lc On line(*Upper and lower case: The International Journal of Graphic Design and Digital Media*) (ITC), 262,
Uppsala, 5, 6, 37, 41, 43, **95**, **231**,
Usherwood, Leslie, 34, 41, 264,
ITC Usherwood, 41, 264,
USA, magazine, 240,
Utopia (More), **223**,
Adobe Utopia, 6, 41,43, 232, **234**,

V

Vacher & Sons, printing firm, 193,
Vale Press, London, 141,
Van Blokland, Erik, 41,
Vanderburg, Wells & Company, 207,
VanderLans, Rudy36, 182, 183,
Van der Ploeg, Jan, 178, 179,
Van de Velde, Henri, 24,
Van Dijck, Cristoffel, 14, 15,
Van Dijck Roman, 26, 27, 39,
Van Doesburg, Théo, 25, 34,
Van Krimpen, Jan15, 26, 27, 39, 40, 104,
Van Rossum, Just, 41,
Vanity Fair, magazine, New York, 28,
Variex, 41, 182,
Vario, 41,
Vatican Library, Vatican, 94,
Veljovick, Jovica, 34, 41, 226, 264,
ITC Veljovick, 41, 264,
Vellvé, Tomàs, 40,
Vellvé, 40,
Vendôme, 30, 40,
Venezia,26, 266,
Venture, 40,
Venturi, Robert, 12, 33,
Venus, 24, 38,
Venus and Adonis (Shakespeare), 220,
Verdana, 104,
WTC Veritas, 43, **45**,
Vermilyea, Thomas, 254,
Ver Sacrum, magazine, 22,
Versailles, 41,
Vertical Writing, 216,
Vest-pocket editions (Elzevir family), 14,
Vicenza / Arrighi, 252,
Victor Bicycles, Boston, **97**,
Queen Victoria, Alexandrina, 18,
Victoria & Albert Museum, London, 24, 37, 104,
Victorian, 40,
Victorian Era, 29, 149, 269,
Victorian typefaces, 33,
Victory, magazine, 240,
Videc, electronic products, 35,
Videocomp (RCA), 33,
Video series, sans serif typefaces, 104,
Videotaped artwork, 12, 34,
Video terminals, 12, 35,
Vidifont, electronic type generator (CBS), 34,
Vienna Akademie der bildenden Künste (Academy of Fine Arts), 22, 154,
Vienna Academy of Fine Arts, 22, 154,
Vienna Secession, 22, 226, 229,
Vignelli, Massimo, 29, 100,

Vignettes, **97**, **131**, **142**, **223**,
Viking Press, New York, 91,
Village, 5, 23, 38, 43, **144**, 220, 260,
The Village Press, Park Ridge, Illinois, 23, 24, 116, 129, 141, **142**, 144, 220, 260,
Village Type Foundry, Marlborough-on-the Hudson, New York, 26, 29, 260,
ITC Vintage, 264,
Virgil, 16,
Virginia Commonwealth University, Richmond, 36,
Virginia Quarterly Review, 110,
Virtuosa, 40,
Visage, 92,
Visible Language, journal, 35, 84,
Visigoth, 5, 41, 43, **52**,
Vision, magazine, 100,
Vision in Motion (Moholy-Nagy), 30,
Visual Art Gallery, Athens, 44,
Visual Graphics Corporation, Tamarac, Florida, 44, 46, 49, 188, 202,
"Visual language", 37,
Visual Thinking (Arnheim), 31,
Viva, 6, 13, 37, 41, 43, 244, **249**, 262,
Vivarelli, Carlo, 32,
Vive le Font, digital display typefaces, 92,
Vogel, Ernst, printer, New York, 21,
Vogue, magazine, New York, 11, 28, 71, 75,
Vogue, 11, 27, 28, 39,
Vogue (Stephenson, Blake & Co.), 27,
Voirin, Henri, 19,
Volkswagen, 31,
Voltaire, 27, 78, 81,
Vortex, 41,
Voskens, Dirk and Bartholomew, 14,
Vostell, Wolf, 32,
Vox, Maximilien (pseud. of Samuel Théodore William Monod), 26, 31,
Voysey, C. F. A., 96,

W

Wagner & Schmidt, type foundry, Germany, 24, 25, 38,
Walbaum, Justus Erich, 38,
Walbaum, 26, 38, 39,
Walbaum Buch, 40,
Waldo, Robert V., 62,
Walden (Thoreau), 224,
Walker, 5, 13, 37, 41, 43, 105, **109**,
Walker, Albert H., 217,
Walker, Emery, 21, 23, 38, 220, 222,
Walker Art Center, Minneapolis, 13, 25, 30, 37, 78, 104, 109,
The Wall Street Journal, New York, 72,
Wallau, 39,
Wang, electronic products, 35,
Warde, Beatrice, 27, 31, 268,
Warde, Frederic, 6, 11, 26, 27, 28, 36, 39, 42, 91, 110, 161, 222, **252**, 268,
Warhol, Andy, 32,
Warnock, John, 12, 36, 262,
S. D. Warren & Co., paper manufacturers, Boston, 126,
Warwick Typographers, Inc., Washington, 179,
Washburn College, Topeka, 240,
The Washburn College Bible (Thompson, designer), 240, **241** (symbol),
Washburn University, Topeka, 240,
George Washington University, 127,
Washington Calligraphers Guild, 49, 51,

Washington Hand Press, letterpress, 18,
Washington Irving (Ruzicka, illustrator), 224,
Washington Metro, map, (Vignelli), 28,
The Washington Post, 104, 178,
Waters, Julian, 226,
Watch Hill Press, Westchester County, 252,
Watt, James, 15,
Waxed tablets, 8,
Wayne State University, Detroit, 172,
Wayside Press, Springfield, 22, 96, 114,
Weavings, 228,
Web printing presses, 18, 19,
Webb, Ebenezer Russell, 254,
E. R. Webb & Company, wood manufacturers, 255,
Webendorfer-Wills Company, 263,
Weber, Christian Emil, 19,
Weber, Richard, 40,
Weber, type foundry, Stuttgart, 19,
Webster, Noah, 18,
Wedding Text, 242,
The Weekly Tribune, newspaper, Snohomish, Washington, 220,
Weingart, Wolfgang, 12, 33, 34, 35,
Weisert, Otto, type foundry, Germany, 38,
Weiss, Emil Rudolf, 18, 21, 25, 39, 91,
Weiss Initials I, II, III, 39,
Weiss Roman, 39,
Weiss Rundgotisch, 39,
Weithas, Arthur, 242,
Wells, Darius, 6, 9, 18, 19, 38, 42, 43, 209, **254**,
Wells, H(erbert) G(eorge) 11, 24, 124, 130, 141, 142, 144, 145, 260,
Wells College, Aurora, 154, 155,
Wells College Press, Aurora, 154,
D. Wells & Company, New York, 254,
Wells & Webb Company, Paterson, 254, 255, 256, 257, 258,
Werner, Nicolas, 38,
Wertheimer, Max, 11, 24, 26, 29, 31,
F. Wesel Manufacturing Company, New York, 99,
West Virginia Pulp and Paper Company, 29, 240,
Western PostScript font, 37,
Western Type Foundry, Chicago, 260, 261,
Westinghouse Electric Corp., 32,
Westvaco Inspirations for Printers, 11, 29, 114, 240, **241**,
White, Hagar & Company, type foundry, 207,
White Consolidated Industries, 263,
Whitin Machine Company, 263,
Whitin Machine Works, 263,
Whitman, Walt, 225,
The Whole Booke of Psalmes (Daye, printer), 14,
"The whole is more important than the parts", principle, 24,
Who's Who in Graphic Art (Amstutz, publisher), 100,
Wiebking, Hermann, 260,
Wiebking, Robert, 6, 9, 10, 11, 25, 26, 27, 38, 42, 43, 141, 145, 190, 194, 220, 222, **260**, 167,
Wiebking, Hardinge & Company, type founders, Chicago, 260,
Widmer, Jean, 36,
Wiegand, Willi, 91,

Wienner Werkstätte, Vienna, 23,
Wienner Werkstätte principles, 186,
Wilde, Oscar, 96, 220,
Wilhelm-Klingspor-Schrift, 39,
Williams, Gluyas, 170,
Williams, William Carlos, 91,
Alexander Wilson, type foundry, Glasgow, 16,
Wilson, Wes, 33,
Winchester, 23,
Winchester School style, 245,
Windings 1, 2, 3, 164,
Windows (computer), 36,
Windsor, 38,
Winkow, Carlos, 25, 39, 40,
Wire, magazine, 104,
Wise, Robert, 188,
Wissing, Beno, 33,
Wolf, Henry, 20,
Wolf, Rudolf, 26, 28, 39, 153, 198,
Wolpe, Berthold, 25, 29, 30, 32, 37, 39, 110, 136,
The Wonderful World of Insects (Gaul), 31,
Woodcuts, 14, 22, 23, 24,
Woodcut poster, 24,
Wood engraving, 9, 16, 18, 19, 20, 30, **225**, 254, **255**,
Wood Letter Cutting business, 254, **255**,
Wood pulp paper, 19,
Wood pulp paper mill, 19,
Wood type, 8, 10, 18, 20, 34, **205**, **206**, **207**, **208**, **209**, **210**, **211**, **212**, **213**, **255**, **256**, **257**, **258**, **259**,
Wood type posters, 18,
Wood type specimen books, 18, 20,
Robert Woods Bliss (bookplate), **225**,
Woodworth, Laurence, 220,
Woolford , H. Clay, 203,
Word processors with video terminals, 35,
Word 97 (Microsoft), 37,
Workshop School of Advertising, New York, 54,
The Works of Geoffrey Chaucer (Chaucer / Burne-Jones), 22,
Works Progress Administration (WPA), 29, 136,
World War I, 11, 24, 25, 78, 91, 129, 154, 242,
World War II, 11, 29, 95, 169, 220, 230, 231,
XX World Olympic Games, Munich, 35,
1893 World's Columbian Exposition, Chicago, 21, 22, 180, 268,
1878 World's Fair Exhibition, Paris, 19,
World Publishing Company, 156,
World Type Center, New York, 45, 100, 101,
Wove calendered paper, 15,
Wozencroft, Jon, editor, 37,
Wozniack, Steve, 12, 35, 36,
Wren's City Churches (Macmurdo), 20,
Wright, Frank Lloyd, 18, 96,
Frank Lloyd Wright Building Conservancy, 100,
Writing and Illuminating and Lettering (Johnston), 23, 24, 143,
The Writing Book of Gerardus Mercator (Mercator), 252,
Wyler, William, 31,

X

Xenon flash tube, 32,
Xerography, 12, 29, 30, 32,
Xerox Corporation, Rochester, 30, 49,

Xerox 9700, electrophotographic printer, 35,
Xerox Palo Alto Research Center, 262,
Xerox PARC Computer Science Laboratory, 262,

Y

Yale University, New Haven, 7, 26,
Yale University Composing Room Award for Typographical Excellence, 44,
Yale University Design Department, 31,
Yale University Graphic Design Faculty, 44, 104,
Yale University Graphic Design Program, 31,
Yale University Press, New Haven, 20, 25,156,
Yale University School of Art and Architecture, New Haven, 33, 240,
Yamashita, Yoshiro, 33,
The Yellow Book, magazine, London, 22,
Yellow Kid (comic strip) (Outcault), 22,
Young, Edward, 29,

Z

Zahn, Carl, 202,
Zapf, Hermann, 7, 11, 22, 23, 26, 28, 31, 32, 34, 35, 36, 40, 41, 92, 134, 164, 197, 232, 238, 240, 264, 266,
ITC Zapf Book, 40, 264,
ITC Zapf Chancery, 40, 264,
Zapf Civilité, 40,
ITC Zapf Dingbats 100, 35, 40,
ITC Zapf International, 40, 264,
Zapf Renaissance Roman, 41,
Zapfino, 41,
Zapf-von Hesse, Gudrum, 40, 41,
Zarte Bernhard / Bernhard Roman, 78,
Zebrawood, **259**,
Das Zeichenbuch (*The Book of Signs*) (Koch), 26,
Zeno, 29,
Zeppelin, 24, 39,
HTF Ziggurat, 6, 43, **162**,
HTF Ziggurat Italic, 160,
Zinc, metal, 18, 20,
Zinc line blocks, 20,
Zurich School of Arts and Crafts, 84,
Zwart, Piet, 34,
Zwart Vet, 41,
Zwart Vet lowercase, 41,
Zworykin, Vladimir, 29,